A HISTORY OF MODERN FRANCE

THIRD EDITION

A HISTORY OF MODERN FRANCE

JEREMY D. POPKIN

University of Kentucky

UPPER SADDLE RIVER, NEW JERSEY 07458

Library of Congress Cataloging-in-Publication Data

Popkin, Jeremy D., (date)
  A history of modern France / Jeremy D. Popkin.— 3rd ed.
    p. cm.
  ISBN 0-13-193293-4
  1. France—History—18th century. 2. France--History—1789– I. Title.

DC110.P67 2005
944—dc22

2004029594

Editorial Director: Charlyce Jones Owen
Executive Editor: Charles Cavaliere
Editorial Assistant: Shannon Corliss
Marketing Director: Heather Shelstad
Marketing Assistant: Cherron Gardner
Production Liaison: Marianne Peters-Riordan
Manufacturing Buyer: Ben Smith
Art Director: Jayne Conte
Cover Design: Bruce Kenselaar
Director, Image Resource Center: Melinda Reo
Manager, Rights and Permissions: Zina Arabia
Manager, Visual Research: Beth Brenzel
Manager, Cover Visual Research & Permissions: Karen Sanatar
Image Permission Coordinator: Carolyn Gauntt
Composition/Full-Service Project Management: Jan Pushard/Pine Tree Composition, Inc.
Cover Printer: Phoenix Color Corp.

Credits and acknowledgments borrowed from other sources and reproduced, with permission, in this textbook appear on the appropriate page within text.

Pearson Education LTD.
Pearson Education Singapore, Pte. Ltd
Pearson Education, Canada, Ltd
Pearson Education–Japan
Pearson Education Australia PTY, Limited

Pearson Education North Asia Ltd
Pearson Educación de Mexico, S.A. de C.V.
Pearson Education Malaysia, Pte. Ltd
Pearson Education, Upper Saddle River, New Jersey

10   9   8   7   6   5   4   3
ISBN 0-13-193293-4

To my parents, who first introduced me both to France and to teaching; to my wife and children, who have shared many trips to France with me; and to my French friends, who have helped me to better understand their country's history and culture.

CONTENTS

PREFACE

As I write the preface to this new edition of *A History of Modern France* in October 2004, official relations between that country and the United States are at a low point. The French government's role in opposing President George W. Bush's decision to invade Iraq in March 2003 angered American leaders and many ordinary Americans as well. Secretary of Defense Donald Rumsfeld dismissed France and Germany as remnants of an "old Europe" unwilling to accept the realities of a new era. For historians in North America who study and teach about France, and for students who take our courses, this crisis in Franco-American relations raises in acute form the question of why we should still care about the history of a medium-sized European country with a population barely twenty percent of the size of the United States. Fifty years ago, the reasons for studying French history seemed obvious. On two occasions in the first half of the twentieth century, the destinies of the two countries were linked, as American troops fought and died to liberate French soil. A knowledge of French history was essential to understand-

ing the origins of those crises. At that time, French culture, more than that of any other European country, represented the epitome of taste and sophistication. French artists, French philosophers, French novelists, and French filmmakers often seemed more profound, more original, and more liberated from confining conventions than our own.

At the start of the twenty-first century, the connections between American and French life are no longer so evident. The prospect of another major American military engagement in France is far-fetched, and French culture no longer occupies the special position it held for previous generations. Yet the sharp division between the American and French governments in 2003 was, among other things, a reminder that France does still matter to the world, and to the United States. French criticism stung American leaders because the relationship between the two countries is such an old and strong one. In the twenty-first century, it may seem irrelevant to recall that French military aid was vital to the winning of American independence in 1783, and that Napoleon's sale of the Louisiana Territory to the young American republic in 1803 cleared the way for the country's westward expansion. Even today, however, France and the United States remain linked as the twin birthplaces of the modern model of democratic society. As recently as 1914, they were the only two major countries in the Western world with republican governments. If the effort to introduce Western-style democracy in Iraq succeeds, Iraqis will have embraced principles that are as much "French" as they are "American." Indeed, the history of France, where democratic ideas have often faced strong resistance, may have more lessons for understanding countries like Iraq than that of the United States, where alternative visions of how a society might be structured have rarely found much support.

Those of us who devote our lives to studying and teaching French history naturally hope that relations between the United States and France will improve, as they have after previous disagreements. For many of us, the current Franco-American diplomatic dispute raises fewer questions about the justification for courses in French history than another more fundamental issue: is the French nation-state still an appropriate framework for understanding major historical issues? In 2002, France joined eleven other European countries in abandoning its national currency, a symbol of its national identity for over hundreds of years, in favor of the euro. As members of the European Union, which expanded in 2004 to include most of that continent, French citizens travel with passports identical to those held by their neighbors. Decisions affecting the French economy, environmental policy, and many other vital measures are increasingly taken in the Belgian city of Brussels, home of the Union's governing commission, rather than in Paris. As it becomes part of a larger European community, France is also changing its cultural identity. A walk through the streets of any

French city will show that the population has become increasingly diverse. Descendants of immigrants have turned Islam into the second religion of this traditionally Catholic country. The Euro-Disney theme park, opened in 1992, has replaced Gothic cathedrals and royal palaces as France's most popular tourist attraction. Despite laws to block it, the English language is steadily infiltrating French daily life. France today bears less and less resemblance to the compact, relatively homogeneous nation-state whose history is described in this book.

The biggest change in this new edition of *A History of Modern France*—greatly expanded coverage of the history of France's overseas empire—reflects a growing awareness among French historians that, in a global era, a history of events limited to what took place within France's European borders risks seeming (to use a favorite French expression) increasingly provincial. Integrating the history of "greater France" with that of the metropole underlines one of the important ways in which France contributed to the rise of the modern world. Even as I have tried to give more attention to the interaction between France and its farflung colonies, I remain convinced that the past two-and-a-half centuries of the country's history constitute a story whose fascination is still strong. The dramas of the French Revolution and the "dark years" of German occupation during World War II pose great questions about politics and morality. Personalities such as Napoleon, Honoré de Balzac, Charles de Gaulle, and Simone de Beauvoir evoke interest far beyond France's borders. The artistic achievements of Eugène Delacroix and of the Impressionists make us want to know about the country and the times in which they lived.

The pages that follow are one American historian's effort to communicate the passion and the stimulation that he has experienced in studying the past two and a half centuries of French life. They do not pretend to give a definitive account of modern French history: the subject is too vast and the controversies concerning it too deep to permit such a thing. They do attempt to provide a basic framework for the understanding of modern French history and—on issues where historians disagree—to outline fairly the competing interpretations that that history has inspired. This book reflects the contributions of hundreds of historians who have devoted themselves to the subject, both in France and in the many other countries where French history has inspired devoted scholars. Without this community of colleagues, a synthesis like this could never have been written. If this book helps teachers to transmit the pleasure that the author has found in striving to understand the history of the French nation and people, and if it encourages students to explore the subject further, it will have served its purpose.

In preparing this new edition, I have tried to take into account major developments in historical research since the previous edition. In addition to expanded coverage of the history of the French empire and its impact on European France, readers will find sections drawing on recent publications in almost every subfield of French history, from women's history to the history of the Michelin tire company. The concluding chapter has been revised to cover events up to mid-2004, including the dramatic national elections of 2002, the Franco-American split over the Iraq war in 2003, and the passage of a law banning Muslim headscarves in public schools in 2004. Making room for new material has meant some tightening up of the narrative, particularly in sections covering domestic politics. The basic chronological plan of the book remains intact, however, and the number of chapters remains the same as in the previous edition.

ACKNOWLEDGMENTS

In thanking all the Prentice Hall reviewers who have helped me improve this book over the years, I would like to pay special tribute to William B. Cohen of Indiana University, whose premature death in 2002 deprived our field of one of its most dedicated members. Other readers have included Leslie Derfler, Florida Atlantic University; Michael S. Smith, University of South Carolina; Herrick Chapman, New York University; Michael Hanagan, New School for Social Research; Patricia O'Brien, University of California, Irvine; and Stephen L. Harp, University of Akron. My colleague Ellen Furlough offered valuable advice on the changes in this edition.

Jeremy D. Popkin

A HISTORY OF MODERN FRANCE

France, Principal Geographic Features

CHAPTER 1

"THE OLDEST NATION OF EUROPE"

In the year 486, one Clovis, the leader of the Franks, one of the barbarian groups that had settled in the territories of the collapsing Roman Empire, gained control of most of the lands the Romans had called Gaul. With Clovis's reign, these lands became an independent kingdom separated from the empire, with its capital at Paris, and loyal to the Catholic religion, which the king embraced in 496. Clovis's kingdom became the ancestor of the modern French state, making France "the oldest nation of Europe." Over the centuries, the boundaries of the territory ruled by Clovis's successors changed many times. Under Charlemagne at the start of the Middle Ages, and again under Napoleon a thousand years later, France ruled much of the rest of Europe; at other times, the territories controlled by the kings of France shrank to a small region surrounding Paris. The political entity Clovis had created never disappeared, however, and its core always remained the territories along the Seine and Loire rivers that had been the center of the original kingdom.

A VARIEGATED HEXAGON

By 1750, the shape of the kingdom was fairly similar to that of the France of our own day. Then as now, its borders formed a roughly six-sided figure, which modern French citizens call "the Hexagon." Although the kingdom's boundaries were the result of centuries of conflict with neighboring states, they had become established by 1750 in positions where natural features appeared to have dictated five of the sides. In the west, the English Channel, which the French call "la Manche" (the sleeve), forms a slanting diagonal, running southwest from Dunkerque to the tip of the Brittany peninsula. There, France's Atlantic coast turns sharply inward, forming a great arc called the Bay of Biscay, which ends abruptly where the mass of the European continent meets the Iberian peninsula.

Separating France from Spain, a high chain of mountains—the Pyrénées—forms a straight line across the base of the French Hexagon, from the Atlantic to the Mediterranean, where the fourth "side" of France (its Mediterranean coast) begins. It runs east past the mouth of the Rhône until it meets the southwestern corner of the Alps. The eighteenth-century French border then turned north, twisting and turning through the mountains east of the Rhône valley (the annexation of Nice and Savoy in 1860 has moved the present-day border with Italy further to the east). North of Switzerland, Louis XIV's conquests, relatively recent in 1750, had extended the kingdom into German-speaking territory along the Rhine river. North of this region of Alsace, the frontier turns sharply to the northwest. The hazards of centuries of wars have left an irregular line through the hills of the Ardennes and the plains of Flanders to the Channel coast; this is the only edge of the Hexagon with no relation to any prominent geographic feature.

These boundaries defined a territory marked more by its diversity than its unity. In the west, three large rivers—the Seine in the north, the Loire in the center, and the Garonne in the south—form natural highways leading to the ocean, but their basins have few natural interconnections. The long projection of the Brittany peninsula makes the trip from the mouth of the Seine to the mouth of the Loire a long and difficult voyage. The flat lands of northern France form part of the north European plain that sweeps across Germany and Poland into Russia, but the Ardennes, Vosges, and Jura mountain chains separate French territory from neighboring regions. South of the Loire, the worn-down volcanic peaks of the Massif Central form a rugged landscape extending almost to the Mediterranean coast. In this region, travel remains slow and difficult even today. Movement has always been easier along the Rhône river, whose valley forms a narrow corridor linking Switzerland to the Mediterranean, but communications between this region and the rest of France are difficult: in the 1600s, it took six horses and eight oxen to pull a carriage over the pass separating the Rhône from the Loire near Roanne.

The simple appearance of the Hexagon is deceptive: the creation of a unified France has been a long struggle against geographic obstacles. In the eighteenth century, neither France nor any other European state was a compact territorial mass, sharply separated from its neighbors. Within France's frontiers, there were small enclaves of territory belonging to foreign rulers, such as the southeastern city of

Avignon, which belonged to the pope. Furthermore, the frontier that marked the limits of the French king's sovereignty did not always coincide with other important boundaries. The great Mediterranean port city of Marseille and much of the territory along the Rhine lay outside of the kingdom's tariff boundaries, able to trade freely with other countries but treated as "foreign" with respect to the rest of France. Important Catholic dioceses overlapped the frontier, so that some French priests owed allegiance to bishops in the Austrian Netherlands (present-day Belgium) or the German states. The border did not follow linguistic frontiers: it took in German-speaking Alsace and Flemish-speaking lands around Lille, but not such French-speaking territories as Liège, Geneva, and Savoy. Nor was the French border in 1750 as fixed and permanent as it now seems. The France of the mid-eighteenth century was still expanding: between 1750 and 1770, it acquired the important eastern province of Lorraine and the Mediterranean island of Corsica.

The territories that lay within the frontiers of France in 1750 differed tremendously in landscape and climate. Lucien Febvre, one of the great French historians of this century, has said that "diversity is the essence of France." In an area not much larger than many American states, it contains low coastal plains and Mont Blanc, Europe's highest mountain peak, areas with some of Europe's richest farmland and others with thin and unproductive soil, regions swept by the storms from the North Sea and others bathed in the sunlight of the Mediterranean. Geologists explain the differences in France's landscape and soil by pointing out that the country is a patchwork of three kinds of formations. Some regions are ancient outcroppings of continental bedrock, covered with thin, poor soil, such as the Armorican Massif in Brittany and the Massif Central in the middle of the country. The flat or rolling countryside one finds around Paris and in the southwest lies above softer sedimentary rock, deposited in geological eras when this part of Europe was under the oceans; these areas include France's richest agricultural regions. Finally, there are the peaks of the Pyrénées and the Alps, high mountains, relatively recently thrust up.

These different geological formations would suffice to make France a variegated country, but they are compounded by marked differences in climate. France is the only European country that is half northern and half Mediterranean. Brittany, Normandy, the Paris basin, and the other northern and eastern provinces share the cool, humid climate of England and Germany. They receive ample rainfall, and their rivers flow steadily all year round. But France's southern regions, such as Provence and Languedoc, are part of the very different Mediterranean world: hot and dry in the summer, with winter rains that can turn small streams into torrents and cause devastating floods. The crops that thrive in the two halves of the country are different, too: climate explains why cooking in northern France is based on the use of butter from cows that thrive on the grain and forage crops suited to the north European climate, whereas the cuisine of the south relies on olive oil, the product of a tree that cannot endure cold winters. The climatic differences between north and south have always tended to divide the country into two great regions, but each of these is subdivided into dozens of smaller lands, or *pays*. Life in the Alpine valleys along the Italian border is quite different from life in the cities in the nearby Rhône valley. The France of 1750 was a mosaic of little territories, each with its own characteristic landscape, crops, and customs.

By 1750, the possessions of the king of France also included overseas territories in the Americas, Asia, and Africa. Although France had been outstripped by other European countries in the race to claim colonies during the years following Columbus's voyages, it had succeeded in claiming much of present-day Canada and the Mississippi valley, several important island colonies in the Caribbean, a strip of land on the coast of South America, island bases for slave trading off the coast of West Africa, and several outposts in India.

THE HISTORICAL HERITAGE

Like the land, the population of eighteenth-century France was diverse, and subsequent history has made it even more so. Modern-day excavations continually add to our knowledge of the prehistoric inhabitants of France, whose monuments include the magnificent cave paintings at Lascaux, often considered the earliest surviving evidence of the human drive for artistic expression. Later, other populations hunted and farmed the territory that has become northern France; in Brittany, they built mysterious structures of great upturned stones, or menhirs, similar to Stonehenge in England. These groups mingled with the Roman conquerors who followed Julius Caesar. Then this largely romanized population absorbed the various Germanic tribes who invaded the area when the Roman Empire gradually disintegrated, as well as the Norsemen or Normans, who gave their name to one of its provinces. Although some homogeneous ethnic minorities maintained their distinct identities and languages—Basques in the southwest, Celtic Bretons in the western part of their peninsula—other groups, including immigrants from neighboring countries, merged into the general population. The conquests of the 1600s and 1700s added new ethnic minorities to the population: Flemings along the northern border, Germans in Alsace. By 1750, the result was a population as diverse in its ethnic heritage as the French countryside was in its appearance.

Diverse in geography, varied in ethnic background, France in 1750 was also a country of many languages. French was the language of the educated throughout the country, the language of law, government, and religion, but it was not the everyday speech of most of the population. The ethnic fringes of the country clung to their own languages which were unrelated to French: Basque, Breton, Flemish, and the German dialect of Alsace. The entire southern half of the kingdom resisted the spread of the king's French: this was the region of the *langue d'oc,* a variety of dialects derived from the same Romance roots as French but significantly different in sound and vocabulary from the *langue d'oïl* of northern France. Even in the provinces close to Paris, regional dialects such as Picard remained common. Differences in language were closely related to differences in culture, for each French region had its own characteristics. Gascons, according to folklore, were boastful—hence the French word *gasconnade* for empty talk— and quick-tempered; Normans were stingy and cautious.

To these differences were added others derived from the distinctive historical experiences of France's different regions. Over the centuries, people in different parts of the country had often lived very different lives. Successive monarchs had acquired new domains, whose historical experiences had often been very different from that of the kingdom's heartland. Many eighteenth-century French provinces had once been independent duchies and principalities, like Brittany, Burgundy, and Provence. Some had been brutally conquered: the memories of the thirteenth-century Albigensian crusade that subjected Languedoc to Catholic orthodoxy and rule from Paris took centuries to fade. Others, like the Habsburg-owned Franche-Comté around Besançon, had lived for centuries under non-French rulers. All had their own customs and local laws. To many of the French kings' subjects, the government was an alien presence that had imposed itself on their region from the outside.

Church and Monarchy

Over the centuries, two institutions—the church and the monarchy—served to overcome linguistic and provincial boundaries, although both also functioned at times to create additional divisions that threatened French unity. Christianity had entered France during late Roman times, and by the Middle Ages only a small Jewish minority, officially expelled from the kingdom in 1306, had refused to accept it. The country was one of the main centers of medieval Christianity. It was near Paris that the first cathedrals in the distinctive Gothic style that later spread to most of Europe were built, and it was at the University of Paris that Thomas Aquinas gave medieval scholastic philosophy its most comprehensive form. But uniform orthodoxy was hard to impose throughout the kingdom, and disputes between opposing sects were the occasion for some of France's bloodiest internal conflicts. In the early 1200s, King Louis VIII brought an army from northern France to stamp out the heretical Albigensians. In the sixteenth century, a powerful Protestant movement, whose followers became known as Huguenots, challenged the dominant church. From 1560 to 1598, France was torn by a religious civil war, and even after its end, pockets of Protestant militants in areas such as the port city of La Rochelle and the southern mountains of the Cévennes continued to resist Catholicism and, on occasion, royal authority. In the eighteenth century, the Catholic church was a major national institution, present in every region of the country, and most of the population had more contact with the church than they did with the royal government.

The other institution that served to bind the diverse parts of France together was the monarchy. France's kings traced their ancestry to Clovis, who had succeeded in conquering the territory from the Pyrénées to the Rhine river and beyond by the time of his death in 511. Two hundred years later, a new dynasty, the Carolingians, replaced Clovis's Merovingian heirs. Under the greatest of the Carolingian kings, Charlemagne, France became part of an empire that took in most of western Europe, but this overextended empire soon broke apart. The treaty of Verdun in 843 divided Charlemagne's territories into three kingdoms, one of which roughly corresponded to modern France. In 987, a third dynasty, the Capetians, took the place of Charlemagne's heirs. By this time, much of the kingdom had been carved up into baronies whose rulers gave only token loyalty to the king. Hugues Capet, the first Capetian monarch, and his immediate successors, directly controlled only a small territory around Paris, the "Ile de France."

The Capetians, though they began with only a modest kingdom, set in motion a process that eventually created a large territorial state. Although threatened with disintegration many times throughout the centuries, the monarchy gradually extended its territorial reach and the scope of its power over its subjects. The king's courts superseded those of local feudal lords for important cases; the crown extended its taxing powers, and the right of great lords to maintain private armies was curtailed. The defeat of the English at the end of the Hundred Years' War in the 1430s (thanks in part to Joan of Arc—an illiterate peasant girl— whose role in inspiring the French forces made her a legendary figure), and the smashing of the neighboring Burgundian state in the 1470s, removed two dangerous rivals who could have prevented the growth of a large French monarchy. France was now set on a course of steadily growing power and territorial expansion which continued until the nineteenth century. Although the disparate territories that made up the kingdom clung to their historic privileges, they all acknowledged a common ruler, one whose agents whittled away steadily at local rights. Generations of jurists, from sixteenth-

century author Jean Bodin onward, elaborated a doctrine of royal sovereignty, imbuing French culture with the notion that the state should have one all-powerful authority at its center. In the realms of both practice and theory, the French monarchy bequeathed the country a powerful impulse toward centralization. The strong monarchy of 1750, like the country's boundaries, was the deceptively natural-looking result of many conflicts. French domestic history had been a long saga of power struggles and conspiracies; its lesson was that rulers were never secure and that power had to be jealously guarded, sometimes by the harshest means. The persistent legend that Louis XIV had kept a close relative and possible rival for the throne imprisoned in an iron mask testifies to the dark undercurrent that history had implanted in the French political imagination.

The Capital

Closely connected to the rise of the centralized monarchy was the development of a great capital city. Until the sixteenth century, the French kings moved frequently from one palace to another, but in the 1500s they gradually settled in Paris. The growing royal bureaucracy and the wealthy nobles attracted to the court swelled the city's population, which was more than 300,000 in the time of Louis XIV and around 600,000 by the time of the French Revolution in 1789—making it, after London, the largest metropolis in the western world. Louis XIV, fearing the restlessness of the urban population, installed himself and his courtiers at Versailles, twenty kilometers outside the city, but Paris continued to be the real center of the kingdom. The demands of its inhabitants made it the economic motor of all of northern France. From Paris emanated all political authority, and it was also the country's cultural and intellectual center, home of the royally supported academies for literature, science, and the arts, focus of theater and music, location of the major publishers. The concentration of so many different activities in a single location created a permanent opposition between the capital and the rest of the country—the provinces. To the present day, this centralization of authority in Paris and its attraction for the liveliest and most ambitious minds of the country have continued to characterize French life. So, too, has a certain fear of the great city and its restless population: Louis XIV has certainly not been the only French ruler to be preoccupied with keeping the capital under control.

Cultural Heritage

The church, the monarchy, and the influence of the capital worked to draw the different parts of France together; the country's high culture served not only to unite its educated elites but to suggest that France was the center of a larger European civilization. French had emerged as a literary language in the Middle Ages in texts such as the *Song of Roland* and *The Romance of the Rose* and, by the eighteenth century, French literature had accumulated a rich heritage of poetry, drama, and philosophy. Only French writers, Voltaire claimed, especially the dramatists and poets of the age of Louis XIV, had achieved the same harmony and perfection of form as the great Greek and Latin authors. Even if French had not yet conquered the other languages spoken within the kingdom, by the eighteenth century it was spreading throughout the European world, bidding to replace Latin as the universal language of educated men and women. French "can be called the language of all nations, equally useful to the nobility, to merchants, and above all to people travelling for business or pleasure," one of the many eighteenth-century journalists working outside the country wrote.[1] By the beginning of the eighteenth century, French styles of art, dress, cooking, and etiquette were being imitated by rulers throughout the rest of Europe. To France's elites, the superiority of their highly developed culture and its vocation to spread far beyond the country's borders seemed obvious.

Part of the reason for French culture's broad appeal was its enormous variety: rather than expressing a unified national spirit, it incorporated many conflicting impulses. The bawdy works of the early sixteenth-century novelist François Rabelais, drawing on the earthiness of popular culture to mock learned traditions in philosophy and theology, contrasted with the thoughtful essays of Michel de Montaigne, who arrived at a skeptical and relativist view of the world. The seventeenth-century philosopher René Descartes exalted the power of human reason and argued—in a clearly articulated style that brought a new precision to the language—that man could comprehend the workings of God and the universe. A generation later, Blaise Pascal, in equally clear and striking phrases, maintained that reason itself led man to a recognition of his need for religious faith. The conflict among enjoyment of the pleasures of life, a faith in the powers of reason, and a need for belief was deeply woven into French culture.

The past had thus bequeathed to eighteenth-century France a rich and complex legacy. A country of great variety—ethnic, linguistic, and cultural—the kingdom was nevertheless drawn together by common religious and political institutions. Its kings looked to expand their territories as their ancestors had, but it was above all France's thinkers and writers, celebrating the spread of its language, who gave the country a sense of universal mission.

Note

1. Cited in Jeremy Popkin, *News and Politics in the Age of Revolution* (Ithaca, NY: Cornell University Press, 1989), 44.

CHAPTER 2

THE STRUCTURE OF EIGHTEENTH-CENTURY FRENCH SOCIETY

One of eighteenth-century France's most complex inheritances was its social structure. In the Middle Ages, a powerful image of a society divided into three fundamental groups, or estates—"those who pray, those who fight, and those who work," or clergy, nobles, and commoners—had pervaded French thought. But this simple division had never been adequate to describe the reality of French life. In the 1700s, writers used a wide variety of often vaguely defined terms to describe the social world around them. They spoke of "the people" or of "peoples," without specifying whether they meant the whole population of the kingdom or just the poor. Peasants were obviously countrydwellers, but this categorical term covered a range of social conditions, from the direst ignorance and poverty to a condition of relative prosperity. "Bourgeois" could be all the residents of a town or just the wealthier ones. Historians who employ modern categories based on social class—particularly the standard division into peasants, urban workers, bourgeois, and nobles—to describe eighteenth-century French society, risk overlooking the groups that mattered the most to the people of the time. And groups *did* matter, for French society was structured as a mosaic of corporate groups, each with its own status and privileges. Objecting to a reform proposal that would have abolished the legal privileges of many of these groups in 1776, the judges of the *Parlement* of Paris, the kingdom's highest law court, argued that French society should not be turned into a world where every individual was "an isolated being, dependent on himself alone."[1] Yet within these groups, the balance between individual and corporate claims was changing rapidly.

The most fundamental social unit in the eighteenth century was the family. Family imagery pervaded the period's thought: the king was the father of his subjects, and family dramas were a favorite subject for popular painters such as Jean-Baptiste Greuze. French society provided little place for those who were not part of a family household: orphans and widows who could not move in with relatives were likely to live in grinding poverty, and the authorities kept close watch over single men without a fixed residence, considering them potential criminals. For most of the population, the family was above all an economic unit, rather than a focus for emotional ties. This was as true of the ambitious noble royal official Charles-Alexandre de Calonne, writing to his father about the financial resources of his intended, as it was among the poor. Peasant households needed the combined labor of husband and wife, as well as that of their children, to support themselves. The tendency of urban artisan families to send newborn babies to rural wet-nurses so that the mother could continue working shows how economic pressures dominated family decision-making.

Although economic considerations formed much of the basis of family life, other aspects were important, too. A family was bound together in defense of its honor and good name; lingering prejudice still inflicted humiliation on relatives if a family member was convicted of a crime. The *lettres de cachet*, or arbitrary arrest warrants, which struck many critics as evidence of royal tyranny, were in fact most often solicited by family heads to punish relatives whose behavior threatened the family's stability or reputation. The Diamond Necklace Scandal of the 1780s, which involved rumors that Queen Marie-Antoinette had committed adultery, brought a stain of dishonor to the royal family itself and contributed to the undermining of respect for the monarchy.

Wealthy bourgeois and aristocratic families were not as completely shaped by economic necessity, and some of them were more influenced by new cultural models of family life such as those propagated in the best-selling novels of Jean Jacques Rousseau, which stressed the importance of affection between husbands and wives and urged mothers to devote themselves to the raising of their children. But even among the wealthy, the emotionally close-knit family was exceptional. Marriages were more often contracted with a view to keeping the family's wealth and property together and promoting its social standing than because of love between the partners. For the aristocracy, at least, extramarital affairs were considered a normal escape from these loveless matches. French law strongly favored the husband over the wife; legally speaking, marriage was not a union of equals.

VILLAGES

Above the level of the family was that of the local community. For some four-fifths of the kingdom's eighteenth-century inhabitants, this community was the rural peasant village, a compact cluster of houses whose population ranged from five hundred to two thousand inhabitants. A village was made up of households, each farming the scattered plots that it owned or leased in the fields immediately surrounding the village. Aside from the village priest, the *curé*, peasants made up the whole of the village community: to find craftsmen who made their living in their workshops, to go shopping, or to find lawyers, doctors, or government officials, peasants had to trek to the nearest town.

The village community controlled many important aspects of its members' lives. Villagers agreed on when to plant crops and when to harvest them. They shared the use of communally owned pastures for their livestock and forest lands where they gathered firewood. The village was usually coterminous with the parish, and the church served as the center of community life, bringing everyone together for conviviality if not always for prayer. Villagers knew all about each other's lives, and they tended to look on outsiders with suspicion. Young men and women usually married within their own village, or found mates from the closest neighboring villages.

But these close-knit communities were not necessarily harmonious ones. Village life was marked by strong divisions, particularly between the minority of especially prosperous peasant families who tended to dominate the community and the majority of poorer, sometimes landless fellow villagers. The better-off peasants, the *coqs du village,* were often those who leased the estates of local noble *seigneurs.* They owned their own draft animals and rented them out to their poorer neighbors to plow their fields. These wealthy families were the leaders of the community. In his autobiographical novels, the eighteenth-century French writer Restif de la Bretonne, the son of a wealthy Burgundian peasant farmer, described such a household. His father worked hard but reserved for himself the most dignified and prestigious farmwork, such as guiding the plow: humbler tasks, such as caring for the livestock, he delegated to the women of the family or to hired servants. Restif's father, educated enough to read a little, dominated his family dinner table, directing conversation and religious observances. He acted as agent for the local *seigneur* and served as a judge in minor village controversies. He had his clientele of dependents among the poorer peasants of the village, doing them small favors and representing the interests of the community to the outside world in exchange for their loyalty. And he was able to invest in his children's future, sending some of his sons to school and preparing them for careers that would take them out of the ranks of the peasantry altogether.

Most eighteenth-century peasants lived a much less comfortable life. Poor peasants worked as day laborers for the wealthy peasants (who leased noble and clerical estates), farmed as sharecroppers on behalf of urban property owners, or supplemented their farming incomes by doing manufacturing tasks such as spinning and weaving in their own homes. Some migrated to other regions for part of the year, like the masons from the Limousin region who traveled regularly to Paris to work on construction projects. Life was difficult and precarious for such families. A bad harvest could reduce poor peasants to grinding misery; illness or accident could ruin them. At times, as much as one-fifth to one-seventh of the population was homeless or forced to rely on charity for survival. With the benefit of hindsight, historians can recognize that eighteenth-century French peasants were modestly better off

than their ancestors and also than their contemporaries in most other parts of continental Europe. But the peasants themselves were conscious above all of how difficult and insecure their lives were, and of how much of their work went to benefit noble, ecclesiastical, and bourgeois landowners who lived much more comfortably.

CITIES

Urban communities contained less than 20 percent of eighteenth-century France's population. Like peasants, most city dwellers had to work for a living. Just as the villages were divided between wealthy and poorer families, the urban working-class population ranged from prosperous master artisans, owners of their homes and enterprises, to penniless, uneducated day laborers living in miserable rented rooms. Divided by their economic condition, these working town dwellers were nevertheless parts of close-knit neighborhood communities. The men drank together in the neighborhood cabarets, women met in the marketplace, and neighborhood children roamed the streets together in their free hours, building social bonds that transcended family ties and gave a sense of local identity that excluded residents from other parts of town and members of the upper classes.

The skilled tradesmen whose crafts were organized into guilds made up the aristocracy of France's working population. The eighteenth-century Parisian glazier Jacques-Louis Ménétra differed from most of his fellows in that he later wrote his autobiography, but in many ways his experiences were typical of his social milieu. Ménétra entered his profession because his father and several other relatives had been glaziers before him. Like most Paris artisans, he had a certain amount of schooling before he started his apprenticeship. After several years spent learning the specialized skills of his trade in Paris, he spent several more years on his *tour de France*, traveling from city to city, stopping wherever he found work. During these years when he was not part of a stable community, Ménétra belonged to one of France's several journeymen's brotherhoods, or *compagnonnages*. The *compagnonnage* hostels welcomed him in each town he came to and integrated him into local economic and social networks.

Independent master craftsmen like Ménétra were the most privileged members of the urban working population. Women of the artisan classes had very different life experiences. Only a handful of female occupations, such as seamstresses, were organized into guilds, and women never tasted the experience of freedom that was part of the journeyman's *tour de France*. Master artisans did need wives to help run their shops; in addition to helping with some of the regular work, wives often managed the money and provided food and lodging for both their own family and for the apprentices and journeymen who lived with their employer. But women were barred from most guilds, and could usually run a shop only if they survived their husbands. Most male workers were also much less well off than skilled artisans. Guild rules, lack of capital, and government regulations limited the number of masters in many trades, and condemned most journeymen to a lifetime of working for others.

Below the skilled artisans was the mass of the urban population, the day laborers, street vendors—often women, who did most of the marketing of foodstuffs and other domestic goods—unskilled workers, and domestic servants. The truly destitute—beggars, prostitutes, and criminals—made up 10 to 20 percent of the population in France's largest city, Paris, where urban culture was most fully developed. They were outnumbered by the working poor, those who had a more or less permanent home and occupation but who often lived on the edge of poverty. Property inventories performed upon their deaths show that few of Paris's working families owned more than a handful of household utensils and one or two basic pieces of furniture. By the second half of the eighteenth century, city workers were beginning to accumulate a few inexpensive luxuries (a small mirror was a common acquisition), but most of their effort continued to go into paying for food and lodging.

Although most city residents were poor, urban populations also included wealthier groups, the bourgeoisie, and, on occasion, the nobility. Of all the social groups in eighteenth-century France, the bourgeoisie are perhaps the hardest to characterize. Members of the bourgeoisie owned property that went beyond the small plot of land that a peasant might possess or the workshop and tools of an artisan. In contrast to peasants and artisans, the bourgeois did not perform manual labor but, unless he had become wealthy enough to live as a *rentier* (supported by income from property and investments), the bourgeois did work. Unlike the noble, however, the bourgeois lacked a legal guarantee of his social status, which depended on wealth, occupation, and lifestyle. The most numerous category among the bourgeoisie was the merchants, ranging from small shopkeepers in France's innumerable towns and cities whose lifestyle often put them on the same level as prosperous master artisans to heads of great international trading firms. The latter accumulated enough wealth to buy landed estates and live in the same style as the nobility. Compared to the number of merchants, the fraction of the bourgeoisie who could be classified as manufacturers was small. On the other hand, members of the educated professions loomed large in the makeup of the preindustrial bourgeoisie. Lawyers were among the most prestigious of these professionals, considerably more so than doctors. Members of the bourgeoisie filled many lower-level government posts and actively sought local positions, such as churchwarden for their parish. Many of the clergy, especially in cities, were of bourgeois origin as well.

Education and lifestyle served to give this disparate social group a certain degree of unity. Nearly every bourgeois occupation required the ability to read, write, and calculate, and literacy had become almost universal among both the sons and daughters of the bourgeoisie even before it did among the nobility, despite the latter's greater wealth. Bourgeois homes reflected a different style of life than that of the lower classes. Whereas peasants and urban workers generally lived with their family in a single room, bourgeois families had houses or apartments divided into several rooms, and with considerably more furniture. They thus had greater privacy and the opportunity to develop a greater sense of individual identity than did members of the poorer classes.

Not only did bourgeois families own more consumer goods, they also had savings which they could invest and which put them above the economic worries of the lower orders. Prosperous bourgeois families bought rural landholdings and profited by renting their fields to peasants; they invested in royal bonds and thus acquired a strong interest in the solvency of the king. Bourgeois families also invested heavily in promoting their children's social mobility. Sons of successful merchants received an education that qualified them for professional careers, and bourgeois families often invested in the purchase of governmental offices, particularly those whose possession led eventually to a title of nobility. Women from the bourgeois classes also commonly received some education in the eighteenth century, although less than men. Like the wives of artisans, merchants' wives often worked in the family enterprises. But women were excluded from the educated professions, which remained exclusively male preserves.

NOBLES

In many respects, the wealthiest strata of the bourgeoisie resembled the nobles who made up the highest level of France's social pyramid. The distinguishing characteristic of nobility was the possession of a hereditary title and its associated special privileges. Centuries earlier, the nobility had established itself in France as a warrior class, but by the eighteenth century, most titled families were in fact the descendants of successful merchant dynasties who had slowly acquired land, titles, and offices that had enabled them to shed the memory of their lowly origins. Military nobles, the *noblesse d'épée*, or nobles of the sword, often found themselves snubbed by nobles whose titles were based on membership in one of the royal courts, or *parlements*, the so-called *noblesse de la robe*, or by families whose claim to fame was several generations of service in the royal bureaucracy.

Whatever their origins, the wealthy nobles of the eighteenth century were landowners, and the nobility as a class controlled a disproportionate share of France's terrain. Less than 2 percent of the country's population, nobles owned perhaps 25 percent of the land. Noble estates, or *seigneuries*, varied greatly in size—there were poor nobles as well as rich ones—but all nobles enjoyed certain special privileges. Noble landowners were exempt from some of the most onerous taxes; in most regions, they did not pay the *taille*, the basic head tax. By virtue of their noble status, they were entitled to a variety of payments from the peasants who lived on their domains, and nobles sometimes enjoyed lucrative monopolies, such as the right to compel the peasants to grind their grain at the noble's mill. Along with these income-producing privileges went honorific privileges that emphasized the noble's special status: the right to wear a sword; the privilege of engaging in the hunt and of raising doves and rabbits, which frequently devastated peasants' fields; the right to erect a weathervane, which set the noble's house apart from all others; and special seating in the local church.

Most of these special privileges harked back to the medieval past, but the power and prestige of the nobility were rooted in more modern developments as well. Formally or informally, noble status was required for ascent to most high positions in government and church, which meant that noble families profited from the handsome livings that such posts provided. Although nobles were barred from engaging in most branches of trade and manufacturing, they were as likely as wealthy bourgeois to invest in lucrative business enterprises and to buy government bonds. Consequently, the economic interests of nobles were not sharply distinct from those of the bourgeoisie.

Culturally, too, nobles were not sharply cut off from the upper strata of the bourgeoisie. Both groups were well represented among the purchasers of "Enlightenment" works, and in the audience of the latest plays and concerts. Nobles and educated commoners both participated in the activities of provincial academies, a form of intellectual sociability widely implanted in France's larger cities, and in the Masonic lodges that spread even to relatively small towns in the second half of the eighteenth century. In Paris, the salon, a regular meeting place for writers, artists, and wealthy patrons, often brought bourgeois intellectuals together with leading aristocrats. Intermarriage between noble and bourgeois families was not unknown: it frequently served as a discreet mechanism for infusing some of the bourgeoisie's growing wealth into the coffers of impecunious aristocratic families. In law, the distinction between nobles and commoners remained clear, but in the ordinary course of life, members of the two groups often seemed to have much in common: education, ownership of property, an interest in public and cultural affairs.

Noble women, although they did not enjoy all the privileges that male aristocrats did, were in many ways less restricted than their poorer sisters. Their work was not essential to the family, and they had a certain freedom to experiment with new lifestyles. In particular, they were in the vanguard of a new attitude toward family life. Noblewomen were among the most likely to adopt the new model of the affectionate family, devoting themselves personally to the care of their young children, as Jean-Jacques Rousseau had urged, rather than leaving their rearing entirely to servants.

CLERGY

Within French society, the clergy formed a special corporate group with its own social hierarchy and its own gender divisions. Only men could become priests, while the approximately fifty thousand nuns in French convents at the time of the Revolution were largely confined to traditional female functions, such as teaching in girls' schools and ministering to the sick. At the top of the church's hierarchy, a wealthy elite of bishops and abbots, drawn mostly from noble families, monopolized the most prestigious positions. The occupants of these top positions enjoyed substantial incomes from the church's own extensive properties and from the tithes that the laity had to pay to the church. And, like many secular nobles, many of these aristocratic churchmen did almost nothing to earn their income. Some bishops rarely visited their dioceses, and much of the income from tithes went to absentee clerics who performed no real religious functions. The working sector of the church was made up above all of the parish clergy, the *curés* who saw to the spiritual needs of the population and the nuns and monks who ran most of the country's schools and welfare institutions. A clerical career was a common choice for younger sons from prosperous peasant and petty-bourgeois families: a son put into the church would be assured of a relatively prestigious career and would not claim a part of the family estate.

The curé was an important part of community life. In a village, he was often the most educated resident and served as a link between the peasants and the outside world. He kept the register of births and deaths, and his participation was necessary at weddings and funerals. He also exercised a degree of authority over the laity, and indeed often came into conflict with them when he tried to enforce church prohibitions on certain popular festivals and oppose superstitions that the church condemned. Despite his important functions, the curé often found himself shabbily treated by the church hierarchy. Curés in some regions, such as Brittany, could generally live comfortably from their parishioners' tithes and the income from the property attached to their churches. But, in other areas, such as the Alpine diocese of Gap, most of the church's income went to absentee clerics, and the local curés had to make do with a meager salary. The church thus had its own version of the larger conflict between a wealthy privileged elite and a mass of poorer members who often felt unjustifiably exploited by their superiors.

Like the clergy, French society as a whole was also split by multiple conflicts at the end of the eighteenth century. Historians have differed over which social fault lines were most important: that separating nobles from commoners, as the rhetoric of the French Revolution and the Marxist scholarly tradition suggest, or the line separating all the wealthy, both noble and bourgeois, from the rest of the population, as many historians in the last three decades have contended. The empirical evidence that nobles and wealthy bourgeois invested in the same kinds of property, read the same books, and shared some of the same lifestyle is strong; so is the evidence that nobles tried hard to safeguard their exclusive privileges and that, when the crisis of 1789 arrived, much of the population regarded them as a distinct group. By the middle of the nineteenth century, the division between rich and poor had clearly become the dominant social issue in French public life, but in the eighteenth century, the complex differences in inherited social status continued to cloud the picture. The special privileges that separated nobles from the far more numerous members of the Third Estate (commoners) had come to seem increasingly unjustified as the nobility had ceased to perform a distinctive social function. Under the right conditions, protest against those privileges could unite a broad array of groups that otherwise had little in common, from wealthy lawyers and merchants frustrated by the nobles' monopoly on prestigious posts to humble peasants infuriated by the dues they owed the local seigneur.

NOTE

1. Remonstrances of the *Parlement de Paris*, 1776, cited in University of Chicago, *History of Western Civilization Readings* (Chicago: University of Chicago Press, 1977), VII:91.

CHAPTER 3

THE PREINDUSTRIAL ECONOMY

In the middle of the eighteenth century, the European world was just beginning to experience the rapid changes in technology that would eventually be labeled the "industrial revolution." To feed and clothe themselves and provide the other commodities they needed, the French still largely depended on hand tools and on power provided by draft animals, water wheels, and windmills. This preindustrial economy was not a stagnant one, however. In the middle of the eighteenth century, France began to depart from the pattern of the past in several significant ways. Some of these changes, such as the beginning of growth in the overall population and in the productivity of the economy, were hardly noticed at the time. Others, such as the development of a new secular culture and the articulation of challenges to the absolutist monarchy and the traditional social hierarchy, were readily apparent—at least to the educated and literate. In 1750, Jacques Turgot, a young nobleman about to embark on a career in the royal administration, wrote an essay introducing a new concept in French thought: the idea of progress. France and the world were not just bound to change, he predicted, but they were changing for the better: becoming more prosperous economically, better administered, more intelligent. Turgot's criteria of progress were those of a new era, the modern world.

THE GROWTH OF POPULATION

One of the most important changes occurring in the France of Turgot's day was the beginning of a steady, long-term rise in the country's population. In the eighteenth century, neither the French government nor any other European country carried out censuses, although French royal officials of the time were increasingly interested in the population question and used what data they could find to make estimates. Thanks to intensive historical studies, we now know what contemporaries could only guess: France's population was indeed rising markedly. This increase was one of the surest signs that fundamental change was taking place in the country.

From 1500—when it recovered from the devastating losses caused by the Black Death—to 1700, France's population seems to have fluctuated within fairly narrow limits. The total population seems to have been not much more than twenty million in 1700. When Louis XIV died in 1715, however, a new era in French population growth was already beginning. The terrible winter of 1709–1710 turned out to be the last of France's old-style famine crises, marked by a "dismal peak" in the death rate sharp enough to wipe out the population increase of several previous decades. In the twenty years after Louis XIV's demise, France's population reached and probably surpassed the highest level it had ever previously attained. After a brief leveling off in the early 1740s, the kingdom's population began a steady march upward to levels never before reached. By 1770, France's population had probably reached twenty-six million, and, even though the rate of increase then slowed, France of 1789 had a population of around twenty-eight million.

Historians have not reached a consensus on the reasons for this phenomenon, part of a general trend affecting the entire European world. Some have credited it primarily to the reduction in death rates caused by the disappearance of certain diseases, notably the plague, which last appeared in France in 1720, and by medical developments, such as the improved birthing procedures taught to midwives after midcentury. Improvements in hygiene, such as the growing use of cheap undergarments which could be changed frequently, and the movement of cemeteries from churchyards in the middle of towns to areas outside, cut down on some health hazards. Other historians have emphasized changes that raised birth rates. A growing economy, itself partly stimulated by the growing population with its increased demand for goods of all kinds, created more job opportunities and allowed young people to get married earlier than they would have in previous generations, thus increasing the number of births. Improved farming methods and the introduction of new crops may have increased the food supply and thus kept the population healthier. The wars of the eighteenth century were smaller in scale than those of Louis XIV's time, and they were not fought on French soil, which spared the population the devastation that always accompanied military campaigns.

Whatever its causes, the population increase had effects on every area of French life. More people meant a greater demand for food, which pushed the prices of agricultural products upward. Population growth increased the demand for manufactured goods. A growing number of peasants competed for the right to farm the available land. As the French population exceeded any previous level, French society was forced to change in a variety of ways. The larger-than-normal generation born between 1750 and 1770, coming of age around 1789, may have contributed to the restlessness that caused the French Revolution.

THE AGRICULTURAL ECONOMY

The vast majority of France's growing eighteenth-century population worked the land. The rich soil in many of its regions and the temperate climate, suitable to a variety of crops, make it even today one of Europe's major farming areas. In the 1700s, some 75 percent of the French population were peasants, members of families whose main occupation was farming. The diversity of France's countryside made for an equally varied agriculture. Some regions, like the Beauce (southwest of Paris), had over the centuries come to specialize in raising of grain crops for flour for the bread that was the main staple of the French diet. These areas of monoculture developed where the soil was good and the market for their produce large and dependable. Other areas, such as Normandy, had a more diversified kind of farming, raising more livestock and producing meat and dairy products as well as grain crops. Diversified agriculture also characterized poor regions such as the Massif Central and Provence, where the soil did not permit the raising of large amounts of grain. Although these regions were less productive than areas like the Beauce, they were often better protected against large swings in production because they were not so depended on a single crop. Where conditions permitted, grapes were grown to produce the wine for which France was already famous; next to cereal grains, they were the country's most important cash crop.

Eighteenth-century French agriculture depended for the most part on methods that had been used for centuries. In grain-growing areas, the two-field and three-field methods of crop rotation, in which one-half or one-third of the soil was left fallow each year to prevent it from becoming exhausted, continued to be used—often in combination with the open-field system under which individual peasant plots were not fenced in. With peasants under pressure to produce as much grain as possible, pasture land for animals was limited. Since animal dung was the main form of fertilizer available, this in turn restricted the supply of that commodity. This was one of the main limitations on agricultural productivity, which was then considerably lower than it has become in modern times. French grain-growing regions normally produced yields of no more than six bushels for every bushel of seed.

Throughout the eighteenth century, innovative landlords and farmers in England were experimenting with new crops and with methods such as crop rotation and the unification and enclosure of previously scattered holdings. Taken together, these changes constituted what historians have labeled the "agricultural revolution." These new methods raised agricultural productivity and thus permitted rapid population growth and economic expansion. Some French estate owners, royal officials, and intellectuals were aware of the new ideas about farming coming from England, but eighteenth-century France was not experiencing an agricultural revolution. "In England we have been making, for forty or fifty years past, a considerable progress in the allotment and inclosure of open fields," the English agronomist Arthur Young wrote during a visit to France in 1789. "In France, on the contrary, they have not taken the first

step."[1] Young and many other commentators of the period put this down to the backwardness of the French political system. The French economic theorist François Quesnay blamed "restrictions in the trade of wheat, the form of the imposition of subsidies, the bad use of men and wealth for the manufacture of luxuries, continual wars" for the country's failure to profit from its natural resources as it should have.[2] Not all the English innovations were suited to French conditions, but political obstacles did play a major role in preventing changes. The British Parliament, dominated by large landowners, systematically favored the process of enclosure, which made it easier for individual landlords to experiment with new farming methods, whereas French laws, which varied tremendously from province to province, generally made it more difficult for landlords to force change on their poorer neighbors.

Nevertheless, total French agricultural production did grow in the eighteenth century. This increase at least kept pace with the growth of population and may even have outstripped it, allowing most people a slightly better diet. As in the case of growth in population, the increase in farm production resulted from a variety of factors, rather than from a single cause. Some new crops were introduced successfully, such as maize (American corn) in the region around Toulouse. Improvements in roads and canals made it easier to transport crops and provided incentives for greater production, and the growing population led to the use of marginal land that had been neglected in earlier periods.

The benefits of this slow development of agriculture were, however, shared very unequally among the French population. Since the supply of land was limited, whereas the number of potential workers was growing steadily, owners of land enjoyed an advantage over the increasingly numerous peasants who clamored to farm it. Farm wages thus rose more slowly than land rents and crop prices. Large landowners were better placed to adopt new farming methods and to specialize in the production of the cash crops that brought the highest profits. They also tended to keep their land-holdings intact from generation to genera-tion, whereas the growth of peasant popula-tion meant that their holdings became divided into ever-smaller units. The changes in the rural economy thus tended to sharpen social differences in the countryside, increas-ing the gap between the prosperous elites who reaped most of the benefits and the swelling number of poor who had to strug-gle to make a living.

MANUFACTURING AND COMMERCE

Although agriculture dominated eighteenth-century French life, manufacturing and com-merce also had important places in its econ-omy. As in farming, the methods used to make and sell goods in 1750 were traditional ones that had changed only slowly over the previous two or three centuries. Most manu-factured products were made by hand in small workshops, which usually consisted of an owner and a handful of assistants—jour-neymen who had learned their craft but lacked the capital to set up on their own—and apprentices who were being taught the skills of the trade. These small manufactur-ing enterprises were spread throughout the country; the process of concentration that would later lead to the formation of large urban industrial centers had not yet begun. Every small market town had its shoemak-ers, bakers, butchers, and tailors. The limi-tations of France's transportation system, which made it difficult to export goods over long distances, contributed to the dispersal of manufacturing. France's geography meant that water transport could not link it to-

gether as well as England's network of canals, rivers, and coastal trade did. Until the coming of the railroad, France remained divided into relatively isolated regions.

To present-day connoisseurs of an-tiques, the mention of eighteenth-century French manufactures suggests luxury goods like the fine porcelain made in the royally supported factory at Sèvres. But at the time, as in preindustrial Europe in general, the country's largest industry was the making of textiles. Silk weaving made Lyon the coun-try's second largest city and one whose econ-omy was dominated by a single trade, but this was unusual. In other regions, where wool, linen, and cotton cloth were made, the labor force usually consisted of peasants who worked in their own homes in what is known as the "putting-out system." Entre-preneurs brought the raw materials to their workers' homes and collected the finished products from them. Most textile manufac-turing was thus dispersed in the countryside, where spinners and weavers were beyond the jurisdiction of the urban guilds whose regulations often limited entrepreneurs' ac-tivities. Even relatively large-scale industrial enterprises like iron-making were usually lo-cated in rural rather than urban areas.

While French manufacturing grew steadily but not spectacularly over the cen-tury, commerce expanded much more rap-idly. Foreign trade was the fastest-growing sector, increasing more than 400 percent be-tween 1716–1720 and 1787–1789. Trade with France's overseas colonies grew at an even faster rate than overseas trade as a whole. Ships from the Atlantic ports took textiles and other manufactured goods from France and slaves from Africa to the West Indies. Sailing most often to Saint Domingue (modern-day Haiti), France's richest colony, they brought back sugar and coffee grown by slave labor on plantations there. The colonial trade cre-ated an elite of wealthy Creole slaveowners in the West Indies and a similarly prosperous group of traders and shipowners in the trading ports such as Bordeaux, Nantes, and Saint Malo. Domestic commerce also grew in the course of the eighteenth century, as France took the first steps toward becoming a modern consumer society. The grain trade was the most important branch of domestic commerce: a complex network of wholesale merchants, millers, and bakers carried out the transformation of the country's major crop into its daily bread. But the deficiencies of France's transportation system and the limited purchasing power of most of the population kept the internal market from developing as spectacularly as foreign trade. After 1800, when it became clear that France would never overcome Britain's lead in overseas trade, the slow growth of domestic demand would become a major obstacle to its industrial development.

Predominantly agricultural and definitely "preindustrial," the eighteenth-century French economy was nevertheless not backward by the standards of its day. The consensus of modern historical research is that the rate of French economic growth from 1700 to the time of the French Revolution was comparable to that of England, but that this growth was less concentrated in

areas suitable for the adoption of new power-driven machinery and the factory system than England's was. Nor was economic growth smooth and regular. The 1750s and early 1760s were a period of general prosperity for landowners, merchants, and manufacturers. Good harvests kept food prices reasonable for the poor. In the late 1760s, however, a succession of poor harvests sent bread prices soaring. Forced to spend more for food, consumers had less to spend on other goods. This crisis was the prelude to two decades of economic distress in the 1770s and 1780s. The political crisis that led to the French Revolution of 1789 took place against the background of this period of prolonged economic insecurity, which affected the poor most drastically.

NOTES

1. Arthur Young, *Travels in France,* cited in Robert and Elborg Forster, eds., *European Society in the Eighteenth Century* (New York: Harper & Row, 1969), 109.
2. Quesnay, "Grains," in Denis Diderot, ed., *The Encyclopedia: Selections,* Stephen J. Gendzier, trans. and ed. (New York: Harper, 1967), 133.

CHAPTER 4

CULTURE AND THOUGHT
IN EIGHTEENTH-CENTURY FRANCE

Just as historians have analyzed the social conflicts of eighteenth-century France and the ups and downs of its economy in the light of the revolutionary crisis of 1789, so they have studied the thought and culture of the era for clues to the coming upheaval. The Protestant-Catholic quarrel of the sixteenth and seventeenth centuries had died down, but religious issues still played an important role in French life. Increasingly, however, members of the educated classes adopted a critical, rational outlook, which led them to question the authority of the church and to favor reforms in many areas of French life. This spirit of enlightenment was not necessarily revolutionary: many aristocrats and high officials accepted the new ideas but believed that they could be implemented through existing institutions. Meanwhile, old traditions of popular belief remained strong and sometimes had the potential to provoke powerful movements of protest. Between the level of high intellectual thought and that of popular belief, a new cultural force emerged: the power of public opinion. The conviction that government and society should follow the dictates of this invisible authority was perhaps the most important cultural root of the changes that occurred after 1789.

Throughout the first half of the eighteenth century, French public life was dominated by the Jansenist quarrel, a controversy within the Catholic church that had begun in the 1600s. The Jansenists, a dissident Catholic minority who followed the ideas of the seventeenth-century theologian Cornelius Jansen, sought a sterner, more austere faith than that taught by the official church. To defend their interpretation of Catholicism, they did not hesitate to challenge the authority of the religious hierarchy and of the royal government that defended it. Louis XIV had considered them a political threat, and pressured Pope Clement XI to condemn the movement in his bull *Unigenitus* in 1713. Efforts to force the French Jansenists to renounce their convictions continued under Louis XIV and led to intense opposition among clergy and laity alike. The movement had many supporters among lawyers and among the judges of the royal courts. These defenders argued for the Jansenists' right to follow their conscience, even in opposition to the pope and the royal government. Elaborate theological and legal arguments against arbitrary authority, developed over the years by Jansenist advocates, familiarized the French public with such notions as constitutional rights, and the strong millenarian impulse behind many Jansenist condemnations of the corruption of existing institutions contributed to enthusiasm for reforms.

THE FRENCH ENLIGHTENMENT

The Jansenist movement had a broad base of popular support, but by the middle of the century, educated elites were beginning to turn away from religious concerns altogether. The middle of the eighteenth century was the high point of the intellectual movement known as the Enlightenment. The philosophical bases of this challenge to all authority higher than human reason and experience had been set out by a number of European thinkers at the end of the seventeenth century,—such as the French Huguenot exile Pierre Bayle, whose widely circulated *Dictionary* highlighted contradictions in the Bible. In many European countries, such "enlightened" ideas, in watered-down form, penetrated the governing elites without causing great upheavals. In France, however, the intertwined structure of a Catholic church particularly wary of ideological subversion and a royal government wedded to a rigid defense of its theoretically absolute authority made these new ideas unusually controversial. More than elsewhere, the French proponents of the Enlightenment, the self-styled *philosophes*, portrayed themselves as critics of an established order resistant to change.

By 1750, France's major thinkers were strongly identified with the Enlightenment movement. The publications of the best-known of the *philosophes*, Voltaire, showed the full range of their interests. Like the other *philosophes*, he saw the movement as a continuation and extension of the scientific revolution of the seventeenth century. One of his most widely read books was a popularization of Isaac Newton's work. Voltaire was best known as a playwright, poet, and pamphleteer whose literary works always carried a clear-cut social or political message. *Mahomet*, for example, used the story of Islam's founder as a vehicle for an attack on religious intolerance. Voltaire's short novels, the works that appeal most to twentieth-century readers, also dealt with burning philosophical issues of the day. *Candide* ridiculed the teachings of the church, even if it offered no very clear philosophy to replace them, and *L 'Ingénu* used the time-honored device of a noble savage to critique many features of French society.

If Voltaire was the best known of the eighteenth-century French *philosophes*, he was certainly not the only one. The Baron de Montesquieu enjoyed equal prestige. In a youthful work, the *Persian Letters*, published just after the end of Louis XIV's reign, he drew a caustic portrait of France's absolutist monarchy. His masterwork, *The Spirit of the Laws*, published in 1749, had even greater impact. In it, he brought the rational and dispassionate scientific approach to bear on political issues, analyzing the characteristics of the different forms of government and the social preconditions for their development. Voltaire had already contrasted England's intellectual and religious freedom to the situation in France; Montesquieu's eloquent description of the virtues of England's constitutional monarchy, with its balance of powers among the king, the Lords, and the Commons, had a profound impact in France, as did his suggestion that some French institutions—notably the sovereign law courts or *parlements*—could and should play a similar role in restraining monarchical power.

By the middle of the century, the ideas incorporated in the writings of Voltaire and Montesquieu had impregnated a generation of lesser writers. Self-proclaimed disciples of Enlightenment dominated France's cultural life; they formed the milieu of the contributors to the collective project that most completely reflected the spirit of the age, the massive *Encyclopedia* edited by Denis Diderot, whose first volume appeared in 1751. The *Encyclopedia* was intended to sum up and popularize the thought of the Enlightenment and to apply the methods of science and reason to every area of human knowledge. Its heavy emphasis on practical subjects, such as manufacturing processes, indicated its authors' conviction that human happiness depended on secular activities, not spiritual ones. Carefully worded articles on philosophy and theology tried to poke holes in traditional beliefs without bringing down the censors' wrath, while the essays on political subjects gingerly suggested that royal authority needed to be tempered by constitutional limits. The fate of the *Encyclopedia* summed up the difficult relationship between the Enlightenment and France's established institutions. Officially banned for offending religious dogmas, the project had too much support among royal officials to be suppressed altogether; Diderot's volumes were finally allowed to circulate with false title pages indicating that they had been printed abroad.

During the 1760s, the *philosophes* gradually infiltrated the institutions of official culture, particularly the prestigious royally sponsored *Académie française*. The influence of the *philosophes* also spread through the institution of the salon. At these informal but regular meetings in private homes, writers, artists, musicians, and scientists mingled with well-to-do members of the aristocracy and upper bourgeoisie. Many salons were hosted by women, who were able to participate in this way in the prestige of intellectual and artistic activity although they were excluded from the *académies* and most other aspects of intellectual life. Parisian salons played an important role in shaping literary and artistic taste. Through them, the elites of the mind and of society were brought together. In the last decades of the Old Regime, the supporters of the Enlightenment had thus become members of an intellectual "establishment," promoting each

other to comfortable jobs. Their writings remained critical of many aspects of French society, but they had become social insiders, occupying comfortable positions within the structure they were seeking to reform.

The growing influence of the *philosophes* earned them not only followers but also opponents. The groups and institutions that Voltaire and Montesquieu had targeted had their defenders. Catholic writers responded to the Enlightenment campaign against the church, but this traditionalist defense of revealed religious truth had lost much of its force of conviction in the face of the rationalist assault.

The greatest threat to the *philosophes'* intellectual hegemony came not from the church or the proponents of the status quo but from within their own ranks. Enlightenment thought was based on the exaltation of reason as the highest of human faculties. The Catholic and conservative critics had taken the traditional religious viewpoint of human reason as weak and unreliable and had therefore urged respect for authority. Jean-Jacques Rousseau, a writer who had originally shared many of the other *philosophes'* convictions, provided a more persuasive critique of Enlightenment rationalism. As he developed his own ideas, Rousseau became increasingly convinced that the rational society his *philosophe* friends hoped to create would not bring about human happiness.

Rousseau: Nature over Reason

Rousseau signaled his break with faith in progress in his controversial *Essay on the Sciences and the Arts*, published in 1751, in which he argued that "civilized" man was becoming ever further removed from his true nature. In his subsequent works, especially his two best-selling novels, *La Nouvelle Héloïse* (1759) and *Emile* (1762), Rousseau glorified feelings and emotions rather than reason as the best guides to living. He sided with the *philosophes* in rejecting the authority of external institutions. One of the most controversial portions of *Emile* was a chapter entitled "The Confession of Faith of a Savoyard Vicar," in which a country priest put forward an argument for a purely natural religion of the heart. But Rousseau broke with the *philosophes* by downgrading reason and emphasizing sentiment.

Rousseau's rejection of Enlightenment rationalism, together with the bitter personal rift that separated him from his former friends among the *philosophes* after 1758, marked a shift in the French intellectual climate. The *philosophes* had made themselves at home in the upper reaches of French society; Rousseau presented himself as an outcast, more at ease with the common people. He sought no sinecures and lived a modest life. Far from making him a marginal figure, this rejection of the intellectual establishment made him the center of a widespread cult. Women especially responded to the sentimental element in his works and to his claim to have embodied virtue in his own life. Rousseau's popularity with women readers is surprising, because he often argued that women distracted men from the serious virtues needed in public life. In his view, women's proper role was to raise children and take care of their homes; he railed against "unnatural" women who became actresses or otherwise interacted publicly with men. Nevertheless, Rousseau became a rallying point for all those who found both French institutions and Enlightenment culture too artificial and too elitist. He was the herald of a society that would be simpler and more natural.

In the same year that he published *Emile*, Rousseau also set forth his ideas about politics in a book entitled *The Social Contract*. Not widely read until after the French Revolution of 1789, Rousseau's work was nevertheless the most important analysis of the origins of political authority written in the eighteenth century. Unlike Montesquieu's

empirical inquiry into the workings of existing institutions, Rousseau's book sought to analyze the prerequisites for a legitimate political system. He argued that all men had equal rights and that the citizens' consent was the only just base for governmental authority; this democratic ideology undercut all existing institutions. At the same time, however, Rousseau envisioned a utopia in which all members would put aside their private interests for the common good; those who refused to do so would be excluded from the community. Rousseau himself was cautious about the practical implications of his own political ideas; he doubted the possibility of a successful effort to remodel Europe's societies, corrupted by centuries of bad institutions. Once the French Revolution began, however, his caution was forgotten and his ideas were cited both to justify the creation of a more egalitarian society and to defend repressive measures against those who opposed the new government.

THE EIGHTEENTH-CENTURY PUBLIC

It is difficult to measure how widely either Enlightenment values or Rousseau's preromanticism penetrated the bulk of French society. It is certainly true that the French population was becoming increasingly literate. The Maggiolo survey, a pioneering study carried out in the late nineteenth century, showed that the percentage of men sufficiently educated to sign their names to their parish's marriage register rose from 29 percent in 1686–1690 to 47 percent for 1786–1790, whereas the figures for women climbed from 14 percent to 27 percent. Writers and publishers made strenuous efforts to serve this growing market. The number of newspapers and magazines published in France, only nineteen in the decade of the 1740s, rose to seventy-three in the 1780s, and the number of books published also increased greatly. Books and magazines remained fairly expensive and therefore out of the reach of most of the lower classes, but the multiplication of reading rooms gave some people who could not afford to purchase their own books access to a wide variety of reading material at a modest price. An increasing number of theaters and concert halls brought a broader cultural diet to the populations of France's cities.

A growing network of cultural institutions also favored the circulation of new ideas. Throughout the first half of the eighteenth century, *académies* modeled after the institutions set up in Paris during the previous century were established in the major cities of the provinces. Like their more prestigious Parisian counterparts, they recruited a mixed membership of aristocrats, clergy, and wealthy members of the bourgeoisie. They sponsored public sessions at which an elite audience listened to reports about research into local history and natural phenomena and applauded the best efforts of local poets and dramatists.

More widespread than the provincial *académies* were the Masonic lodges that spread throughout France after 1750. Freemasonry was introduced into France from England in the 1720s. The Masonic lodges brought together members of all classes who shared a common devotion to virtue and fraternity. The secrecy of their proceedings was an additional lure for potential members. Eighteenth-century French lodges seem to have spent most of their time enacting elaborate rituals whose symbolic significance was clear only to initiates, listening to edifying speeches, and enjoying lavish banquets; the myth that the Masons were controlled by a clique determined to propagate subversive ideas and bring about the overthrow of the monarchy has no factual basis. But the lodges were receptive to Enlightenment ideas about religious toleration and, as participatory organizations whose members were supposed to treat each other without

regard to their social status, they fostered ideas about representative government and social equality that were at odds with the official values of the Old Regime. By the 1780s, the Masonic movement counted more than thirty-five thousand adherents in France.

The growing reading public and the network of groups of various kinds that met to discuss ideas conveyed in books and periodicals provided the social basis for the rise of a new phenomenon in French society, the force of public opinion. The concept of a "public opinion" based on the exchange of views among private individuals was a new one in the eighteenth century; the term only became common around 1750. The "public" whose opinion increasingly replaced God and the king as the source of authority in eighteenth-century discussions contrasted sharply with all the clearly identifiable social groupings in eighteenth-century France. Membership in the public was open to anyone with a modicum of wealth, leisure, and education, and members of the public were all equal. These private individuals whose collective judgment became the standard of authority claimed no overt political role, but it was inevitable that they would comment on governmental actions as well as on books, plays, and works of art. "Ministers have become the most carefully observed actors on the stage of the great world, and their performance is the most severely judged," the former controller-general Jacques Necker observed in 1785.[1] He and other leading political figures increasingly saw the need to have the intangible force of public opinion on their side if they were to govern effectively.

Although the importance of the public was increasingly acknowledged as the century wore on, its composition remained a matter of dispute. The public, with access to the printed writings of the *philosophes* and of Rousseau, was not identical with the people, the mass of the population. Lacking education and information, the common people could not participate in the process of public discussion that constituted public opinion. Exactly where the social frontier that divided "public" from "people" lay was uncertain, but educated French men and women were certain that the culture they participated in was not that of the mass of the peasantry and the urban lower classes.

Popular Culture

The culture of the ordinary people remained largely oral. There was some printed literature aimed at this audience, but it was far removed from the texts that circulated among the educated. The small, cheap, badly printed paper-bound volumes of the *Bibliothèque bleue*, so named because these books for the poor usually had a blue paper cover, were the basis of popular print culture. They included simplified versions of old folk tales, religious tracts, simple how-to books in a variety of fields, and almanacs that forecast the weather, provided a short summary of the great events of the year just past, and offered practical advice to peasant farmers. Over the course of the century, the titles of the *Bibliothèque bleue* did show some modest evolution: the proportion of traditional works of piety declined somewhat, while the number of practical utilitarian titles rose. But the overall pattern was one of stability, and there was little sign of overt influence from the Enlightenment or other intellectual currents of the time.

Compared to the culture of France's elites, popular culture remained more influenced by religion and by traditions that the upper classes were quick to dismiss as "superstitions." Ironically, church authorities and antireligious Enlightenment writers sometimes found themselves united in condemning popular beliefs, such as the widespread conviction among peasants that the ringing of church bells could ward off destructive hailstorms, a practice officially rejected by the clergy on the grounds that it implied a human ability to control God's

will. Peasants clung to their beliefs, however, because they provided some sense of control over the dangerous forces of nature. For similar reasons, they often preferred folk healers who prescribed herbs and spells over educated doctors who confessed themselves helpless in the face of most diseases.

It would be misleading to categorize the beliefs of the common people in the eighteenth century as irrational or benighted. They reflected a very different world of experience from the culture of France's educated urban elites. The two worlds were not completely separated, however. For all their sophistication, even France's most privileged inhabitants still lived in a world of uncontrollable natural forces: learned doctors were just as unable to save Louis XV from a fatal case of smallpox in 1774 as they were to treat the maladies of the poor. Both rich and poor enjoyed the rough-and-tumble performances in Paris's boulevard theaters. Broadsheets and newspaper reports about the "beast of Gévaudan," a huge wolf blamed for a number of bloody attacks in a remote region of southern France during the 1760s, terrified all sectors of the population and made the animal—as one modern French historian has said—one of the country's first national celebrities. Conversely, the poor were not totally immune to the currents of "enlightened" thought. A massive quantitative study of the religious attitudes expressed in wills drawn up in the southeastern region of Provence over the course of the eighteenth century has shown a clear drop in legacies left for strictly religious purposes among members of the lower classes as well as the elites. Even artisans and peasants in some regions were thus abandoning traditional religious practices in the decades before the Revolution.

Note

1. Jacques Necker, *De l'administration des finances de la France* (N.p., 1785), 1:6.

CHAPTER 5

A GOVERNMENT UNDER CHALLENGE

At the beginning of the 1700s, France's system of absolute monarchy had been a model for much of Europe. By the last decades of the century, it had become unacceptable to most of the French population. Changes in society and culture contributed to the undermining of the absolutist system, but so did the succession of political crises that began around 1750. These confrontations, often dismissed as the irrelevant thrashings about of a doomed system, were in fact the signs of the first efforts to create political institutions adapted to the modern, secular world, and their outcome strongly influenced the direction of French life during and after the Revolution.

THE ABSOLUTIST SYSTEM AND ITS WEAKNESSES

The structure of the French government in 1750 was complex and difficult to describe. Parts of it had begun to resemble a modern bureaucracy, organized around a common center; indeed, the word *bureaucratie*, meaning a government run by clerks who tied up every decision in unnecessary paperwork, appeared for the first time in France in the 1780s. But this rational structure coexisted with a welter of other institutions that were rooted in France's long history and that frequently paralyzed the workings of the more centralized parts of the governing apparatus.

The most obvious fact about France's system of government in the eighteenth century was that it was monarchical. Like so many other aspects of the system, the monarchy was at once ancient and modern. France's eighteenth-century kings, descendants of the Bourbon family that had come to the throne with Henry IV in 1589, continued a tradition whose origins went back to the fifth century of the modern era. Succession to the throne was still regulated by the ancient Salic law, which barred women from inheriting the crown; the kings of France were still crowned and anointed according to medieval rites in the great Gothic cathedral of Reims.

But the eighteenth-century monarchy was far different from that of earlier epochs. In the Middle Ages, the king of France had been a feudal lord, whose vassals pledged him loyalty in return for the right to govern their own fiefs or domains. The kings of the Renaissance and especially those of the seventeenth century had transformed the monarchy into something very different: a so-called absolute monarchy, in which the king claimed to hold full sovereign powers over all his subjects and in which he was no longer bound by the reciprocal obligations of feudal society. The absolute monarch claimed to wield all the powers of the state. Unlike the king of England, who needed the approval of Parliament to enact laws and collect taxes, the French king did not share his legislative power with any other institution. He commanded the army and navy and the entire machinery of governmental administration, and he was also the supreme judge, to whom verdicts in any other court could be appealed.

The process by which the absolutist monarchical state had been built up culminated in the long reign of Louis XIV. Louis XIV succeeded to the throne in 1643 at the age of five, and personally ran the government from the death of his advisor, Cardinal Mazarin, in 1661 until his own death in 1715. This determined and hard-working ruler came close to making government practice correspond to absolutist theory, as it had been articulated by earlier politicians such as the great minister of the early seventeenth century, Cardinal Richelieu. He tamed the independent-minded nobility, integrating them into his system of government and encouraging ambitious aristocrats to spend their time bidding for favors at his court rather than asserting their independence in the provinces. Harsh repression ended the long series of seventeenth-century peasant revolts after 1675, and the revocation of the Edict of Nantes in 1685 deprived the troublesome Protestant minority in the kingdom of its special privileges. Louis XIV ended the tradition of reliance on a single powerful minister: his ministers, although they were often talented men, were definitely his subordinates. Through them, he controlled a more efficient governing machine than his predecessors. Louis XIV could truthfully have said—although he probably didn't—the words often attributed to him: "L'état, c'est moi (I am the state)."

The "Sun King" not only consolidated all political power in his own hands; he also involved the monarchy in almost every area of French life. Through his power to appoint bishops and the heads of monasteries and convents, he controlled the church and the kingdom's religious life; as Europe's most powerful Catholic monarch, he was even able to influence the policies of the papacy. The name of Louis XIV's finance minister, Jean-Baptiste Colbert, came to stand for a policy of active government involvement in economic affairs. Colbert tried to promote French domestic industries and diminish the kingdom's reliance on imports; he organized companies of merchants in a largely unsuccessful effort to promote overseas trade. A complex system of regulation, meant to maintain quality and prevent cutthroat competition, restricted entrepreneurial initiative. The Colbertist tradition of close government involvement in economic affairs left a permanent mark on French life. So did the tradition of governmental involvement in cultural and intellectual life, which also reached a high point under Louis XIV. Cardinal Richelieu had created the *Académie française* in 1635. Its forty members, supposedly the greatest writers in the country, received royal pensions and in return were expected to produce works glorifying the monarchy and to regulate the proper use of the French language. In the 1660s, Louis XIV added new *académies* devoted to history and to the natural sciences, so that the king both supported and controlled almost every aspect of French intellectual life. Theater, opera, ballet, and music all gravitated to the court, the main source of patronage.

The keystone of Louis XIV's governing system was the appointment of a royal representative, the *intendant*, to oversee the administration of each province. The *intendants*, who served at the king's pleasure, gave the monarch real authority over his realm, unlike the noble *gouverneurs* of earlier times, who could not be removed from office and frequently refused to carry out the king's orders. But the *gouverneurs* remained in existence, although without real functions, until the coming of the Revolution. Louis XIV's hesitancy to abolish such offices reflected his instinctive conservatism: he did not abolish older institutions, but simply created new ones alongside them.

It was not only respect for tradition that made it hard for French rulers to simplify the structure of their government. They were also trapped by the fact that most government positions were actually owned by the families whose members occupied them, a system known as "venality of offices." Kings resorted to this system because the sale of offices brought them revenue, and the purchasers were supposedly responsible for carrying out at their own expense functions that would otherwise have had to be done by paid officials. But the owners of an office were largely independent of the king and his ministers: they could not be dismissed or disciplined for failing to perform their functions. A long tradition of respect for the rights of property prohibited the king from abolishing venal offices unless he reimbursed their holders. The system of venal office holding thus limited the king's control of his own government.

Despite this obstacle, Louis XIV succeeded in making the French monarchy reasonably effective. But his success depended on his unique combination of personal energy and force of will; he drove himself to the brink of exhaustion overseeing every detail of the running of the government and keeping his officials in line. His eighteenth-century successors—Louis XV, who reigned from 1715–1774, and Louis XVI, ruler from 1774 until the Revolution abolished the monarchy in 1792—lacked their ancestor's enthusiasm for the "profession of king." Under their rule, two main shortcomings of France's supposedly absolutist monarchy became glaringly obvious. These were the monarchy's inability to reform and control its own bureaucracy and its inability to prevent local and provincial institutions from opposing its policies.

The weakness of France's royal bureaucracy was most evident in the area of tax collection. Rather than employing officials appointed by and responsible to the king to collect its revenues, the monarchy sold the right to collect taxes in different regions to private entrepreneurs, often nobles who turned the actual work over to lesser employees. These tax farmers had every incentive to collect as much money as possible from the king's subjects, but to forward as little as possible to Versailles. Throughout the eighteenth century, successive finance ministers recognized the structural weaknesses of the tax collection system, but they were unable to make major changes in it. The tax farmers jealously guarded the rights they had purchased from the government, and the crown lacked the resources to do without them. As a result, the royal government was chronically short of money and had to rely on borrowing to cover its needs. Even as the kingdom's economy grew, the monarchy fell ever more heavily into debt.

One reason France's eighteenth-century ministers could not discipline the tax collectors and other subordinates effectively was because they faced strong opposition from political institutions that had never been entirely subordinated to the crown. Louis XIV had successfully intimidated these groups by the force of his personality, but they reasserted themselves under his successors. In a number of areas, such as Brittany and Languedoc, provincial Estates continued to meet periodically, bargaining with the royal government about taxes and jealously guarding their region's traditional laws and privileges against centralizing reform. The Catholic church, immune to taxation and reinforced by a governing system of its own, enjoyed considerable autonomy from royal commands. Most importantly, the king's own law courts—especially the thirteen *parlements* which served as appeals courts for France's different provinces, and

Traditional symbols dominate this illustration of Louis XVI's coronation in 1775. The king takes his crown from a saint holding the cross, indicating the divine origin of his powers, while angels behind him carry banners and emblems associated with the French monarchy since the Middle Ages. This engraving gives no hint of the challenges to the church and established institutions that were to lead to the French Revolution a few years later.

(Source: Bibliothèque nationale, Paris.)

several other specialized courts which dealt with taxes and finances—formed a permanent obstacle to absolutist rule. The judges, wealthy nobles whose offices were their own property, asserted their right not only to rule on individual cases but to scrutinize the king's edicts and the actions of his officials to ensure that they conformed to the law. Through their right of sending the king remonstrances or objections, they could suspend the enforcement of new laws.

By the middle of the eighteenth century, the pretensions of the *parlements* had become the central issue in French politics. The judges of the *parlements*, often sympathetic to the Jansenists, argued that their ability to restrain the actions of the king's officials was critical if France was to be a monarchy based on laws, rather than an arbitrary despotism. The greatest French political thinker of the eighteenth century, Montesquieu, was himself a judge in the *Parlement* of Bordeaux; his masterwork, *The Spirit of the Laws*, identified those courts as crucial "intermediate bodies" between the absolute king and his individual subjects, whose existence safeguarded liberty. In a series of confrontations with the crown from 1750 onward, the *parlements* and their defenders argued that the judges were the natural defenders of the rights of the king's subjects, and they familiarized those subjects with ideas of the rule of law and the need for representative government. As long as the *parlements* remained untamed, France's supposedly absolutist system of government was in fact limited by a very real division of powers.

THE BREAKDOWN OF ABSOLUTISM, 1750–1774

The shortcomings of France's disorganized monarchical system became increasingly apparent in the decades after 1750, as the challenges facing the government became more acute. Major wars—the War of the Austrian Succession from 1740–1748 and the Seven Years' War of 1756–1763—forced the ministers to raise more money. Economic distress and religious quarrels added to their difficulties. These pressures made it clear to all concerned that France's political institutions were in need of reform. The pattern of government inherited from the past satisfied no one. The king's ministers found themselves hamstrung at every turn by the inefficient workings of a system based on venal officeholders and restricted by the privileges of the country's innumerable corporate groups. *Parlement* magistrates, lesser officeholders, and ordinary subjects, on the other hand, perceived the government not as too weak but as too strong. In the absence of any representative institutions through which the king's subjects could participate in law-making, government policy was set by the monarch's small group of advisors, made up of the ministers and the king's favorites. Those outside this charmed circle had no institutionalized way to make sure their interests were protected. To all those outside the inner circles of government, the monarchy seemed perpetually in danger of degenerating into what the polemicists of the period labeled a "ministerial despotism," in which a few royally appointed officials would wield all the power.

French politics in the period from 1750–1789 was dominated by a series of controversies generated by successive ministers' efforts to make the government more effective and by determined resistance from opponents who feared that an effective royal government would be a tyrannical one. These controversies failed to produce any major change in the governing system, but they did have a very important result: they gave the king's subjects an education in politics. Partisans and opponents of reform both used a variety of media to appeal to the new public that had matured by mid-century; increasingly, they propagated the idea that the public's approval should be the basis of political authority. Rather than being universally accepted as part of the natural order of things, France's institutions were seen by 1789 as highly questionable. Few educated French men and women at the end of the eighteenth century still saw the king as a sacred figure, or the institutions of the monarchy as inherently legitimate.

Among the issues that led to constitutional disputes after 1750, the most straightforward was the question of taxation. The issue became pressing at the end of the War of the Austrian Succession in 1748. Faced with debts accumulated during the war, Machault d'Arnouville, the controller-general (the minister responsible for royal finances), sought to introduce a new tax. The *vingtième* was to be levied on all owners of property, regardless of their social status. This was an attack on the system of privilege on which French society was based, and Machault's plan generated strong resistance. The outbreak of the Seven Years' War in 1756 allowed the government to impose some new taxes but, after it ended, difficulties arose again. During the 1760s, Louis XV's ministers shifted their strategy to one of reforming the French economy, hoping that general prosperity would generate more revenue for the government. In 1763 and 1764, a set of edicts abolished traditional controls on the grain trade, the most important branch of French commerce. Influenced by the ideas of the Physiocrats, a group of economic theorists who advocated less regulation and more reliance on market forces, the ministry took the risk of letting grain and bread prices rise to encourage landowners to invest in increased production. The members of the *parlements* (themselves often large landowners) did not initially resist these measures, but when grain prices began to rise sharply in the second half of the 1760s as a result of several years of bad harvests, the judges began to oppose royal policy—casting themselves as defenders of the poor and denouncing a ministerial "famine plot" to profit from the public's misery.

Struggle over Religious Issues

By this time, the government and the *parlements* were also in conflict over a second set of equally explosive issues growing out the Jansenist quarrel. In 1750, the archbishop of Paris, Christophe de Beaumont, began an unprecedentedly harsh campaign to stamp out the Jansenists by denying them church sacraments unless they renounced their beliefs. Jansenist sympathizers immediately appealed the archbishop's directives to the *Parlement* of Paris, which saw an excellent opportunity to assert its right to intervene in church-state matters.

This "refusal of sacraments" controversy dragged on for several years and led to a steady radicalization on both sides. The advocates of the *parlements* used the conflict as an opportunity to claim that the judges were the true defenders of French liberty, and that the different *parlements* scattered around the country were in fact one body, representing the French nation. Propagandists loyal to the king's ministers responded that acceptance of *parlements*' claims would amount to converting France into a republic of judges. Louis XV attempted to end the controversy by decreeing a compromise and ordering all parties to observe an "edict of silence" which forbade further discussion of the issues raised by the dispute. But repeatedly the argument about *parlements*' powers flared up again. When an unemployed domestic servant named Robert Damiens stabbed the king in 1757, each side claimed that he had been inspired by the others' religious doctrines.

The issue of whether the *parlements* had a right to challenge royal policies affecting the church heated up again in 1762, when *parlements* began a concerted campaign against the Jesuit order. The Jesuits, the Jansenists' most determined opponents, were a secretive organization, international in scope and sworn to loyalty to the pope. This conflicted with the long-standing French tradition of Gallicanism, the doctrine which required that the French Catholic church demonstrate its subservience to the authority of the king. The *parlements* were able to demand a ban on the Jansenists' Jesuit opponents in the name of upholding royal authority; the king and his ministers, needing *parlement* cooperation to pay for the Seven Years' War, were unable to resist. In 1764, Louis XV signed an edict expelling the Jesuit order from France. The power and prestige of the *parlements* naturally increased.

Other Clashes with the Parlements

Parlement and ministerial authority soon clashed again. As a result of their earlier conflicts, the *parlement* of Brittany had become embroiled with the royal governor of the province, the Duc d'Aiguillon. The *parlement* judges brought charges against him for abusing his authority and threatened to stage a trial that had every prospect of resulting in an order for the punishment of a high royal official. The government, aware that a similar process had set in motion the Puritan revolution in England a century earlier, was determined to block the proceedings. In June 1770, Louis XV issued an edict quashing d'Aiguillon's trial and declaring him absolved of all charges. The judges were, of course, outraged, and they inundated the country with denunciations of the king's arbitrary action. In this situation, Louis XV finally listened to advisors who had been telling him that royal authority could only be maintained by a showdown with the *parlements*. The leading figure advocating this policy was Chancellor René Maupeou who, as minister of justice, had direct responsibility for dealing with *parlements*. In December 1770, Maupeou staged a "coup" against them, issuing edicts drastically curtailing their privileges and warning that any judge who protested would be deprived of his post. The majority of *parlement* judges refused to accept the Maupeou decrees. Maupeou consequently declared them dismissed

from their jobs and appointed new men to replace them; the protesting judges were exiled to remote districts in the provinces.

Maupeou's crackdown on the *parlements* was the final test of the traditional French monarchy's ability to impose its authority by force. Its results were inconclusive. Maupeou succeeded in setting up his new courts, but the supporters of the ousted judges mounted a massive propaganda campaign against him. By 1774, when Louis XV died unexpectedly and Maupeou's whole policy was thrown into question, the new courts had still not overcome the widespread distrust that the circumstances of their appointment had inspired. By then it was clear, however, that Maupeou and his supporters in the ministry had not used the opportunity they had created by taming the *parlements* to deal with the French monarchy's underlying structural problems. Two and a half decades of confrontation between the ministry and *parlements* had served primarily to suggest that—on fundamental issues—France's political system was stalemated, incapable of coping with pressing crises. The politics of the period exhibited many features that have characterized French national life ever since, particularly the tendency for confrontations to take on a dramatic ideological tone and for all parties to reject any idea of compromise. The final two and a half decades of Louis XV's reign were thus a crucial period in the formation of modern France's political culture.

THE REIGN OF LOUIS XVI, 1774–1787

For a few years after the death of Louis XV, the temperature of French politics seemed to cool down. The old king's young and inexperienced grandson, Louis XVI, had been impressed by the unpopularity of measures against the *parlements*. Within a few months, the new monarch's advisors had persuaded him to dismiss Maupeou and his allies, and to recall the judges of the old *parlements* who had been exiled in 1771. Somewhat chastened by their experience, the judges were less combative than they had been in the late 1760s, but the lesson to the monarchy was nevertheless clear. Royal ministers could not expect to carry out measures that involved a fundamental restructuring of France's governmental system.

Turgot and Necker

Even though Louis XVI had begun his reign by retreating from his predecessor's major reform initiative, his ministers were still aware of the government's weaknesses. But for the next decade, Maupeou's successors tried to effect reforms without risking a direct confrontation with the *parlements*. Among Louis XVI's first ministers, the leading figure was Jacques Turgot, an experienced administrator whose ideas were close to those of the Physiocrats. Turgot was determined to revive the liberal economic program first enacted in the early 1760s. In 1775, he once again abolished the restrictions on the grain trade, and in early 1776 he issued a set of edicts intended to clear the way for the transformation of France's entire economy. The most important of these was a law abolishing all the traditional guilds and economic corporations. Had it succeeded, the French economy would have been organized on the basis of virtually unregulated free enterprise. Turgot and his supporters hoped that this would encourage entrepreneurial initiative, promote economic growth, and ultimately enrich the government's coffers.

Like his predecessors, however, Turgot soon found that the monarchical machine could not be relied upon to carry out controversial reforms. The *Parlement* of Paris once again provided a mouthpiece for the privileged groups who opposed the abolition of the guilds and Turgot's other innovations. The liberalization of the grain trade had never been popular with the lower classes in the

cities who had to buy their bread, and they had responded to Turgot's measures with rioting in the "grain war" of May 1775. It was the most serious wave of popular protest in the decades before the Revolution of 1789. By June of 1776, the coalition of resistance to Turgot had become so powerful that Louis XVI decided to dismiss him. Another serious effort at reform under governmental sponsorship, this one explicitly justified in the rationalist and secular language of the French Enlightenment, had been abandoned.

A similar fate awaited Turgot's successor, Jacques Necker. His appointment as controller-general in 1777 was in itself something of an innovation: Necker, a successful banker and a Protestant, was the first commoner to hold such an elevated post. As controller-general, he sought to carry out a variety of piecemeal reforms to reduce expenses, make tax collection more efficient, and decentralize authority by creating provincial assemblies with limited powers in several French provinces. In 1781, he caused a sensation by publishing for the first time a summary of the French government's revenue and expenses, thereby inviting the public to participate in the debate on France's finances. But even these modest efforts involved conflicts with powerful interests, such as the officeholders whose lucrative positions Necker wanted to abolish. In May 1781, he too lost his ministerial post, and the reforms he had tried to introduce were repealed, like those of Maupeou and Turgot.

The institutional reforms attempted by Maupeou, Turgot, and Necker show that the top officials of France's royal government were acutely aware of the system's many weaknesses long before the crisis of 1789. Down to the present day, historians have continued to debate the merits of their different approaches: Maupeou's vigorous authoritarianism, Turgot's sweeping rationalism, and Necker's cautious gradualism. The failure of all three approaches suggests, however, that the absolute monarchy ultimately lacked the resources to reform itself. Its many internal conflicts, coupled with the lack of any real mechanism for associating an increasingly vocal public with the reform process, made it exceedingly difficult to obtain a consensus for real change. Yet the imperatives of France's role in the European state system made reform ever more necessary.

FRANCE AND THE EUROPEAN STATE SYSTEM

Ironically, it was a major foreign policy success in the early years of Louis XVI's reign that pushed the French monarchy into its final crisis. The rise of the French absolute monarchy in the 1600s had coincided with France's rise to the status of the leading power in continental Europe. Glorious success in warfare and the acquisition of new territories had become part of what each French monarch was expected to achieve. In this, as in so many other ways, Louis XIV had left his successors a hard example to match. The many long conflicts of his reign—particularly the war of the League of Augsburg (1688–1697) and its continuation, the war of the Spanish Succession (1701–1713)—had been bitter, costly conflicts in which French armies suffered many reverses. But in both wars it had taken a coalition of almost all other European powers to equal France's might. At their close, Louis XIV had established France's border firmly on the Rhine through the annexation of the crucial province of Alsace, and gained new territory along France's northern and southern frontiers. During Louis XIV's reign, France had become increasingly active in the pursuit of territories and influence in the non-European world as well. In place of Spain and the Netherlands, France became England's main rival for trade and influence in North America, the Caribbean, and India.

For a generation after the great wars of Louis XIV's reign, Europe enjoyed relative peace. The cautious Cardinal Fleury, Louis XV's principal minister until his death in 1743, avoided risky conflicts. Shortly before Fleury died in 1743, Prussian king Frederic II, "the Great," inaugurated a new series of wars with his attack on Austria in 1740. The resulting war of the Austrian Succession followed the pattern of Louis XIV's wars: France, allied with Prussia, fought against Austria and England. At its conclusion, in 1748, the major issues between France and England, particularly the question of who would dominate North America, remained unsettled. On the continent, France's Prussian ally made a major gain, acquiring the valuable province of Silesia, while Louis XV's government obtained nothing comparable. Deprived of Fleury's capable guidance, Louis XV took a more active but not necessarily well-thought-out role in shaping French foreign policy. With renewed conflict with England virtually inevitable, the stage was set for diplomatic confusion and for a startling reversal of alliances.

France Versus England in North America and the Caribbean

In 1754, a series of incidents in North America ignited a new round of Anglo-French fighting, known in the United States as the French and Indian War. Britain cast about for potential continental allies; Prussia, fearful of an Austrian effort to recapture Silesia, was more forthcoming than Austria. Once Britain and Prussia had concluded a treaty, Austria and France, traditional enemies, were driven together. Their formal alliance, signed on May 1, 1756, completed the "diplomatic revolution" that reversed three-quarters of a century of European power politics. Unfortunately for the architects of France's new policy, the Seven Years' War that began with Prussia's preemptive invasion of Saxony in August 1756 quickly turned into a costly disaster.

French forces had to fight the British on the seas, in distant North America, and on the Indian subcontinent and, at the same time, meet Frederic the Great's armies in Germany. Frederic, the greatest military commander of his day, inflicted a painful defeat on the French at Rossbach in 1757. In North America, the British captured all of French Canada in 1760, and their naval forces seized key French colonies in the Caribbean. The British also gained control of the French possessions in India. Whereas wars had traditionally been regarded as the king's private affairs, the French government tried to encourage patriotic enthusiasm for this conflict, thereby beginning a process that would lead to the bellicose nationalism of the revolutionary era. But this effort was only partly successful. The *philosophes,* many of them admirers of Prussia's Frederic the Great, openly favored France's enemies, and many army officers were unhappy about fighting in alliance with their traditional Austrian enemies. The Seven Years' War was also the costliest conflict France had engaged in for half a century. The need to raise new taxes to pay for loans needed to fight it was one of the main causes of the French monarchy's desperate financial crisis in the last decades of the Old Regime.

The Treaty of Paris, signed in February 1763, set the seal on a defeat that cost the French monarchy dearly in money and prestige. France regained the vital sugar islands of Guadeloupe and Martinique, but only at the cost of abandoning all its territorial claims in Canada, North America, and India to the British. As a result of this treaty, the French province of Québec came under British rule. Ironically, Québec, the largest overseas settlement founded by French immigrants and even today a bastion of French language and culture, has had no political ties with France since 1760. Louis XV's energetic foreign minister, the Duc de Choiseul (who had guided policy since 1758), set in motion military reforms that eventually benefited the armies of the revolutionary period,

but he lost his post in 1770 before the opportunity to take revenge on the British arose. With its government preoccupied with the domestic repercussions of the Maupeou "coup" after 1770, France stood by while Prussia, Austria, and Russia carved out gains for themselves in the First Partition of Poland (1772–1774). Since Poland had traditionally been one of France's allies, this was another blow to France's standing among the Great Powers.

Louis XVI, the young monarch who succeeded to the throne in 1774, had neither the thirst for glory that had driven his ancestor, Louis XIV, nor the appetite for diplomatic intrigue of his immediate predecessor. The foreign minister he appointed, the Count de Vergennes, was a cautious career diplomat who had no far-reaching plans to increase France's power. But in 1776, when Britain became embroiled in a fight with its rebellious colonists in North America, Vergennes decided that the opportunity to pay the British back for their successes in the Seven Years' War was too good to resist. By 1778, France was once again at war with its traditional enemy. Through this decision, made in accordance with the monarchy's customary foreign policy, Vergennes—one of the most conservative of Old Regime officials—helped bring about two revolutions, the American and the French.

This time, the conflict did not spread to the European continent. The French were able to concentrate on a naval campaign against Britain, supplemented by the dispatch of a small expeditionary force to aid the American rebels. This French aid may not have been decisive, but it was certainly of great value to the American cause. French Admiral de Grasse's ships were crucial in cutting off General Cornwallis's forces and compelling their surrender to the American army at Yorktown in 1781. But the peace treaty that ended the war in 1783 gave France little more than prestige; hopes that the newly independent Americans would become a major market for French goods were soon dashed. Meanwhile, the war—which the controller-general Necker had financed by extensive borrowing rather than risking controversial tax increases—had driven the French government further into debt. Britain, with its more robust economy and system of credit, quickly recovered from its defeat. The French monarchy's single foreign policy success during the final decades of the Old Regime thus produced no tangible benefits.

By the mid-1780s, the aged Vergennes had come to recognize that France's creaky domestic institutions were crippling its ability to sustain the role of great power. The French monarchy was so short of money that it had to stand by helplessly while its rivals Britain and Prussia intervened in the Dutch Republic. The conservative Vergennes thus became one of the main backers of Controller-General Calonne's renewed effort to reform the tax system, which set off the process leading to the French Revolution.

Some modern historians have concluded that the French monarchy thus fell victim to its own excessive ambitions abroad. The revolutionary and Napoleonic era would show that France actually had resources to sustain a far more extensive foreign policy, if these resources were used effectively. Before that was possible, however, barriers to domestic reform had to be broken down.

CHAPTER 6

COLLAPSE OF THE OLD MONARCHY

France in the mid-1780s presents the historian with a puzzle. With the benefit of hindsight, we know that the country was on the brink of a revolutionary crisis. But it is not so simple to decide which of the many strains and tensions in prerevolutionary French society led to this explosion. Demographic expansion and economic change had led to pressure on the land and a widening gap between rich and poor, but living conditions for most of the population were better by the 1780s than they had been at the death of Louis XIV in 1715. Bourgeois resentments against the special privileges of the nobles were strong, but at the same time, the scramble to acquire noble status continued unabated. New cultural and intellectual values that undermined faith in traditional institutions ranging from the church to the guilds had spread, even among some of the lower classes, but these had not led to any overtly revolutionary movement. Since 1750, France's political system had teetered from crisis to crisis, but it had survived more than three decades of such episodes without reaching the point of breakdown. What happened in 1789 was different, because the crisis that broke out that year brought all the social, cultural, economic, and political conflicts of eighteenth-century France to a head simultaneously.

If the long-term causes of the French Revolution remain difficult to disentangle, its immediate origins are easy to trace. In August 1786, the controller-general, Charles-Alexandre de Calonne, reported to Louis XVI that the royal government was on the brink of insolvency. The immediate problem was the need to repay loans floated to pay the cost of France's participation in the American War of Independence; the fiscal crisis was thus directly linked to the effort to maintain France's role as a world power. But Calonne now advised Louis XVI that "the only way to bring real order into the finances is to revitalize the entire state by reforming all that is defective in its constitution."[1] His predecessors' failures had convinced Calonne that he could not accomplish his aims through the normal institutions of the monarchy. And so he took the first step that was to lead to a revolution: he announced the convocation in January 1787 of an Assembly of Notables to discuss fundamental changes in the structure of French government.

By convening an assembly of leading noblemen, clergy, and high officials to examine his reform proposals, Calonne believed that he could enlist the force of public opinion in favor of his most important proposals and outflank the *parlements'* resistance to change. He wanted a new land tax to be levied on all property owners—nobles, clergy, and commoners—and the establishment of consultative assemblies in all of France's provinces. The land tax implied the breaking down of deep-rooted distinctions between social classes and corporate groups; the provincial assemblies suggested an abandonment of the fundamental principle of absolutism, that authority should flow from the top down. But the 142 delegates who arrived at Versailles in January 1787 reacted to Calonne's projects with suspicion, demanding a precise accounting of revenue and expenditures to demonstrate the necessity for new taxes.

By April 1787, it was clear that Calonne's gamble had failed. Louis XVI replaced him with one of his chief critics among the notables, the archbishop of Toulouse, Loménie de Brienne. Brienne sought to have the *parlements* approve modified versions of Calonne's proposals, but without success. Compromise with the *parlements* having failed, Brienne and his fellow ministers decided to adopt a policy of confrontation similar to Maupeou's "coup" of 1770. On May 8, 1788, they promulgated a set of edicts that abolished the *parlements*, replacing them with a single high court for the whole country. They accompanied this radical measure with other reforms designed to make the elimination of the *parlements* more palatable, such as the abolition of fees that litigants had to pay judges to have their cases heard. But these reforms did little to soften the shock of their actions, which revived the fear of an all-powerful despotism that had been raised earlier by Maupeou's measures.

From Failed Reforms to Revolutionary Crisis

Although the issues raised by the 1788 reforms were similar to those posed in 1770, the outcome of this crisis was very different.

Nearly two decades of unsuccessful reform efforts from above, and the unprecedented severity of the financial crisis, had dangerously eroded the government's standing. The successful creation of a republic based on popular sovereignty in the United States provided a thought-provoking new political model. Furthermore, the political crisis was compounded by other problems. For nearly two decades, the French economy had struggled. The government's attempt to stimulate trade through a treaty with England in 1786 had hurt many manufacturers. In the summer of 1788, a devastating hailstorm damaged grain crops in much of northern France, provoking a steep rise in bread prices that continued until the following summer.

In this tense context, the attempt to abolish the *parlements* opened a debate that went beyond the issues of new taxes or court reform and raised the question of who had the sovereign power to make fundamental laws for the kingdom. Supporters of the *parlements* maintained that this power could be exercised only by the nation itself, not by the king and his ministers. Inspired in part by the examples of England and the United States, these protesters demanded a form of representative government for France. French historical tradition offered an example of such a body: the Estates-General, a body of representatives chosen from the three traditional Estates with power to present grievances to the king and offer advice on taxes and laws. France's absolute monarchs, reluctant to share their hard-won power, had not summoned a meeting of the Estates-General since 1614.

As resistance to the abolition of the *parlements* and demands for a representative assembly mounted, the king and his ministers finally saw no alternative to convening the Estates-General. Royal authority was breaking down in several provinces, notably in Dauphiné—where an unauthorized assembly had met to plan reestablishment of the province's long-dormant Estates—and in Brittany, long a stronghold of resistance to ministerial authority. On July 5, 1788, to head off these menaces, Brienne announced that the Estates-General would be convened. The announcement made government authority crumble even further. By early August, the treasury was virtually empty, and Brienne had to resign in favor of the popular former minister Jacques Necker.

MEETING OF THE ESTATES-GENERAL

The summoning of the Estates-General raised new and divisive questions. How were the deputies to be chosen? And how was the Assembly to be organized when it met? In the past, the Estates-General had met in three separate chambers representing respectively the clergy, the nobility, and the Third Estate, or commoners. The two privileged estates, the clergy and the nobles—who collectively amounted to less than 3 percent of the population—thus controlled two of the assembly's three chambers and could dominate its proceedings. This perspective suited many of those who had opposed arbitrary ministerial authority under Louis XV and his successor. They saw the nobles, particularly the aristocratic judges of the *parlements,* as the natural leaders of the nation and its protectors against the king's arbitrary power. But articulate members of the Third Estate feared their interests would be ignored.

Movements in the provinces offered two new models for the Estates-General. In Dauphiné, reformers drafted a plan to restore its long-dormant Estates in the form of a single assembly in which half the deputies would represent the two privileged orders, and half the Third Estate. They defended their plan on the grounds that, like the English constitution, it would ensure harmony among the three Estates by giving the privileged orders a stake in the new system.

Events in Brittany pointed in a very different direction. In this province, dominated by impoverished petty noblemen who feared seeing themselves displaced by wealthy urban commoners, the privileged orders rejected any concessions to the Third Estate. Their opponents countered by urging the Third Estate to set itself against them and claim all authority for itself.

The radical Breton argument was transferred to the national level in one of the most influential pamphlets written in the late fall of the 1788—the abbé Sieyès's *What Is the Third Estate?* Sieyès began with a ringing declaration: "The plan of this work is very simple. We have three questions to ask: First, What is the Third Estate? Everything. Second, What has it been in the political order up to now? Nothing. Third, What does it demand? To become something." The Third Estate, Sieyès asserted, "has . . . within itself all that is necessary to constitute a complete nation," since its members did all the useful work in the country. "If the privileged order were abolished," he concluded, "the nation would be not something less but something more." He called for a single assembly representing those who made real contributions to the public welfare, from the humble peasant to the wealthy merchant and the learned lawyer. This group, Sieyès maintained, had a single common interest: "It is the nation." Its representatives had every right to legislate on their own, disregarding any objections of deputies from the privileged orders.

As the elections to the Estates-General proceeded in the first four months of 1789, Sieyès's radical arguments seemed to have limited support. Necker had managed to get Louis XVI to defuse some opposition by announcing the "doubling of the Third" on December 27, 1788: as in Dauphiné, the commoners would elect twice as many deputies as each of the other two orders. But this decree said nothing about whether the deputies from the three orders would meet together in a single assembly or in separate chambers, in which case the Third Estate's predominance would be meaningless.

The elections to the Estates-General transformed the notion of governing according to public opinion from an abstract slogan into a living reality. In every parish and district of the country, all adult men were called together and asked not only to choose representatives but also to voice their views on what issues the Estates-General should consider by drawing up *cahiers de doléance* (lists of grievances). Few of these *cahiers* expressed revolutionary demands, but they showed that there was a strong consensus in favor of the creation of some form of representative government, the abolition of tax privileges and other forms of legal inequality, and a number of other important reforms. The *cahiers* thus gave the deputies a mandate for significant reforms, but they also revealed important differences between the country's main social groups. Peasants expressed numerous complaints about the seigneurial rights that weighted directly on them. *Cahiers* drawn up by urban members of the Third Estate voiced more general demands for reform and social equality. The nobles' *cahiers* criticized arbitrary government authority but offered few concessions on the issues raised by the peasants.

THE PARLIAMENTARY REVOLUTION

On May 3, 1789, the approximately twelve hundred deputies to the Estates-General assembled in Versailles. They included well-known participants in the public debate that had occupied the country ever since Calonne had convened his Assembly of Notables more than two years earlier. Also included were obscure parish priests, backwoods noblemen, and small-town lawyers. Contrary to the allegations of critics then and since, many of the members of the Estates-General had practical experience in public affairs as royal officials, in local government, or as administrators in the church. Among the assembled deputies, there was an articulate minority of self-proclaimed patriots, bent on a sweeping transformation of French public life. Their program included a fixed, written constitution for France which would severely limit the king's powers, the abolition of legal privileges, a representative assembly, religious toleration, and press freedom. Initially, however, most of the deputies rejected the patriots' radicalism and looked for leadership to Louis XVI, whose popularity had soared since he had agreed to the convocation of the Estates-General, and to the chief minister, Necker.

The king and Necker proved unprepared for a revolutionary situation. Louis, an honest and well-meaning man, lacked the vision and determination to take the lead in a reform movement; Necker had little sense of how to handle a crisis. Charged with presenting the government's program to the Estates-General in its opening session, he exhausted the deputies with a long-winded account of the monarchy's fiscal problems but offered no specific proposals to debate. The king and Necker left the Estates-General itself to decide whether it would vote by head or by order.

With no commitment to significant reform from the king, the deputies of the Third Estate had every reason to fear that subsequent proceedings would be dominated by the two privileged orders. This fear drove the moderate members of the Third Estate to support a radical decision: the Third Estate paralyzed the assembly by refusing to organize itself and begin work unless the other two orders immediately agreed to meet and vote in common. The underlying issue was fundamental: was France to become a country of citizens enjoying equal rights, or was it to remain divided into different status groups with differing privileges?

On June 10, after five weeks of futile negotiations, the Third Estate deputies had become sufficiently impatient to endorse Sieyès's motion to send a final invitation to the nobles and the clergy to form a single assembly, and to proceed without them if they declined. Joined by a handful of deputies from the clergy, they then voted on June 17, 1789, to assume the new name of National Assembly—thus proclaiming they were speaking for the national community as a whole. News of their actions reached a wider public through the regular letters that many of the deputies sent home and via hastily created newspapers that summarized the Estates-General's debates. In coffeehouses and other public places throughout the nation, ordinary citizens, living embodiments of the public opinion that had taken on a new level of importance with the monarchy's virtual abdication of power, eagerly followed the debates.

The Third Estate's decision to transform itself into a National Assembly was a challenge not only to the other two orders, but to the authority of Louis XVI. Three days later, he announced a special royal session of all three orders to take place on June 23. In the meantime, royal officials locked the deputies of the National Assembly out of their regular meeting hall. Fearing the king would try to quash their decisions, the members of the Assembly held an emergency session in the only building they could find that was large enough to accommodate them, the king's indoor tennis court. There, they swore the dramatic "Oath of the Tennis Court," pledging not to allow themselves to be dissolved until they had given France a new constitution.

The king's speech on June 23, 1789, failed to halt this defiance of royal authority. When royal officials ordered the deputies to disperse after the king's speech, Count Mirabeau—a renegade nobleman who had been elected to represent the Third Estate of his native Provence—defiantly replied, "We are here by the will of the French people, and we will only be dispersed by the force of bayonets." Faced with the intransigence of the Third Estate deputies, the king was forced to back down: on June 27, 1789, he himself ordered the deputies of the clergy and the nobility to join the National Assembly. The former deputies of the Third Estate seemed to have won, and the National Assembly began drafting a constitution. But the bayonets Mirabeau had referred to were not out of the picture. The ministers had begun to assemble troops near the capital; the incipient revolution still risked being put down by force.

The Storming of the Bastille

While the troops assembled and the deputies debated, the rest of the French population began to take a hand in determining the country's fate. The agitation accompanying the elections to the Estates-General and the unrest stemming from difficult economic conditions had already led to outbreaks of violence in several parts of the country. In April 1789, artisans and workers in Paris's populous *faubourg* Saint-Antoine had sacked the mansion of a wallpaper manufacturer, Reveillon, who had been accused of trying to lower wages. This incident was a warning of the height social tensions had reached. Political excitement was even more visible in Paris than social unrest. Crowds gathered every day in open spaces like the gardens of the Palais-Royal to listen to reports from Versailles and speeches by self-appointed orators. Popular sympathies were overwhelmingly with the leaders of the Third Estate, and hostile to the "aristocrats" of the other two orders. Political agitation affected even the soldiers stationed in and around Paris, some of whom openly expressed their sympathies for the National Assembly.

In Versailles, the king's most conservative advisors had now gained the upper hand. On July 11, 1789, Louis dismissed Necker who, in spite of his ineffectual performance at the opening of the Estates-General, was still regarded as an advocate of reform. Even before the deputies in Versailles could respond to this move, the people of Paris took to the streets in protest. As fears of an armed intervention to put down the movement grew, the crowd besieged several royal arsenals in the city demanding arms. Meanwhile, army commanders warned Versailles that they could not count on their men to fight against the Parisians.

On July 14, 1789, a large crowd drawn from all levels of the Paris population surrounded the Bastille, an imposing medieval fortress-prison that had become a symbol of despotic authority. Defended by only a few hundred troops, and housing at that moment only seven prisoners, the Bastille had little real significance. But when the Parisians, infuriated by the commander's refusal to give up the weapons it contained, stormed and captured it, their victory became an immediate symbol of the newly born popular revolutionary movement. The "victors of the Bastille" had defeated the forces of the old government and of the privileged groups that had depended on it; the aroused populace had shown its strength.

The storming of the Bastille was only the most publicized episode in a wave of revolutionary uprisings that swept over France in July 1789, some before and some after the Parisian events. In provincial cities, crowds forced the royal intendants and the appointed municipal officials to yield power to improvised councils of men loyal to the National Assembly. Artisans and workers destroyed machinery that they blamed for creating unemployment. In many rural regions, peasants terrified by rumors that "brigands" in the pay of unidentified opponents of the Revolution were about to devastate their crops, turned on the manor houses of local nobles in a mass movement that came to be known as the "Great Fear." Everywhere, royal authority dissolved and power rested in the hands of those who declared their loyalty to the Assembly and adopted the new symbols of patriotism, such as the red, white, and blue tricolor cockade that the Paris patriots had created. This largely uncoordinated movement from the masses ensured the success of the National Assembly and of what was now openly proclaimed to be a revolution.

NOTE

1. Cited in Jean Egret, *The French Pre-Revolution, 1787–1788*, Wesley D. Camp, trans. (Chicago: University of Chicago Press, 1977), 2.

CHAPTER 7

SUCCESSES AND FAILURES
OF THE LIBERAL REVOLUTION

THE "ABOLITION OF FEUDALISM" AND THE DECLARATION OF RIGHTS

In the wake of the Paris crowd's storming of the Bastille on July 14, 1789, the 1,200 deputies to the National Assembly in Versailles found themselves in an extraordinary position. The danger from the king was gone: his army and his bureaucracy had ceased to function. They could count on a national groundswell of popular support. But the violence that had resulted in the lynching of the Bastille's commander and of the head of the royally appointed municipal government in Paris on July 14, and the wave of reports of peasant revolts in the countryside, showed that the revolutionary process could easily get out of control. The deputies needed to establish principles of a new social and political order before the disintegration of the old one plunged France into chaos.

In the six weeks after the fall of the Bastille, the Assembly took two decisive steps that defined the ways in which the new society and the new government would differ from the old. The first was to eliminate the dense thicket of special privileges that had blocked all previous efforts at change. On August 4, 1789, the Assembly, alarmed by reports of rural insurrection arriving from around the country, held a special session to consider abolishing some of the nobility's special privileges. This limited reform was unexpectedly upstaged by a sweeping proposal to do away with the whole complex of "feudal" privileges that had distinguished nobles from commoners. The success of this motion launched a chain reaction of further renunciations. Representatives of the clergy moved to abolish tithes; deputies from the provinces and privileged cities gave up their immunities from taxes, customs fees, and other regulations. The sale of government offices was done away with, and recruitment to church, government, and military positions was thrown open to all citizens, regardless of status. By the time the exhausted deputies staggered out into the dawn on August 5, they had gone far to "abolish the feudal regime entirely," as the preamble to their edicts promised.

The deputies later qualified much of the language they had initially voted for. Peasants soon discovered, for instance, that the deputies had made distinctions between "feudal" obligations derived from medieval serfdom and "real" obligations considered analogous to rent; peasants were to pay their landlords compensation for the latter. Nevertheless, the basic thrust of this radical package of reforms remained intact. The Assembly had repudiated the corporate-group basis of prerevolutionary society and decided that France would henceforth be a community of legally equal citizens. No subsequent French regime has been able to reverse this fundamental accomplishment.

Having dismantled the old order, the National Assembly turned to establishing the new. On August 27, 1789, it endorsed a seventeen-article "Declaration of the Rights of Man and Citizen," a statement of principles for the future constitution. The declaration, broader in scope than the American Bill of Rights, was formulated in abstract and universal terms, suggesting that the principles it contained were valid not only in France but throughout the world. Its first article echoed the opening sentence of Jean-Jacques Rousseau's *Social Contract* in proclaiming that "men are born and remain free and equal in rights." Article Two stated that government existed only to protect the rights of "liberty, property, security, and resistance to oppression." Article Three asserted that "the source of all sovereignty resides essentially in the nation," thereby abolishing the king's claim to supreme authority. Article Six, again borrowing language from Rousseau, proclaimed that "law is the expression of the general will" and promised all citizens a right to participate in the making of it. In passing the Declaration, the Assembly encouraged the French people to think of themselves in a new way: as active individuals, endowed with rights they were entitled to protect through political participation.

At the same time, however, the Declaration of the Rights of Man and Citizen, like the decrees of August 4–5, 1789, incorporated significant ambiguities. Did the term *man* include all human beings or only members of the male sex? Did the Declaration's promise of freedom apply to the slaves in France's overseas colonies? How was the document's promise of equality to be reconciled with its explicit defense of private property, the unequal distribution of which left some citizens better off than others? Did the promise of liberty include the liberty to oppose the Revolution itself? And who was entitled to speak for the nation, the new source of political legitimacy? Much more than the American Revolution, the French movement raised fundamental questions. The men of the National Assembly have often been blamed for this, and for not trying harder to salvage what they could from the French past. Their optimistic faith that France was uniquely suited to give the world an example of enlightened political reform proved excessive, but in the face of the Old Regime's inability to reform itself before 1789, their actions are understandable.

THE OCTOBER DAYS

Although he had appeared ready to bow to the power of the Revolution after the fall of the Bastille, Louis XVI was not prepared to endorse the drastic restructuring of government and society implied by the August 4 decrees and the Declaration of Rights. Throughout the month of September, the king refused to make a public statement accepting the Declaration. Louis's foot-dragging raised public suspicions, not only among the deputies, but in the general population. In Paris, the high bread prices that had provoked public unrest earlier in 1789 exacerbated discontent. When reports reached Paris that an army regiment recently summoned to Versailles had held a raucous banquet in which the patriotic tricolor cockade was supposedly trampled on the floor, popular anger exploded. On October 5, a large crowd of women assembled at the Hôtel de Ville to demand that the city government take action to protect the Revolution. Dragging cannon, and accompanied by male members of the National Guard, the women set out to march on the royal palace.

The guard commander, Lafayette, although opposed to direct popular action, joined the expedition to avoid losing control over his own troops.

The marchers reached the royal palace late at night. To avoid a bloody confrontation between the crowd and the palace guards, the king agreed to demands that he and his family come to Paris; the National Assembly, relegated to the sidelines during the confrontation, had no choice but to agree to follow. On October 6, 1789, the royal family set off, accompanied by the marchers, who were carrying the severed heads of some of the royal guards on pikes and noisily celebrating their success in bringing "the baker, the baker's wife, and the baker's boy" (the king, queen, and their son) back to the city. Like the storming of the Bastille on July 14, the "October Days" showed that popular violence could have major political effects: the king and the Assembly, brought to Paris by force, were now much more exposed to organized pressure from the populace. The uprising demonstrated that women, normally excluded from politics, could influence the course of events. Paris became calmer as the king and the Assembly settled into new quarters in the heart of the city, but the threat of organized popular violence hung over all subsequent episodes of the Revolution.

A New Political Culture

As the deputies to the National Assembly debated the provisions of the new constitution, the citizens they claimed to represent were creating the forms of a new participatory political culture. Three fundamental features of this new political culture were newspapers, political clubs, and public festivals. The periodical press was the most important medium by which the public at large could follow the proceedings of the National Assembly and other events of the Revolu-

tion. Prior to 1789, France's domestic newspapers had been tightly controlled by censorship. As soon as the Estates-General convened, this system broke down. Over 130 new journals were launched before the end of 1789. The new papers came out daily and gave readers the sense of being in the midst of great events that were moving forward at tremendous speed. The new medium was no monopoly of the Revolution's supporters; counter-revolutionary polemicists used it just as skillfully as did advocates of change. Throughout the Revolution, the press was a cacophonous chorus of conflicting voices, commenting on events and frequently undermining the legislators' efforts to bring them under control.

Clubs channeled and organized the public's participation in the new politics. The first ones grew out of the informal gatherings in coffee-houses and other public places accompanying the elections to the Estates-General. By November of 1789, a group of patriot deputies had founded a club that met regularly to plan common strategy in the Assembly. In January 1790, this club—which now included a growing number of private citizens as well as legislators—named itself the Society of Friends of the Constitution. But it was more commonly referred to as the Jacobin Club, because it met in a church formerly owned by the Jacobin order. The Paris Jacobins and the numerous provincial clubs that affiliated with it became a vast political machine to support the Revolution. By mid-1791, there were 434 Jacobin clubs, and the number grew into the thousands during the Revolution's radical phase in 1793–1794. These clubs brought supporters of the Revolution together to hear the latest news from the Assembly, discuss the issues of the day, and plan local political initiatives. Until 1791, membership was restricted by a relatively high admission fee, and the early Jacobins tended to be substantial members of the middle classes who distrusted radicalism. In later years, however, as membership in the Jacobins was opened up to poorer citizens, the club network supported increasingly radical policies. Clubs in popular neighborhoods like the *faubourg* Saint-Antoine spread new political ideas among the capital's working classes. Women, excluded from the electoral politics of the Revolution, participated in many of the clubs and formed their own in at least sixty towns. Patriot hostility obstructed the spread of counter-revolutionary groups; in some instances, violent demonstrations broke up their meetings.

Public festivals provided a symbolic representation of the movement's achievements that all groups could participate in. The first of these revolutionary celebrations were largely spontaneous, like the "liberty trees"—poles festooned with revolutionary symbols—that sprouted in many towns in 1789. Toward the end of the year, local patriotic groups and units of the National Guard began organizing "federations," bringing together groups from several towns or regions for ceremonies honoring the new constitution. This movement culminated on July 14, 1790, in a national Festival of Federation celebrated on Paris's *Champ de Mars,* now the site of the Eiffel Tower. Before an enormous crowd, the king and the leaders of the Assembly and the National Guard swore loyalty to the new constitution. Press reports and the accounts of those who had come from the provinces gave the entire country a sense of having participated.

THE ACCOMPLISHMENTS OF THE NATIONAL ASSEMBLY, 1789–1791

After the October Days, the political tension in Paris declined. For the next year and a half, although violent episodes affected the provinces, the capital was relatively calm, and the National Assembly's deputies were able to concentrate on their task of constitu-

tion making. Many historians have called this period the "liberal revolution," because it was characterized by the enactment of fundamental legislation incorporating the principles of individual liberty announced in the Declaration of Rights. But this phase of the movement has also been labeled the "bourgeois revolution," because the Assembly's interpretation of liberty favored educated property owners. Only they could fully exercise the rights of citizens, as the new constitution outlined them. The new order did open many new possibilities for members of the bourgeoisie, but to define the liberal phase of the Revolution as the capture of the movement by a self-interested minority overlooks the extent to which the revolutionary legislators were actually striving to transform the entire French population into something new: a community of civic-minded citizens fit to make the new system work.

By the fall of 1789, the twelve hundred men who had arrived in Versailles at the beginning of May, uncertain about their role and for the most part unacquainted with one another, had found leaders and organized into informal parties. Those who considered themselves the most determined supporters of the Revolution stationed themselves in seats on the left side of the speaker's desk; the most vehement opponents of the Revolution claimed the right side of the room. Ever since, the terms *left* and *right* have served to characterize radicals and conservatives, not only in France but throughout the world.

The size and diversity of the Assembly made it difficult for any one figure to dominate it. The strongest potential leader was the Comte de Mirabeau. He was a master of the spoken word and also one of the first to sense the importance of the newspaper medium. But his transparent ambition, his dissolute private life, and the apparent inconsistency of his policy (after challenging royal authority in the Estates-General, he defended a strong executive branch in the constitutional debates), made many other deputies distrustful of him. No other deputy came close to obtaining sway over the Assembly and the revolutionary movement. Some—such as Maximilien Robespierre, a small-town lawyer from northern France who became the leading advocate of the common people's interests in debates, or abbé Maury, a clergyman from humble origins who proved to be the most eloquent defender of royal authority and church interests—established themselves as representatives of minority viewpoints. But the National Assembly, setting a precedent that has had lasting influence in France, made its decisions collectively through debate and bargaining, and blocked the emergence of strong leaders.

Certainly the king was no longer in a position to fill the leadership vacuum. Louis XVI stubbornly resisted Assembly measures that he regarded as undermining royal authority or religion, but he put forward no positive program. The queen, Marie-Antoinette, had a firmer character, but a limited comprehension of the revolutionary situation. Her widely rumored efforts to get the government of Austria, her homeland, to intervene against the Revolution made her and the monarchy increasingly unpopular. With real power concentrated in the National Assembly, the king's ministers—so influential under the Old Regime—no longer had much authority.

In the fall of 1789, the Assembly debated the question of what powers the king should have in the new constitution. At first, a moderate group, the *monarchiens*, dominated the Assembly's constitutional committee. They epitomized the fusion of property-owning elites that had seemed poised to govern the country at the end of the Old Regime; their proposed constitution represented a compromise between the old order and the principles of the Revolution. It gave the king extensive powers; he would have a large budget to spend as he pleased and the right to veto laws he disapproved of. The legislature would have consisted of two houses as in England, one of peers and one representing the common people. More radical deputies, including Mirabeau, rejected this scheme. They feared that the king would use his veto to paralyze the Assembly and that the division of the legislature would leave the aristocracy too much power. The Assembly settled instead on a plan that gave the king much reduced authority and put real power in the hands of an elected one-house legislature, free to act without restrictions because it directly represented the will of the people. The king was given only a suspensive veto—the right to delay legislation for three two-year sessions of the Assembly.

The Right to Vote

Another contentious issue concerned the right to vote. Most deputies accepted the argument that only voters who owned a certain amount of property and thus had tangible individual interests to defend could be expected to make intelligent political choices. In December 1789, they voted to restrict the franchise to adult males who paid taxes equivalent to three days of an ordinary laborer's wage, with an even higher wealth qualification for deputies. By the standards of the time, the property qualification for voting was quite modest. It would have allowed well over half the adult male population to vote in national elections—a group that extended well beyond the narrow bounds of the bourgeoisie. The restriction on eligibility to the legislature was much tighter; only about seventy-two thousand men, many of them nobles rather than bourgeois, met the qualifications. Having declared that all French citizens were equal, defenders of both provisions were hard put to answer Robespierre's challenge, "Can the law be termed an expression of the general will when the greater number of those for whom it is made can have no hand in its making?"[1]

Although the majority of the Assembly voted to bar the poorest citizens from any direct participation in politics, the deputies were concerned about the needs of the lower classes. The Assembly's Committee on the Needy made a full-scale inquiry into France's social problems and proposed that the government assume responsibility for assuring a decent standard of living for orphans, the poor, the ill, and the elderly. The new constitution included provisions for a permanent Committee of Public Instruction, with a mandate to make elementary education available to all citizens. Unfortunately, neither the National Assembly nor any subsequent revolutionary government ever had the resources to implement these sweeping proposals. And in some areas, the laws it drafted did adversely affect the poor. The Le Chapelier law of June 1791, for example, which barred all "coalitions" aimed at affecting wages and prices, made workers' organizations and strikes illegal.

Individual Liberty

Unable to make significant improvements in the lot of the poor, the National Assembly was more successful in extending the definition of individual liberty. Religious minorities—first Protestants, who had already obtained legal recognition in 1787, then the wealthy Jewish communities of southwestern France, and finally (after considerable controversy) the poorer Jews of Alsace—were granted political rights and full access to all public employments. For the first time in Europe, religious belief was thus separated from citizenship. Influenced by representatives of colonial interests, who warned that the abolition of slavery would destroy France's flourishing overseas trade, the Assembly avoided the issue. In May 1791, however, it did grant rights to the handful of people of color in France and to some of the mixed-race inhabitants of the colonies, thus taking a first step to dismantle racial hierarchies. The legal system was reformed to abolish arbitrary detention without trial and to give defendants a better chance of proving their innocence. The censorship system had collapsed in the summer of 1789; the Assembly debated several proposals to limit the "excesses" of the press, but in practice left it completely uncontrolled. In March 1791, the Assembly voted to abolish the guilds and to give all citizens equal access to all trades, thus consecrating economic individualism.

With a few exceptions, the Assembly's legislative measures making all male citizens equal in rights proved to be part of its enduring accomplishments. So was its division of France into new administrative districts, called departments. These units, of approximately equal size and named after prominent geographic features such as rivers or mountains, were intended to rationalize France's administrative system and also to break down provincial loyalties that might conflict with loyalty to the nation as a whole. With minor modifications, they have survived to the present day. The decentralized system of local government initially set up in 1790 proved far less enduring. Local officials were to collect taxes, administer justice, and enforce laws. The central government became almost totally dependent on the good will of these local authorities, whom it could not control, to carry out its directives. In the first flush of revolutionary enthusiasm, the system seemed attractive, but before long, conflicts between local and national officials proved that it contained dangerous weaknesses. The Assembly also abolished all the various tolls and customs boundaries that had divided France economically. The entire country thus became a unified market, which the deputies hoped would encourage commerce and manufacturing.

THE REVOLUTION AND THE REFORM OF THE CHURCH

The liberal legislation enacted by the National Assembly had the potential to create a conflict between the wealthy bourgeoisie, who stood to benefit most from the new system, and the mass of the population; the Third Estate was no longer a united block. But the issue that most visibly threatened the liberal revolution grew out of the Assembly's attempt to reform the French Catholic church. The Assembly had first faced this issue in November 1789, when it voted to expropriate the church's accumulated property and sell it to private owners. Decades of denunciation of the clergy's mismanaged wealth had paved the way for this idea. Furthermore, since the Assembly intended to have the civil government take over many of the functions traditionally performed by the church, such as schooling and aid to the poor, it was logical that the government inherit the resources that the church had used to pay for these services. Even many of the clergy, particularly the underpaid parish priests who were now to receive salaries from the state, supported the move.

The expropriation of church property led to a controversy about the restructuring of the church. Church reform had been a widespread demand throughout the eighteenth century, and numerous *cahiers* had encouraged the Estates-General to carry it out. "Establishments without any purpose, useless men highly salaried, useful men without recompense"—so the deputy Jean-Baptiste Treilhard summed up the revolutionaries' view of the Old Regime church.[2] Even most of the clergy recognized that reform was long overdue. It was the nature of the reforms imposed, and the lack of consultation with the church, that caused conflict. For many Catholics, the granting of full civil and political rights to religious minorities was a jarring change. In regions where Catholics and Protestants had long been in conflict with each other (such as the southern city of Nîmes), violence broke out, and some Catholics came to regard the Revolution as a Protestant plot against their faith.

More conflicts resulted from the deputies' internal restructuring of the church. The Assembly redrew the boundaries of dioceses to correspond to the boundaries of the departments it had established, abolishing more than a third of the prerevolutionary bishoprics. More controversial was the decision to have departmental electoral assemblies choose priests and bishops. French kings had long had the right to choose bishops. Now that authority was vested in the people rather than the king, it seemed logical to the legislators that this power should pass to the voters. But the reform overturned the hierarchical structure of the church, under which authority descended from God through the pope to the bishops, who in turn consecrated priests. Devout Catholics objected that the electoral assemblies charged with selecting priests included Protestants, Jews, and atheists.

Disregarding these criticisms, the Assembly enacted its Civil Constitution of the Clergy in July 1790. Every French priest soon had to make a public choice. To accept these reforms was to endorse the Revolution and the nation; to refuse them was to challenge both. The issue split France almost in half. Slightly more than 50 percent of the parish clergy took the oath, but the remainder, along with all but seven French bishops, refused. Where parish priests refused the oath, the government sought to install newly promoted priests who had accepted it, often in the face of violent local resistance to the "intruder." The imposition of the Civil Constitution thus raised in acute form the issue of how far the revolutionary government could go in imposing its decisions on citizens who opposed them in the name of their individual freedom.

Provinces and Departments

In dividing France into departments of roughly equal size, the National Assembly attempted to follow the boundaries of the prerevolutionary provinces as much as possible. This map shows present-day departmental boundaries.

THE KING'S FLIGHT AND THE CRISIS OF 1791

The religious conflict led directly to the undermining of the National Assembly's constitutional system because it helped Louis XVI decide to make an open break with the Assembly in June 1791. The king's antipathy to the Revolution had been clear from the outset. He had repeatedly delayed giving his official sanction to the Assembly's major measures and often acted only under intense pressure. He also had refused Assembly demands for strong measures against nobles and members of the royal family who fled abroad after July 1789. From their refuges across the border, these emigrés lobbied foreign powers to invade France and free the king. Louis issued token appeals to his relatives, but failed to convince the supporters of the Revolution that he meant them. In any event, the emigrés retorted that the king was acting under duress and ignored his injunctions.

On June 20, 1791, the king finally decided to break out of his increasingly awkward situation by fleeing. By the time the king's disappearance was discovered, he and his family had already escaped from the capital. A nervous National Assembly immediately sent couriers in pursuit, while announcing to the public that the monarch had been "abducted." The discovery that Louis had left behind a manifesto denouncing the Revolution which had replaced "the monarchical government under which the nation has prospered for fourteen hundred years"[3] discredited this story, but the Assembly hesitated to condemn the king and commit itself to replacing him. The entire constitutional edifice so painfully erected since July 1789 would be called into question by such action. For the royal family, the attempted flight turned into a tragedy of errors. Delays caused them to miss their rendezvous with troops who had been recruited to escort them. In the small town of Varennes, the fugitives were recognized, and the local authorities halted their coach. Heavily guarded, the royal party traveled back to Paris.

The flight to Varennes was a clear indication that the Revolution had reached a crisis. For the first time, there were open calls for the creation of a republican government and the abolition of the monarchy; the absence of popular support for the king showed that much of the population was ready to accept such a move. The leaders of the National Assembly quickly decided, however, that they needed to preserve the monarchy in spite of the king's actions. Barnave, one of the most eloquent spokesmen for the Third Estate in June 1789, now became the leading defender of this policy. If France was to become a stable country in which the rights of property owners were secure, he argued, there had to be a strong executive authority, independent of public opinion, to maintain the laws. To remove the king from office would be to "begin the Revolution anew," and it would invite demands for complete democracy and the redistribution of property.

Barnave and his followers prevailed in the National Assembly, which voted to absolve the king for his flight, but they also split the revolutionary movement. On July 16, 1791, Barnave and most of the other deputies quit the Jacobin club, leaving a small rump organization in the hands of Robespierre, and founded a rival club, the Feuillants. On the following day, Paris radicals called for a mass demonstration to protest the Assembly's decision. When disorders broke out, the National Guard commander, Lafayette, and the mayor of Paris, Sylvain Bailly—both sympathetic to the Feuillants—sent in the National Guard. About sixty demonstrators were shot down in the "massacre." This repression appeared to confirm the radical claim that the Assembly despised the common people. A constitution put into effect under these conditions rested on shaky foundations.

With the king's fate resolved and the radicals temporarily silent, the National Assembly hastened to conclude its work. In August and September 1791, the deputies "revised" the entire constitution, altering a number of clauses to strengthen the safeguards for property owners. The conflict over the Civil Constitution of the Clergy, the king's flight, and the massacre of July 17, 1791, were clear evidence that grave difficulties threatened the new liberal order, but the deputies could be forgiven for taking pride in what they had accomplished. They had broken the political deadlock that had prevented necessary political reforms for decades before 1750. They had given France a complete new constitutional system, based on the principles of legal equality for all male citizens and individual liberty. If they failed to solve some of the most pressing problems they had come up against—such as poverty and education—they had at least proclaimed principles that, a century or more later, would become the basis for effective legislation.

Critics at the time and since have blamed the National Assembly for trying to do too much at once, and for failing to provide sufficient checks and balances in their constitutional system. To the revolutionaries of 1789, however, well aware of the decades of unsuccessful reform efforts that had preceded the summoning of the Estates-General, the opportunity that appeared in July 1789 was too valuable to be passed up, and the danger of political deadlock too serious to permit a real division of powers. The first two years of the Revolution had been accompanied by a certain amount of violence, but, in view of the scope and complexity of the issues the movement had raised, the amount of overt conflict had been relatively modest. Had the Revolution been successfully stabilized in 1791, France would have had a constitution incorporating liberal and democratic principles that were not to be adopted in most other European countries until a hundred years later.

Notes

1. Cited in George Rudé, ed., *Robespierre* (Englewood Cliffs, NJ: Prentice Hall, 1967), 14.
2. Cited in Paul H. Beik, ed., *The French Revolution* (New York: Harper & Row, 1970), 138.
3. Ibid., 167.

Chapter 8

The Radical Revolution

If the Revolution had been stabilized in 1791. . . . But chances of such an outcome were few. The new system of constitutional monarchy was not inherently unworkable. But the attempt to implement it with a monarch who had proven his ill will would have been difficult at best. In addition, the National Assembly had declared its own members ineligible for reelection. This left power to new legislators, bent on enforcing controversial policies such as the Civil Constitution of the Clergy, in the face of a growing challenge to the principle of limiting political rights to the propertied classes. This risky political gamble failed, and the liberal phase of the Revolution gave way to a far more radical one in which a republic replaced the monarchy, and the principle of democratic suffrage replaced the effort to limit political participation to those with property. The violence that had been more or less controlled during the movement's liberal phase now came to dominate the scene, creating deep divisions in the country that had a lasting effect on its history.

The Legislative Assembly and the War

Fewer than 25 percent of the "active" citizens entitled to vote under the new constitution actually took part in the 1791 elections.

Most of those who voted were supporters of the Revolution, and the deputies they elected were probably more enthusiastic about the Revolution than the population as a whole. Most of the 745 deputies elected to the new Legislative Assembly that opened its sessions in October 1791 were from the bourgeois groups that had gained the most from the National Assembly's reforms. The moderate Feuillant group started out with more supporters in the new assembly than the radical Jacobins, but Robespierre and his allies had managed to hold the loyalty of most of the provincial club network. Meanwhile, outspoken royalist journalists openly urged army officers to join the emigrés and looked forward to a foreign invasion that would quash the Revolution.

The Revolt Against Slavery

The Legislative Assembly immediately had to deal with a major revolt in France's most valuable colony and with the threat of war in Europe. News of a massive slave revolt in the Caribbean sugar island of Saint-Domingue reached Paris in October 1791. The rebels burned plantation buildings and massacred slave owners. Deputies such as Jacques-Pierre Brissot, a leading opponent of slavery and racial discrimination, blamed the revolt on the stubbornness of the whites in the colony, who had resisted the May 1791 law giving rights to a few men of mixed race and had even succeeded in having it repealed just before the National Assembly had finished its work in September 1791. The Legislative Assembly did send troops to fight the rebellious slaves, but in March 1792, it voted to extend citizenship rights to the entire mixed-race population in the colonies. Desperate though they were for military aid, the whites in Saint-Domingue remained violently opposed to such a step. Some of them began negotiations to encourage the British and Spanish to occupy the colony, thereby justifying the French revolutionaries' accusations that its opponents were prepared to commit treason to stop it.

The Legislative Assembly had to cope with spreading social unrest closer to home as well. The 1791 grain harvest was a poor one, and by the fall there were outbreaks of social violence in a number of rural areas. In February 1792, crowds in Paris, angered by the high price of sugar, attacked merchants' shops. The deputies, who saw the Revolution as a movement on behalf of the people, could not understand why ordinary men and women would blame the Revolution for economic problems. They found it easier to claim that members of the former privileged orders had incited these disturbances. Although the deputies supported a political system based on individual rights, many of them were now ready to back laws curtailing the rights of groups blamed for obstructing the new order. In November 1791 the Legislative Assembly voted stringent laws against refractory priests and emigrés.

THE MOVE TOWARD WAR

The issue of the emigrés was one of the main factors that drove the Legislative Assembly to its most important decision: its vote on April 20, 1792, to declare war against Austria. The revolutionaries of 1789 had been persuaded that war, the result of kings' greed for conquests and glory, was one of those evils of the Old Regime they could abolish. They had proclaimed France's intention to renounce territorial expansion, and had stripped the king of his right to declare war. For their part, Europe's other governments had initially shown little hostility to the Revolution; some were pleased at the weakening of France's power. Louis XVI's flight to Varennes finally stirred Europe's rulers to make verbal gestures on behalf of their fellow monarch. Leopold II and the king of Prussia met in Pillnitz in August 1791 and issued a vague declaration threatening action if Louis XVI was harmed, fueling the French patriots' contention that the Revolution was in danger from abroad.

In France, support for war came from the extremes of right and left. A majority of the radical Jacobin supporters of the Revolution openly favored hostilities. According to their leading spokesman, the journalist-deputy Jacques Pierre Brissot, war would exalt patriotic fervor and expose traitors who hoped for the defeat of the Revolution. The Jacobin war party found an unlikely ally in the king. Once war was declared, the king, as commander-in-chief of the army, would have expanded powers. If France was successful, his position would be strengthened; if the French army was defeated, the foreign powers would do away with the revolutionaries. When the Austrian government rejected a French ultimatum to expel the emigrés from German territory, the king asked the Assembly to declare war, and so, on April 20, 1792, France entered into a conflict that would last for more than two decades.

The outbreak of war focused attention on the condition of the French army. Until July 1789, the army had been the king's, not the nation's. It consisted primarily of long-term professional soldiers, many of them from abroad. The officer corps was entirely aristocratic; regardless of merit, rank-and-file soldiers could not hope to rise above the rank of noncommissioned officers. The National Assembly had undertaken to reform the army, like every other French institution. Soldiers and officers were given the same rights as other citizens, and the officer corps was opened to commoners. By 1792, these reforms had been only partially successful in creating an army in accordance with the Revolution's new concept of the nation. Many aristocratic officers' loyalty to the new revolutionary order was less than certain, and relations between the officers and their men were strained, as a bloody soldiers' mutiny at Nancy in August 1790 had shown. At the start of the war, army morale was low. The troops were quick to blame their commanders for any reverses they suffered; at Lille, panicked French soldiers massacred their own commander. In Paris, news of these defeats plunged the institutions of the constitutional monarchy into a fatal crisis.

THE OVERTHROW OF THE MONARCHY

By the start of the war, the constitutional system put into effect in 1791 was already coming apart. Particularly in Paris, the large population of artisans and shopkeepers who had made up most of the crowd that stormed the Bastille had never accepted their exclusion from politics. In the spring of 1792, prorevolutionary political activists had mobilized strong support among these *sans-culottes*—so called to distinguish them from the educated classes who wore elegant knee breeches, or *culottes*, instead of workers' long trousers. By mid-1792, *sans-culotte* activists had begun to mobilize against both the king and an Assembly that seemed indifferent to the Austro-Prussian army's advance into France.

At the beginning of July 1792, a small group of revolutionary militants, including both radical members of the Assembly and *sans-culotte* leaders, evolved a plan for an uprising that would lead to the summoning of a National Convention, which would remove the king, take emergency measures to defend the country, and give France a new constitution. As a spearhead for the insurrection, the plotters relied on the armed *fédérés*, volunteer units from all over the country that had come to Paris for the celebration of July 14. The unit from Marseille was especially noted for its revolutionary ardor; its members had arrived in Paris singing a rousing marching song, composed a few months earlier, whose verses called on all "children of the fatherland" to take arms and let "the blood of our enemies water our fields." This "song of the Marseillais" became a rallying cry for the assault on the monarchy.

On July 28, 1792, the commander of the allied forces, the Duke of Brunswick, issued a proclamation holding the inhabitants of Paris responsible for any attack on the king. When the news reached Paris, the insurrectionary leaders decided to act. By 9:00 A.M. on August 10, thousands of them were converging on the Tuileries. The king and his family took refuge with the Legislative Assembly, leaving behind their loyal Swiss guards. In the course of the day, fighting broke out; the outnumbered guards killed at least one hundred of the insurgents. The *sans-culottes* retaliated by massacring the guards who fell into their hands. The 10th of August thus became by far the bloodiest of the revolutionary *journées* (days of violence). It was also among the most decisive politically. The Legislative Assembly suspended Louis XVI from his functions and voted to call nationwide elections for a Convention that would determine the fate of the monarchy; it thus scrapped the Constitution of 1791. By declaring that all adult males were eligible to vote for the Convention, the Assembly abandoned the effort to keep power in the hands of the propertied classes. The liberal or bourgeois Revolution had ended; the democratic and radical Revolution had begun.

THE CONVENTION AND THE REPUBLIC

Like the National Assembly, the National Convention that convened in September 1792 made comprehensive and fundamental changes in French life that broke radically with the past. Even more than the National Assembly, its work has been controversial. To some in France, this first attempt at the creation of a popular republic laid the groundwork for the basic institutions that make France a democratic society today. To others, the Convention was a violent and destructive regime comparable to the totalitarian dictatorships of the twentieth century. However it is viewed, no historian can deny that the three years of the Convention's session were among the most event-filled in all of French history.

The National Convention was born in crisis, and its entire three-year existence was shaped by a series of urgent problems. The deputies elected in September 1792 had to deal with both the Austro-Prussian invasion and the issue of constitution making. The 749 new deputies were on the whole similar to the members of the outgoing Legislative Assembly. Lawyers and former government officials still predominated, and the deputies were still overwhelmingly members of the bourgeoisie. They were young (two-thirds were under forty-five) and strongly committed to the Revolution.

These deputies had little in common with the Parisian *sans-culottes*. The deputies still wanted to govern through orderly processes, whereas the *sans-culottes* were men and women of direct action, who considered the crisis facing the Revolution too grave to be dealt with through slow-moving legislative debates. To appease them, the Legislative Assembly had set up a Revolutionary Tribunal on August 17, 1792; its procedures superseded many of the guarantees in the Declaration of the Rights of Man. There was no appeal from its sentences, and those condemned to death were executed with a new mechanical beheading device that experts had created for the National Assembly. Supposedly painless and efficient, the guillotine was named for Dr. Guillotin, a legislator who had wanted to abolish cruel punishments.

The establishment of the Revolutionary Tribunal was not enough to satisfy the *sans-culottes'* demand for immediate measures to defeat the counter-revolution. On September 2, 1792, reacting to news that the key fortress of Verdun was about to surrender, crowds surrounded the principal Paris prisons where political suspects were being held. They set up improvised tribunals and forced the jailers to bring out the prisoners. In all, some thirteen hundred—most of them guilty of nothing more tangible than having held privileged status before 1789—were killed. The September massacres stained the Revolution's reputation throughout Europe; they also made the Convention acutely aware of the need to convince the *sans-culottes* that it was doing everything necessary to defend the Revolution.

Military successes soon gave the Convention some breathing room. On September 20, 1792, the day the Convention first assembled in Paris, the revolutionary army met the invaders at the village of Valmy. The French, now better organized than in the first battles of the war, profited from their superiority in numbers and their artillery to halt the Austro-Prussian advance.

GIRONDINS AND MONTAGNARDS

Even before the arrival of news from the battlefield at Valmy, the Convention had set its political course. At its opening session on September 20, 1792, it immediately voted to proclaim France a republic and thus cut the last institutional link between the Revolution and the Old Regime. But what was to be done with Louis XVI? The debates on his fate revealed that the Convention was deeply divided. The two main groupings that emerged in the Convention during these debates have gone down in history as the Girondins and the Montagnards. The Girondins, so called because several of them represented the Gironde department around Bordeaux, were a loose group of sixty or so deputies. Their most prominent spokesman was Brissot; their true leader was Madame Roland, the spirited wife of another leading member in whose salon the Girondin deputies regularly met. The Girondins tended to be talented and ambitious individualists, who had made their way in the world by virtue of their own abilities. No friends of the Old Regime, they were nevertheless susceptible to the concerns of France's bourgeois elites; many of them represented the country's big trading cities, such as Bordeaux and Marseille.

The Montagnards, who now controlled the Jacobin club, were just as bourgeois as the Brissot group, but they were often from more modest origins. The most prominent was Maximilien Robespierre, the small-town lawyer whose numerous speeches on behalf of the less privileged during the National Assembly had given him a national reputation. In the Convention, his main allies were the popular agitator, Danton (one of the leaders of the August 10 movement), and the radical journalist Marat. Compared to the Girondins, the Montagnards voiced greater concern for the lower classes. Their rhetoric tended to be more moralistic than the Girondins', their political positions more uncompromising.

The two rival groups clashed regularly from the first weeks of the Convention's sessions, with the Girondins accusing the Montagnards of plotting to establish a dictatorship and the Montagnards responding that their opponents were in collusion with the imprisoned king. Indeed, the Girondins did believe that trying and executing the king would create new difficulties for the Revolution. But the Montagnards' most effective orator, the twenty-five-year-old Louis Antoine Saint-Just, responded that "those who worry about whether it is fair to punish a king will never establish a republic."[1] In the end, the Montagnards' harsh logic prevailed. After considerable debate, the deputies voted overwhelmingly to find Louis guilty of treason. By a narrower majority—380 to 310—they endorsed the Montagnard demand to execute him, and he was guillotined on January 21, 1793. The Convention had irreversibly cut itself off from any compromise with the Revolution's opponents.

There was also no compromise in the party struggle that divided the Convention. The resulting instability became more and more dangerous as the problems facing the Convention became more critical. After some temporary successes in late 1792, the French armies had to face new foes, most notably Britain and Spain. By March 1793, the Austrians had regained the initiative in Belgium and the Rhineland, while the Spaniards launched an invasion in the south. Dumouriez, the defeated French commander in Belgium, tried to lead his troops against the Convention and then went over to the Austrians, leaving the main French army in disarray.

Opposition was mounting at home, as well. In March, an attempt to draft new troops for the army set off a peasant uprising in rural western France, centered in the department of the Vendée. This rebellion grew into a veritable civil war, waged with unrelenting cruelty on both sides. Although resistance to the draft set off the uprising, the Vendéans had much broader grievances against the Revolution. The deeply Catholic rural population in western France resented the Civil Constitution of the Clergy, and many peasants had had to watch as the prorevolutionary towndwellers in their region reaped most of the benefits from the abolition of feudal dues and sale of church lands. The Vendée peasants' proclamation of a war for the restoration of king and church found little echo elsewhere in the country, but their complaints about the Revolution's failure to address their problems were shared in many other regions.

In addition to the war and the Vendée rebellion, the Convention had to deal with a worsening economic crisis. A poor grain harvest in 1792 sent food prices soaring again; this inflation undermined the *assignats,* the paper currency supposedly backed by the value of nationalized church lands that the National Assembly had begun to issue in 1789. Wages failed to keep up with the rise in prices, leading to *sans-culotte* protests. To calm the unrest, the Convention passed a law setting maximum prices for wheat and flour, and giving the government the right to requisition supplies from reluctant growers. This measure showed the Convention's growing tendency to meet crises by restricting individual freedoms guaranteed in the Declaration of the Rights of Man, and by strengthening the powers of the national government.

The political crisis in the Convention had echoes throughout the country, as moderates and radicals struggled for control of local governments. To the Montagnard leaders in Paris, the situation cried out for action; only if they could gain firm control of the Convention could they deal with the country's pressing problems. On May 31, 1793, the Montagnards organized a repetition of the August 10, 1792, insurrection. National Guard units from the sections surrounded the Convention, and two days later the intimidated assembly suspended twenty-nine Girondin deputies. The defeated Girondin leaders fled to the provinces; the Montagnards were left in control of the Convention, which itself was clearly at the mercy of whoever could rouse the armed *sans-culotte* battalions.

The Montagnards had gained control of the Convention, but they seemed likely to lose much of the rest of the country. France's foreign enemies continued their advances, the Vendée rebels remained a threat, and there was a new danger—a series of revolts against the Jacobin-dominated Convention in some of the major provincial cities. These uprisings, known as the "federalist movement," often took place in towns whose deputies had been among the purged Girondins, such as Caen, Bordeaux, and Marseille. Unlike the Vendée rebels, the federalists proclaimed their loyalty to the Revolution and the Republic. But they condemned the influence of the radical *sans-culotte* movement and the centralization of authority in Paris.

Luckily for the Convention, the revolts in different parts of the country remained uncoordinated and the federalists' essentially negative program failed to rally widespread support, whereas the Convention had the advantage of being the focus of patriotic resistance to foreign threats. The federalist movement, together with the assassination of the journalist-deputy Marat on July 13, 1793, added to the Montagnards' sense of being under siege and made them even more reluctant to compromise with opponents. At Lyon, cannon loaded with chain shot were used to mow down hundreds of captured rebels in a mass execution that was intended to dramatize the Revolution's determination to stamp out its enemies. The Convention even tried to expunge the rebel cities' names from the map: Lyon was to be renamed "Liberated Commune."

THE DICTATORSHIP OF THE JACOBINS

The Convention's vote to impose a new name on a major city reflected its conviction that the Revolution could only succeed if it truly remade French society from top to bottom. Between the summer of 1793 and the summer of 1794, under the leadership of the Jacobin Montagnards, a powerful centralized government was created that simultaneously dealt with pressing practical problems and tried to create a totally new republican society. To meet the immediate crises it had to deal with, the Convention for the first time found strong and capable, if ruthless, leadership. Both contemporaries and historians have recognized Maximilien Robespierre as the leading figure among the Jacobins. It would be hard to imagine a politician more different from Mirabeau, the strongest personality in the National Assembly. Mirabeau had been passionate, profligate, a whirlwind of energy who loved crowds and intrigue. Robespierre was cold, restrained, happiest among a small circle of intimates. In his own way, however, Robespierre was as skillful a politician as Mirabeau. His reputation for disinterested devotion to the public good gave him the nickname "the Incorruptible." In the end, Robespierre would be brought down by his obsession with his vision of the ideal republic and his indifference to the human cost of installing it. But historians who see him as merely a ruthless fanatic overlook the complexity of his conduct and of the challenges he faced.

Although Robespierre was the best known of the Montagnard leaders of 1793–1794, he was never a dictator in his own right. Rather than entrusting executive power to a single person, the Convention in the fall of 1793 had given day-to-day authority over the government to its Committee of Public Safety, a group of twelve deputies who oversaw the ministries and the conduct of the war. Robespierre's colleagues were strong-minded men who never hesitated to argue with him. To meet the multiple crises it had to deal with, the Committee of Public Safety improvised a new system of government whose main features were a concentration of power in the hands of the national

government, and the elimination of all potential opposition. Robespierre justified this system of revolutionary government in one of his most celebrated speeches, delivered in December 1793. The object of the Revolution, he said, was to guarantee individual freedom, as the men of the National Assembly had attempted to do. But before a constitution based on civil liberty could be put into effect, the enemies of liberty had to be defeated, and this could only be done by a government free to act without restrictions— a revolutionary government.

This doctrine clearly reflected the circumstances of 1793, in which the men of the Convention had had to combat armed enemies on all sides and take extraordinary measures to keep the population fed. But the idea of using the instrument of government to remake the French people tempted the radical leaders. In a manuscript he left unpublished, Robespierre's young colleague Saint-Just planned an austere modern-day Sparta, in which children would be taken from their parents at the age of seven and raised in state schools, so that their only loyalty would be to the nation. Robespierre, for his part, talked of a Republic of Virtue, from which private selfishness would be banished.

Although the dictatorship of the Committee of Public Safety did have some of the characteristics of twentieth-century totalitarian governments, it remained much more directly connected to real and urgent problems around it. After the defeat of the federalist revolts, the Convention turned its attention to the foreign threat. On August 23, 1793, it decreed a *levée en masse*, or mass mobilization. According to the terms of the decree, "The young men shall go to battle; the married men shall forge arms and transport provisions; the women shall make tents and clothes. . . . The children shall turn old linen into lint [for bandages]; the old men shall repair to the public places, to stimulate the courage of the warriors."[2] The conscription order was never universally obeyed—thousands of potential draftees rushed to get married, and a third or more of those drafted never reported—but it swelled the Republic's forces sufficiently to halt the foreign invasions. At the front, the Convention ruthlessly weeded out unsuccessful commanders, executing several defeated generals and promoting young, determined officers. By the end of 1793, the tide of the war had begun to turn in France's favor.

Controlling the home front remained difficult. The Parisian *sans-culotte* movement remained restive: food prices continued to climb, and the Convention's policies seemed to have no effect on the economic crisis. Unable to restore the economy, the Committee of Public Safety took measures to create a system of government that would bring *sans-culotte* protesters and all other potential foes under control. By giving the Committee of Public Safety the authority to nominate members of all its other committees, the Convention made it the real center of the government. The Law of Suspects, passed on September 17, 1793, allowed the imprisonment of anyone whose conduct, talk, or writings could be interpreted as having opposed the Revolution, as well as anyone who had no regular source of income or whose relatives had emigrated. Local revolutionary militants were organized into surveillance committees to identify suspects, and the number of prisoners rose to as many as 100,000. Show trials in October 1793 ended with the execution of the queen, the leading Girondin deputies as well as their political muse, Madame Roland, and Antoine Barnave, the main defender of the constitutional-monarchist 1791 constitution. While the Law of Suspects organized the system of political repression, the General Maximum law of September 29, 1793, extended controls to most of the economy. The prices of most basic commodities were fixed at a level one-third higher than in 1790,

while wages could not exceed a level one-half above the 1790 rate.

Armed with these new powers, the Committee of Public Safety was able to do what no previous revolutionary government had been capable of: govern the country. To enforce its authority outside of Paris, it dispatched trusted Convention deputies on missions, giving them full power to overrule or even replace local elected authorities. A law passed on December 4, 1793, specified that the Convention's decrees took precedence over all local measures and gave the central government authority to remove and replace local administrators. This centralized power was enhanced by the tremendous growth in the government's bureaucracy: hundreds of new clerks were hired to see that the new laws were carried out. In the provinces, local militants, charged with enforcing the Maximum and rounding up suspects, found themselves converted into public officials under Parisian control.

REVOLUTIONARY CULTURE

Determined to exert administrative and economic control over the whole country, the Convention's leaders were also determined to create a new revolutionary culture. On October 5, 1793, the Convention replaced the Christian calendar with a new revolutionary one, meant to show that the Revolution had begun a new era in human history. Years were to be counted from the establishment of the French Republic on September 22, 1792, so that 1793–1794 became the Year II. The year was divided into twelve months, each given a poetic name based on its weather—*nivôse* was the month of snow, *floréal* the month when flowers bloomed—and each month was divided into three ten-day weeks, or *décades*.

The new calendar was part of a program of rationalization that included the introduction of the metric system (a reform that lasted), and the division of the day into ten hundred-minute hours (which did not). But it was also related to the dechristianization campaign that reached its height in late 1793. Whereas the National Assembly had intended to reform the church, the dechristianizers aimed to abolish it altogether. Initiated by revolutionary militants in some provincial areas where anticlerical attitudes were already strong at the end of the Old Regime, dechristianization became a part of the *sans-culotte* program. Activists intimidated priests into renouncing their vows and marrying. They destroyed religious statuary and confiscated church buildings for granaries and other secular purposes. In November 1793, the dechristianizers turned Paris's Notre-Dame Cathedral into a Temple of Reason and staged a ceremony in honor of a Goddess of Liberty, impersonated by an actress from the Opera. Robespierre and the leaders of the Convention stood aloof from the dechristianization campaign, and eventually reined it in; they feared its potential for further inflaming religious conflict. But to much of the French population, dechristianization became synonymous with the Revolution. The split between Catholics and their opponents was to remain one of the main divisions in French life for well over a century. The revolutionaries also undertook to root out dialect languages and regional cultures, which they saw as threats to national unity.

In place of France's traditional culture, the revolutionaries of the Year II propagated new symbols and new values. Plays like Sylvain Maréchal's *Last Judgment of Kings* used melodramatic techniques to portray the war as a crusade for the welfare of humanity. On public buildings and government agencies' letterheads, slogans like "Liberty, Equality, Fraternity or Death" and icons like an all-seeing eye—a reminder of the vigilance every patriot was expected to maintain—replaced the symbols of Catholicism and the monarchy. Revolutionary militants encouraged

their fellow-citizens to address each other with the familiar *tu* rather than the more formal *vous* that had traditionally been used to show respect for social superiors. This revolutionary culture reinforced the consciousness of a break with the past at the level of everyday life, but its enforced nature created much resentment against the new regime.

Along with their program of cultural transformation, the Montagnards also enacted a number of measures meant to favor the lower classes. In the countryside, the Convention settled disputes about the interpretation of the National Assembly's decrees of August 4, 1789, in favor of the peasants, rather than the landlords. Redemption payments for feudal dues were abolished (in most areas, the peasants had refused to pay them anyway) and the Convention ordered that church and emigré lands put up for auction be divided into smaller lots so that peasant bidders would have a better chance of purchasing them. In February 1794, the Convention passed its most radical social legislation, the so-called *ventôse* decrees. They called for the confiscated estates of counter-revolutionaries to be divided up and distributed free to indigent patriots.

It was during the period of the Convention's dominance that the nature of the Revolution's impact on women became clearest. In the Declaration of the Rights of Man and Citizen, the word *man* was used in its general sense, including both sexes, but the revolutionary constitutions reserved political rights exclusively for males. The abolition of noble privileges eliminated the wealthy female patronesses who had often played a major role in French culture. The breakup of convents abolished a sphere in which religious women had been able to live largely outside of male control. Some revolutionary legislation went against this trend; the 1792 divorce law gave both sexes the right to initiate proceedings. In general, however, revolutionary reforms changed a situation in which

VUE DE LA MONTAGNE ELEVÉE AU CHAMP DE LA REUNION.
pour la fête qui y a été célébrée en l'honneur de l'Etre Suprème le Decadi 20 Prairial de l'an 2.ᵉ de la Republique Française
A Paris chez Chéreau Rue Jacques, aux deux Colonnes, près la Fontaine Severin, Nᵒ 257.

Revolutionary festivals gave citizens a sense of participating in the making of new world and allowed revolutionary leaders to communicate the values of the new order they were striving to create. In this engraving of the Festival of the Supreme Being, held on June 8, 1794, an artificial mountain represented the radical Montagnard Jacobin movement. The powerful male figure atop the pillar stood for the French people, while a female figure representing nature rode a wagon pulled by oxen. Robespierre led a procession of Convention deputies, who can be seen scaling the mountain.
(Photo credit: Library of Congress.)

some privileged women had enjoyed more freedom than most unprivileged men into a society in which all men enjoyed more rights and freedom than all women.

Women did participate in many of the revolutionary *journées*, particularly the October Days of 1789. They were especially likely to turn out in the streets to protest against high bread prices, since they were traditionally responsible for the feeding of their families. A few feminist militants, such as Olympe de Gouges, a self-educated playwright, saw liberating possibilities in the Revolution's

principles. In 1791, she published a "Declaration of the Rights of Woman," proclaiming that "woman is born free and lives equal to man in her rights."[3] In the summer of 1793, when radical agitation in Paris reached its height, militants organized the Society of Revolutionary Republican Women and took a leading role in public demonstrations. Far from favoring this involvement in revolutionary politics, however, male revolutionaries sought to limit it. In November 1793, the Society was banned for promoting street agitation. A Convention spokesman laid down the official revolutionary line: nature itself had destined men and women for separate roles. As Rousseau had urged, women were to confine themselves to the home, where they could serve the nation by raising their children as patriots.

Excluded from the revolutionary movement, many women turned against it. Female participation in bread riots had served to radicalize the Revolution in 1789, but by 1794 such protests often expressed counter-revolutionary sentiments. Women were prominent in many protests against the Civil Constitution of the Clergy. It was during the revolutionary period that the division between a male population attracted to liberal and rationalist ideas and a female population loyal to traditional religious beliefs—which was to characterize France throughout the nineteenth century—first emerged.

Although the radical revolutionaries limited women's rights, they took important steps on behalf of people of color. These actions were prompted by developments in France's embattled Caribbean colony of Saint-Domingue, where most of the white population had turned against the Revolution. Desperate for support, the French republican commissioner in the island, Sonthonax, turned to the former slaves who had been fighting against the whites since 1791. In June 1793, Sonthonax offered freedom to slaves who joined the French army, and in August 1793, he extended this emancipation to the whole black population. In February 1794, three deputies from Saint-Domingue—a white, a member of the mixed-race group, and a black—arrived in Paris and urged the National Convention to endorse Sonthonax's decree. The resulting law of 16 pluviôse II made France the first western nation to abolish slavery, and the former slave J. B. Belley became the first black man to sit in a European legislature. In Saint-Domingue, the most effective of the black military commanders, Toussaint Louverture, joined the French forces in May 1794. Under his leadership, the French were eventually able to drive back the British and Spaniards.

THE GREAT TERROR AND *THERMIDOR*

Obsessed with maintaining national unity, the Montagnard leaders engaged in a constantly intensifying hunt for hidden conspirators whose activities they blamed for the Revolution's continuing difficulties. In the provinces, some of the deputies on mission interpreted their mandate to "make terror the order of the day" in extreme terms. At Nantes, Jean Baptiste Carrier, sent to crush the peasant guerrilla war that had continued even after the defeat of the Vendéan army in the summer of 1793, rid himself of several thousand suspected rebels crowding the prisons by mass executions in which victims were thrown into the Loire River. To end rural resistance, "infernal columns" of republican troops scoured the countryside, burning villages and fields. The guerrillas retaliated by massacring local republican loyalists and government troops. The total loss of life in the region, where fighting continued for several years after the fall of Robespierre, may have exceeded 100,000.

Another spectacular feature of the Terror was its use against an increasing number of the Revolution's most dedicated supporters. By 1793, the arrested Girondin deputy Vergniaud had commented prophetically that "the Revolution, like Saturn, is devouring its children." In early March 1794, the Committee of Public Safety tried and executed the most prominent spokesmen of the Paris *sans-culotte* movement. The journalist Hébert, author of *Père Duchêne*, the pamphlet-journal that had become the symbol of radical patriotism, fell victim to trumped-up charges.

The Committee then turned against a group of Convention deputies who had raised their voices against extension of the Terror. Whereas Hébert and his followers had been *Ultras* who wanted to push the Revolution too far, Robespierre charged, these men—particularly the famed orator Danton and the journalist Camille Desmoulins (who had criticized the Committee in his paper, the *Vieux Cordelier*)—were *Citras* who wanted to stop the Revolution before it had gone far enough. Danton's group's fate was proof that even the most prominent supporters of the Revolution were not immune to the Terror.

Rather than reassuring the Committee, the executions of the Hébertists and Dantonists merely accelerated the pace of the Terror. The atmosphere of enforced conformism and the evident lack of genuine enthusiasm that the Terror itself had engendered made the movement's leaders even more fearful. Saint-Just complained that "the Revolution has become frozen" and called for ever more drastic measures against hidden counter-revolutionaries. Two days after his elaborately staged Festival of the Supreme Being, organized to demonstrate the nation's spiritual unity and adherence to revolutionary principles, Robespierre rammed through the Convention a law that stripped suspects sent before the Revolutionary Tribunal of all rights to defend themselves. Convention deputies no longer enjoyed any special immunity from arrest. This law unleashed the so-called Great Terror of the summer of 1794. In six weeks, the guillotine decapitated over thirteen hundred victims in Paris alone.

The Great Terror took place just as the real dangers to the republican government's security were fading. At the battle of Fleurus on June 26, 1794, the French armies in the north decisively defeated the Austrians, who withdrew from Belgium. The French occupied Brussels on July 10, 1794, the beginning of a twenty-year period of territorial expansion. As the crisis atmosphere of 1793 faded, a number of deputies in the Convention and even within the Committee of Public Safety began to turn against Robespierre's Terror policy. On the ninth day of *thermidor* (new calendar), they unexpectedly took the floor in the Convention to accuse Robespierre of plotting to make himself dictator. The Convention shouted Robespierre down when he tried to reply, and then voted overwhelmingly to arrest him and several of his supporters. Robespierre and his fellow arrestees briefly escaped from their captors and rallied some supporters at the Hôtel-de-Ville, the seat of Paris's city government. But the mass of the Paris *sans-culottes*, alienated from the Montagnards by the execution of the Hébertists and the repression of the popular movement, made no effort to support them. Early the next day, the Convention's troops captured the escaped prisoners and hustled Robespierre, Saint-Just, and over one hundred of their supporters to the guillotine. Once again, the mechanism of the Revolution had turned against those who had set it in motion. But the ninth of *thermidor* marked a turning point; instead of intensifying the revolutionary process, the victors—no longer pushed along by organized popular protest—began to dismantle the machinery of revolution.

Notes

1. Saint-Just, *Oeuvres choisies* (Paris: Gallimard, 1968), 76.
2. Cited in J. H. Stewart, *Documentary Survey of the French Revolution* (New York: MacMillan, 1951), 473.
3. Cited in Darline Gay Levy, Harriet B. Applewhite, and Mary D. Johnson, eds., *Women in Revolutionary Paris, 1789–1795* (Urbana, IL: University of Illinois Press, 1979), 90.

CHAPTER 9

THE RETURN TO ORDER

THE THERMIDORIAN REACTION

To a remarkable degree, the first five years of the Revolution, from 1789 to 1794, had set the shape of French society for decades to come. The revolutionaries had eliminated corporate privileges and given equal rights to all male citizens; they had established a strong central government; they had strengthened the position of the property-owning bourgeoisie and of peasant landholders, and sharpened the gender division between men and women. They had established a secular society, and they had created a formidable military machine. What they had not been able to do was to assure political stability. The many regimes that followed the republican Convention between 1794 and 1870 can all be seen, in various ways, as attempts, none of them fully successful, to resolve this problem without returning to the democratic and republican principles of the radical revolution.

The thermidorian conspirators were the first group to confront this difficulty. Initially it was not clear whether they wanted to eliminate Robespierre's methods, or just the man. But *thermidor* unleashed a reaction against the Terror and the radical revolution that they could not control. For the next five years, the question of how to repudiate the

worst excesses of the Revolution without endangering the new principles it had articulated, and the new elites it had brought to power, dominated French political life.

Since they had overthrown Robespierre because he had tyrannized the Convention and the people, the *thermidor* plotters found themselves compelled to dismantle the dictatorial apparatus of the Terror. Hundreds of prisoners arrested under the Law of Suspects were released from prison, and several of the most prominent architects of the Terror—including Carrier, who had overseen the massacres of rebels in Brittany, and Fouquier-Tinville, the prosecutor of the Revolutionary Tribunal—were tried and executed. This occurred despite their protests that they had simply carried out policies approved by the Convention as a whole. In November 1794, the Convention ordered the closing of the Paris Jacobin Club. Bands of elegantly dressed young men, the *jeunesse dorée*, or "gilded youth," chased down former *sans-culotte* activists and destroyed symbols of the radical revolution, such as the busts of Marat that had been placed in all public buildings after his assassination. In the provinces, similar groups were even more violent; there were numerous killings of former Jacobin militants in Lyon, Marseille, and other areas where counter-revolutionary sentiment was strong.

The "thermidorian reaction" also turned against the Revolution's social and economic policies. The Convention dismantled the Maximum system and left prices free to find their own levels. Without the threat of the guillotine to sustain it, the *assignat* rapidly lost all value. This runaway inflation benefited peasants with grain reserves and middle-class speculators, who scooped up national lands at bargain prices. But it was devastating to the poor, whose wages lagged far behind the skyrocketing price of bread. The hungry Paris *sans-culottes* reacted by staging two massive protest demonstrations in April and June 1795; during the latter, they invaded the Convention and murdered one of the deputies. As always when food prices were an issue, women made up much of the crowd in these protests. But these uprisings lacked the clear-cut program and leadership that had made popular mobilization effective in 1792 and 1793. Aided by troops and the *jeunesse dorée,* the Convention dispersed the crowds and proceeded even more determinedly to eliminate the democratic elements of the Revolution.

The new attitude toward the lower classes was reflected in everyday life and in politics. Instead of dressing to look like *sans-culottes,* the wealthier classes reverted to elegant, sometimes extravagant costumes that emphasized their special status, such as the provocative see-through dresses worn by some fashionable Parisian women. While the poor struggled to afford bread, the wealthy crowded cafés, restaurants, and theaters where they applauded plays that denounced the horrors of Robespierre's reign and presented the *sans-culottes* as bloodthirsty monsters. In the streets, the honorific term *Monsieur* ousted the revolutionary *Citizen* as the preferred form of address, and the polite form *vous* regained its ascendancy. Objects of sympathy during the early revolutionary years, the poor were now seen as violent and dangerous, needing to be disciplined by the rigorous workings of economic laws.

By mid-1795, the thermidorian Convention was ready to scrap the democratic constitution enacted but never put into effect in 1793. In the new constitution, the deputies sought to accomplish three main goals: to protect the interests of middle-class supporters of the Revolution, to prevent the rise of another dictatorial government, and to exclude the common people from politics. The new Constitution of 1795 limited the right to vote and to hold office to the wealthiest taxpayers; only about thirty thousand met the requirements to serve in the departmental electoral colleges where deputies were to be chosen. All references to social rights were eliminated from the constitution, and the deputies added a "declaration of duties" designed to remind the poor of their obligation to respect the rights of property and the authority of the law. The administrative system remained highly centralized, but the powers of the central government were carefully divided. The five-member Directory, the executive branch, was held in check by a two-house legislature made up of a Council of 500 and a smaller Council of Elders (limited to deputies over age forty). To make sure that the new government did not suddenly turn against the deputies who had served in the Convention and who were now often accused of having permitted the excesses of the Terror, an accompanying decree required voters to choose two-thirds of the deputies for the new councils from the outgoing members of the Convention.

The new constitution inspired none of the enthusiasm that had greeted the first revolutionary constitution of 1791. In Paris, counter-revolutionary activists in the section assemblies seized on the law forcing voters to choose two-thirds of the new deputies from the Convention to mobilize an armed assault on that body just before it was due to dissolve. To suppress this uprising of 13 *ven-démiaire* (October 5, 1795), the Convention called on troops from the regular army. This use of the army to maintain the regime set a dangerous precedent, particularly since one of the officers employed was the young general Napoleon Bonaparte.

THE DIRECTORY

A nineteenth-century French journalist once remarked that the Directory was the only regime in the country's history for which no one ever expressed nostalgia after it fell. It has been remembered as a period of flagrant corruption, unscrupulous intrigue, and fruitless confrontation. Recent historians have demonstrated that the Directory years were not as chaotic as this stereotype suggests. Perhaps the regime's greatest weakness was that it failed to inspire loyalty even among its own leaders: their betrayal eventually destroyed it.

The political leaders of the Directory lacked the stature of their predecessors under the National Assembly and the Convention. Paul Barras, a corrupt thermidorian Convention deputy who served on the five-man Executive Directory throughout its existence, symbolized their shortcomings. Barras had no commitment to revolutionary ideals, but he had a single-minded devotion to keeping himself and men like him in power, even at the cost of disregarding the republican constitution he had helped to create. Most of his fellow politicians were successful members of the bourgeoisie who had been active in local affairs during the early years of the Revolution. Having held public office after 1789, and often having invested in national lands, they had good reason to support the republican regime against any counter-revolution. In general, however, they had avoided taking strong positions on controversial issues prior to 1794. Their caution enabled them to survive the Terror, but the result was that France was governed during the Directory years primarily by men concerned with not sticking their necks out. In a crisis, these men were easily pushed aside by cynical revolutionary veterans like Barras.

Despite this weakness at the top, the Directory succeeded in restoring a certain degree of order to a country racked by six years of revolutionary upheaval. The regime benefited from a favorable economic climate due to a series of good harvests. After an unsuccessful effort to replace the worthless *assignats* with another form of paper money, the Directory reverted to metallic currency. By 1798, monetary stability had been achieved and economic growth resumed. The Directory also resolved the government debt problem that had forced the calling of the Estates-General in 1789, and that had dogged every subsequent revolutionary government. In 1798, it "consolidated" the public debt, writing off two-thirds of it. This partial bankruptcy freed subsequent governments from a painful burden. To put the government on a sound financial footing, the Directory systematized the collection of the taxes on land and on business activity imposed by the National Assembly, and added new taxes on luxury items plus a real estate tax calculated according to the number of doors and windows in each taxpayer's house. Easier to collect than the multiplicity of Old Regime taxes, these four taxes remained the main bases of French government revenue for a century. To enforce its policies, the Directory continued the centralization of authority begun during the Terror, sending appointed officials, called commissioners of the executive power, to oversee departmental administrations.

An important aspect of the Directory period was the consolidation of a new set of institutions to organize France's intellectual life. The Convention had already begun to replace the aristocratically dominated royal academies of the old regime with new, more professionally oriented institutions for research and teaching. Examples were the Museum of Natural History, founded in 1793, the *Ecole normale* for teachers, and the *Ecole polytechnique* for engineers, both the latter set up to teach an elite of outstanding students from all over the country in 1794. New medical schools, organized along scientific lines, were also opened that year, and the *Institut* replaced the abolished academies in 1795. These new institutions made Paris the world's center in science and medicine for the next several decades. To a greater extent than in any previous era of French history, professors and scientists held positions of political responsibility. They hailed the Revolution for having cleared the way for the triumph of rationalism by its destruction of the old academies and the church. Furthermore, the Directory period saw the publication of important works that summed up the Enlightenment's world view in a new, more rigorously scientific manner, such as the astronomer Laplace's *Exposition of the System of the World*. Leading philosophers and social thinkers formed a group known as the *Idéologues* and elaborated the science of *idéologie*, the analytic study of human thought, which they attempted to relate to new advances in medicine and anatomy.

The Directory and Foreign Affairs

While the Directory thus took some important steps to stabilize conditions inside France, its most striking achievements were in the realm of foreign affairs. Even before the fall of Robespierre, the French armies had regained the initiative in the war. In the fall of 1794, the revolutionary armies swept through Belgium and the Rhineland. In the first months of 1795, they occupied the Netherlands, where they sponsored a "Batavian revolution" in which the old ruler, the *Stadholder*, was expelled and a republican constitution on the French model was drawn up. For their services in liberating the country and protecting its new government, the French imposed a heavy indemnity on the Dutch. The revolutionary war began to change into a war of conquest, undertaken for the profit of republican France. The army and its leading generals also acquired a growing influence in domestic politics.

Under the Directory, France continued this expansion. In 1796 and 1797, French armies penetrated deep into Germany and Italy, where the young General Bonaparte scored spectacular successes, occupying the peninsula as far south as Rome. He applied the policies pioneered in the Netherlands, backing local movements to set up "sister republics," which were required to pay heavy indemnities to their liberators. In many areas, these exactions alienated the local populations, which came to consider French-style reforms a smokescreen for exploitation.

By the summer of 1797, with Bonaparte's army having crossed the Alps and threatening Vienna, the Austrians seemed ready to make peace, as Prussia had already done in 1795. Bonaparte, acting on his own, without approval of the Directory, negotiated a treaty in which Austria ceded its claims to Belgium and recognized the French-sponsored republics in Italy. In exchange, he presented them with Venice, which his troops had conquered. This exchange of territories, carried out without any regard for their inhabitants' wishes, showed how completely France had abandoned any pretense of extending the principle of national self-determination to other peoples. With Austria out of the war and Britain limited to naval operations and the capture of France's overseas colonies, the French tide of conquest rolled on. In 1798, Switzerland (renamed the Helvetic Republic) was added to the belt of satellite states surrounding the "Great Nation," as the French referred to themselves. In early 1799, a short-lived Parthenopean Republic replaced the Kingdom of Naples in southern Italy. Meanwhile, the Directory, fearful of its leading general's growing popularity, sent Bonaparte on an expedition to Egypt, an idea that attracted him because of the possibility of founding a French empire in a region rich in history. The French landed and defeated the Turks, opening the era of European expansion into the Islamic world, but British admiral Horatio Nelson's destruction of the French fleet at Aboukir left their army cut off from France.

Discord at Home

Although it consolidated French power abroad, the Directory could not achieve political peace at home. The popular *sans-culotte* movement had been crushed, and peasant discontent had died down; but the middle-class landowners, businessmen, and professionals whom the constitution makers of 1795 had expected to form the base of support for the regime remained bitterly divided. Many of these men, including a number who had profited from the Revolution by buying national lands, had been deeply shaken by the Terror and remained hostile to the republican government. They supported politicians who hinted broadly at the restoration of the monarchy and a purge of all those who had held important political positions during the Revolution. On the other hand, a significant number of former Jacobins remained politically active, denouncing the Directory government for being insufficiently dedicated to the principles of liberty and equality. The religious issue remained divisive: militant republicans and *Idéologue* intellectuals continued to identify Catholicism with counter-revolution and obscurantism, while the faithful denounced the regime's restrictions on worship and religious education.

Rather than taking a firm position, the government of the Directory strove to remain above politics. Its policy consisted of a series of alternating blows aimed against the royalists and the neo Jacobins. This "balance-beam policy" multiplied the regime's enemies without gaining it substantial support. In May 1796, the government attacked the radical left. It arrested the agitator Gracchus Babeuf, an agrarian radical who advocated communal ownership of property, and a number of former supporters of Robespierre. Babeuf had tried to organize a conspiracy to overthrow the Directory and install a dictatorship that would carry out his communist program. His plan had never had much chance of success, but his arrest presented the Directory with a chance to pose as the firm defender of social order and the rights of property. The breakup of a plot to restore the Bourbon monarchy in February 1797 allowed the government to show that it was equally opposed to any return of the Old Regime.

Rather than rewarding the Directory for its balanced policy, voters in the first regular parliamentary elections in April 1797 elected conservative deputies. Split among themselves on whether to work for a constitutional monarchy or to do what they could within the republican constitution, these new deputies spent the summer of 1797 arguing while the three firmly republican members of the five-man Directory planned countermeasures. With support from the army, whose leading generals were mostly militant republicans, this "triumvirate," headed by Barras, staged a coup on the eighteenth day of *fructidor* (September 4, 1797), expelling their two more moderate colleagues from the Directory and purging the prominent right-wing deputies from the Councils. This encouraged the militant republicans or neo-Jacobins who scored important gains in the elections of April 1798. The Directory responded by "correcting" the voters' decisions in the coup of the twenty-second day of *floréal* (May 11, 1798), installing its own henchmen in contested races. The *fructidor* and *floréal* coups showed that political power had become concentrated in the hands of a self appointed group of professional politicians who identified the survival of the Republic with their own tenure in office.

Whether a regime with such a narrow base of support could have survived thanks to economic prosperity and military success is hard to say. But the Directory was certainly poorly placed to cope with a crisis, and by the end of 1798 it was confronting one. A new foreign coalition had assembled against France. It included the intransigent British, the Austrians who hoped to reverse the unfavorable treaty of Campo-Formio of 1797, and the Russians, whose new ruler, Tsar Paul, harbored a fanatical hatred for the Revolution. In the first half of 1799, the French armies reeled backward on every front. The sudden military collapse discredited the Directory at home. The directors once again failed to control the spring parliamentary elections, and a broad coalition of discontented deputies reversed the procedure of the coups of *fructidor* and *floréal,* purging the Directory itself in the coup of the thirtieth day of *prairial* (June 18, 1799).

The *prairial* victors represented two tendencies. Some were neo-Jacobins who believed that the military crisis required a revival of the emergency measures and the patriotic spirit of 1793. Others, led by Sieyès (now a member of the Directory), intended to "revise" the Constitution of 1795 so that it would no longer be vulnerable to periodic challenges from either right or left. At first, the neo-Jacobins seemed to hold the upper hand. They pushed through a new draft law, a forced loan to levy money from the rich, and the "law of hostages," which allowed local officials to deal with counter-revolutionary unrest by arresting relatives of nobles and emigrés. These measures revived unhappy memories of the Terror, and provoked considerable resistance. Meanwhile, Sieyès and his group conspired to rid themselves of their neo-Jacobin allies. Recognizing their lack of organized public support, the plotters looked for a popular military figure to serve as their figurehead.

As Sieyès was casting around for a suitable general, the most celebrated of the Directory's commanders unexpectedly reappeared in Paris. Having learned of France's defeats in Europe, and alarmed by letters about his wife's infidelities, Napoleon Bonaparte had abandoned his stranded army in Egypt and arrived in France at the beginning of October. Large crowds turned out to cheer him as he traveled from the Mediterranean to Paris; his remarkable military accomplishments had made him genuinely popular. Napoleon had abandoned the revolutionary radicalism that had once made him a friend of Robespierre's younger brother and had led to his arrest after *thermidor.* During his years in Italy, he had supported pragmatic, socially conservative republicans rather than passionate idealists. He quickly cast his lot with the Sieyès group, who arranged for his appointment as commander of the troops in Paris. In three weeks, the coup plan was completed; on the eighteenth day of *brumaire* (November 9, 1799), it was put into effect.

Deputies sympathetic to the *brumaire* plotters invoked a constitutional provision allowing for an emergency convocation of the legislature outside of Paris in case of a crisis. By the time the two Councils met on the nineteenth day of *brumaire,* however, many deputies had become suspicious, and angry debate broke out while troops assembled to intimidate the politicians waited restlessly outside. Finally, the plotters used force to coerce the reluctant legislators into voting full powers to Sieyès and his group to prepare a new constitution. France's first postrevolutionary government had collapsed, and the lack of public reaction showed how little support the Directory had had.

CHAPTER 10

THE NAPOLEONIC YEARS

The conspirators who overthrew the Directory in November 1799 claimed to be protecting the achievements of the Revolution. Officially, France remained a republic, governed by men who had established their careers after 1789. But it quickly became obvious that the *brumaire* coup had produced a fundamental change. The participatory politics inaugurated in 1789, already robbed of much of its substance by the Jacobins and then by the Directory, disappeared, and one man concentrated all real power in his own hands. As First Consul and then as emperor, Napoleon Bonaparte exercised greater authority than any other French ruler before or since. The dramatic story of his rise and fall is probably more widely known than any other chapter of French history. And yet many historians have concluded that, despite his ceaseless activity and his lasting impact on the French imagination, Napoleon's accomplishments were relatively modest. Napoleon's most substantial achievement was not to initiate anything, but to consolidate the new society created during the Revolution.

THE CONSUL AND THE CONSULATE

The coup of the eighteenth of *brumaire,* which brought Napoleon Bonaparte to power, was more the work of Sieyès, the veteran politician who had done so much to launch the Revolution ten years earlier, than of the man who reaped the main benefit from it. Sieyès's intention was the same as that of the authors of the 1795 constitution: to consolidate the power of moderate republican politicians and bourgeois propertyholders, and to prevent any revival of either royalism or Jacobinism by a complex division of powers. The main innovation in Sieyès's scheme was the abolition of the parliamentary elections which had troubled the Directory so much. Instead, he proposed a system of cooptation, in which politicians already in power would pick their own successors from lists of property-owning "notables" drawn up by local electoral assemblies. Before Sieyès could implement his ideas, however, he had to negotiate with the young general he had been forced to bring into the coup plan. He quickly discovered that Napoleon Bonaparte had definite ideas of his own about how France should be governed. The rest of France soon learned the same lesson: the coup of *brumaire* had brought a dominating new leader to the fore.

More has been written about Napoleon Bonaparte than about any other figure in France's long history. He has been hailed as a political and military genius and condemned as the first modern totalitarian dictator, credited with consolidating the achievements of the Revolution and damned for destroying it. In the nineteenth century, with its cult of romantic genius, Napoleon was often seen as a colossus, a unique figure who changed the course of his era. Twentieth-century historians have tended to downplay both his personal impact and the importance of the changes that occurred in France during the fifteen years of his rule. Regardless of how one evaluates the impact of Napoleon's actions, however, he has certainly haunted France's collective memory. The "Napoleonic legend," planted in Napoleon's own propaganda and memoirs and cultivated by a host of subsequent artists, historians, and memoirists, has been an essential part of French culture.

Napoleon, it has often been said, was a "child of the Revolution," who owed his career to the upheaval of 1789. Born in 1769 to a poor noble family on the island of Corsica (a territory annexed to France just a year earlier), the young Bonaparte had been educated as an artillery officer, the least prestigious branch of the prerevolutionary army. Teachers and fellow cadets had noted the young man's intelligence and fierce willpower, but because of his modest background, his prospects for promotion in the prerevolutionary army were not dazzling. A young lieutenant at the time of the Revolution, he enthusiastically embraced its promise of "careers open to talent."

The emigration of many aristocratic army officers after 1789 and the outbreak of war in 1792 turned those possibilities into realities. By 1793, Bonaparte had been promoted to captain. The federalist revolt gave him the opportunity to show his mettle. His skillful use of artillery at the siege of Toulon won the day for the Convention's forces and brought him promotion to the rank of general. Augustin Robespierre, a deputy on mis-

sion in the area and the younger brother of the Montagnard leader, became his patron and had him draft plans for an invasion of Italy. As a result of this association, Napoleon nearly fell victim to the purge that followed the ninth of *thermidor;* he remained unemployed until the Convention called on him for help in putting down the counterrevolutionary uprising of the thirteenth of *vendémiaire* (October 1795). This gained him entry into Barras's political circle, where he met and hastily married Josephine Beauharnais, the attractive widow of an officer executed during the Terror. As a reward for his services on the thirteenth of *vendémiaire*, he was given command of France's most demoralized troops, the Army of Italy.

In the Italian campaign of 1796, Napoleon immediately demonstrated the qualities that were to carry him to glory. He had a remarkable ability to sense the decisive point at which victory could be obtained, and he acted quickly and boldly to achieve it. Outnumbered by the combined Austrian and Piedmontese forces opposing him, Bonaparte succeeded in splitting his foes and overwhelming them separately. In two months, he had knocked the Piedmontese out of the war, occupied their entire kingdom, and chased the Austrians from Milan. Only twenty-six years old, he had established himself as the most brilliant of the French Republic's generals. As commander of the French occupation forces in northern Italy, he showed himself an adept politician as well. He stage-managed the creation of carefully controlled sister republics, enriched both himself and the Directory from the levies he raised, and successfully courted the Catholic church, avoiding the religious conflicts that had dogged the Revolution at home.

The Directory recognized Bonaparte's driving ambition and kept him at arm's length after he negotiated his own peace treaty with the Austrians in 1797. After the *brumaire* coup, Sieyès had intended to give Bonaparte a high-sounding title but little real power. But the general had other ideas. Despite his lack of political experience, he proved more than a match for Sieyès in the constitutional negotiations. He was unconcerned with most of the document's details. A constitution, he remarked, should be "short and obscure." But he insisted that real power, instead of being carefully divided, should be concentrated in the hands of a single person. He accepted those parts of Sieyès's draft that weakened parliamentary government and sabotaged the electoral principle, but he insisted on the creation of a strong executive body of three consuls. The First Consul was to have much greater powers than his two colleagues; in case of a disagreement among them, his decision would prevail. Once Bonaparte's definition of the First Consul's role was accepted, it was inevitable that he would be entrusted with the office; no one else had the prestige and popularity to fill it. Two relatively unknown political figures were appointed as the other consuls, and Sieyès found himself relegated to the presidency of the largely powerless Senate that he had designed.

The *brumaire* plotters submitted this hastily drafted Constitution of the Year VIII (new calendar) to the voters for ratification. This plebiscite enabled the new strongman to maintain that he had a popular mandate to govern. The often-quoted story of the voter who, when asked what was in the constitution he was approving, said it was enough for him that " there is Bonaparte" was a creation of the new leader's propaganda machine. Participation was low and officials were told to pad the figures to make them more impressive, but only fifteen hundred voters risked casting a negative vote. Bonaparte understood, however, that his support was less overwhelming than it seemed. France was weary of political turmoil and disenchanted with revolutionary

ideals; it remained up to him to show that he could do better.

Napoleon's Consolidation of Power

To consolidate his power, the new First Consul—increasingly referred to by his first name, Napoleon, rather than his family name of Bonaparte—moved quickly to break up the political factions created by the Revolution. He muzzled the political press and used the police to harass prominent neo-Jacobins and die-hard royalists. But all those political figures between the extremes were welcomed into the system. By choosing collaborators regardless of their attitude to the Revolution, Napoleon did much to defuse the bitter conflicts of the previous decade.

The second key feature of the Napoleonic system was the creation of a streamlined system of government that could act swiftly and effectively. Napoleon strengthened the already-centralized bureaucracy by the creation of prefects, administrators appointed in Paris and dispatched to the departments to oversee local administration. The prefects bore some resemblance to the prerevolutionary intendants and to the Directory's commissioners, but they had more extensive powers in the field, while being more strictly controlled from Paris. Thanks to the Revolution, they faced no institutional opposition in their local regions. The reforms of 1789 had abolished all the traditional privileged bodies that had obstructed the monarchy's officials. Appointed from Paris and rotated from post to post after a few years to keep them from developing too many attachments to local interests, the corps of prefects, which included men drawn from a variety of political backgrounds, gave the central government a powerful mechanism for imposing its will on the country.

The laws the prefects enforced were no longer the result of stormy public legislative debates as they had been throughout the

Revolution. Napoleon concentrated real law-making powers in a new body, the *Conseil d'Etat*, or Council of State, which he appointed himself and whose meetings were held in private. To it, Napoleon appointed competent and articulate councilors, drawn—like the prefects—from diverse political camps, and whom he urged to engage in free-wheeling debate. Once he had approved a proposal hammered out in the council, however, public debates were largely a formality. The deputies—divided under Sieyès's complex scheme into a Tribunate which debated proposals without voting on them, a legislative body which listened to the debates and voted without speaking, and a senate supposedly charged with preventing violations of the constitution—generally accepted the government's proposals.

With all real power in his own hands, and with the new administrative and law-making machinery at his control, Napoleon was able to govern more effectively than any previous French regime. The economic revival that had begun under the Directory continued, benefiting merchants and manufacturers and providing jobs for workers. The establishment of the Bank of France in 1800 made it easier for the government to borrow money and supplied credit for business needs. New gold coins issued in 1803 set the value of France's currency for a century to come. Napoleon reassured the purchasers of the national lands sold under the Revolution that their acquisitions would be protected, even though he allowed many of the emigrés whose estates had been confiscated and sold to return to the country. This "Napoleonic settlement," under which properties and positions attained during the Revolution were guaranteed in exchange for acceptance of Napoleon's one-man rule, satisfied much of the population. The efficient spy network set up by Joseph Fouché, a former Jacobin terrorist turned minister of police, kept grumblers under surveillance.

Ending the Religious Conflict

To complete his policy of liquidating the conflicts engendered by the Revolution, Napoleon needed to resolve the religious struggle that had begun with the imposition of the Civil Constitution of the Clergy in 1790. Napoleon had no firm religious beliefs of his own; in Egypt, he had made a great show of courting Muslim leaders. But he considered religion a useful instrument of social control and was determined to end the conflict that had grown out of the Revolution's religious reform efforts. His strategy was to go over the heads of the counter-revolutionary French bishops, most of whom had gone into exile during the 1790s, and deal directly with Pope Pius VII, a man who had shown some sympathy for revolutionary reforms during Napoleon's first occupation of Italy.

Negotiations for a Concordat between the French government and the papacy were successfully completed in July 1801. Under this agreement, Napoleon recognized Catholicism as the religion of the majority of the population in France and authorized the resumption of public worship. The government would pay priests and bishops; as under the Old Regime, it would nominate bishops, who would receive their consecration from the pope. To end the schism resulting from the Civil Constitution, the pope called on all French bishops, both emigrés and constitutionals who had remained in France, to submit their resignations and appointed a new hierarchy including some members of both factions. The church had to accept the permanent loss of its confiscated lands and the legalization of other religions, as well as government control of education and tight regulation of religious orders and charitable activities. To Pius VII and to most French Catholics, the price was acceptable in order to restore regular public worship. Many prominent ex-revolutionaries objected to the Concordat; they blamed Napoleon for

Jacques Louis David's painting Napoleon Crossing the Alps *represents the First Consul as a hero larger than life, surpassing the achievements of Hannibal and Charlemagne, whose names appear carved in the rocks under the horse's hooves. The style of the painting is typical of the romantic spirit that came to dominate the creative arts during the early nineteenth century. In reality, Napoleon crossed the mountains riding on a sure-footed mule.*

(Source: Kunsthistorisches Museum, Vienna.)

abandoning the Revolution's hard-won triumph over what they saw as outmoded superstition. But the majority of the population welcomed the Concordat and the end of the conflict that had begun with the imposition of the Civil Constitution of the Clergy. The Protestant and Jewish religious minorities still enjoyed the legal protection they had been granted after 1789.

In 1807, Napoleon took the extraordinary step of convoking an international congress of Jewish religious leaders, the *Sanhedrin,* to discuss the relationship between French and Jewish law. Together with the granting of citizenship rights to Jews in 1791, the meeting of the *Sanhedrin* constituted a remarkable departure in the relations between Jews and the world around them. Not even Napoleon's imposition of discriminatory regulations on the Jewish money-lenders of Alsace in 1808 destroyed the impression made by his earlier initiative.

To round out the changes taken to consolidate his regime, in May 1802 Napoleon announced the creation of the Legion of Honor, an award to be given to those who had rendered special service to the country. Giving special distinctions to certain citizens struck many as a violation of the Revolution's promise of equality, but Napoleon maintained that he was not creating a new privileged class. Membership was not hereditary, and any French citizen could earn the coveted cross. In practice, the Legion became composed primarily of military officers; it served to bind them and the small elite of civilian members to their leader.

The Peace of Amiens and the Saint-Domingue Expedition

In addition to establishing firm control at home, Napoleon also needed to show that he could defend France's international position. Even before the *brumaire* coup, the French armies had stopped the tide of Coalition victories that had threatened France in early 1799, but France had lost much of the territory gained under the Directory. With the Russians having quarreled with their allies and withdrawn from the war, Napoleon turned his attention to Austria. His dramatic victory at Marengo in June 1800 restored French control of northern Italy. General Moreau's victory at Hohenlinden in southern Germany in December 1800 completed the demoralization of the Austrians; in February 1801, they accepted the treaty of Lunéville, which gave France even greater gains than the 1797 Campo-Formio treaty. In addition to Belgium and Luxemburg, France now annexed the German territories west of the Rhine River that it had occupied since 1795, setting in motion a reshuffling of borders throughout the Holy Roman Empire, as rulers who had lost lands to France sought compensation elsewhere. French-dominated regimes were installed throughout the Italian peninsula and in the Netherlands and Switzerland.

With Austria out of the war, Britain—France's most implacable enemy—made overtures for peace as well. In the treaty signed at Amiens in March 1802, England made a few colonial gains but had to acknowledge France's continental predominance. With this treaty, Napoleon appeared to have brought the ten years of war in Europe to a glorious conclusion. He could boast that revolutionary France had expanded far beyond the limits dreamed of by its Bourbon kings. The other European powers had had to recognize France's "natural frontiers" along the crest of the Alps and the Rhine River.

The peace of Amiens allowed Napoleon to dream of restoring France's colonies in the Caribbean and using Louisiana, acquired from Spain, as a base for expansion on the American continent. First, however, he had to reassert French authority in Saint-Domingue. After the National Convention had abolished slavery in 1794, the black ex-slave, Toussaint Louverture, had used his military skills to make himself the virtual ruler of the island.

In 1798, he negotiated the withdrawal of the British, and by 1801, he had brought the island to the brink of independence. The French succeeded in landing twenty thousand troops in Saint-Domingue in February 1802; Toussaint was arrested soon afterward and shipped to France, where he died in prison. Fear of the barely concealed French intention to restore slavery—which Napoleon did in the other colonies—inspired the black population to furious resistance. Disease decimated the French troops, and the resumption of war with England in 1803 cut off reinforcements; in November 1803, the French conceded defeat.

The failure of the Saint-Domingue expedition had profound historical consequences. Once he saw that the loss of Saint-Domingue was inevitable, Napoleon realized that he could not hold on to France's claims in North America and offered to sell them to the United States. This "Louisiana Purchase" of 1803 doubled the size of the United States and opened the way for the country's westward expansion. Saint-Domingue became the independent republic of Haiti, and its example encouraged the countries of Latin America to free themselves from Spanish rule. This first triumph of a non-white population over a European power has remained an inspiration to anti-colonial movements for the past two centuries.

One-Man Rule and the Code Napoleon

The Peace of Amiens, the Concordat, and the successful restoration of domestic order brought Napoleon to the height of his popularity. He followed up by carrying out various modifications of the constitution that strengthened his power and virtually silenced all opposition. In a plebiscite, more than 3.5 million voters approved Napoleon's being named First Consul for life; only 8,000 cast negative votes.

The loss of Saint-Domingue in 1803 had little effect on Napoleon's popularity, and did not prevent him from transforming the Consulate for Life into a hereditary Empire in 1804, after another plebiscite. The promulgation of the Civil Code, often known as the *Code Napoleon,* in 1804, completed Napoleon's program of domestic reforms. Since 1792, France's revolutionary legislators had labored to replace the hundreds of prerevolutionary local law codes with a single national system of civil law. The project, carried to completion at Napoleon's urging, implemented the Revolution's major principles at the level of everyday life. It gave property owners the clear right to use their wealth as they saw fit, eliminating the last vestiges of feudal dues on land and guild restrictions on business. It modified the revolutionary inheritance law, which had forced parents to divide their property equally among their children, but maintained the ban on the system of primogeniture, which had consolidated the wealth of noble families. Its harsh restrictions on women's rights codified male superiority. The husband had full control of the family's property and the fate of his children. Divorce was sharply restricted, though not completely abolished, and the husband had greater latitude to start proceedings than the wife. The Civil Code provided a clear and systematic framework for the society of autonomous individuals and private families that the Revolution had created. With modifications, it has remained the basis of French civil law down to the present. Introduced in most of the territories the French occupied during the Napoleonic era, including Louisiana, it proved to be one of the most influential results of the French Revolution.

THE NAPOLEONIC EMPIRE

For all of its accomplishments, Napoleon's regime continued to face one central problem: its fate depended entirely on Napoleon's personal authority. By crowning himself emperor in 1804 and making his power hereditary, Napoleon tried to institutionalize his system of one-man rule. But his marriage to Josephine was childless, and it was by no means clear that the country would accept his designated heir as his eventual successor. To maintain his authority, Napoleon felt compelled to be constantly active, reminding the French of his indispensabilty. When the fragile Peace of Amiens collapsed in 1803 and war resumed, he directed his energies particularly to winning new conquests. In doing so, he took the risk of making the continuation of his own rule dependent on his military successes.

Neither side had been fully satisfied with the 1802 treaty: Napoleon still considered British sea power a threat, and the British were unwilling to accept France's domination of its neighbors and the loss of European markets. But Napoleon lacked any immediate way to strike at the British. Cartoonists imagined French troops crossing the Channel by balloon, but Britain's naval supremacy foiled Napoleon even before Admiral Nelson's crushing victory at Trafalgar in October 1805 permanently ended any hopes for a seaborne invasion.

Britain's ability to defeat France depended on finding allies on the continent to challenge Napoleon's land forces. The obvious candidates were Austria (which had lost both territory and prestige in its previous campaigns against France) and Russia (which had never accepted France's revolutionary conquests). British subsidies helped both nations renew the fight in August 1805.

Napoleon promptly marched the forces he had been training for a possible invasion of England toward the Danube. By this time, he had turned his Grand Army into a fighting machine that combined mobile artillery developed after the Seven Years' War with mass attacks made possible by the size and enthusiasm of the revolutionary citizen armies.

Over a decade of campaigning had given him a galaxy of tested generals and a large core of experienced professional soldiers strongly devoted to their brilliant commander.

Austerlitz and Jena

At Austerlitz, close to Vienna, Napoleon won perhaps his most celebrated battle, completely crushing the Austrian forces. The Austrians hastened to make peace, ceding even more territory to France and its satellite states. The following year, Prussia, which had remained neutral during the Austerlitz campaign, unexpectedly joined Russia and resumed the fight against Napoleon. At the battles of Jena and Auerstädt, French forces annihilated the famous Prussian army. Napoleon occupied Berlin. The Russians continued the war in 1807, as Napoleon advanced into Poland. At Eylau, in February, the two armies fought to a bloody draw, but in June 1807 Napoleon caught the Russian forces in a trap at the battle of Friedland and inflicted decisive casualties on them. Russia, too, sued for peace.

Napoleon met the young Russian emperor Alexander I personally at Tilsit, in Poland, to conclude a settlement. The Peace of Tilsit in 1807 went well beyond a mere end to hostilities. The charismatic French emperor persuaded Alexander to become his partner in a grand plan by which the two powers would divide Europe and Asia into spheres of influence, and work together to defeat England. With Russia on his side, Napoleon appeared to have achieved total control of the European continent. He had already converted the sister republics established in the Directory period into satellite kingdoms, ruled by members of his family. Hapless Prussia and Austria had to accept Napoleon's orders.

Economic Challenge to England

Unable to challenge Britain's naval power directly, Napoleon planned to defeat her through a program of economic warfare that he called the "Continental System." In essence, this amounted to a boycott of trade with Britain, whose rapidly industrializing economy depended on overseas outlets to sell its goods. The Continental System was also aimed at promoting the growth of French industry, which Napoleon hoped would capture the European markets Britain would lose. With his encouragement, cotton-spinning plants sprang up in Paris, which became France's largest industrial center. To replace cane sugar, normally imported from the West Indies, the Napoleonic regime encouraged the planting of sugar beets in northern France and the Belgian departments, and sponsored the growth of a refining industry.

French manufacturers benefited from the hothouse atmosphere of the Continental System, but the port cities—cut off by the British naval blockade—suffered. Those in France itself could do little more than grumble but, in the French-occupied areas, illegal trade with Britain flourished, undermining the boycott and driving authorities to ever-harsher measures against the local population. To stop the leaks, Napoleon felt driven to impose tight controls on one territory after another. In 1808, he replaced Spain's Bourbon king with his brother Joseph; this insult to Spanish national pride triggered a guerrilla insurrection which tied down considerable numbers of French forces. The following year, he took over the Papal States in Italy, starting a test of wills with Pius VII that lasted until Napoleon's downfall. In 1810, Napoleon annexed directly to France northern Germany, the Netherlands, and Italy as far south as Rome, installing French prefects and French police.

The Domestic Scene

The counterpart to Napoleon's bid for control over Europe was a steady expansion of government authority in France itself. After the declaration of the Empire in 1804, the vestigial powers of the legislature were still further curtailed. Napoleon used the compliant Senate to implement constitutional changes without resorting to the plebiscite mechanism. A law of 1807 formally reinstated a system of censorship, which had already been carried out by other means since Napoleon came to power. In 1808, Napoleon created the Imperial University, a bureaucratic arrangement giving the government a monopoly over secondary and higher education throughout the country. Under the Concordat, the church was turned into an instrument of political indoctrination; the Imperial Catechism, issued in 1807, required priests to teach that loyalty to the emperor and military service were religious obligations.

Determined to prevent the emergence of lower-class protest, Napoleon strengthened employers' powers over their workforce. An 1803 law required every worker to have a *livret*, or "work book"; workers needed their employer's signature to change jobs, and, in case of conflicts, the employer's testimony was to be accepted in court. Workers did have some representation, but not an equal voice, on the *conseils de prud'hommes*, or arbitration panels, set up after 1806 to resolve conflicts between employers and employees in various trades.

Art and cultural life were regimented to serve the regime: Jacques Louis David, who had organized republican festivals under the Terror, now devoted himself to huge canvases of Napoleon's coronation and his military successes. Napoleon set in motion plans to make Paris a monument to his glory. A long, straight boulevard, the *rue de Rivoli*, was to traverse the city, and two arches of triumph were to mark his conquests. To reward his followers, in 1808 Napoleon created a new nobility, handing out titles of baron and count and endowing his favorites with landed estates.

ELEMENTS OF OPPOSITION

As long as Napoleon marched from victory to victory, there was little visible opposition to him at home. Under the surface, however, there was quiet resistance to the regime's increasing authoritarianism. Small circles of devoted royalists and disgruntled republicans continued to exist. Napoleon could hire artists to glorify him and pamphleteers to praise him, but he was unable to win over the country's major thinkers. The leading members of the rationalist *Idéologue* group that had formed during the Directory period became the hard core of the opposition to him during the Consulate. In 1802, Napoleon had eliminated them from the legislative councils. In 1803, he suppressed their institutional stronghold, the Third Section of the Institute. But he remained uneasily aware of their silent disapproval of the regime.

Paris continued to be a center of scientific activity, but imperial policy favored applied research over theoretical investigations, and leadership in the latter area began to shift from France to less restricted universities in Germany. Napoleon maintained the *grandes écoles,* such as the *Ecole polytechnique,* set up during the revolutionary decade to train the nation's intellectual elite. But he imposed a quasi-military discipline that the most independent-minded students resented.

Napoleon himself thought for a time that he might find support among the thinkers associated with the revival of Catholicism that had begun even before the Concordat. As a result of the controversy over the Civil Constitution of the Clergy and the dechristianizers' attacks on the church, those priests who lacked a real commitment to the faith had left the church. Those who stayed formed a clergy far more serious about its beliefs than most of their prerevolutionary predecessors. The laity's faith had also been renewed. During the Terror, many formerly free-thinking nobles and other victims of persecution had embraced Catholicism, and many of the emigrés had found consolation in religion during their years in exile.

It was an emigré, François René de Chateaubriand, who captured this mood of religious revival in his *Genius of Christianity.* The book appeared in April 1802, coinciding with the first Easter celebration in Paris's Notre-Dame Cathedral since 1793. Chateaubriand's lyrical evocation of religion's aesthetic and emotional appeal made Catholicism fashionable, particularly among the upper classes who had frequently distanced themselves from it before 1789. The success of his book marked a shift in the intellectual climate. He and other apologists for religion challenged representatives of the rationalist Enlightenment tradition that had dominated French public life since the time of the *Encyclopédie.*

Chateaubriand marked a break with the Enlightenment not only because of his embrace of Catholicism but also because of his emphasis on the superiority of sentiment and emotion over reason. He was one of the first writers of the French romantic movement; his novel *René* was one of the first to sound the characteristic romantic themes of introspection and melancholy. Romanticism was not a monopoly of conservative writers during the Napoleonic period. Liberals frustrated with the stifling of public life during the Empire, such as Benjamin Constant, also wrote novels exploring psychological issues—implicitly suggesting that private life was more important than what went on in the regimented public sphere. Madame de Staël, driven into exile for her liberal views, became France's contact with the lively world of German romanticism, quite different from the regulated intellectual life of Napoleonic Paris. Artists accepted commissions to celebrate Napoleon's victories, but expressed their feelings most fully in more personal works, such as Pierre Paul

Prud'hon's subdued portrait of a pensive Empress Josephine or his mythological works on the theme of love.

Like the romantic artists, social thinkers of the period were united only by their distaste for the imperial regime. The thinkers of the *Idéologue* tradition continued to defend the rationalist individualism of the Enlightenment, implicitly condemning the Concordat and the Empire's tight controls on intellectual activity. The economist Jean Baptiste Say was a typical representative of this tradition. His *Treatise of Political Economy,* published in 1803, adapted and systematized Adam Smith's doctrines of economic liberty. The latter were in sharp contrast to Napoleon's policies of state intervention.

More original was the conservative Catholic thinker Louis de Bonald. During his years in emigration, this provincial nobleman had elaborated a far-reaching critique of rationalism and individualism, on which he blamed the horrors of the Revolution. He argued that society needed an unquestioned principle of authority, which he found in the Catholic church. The truth of its doctrines was confirmed, he argued, by the testimony of tradition. A body of beliefs that had endured for eighteen hundred years was more reliable than the speculations of modern philosophers. Society, according to Bonald, was a living organism that needed to be governed by a single head, not an agreement among private individuals. Until France returned to a society in accordance with divine will, with authority flowing from God, through the pope and the king to the aristocracy and finally down to the common people, it would continue to be racked by turmoil. Bonald's organic conception of society made him one of the ancestors of modern sociology. The authoritarian cast of his doctrines attracted Napoleon, but he could not wean the stubborn marquis away from his loyalty to the Bourbon monarchy.

Bonald was only one of a number of writers who contributed to the revival of royalist sentiment under the Empire. He and many others contributed occasional articles to the *Journal des Débats,* the most widely read newspaper of the period, whose sympathy for the Bourbon monarchy was barely disguised. Unable to raise the issue directly, the paper's contributors turned to literary and theatrical criticism, condemning the writings of Voltaire and the *philosophes,* and glorifying the classic seventeenth-century works of Corneille and Racine, with their royal heroes.

Other royalists tried more direct means of undermining the Empire, staging several assassination attempts against Napoleon and driving him in 1804 to take a drastic action. French troops invaded neutral Baden to capture the Duc d'Enghien, a Bourbon prince Napoleon thought was implicated in a plan to restore the monarchy. Napoleon had him tried in secret and executed. Even many of the former emigrés who had reconciled themselves with the Napoleonic regime never forgave this direct assault on the Bourbon family. Napoleon's foreign minister, Talleyrand, said, with reason, "it is worse than a crime, it's a blunder."

These elements of discontent did not threaten the regime as long as Napoleon could count on military success and economic prosperity. Up to 1810 at least, the war did not weigh too heavily on French society. Napoleon recruited a large proportion of his troops from his non-French territories and his satellite kingdoms. He financed his conquests from tribute levied on his defeated foes. Even after his final defeat in 1814, he left his successors a healthy treasury. Most of his common soldiers came from the French peasantry and, for many, military service proved to be a road to social mobility. There were many opportunities for enrichment during the campaigns, and Napoleon continued to adhere to the principle of promotion according to merit. His personal hold over his troops remained strong.

THE END OF THE EMPIRE

The year 1810 marked a turning point for Napoleon's regime. The emperor found himself bogged down in a growing number of conflicts that seemed to defy resolution. The "Spanish ulcer," the revolt against French domination that had begun in 1808, had turned into a bloody peasant war, as brutal as the Vendée rebellion. It ate up increasing numbers of French troops, and provided an opening for the British, who landed an expeditionary force under General Wellington in Portugal. Pius VII, placed under arrest on Napoleon's orders, refused to bow to French pressure. Austria made yet another bid to shake off French domination in 1809; although Napoleon's victory at Wagram smashed Vienna's military hopes, he himself was well aware of how thin his forces had been stretched. In 1810, to shore up his ties with the defeated Austrians and in the hope of putting his dynasty on a firmer footing, he divorced the childless Josephine and married an Austrian princess, Marie-Louise, who bore him a son in 1812.

Napoleon's rapprochement with Austria failed to solve his mounting problems. The Continental System had begun to unravel; Napoleon himself connived at violations of it, selling licenses for trade with Britain as a means of raising money. In December 1810, Russia abruptly withdrew from the System and resumed trade with Britain, convincing Napoleon that Alexander intended to turn against him. At home, the year 1810 was marked by the beginning of a sharp economic crisis that persisted into 1811. French manufacturing slumped, and factory owners joined the merchants of the port cities in blaming the regime for their troubles. Peasants showed increasing resentment about the weight of taxes and the growing draft calls needed to keep the army up to strength.

The Russian Campaign

Napoleon responded with his tried-and-true formula, a daring military campaign to silence his foes. But this time his gamble—an invasion of Russia to force Alexander back into the Continental System—failed. He advanced as far as Moscow, but could not catch and destroy the Russian army. Alexander refused to negotiate, and Napoleon finally had to begin a retreat in the harsh Russian winter. Cold, hunger, and Russian harassment decimated his troops; less than one-tenth of the men who had set off for Moscow returned. In Paris, conspirators spread the rumor that Napoleon himself had been killed in Russia. In the hours of confusion caused by the coup attempt, Napoleon's top officials failed to put into effect plans to declare his infant son emperor, revealing how shaky the regime's support had become.

Even after the defeat in Russia, Napoleon still thought that his own military genius and the potential divisions among his foes would allow him to reverse the situation. He pulled together a new army, made up mostly of raw recruits and men previously rejected as unfit, but he was unable to prevent first Prussia and then Austria from joining forces with the Russians. In October 1813, the combined allied forces defeated him at the battle of Leipzig, and Napoleon had to retreat across the Rhine. Meanwhile, British and Spanish forces under the Duke of Wellington advanced toward the Pyrénées. As the enemy forces penetrated into France in the winter of 1814, Napoleon fought a brilliant rearguard campaign; but he was hopelessly outnumbered. The French population, whose patriotism had enabled the revolutionary armies to fight off invaders in 1792 and 1793, now refused to heed Napoleon's summons to rise to the nation's defense. For too long, he had smothered all real participation in public affairs. At the end of March 1814, allied forces reached Paris.

Although military defeat was now certain, it was not clear that the Napoleonic regime would also fall. Royalist conspirators' efforts to set off demonstrations in favor of a Bourbon restoration enjoyed only limited success, and the victorious allies wanted to be sure that France had a stable government that would not be totally dependent on them for support. The Napoleonic regime's fate was sealed by Napoleon's own top officials, led by his foreign minister, Talleyrand. Determined to keep their own positions, they prepared to reinstate the Bourbons, but on their own terms. Louis XVI's long-exiled brother would be put on the throne, but he would have to accept a written constitution limiting his power and maintaining the principal features of the "Napoleonic settlement." Those who had obtained high governmental positions under Napoleon would keep them, and purchasers of church and emigré property would not be disturbed. The slippery diplomat Talleyrand, who had served every successive French government since the Old Regime, and the much-feared police minister Fouché retained their offices.

Napoleon, betrayed by his own ministers and warned by his generals that the army would not continue the fight, abdicated his throne on April 6, 1814. The victorious allies dealt generously with him, allowing him to retire as ruler of the island of Elba off the coast of Italy. His departure brought to an end an extraordinary twenty-five years of French history. In one respect, 1814 really did mark the end of an era. For nearly two centuries, France had threatened to dominate the European continent through its military might. The revolutionary and Napoleonic armies had come closer than any of their predecessors to conquering all of Europe. But Napoleon's defeat ended the possibility that France might achieve lasting control over its neighbors.

In domestic affairs, however, Napoleon's fall left more uncertainties than answers. Would the restoration of the Bourbon monarchy mean a full-fledged restoration of the Old Regime, with its privileged classes and its state-imposed religion? If not, which aspects of the revolutionary and Napoleonic periods would be incorporated into the new system?

CHAPTER 11

THE RESTORATION

FRANCE IN 1814

With Napoleon's defeat in 1814, the twenty-five-year cycle of political upheavals that had begun in 1789 seemed to have returned to its starting point. A Bourbon prince, the closest male heir of Louis XVI, restored the monarchy; the nobles who had emigrated returned. The dream of a return to the hierarchical society of the past, harbored by counter-revolutionary intellectuals and by many of those who had lost positions or property after 1789, did not appear completely impossible. In reality, however, the Revolution had caused too many changes to permit a simple return to the former status quo. And, in many respects, the restored king, Louis XVIII, had no real desire to do so.

THE RETURN OF THE BOURBONS AND THE HUNDRED DAYS

Louis XVIII did not owe his restoration to a broad popular movement. His return was arranged by a small group of politicians and a small band of devoted royalists. For the political elite of the Napoleonic regime and their spokesman Talleyrand, a deal with the long-exiled Bourbon pretender offered a chance of preserving their own positions. For the victo-rious allies, the restoration promised to give France a stable government that could be depended on not to provoke another European war. And for Louis XVIII himself, agreement with Talleyrand appeared to be the only way to regain the French throne. Hasty negotiations produced a constitutional document, called the *Charte,* or "charter," to avoid the use of the word *constitution,* with its revolutionary connotations. The king asserted that he had granted the *Charte* of his own free will; he rejected the doctrine of popular sovereignty. Its provisions, however, reflected the impact of the Revolution. The *Charte* made France a limited monarchy, with the king sharing power with a bicameral legislature consisting of a hereditary Chamber of Peers and an elected Chamber of Deputies. Voting eligibility was restricted to the wealthy, a group of perhaps 100,000, but this group included many members of the bourgeoisie who had enriched themselves during the Revolution. The special privileges of the hereditary nobility were not restored, and the highly centralized Napoleonic administrative system remained in place.

To the die-hard emigrés and royalists who had hoped that Louis XVIII would truly bring back the prerevolutionary order, the *Charte* was a disappointment. It maintained the basic features of liberalism, such as legal equality of all citizens, religious freedom for Protestants and Jews, and freedom of the press, subject to certain controls. Louis XVIII upheld the Napoleonic land settlement, promising that property acquired since 1789 would be secure and thereby dashing emigrés' hopes of regaining their confiscated estates. He also vowed not to inflict reprisals on anyone for political actions during the Revolution. His ministerial cabinet included Talleyrand and Fouché, both of whom had voted for the execution of his brother in 1793. But the new regime did not really satisfy former revolutionaries and supporters of Napoleon either. Emigrés, including some who had borne arms against France, occupied key political positions. The new regime ostentatiously favored the Catholic church. In May 1814, at the peace conference assembled at Vienna, Talleyrand agreed that France would return to its borders as they existed at the start of the war in 1792, giving up all territorial gains for which its armies had fought. Massive layoffs in the army and the bureaucracy created a large pool of discontent.

The Restoration also had little impact on laws governing commerce and manufacturing. No one wanted to restore the domestic tolls and other economic restrictions eliminated after 1789 or to limit the open national market the Revolution had created. Some Catholics hoped for a revision of the Napoleonic Concordat, which had given the government firm control over the church, but the new ministers had no desire to see their influence over this important institution weakened. The Revolution's social effects also proved permanent. There was no effort to restore the nobility's legal privileges. Though bearers of titles reoccupied top government positions, they could not completely oust the numerous members of the bourgeoisie who had entrenched themselves since 1789, nor could they monopolize future openings. The institutions of the revolutionary and

Napoleonic period had established the principle of careers open to talent, although they certainly favored the sons of wealthy families. The prestigious *grandes écoles,* such as the *École polytechnique,* were open in theory to all on the basis of merit but in fact served primarily to promote the children of families who could afford expensive preparatory courses.

Despite the Restoration's efforts to repress the memory of the Revolution, its legacy pervaded the period's thinking. The myth of the Revolution—whether it was seen as a model to be reenacted in the future or as a destructive cataclysm that needed to be warded off—as well as the memory of Napoleon lived on as major features of French culture. So did the conviction that the revolutionary experience made France unique and gave its history a universal significance. Successive ruling elites down to the present have all acted as if certain political principles enunciated after 1789 were too fundamental to be ignored. Thus, no subsequent French regime has felt able to dispense with a written constitution. The religious conflict also had lasting effects. Regions that had resisted the Civil Constitution of the Clergy and dechristianization (which included much of rural western France and parts of the south) became permanent bastions of conservatism—often remaining hostile to liberalism and change down to the present day. In other rural areas, dechristianization had a lasting impact, providing a base for the later implantation of radical political ideas. The social and legal divisions between men and women, underlined in the *Code Napoléon,* remained powerful. In many ways, the French of 1814 no longer thought or behaved like their ancestors before 1789.

The Hundred Days

Events quickly demonstrated the shakiness of this First Restoration. In March 1815, encouraged by reports of unrest in France, Napoleon eluded his guards and sailed from

Elba to the southern French coast. With a handful of followers, he set out for Paris. Troops sent to arrest him en route went over to the side of their former commander, and crowds cheered the emperor as he neared the capital. Louis XVIII, who had initially promised to die rather than abandon his throne, prudently changed his mind and departed for Belgium. On March 20, 1815, Napoleon entered Paris unopposed. Aware that his own authoritarian regime no longer had much support, Napoleon proclaimed that his restored Empire would be different. He issued amendments to the Constitution that guaranteed basic political freedoms. His gesture won over some leading liberals, such as the writer Benjamin Constant, who had formerly opposed him.

Napoleon's chances for success depended as much on the reaction of the allied coalition that had defeated him in 1814 as on his ability to find support at home. Only a quick military victory would compel the other European powers to accept his return. As the allies scrambled to gather their forces, Napoleon invaded Belgium. There, at Waterloo, allied forces under the British commander Wellington ended the saga of the Hundred Days on June 18, 1815. Rather than pursue a hopeless campaign, Napoleon surrendered to the British, who dispatched him to the remote South Atlantic island of Saint Helena, too far away from France to threaten another escape. The Hundred Days was not just another dramatic chapter added to the Napoleonic legend, however. Napoleon's easy success in toppling Louis XVIII was a lasting reminder of the Restoration's lack of genuine popular support.

THE CONSOLIDATION OF CONSTITUTIONAL MONARCHY

Ironically, the enduring political institution implanted by the Restoration was not the monarchy, but the practice of parliamentary

government that so many enthusiasts for the Bourbons initially condemned as a vestige of the Revolution. Such an outcome would have been hard to predict in the aftermath of Waterloo. Neither the victorious allies nor France's political elites saw any better alternative than putting Louis XVIII back on the throne. The king took advantage of his situation to punish former revolutionaries who had supported Napoleon during his brief return. In this way, many of the Convention deputies who had been pardoned for voting to execute Louis XVI were now forced into exile. In southern France, the settling of political accounts turned violent, as royalist gangs murdered former republicans in a "white Terror." Louis XVIII modified the *Charte* to make it somewhat more authoritarian. Well aware of the weakness of his regime, however, he did not touch the fundamental features of this compromise with the Revolution. The Restoration government remained an uneasy hybrid of liberal and counter-revolutionary principles.

The trend toward strengthening of parliamentary institutions first emerged when the royalists who criticized the king for being too tolerant toward supporters of the Revolution and Napoleon won an unexpected victory in the legislative elections of October 1815. With their opponents temporarily intimidated into silence, the die-hard royalists, or *Ultras*, took most of the seats in the new Chamber of Deputies. Stunned by this unexpected victory for royalist principles so soon after the monarchy's humiliating collapse, Louis XVIII dubbed the legislature the *chambre introuvable*, the "unimaginable Chamber," an ambiguous label that suggested his mixed feelings about its leaders' intransigence. For his part, he continued to avoid policies that would revive quarrels from the revolutionary era. In the face of the *chambre introuvable*, however, he could hardly keep former revolutionaries like Talleyrand and Fouché as ministers. The *Ultras* thus imposed the principle that the ministry had to take account of the legislative balance of power. The new ministry, it is true, still reflected the king's caution more than the *Ultras'* zeal. Although it was headed by an emigré noble, the duc de Richelieu, its dominant figure was a young official of the Napoleonic regime, Decazes. Decazes, who had become the king's personal favorite, was determined to steer a middle course between the *Ultras* and beneficiaries of the "Napoleonic settlement." In the Chamber, a group of deputies known as *Doctrinaires* provided the strongest support for this middle course. The most prominent of the *Doctrinaires,* Pierre Paul Royer-Collard, articulated a theoretical justification for the *Charte,* saying that, by giving both the king and the legislature real powers, it provided a balance of power that would guarantee individual civil rights and political stability.

Decazes's policies and the *Doctrinaires'* ideas were challenged from both the right and the left. The *Ultras* denounced any compromise with the principles that had governed the French Revolution. They insisted that no stable society could be created out of an assemblage of individuals assumed to have equal rights. Society required a hierarchy headed by a single monarch and based on the principle of obedience, and it needed the binding glue of a universally accepted religious faith. *Ultra* spokesman Louis de Bonald insisted that it was necessary to replace talk of the "rights of man" with an emphasis on the "rights of God," and to restore the power of the Catholic church. Liberals like Benjamin Constant and Madame de Staël countered by arguing that the events of the French Revolution did not discredit the ideals of individual freedom and representative government. Constant sought to ward off the claim that the doctrine of natural rights led inevitably to the dictatorial democracy of the Jacobins by asserting that freedom in modern societies really meant "the security to pursue private interests" and that this

security was best guaranteed for all citizens when political functions were exercised by a wealthy elite within a constitutional system.[1] He criticized the *Doctrinaires* for following a policy of pure pragmatism and separating themselves from the positive aspects of the revolutionary heritage. The Restoration years thus saw the articulation of clearly defined doctrines of conservatism and liberalism.

Parliamentary elections in the years after 1815 showed that Louis XVIII's skepticism about the political strength of the *Ultras* had been more than justified. The *chambre introuvable* was dissolved in September 1816, and the electors returned a much less intransigent group of deputies. By 1817, an outspoken liberal opposition determined to defend many of the basic principles of 1789 had gained a number of legislative seats. Its leaders included prominent former revolutionaries such as Lafayette. The middle course steered by Decazes and the *Doctrinaires* seemed to be the safest path for the government, which succeeded in convincing the allied powers to withdraw their occupying troops as scheduled in 1818, returning France to full sovereignty over its own affairs.

The Ultras in Power

The assassination in February 1820 of the duc de Berry, the presumptive heir to the throne, opened a crisis that brought down Decazes and his compromise policy. Enraged royalists blamed the government for not dealing more firmly with the enemies of the monarchy. Even the discovery that the duchesse de Berry had become pregnant before her husband's death and that the Bourbon line had escaped extinction did not calm their fury. When the government sought to appease the right by revising the election laws in June 1820 to reduce the liberals' chances, it drove the left-wing opposition to resort to underground political conspiracy. A network of activists, known as the Carbonari after a similar subversive group in Italy, brought together ex-revolutionaries with young students and discontented military officers. Louis XVIII tried to satisfy the right by dismissing Decazes and bringing back the duc de Richelieu, who formed a cabinet including some of the more conservative royalists. But the *Ultras* in the Chamber continued to assail him for his inability to stamp out republican agitation. Finally, at the end of 1821, the king had to replace Richelieu with a minister who had the confidence of the *Ultra* deputies, a provincial nobleman named Joseph Villèle.

The conservative Villèle proved in many ways the most capable of the Restoration's politicians. Backed by a strong majority in the Chamber, Villèle gave France such a successful experience of parliamentary government that he inadvertently weakened the claim that only a king with broad powers could govern the country. Domestically, he concentrated particularly on putting the government's finances in order and avoiding the fiscal irresponsibility that had doomed the Old Regime. Determined to show that France was once again a major European power, Villèle sent troops to put down a liberal revolt against the Spanish monarchy in 1823. Where Napoleon's army had bogged down in a bloody guerrilla war, the Restoration's troops achieved an easy success against the Spanish liberals.

Charles X

But Villèle's parliamentary skills could not paper over the political divisions that threatened the regime. These were exacerbated when Louis XVIII's death in 1824 brought his brother to the throne as Charles X. During his years in exile, Louis XVIII had become cautious and open to compromise; his brother had become more intransigent and devoted to Catholicism. On ascending the throne, he immediately challenged liberals and moderates by reviving the elaborate coronation ceremonies at Reims cathedral, which Louis XVIII had omitted for fear of

being seen as trying to bring back the past. Even as Villèle was showing that monarchy and parliamentary government were not incompatible, Charles X continued to regard the *Charte* as an unacceptable limitation of his powers. His attitude encouraged the *Ultra* party to demand legislation that widened the gap between former supporters and former opponents of the Revolution.

Some of the new laws passed under Charles X ultimately proved successful, particularly an 1825 measure that compensated emigrés for property confiscated under the Revolution and thus put an end to their agitation against the postrevolutionary land settlement. For the most part, however, the *Ultras'* pet measures provoked increased opposition to the regime. A law authorizing the death penalty for desecration of Catholic churches outraged liberals, who also objected to the church's growing influence on the schools. A strict censorship law proposed in 1827 seemed designed to silence opposition to the *Ultras*. Opposed both by the liberals and by dissident royalists grouped around the famous author Chateaubriand, whom Villèle had dismissed from the ministry in 1824, the government lost badly in the 1827 parliamentary elections. Villèle was forced to resign. Charles X reluctantly appointed a moderate ministry headed by the vicomte de Martignac. Lacking real support from either the king or the Chamber, Martignac achieved little. With an electorate unwilling to tolerate any more concessions to the *Ultras* and the church, and a king unwilling to accept a prime minister representative of the Chamber, the Restoration political compromise was rapidly unraveling.

Postrevolutionary France

In the Countryside

Napoleon's downfall left an unstable political situation, but it ushered in a period of relative stability in social and economic life.

Despite Napoleon's highly publicized efforts to encourage manufacturing, France in 1815 and for many years afterward remained a primarily agricultural country. The sale of national lands, begun under the Revolution, had continued throughout the Napoleonic period. Although the initial sales had benefited well-to-do bourgeois buyers, these purchasers had frequently divided their new properties and resold them to peasants. The revolutionary inheritance laws, which dictated the equal division of property among heirs, had furthered the tendency toward the multiplication of small peasant landholdings already evident in the eighteenth century. This ensured that France would not follow the example of England, where enclosure laws had allowed large landowners to force small farmers out of business. Despite revolutionary legislation, many communal controls over land use remained in effect. Gradual improvements in agricultural productivity continued sufficiently to keep pace with a still-growing population. But, in many respects, rural life—still the life of the vast majority of France's population—remained much as it had been before the Revolution.

Population trends underlined the continued vitality of France's peasant economy. The overall birth rate had begun to fall during the Revolution, indicating that even peasant families were beginning to adopt some birth control practices. But population had continued to grow as the large cohort of men and women born in the decades before 1789 had married and completed their families. Throughout the Restoration, population growth remained fairly evenly distributed across the country. There was no large-scale migration from the countryside to the towns. As a result, France's rural population reached an all-time peak in the 1830s and 1840s. In the late eighteenth century, growing rural population had generated competition for land and social unrest that had fi-

nally exploded in 1789. In the first half of the nineteenth century, however, peasants generally enjoyed favorable economic conditions. Although the revolutionary reforms had favored bourgeois landowners more than peasants, they had eliminated some of the most resented seigneurial rights and given peasants more legal protections. In retrospect, the Restoration years were the high point for traditional peasant agriculture.

Manufacturing

France's manufacturers had been more severely affected by the turmoil of the revolutionary period than her farmers. Even the consolidation of Napoleon's regime had not fully restored favorable conditions. Each new episode of war had disrupted economic life severely, and the collapse of the Continental System had exposed industrialists to competition from British rivals who had gained a long lead in adopting new methods while France had been in turmoil. The Restoration brought more favorable conditions. Assured of peace and protected by a high wall of tariffs aimed at keeping British goods out, manufacturers of textiles, metal goods, and other products could plan investments with greater security. Throughout the period, the government made modest efforts to encourage the growth of industry. It maintained a stable currency and, blissfully unaware of the pending arrival of the railroad era, invested in a network of canals meant to improve transportation and broaden markets.

Like French farmers, however, French manufacturers continued to rely primarily on traditional methods. Tariff protection meant that they did not have to invest in the new, efficient power-driven machinery that British industrialists had begun to adopt. Rather than building large factories, most French entrepreneurs continued to rely on the putting-out system. The textile industry, still France's largest trade, learned to exploit its market more effectively. By the 1820s, manufacturers were consciously promoting periodic changes in fashion that allowed them to exploit the growing number of middle-class consumers. They were also learning to cope with the periodic ups and downs of a business cycle that was less directly linked to annual harvests than in the eighteenth century. A particularly marked business downturn after 1827 drove some manufacturers to make a more determined effort to rationalize their operations and reduce their costs. It also contributed to middle-class dissatisfaction with Charles X's government.

Culture

Intellectual and cultural life presented a very different spectacle from the slow evolution of population, agriculture, and manufacturing. The Napoleonic regime had imposed a stifling conformity on writers and artists; the Restoration, despite the maintenance of some restrictions, permitted lively debate. Intellectuals of all persuasions meditated on the significance of the country's dramatic experiences since 1789 and shared a conviction that ideas were of decisive importance in national life. And both the *Ultras* and the governments of the period made cultural issues central by their insistence on a symbolic restoration of the role of religion in public life.

The Church

Napoleon's Concordat of 1801 had permitted the resumption of religious life, but his regime had kept the church under strict control. Although the first Restoration monarch, Louis XVIII, retained the eighteenth-century Voltairean skepticism about religion, the *Ultra* party made promotion of the faith a central part of its program. Initially, they campaigned against the Concordat, which restricted church activities, and were disappointed when Louis XVIII's ministers decided to maintain the Napoleonic system

and its controls over the clergy. Spokesmen for militant Catholicism, like the intense young Breton priest Félicité de Lamennais, made vehement arguments in favor of a society built on traditional religious values. Lamennais argued that the only answer to the ideological chaos left by the Revolution was adherence to a dogmatic creed enforced by an authoritarian church. He and the other Catholic apologists of the period abandoned the Gallican tradition of independence from papal authority and exalted the pope's powers. The *Ultras*, building on the tradition established by the clergy who had emigrated rather than accept revolutionary reforms, identified Christianity with opposition to all the changes stemming from 1789.

The revival of Catholicism found a genuine echo in some parts of French society. Catholic preachers, adopting revivalist techniques first seen in the "Great Awakening" movement in the United States after 1800, held fifteen hundred meetings between 1815 and 1830 that inspired at least a temporary return to religious observance. Religious monuments destroyed during the Revolution were restored, new ones erected, and public celebration of religious holidays resumed. Especially after Charles X came to the throne in 1824, church influence in the educational system increased. Bishop Denis Frayssinous, Grand Master of the university system from 1824 to 1828, was particularly assiduous in combing out irreligious professors and trying to replace them with believers. By 1825, Catholic educational efforts began to produce a noticeable upswing in ordinations to the priesthood.

Although the reinvigoration of Catholic faith under the Restoration was unmistakable, the church's vehement condemnation of everything that had happened during the Revolution and the Napoleonic period limited its ability to reach much of the population. Restoration government officials worried that the priests' attacks on purchasers of former church lands and on soldiers who had served in the Napoleonic armies would cause unrest. Free thinkers countered religious revivals by sponsoring productions of the seventeenth-century playwright Moliére's *Tartuffe*, which condemned religious zealots as hypocrites. Publishers flooded the market with inexpensive editions of the leading Enlightenment writers, such as Voltaire, with special emphasis on their polemics against traditional Christianity. Liberal politicians campaigned against the insidious influence of the Congregation of the Faith—a shadowy Catholic organization accused of secretly influencing government policy—and against the government's toleration of unauthorized Catholic seminaries forbidden under the Concordat. The religious quarrel that had been so bitter during the Revolution thus was revived in a new form under the Restoration.

The Romantic Movement

In the early years of the Restoration, the cause of monarchical and religious revival had attracted the enthusiasm of many young students and intellectuals. One was the teenaged Victor Hugo, soon to become the leading representative of the romantic movement in France. Hugo and his peers, born during the Revolution and schooled in the regimented atmosphere of the Empire, welcomed the Restoration as a promise of freedom. Hugo won his first literary prizes for poems celebrating the glories of the old French monarchy. But as the regime quickly moved to substitute a rigid religious doctrine for the authoritarianism of the Empire, France's leading young thinkers turned against it. When the government banned the popular philosophy professor Victor Cousin's public lectures after the assassination of the duc de Berry in 1820, it opened an irreparable rift between itself and the new intellectual and artistic elite that had grown up since the Revolution.

Although they now joined older liberal spokesmen like Benjamin Constant and La-fayette in opposition to the regime, these younger men did not adopt the rationalist philosophy of the Enlightenment. The most eloquent, like Hugo and the poet Alphonse de Lamartine, identified themselves with romanticism. This artistic movement had flourished in England and Germany since the turn of the century. In France, Chateaubriand had exemplified its new appreciation of the beauties of nature, its sympathy for the organic, religious society of the Middle Ages, and its glorification of individual emotional experience. But the Napoleonic regime had favored artists and authors who worked in more traditional modes, and romanticism never evoked as strong a response in France as it did in other European countries. The strong rationalist tradition in French intellectual life militated against it, as did the fact that the most powerful models of romantic art and literature came from abroad.

By the early 1820s, the romantic spirit had nevertheless made significant inroads into French culture. Walter Scott's historical novels enjoyed great popularity in French translation. Eugène Delacroix, whose paintings translated the romantic spirit into visual art, produced canvases glorifying the Greek revolt against Turkey in the late 1820s, a cause that the romantics saw as a heroic struggle for freedom. His *Death of Sardana-palus,* exhibited in 1828, contained a disturbing mixture of sensuality and cruelty that was alien to classical sensibilities. Though it had no immediate reference to politics, it was most emphatically a painting meant to shock conventional opinion. In music, the young composer Hector Berlioz's *Symphonie fantastique,* first performed in 1830, showed similar tendencies.

Socialism

The beginnings of French socialism had links with artistic romanticism. Like the romantics, the early socialists rejected conventional values and proclaimed the need for a society that paid heed to human beings' varied psychological needs. The socialists opposed not only the Restoration government, but also the individualistic society inspired by Enlightenment thought and structured according to the rules of the *Code Napoleon.* The most influential socialist thinker of the Restoration period was Henri de Saint-Simon, an eccentric former nobleman of the prerevolutionary generation, whose writings attracted a following of young people in the 1820s. Saint-Simon preached a return to an organic, communitarian society in which all would work together for the common good, instead of pursuing selfish individual interests. Rather than joining the *Ultras* in calling for a return to traditional religious beliefs, however, he embraced science and technology and envisioned a society organized by a priesthood of dedicated engineers and technologists, who would replace the unproductive elite of politicians and aristocrats who governed Restoration France. Saint-Simon's teachings spoke powerfully to many intelligent and restless young people dissatisfied with the society they saw around them, and eager to devote themselves to improving the world.

Another influential socialist thinker of the period was Charles Fourier. A stubborn eccentric whose ideas were couched in a dense jargon of his own creation, Fourier was an acute critic of France's individualist society and of the bourgeois family, which he claimed condemned men and women alike to lives of frustration and boredom. In the ideal communities, or *phalansteries,* that he proposed, personality types would be combined in proper proportions so that no one would have to do tasks he or she found unpleasant, and those who found exclusive monogamous relationships confining could have multiple partners. Like Saint-Simon, Fourier attracted devoted disciples. Whereas Saint-Simon's ideas appealed especially to youths from well-to-do families who saw themselves as part of an educated elite with a vocation to lead society, Fourier's doctrines—simplified by followers like Victor Considérant—were taken up by some of the working class. His criticism of monogamous marriage also influenced later feminists.

THE REVOLUTION OF 1830

Instead of successfully unifying postrevolutionary society under the banner of a revived Catholic faith, the Restoration saw a proliferation of intellectual and cultural currents, many of them overtly hostile to the regime or at least to the policies adopted under Charles X. This lively debate might not have posed a real threat to political stability if a government sensitive to the opinions of the electorate and open to compromise on practical issues had been in power. However, Charles X listened to advisors who steered him toward political and ideological confrontation. In August of 1829, he dismissed the cautious Martignac and appointed a ministry of die-hard *Ultras* headed by Jules de Polignac, son of one of Marie-Antoinette's favorites and a man whose very name recalled the most discredited aspects of the Old Regime.

The Polignac ministry seemed to be bent on altering the constitution to avoid bowing to the majority in the Chamber. But in fact it took no decisive action for more than half a year. Polignac's only major initiative was to send French troops to occupy the coast of Algeria, hoping that a spectacular military success would boost the regime's popularity. During this time, the ministry's opponents had ample opportunity to prepare themselves. Since 1827, the historian and liberal leader François Guizot had organized liberal political efforts under the banner of a society called *Aide-toi, le ciel t'aidera* (roughly, "God helps those who help themselves"). His group had assured the election of a large block of liberal deputies in 1827 and, when 221 deputies rejected the Polignac ministry in March 1830 and Charles X used his power of dissolution to force new elections, Guizot's society went to work again. Backed by a number of newspapers, not only were the "221" reelected, but the liberals also picked up another fifty seats.

Rather than bow to the will of the voters, Charles X's ministers reacted by preparing a set of ordinances to muzzle the press and to alter the voting laws in such a way as to guarantee victory for their party. The regime's liberal opponents were prepared to fight back. As soon as the "July Ordinances" were posted on the morning of July 26, 1830, the young writer Adolphe Thiers (who was beginning what would prove to be a long career as one of nineteenth-century France's most important politicians) organized a journalists' protest against violation of the *Charte*. The protest was published in several papers despite the new censorship laws. Leading liberal parliamentary deputies, including Guizot and the banker Casimir Périer, hoped that this moral appeal would be sufficient to thwart the ministry's plans and force it to resign. These men, solid members of France's social and political establishment, had no interest in triggering a revolution aimed at toppling the Bourbon monarchy. But they were willing to risk a crisis in order to maintain the system of parliamentary government.

By the second day of the crisis, events began to escape the liberal leaders' control. Many Paris employers had closed their shops, leaving their workers to congregate in the streets, where agitators stirred them to defend the cause of liberty. By the evening of July 27, a popular insurrection was under way, as barricades were thrown up in many neighborhoods. The troops ordered to put down the unrest were, in many cases, more in sympathy with the rebels than with the government. After three days of street fighting, the "Three Glorious Days," Charles X abandoned the struggle. Rather than risk the fate of his older brother, Louis XVI, he fled to England. His departure marked not only the end of his reign but of the Restoration itself. Power now lay with the liberal politicians who had sparked resistance to the July ordinances and with the popular crowds who had battled the king's troops.

NOTE

1. Constant, *De la liberté chez les Modernes* (Paris: Livre du Poche, 1980), 502.

CHAPTER 12

THE JULY MONARCHY AND ITS CRITICS

Because it was brief and relatively bloodless, and because the constitutional regime that replaced the Restoration closely resembled its predecessor, the Revolution of 1830 has often been classed as a minor episode in nineteenth-century French history, less dramatic and less significant than the revolutions of 1789 or 1848. In recent decades, however, historians have come to better appreciate its importance. The "Three Glorious Days" were only one episode in a broader revolutionary cycle. The social and political unrest that had surfaced in the late 1820s remained strong for several years after Charles X's flight. Until 1835, there seemed to be a real possibility that the constitutional-monarchist regime precariously installed in power in July 1830 would fall to a more radical replacement, as the constitutional monarchy created in 1789 had. Even though this did not happen, the Revolution of 1830 allowed a permanent expansion of France's sphere of public debate.

Until 1830, the political language of France had been that of the revolutionary decade of the 1790s, the language of constitutionalism and of individual rights. After 1830, new issues came to the fore: industrialism, social problems, the "woman question." The political "families" that some historians have argued dominate French political life

even today took shape. These changes coincided with a new period in the history of the French economy, symbolized by the appearance of the railroad, a product of the technology of the industrial age that was in itself a major agent of change. Increasingly, 1830 has come to strike historians as one of the major milestones in modern French history.

THE BOURGEOIS MONARCHY AND ITS FOES

Romantic artist Eugène Delacroix's famous painting of the Revolution of 1830, *Liberty Leading the People,* dramatically captures the ambiguity of the events that toppled the Bourbon Restoration in July 1830. The heroic female figure in the center of the composition wears the red cap of liberty, the symbol of the radical Jacobin republic first proclaimed in 1792. But she holds aloft the tricolor flag, a banner that united liberals whose ideal was the moderate Revolution of 1789 as well as admirers of Napoleon—for whom the flag symbolized above all French national pride. Liberty is flanked by three armed insurrectionists: a man dressed in the costume of a respectable bourgeois (whose top hat remains firmly in place even as he surveys the insurrectionary barricade), a worker brandishing a cutlass, and a child waving pistols in both hands—who can be seen as a symbol either of youth and energy or of the violence the Revolution threatened to unleash. As Delacroix's composition suggested, the revolutionary movement enjoyed support from members of both the middle and lower classes, and from the young, but it was by no means clear that all participants in the movement were fighting for the same thing.

The liberal deputies and journalists who had taken the lead in denouncing the July ordinances were mostly concerned with bringing the revolutionary interlude to a close before events got out of hand. Led by Adolphe Thiers, most of them quickly rallied to the support of a new monarch who would accept the principles of constitutional and parliamentary government wholeheartedly, unlike the recalcitrant Charles X with his dream of returning to the prerevolutionary past. The new candidate for the throne was Louis-Philippe, the duc d'Orléans, head of a younger branch of the Bourbon family. Louis-Philippe had served with the revolutionary army in 1792–1793 and had only emigrated during the Terror. He had returned to France during the Restoration and lived quietly until 1830. His career made him uniquely qualified to lead a French version of the "Glorious Revolution" of 1688 in England, guaranteeing constitutional liberty without drastically changing political institutions. Thiers drafted a widely circulated proclamation touting the duke as a "citizen king," whose rule would save the country from the divisions that any attempt to install a republic was bound to cause. The aged General Lafayette, one of the great names of 1789 and a leader of the republican movement during the Restoration, gave the Orléanist solution his support, defusing radical opposition.

The Chamber of Deputies hastily revised the constitution, and on August 9, 1830, Louis-Philippe was officially installed as king. Whereas Louis XVIII and Charles X insisted that they had granted a constitution of their own free will, Louis-Philippe accepted the principle of national sovereignty. He also restored the tricolor as the national flag, replacing the white banner of the Bourbons that Louis XVIII had brought back in 1814. The Orléanist solution appeared to satisfy the demands that the leaders of the French Revolution had made in 1789. After more than forty years of political conflict, France would now be a constitutional monarchy, similar in many ways to its British neighbor.

THE REGIME'S OPPONENTS

Although the "July Monarchy" created by the Revolution of 1830 appeared to middle-class liberals as a near-perfect solution to the nation's needs, it left many other groups unsatisfied. On the right, a legitimist opposition refused to acknowledge the new dynasty and retained its loyalty to Charles X's young grandson, who was proclaimed heir to the throne after Charles X officially abdicated. The legitimists remained loyal to an intransigent Catholicism and continued to denounce the whole panoply of liberal institutions. Defeat, rather than discouraging them, strengthened their loyalty to an idealized vision of the past. In many rural areas, legitimist landowners, often allied with conservative clergy, dominated local politics and harassed July Monarchy officials. Often, they posed as defenders of the poor against the middle-class–oriented policies of the new regime.

In Paris, republican activists had been in the forefront of the street fighting during the "Three Glorious Days." Louis-Philippe's elevation to the throne and the limited revision of the *Charte*, which extended the right to vote only to wealthy members of the middle classes (the electorate was enlarged only from 90,000 to 166,000 voters in 1831), struck them as a betrayal. Although they disassociated themselves from the violence of the Reign of Terror, the republicans identified themselves with the democratic and patriotic ideals of the Jacobins, calling for a regime based on universal manhood suffrage. Republican idealists also criticized the new government for refusing to extend aid to revolutionary movements that broke out in Poland and Italy after the French uprising. The main republican organization, the Society of the Rights of Man, made a special effort to broaden the base of the movement by winning followers among the workers of France's major cities. Popular republicanism was often tinged with nostal-

gia for Napoleon. Among the lower classes, Napoleon's authoritarianism was forgotten. He was remembered for having made France respected throughout Europe and for providing opportunities for commoners.

The lifting of the Restoration's rigorous press laws allowed political dissent greater freedom. The republicans took special advantage of this freedom, notably in the realm of political caricature. The satirist Charles Philipon's depiction of the fat-cheeked Louis-Philippe as a pear (a slang term for "dimwit")

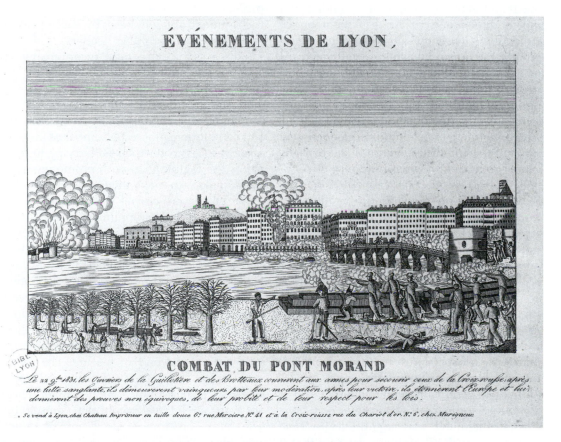

The November, 1831, silkworkers' insurrection in Lyon was interpreted as evidence of a developing conflict between social classes. It had inspired hopes among workers and deep fears among the property-owning classes. The dark-skinned figure in the center of the picture is probably Etienne Stanislas, "the Negro," a black man who was later tried for his role in the uprising.
(Photo credit: Bibliothèque municipale de Lyon, Fonds Coste no. 716.)

created an image the regime never managed to shake off. Among Philipon's young associates, the most talented was Honoré Daumier. Often considered the greatest genius in the history of political cartooning. His famous cartoon of "The Legislative Belly," showing well-known politicians yawning and gossiping in the Chamber, was a condemnation of the constitutional monarchy as a whole. The well-fed but obviously incompetent deputies stood condemned as a selfish elite running public affairs in their own interests.

Popular protests in many parts of the country encouraged republican hopes that the 1830 Revolution might be extended in a radical direction. In rural areas, outbreaks of violence had become increasingly common toward the end of the 1820s. Many of them were directed against the new forest code introduced in 1827. It had put an end to traditional rights that peasants had often enjoyed to exploit wooded areas and marked a widening of liberal notions of property rights. In urban areas, workers and artisans were primed to protest because of the economic depression that had gripped the country since 1827. In the textile center of Rouen, workers responded to the news from Paris by demonstrating against the introduction of new machinery that threatened their jobs and new work rules that gave employers more control over the production process. The slogan adopted by insurgent Lyon silk workers in 1831—"Live working or die fighting"—dramatized the intensity of the emerging social problem: the difficulty of providing urban workers with a good life in the framework of a liberal economy.

Popular dissatisfaction also surfaced in the form of attacks against the church. The clerical hierarchy had identified itself so strongly with the Bourbon monarchy that it inevitably became a target after the Revolution. In February 1831, Parisian rioters, angered by a church service in memory of the Bourbon duc de Berry, sacked the palace of the archbishop. The new regime, quick to put down workers' protests, showed less zeal about protecting the church. The wave of anticlerical protests suggested that the Revolution might indeed take on a more radical character.

The cholera epidemic that struck France in 1831–1832 added to the atmosphere of fear and instability that had persisted since the Revolution. Among its victims was the banker and prime minister Casimir Périer, a forceful leader with broad parliamentary support who might have dealt more effectively with the regime's problems than his successors. Attacked from the right and the left, beset by social protest, and bereft of popular leaders, the July Monarchy's future seemed uncertain at best.

PROPHETIC VOICES

The more open atmosphere created by the July Revolution allowed a number of thinkers who were less concerned with trying to overthrow the regime than with promoting alternative values to make themselves heard. The early 1830s were crucial years for the development of socialism, feminism, and new notions about the place of religion in society. The followers of Henri de Saint-Simon, who had died in 1825, contributed to the development of both socialist and feminist movements. His circle of young disciples had continued to meet and elaborate his doctrines, especially the antiindividualistic "new Christianity" that Saint-Simon had begun to propagate toward the end of his life. The movement came under the leadership of Prosper Enfantin, a charismatic young man who built up a quasi-religious cult around himself, but who also encouraged discussion of radical new ideas about sexual morality and gender roles. Enfantin himself had few original ideas, but the Saint-Simonian circle continued to attract many of the brightest young men and women in Paris. The group's writings won converts as far away as Russia. In opposition to the July Monarchy's enthusiasm for *laissez-faire* economics, the Saint-Simonians stressed the necessity of economic planning to assure that industrial development benefited all classes. They were also pioneers in asserting that women had a positive role to play in the transformation of society, and in criticizing the effect of the monogamous bourgeois family on women's lives. By 1831, Enfantin had appointed several women to significant positions in the Saint-Simonian hierarchy. When he changed his policy and demoted them, frustrated female members of the movement broke away in 1832 and founded the first all-women's feminist group in French history. In their journal, *La Femme libre (The Liberated Woman)*, Pauline Roland and others proclaimed that the liberation of women and the redemption of the working class had to go together. They developed the Saint-Simonian challenge to the monogamous family from a feminist perspective, putting forward arguments to liberate women from the control of husbands by allowing free love and communal childrearing.

Both the Saint-Simonian movement and its feminist offshoot disintegrated within a few years. In 1832, Enfantin and a number of his followers, who had formed a commune to practice the movement's ideas about free love and collective living, were prosecuted for outraging public morals. The highly publicized trial broke up the movement; many of its young adherents disavowed their leader and his more radical doctrines. Enfantin and a few faithful loyalists contributed to the breakup of the movement by leaving for Egypt to search for a "female Messiah" who was to share the leadership of the movement and usher in a new age for humanity. Their quest made the movement an easy target for ridicule, and Saint-Simonianism as an organized force disintegrated. The impact of its teachings about the need for social harmony and the importance of an organized approach to economic development remained alive in the minds of former members, however, influencing French public life down to the time of the Second Empire and beyond.

The feminist group associated with *La Femme libre* also faded out after 1834. Its leading members were overwhelmed by the difficulties of supporting themselves as working women. Some came to question the practicality of abolishing marriage if it meant leaving mothers with the burden of supporting themselves and their children. A more middle-class publication, the *Gazette des Femmes*, founded in 1836, campaigned for changes in the legal system rather than questioning the institution of marriage. The only women who seemed able to live out the feminist dream of choosing their own lovers and careers and mingling with men on an equal basis were intellectuals from well-to-do family backgrounds, such as the novelists George Sand (Aurore Dupin) and Daniel Stern (Marie d'Agoult). In the 1830s, both scandalized polite society by their public extramarital liaisons with prominent male artists and writers, but their talents and personalities made them important figures in Parisian literary and political circles.

Lamennais

Another prophetic figure whose influence was at its peak during the first years of the July Monarchy was Felicité de Lamennais, the most original Catholic thinker of the nineteenth century. At the beginning of the Restoration, Lamennais had been among the most vehement advocates of an authoritarian Catholic church that would be a close ally of the monarchy. During the 1820s, however, he had become disillusioned with the results of the union of throne and altar. Rather than shaping a purified society inspired by Christian values, the Restoration government turned the church into a bureaucratic tool for its own purposes. By the end of the decade, Lamennais had become convinced that the spiritual welfare of the church required that it separate itself from the state.

The 1830 Revolution gave Lamennais the opportunity to promote his new, liberal ideas. Like Saint-Simon, he had gathered around him a group of energetic young disciples. With their help, he founded a newspaper, *L'Avenir,* to disseminate his views. Articles in this short-lived publication sowed the seeds for what came to be known as liberal Catholicism (which argued that the church could use the freedoms guaranteed by a liberal constitution for its own purposes) and social Catholicism (which insisted on the church's duty to ameliorate the devastating consequences of economic liberalism and unrestrained industrial development). The French Catholic hierarchy, staffed with clergy promoted during the Restoration, was horrified by Lamennais's ideas, and in August 1832, Lamennais found his doctrines condemned in the papal encyclical *Mirari vos.* Lamennais's followers bowed to the pope's orders, staying within the church and gradually gaining support for some of his suggestions. Lamennais himself took a different course. In April 1834 he published an explosive book, *Paroles d'un croyant (The Words of a Believer),* using biblical language to predict the downfall of existing governments and the eventual triumph of a religiously inspired democracy. *Paroles d'un croyant* was a bestseller, but it sealed Lamennais's break with Rome. The pope condemned the book, and Lamennais found himself outside the church. He continued to write throughout the 1830s and 1840s, and his advocacy of a democratic faith helped infuse much of the social protest of the period with a religious aura.

Writers

Lamennais's writings showed the continuing influence of the romantic current that had begun to dominate French literature in the 1820s. The Revolution of 1830 had given

a powerful boost to this tendency. For Parisians, the months preceding Charles X's overthrow had been enlivened by a running controversy over the *Comédie-française* production of Victor Hugo's drama *Hernani,* in which the young romantic playwright defied the conventions of French classical drama. Youthful liberals took up the play as a cause, and engaged in pitched battles inside and outside the theater with outraged partisans of cultural conservatism. Hugo's triumph on the stage coincided with the liberal victory over the Restoration monarchy. Hugo's assertion, in his preface to his play, that "romanticism . . . is nothing but liberalism in literature" underlined the close connection between the two movements. Another literary masterpiece closely associated with the 1830 Revolution was the novelist Stendhal's *The Red and the Black,* a scathing indictment of Restoration society that appeared just after the July Days. Older than most of the romantic generation, Stendhal had associated himself with their cause in the 1820s, but the clear-eyed, ironic psychological insights of his novels set his work apart from the romantic mainstream. As he himself had anticipated, the greatness of his achievement only came to be appreciated many years after his death.

At the time, the educated public paid more attention to a cluster of young writers, the "generation of 1830," who also burst into the public eye with the July Revolution, including such romantic poets and writers as Gérard de Nerval and Théophile Gautier. Publishers, whose business had suffered from the general economic slump of the late 1820s, found in these new authors a solution to their economic problems. A host of less talented writers copied the techniques of the great romantics and produced a "popular romanticism," tailored to less sophisticated readers, that enjoyed a great vogue in the early 1830s. Although the Revolution of 1830 had created the atmosphere in which interest in their works flourished, the romantics' intense cultivation of private sensibility and aesthetic emotion soon separated them from a regime whose public values were those of economic success and bourgeois order. The young romantics of the 1830 generation turned to a cult of "art for art's sake," denying that the artist should have any political role and condemning the "philistinism" of bourgeois society in the name of higher artistic values.

ORLÉANIST LIBERALISM

Rather than convincing the other leaders of the new regime to make broader reforms, the agitation of the early 1830s drove them to take an increasingly rigid conservative stance, and to give the doctrines of liberalism a clearer form. The regime's most prominent spokesman (although he did not obtain the prime ministership until 1847) was François Guizot. Guizot came from a Protestant family; his rise to high office under the July Monarchy reflected that regime's break with the Restoration's alliance of church and government. Under the Restoration, Guizot became one of France's best-known historians. In his writings and lectures, he argued that the liberal ideals of 1789 were products of many centuries of historic development, going back to the emergence of free urban communes in the Middle Ages. He stressed the positive role of the nonnoble middle classes in developing the ideal of freedom. In politics, Guizot was part of the *Doctrinaire* group that had hoped to build a stable constitutional monarchy on the basis of the *Charte*, until Charles X's rigidity disillusioned them. Firm in his adherence to liberalism, Guizot had not the slightest sympathy for revolutionary violence. Once the installation of Louis-Philippe had consolidated constitutional monarchism, he was determined to prevent any further political upheaval. The political task of the new regime, he told

the Chamber in 1831, was to find the *juste milieu*, the proper balance point that would allow it to "establish definitively, not order alone, not liberty alone, but order and liberty at the same time."[1]

For Guizot, the limitation of the electorate to the wealthiest fraction of the property-owning classes was essential to social order. This elite of notables—influential and property-owning community leaders—fairly represented the interests of all classes, he argued. They alone had the intelligence and the experience to make informed political judgments. For those whose income precluded them from voting but who wanted to participate in the political process, he had a simple recommendation: *"Enrichissez-vous!"* ("Make yourself wealthy!") The possibility to do so, he argued, was open to anyone with the necessary talent. Guizot was not blind to the distress of the lower classes, but he was convinced that the only way to improve their condition was for the government to eschew interference in the economy. He did believe in universal education, which he thought would serve the cause of social stability. The poor could be taught the economic reasons for their condition and be given the lesson that hard work would lead to improvement. As a result, Guizot was the main architect of the 1833 law that called for the establishment of public elementary schools in every French *commune.* Implementation of the law was slow, however. It took more than a generation before it became fully effective.

Guizot's main rival for political prominence throughout the July Monarchy was the slightly younger Adolphe Thiers, one of the key strategists of the Orléanist triumph in the 1830 Revolution. Thiers, a hard-working and intensely ambitious man, had, like Guizot, established himself with his pen during the 1820s. He had become a prominent journalist and had written an influential history of the French Revolution, in which he praised the early, reforming phase of that movement but strongly condemned Robes-pierre and the Terror. In the 1830s, Thiers, like Guizot, strongly defended law and order and opposed all protest movements from below. He was somewhat more flexible than Guizot, however, and advocated gradual reforms that would give more modest sectors of the middle class the right to vote. He also advocated a more assertive foreign policy. During the second of his two brief terms as prime minister, in 1840, he negotiated the return of Napoleon's remains from Saint Helena to France, where they were buried with great ceremony in the *Invalides* church. In this way, Thiers claimed for France the right to aspire to the dominant role in Europe she had enjoyed under the emperor.

Repressive Measures

To maintain its conservative policy of limiting political representation to the wealthy in the face of such widespread criticism and unrest, the July Monarchy had to adopt increasingly repressive measures. From the outset, the government harassed oppositional newspapers and caricaturists and, as early as April 1831, it pushed through the Chamber a severe new law against public demonstrations. In June 1832, republican groups in Paris tried to turn the funeral of one of their leaders, General Lamarque, into an uprising. The government responded by imposing a state of siege on the capital. By the time the Lyon silk workers rose up in an insurrection that combined republican and working-class slogans in April 1834, the forces of repression were well prepared. About three hundred were killed in the two days of fighting that ended the largest outbreak of mass violence under the July Monarchy. The fears inspired by an unsuccessful assassination attempt on the king in 1835 led to the passage of the "September laws" later that year. They gave the government stricter control over the press and made convictions for political agitation easier to obtain. The "September laws" drove republican opposition underground. Armed with these new weapons, the police succeeded in putting an end to most public protest against the regime. The revolutionary cycle that had begun in 1830 was finally closed. Subsequent movements like a republican conspiracy to overthrow the regime in 1839, organized by the veteran plotter Louis Blanqui's secret "Society of the Seasons," and two amateurish efforts in 1836 and 1840 by Napoleon's nephew and heir, Louis Bonaparte, to rally the army to the imperial banner were easily suppressed.

Although the government of the July Monarchy defended itself successfully against agitation from below, it failed to produce a stable parliamentary government during the 1830s. Between 1830 and 1840, fifteen different ministries held office. Louis-Philippe, who had been expected to confine himself to the role of a constitutional figurehead, proved instead to have a taste for political intrigue. He encouraged rivalries among the ministers and, by preventing the emergence of strong party leaders, maintained his own influence. Throughout the 1830s, Guizot was confined to minor ministerial posts. His rival Thiers obtained the prime ministership for two short periods, in 1836 and 1840, but both ministries quickly disintegrated. Thiers's second passage in power resulted from an agreement among the leading parliamentarians to unite and impose real legislative rule on the king; Guizot gave Thiers his support. But Thiers soon brought his ministry down through his aggressive foreign policy. In the summer of 1840, when an Egyptian leader, Mehemet Ali, led a revolt against Turkish rule, Thiers backed him. The British and other European powers prepared to defend the integrity of the Ottoman Empire, however, and France found itself dangerously isolated. Thiers talked of war; his threat to invade Germany inspired the composition of the German patriotic anthem "The Watch on the Rhine." His bellicose policy alarmed the king and the Chamber, and Thiers had to resign in October 1840.

Thiers's departure finally opened the way for François Guizot to take control of the ministry. For the next seven and a half years, Guizot determined government policy, although the aged Marshal Soult remained the nominal head of the cabinet until 1847. The Guizot government reversed Thiers's adventurous foreign policy, emphasizing good relations with Britain, whose parliamentary regime he admired. Queen Victoria's state visit to France in 1843 marked the high point of this rapprochement. Rivalry with Britain did lead France to claim the island of Tahiti as a colony in 1842, beginning a process of expansion in the Pacific. The British decision to abolish slavery in their colonies in 1833 revived concern about this issue in France, where the 1794 revolutionary law abolishing the institution had been reversed under Napoleon in 1802, but opposition from plantation-owners and Louis-Philippe's fear that granting any reform would lead to demand for other changes prevented any action.

The Guizot government did take a major decision regarding Algeria, where a young leader, Abd el-Kader, had claimed the title of "sultan of the Arabs" and proclaimed a *jihad* or holy war against the French in 1834. Some critics questioned whether France should aim at permanent occupation of Algeria. A commission appointed to study the issue in 1840–1842 convinced the government that the territory could be pacified and become a home for European settlers, and that the indigenous population could be won over and assimilated to French ways of life. French troops under General Bugeaud used brutal tactics, including the suffocation of eight hundred Arabs trapped in a cave at Dahra, and finally forced Abd el-Kader to surrender in December 1847. The methods used to bring Algeria under control raised questions about the supposed benefits that the extension of French control would bring to its population. Speaking for a parliamentary commission in 1847, Alexis de Tocqueville wrote, "We have made the Muslims more miserable, more disorganized, more ignorant, and more barbarous than they were before we encountered them."[2] The July Monarchy's first effort at building a new overseas empire thus raised issues that were to arise again for as long as France continued to maintain colonies. At home, Guizot's policy was one of principled immobility. He stood steadfast against any efforts at reform, and above all he opposed any extension of the right to vote in national elections. To maintain himself in office, Guizot perfected tactics of electoral manipulation that had already been used throughout the 1830s. The government sponsored candidates, often public officials who could be counted on to vote as their superiors told them (in 1846, 40 percent of deputies held government jobs), and used the prefects to put pressure on the voters. With legitimist, republican, and Bonapartist critics largely silenced, the main public opposition to Guizot came from the deputies of the "dynastic opposition," led by Odilon Barrot, who accepted the main features of the regime but called for a broadening of the franchise. But the gravest threat to Guizot came from his own success in stifling all change. By the late 1840s, Lamartine (the poet turned politician) warned, "France is bored."

NOTES

1. Cited in Thomas C. Mendenhall et al., eds., *The Quest for a Principle of Authority in Europe, 1715–Present* (New York: Henry Holt, 1948), 144.
2. Cited in C.-R. Ageron, *Histoire de l'Algérie contemporaine* (Paris, 1969), 20.

CHAPTER 13

A NEW SOCIAL WORLD

If the French public found the maneuverings of the July Monarchy's politicians boring, it was largely because their refusal to act seemed to reflect their inability to understand the striking changes occurring in the country during the 1830s and 1840s. During these decades, France felt the first effects of industrialization. The rapid growth of the urban population created a sense of social crisis, and writers and artists felt increasingly driven either to directly address what they saw as their society's urgent problems, or to distance themselves from a world whose values they condemned as antithetical to real art.

THE BEGINNINGS OF FRENCH INDUSTRIALIZATION

By the 1830s, French observers had become acutely aware of the industrial revolution that was transforming the economy and the very landscape of some regions of neighboring Britain. Travelers like the social philosopher Alexis de Tocqueville described the new wealth and the new poverty generated in Manchester and other burgeoning factory cities. Although French industrial development lagged behind Britain's, by the 1830s similar processes were underway in some regions of the country. Economic historians

have long argued over whether the concept of "industrial revolution"—a rapid and dramatic transformation analogous to what occurred in England at the end of the eighteenth century—is applicable to the slower and more gradual way in which France entered the industrial era. There is general agreement, however, that the years after 1830 saw the first significant development of modern factory-based industry in the country and the beginnings of profound social changes that accompanied it.

Industrialization meant first of all the adoption of new, mechanized methods for producing goods. In the textile industry (the first to mechanize), power-driven spinning jennies and "mules" copied from English models replaced the hand-operated spinning wheel, and power looms took over weaving. This allowed production to become faster and cheaper. Instead of contracting with workers who produced goods at home, using simple machinery like hand looms, entrepreneurs began to concentrate production processes in large factory buildings. As the machines they employed became larger, more expensive, and more complicated, they increasingly depended on the power of water wheels or steam engines. And, for a variety of reasons, factories tended to cluster in particular regions, creating centers of industrial development and ending the centuries-old pattern in which manufacturing enterprises were scattered throughout the country to serve local markets.

Textile manufacturing was the largest French industry during the July Monarchy. Factory-based production developed primarily in the north and northeast, in cities such as Rouen, Lille, and Mulhouse. Mulhouse and its surrounding region of Alsace were the most dynamic center. Starting in the 1820s, a small coterie of largely Protestant manufacturers invested heavily in modern machinery to spin and weave cotton, a new product whose production was not hampered by traditional restrictions. The increasing availability of high-quality raw material, first from Egypt and, after 1840, from the southern United States, encouraged the growth of the industry. Its inexpensive products were marketed to a rapidly growing middle class with an increasing desire to keep up with changing fashions. The streams of the hilly Vosges region around Mulhouse provided water power for the mills, and the growing population provided an ample number of workers. By the mid-1840s, Mulhouse was as up-to-date and efficient a manufacturing region as any to be found in Europe.

The determination of Mulhouse's industrialists to use the latest machinery and methods was not typical of French industry, however. Textile manufacturers elsewhere often continued to subcontract much of their work to independent artisans, in effect renting out the machines in their factories rather than controlling the production process themselves. Cautious about borrowing money to enlarge their operations, French entrepreneurs generally built small factories and relied on machinery that the British had already discarded as outdated. In any event, they had trouble challenging England's firm grip on the world market. In 1845, the peak year for French cotton goods production in the first half of the century, the country imported 60,000 tons of raw cotton for its mills. In the same year, Britain imported 276,000 tons—more than four times as much.[1]

Economic historians have advanced many explanations for the slow transformation of French industry in comparison with the British. France lacked some of Britain's natural economic advantages, such as the coal and iron deposits conveniently located together that furthered iron making across the Channel. France also lacked the ability of British manufacturers to ship raw materials and manufactured products by boat throughout the island. However, most historians who have suggested that France's economy could have industrialized more rapidly have stressed differences in French entrepreneurs' attitudes more than objective factors. In general, French manufacturers were conservative in their investment strategies and not overly optimistic about the prospects for making large profits by expanding production. They preferred to keep their enterprises under family control, and to avoid selling stock to outsiders or borrowing heavily from banks. Bankers, in any event, shared the conservatism of the manufacturers and were reluctant to lend money for industrial investment. As a result, French factories usually remained relatively small in size and therefore achieved smaller gains in productivity than their British rivals. French workers, too, acted in ways that slowed the adoption of new industrial methods. More strongly than British workers, they clung to their self-image as independent producers, even when they did their actual work on machines belonging to a manufacturer and housed in a factory building. Handloom weavers accepted reduced piece rates rather than abandoning their traditional autonomy for factory work. In many areas, factory workers were peasants who also continued to farm their plots part-time, thereby maintaining a margin of economic independence that made it difficult for employers to regiment them.

Finally, the French government, even in the July Monarchy period when it was officially committed to *laissez faire*, regulated and controlled economic activity more than the British, sometimes discouraging innovation.

The introduction of the railroad, which took place during the July Monarchy, offered an opportunity to break through one of the major obstacles to industrial development, the limitations of France's transportation network. The huge job of constructing a national rail system also provided an important stimulus to the growth of French industry. The first successful rail line using steam locomotives had been opened in England in 1830. French industrialists and experts from the government's *Corps des Ponts et Chaussées* followed this British experiment with great interest, but with some doubts about its long-term success. The government, which had invested heavily in canal-building projects, was in no hurry to change technologies. Concessions for a few short local lines were given out starting in 1835, but political leaders remained unsure about the invention's future. Voting to allow construction of a rail line from Paris to Versailles, Adolphe Thiers is said to have remarked, "Paris has to have this toy; but it will never carry a passenger or a package."[2]

In Britain, private entrepreneurs had taken the initiative in creating the rail system, but in France the government played a larger role. Trained government engineers, traditionally responsible for the design of France's roads and canals, opposed letting private companies dictate the shape of the future French transport system. In 1842, they persuaded the Chamber of Deputies to vote for a centrally planned system, the "Legrand Star," named for its designer, civil engineer Victor Legrand. Legrand's plan called for trunk lines connecting Paris to the major provincial cities. The government was to provide the roadbeds, and the private companies that were to be given concessions to build the actual railroads had to follow state-imposed specifications much stricter than those in other countries. When the system was finally completed in the 1850s, France had a rail network that was better built and able to accommodate faster trains than her neighbors'. But the French system had also been more costly to build and had taken longer to finish. The routes were chosen more for administrative and military purposes than for economic ones. The centralization of the system in Paris, together with the neglect of lines connecting major provincial cities, slowed the development of a true national market.

Whatever shortcomings the Legrand plan may have had, the heavy investment in railroad construction in the 1840s spurred overall French economic development. Initially, locomotives had to be imported from England, but French firms soon began producing their own equipment, and the growth of railroads spurred the development of iron making. Railroad projects were too costly to be handled by traditional family firms; they demanded joint-stock companies and encouraged the growth of the capital market—along with a great deal of speculation, corruption, and fraud. Thanks in large part to the start of large-scale railroad construction, France enjoyed its first true industrial boom from 1842–1845. Lines linking Paris to Orléans and Rouen were completed in 1843, and the route to the Belgian border was finished in 1847. By then, however, the feverish railroad boom was over. A severe economic depression in 1846–1847 slowed the completion of the system. Many of the private rail companies had run out of money to complete their projects. Only after 1850 would France begin to reap the real benefits of the railroad revolution.

BOURGEOIS SOCIETY

The shift from Charles X to Louis-Philippe and the July Monarchy symbolized a major social transformation. The new regime was seen from the start as a "bourgeois monar-chy." The tendency of many aristocrats to withdraw from court life in protest against the overthrow of the Bourbons accentuated the symbolic social cleavage caused by the July Revolution. But the ruling elite of the period was by no means a cross section of the former Third Estate. The leaders of the "bourgeois monarchy" included many with aristocratic titles—some from old families that accepted the new order, like Alexis de Tocqueville, and others who had been en-nobled under Napoleon or were elevated to the peerage by Louis-Philippe himself. Land ownership remained a major source of wealth for most of this elite, but it also included many people whose fortunes were based on other activities. Bankers were es-pecially prominent in the early years of the regime, and the economic expansion of the period propelled many industrialists into the ranks of the dominant class. The ascen-dancy of the Jewish banker James Roth-schild, whose investments extended to every area of the new industrial economy, symbolized the degree to which wealth al-lowed successful individuals to transcend old barriers of religion and status. Lawyers, magistrates, and high-ranking government officials made up another important com-ponent of the bourgeoisie. And, as the cases of Guizot, Thiers, and the regime's semi-official philosopher Victor Cousin demon-strated, there was a place in this group for men who distinguished themselves by ex-ceptional intellectual talents. The governing stratum of the bourgeoisie under the July Monarchy was no longer a hereditary privi-leged group, like the nobility of the Old Regime, and its economic position was no longer based solely on ownership of land. But this *haute bourgeoisie* (those rich enough to vote in national elections) remained a small minority, set off from the rest of French society by its wealth and its style of life.

The new king and his family were prime representatives of this shift in values. Whereas Charles X had revived many aristo-cratic traditions of the old court, Louis-Philippe lived the life of a wealthy bour-geois. Court etiquette was greatly simplified. The king adopted bourgeois norms of family life, and became the first monarch to have his sons educated in the state-run *lycées*, rather than entrusting them to private tu-tors. As the most prosperous bourgeois be-came richer, they invested in landed prop-erty and took on some of the lifestyle of the aristocracy, but their political values and outlook on life remained different. Rather than looking nostalgically to the past, they looked forward to a future of economic growth. Rather than adhering to a conserva-tive Catholicism, the male members of these bourgeois clans were usually resolutely sec-ular in outlook.

Below the level of the *haute bourgeoisie* was a large and diverse middle group, clearly better off than artisans and peasants but distinctly less privileged than those at the top. This middle class included educated professionals—lawyers, doctors, notaries, professors, journalists—as well as small businessmen and rural landowners. At the lower boundary of the middle class, shop-keepers and master artisans struggled to dis-tinguish themselves from the urban working classes. Dazzling ascents from rags to riches were the exception, but access to the more modest levels of the middle class in the first half of the nineteenth century was fairly open. Hardworking and successful shop-keepers could hope to rise to the status of merchants, and owners of small workshops had the opportunity to become factory own-ers. Thrifty small-town families, who could afford advanced schooling for their sons, could hope to see them established as lawyers in bigger cities.

The common characteristics shared by the *haute bourgeoisie* and the middle classes

Main Rail Lines in France, 1878
The French rail system, largely completed during the Second Empire, centered on the capital. Thickness of lines indicates volume of traffic.

were the possession of some form of property, or *patrimoine*, a certain degree of education, and a style of life that increasingly set them apart from the poorer sectors of the population. The basis of most bourgeois fortunes was the family business, whether it was a small shop or a large factory. If the business prospered, the typical bourgeois would plow the profits into conservative investments—land, government bonds, shares in railroads and mining enterprises—that would guarantee the family's financial status. Successful bourgeois families also spent money to acquire the proper trappings for their preferred style of life. In Paris, old noble *hôtels* that had housed a single aristocratic clan were now subdivided into apartments for the increasingly numerous bourgeois, who filled them with a clutter of furniture and decorative objects. When possible, they also bought themselves country houses or estates.

Education was another form of bourgeois investment. Sons were sent to the state-run but tuition-charging *lycées* established under Napoleon, where they received training that would set them apart from the less privileged. The curriculum, which stressed the study of Latin, had little to do with the careers most of these men later pursued, but it gave them a common culture and a sense of their superiority and right to lead. Those destined for the professions—particularly teaching, the law, and state administration—undertook further studies after obtaining the *baccalauréat* at the end of their *lycée* days. The system of *grandes écoles*, national schools that prepared outstanding students for careers in teaching or the technical professions, had been established under Napoleon. Admission was by open competition, but in practice only students from wealthy families could afford the lengthy preparation necessary for success.

The memoirs of Jean-Baptiste Monfalcon, a doctor, writer, and librarian from Lyon, provide insights into the world of the nineteenth-century bourgeoisie. Like many members of this group, Monfalcon had risen above humble origins thanks to his parents' determination to give him an education. His medical training and the taste for literature that he acquired during his student years cut him off from his family roots, however. Bourgeois life had its attractions but also its drawbacks. Monfalcon himself commented on his own limited sexual experience, and his devotion to the code of honor of bourgeois men meant that he had to risk fighting several duels during the years when he wrote regularly for local newspapers. Monfalcon did try to improve the lives of the poorer classes from whom he had come, through his work as a doctor at Lyon's char-

ity hospital and through efforts to improve urban sanitation, but he was convinced that the poor and uneducated should not play any role in public life. He wrote several books to convince them that they should better themselves through hard work and patience rather than through collective action. Monfalcon sincerely believed that the educated classes had a mission to support culture and improvement, but he did not think that most of the population would ever be able to participate in intellectual activities. Appointed as municipal librarian in the 1840s, Monfalcon was less interested in spreading the habit of reading than in acquiring expensive editions that would make the city's collection a symbol of its status.[3]

While bourgeois men engaged themselves in the rough-and-tumble of business and politics, the bourgeois home came to be increasingly a woman's domain. Bonnie Smith's case study of bourgeois women in the textile manufacturing region around Lille shows how this new domesticity developed in the first half of the nineteenth century. Up to 1820, it was still common for the wives of entrepreneurs to take an active role in the family business enterprise—sometimes even traveling extensively to deal with suppliers and retailers. As industry developed, however, the wives of prosperous mill owners were excluded from their husbands' businesses, where hired male employees took over their functions. These "ladies of the leisure class" accepted a new pattern for living based on the division of life into a male public sphere of business and politics, and a female private sphere of family life.

Bourgeois women's lives were supposed to be centered on their families. Children occupied a central place in bourgeois domestic life. The period saw a marked increase in the sale of commercially marketed toys and of books and magazines for young people. The passage in 1841 of a law limiting child labor—the French state's first

LES DIFFÉRENTES POSITIONS SOCIALES DE LA FEMME

This mid-nineteenth-century engraving of "the different social roles of women" reflects a recognition that French women performed many different functions besides those of wife and mother. (Source: Edimedia, Paris, all rights reserved.)

intervention in the workplace—signaled the growing concern for child welfare. Family identity was also maintained through a new cult of family gravesites. A Napoleonic law of 1804 entitled every citizen to purchase an individual cemetery plot and a decorated tombstone. (Previously, bodies had been buried in mass graves without individual markers.) Visits to the burial sites of loved ones became an important family ritual in the nineteenth century.

As the mid-nineteenth-century illustration of "the different social roles of women" reproduced here shows, many women, including some from the middle classes, were active outside the home. Although the women shown are all in occupations that were traditionally considered appropriate for their sex, the picture conveys a clear impression of the variety and importance of women's work. Catholic nuns continued to staff the country's hospitals, and midwives continued to deliver the majority of babies. The growing number of girls' schools created a need for teachers, and therefore for women who had more than an elementary education themselves. Despite the Napoleonic Code's restrictions on women's control of money and property, some women did run businesses, like the fashion-shop owner shown at the top of the pyramid in the illustration. The three figures on the right-hand side of the picture—a household servant, a weaver, and a peasant—are reminders that women also performed a good share of the manual labor on which the French economy depended. Bourgeois life depended on the availability of maids, cooks, and nannies to free wealthier women from household chores, while factory-owners often preferred women as workers. As in previous centuries, all members of peasant households had to help with farming tasks.

Peasant Life

The new social patterns pioneered by France's small bourgeois elite were held up as models for the lower classes, but few workers or peasants could hope to emulate them in real life. Peasant life changed most dramatically in areas where new industries were penetrating the countryside. In the large rural villages of Provence, for example, where public sociability was extensive, peasants influenced by their more bourgeois fellow citizens developed new political attitudes and new habits of social behavior, such as drinking in public at a neighborhood cabaret or *chambrée* (drinking club). In more isolated rural areas, however, bourgeois models of behavior had less impact. Not all changes in the countryside reflected imitation of urban patterns. Deliberate control of births in order to keep the number of children in the family down was more common among peasants than among urban groups in the first half of the nineteenth century. It was partly a reaction to the new inheritance laws passed during the revolutionary period, which required the equal division of family property among heirs. Peasant property owners feared the splitting up of their land into uneconomically small units. Rural overcrowding was serious in some regions. The July Monarchy was the first period in which some poorer farming areas began to witness an actual decrease in population as young people left to find employment in the cities.

THE NEW URBAN WORLD

Changes in urban living patterns were more visible than those in the countryside. Urbanization was not simply a result of industrial development, although industrial cities like Lille and Mulhouse experienced the highest rates of growth. The growing wealth of the urban bourgeoisie created new employment opportunities even in traditional, nonindustrial occupations, such as domestic service. Rural overpopulation left many young people with no alternative but to seek their fortune in the nearest town. Growth in Paris outpaced that in most other urban areas, reflecting the capital's expanding role as a center of administration, finance, and culture. The city's population doubled in the first half of the century, reaching a level of over a million.

Most new urban migrants arrived with little money, and were forced to live in crowded, unhealthy conditions in the poorer sections of the big cities, such as the *Ile de la Cité* in Paris and the Saint-Sauveur district in Lille. Bourgeois observers like Louis-René Villermé, whose book on the living conditions of French textile workers was published in 1840, spread alarm about the impact of industrialization and urbanization. They described in graphic detail the squalid conditions in France's worst urban slums and the disease and signs of social breakdown that accompanied them. "A single, bad straw mattress for the whole family, a small stove which serves for cooking and for heating, a crate or large box masquerading as a cupboard, a table, two or three chairs, a bench, some dishes—these make up the normal furnishings of the rooms of the workers," Villermé reported from Mulhouse.[4] The cholera epidemics of 1832 and 1849, which struck especially hard in the poorer quarters of the large cities, underlined this message. Respectable property owners lived in fear of the "dangerous classes" crowded together in poor urban neighborhoods. Poverty went together with crime and evidence of social breakdown, such as the spread of prostitution—an inevitable by-product of the fact that most migrants were young single men and that poor urban women often found themselves with no other resource to sell but their bodies. Bourgeois fears led to demands for better policing and the more efficient registration of prostitutes. Despite the extensive discussion of urban problems, the budget-conscious July Monarchy government made no systematic effort to improve conditions.

In the minds of bourgeois observers, the increasingly visible problems in France's cities were linked to the rapid growth of a new industrial working class, a creation of the new age of machines. In fact, this impression was misleading. Large factories remained relatively rare in France, and most urban workers continued to be employed in small workshops, using hand tools. Indeed, many artisans were still small, independent entrepreneurs, like the master silk weavers, or *canuts*, of Lyon, who played leading roles in the workers' insurrections of 1831 and 1834. Where there were factories, employees were likely to include more women and children than men, since their salaries were lower and they were less likely to object to industrial discipline. Much of the urban working population had no connection to mechanized industry. Domestic service continued to be the most common occupation for urban women, and the retail sector also absorbed a significant fraction of the workforce.

If the rhetoric of the period nevertheless tended to describe urban society as being divided into two alien blocs of bourgeois and proletarians, it was in part because the laboring classes themselves were becoming more conscious of what divided them

from the rest of society. The characteristic forms of working-class organization that developed during this period underlined the division. Forbidden to organize collectively to bargain with their employers by the Le Chapelier law of 1791, urban workers nevertheless refused to be reduced to a mass of isolated proletarians, living solely by the sale of their labor. In some of the more skilled trades, the prerevolutionary *compagnonnages,* or journeymen's leagues, remained powerful. Throughout the period, the authorities tolerated the formation of mutual aid societies which collected dues from members and maintained a fund to aid the sick and unemployed, and meet expenses of members' funerals. Unlike the prerevolutionary guilds, mutual aid societies included only workers, not their employers. Their spread showed that workers were coming to see themselves as a separate social group with distinct interests. Another way in which workers contested the developing capitalist system was the development of consumer cooperatives. The first French cooperative store opened in Lyon in 1835. Women took an active role in many of the early French cooperative experiments.

Mutual aid societies, which became increasingly numerous in the 1830s and 1840s, often served as a cover for collective agitation against employers. When waves of strikes did break out, the police invariably found members of mutual aid societies among their leaders. Strike action, like the formation of unions, was illegal, but this did not prevent workers from resorting to it when they found themselves sufficiently hard-pressed. The 1830 Revolution—in which popular mass action had toppled a government—and republican agitation both encouraged worker militancy. The strikes of the period were usually spontaneous outbursts, poorly planned from the point of view of bringing economic pressure on particular employers. They generally affected all the enterprises in an industry in the region where they occurred and often spilled over into violence. Naturally, the prefects and the police tended to intervene on the side of the employers, and the most serious outbreaks of worker militancy—such as the Lyon silkworkers' uprisings of 1831 and 1834—often ended bloodily. But these militant protests were clear evidence of workers' growing self-consciousness and discontent.

The period saw repeated efforts to give workers a voice and to improve their conditions. There were several periodicals written for and to some extent by workers, including Lyon's *Echo de la Fabrique* in the early 1830s and the longer-lasting *Atelier* in Paris from 1840 onward. The courageous militant Flora Tristan was one of the first to try to organize a nationwide working-class movement, *L'Union ouvrière.* Through speeches and writings, she tried to combine improvements in workers' conditions with equality for women. She died during an organizing tour in 1844.

CULTURAL TRENDS

Under the Restoration, writers and artists had struggled against the imposition of a Catholic-oriented official culture. The July Monarchy, committed to a policy of *laissez faire,* permitted a wider range of cultural freedom. If it harassed caricaturists who ridiculed the king and handed out public commissions to conformist painters, it nevertheless tolerated a wide range of cultural tendencies. An increasingly educated population and France's growing prosperity provided a wider audience for books, periodicals, art exhibitions, and other cultural manifestations. Publishers and other cultural entrepreneurs became increasingly adept at exploiting this enlarged market. Rather than endorsing a regime and a society that permitted them to operate so openly, however,

French writers and artists showed an increasing tendency to take an oppositional stance, both to the regime and to the bourgeois society with which they identified it.

The populist romanticism that suffused Lamennais's writings also colored the works of the historian Jules Michelet, whose books on the Middle Ages and the French Revolution stressed the creative role of the common people. In his best-selling volume *Le Peuple (The People),* published in 1846, Michelet contrasted the cultured but dessicated upper classes with the common folk, "full of a new sap, life-giving and rejuvenating," whose energy would give France the dynamism it needed to fulfill its role of promoting freedom in the world.[5] The romantic movement remained strong into the 1840s, but as memories of the July Revolution faded and the new regime put down firmer roots, a new realist current surfaced among artists and writers who sought to depict the society around them. The best known of France's realistic novelists was Honoré de Balzac, who enjoyed his first major successes in the 1830s. Balzac conceived his many novels as part of one overarching *Comédie humaine,* a "human comedy" portraying all aspects of French society, just as Dante's *Divine Comedy* had portrayed heaven and hell. Many of his stories revolved around the theme of how the unbridled pursuit of money and individual success ultimately degraded human life and led to tragedy. Balzac's jaundiced view of the world was incarnated in his fictional characters: Lucien de Rubempré, the ambitious young man from the provinces who rose and fell in the whirlwind of Parisian politics; and Old Goriot, the honest vermicelli maker who married his daughters off to husbands with titles, only to have them abandon him in poverty. A conservative, Balzac contrasted this world unfavorably with the ordered, religious world he imagined to have existed in the past. Despite his professed distaste for the world of Guizot and Rothschild, however, his novels themselves conveyed the energy and dynamism of the new society. His ceaseless energy as a writer made him an exemplar of the new credo of productivity. In the fine arts, the caricaturist and painter Honoré Daumier exemplified the new realist atmosphere. He targeted not only politicians but the full range of French social types. His series of drawings based on the fictional character Robert Macaire, the consummate con man who knew how to succeed in the rough-and-tumble of the July Monarchy's *laissez-faire* world, constituted a visual pendant to Balzac's word portraits, even though Daumier's political sympathies were on the left rather than the right.

Balzac's stories and Daumier's drawings were just two of the many cultural products that reached an ever-growing audience as culture became increasingly commercialized during the 1830s and 1840s. A growing number of museums, public concert series, public lectures, and magazines brought art, music, and ideas to a larger audience. Privately owned reading rooms and lending libraries made periodicals and books available to those who could not afford to purchase them. There were as many as 400 *cabinets de lecture* in Paris under the July Monarchy. The launching of Emile Girardin's low-priced newspaper, *La Presse*, and its imitator and rival, *Le Siècle*, in 1836, as well as the introduction of cheap paperback books in 1838, were milestones in this commercialization of culture. These new-style newspapers were sold at half the price of Paris's existing daily papers, so that ordinary members of the middle class could afford them. Unlike the politically oriented titles they sought to replace, *La Presse* and *Le Siècle* eagerly sought out commercial advertising, using the revenue generated this way to compensate for their reduced price. They also tailored their content to an audience with less literary and political sophistication

than the small elite of notables who read the more expensive political dailies.

The new papers found a particularly successful way to boost their circulation when they began publishing novels in serial form. These *romans-feuilletons* were an immense success. Readers rushed to newsstands to get each new installment, boosting the newspapers' circulation and allowing them to pay unheard-of sums to the most popular authors. Balzac and George Sand, the most successful woman author of the period, were among the literary notables who profited from the demand for *romans-feuilletons*. But the master of the genre was Eugène Sue, whose melodramatic stories of life among the Paris poor made the fortune of several different newspapers. He received 100,000 francs for the rights to his *Wandering Jew*, which appeared in installments over thirteen months in 1844 and 1845. Critics deplored the debasement in literary taste they associated with the vogue of the *romans-feuilletons*, but these works and the inexpensive newspapers that carried them greatly broadened the French reading audience.

Press barons like Emile Girardin embraced the new, business-oriented world of the July Monarchy, but undercurrents of resistance against it remained strong throughout the 1840s. In contrast to the Saint-Simonians and Lamennais, however, protest movements in the 1840s tended to become more pragmatic in their language as they adjusted to the new realities of social and economic life. The liberal Catholicism developed in the late 1830s and 1840s by some of Lamennais's former followers was one example of ideals being tempered to fit the reality of mid-nineteenth-century France. Charles de Montalembert, an aristocratic layman who had accompanied Lamennais on his unsuccessful trip to Rome in 1833, urged Catholics to abandon their dream of an integral Catholic society in return for freedom to organize their own institutions.

The liberal Catholic movement focused particularly on educational issues. Guizot's 1833 primary education law had provided for a state-run school system. Tax-supported public schools threatened to replace the Catholic institutions that had long provided most of the elementary education in many regions and, in the interests of promoting national unity and equality, the church was forbidden to set up its own system of secondary schools. Montalembert and his supporters denounced this as a violation of their rights as citizens, and their agitation made the Catholic schools issue one of the dominant themes of public debate in the early 1840s. The issue was still unresolved, however, when the Revolution of 1848 overthrew the July Monarchy.

Although the July Monarchy government continued to oppose religious schools, attitudes toward religion were changing by the 1840s. Many socialist and democratic movements followed the example of Lamennais and contended that Jesus would have endorsed their calls for equality and social justice. Feminists also put their arguments in religious terms. These groups often called for a simple, popular version of Christianity, but much of the French population still remained loyal to the Catholic church. Several visionaries who reported that Mary had appeared to them and given them special messages for France attracted large followings, foreshadowing the response to the most famous of these apparitions, that of Bernadette de Soubirous at Lourdes, which occurred in 1858.

Socialists and Other Critics

French socialism began to evolve from an idealistic bourgeois rejection of liberal society into a working-class movement fueled by protest against economic conditions. Socialist thinkers increasingly addressed themselves directly to the growing number of discontented workers in France's cities, urging them to see themselves as victims of an industrial society that measured their worth in purely economic terms. Utopian elements remained strong in many of these socialist doctrines, such as those of Etienne Cabet, whose Icarian movement was the first to attract a mass following (perhaps as many as 100,000) during the 1840s. Cabet appealed to workers with his vision of a communistically organized society in which private property would be abolished and individuals would cooperate voluntarily to meet social needs. Cabet, a pacifist, opposed violence and eventually threw his energies into organizing an unsuccessful community to be founded in Texas. The Revolution of 1848 left his movement behind. Other socialists who had emerged during the 1840s were destined to play a larger role in that upheaval, however. The most important of these was Louis Blanc, whose book *The Organization of Labor,* published in 1840, had made him one of the best-known socialist writers in France. Blanc's socialist ideas were cast in a more pragmatic mold than Cabet's. He proposed to resolve the problems of the working class through state-sponsored workers' cooperatives. Universal suffrage would guarantee a government sensitive to workers' needs. Blanc's combination of democracy and socialism had considerable influence on the subsequent evolution of French left-wing movements, although the 1848 Revolution was to show that even his pragmatic proposals for change were hard to put into practice.

Socialists were not the only ones to take a hard look at the realities of nineteenth-century life during the July Monarchy. Frustrated by the Guizot government's inaction on slavery, abolitionists like Cyrille Bissette, who had founded the first French periodical edited by a black writer in 1834, and Victor Schoelcher stepped up their campaign against the institution in the late 1840s; for the first time since the 1790s, they succeeded in winning considerable public support. Conservative critics who blamed the liberal July Monarchy for encouraging the unbridled pursuit of profit did as much as the socialists to spread the misleading impression that France's cities were becoming the home of a massive and impoverished industrial proletariat. The most insightful liberal thinker of the period, Alexis de Tocqueville, was one of many who made a pilgrimage to the industrial cities of Britain to learn first-hand about the effects of economic development. More significant, however, was Tocqueville's decision to visit the United States and describe the workings of its democratic political system. His *Democracy in America,* whose first volume appeared in 1835, noted both the benefits and the costs of the egalitarian society Tocqueville was sure would eventually spread to Europe. Implicit in Tocqueville's admiration for the vigorous American citizenry was a critique of the French lack of civic-mindedness. But his criticism of the conformism of American life and the lack of a genuine cultural tradition conveyed a regret about aspects of European civilization that he feared were doomed by the progress of democracy.

As the regime created in 1830 neared the end of its second decade, French society had clearly begun to take on a new shape. The ascendancy of the bourgeoisie, first proclaimed in 1789, had become a reality, as the values and lifestyle of this class replaced those of the landed aristocracy. Although few French workers were employed in large factories, the organization of French industry had changed; new machines had become commonplace, and the rapidly expanding railroad system provided clear evidence that the country was entering a new era. The new cultural climate directed the public's attention to these social changes, and a growing culture industry of newspapers, reading rooms, and other enterprises ensured the broad circulation of new ideas. Politics remained, however, the preserve of a narrow elite. The number of men wealthy enough to vote in national elections did grow steadily in the 1840s, going from around 170,000 in 1830 to over 266,000 in 1846, but this remained a small fraction even of those who had the wealth and education to feel entitled to a voice in public affairs. The growing working class, ever more conscious of its problems, remained entirely excluded from politics. Unwilling to bring a broader segment of French society into the political system, Guizot's political system rested on a perilously narrow base.

Notes

1. Figures from David Landes, *The Unbound Prometheus* (Cambridge: Cambridge University Press, 1969), 165.

2. Cited in J. H. Clapham, *Economic Development of France and Germany* (Cambridge: Cambridge University Press, 1955), 144.

3. Jean-Baptiste Monfalcon, *Souvenirs d'un bibliothécaire, ou Une vie d'homme de lettres en province* (Lyon: Nigon, 1853).

4. Cited in William Reddy, *The Rise of Market Culture* (Cambridge: Cambridge University Press, 1984), 177.

5. Cited in Paul Vialleneix, ed., *Michelet Cent Ans Après* (Grenoble: Presses Universitaires de Grenoble, 1975), 31.

CHAPTER 14

THE REVOLUTION OF 1848: THE CRISIS OF BOURGEOIS SOCIETY

Had the rapid economic and social changes of the 1830s and 1840s made a new revolutionary upheaval inevitable in France? Alexis de Tocqueville, the liberal nobleman famed for his book on American democracy, warned the Chamber of Deputies in January 1848 that the growing division between rich and poor in France and the spread of socialist ideas were making a revolution inevitable: "We are lulling ourselves to sleep over an active volcano."[1] When a popular uprising overthrew the July Monarchy a few weeks later, he gained a reputation as a prophet. But the Revolution of 1848 was a more complicated affair than the social civil war Tocqueville had warned of. It was made possible by widespread discontent among the educated classes as well as among the urban poor. The bloodiest moment of the Revolution—the war of barricades in Paris in June 1848—pitted the city's underclass against equally poor soldiers recruited from the countryside. And although the revolutionary upheaval of 1848 failed to produce a stable new form of government, it did plant the seeds for the eventual success of democratic republicanism in France.

THE FEBRUARY REVOLUTION

The July Monarchy's sudden collapse came as a surprise. A revolution would have seemed more likely in 1846 or 1847, when France had been hit by a sharp economic depression. The boom fueled by the 1842 railroad-building program had burst, and agriculture had been hard hit by crop failures, especially the potato blight—the same plant disease that caused deadly famine in Ireland in 1846. Guizot's government had done little to alleviate the resulting unemployment and misery, but the economic crisis had actually dampened worker agitation. Concern about eking out a living and fear of unemployment discouraged organized protests.

The most visible opposition to the July Monarchy at the beginning of 1848 came not from the lower classes but from upper- and middle-class groups who felt excluded from the political system. The long-standing school conflict alienated even many wealthy Catholics from the regime. Aristocratic landowners continued to regard Louis-Philippe as a usurper. Students protested against the government's silencing of outspoken professors, such as the romantic historian Michelet. Most seriously, the "bourgeois monarchy" continued to deny much of the bourgeoisie itself any political role. Guizot, who had dominated the ministry since 1840, remained rigid in his opposition to any modification of laws that limited the right to vote to the wealthiest strata of the population. The theme of electoral reform provided a basis for the development of an eminently respectable opposition movement that was not overtly revolutionary. Indeed, the deputies and bourgeois notables who organized this national campaign would never have begun to agitate unless they had been confident that they could do so without unleashing dangerous unrest.

The electoral reformers' strategy was to hold banquets in major provincial cities, charging admission fees to limit the attendance to respectable members of the middle class. By providing a focus for public protest, however, the banquet campaigners set in motion a much broader movement. As the campaign moved from city to city, workers, artisans, and small shopkeepers turned out in the streets to cheer the bourgeois opponents of the regime and express their own discontent. By the time the banquet campaign's planned climax in Paris in late February approached, both the government and its organizers had begun to fear that matters were getting out of hand, and the organizers were almost relieved when the government announced that it was banning the meeting.

But it was now too late to prevent crowds from gathering in the streets. Large and noisy demonstrations on the evening of the planned banquet, February 22, 1848, continued on the following day. The National Guard, charged with maintaining order but made up of citizen volunteers, many of whom came from the same middle-class groups whose frustration had guaranteed the success of the banquets, showed little energy in controlling them. On the evening of the twenty third, the demonstrators clashed with army troops, who opened fire and killed a number of protesters. For militants of the various republican and socialist groups that had suffered under the Guizot regime's repression, these killings provided the means to turn reform protests into a revolution. The victims' bodies were loaded onto carts and hauled around the city. The

sight of the corpses spurred the population's anger, and during the night of the twenty-third to twenty-forth, barricades blocked the streets in the city's poorer neighborhoods. Louis-Philippe, alarmed by the tide of unrest, had already jettisoned Guizot. But by the time he persuaded Odilon Barrot, a leader of the banquet campaign, to accept the prime ministership on February 24, events had outstripped him. Like Charles X in 1830, he tried to abdicate in favor of the young heir to the throne, but the crowds in the streets had already rallied to the slogans of republicanism.

THE PROVISIONAL GOVERNMENT

Even as the Chamber of Deputies was discussing Louis-Philippe's abdication, a provisional republican government headed by the romantic poet Alphonse de Lamartine, author of a best-selling history of the Revolution of 1789, was being proclaimed at the Hôtel-de-Ville. Although the provisional government's eleven-member council included a number of bourgeois reformers and only two spokesmen for the lower classes—the socialist writer Louis Blanc and the artisan Albert, a member of one of the secret republican societies—its accession to power meant a sharp break with the constitutional monarchy. As in 1792, the proclamation of the republic meant that France's future would be entrusted to a constituent assembly chosen by universal suffrage. There would be no repetition of 1830, when a small group of politicians and journalists had replaced one regime with another. And the appeal to universal suffrage meant that peasants, artisans, and workers would far outnumber the educated, property-owning bourgeois voters. The February Revolution suddenly threw the whole future of liberal, bourgeois society into question.

At first, the bourgeoisie seemed resigned to its fate. In Lyon, the bourgeois librarian and well-known local Orléanist Jean-Baptiste Monfalcon wrote a cringing letter to the newly installed republican mayor, assuring him of "my sincere adherence to the Republic" and asking, "Will the Republic, which has solemnly guaranteed bread to hard-working laborers, take away that which thirty years of hard toil has gotten me?"[2] The insurrection had been confined to Paris, Lyon, and a few other major cities. In most of the country, the Provisional Government retained the previous regime's officials, and local landowners and notables were initially undisturbed. But the overthrow of the July Monarchy did unleash a torrent of popular political activity. By mid-April, less than two months after the uprising, over 200 clubs, with a total membership of over 100,000, were meeting in Paris, some as often as six times a week. The different factions represented in the Provisional Government each tried to unify the club movement behind its own program. Meanwhile, militants who had been in the clandestine opposition before February, such as Blanqui, tried to create a powerful popular socialist movement. Dozens of hastily founded newspapers, many of them closely associated with clubs, broadcast new ideas to the country at large. Republicans of all persuasions, socialists, feminists, and promoters of Christian democracy all competed for attention. Conservative groups, especially in the provinces, warned of the dangers of disorder and predicted that the new democratic order would soon collapse.

All across the political spectrum, there was agreement that the new revolution required policies that would resolve "the social question" and prevent a civil war between hostile classes. The Provisional Government's efforts to aid the working class while reassuring nervous property owners showed how difficult it was to achieve this objective, despite the apparent consensus on the need to do so. To deal with unemploy-ment, which rose sharply because of the uncertainty following the February revolution, the Provisional Government opened National Workshops, where Paris workers were paid a modest wage but frequently had little to do. Conservatives attacked the workshops as a waste of money and as a political danger, since the workers appeared to spend much of their time reading newspapers and discussing socialist ideas. The Provisional Government delegated Louis Blanc to hold public hearings on workers' problems. He headed a commission that met at the Luxembourg Palace and took extensive testimony from members of a wide variety of trades. To conservatives, the Luxembourg Commission was a dangerous concession to socialism, encouraging the workers to imagine they could bring pressure on the government to solve their problems. To the radical socialist Karl Marx, however, the Luxembourg Commission served merely to ensure that "the representatives of the working class were exiled from the seat of the Provisional Government," which was left in the hands of the bourgeois republicans.[3]

The revolution sparked debate on the role of women as well as that of workers. Feminist groups, largely silenced since the early 1830s, reappeared, forming clubs and publishing newspapers—some demanding the right to vote and others linking the cause of women to a general call for social restructuring. Male republicans, and even some prominent women such as George Sand, a close associate of the Provisional Government's interior minister, Ledru-Rollin, opposed such demands. In Lyon, unemployed female workers demonstrated to be admitted to the National Workshops. But the republican authorities limited them to organizing a door-to-door fundraising drive, accompanied by charitable and respectable bourgeois women. The caricaturist Daumier turned his crayon against the radical feminists, mocking their club meetings and lamenting the plight

This illustration shows armed workers in Lyon carrying a bust of "Marianne," the female personification of the Republic, in a parade celebrating the overthrow of the Orléanist monarchy. Street demonstrations gave members of the lower classes a sense of political power, but they scared and angered conservatives, who were determined to restore "order."
(Source: Bibliothèque municipale de Lyon, Coste 729.)

of fathers left at home with crying children. A conservative female author rushed a story entitled "The Young Republicannesses" into print to convince readers that "to be the worthy companion of a true and pure republican" a woman should devote herself above all to being "a wife, a mother . . . the good angel of the home."[4]

The revolution had immediate effects on France's colonies. In Algeria, civilian settlers demanded an end to arbitrary government by the French army. General Bugeaud's troops had crushed Abd el-Kader's revolt in 1847, but the military regime, concerned about maintaining order, tried to restrain the settlers from taking over most Arab lands. The Provisional Government sided with the settlers, promising that Algeria would eventually be put under the same laws as metropolitan France. Although this policy of "assimilation" to French conditions would not be fully implemented until the Third Republic, it had major implications for the future of the colony: carrying it out would mean eliminating the traditions and institutions of the territory's Arab and Berber populations. The abolitionist Victory Schoelcher persuaded the Provisional Government to decree the immediate end of slavery in France's overseas colonies on April 27, 1848. By the time the decree reached the Caribbean islands of Martinique and Guadeloupe, the local populations had already risen up to demand their freedom, an event vividly recounted in Patrick Chamoiseau's 1992 novel, *Texaco.* The Provisional Assembly's action kept France's new republican government from having to send troops to uphold slaveowners' rights, and ensured that the "old colonies" where slavery had existed would remain loyal to France.

The Provisional Government's most fateful and most controversial decision was to hold national elections for a constituent assembly just two months after the overthrow of Louis-Philippe's government. As they began to organize for the election campaign, the radical and socialist groups in Paris quickly realized how difficult it was to gain support for their ideas across the country in the few short weeks they were allowed. Even within the government, dedicated republicans like Ledru-Rollin—who occupied the crucial Interior Ministry and was in charge of organizing the elections—argued for a postponement so that the millions of new voters could be educated enough to make intelligent choices. But the republicans were trapped by their own political principles. They needed a popular mandate to justify the legitimacy of their own government. And conservative critics denounced the Paris radicals' call for postponing the vote as an effort to install a revolutionary dictatorship. Mass demonstrations organized by the Paris political clubs on March 17 and April 16, 1848, seemed to show the danger of a lower-class insurrection if a government with a firm claim to authority was not quickly installed.

The voting on April 23, 1848, confirmed the Paris radicals' fears. In most rural districts, still the home of the overwhelming majority of the population, the voters turned to local dignitaries who were often the only men with any previous political experience. The liberal noble Alexis de Tocqueville wrote a classic description of how he swayed the peasants from his Normandy estate, which gives a vivid sense of how local notables in conservative regions succeeded in influencing the vote: "A circle formed around me, and I said a few words appropriate to the occasion. I reminded these good people of the seriousness and importance of the act they were going to perform; I advised them not to let themselves be accosted or diverted by people who might, when we arrived at the town, seek to deceive them."[5] In any event, peasant voters needed no coaching from the rich to react against the one measure of the Provisional Government that had affected them the most. To pay for the many expenditures the crisis situation after February had required, the government had imposed a stiff tax increase of forty-five centimes for every franc.

The result of the voting in this, France's first genuinely free election under universal male suffrage, was thus paradoxical. The voters picked about 270 moderate republicans pledged to draft a democratic constitution that would respect the rights of private property, and about 70 to 80 radicals and socialists. But the mostly rural electorate returned over 400 deputies whose real loyalties were to one or another of France's banished ruling dynasties. Supporters of the fallen Orléanists were the most numerous, but there were a number of legitimists loyal to the Bourbons and a few Bonapartists bent on restoring the Empire. For the moment, most of these conservative deputies put aside their divisions over the question of which dynasty to support and coalesced into a "Party of Order," united in their opposition to socialism and concessions to the workers.

THE JUNE DAYS AND THE CONSERVATIVE REPUBLIC

Although the "Party of Order" dominated the newly elected assembly, more radical groups remained active. Left-wing candidates had won the elections in Paris, and the conservative deputies had to meet in the midst of a restless urban population. The Assembly's conservative majority showed its colors by ousting Louis Blanc and the artisan Albert from the Executive Commission, but the deputies hesitated to close the National Workshops, for fear of sparking a popular uprising.

The radical militants of the Paris clubs, disappointed by the election results, cast about for a way to rally their forces and found it in the sphere of foreign policy. In the wake of the February Revolution, democratic and nationalist uprisings had broken out all over central Europe. The republican and socialist groups in Paris saw an opportunity to counter the conservative tide in France by pressuring the government to put the country at the head of an international crusade for democracy. Republican France would regain the leadership it had exercised during the 1790s. On May 15, 1848, the clubs staged a mass march to demand French aid for the nationalist movement in Poland. Some of the marchers broke into the Assembly's meeting hall, took over the rostrum, and declared the Assembly dissolved, while another group seized Paris's town hall, the Hôtel-de-Ville. The National Guard, largely dominated by middle-class volunteer soldiers, soon regained control of the city, and the radical movement was disrupted by the arrest of many of its leaders. But the incident increased tensions in the capital, convincing both sides that a further showdown was inevitable.

Although the surviving club leaders tried to avoid provoking the authorities after May 15, they were rapidly losing control of their own followers. By-election results showed that the situation was becoming increasingly polarized, with the moderate republicans losing strength to conservatives on one side and socialists on the other. Urban crowds demonstrated against the government in numerous provincial cities, including Limoges, Nantes, and Marseille. Meanwhile, the Bonapartist pretender, Louis-Napoleon, still in exile in England, had allowed his name to be put forward for an Assembly seat and had shown that he could draw votes from both conservatives and radicals for his vaguely outlined program of a strong government independent of all parties. Talk of resolving the social problem gave way among conservatives to an obsession with proving that the government could maintain public order and break the socialist and working-class opposition. On June 21, 1848, the Assembly voted to close the National Workshops in Paris. Unmarried workers would be sent from the capital to work on swamp-draining projects in the Sologne, a notoriously unhealthy region.

The Assembly's action was too much to bear for many Paris workers and artisans. The democratic republic their uprising had created in February 1848 was turning against them. As in February, barricades went up in the narrow streets of the capital's crowded working-class quarters. Arrest statistics show that the rebels were a cross section of the city's poorer classes. Some came from the lower reaches of the petty bourgeoisie, some were skilled artisans whose trades were feeling the pressure of industrial competition, some were factory workers, and some were casual laborers or unemployed. Engravings from the period emphasize the fact that women fought alongside the men. Altogether, fifty thousand may have taken an active part in the struggle.

The government's strategy was to avoid a repetition of the confused fighting that had allowed the February movement an easy triumph. The revolt was allowed to spread while army troops and artillery were readied for a systematic assault. By June 24, most of the poorer neighborhoods in eastern Paris were covered with barricades. But the rebels, whose most capable leaders had been arrested after May 15, lacked direction, and they had been unable to capture key government buildings such as the Hôtel-de-Ville, the symbolic center of the city's government. On the twenty fifth, the army began a systematic and bloody reconquest of the city. In several days of fierce fighting, some three thousand people were killed; the victorious forces of order arrested some fifteen thousand others, many of whom were deported to prison camps in Algeria.

Emboldened by their victory, the conservatives in the Assembly voted repressive measures against clubs and newspapers, and tried to pin the blame for the uprising on prominent socialist and republican leaders.

Although the June Days movement had been confined to Paris, provincial authorities now assumed that they had a mandate to harass republican militants and journalists.

To the majority of deputies in the Assembly, the June Days showed the need for a "strong government" that could be trusted to keep the lower orders in their place. They turned leadership of the government over to General Eugène Cavaignac, who had commanded the repression of the June uprising. Ironically, the firmly republican general proved less conservative than most of the deputies. The deputies of the "Party of Order" turned to the church as well as the army, forcing Cavaignac to appoint an education minister sympathetic to religious influence in the schools. Above all, they sought to institutionalize order by designing a constitution that featured a strong executive branch. Inspired in many ways by the model of the United States, they provided for an elected president with extensive powers, to be balanced by a one-chamber assembly. The president's powers would be limited because he could not run for reelection. The deputies' only concession to democracy was the retention of universal male suffrage. They hesitated to provoke another desperate uprising by repealing the one essential achievement of the February revolution.

The Constituent Assembly's leaders had assumed that the president elected in the voting called for in December 1848 would be a man loyal to the new system. There was one serious threat: Louis-Napoleon, after scoring several successes as a symbolic protest candidate in by-elections, announced plans to run. The various monarchist factions, determined to keep him out and to defeat the democratic left, put aside any hope of an early restoration and agreed to support General Cavaignac. The left-wing republicans' candidate was Ledru-Rollin, a member of the original Provisional Government who had avoided association with the June Days uprising. The veteran socialist Raspail represented the extreme left. Lamartine, the poet who had headed the Provisional Government in February, also put himself forward.

Despite the upheavals and violence earlier in the year, the election campaign was peaceful and relatively orderly. Cavaignac, with the combined support of the "Party of Order" and the moderate republicans, seemed to be the overwhelming favorite. But the results of the voting on December 10, 1848, were a surprise—indeed, the greatest electoral surprise in French history. As anticipated, the figures identified with the February revolution did poorly. Ledru-Rollin ran a distant third with fewer than 400,000 votes, and the hapless Lamartine drew an embarrassing 8,000. But Cavaignac and the "Party of Order" were also rejected; the general won only 1,400,000 votes. The overwhelming victor was Louis-Napoleon Bonaparte, the nephew of the emperor, who received more than 5,400,000 ballots. Even today, the reasons for his triumph remain elusive. His name was, of course, recognizable to even the most poorly educated voter, and it summoned up memories of a time when France's glory had been at its peak. He had the advantage of not having taken part in any of the earlier events of the 1848 Revolution, so that he was identified neither with radicalism nor with repression. His vaguely worded proposals reflected some Saint-Simonian influence and a concern for both business and workers. And, in the Bonapartist tradition, he claimed to stand for both order and democracy. Above all, however, the vote for Louis-Napoleon seems to have reflected a popular rejection of all the politicians of 1848, the conservatives as well as the radicals.

THE TROUBLED REPUBLIC

Three main issues dominated the three years following Louis-Napoleon's election victory:

the conservative legislature's continuing effort to protect the interests of the wealthy elites that it represented, the steady growth of democratic republicanism in spite of the setbacks of 1848, and the new president's effort to find a way to remain in office after his four-year term expired in 1852. Initially, the president and the "Party of Order" appeared to be in agreement, although Louis-Napoleon moved quickly in January 1849 to assert that he could pick his own ministers, even if their policies failed to win a majority in the Assembly. The machinery of government continued to be used to repress democratic and socialist propaganda. In the spring of 1849, elections for a new Assembly to replace the Constituent Assembly produced another victory for the "Party of Order." But radical democratic deputies still formed a significant opposition group, dubbed the *Montagne* in memory of the radical Jacobins of 1793. The radicals, or *démoc-socs* (democratic socialists), did particularly well in urban areas, but the election returns showed that they were now finding support in some rural regions as well. This was particularly true in Alsace, in the Rhône valley, and in some parts of the Massif Central.

In May 1849, Louis-Napoleon consolidated his alliance with the conservatives when he sent French troops to protect the pope from a republican revolution in Rome, thus placing himself squarely on the side of the Catholic church. The move outraged the *démoc-soc* minority in the Assembly. Led by Ledru-Rollin, 120 deputies signed a manifesto urging a protest demonstration on June 13, 1849. In Paris, the police easily controlled the demonstration, but in Lyon the protest turned into an uprising with barricades and deaths. The government used this pretext to make another wave of arrests of radical and socialist leaders. But the movements in Paris and Lyon showed that there was still strong support for the *démoc-soc* movement. Conservatives obviously could not rest easily.

The Falloux School Law

Aside from outright repression, the conservatives' main response to the spread of democracy involved a systematic effort to inculcate the values of respect for order and social hierarchy into the population. The most significant effort of the "Party of Order" to do this was the passage of the Falloux school law in March 1850. The Falloux law conceded to Catholics the privilege of creating their own schools, thus settling the long-running dispute that had divided religiously minded conservatives from other members of the upper classes throughout the 1840s. Inasmuch as almost all girls' schools were already run by the church, the Falloux law allowed Catholics to create a school system almost as extensive as the public schools. The Falloux law also introduced Catholic religious education in the public schools, breaking with the secularist tradition inaugurated during the Revolution. Children of religious minorities— Protestants and Jews—could be exempted from these classes, but the law signaled a new alliance of the church and the French state. Although the Falloux law gave much to the church, it also gave new powers to the government. Control over the school system was firmly centralized in Paris, preventing communes dominated by the left-wing opposition from using the schools to propagate democratic ideas. And it also contributed to the professionalization of teaching by granting instructors a major pay increase.

Suffrage

In the face of continuing *démoc-soc* successes in off-year elections, the Assembly's conservative majority tried to curtail universal suffrage. A new election law, enacted in May 1850 and aimed at excluding what Thiers called "the vile multitude," required voters to be registered taxpayers and to have had a fixed address for three years. It reduced the number of eligible voters from 9,600,000 to 6,800,000, and marked a retreat from the principles of democracy adopted in 1848. The message to the *démoc-socs* was clear: they would not be allowed to come to power through the electoral process. As a result, many militants began to revert to the clandestine tactics they had practiced before 1848. Louis-Napoleon also changed tactics in response to the law. Recognizing its unpopularity among the lower classes, he ostentatiously distanced himself from it, making it clear that it represented the wishes of the deputies, not his own.

According to the constitution enacted in 1848, the year 1852 was to see two national elections: one for a new Assembly in May and one for the presidency in December. Buoyed by their steady gains in partial elections in 1850 and 1851, the *démoc-soc* forces still expected to take control of the Assembly, a prospect the conservative "Party of Order" anticipated with corresponding alarm. As for Louis-Napoleon, he remained frustrated; repeated efforts to persuade the deputies to amend the constitution to permit him to run for reelection had failed. But the conservatives' fear of the radical republicans offered Louis another possibility: a coup d'état that would forestall the elections at the price of overturning the constitution. In preparation for such a showdown, the president systematically put men loyal to him in key positions in the government bureaucracy and the army. Lacking a strong party of his own in the Assembly, he worked cleverly to keep the conservatives and the republicans divided. He also used his considerable talents as a propagandist to discredit the deputies and put himself forward as the one figure who could give the country strong and stable government.

After long months of preparation, Louis-Napoleon finally struck on December 2, 1851, the anniversary of his uncle's great military victory at Austerlitz. In a proclamation posted on the walls of Paris at dawn that day, he justified his action by condemning the incompetence of the divided Assembly, and recalling the successes of the First Empire. In a bid to give his new regime an air of legitimacy, he announced that a new constitution would be drawn up and restored universal manhood suffrage, curtailed by the law of May 31, 1850. The police arrested a number of deputies, both leading republicans and prominent Orléanists and legitimists, and top military officers who were not loyal to the president. A small group of parliamentarians succeeded in evading the dragnet. Led by Victor Hugo, they issued a call for an insurrection to defend the Republic. For a day, the success of the coup seemed in doubt. Residents of some of the city's poorer neighborhoods built barricades, and respectable bourgeois ostentatiously refused to support the troops. But the army, under the orders of commanders hand-picked by Louis-Napoleon, followed orders to destroy the barricades, and the resistance was much more limited than in June 1848. The common people of Paris were not prepared to fight to the death for the conservative Republic.

Triumph in the capital was not enough to assure Louis-Napoleon's success, however. News of the coup set off a major insurrection in the south of France, revealing how extensively republican ideas had penetrated among the peasants and villagers of Pro-vence. At its height, this rural insurrection may have involved more than 100,000 people. Enthusiastic but disorganized, the republicans armed themselves as best they could and marched on the nearest towns, hoping to spread the movement. Hastily summoned troops soon dispersed these columns and arrested hundreds of participants, but the extent of the insurrection showed that the brief interval of the Second Republic had made a lasting change in the political attitudes of the common people in much of rural France. Republican, democratic, and even socialist ideas were no longer confined to the large cities. On the other side, the harsh repression of the uprising identified Louis-Napoleon's regime with conservatism. His gesture in restoring universal suffrage had not been sufficient to capture the support of the lower classes.

NOTES

1. Alexis de Tocqueville, *Recollections,* George Lawrence, trans. (Garden City, NY: Doubleday, 1970), 14.
2. Monfalcon to mayor, 13 Mar. 1848, in *Bibliothèque municipale de Lyon,* Ms. Fonds Coste 1129.
3. Karl Marx, *The Class Struggles in France 1848–1850* (New York: International Publishers, 1964), 41.
4. Mme. Adèle Cleret, "Les Jeunes républicaines," in *La Providence, Journal des peuples.*
5. Tocqueville, *Recollections,* 95.

CHAPTER 15

THE SECOND EMPIRE'S DECADE OF PROSPERITY

In 1851, as in 1799, a Bonaparte overthrew a discredited republican regime and replaced it with a system that gave him a firm grip on power. Like his uncle, Louis-Napoleon was initially able to rely on fairly broad popular support because he promised to put an end to the futile squabbling of the politicians he ousted. The new Napoleon benefited during the first half of his reign from a favorable economic climate, but he also strengthened his position through innovative domestic policies and successful ventures abroad. Not everyone accepted the new Napoleonic order; the regime's police kept a strict watch on the unrepentant republicans, socialists, and legitimists who refused to renounce their ideas. For some ten years, however, the revived Bonapartist regime seemed to have resolved many of the dilemmas that had weakened all the previous postrevolutionary governments.

THE EMPIRE'S NEW CLOTHES

With the resistance to his coup quickly crushed, Louis-Napoleon and his supporters turned to the erection of new institutions that would guarantee his grip on power. The abortive resistance in Paris and the *Midi* insurrection served as pretexts for the arrest of thousands of republican activists throughout the country, the most important of whom were imprisoned or deported to the French colonies. A plebiscite, called for December 20, 1851 and organized by prefects who had been ordered to produce impressive results, duly provided an overwhelming majority in favor of a new constitution. Under it the president would remain in office for ten years and the powers of the legislature, divided once again into two houses, would be greatly curtailed. Parliamentary elections in the spring of 1852 produced a compliant Chamber of Deputies, from which the regime's opponents were excluded.

Not since the first Napoleon had one man held so much power in France. Raised in exile, Napoleon III was an outsider to his own country. Before 1848, his only period of residence there had been a term in the prison-fortress of Ham after his unsuccessful coup attempt in 1840. Years in exile and in prison had taught him to keep his true thoughts to himself and to rely on a small group of loyal followers. The future emperor was not lacking in intelligence, and the pamphlets he had written before 1848 had shown that he was interested in new ideas, particularly Saint-Simonian proposals for overcoming poverty and social conflict through planned economic expansion. His successful campaign in 1848 and his ability in outmaneuvering the parliamentary politicians afterward revealed a combination of unscrupulousness and genuine political skills. To the end of his reign, however, he kept his true intentions to himself, making it difficult for contemporaries and historians to make sense of what often seemed to be contradictory policies.

Freed from concern about political opposition, Louis-Napoleon sought to demonstrate that his authoritarian, one-man rule could produce results that the parliamentary Republic had been unable to achieve. In particular, he wanted to restore business confidence and promote economic prosperity. The government took an active role in encouraging negotiations between the railroad companies (many of which had been in severe difficulty since the mid-1840s) and bankers, with an eye toward pushing the national rail network toward completion. Government assurances to business revived the stock market, too, and made capital for industrial expansion more available. The modest economic recovery that had begun after the crisis of 1848 turned into a sustained boom that continued through most of the 1850s. This wave of prosperity helped reconcile both businessmen and workers to the Bonapartist regime.

The revised constitution approved in December 1851 and the title of Prince-President did not satisfy Louis-Napoleon's ambitions to make his regime permanent. In 1852, he undertook an extensive speaking tour of the French provinces to lay the groundwork for the restoration of the Napoleonic empire. To the French people, Louis-Napoleon claimed that he alone could bring unity, "because I don't belong to any family of ideologues." To governments in the rest of Europe, whose memories of the first Napoleon were anything but reassuring, the president promised that "the Empire means peace": France had no desire for conquests. The nation's energies would be fully occupied, he claimed,

with a massive program of public works.[1] On November 20, 1852, a second plebiscite—by a vote of 7,800,000 yes to 250,000 no—approved the restoration of the hereditary Napoleonic Empire. Louis-Napoleon, out of respect for Napoleon I's son who had died in 1832, took the title Napoleon III.

The prefects' success in producing an overwhelming vote in favor of the new Empire could not mask the persistence of opposition to the regime. Throughout his reign, Napoleon III never enjoyed deep support. Many of the business-minded bourgeois notables who had held power under the July Monarchy accepted positions under the Empire, but their true loyalties remained with the Orleans dynasty and the parliamentary system under which they had monopolized political power. Similarly, the wealthy legitimist landowners who dominated many regions of the west continued to dream of a Bourbon restoration. The urban working class, unrepresented in the government, kept its faith in republican and socialist ideas, and the petty-bourgeois supporters of the 1848 republic were equally unpersuaded by imperial propaganda. A few prominent Orleanists and moderate republicans, such as Adolphe Thiers and Victor Hugo, were driven into exile. Intellectuals such as Tocqueville and Michelet retreated into opposition to a regime whose power, they claimed, was based on naked force. Over the course of his reign, Napoleon III alternated between efforts to win over devotees of different opposition groups and policies of repression. He succeeded at times in converting many opponents to a pragmatic acceptance of his policies, but he never won them over to genuine loyalty to himself and his system.

Prosperity

During the 1850s, the emperor had two major advantages in seeking to consolidate his power. The institutions he had re-created allowed him to act with considerably more decisiveness than the parliamentary governments of the July Monarchy and the Second Republic. In both domestic and foreign affairs, the Second Empire was more dynamic than its predecessors. The Empire also benefited during the 1850s from a surge of economic prosperity. The causes of this were partly fortuitous. Major gold discoveries in California and Australia gave the entire world economy a much-needed stimulus. But Louis-Napoleon's policies provided additional impetus to business expansion during the 1850s. Only after 1860 did business confidence begin to flag. While industrial growth was the most prominent feature of the Second Empire, the period was also one of sustained prosperity for French agriculture. Even though French farmers clung to traditional methods, they enjoyed a succession of mostly good harvests and a period of high prices that contrasted sharply with the severe difficulties that were to descend on the countryside after 1870.

The economic expansion of the 1850s was in most respects a continuation of the process of industrialization that had begun in the early 1840s, before the interruption of the 1845 depression and the Revolution of 1848. Even before the coup d'état, the government had provided a boost to growth by lending support to the large railroad companies whose projects had stalled for lack of credit in the late 1840s. The completion of the major trunk lines in the 1850s provided a massive stimulus for the economy as a whole. Industrial expansion, which was most dramatic in such basic industries as iron making, averaged 3.9 percent a year between 1850 and 1855, a pace only slightly lower than that of the boom years in the early 1840s. The railroads needed iron and coal, machinery, and labor. Their completion lowered transportation costs, encouraging growth in other branches of industry as well. When the railroad reached the porcelain

manufacturing city of Limoges in 1856, for example, it enabled local manufacturers to lower their costs by importing coal for fuel in place of wood. It also enabled them to aim at a national and even an international market. As a result, formerly cautious entrepreneurs began to invest aggressively to expand and modernize their factories.

To what extent was this economic growth the result of Napoleon III's policies? The emperor frequently spoke about the importance of promoting prosperity, and his youthful writings showed the influence of Saint-Simonian ideas about centralized economic planning. His advisors included a number of men who had participated directly in the Saint-Simonian movement, such as the economist Michel Chevalier. In 1852, Louis-Napoleon decreed the construction of a Palace of Industry to showcase French technological achievements, and the lavish international expositions held in Paris in 1855 and 1867 gave pride of place to French manufactures.

Private Enterprise

Unlike some twentieth-century French governments, however, Louis-Napoleon's regime did not attempt to create a planned, government-directed economy. Like the July Monarchy, it essentially relied on the initiative of private entrepreneurs. Even the Palace of Industry, encouraged by the government, was run by a private corporation. But the Second Empire did stimulate private economic initiative in a number of ways. Prior to 1848, the French banking system had remained conservative and old-fashioned. Businessmen had often had trouble borrowing money for plant expansion. The imperial regime encouraged the establishment of new banks, more attuned to business needs, such as the *Crédit Mobilier*, the creation of the Pereire brothers, two aggressive entrepreneurs and former Saint-Simonians. Government guarantees encouraged private bankers to lend to the

In the 1850s, the Schneider ironworks at Le Creusot was the largest industrial enterprise on the European continent. Located in a rural setting, the plant depended on the growing French railroad network to distribute its products. Le Creusot represented the modern sector of the French economy, but older patterns of manufacturing persisted well into the twentieth century.
(Source: Bibliothèque nationale, Paris.)

railroad companies and thus fostered their growth. And the government spent heavily on public works projects, most notably in the capital, thus creating employment and a demand for building materials.

HAUSSMANNIZATION AND OSTENTATION

The rebuilding of Paris illustrated the extent and the limits of Napoleon III's promotion of economic modernization and development. Napoleon III, who fancied himself something of an architect, personally sketched plans for massive rebuilding projects and a network of widened boulevards. But the actual execution of his projects was carried out by Georges Haussmann, a civil engineer and career administrator who had caught the emperor's eye by his help in promoting the plebiscite in favor of the Empire in October 1852. In June 1853, Haussmann took over as prefect of the Seine Department, and over the next decade and a half, he oversaw the transformation of the capital. Working from the bottom up, Haussmann installed underground storm sewers and water pipes to prevent the periodic flooding of Paris's low-lying neighborhoods and to provide clean water, brought via aqueduct from rural areas as much as sixty miles away. At ground level, Haussmann gave the city wide new boulevards. They not only facilitated traffic movement, but also served as a pretext for the demolition of some of the city's worst slum neighborhoods. Haussmann imposed regulations that required that buildings constructed along the new boulevards be of uniform height and design. He thus gave modern Paris its characteristic appearance. Along with new streets, Haussmann dealt with many other urban problems. For example, he oversaw the construction of a great central food market, *Les Halles,* one of the first major building projects to use iron-frame construction. It allowed for better supervision of the city's food supplies and the reduction of health hazards.

Critics at the time and since have pointed out, however, that Haussmann paid little attention to upgrading the quality of housing provided in the new buildings along his boulevards. He did not even make installation of indoor plumbing mandatory, and many tight-fisted landlords refused to pay for it. Nor did he do anything to mitigate the social effects of his massive rebuilding scheme. Poor Parisians forced to relocate found themselves unable to pay the increased rents in new buildings and were forced into cheap housing on the outskirts of the city. Haussmann's operations thereby brought about an increase in social segregation. The grumbling of the poor and of city dwellers who lamented the disappearance of the colorful older neighborhoods in the city center did not affect Haussmann; but the methods by which he financed his projects and the profits raked in by real estate speculators—whose connections allowed them to acquire property along the new boulevards—left him open to criticism. By the late 1860s, Haussmann's financial arrangements had become the subject of intense political controversy. Jules Ferry, a future leader of the Third Republic, published newspaper articles denouncing the scandal of "so many millions in the hands of a single man,"[2] and, although he was never proven to have done anything wrong, Haussmann was finally removed from office in January 1870 as the regime sought to refurbish its image. The story of Haussmann's work in Paris was representative of many aspects of the Empire as a whole. In retrospect, Napoleon III and Haussmann could claim credit for taking crucial steps to make Paris a modern, livable city. But they had done so without much concern for social consequences. And the rebuilding of the capital had favored the rich and increased the gap between workers and bourgeoisie.

The Accumulation of Wealth

The social divisions exacerbated by the rebuilding of Paris were characteristic of the Second Empire. It was a period in which society was more dominated by unabashed wealth than at any other time in French history. The tone was set in part by the emperor's immediate entourage. From his days in exile, he had relied heavily on a small circle of faithful supporters, such as his half-brother the duc de Morny and his faithful henchman Persigny. These men, social outsiders who had cast their lot with Louis-Napoleon at a time when the Bonapartist cause seemed hopeless, were none too scrupulous about enriching themselves once they came to power. The emperor's determination to encourage the growth of industry favored the enrichment of the bourgeoisie, too. Alexis de Tocqueville, the liberal noble who had forecast the 1848 Revolution, complained that the Napoleonic regime fostered "love of gain, a fondness for business careers, the desire to get rich at all costs, a craving for material comfort and easy living."[3] Certainly wealth became the most important criterion of social status. Like his uncle, Napoleon III made no distinction between families whose fortune was rooted in the past and those who had only recently enriched themselves.

The bourgeois elite who dominated the Second Empire tended to become an increasingly closed group after 1848. Earlier in the century, it had been easier for men from humble backgrounds to accumulate the wealth that would allow them to claim bourgeois status, but now inherited positions became more significant. The growing importance of secondary education, for example, favored the sons of families who were able to afford long years of education for their children. As the size of industrial firms became larger and the capital invested in them greater, it became correspondingly more difficult for newcomers to compete with established "bourgeois dynasties." Carefully arranged intermarriages among wealthy families preserved fortunes and ensured their transmission from generation to generation.

While their menfolk concentrated on building the family fortune, the women of this bourgeois elite, freed from the economic responsibilities their grandmothers and mothers shared with their husbands, surrounded themselves with expensive furnishings and possessions in the ever-more-ornate homes that were a sign of bourgeois status. Napoleon III's consort, the beautiful and intensely Catholic Eugénie, whom he had wooed and married in 1853, set a tone that other women sought to imitate. Constructed in new neighborhoods removed from the squalor of working-class slums and the grime of factories, the homes of the wealthy advertised the status of their inhabitants. In them women could live out the domestic, family-oriented lifestyle associated with bourgeois rank, devoting themselves to the rearing of their children and the supervision of servants who did the actual work of the household.

While the bourgeoisie was thus accumulating and displaying wealth on an unprecedented scale, the industrial working class continued to live in poverty. The short-lived revolutionary episode of 1848 had done much to convince urban workers that they were a coherent group with distinct interests and to alienate them from a society that seemed indifferent to their problems. The imperial regime proclaimed its sympathy for workers and encouraged paternalist initiatives such as employer-sponsored model housing projects (few of which were built). It also encouraged the formation of mutual aid societies, which attracted primarily better-paid workers in the more skilled industries. But these initiatives failed to win the workers' loyalty.

Socialism Gains Support

Despite governmental repression, socialist ideas continued to gain adherents among the workers. The most important socialist theorist of the Second Empire period was Pierre Joseph Proudhon. Proudhon denounced the exploitative capitalist and industrial system, and called for a "mutualist" society based on workers' cooperatives which would exchange goods and services with one another. "Society," Proudhon wrote, "must be thought of . . . as a system of free forces balancing each other; a system in which all individuals are guaranteed the same rights provided they perform the same duties, one in which they will receive the same benefits in return for the same services rendered."[4] A mutualist society would have no need for a bureaucratic state, and Proudhon ridiculed those socialists, such as Louis Blanc, who had tried to improve workers' conditions through political action in 1848. Under Blanc's system of state workshops, Proudhon wrote, "we would simply have exchanged our present chains for others."[5]

Proudhon's mutualist and anarchist ideas spoke to those French workers who still saw themselves as economic individualists, needing only protection from the unfair competition of large industries and banks. The Proudhonists were strongly opposed to the "scientific" socialist doctrines being articulated at that same time by the German socialist Karl Marx from his London exile. Marx, unlike Proudhon, accepted the progress of industrialization and urged workers to engage in mass political action. As Marx's ideas began to penetrate into France during the 1860s, French socialism became increasingly divided over these basic issues.

Socialist doctrines promised workers a better future, but conditions in the 1850s drove them to find ways to protect their immediate interests. Despite efforts to teach their workers "proper" habits of timeliness, thrift, and sobriety, employers complained that all too many of them behaved like *sublimes,* a term for employees who refused to submit to workplace discipline and showed an incorrigible contempt for bourgeois values. Manufacturer Denis Poulot (a self-made man) wrote a book of that title, first published at the end of the Second Empire. It gave a highly colored account of the outrages these independent-minded workers perpetrated on their uncomprehending employers. Behind Poulot's litany of complaints we can see the reality of a working-class world that held to its own values and its own ways of life.

Entertainment and Culture

In the cultural domain, the Second Empire was marked by two significant tendencies. The official culture of the day stressed elegantly crafted entertainment and lavish spectacle, divorced from any consideration of the period's social problems. In the shadow of this glittering carnival, small coteries of writers and artists created a counter-culture that challenged the values of the regime and of the wealthy bourgeoisie who benefited from it. Jacques Offenbach's successful operettas, such as *La Belle Hélène* and *La Vie Parisienne*, which combined theater, singing, and dance in a looser manner than traditional grand opera, typified the conventional culture of the period. Featuring sprightly melodies and humorous plots, Offenbach's works were the antithesis of the ultra-serious operas that German composer Richard Wagner was creating in the same period. They seemed to confirm the stereotype of French culture as frivolous and slightly immoral. Wagner initially appealed only to a small public, however. Offenbach's works, like many creations of the Second Empire period, aimed at a much broader audience.

The desire to appeal to a wide audience was especially evident in the press. In the 1830s, lower-priced newspapers such as Emile Girardin's *La Presse* had given the middle classes access to the news. In the 1860s, Polydore Millaud's even cheaper *Petit Journal* made the daily newspaper accessible to workers and peasants. The *Petit Journal* emphasized

sensational crime stories and other apolitical events. Its price of five centimes allowed it to reach a level of circulation no previous French periodical had ever enjoyed (259,000 sales per day by 1865) and to inaugurate the age of the mass press and mass culture in France.

Alongside these triumphs of mass entertainment and mass culture, the Second Empire saw a growing estrangement between serious writers and artists and society. The regime was not hospitable to innovative experiments, although some of the emperor's entourage, such as his cousin Mathilde—who kept a lively salon—cultivated contacts with intellectuals who refused to embrace orthodoxy. In 1857, government officials sought to ban the novelist Gustave Flaubert's realistic depiction of provincial bourgeois life, *Madame Bovary*, because of its supposed immoral influence. Flaubert's heroine, driven first to adultery and then to suicide by the boredom and superficiality of her life as the wife of a rural doctor, challenged the conventional values of French society, and the author and publisher paid the price. A similar fate descended on Charles Baudelaire, the period's most original poet, after he published *Fleurs du Mal*, in which many of the poems dealt overtly with sexual themes. Visual artists fared no better. Gustave Courbet, the master of realism, had to set up a private exhibition of his two large paintings, *Funeral at Ornans* and *The Artist's Studio*, after they were excluded from the official exhibition held in conjunction with the 1855 international exposition.

FOREIGN ADVENTURES

From the outset of his reign, Napoleon III had counted on successes abroad as one way to solidify domestic support. Acquiring colonies outside of Europe was not his highest priority, but he continued to send troops to strengthen French control of Algeria, where resistance against French occupation remained strong throughout the 1850s. The European population had increased, in part as a result of the deportation of political prisoners from France. French expansion in Algeria during this period resembled the process of westward expansion in the United States. Like American pioneers, French settlers wanted to push the supposedly uncivilized "natives" out of their way and grab their land. In 1861, a pro-colonist newspaper wrote, "In our view, there is only one interest in Africa that deserves respect: that of the colonist."[6] Visits to Algeria in the 1860s led Napoleon III to express a certain sympathy for the Muslim population, an attitude that put him at odds with the European settlers and led most of them to sympathize with the republican opposition movement. Algeria was not the only area of French colonial expansion under the Second Empire. In 1853, France took control of New Caledonia, in the South Pacific, which was used as a penal colony. Starting in 1856, French forces also began establishing control over Annam and Cochinchina, territories that are now part of Vietnam. The French hoped, unrealistically, that they could make the region's rivers major routes for trade with China. Together with France's older colonies in the Caribbean, South America, the west coast of Africa, the islands of Saint-Pierre and Miquelon in the North Atlantic, and Réunion in the Indian Ocean, these new acquisitions meant that France now occupied territories in all major regions of the world. A law passed in 1854 created the legal framework that would govern French colonial rule until 1946. It specified that French domestic laws did not apply overseas, and gave the government freedom to impose taxes and regulations in the colonies as it saw fit.

In Europe, Napoleon III had promised his neighbors that "the Empire means peace," but it certainly did not mean caution. He moved quickly to show that France would no longer accept the limitations imposed by the 1815 peace settlement. In 1853, Russia alarmed both Britain and France with its bid for increased influence over the Ottoman Empire. Concern for the balance of power in that region and traditional conflicts over which of the Christian powers should represent European interests at the holy sites in Palestine created friction between France and Russia. Although his cooperation with the traditional enemy, England, was not popular in France, Napoleon III seized the opportunity to demonstrate France's strength. London and Paris declared war in March 1854, and dispatched an expeditionary force to the Crimea, in the Black Sea. Napoleon III, who had initially planned to command his troops in person, had hoped for a quick and striking victory. Instead, the allied forces bogged down in a prolonged siege of the fortress city of Sebastopol, which finally fell in September 1855. By then, fear of a widened conflict made Paris and London eager to take up Russian offers to negotiate. Even if the war failed to produce a dramatic military success like the first Napoleon's campaigns, French forces were victorious, and in January 1856, the emperor was able to convene a great peace conference in Paris. France obtained no territorial gains from the Crimean War, but Napoleon III had reasserted France's claim to be Europe's leading power.

One important feature of the Paris peace conference was a discussion of the possibility of creating a unified Italy. Napoleon III, who had spent much of his youth on the peninsula, had made the small Kingdom of Piedmont part of the wartime alliance. At Paris, the Piedmontese leader, Camillo Cavour, had the opportunity to state his case for unification, although the Austrians, who controlled much of northern Italy, blocked any action on the issue. For Napoleon III, support for Italy offered an opportunity to identify France with the forces of nationalism and liberalism throughout Europe, and a way to overturn the international order created by the Congress of Vienna without reviving France's image as a ruthless conqueror. The Italian nationalist movement was identified with hostility to the pope and the Catholic church, however, because unification implied abolition of the Papal States. French conservatives thus opposed support for Cavour. For several years after the Paris peace congress, Napoleon III hesitated to take any clear initiatives in Italy.

In January 1858, an Italian nationalist exile, Felice Orsini, made an unsuccessful attempt to assassinate the emperor outside the Paris Opera. Orsini was captured and condemned to death, but Napoleon III decided the moment had come to force the Italian issue. He arranged to have the condemned assassin sign a letter promising the emperor that if he aided Italian unification, "the blessings of its 25 million citizens will follow him through the ages."[7] In July 1858, Napoleon III held a secret meeting with Cavour at the French summer resort of Plombières. The two agreed to an eventual war against Austria that would lead to formation of a Kingdom of Italy in the northern half of the peninsula. In exchange, France would receive the Piedmontese territories of Nice and Savoy. The two governments signed a secret treaty in January 1859. The Austrians, targets of this plotting, recognized that combat was inevitable and took the initiative in April 1859. Napoleon III hastened to the battlefront in northern Italy, determined to show that he, like his uncle, could be successful at war as well as at politics.

As in the Crimea, French forces were successful but not overwhelmingly so, and Napoleon III certainly did not impose himself as a military genius. At Magenta, the Franco-Piedmontese forces won an initial victory that gave them control of the Lombard capital of Milan. The subsequent battle of Solferino, the costliest encounter of the war, was another French victory. But the number of deaths, the threat of Prussian intervention, and the lack of firm public support for the war in France convinced the emperor to bring the campaign to an end. On July 11, 1859, Napoleon III and the Austrian emperor Franz Joseph negotiated the armistice of Villafranca. Austria agreed to Piedmontese annexation of Lombardy and several other north Italian states, and France withdrew from the war. Cavour was outraged; Napoleon III had promised him to continue fighting until Austria was entirely driven out of northern Italy, but Villafranca left the city of Venice in Austrian hands. Events soon outran Napoleon III's plans, however. By the middle of 1860, a popular insurrection in southern Italy sparked by the nationalist hero Giuseppe Garibaldi gave Cavour the opportunity to add both the Papal States and the Kingdom of Naples—territories excluded from the agreement with France—to the new Kingdom of Italy. French intervention had been decisive in breaking Austria's hold on the Italian peninsula, but the end result showed that Napoleon III, rather than controlling events and demonstrating French power, had set in motion forces that he could not restrain. In many ways, the Italian conflict was symbolic of the problems in which the regime found itself increasingly trapped in the 1860s.

NOTES

1. Cited in Maurice Agulhon, *1848 ou l'apprentissage de la république* (Paris: Seuil, 1973), 222.

2. Cited in David Pinkney, *Napoleon III and the Rebuilding of Paris* (Princeton, NJ: Princeton University Press, 1958), 200.

3. Tocqueville, *The Old Regime and the Revolution*, Stuart Gilbert, trans. (New York: Doubleday-Anchor, 1955), xiii.

4. Proudhon, *On the Political Capacity of the Working Classes*, cited in S. Edwards, ed., *Selected Writings of P.-J. Proudhon*, E. Fraser, trans. (New York: Doubleday-Anchor, 1969), 59.

5. Ibid., 61.

6. Cited in C.-A. Julien, *Histoire de l'Algérie contemporaine* (Paris, 1964), 1:406.

7. Cited in J. M. Thompson, *Louis Napoleon and the Second Empire* (New York: Norton, 1955), 179.

CHAPTER 16

THE SECOND EMPIRE IN DIFFICULTIES

In 1860, Napoleon III's Empire appeared to be the most successful regime France had known since 1815; ten years later, it crumbled in a single day. Long before then, however, difficulties had begun to accumulate for the emperor. Just as Napoleon III's achievements in the 1850s had resulted from a combination of his policies and favorable conditions, so the problems of the subsequent decade were partly the result of the regime's own failings and partly due to circumstances beyond its control. Not that the emperor's policy initiatives after 1860 were all ill-advised. Many of his problems resulted, in fact, from controversial reforms meant to adapt France more quickly to the modern world. But the painful national humiliation that ended the Second Empire has colored attitudes toward it ever since, and Napoleon III cannot be entirely cleared of responsibility for the disaster that ruined his regime's reputation.

DOMESTIC POLICIES IN THE EMPIRE'S SECOND DECADE

In the 1850s, economic prosperity and foreign policy successes had given the regime a firm base of support, particularly among the wealthier classes. After 1860, a more troubled economic climate, a less favorable interna-tional situation, and a widening gap between the articulate members of French society and the government contributed to the weakening of Napoleon III's regime. Unlike many authoritarian rulers, the emperor responded to these challenges with some genuine reform-ing initiatives until, by 1870, the Empire had taken on the form of a democratically based constitutional monarchy. Paradoxically, these reforms gave the regime's opponents greater opportunities to attack it, and its prospects of long-term survival remained unclear.

The end of the economic boom of the 1850s coincided with one of Napoleon III's most controversial initiatives, a liberal trade treaty with England. The treaty had been worked out in secret negotiations between the two trade representatives, Richard Cob-den and Michel Chevalier, and implemented in 1860. The Cobden-Chevalier treaty repre-sented a major shift in French economic pol-icy. From the time of the Restoration, high tar-iffs had sheltered French manufacturers from low-priced foreign competition, particularly that of the British with their rapidly growing factories. In France, economists of the liberal school and Saint-Simonian advocates of in-dustrial progress—Chevalier being notable among them—had consistently argued that this protectionism favored inefficient producers and discouraged the adoption of modern production methods. Napoleon III, who had been impressed with the virtues of free trade during his stays in England, was sensitive to these arguments, and during the 1850s the government had created loopholes in France's protectionist wall to allow import of low-priced English iron products needed to build the French railroad system.

In general, however, French manufacturers opposed free trade. They argued that the British edge in manufacturing technology was so massive that French firms could not compete successfully against them and that the 1860 treaty was put into effect without being submitted to the Chamber of Deputies. French businessmen complained that its benefits went disproportionately to the British, who exported more to France but did not increase their purchases of French products. The Cobden-Chevalier treaty thus alienated a good part of the business class from the regime, even though the government continued to carry out important reforms that benefited manufacturers. Old laws that had restricted the formation of joint-stock companies and thereby hindered industrial expansion were reformed in 1863 and 1867, encouraging greater use of the stock market to generate capital. But the regime, beset with difficulties in other areas, faced increasingly severe economic problems by the end of the 1860s. The 1867 bankruptcy of the Pereire brothers' *Crédit Mobilier,* the symbol of the Empire's devotion to economic expansion, was a particularly embarrassing failure.

The regime's gestures in favor of the industrial working class after 1860 were another reason why it lost some of its popularity among businessmen. Napoleon III, the one-time admirer of Saint-Simonianism, had always claimed that his regime would produce benefits for the poor. During the 1850s, he had done little beyond promoting economic growth, which meant more jobs and somewhat higher wages. In the 1860s, however, the regime took several initiatives that helped promote the growth of an autonomous workers' movement. The French government paid for several French workers' delegates to attend the 1862 International Exposition in London. There, they met with English socialists, came into contact with Marx's doctrines, and helped pave the way for formation of the latter's International Working Men's Association in 1864. Aware of the imbalance between the power of employers and that of their workers, Napoleon III legalized the formation of unions in 1864. Although various forms of worker organizations had existed throughout the nineteenth century, the Le Chapelier law of 1791 had made them all technically illegal. The new law regularized their existence, although it did not require employers to bargain with them. The year 1864 also saw French workers' first effort since 1848 to run their own election candidates, with the issuing of the "Manifesto of the Sixty" in Paris's municipal elections. As the 1860s drew to a close, workers made increasing use of their right to organize and staged a growing number of labor strikes, the largest wave of economic protest France had known up to that time. Rather than winning workers' loyalty, Napoleon III's timid efforts at reform had served primarily to encourage them to be more aggressive in promoting their own interests.

The Republican Counterculture

The collapse of the Second Republic in 1851 was a setback for those who believed in the ideal of republican government, but few of them were won over to Bonapartist authoritarianism. In the more liberal atmosphere of the early 1860s, a republican counterculture hostile to the Empire gained strength in a number of institutions that were not completely under government control. Freemasons, university students in Paris's Latin Quarter, small businessmen who felt unrepresented by the conservative elite that dominated the official Chamber of Commerce, Jews, and liberal Protestants were among the groups that both espoused republican ideas and adopted democratic and antielitist practices within their own organizations. Lawyers, who had successfully resisted the regime's efforts to regiment their profession in the 1850s, were a hotbed of opposition. Léon Gambetta, who would become the main architect of the republicans' rise to power in the 1870s, was just one of many future politicians who launched their careers representing opponents of the Empire in court cases during the 1860s. Dissident artists barred from the government-sponsored official *salons,* or exhibitions, including many of the impressionists, were another group that showed strong republican sympathies.

The republicans argued that the authoritarian imperial regime stifled freedom and creativity in every aspect of French life. By putting control of the university in the hands of advocates of Victor Cousin's outdated eclectic philosophy, the regime was preventing the teaching of modern scientific theories. Its patronage of conservative painters ignored the experiments of original artists like Edouard Manet and Claude Monet, whose art reflected the realities of modern life. The republicans argued that the luxury of the imperial court and the extravagances of the Empress Eugénie spread immorality. By contrast, they called for a reform of family life. Women should be given a secular education that would allow them to be intelligent companions to their husbands, and husbands, while retaining dominant authority in their families, should show consideration for their wives and affection for their children.

The Legislature and Elections of 1863

The different currents of opposition to the Empire were able to express themselves with increasing force after 1860 because of a process of liberalization that the regime itself had set in motion. An opposition group had appeared in the Chamber of Deputies in 1857, when five deputies hostile to the regime had nonetheless sworn the constitutional oath and taken their seats—using their positions to criticize the government. In 1859, the emperor granted an amnesty to republican militants who had opposed him in 1851. The following year, he granted several important new rights to the legislative body. The deputies were permitted to hold a public debate in response to the emperor's speech setting out the government's program at the beginning of each session, and newspapers were allowed to publish accounts of legislative debates which had previously been held in secret. An edict in 1861, a response to criticism of the regime's free-spending habits, gave the legislature some real ability to impose restrictions on expenses. The Second Empire was beginning to evolve from an authoritarian to a parliamentary regime.

The national parliamentary elections held in 1863 showed that the main beneficiaries of this evolution were the government's opponents. Various opposition groups—Catholic conservatives angered by the government's support for an anticlerical regime in Italy, businessmen resentful about the Cobden-Chevalier treaty, republicans who wanted a genuinely democratic government—won three times as many votes as they had in the previous elections of 1857. The republican movement scored striking successes that embarrassed the regime severely in Paris and France's other major cities where traditional methods of influencing voters had lost most of their efficiency. Adolphe Thiers, the former Orléanist leader, who favored the restoration of a genuinely representative parliamentary government, won a seat. Among the emperor's closest advisors there was disagreement on what to do. The duc de Morny (Napoleon III's illegitimate half-brother and one of the more imaginative Bonapartists) advocated an effort to rejuvenate the regime by winning over some of the opposition leaders, particularly the pragmatic young liberal Emile Ollivier. Ollivier was one of the five regime opponents first elected in 1857. Morny's death in 1865 left the emperor under the sway of more cautious advisers who refused to embrace the logical consequences of the liberalizing reforms and give members of the opposition positions of responsibility. The regime thus remained suspended uneasily between conflicting policies of reform and authoritarianism.

THE CULTURAL CLIMATE

The gradual loosening of political restrictions imposed in the 1850s was reflected in the increasing vitality of the period's artistic and intellectual currents. Paris in the 1860s was the birthplace of what is now recognized as modern painting. By the middle of the decade, a group of experimentally minded painters emerged, led by Edouard Manet. Manet's paintings challenged artistic conventions both in their style and subject matter—the female nudes in his *Picnic on the Grass* and *Olympia* were depicted realistically and in modern settings, rather than being idealized figures in classical or exotic frameworks that distanced them from the viewer. Critics objected to the flatness of Manet's figures and his bold and sometimes arbitrary use of color. It was precisely these controversial characteristics that made Manet one of the founders of modern art. By the end of the 1860s, he had become the center of a group of painters that included many of the future leaders of the impressionist school, such as Claude Monet and Camille Pissarro.

At the same time as artists were challenging aesthetic conventions, intellectuals were undermining accepted philosophic certainties. The sentimental and quasi-religious romanticism of the 1840s gave way to a new faith in science, often labeled "positivism." The doctrines of positivism had been elaborated in the 1830s and 1840s by Auguste Comte, a highly original disciple of Saint-Simon. Comte maintained that human thought had progressed from a primitive, mythological stage (in which natural and social phenomena were explained in religious terms), to a more sophisticated metaphysical stage, in which they were attributed to abstract causes. The final stage of human development, which Comte saw emerging in the nineteenth century, was what he labeled positivism, in which metaphysical doctrines gave way to precise, scientific explanations. Comte himself, after his early flirtation with Saint-Simon, had become a conservative defender of social hierarchy and a firm supporter of the Second Empire. During the 1850s, he even promoted his own positivist religion, with himself in the role of pope. But his ideas about the inevitable progress of scientific knowledge attracted many radicals, who saw in them a weapon against religious obscurantism. Among the most prominent of these radical positivists were the linguist Emile Littré, whose writings influenced the generation of republican politicians who would eventually consolidate the Third Republic after Napoleon III's downfall, and the philosopher Ernest Renan. Renan caused one of the period's great public scandals when, at his inaugural lecture at the *Collège de France* in 1862, he proclaimed that Jesus should be seen as "a remarkable man," but not as a divine being. Renan's humanistic interpretation of the founder of Christianity, incorporated in his best-selling *Life of Jesus* (1863), led to dismissal from his post in 1864. The government's treatment of men such as Littré and Renan seemed to argue that support for the Second Empire was incompatible with independent, critical thinking. Positivism became associated with opposition to the government.

The success of positivism was related to the very real progress in scientific knowledge that marked the period. Although French science was no longer as dominant as it had been at the beginning of the century (French researchers regularly lamented that they lacked laboratories to rival those at the leading German universities), men like biologist Louis Pasteur continued to make major contributions to knowledge. Pasteur's first great discoveries were made in the 1850s, and he continued to work until the 1880s. His demonstration that processes of fermentation and decay were caused by microscopic organisms had important practical consequences for brewers and wine makers. His conclusive proof that living organisms were not the result of spontaneous generation ended a centuries-old debate among biologists. A deeply religious man himself, Pasteur nevertheless contributed to a growing sense that the human mind was capable of explaining and controlling the forces of nature.

In its early years, the Napoleonic regime had strongly supported the Catholic church, maintaining the Falloux law that provided for religious education in the public schools and keeping French troops stationed in Rome to defend the pope against the Italian nationalists. The Revolution of 1848 had turned the church in a conservative direction. The generation of Catholic liberal leaders who had represented it under the July Monarchy was increasingly challenged by proponents of a more militant Catholicism that rejected any compromise with modern political and intellectual ideas. Journalist Louis Veuillot's *L'Univers* was the main organ for this Ultramontane group. The group was often in closer agreement with the highly conservative Pope Pius IX than with leading members of the French clerical hierarchy. Pope Pius IX's *Syllabus of Errors*, a vehement condemnation of liberal, democratic, socialist, and positivist principles, issued in 1864, was aimed specifically

at French Catholic liberals, whom the pope condemned for too easily accepting modern ideas that went counter to traditional Catholic teachings.

While educated Catholics argued over the degree to which the church should accommodate to new realities, the faithful—especially women, who made up the bulk of Catholic congregations—were drawn to forms of worship that emphasized direct and emotional contact with Jesus, through the cult of the Sacred Heart, and with the Virgin. In 1858, a peasant girl in southern France, Bernadette Soubirous, had a series of visions of the Virgin in a grotto near the town of Lourdes, which soon became the site of mass pilgrimages. Shrugged off by skeptical males, the Lourdes cult appealed strongly to female worshippers whose emotional needs were ignored in the positivist doctrines of the period. By the end of the Second Empire, the Catholic church, which had at times seemed open to an alliance with the democratic movement during the July Monarchy, had defined itself in clear opposition to the new ideas associated with the Revolution of 1789 and the rise of modern science and thought.

Napoleon III's government, while never hostile to the church, found itself increasingly driven to separate itself from the antimodernist thrust of Ultramontanism. From 1863 to 1869, Victor Duruy, the minister of education, made a major effort to modernize every level of French schooling. He updated the secondary school curriculum for boys, trying to put more emphasis on understanding than on memorization and introducing new subjects, such as modern history, that were directly related to the problems of contemporary life. In 1867, he challenged the church and much of public opinion by attempting to introduce state-supported secondary schools for girls. This reform was soon scuttled, but another Duruy law did make the establishment of girls' elementary schools obligatory. It would be left to the Second Empire's successors to introduce compulsory free public education for all French children, but Duruy had gone a long way in that direction by the time he left office.

THE GAMBLE OF THE LIBERAL EMPIRE

The controversies aroused by Duruy's school reforms and Napoleon III's unwillingness to stand by his minister showed that the regime had lost much of its decisiveness by the late 1860s. One reason for the government's troubles was the embarrassing series of failures it suffered in foreign affairs. When the American Civil War cut off supplies of raw cotton from the southern states and plunged the textile industry into crisis, Napoleon III talked about diplomatic intervention to impose an end to the fighting, but did nothing. In 1862, he sent French forces to intervene in Mexico, an area that had attracted some French business interests. He hoped to establish a French-backed government under the Austrian Archduke Maximilian, but the effort ended in calamity in 1867 when Mexican republicans led by Benito Juarez defeated the French-backed forces and executed Maximilian. In Europe, too, the situation was increasingly menacing for France. The dynamic Prussian prime minister, Otto von Bismarck, had engineered a successful war against Austria in 1866 that led to the creation of a North German Confederation under Prussian domination in 1867. Faced with the very real possibility of a powerful united Germany on its eastern frontier, the French government sought to demonstrate its ability to control matters by claiming territorial compensation for itself. But Bismarck blocked French efforts to annex Luxembourg in 1867.

Shaken by these reverses abroad, Napoleon III sought once again to regain support at home by further measures of liberalization. New reforms in 1867 gave the legislature the right to summon the ministers to defend their policies. Several measures gave public opinion new weight in politics. Most restrictions on the press were abolished, as were laws that had hampered the holding of public meetings and the conduct of election campaigns. Rather than mollifying the regime's opponents, these changes unleashed a torrent of attacks on the government. Perhaps the most successful of the regime's new critics was journalist Henri de Rochefort, who took advantage of the end of press censorship to launch a weekly journal called *La Lanterne*. His virulent personal attacks on the emperor and on the tottering regime's bureaucratic authoritarianism won him an immense circulation. The government's inability to counter him and the many other journalists and caricaturists who quickly followed his example showed how badly its base of support had eroded.

Parliamentary elections in 1869 confirmed the steady rise of the opposition. As the possibility of actually coming to power increased, however, the political spectrum began to shift. Fearful of the rise of more extreme groups, such as the socialists, a number of liberals muted their traditional hostility to cooperation with the regime. Napoleon III seized on this opening by making the most prominent of these moderates, Emile Ollivier, his prime minister and initiating yet another set of political reforms. These created the so-called Liberal Empire, a genuine parliamentary regime based on universal manhood suffrage. Ministers now had to have the confidence of the legislature to hold their posts, although the emperor still retained the right to choose and dismiss them as well as control of foreign policy. In twenty years, Napoleon III's regime had evolved from a pseudodemocratic dictatorship to what looked like a genuine constitutional monarchy. A plebiscite in May 1870 seemed to indicate that these reforms and the granting of power to a distinguished opposition leader had allowed Napoleon III to regain broad public support. The voters endorsed the Liberal Empire by 7,350,000 to 1,538,000, a margin reminiscent of the early days when the prefects had "made" elections as they pleased. But this apparently massive support was fragile. It depended on the new government's ability to show it could reverse the trend of failures that had marked the decade of the 1860s. Bismarck was not to grant the Liberal Empire that opportunity.

THE FRANCO-PRUSSIAN WAR

The 1866 war had left Prussia in control of all of northern Germany, but Bismarck still sought to annex the south German states which were traditionally suspicious of Prussian domination. He knew no other force united Germans as much as anti-French sentiment, rooted in bitter memories of occupation in Napoleonic days. Bismarck, therefore, took advantage of a complicated imbroglio over Prussian efforts to put a member of the Hohenzollern family on the Spanish throne to create a diplomatic crisis with France. The latter had reacted strongly to the threat of having to face a Prussian ally on its southern border. Prussia actually agreed to withdraw its bid for control of Spain, but Bismarck altered the wording of a telegram drafted by the Prussian king stating the agreement so that it seemed to incorporate a deliberate humiliation of the French. Ollivier and Napoleon III, uneasily aware of Prussia's military power and France's military unpreparedness, nevertheless decided they could not risk appearing to accept the insult contained in the "Ems telegram."

French public opinion, often said to have been strongly pro-war, was in fact divided, with nationalist sentiment strongest in the cities. On paper, France's military forces seemed equal to the challenge. The Prussians had superior artillery, but the French *chassepot* rifle, introduced in 1866, was better than enemy firearms. But the French suffered from critical weaknesses in command. The leading French generals, used to colonial campaigns against weak opponents, had no agreed-upon strategic plan for the war. The Prussian general staff, on the other hand, had been preparing for such a conflict since 1866. The French mobilization effort was chaotic, with plans being changed in the midst of the process and some units being sent to the front before all their men had reported for duty. More than a sixth of the soldiers never appeared at all. The two main French armies were assembled at Strasbourg and Metz, near the border, from where they were supposed to launch an invasion of German territory. The Prussians quickly gained the initiative, however. By August 16, after two weeks of fighting, they had cut off the retreat route of General Bazaine's army in the Lorraine fortress of Metz. Discredited by these unexpected defeats, Ollivier had to resign, and a new ministry headed by a conservative Bonapartist, General Palikao, was named. General MacMahon, commander of the remaining French field forces, was given conflicting instructions—first to protect the capital, then to move east to rescue Bazaine. Accompanied by the emperor, who had unwisely decided to associate himself directly with the army, MacMahon's force slowly moved northeast, giving the Prussians ample time to catch up and corner it at Sedan for a decisive battle. There on September 2, 1870, the Prussian forces inflicted a crushing defeat on the French, capturing 104,000 prisoners including Napoleon III himself. The emperor had ridden into the fray with the idea that, if he died in battle, he might at least generate enough sympathy to keep the country loyal to the regime.

The news of the defeat at Sedan reached Paris early in the morning of September 4. Crowds assembled in the streets demanding the overthrow of the Empire, whether Liberal or not. At Paris's Hôtel de Ville (the traditional locus of popular power), deputies from the legislature's republican opposition, led by skilled orator Léon Gambetta, repeated the procedure of 1848. They proclaimed the Republic, opening a new cycle of revolution. As in 1830 and 1848, the old government collapsed without a struggle. The overwhelming mandate it had received in the plebisicite of May 1870 proved to be worthless in the face of military debacle. But war had only revealed the regime's deeper weakness. In its effort to satisfy all sectors of French society, the Bonapartist regime had never acquired a real social base. Too authoritarian and too favorable to the upper classes to win over the common people, it was nevertheless too reform-minded and too sympathetic to the concerns of workers and peasants to woo the notables away from their Legitimist or Orléanist sympathies.

Under its successor, the Third Republic, the reputation of the Second Empire was consistently negative. Its centralized political structure combined with a pseudodemocratic plebiscitary base led some twentieth-century historians to see Louis-Napoleon as a forerunner of modern totalitarian dictators like Mussolini and Hitler. Only after the Second World War did scholars come to take a more favorable view of a government which had made real efforts to promote economic development and to cope with the problems of urban communities. Charles de Gaulle's Fifth Republic, a government with a powerful president elected by universal suffrage, appeared in some ways to be a reversion to the traditions of the Liberal Empire. Even the artistic taste of the period, long condemned as shallow and showy, came to be seen with greater sympathy in the late 1960s and 1970s. Charles Garnier's elaborately and eclectically decorated opera house (begun under Napoleon III but only completed in 1875), so offensive to modernist architects for whom ornament was crime, appealed to postmodern sensibilities. In the years after 1980, however, the image of what American historian Alan Spitzer called "the good Napoleon III" has again been called into question. Much of the regime's positive reputation rested on the belief that it had spurred economic development. But the most recent research now indicates that France's greatest surge of industrialization in the nineteenth century came in the 1840s under the July Monarchy, and that growth rates declined throughout most of the Second Empire. Social historians have made "Haussmannization" synonymous with the expulsion of the poorer classes from city centers; and a rehabilitation of the nineteenth-century republican movement has led to a harsher verdict on the regime against which it revolted in 1870. These changing images of the Second Empire reflect the ambiguous characteristics of both the regime itself—so much harder to classify than other governments of the nineteenth century—and of its enigmatic leader.

CHAPTER 17

THE PARIS COMMUNE AND THE ORIGINS OF THE THIRD REPUBLIC

The collapse of the Second Empire after the defeat at Sedan allowed republican militants to proclaim the start of a new republic, first in the left-wing strongholds of Lyon and Marseille on September 2, 1870, and then in Paris two days later. No one could have guessed, however, that these hasty actions were laying the basis for the most long-lived regime France has known since the fall of the Bourbon monarchy in 1789. The hastily proclaimed Government of National Defense was barely able to maintain control of a capital boiling with agitation. In the country at large, conservative forces saw their long-awaited opportunity to reassert themselves. French settlers in Algeria seized the chance to overthrow the military regime they had complained about throughout the Second Empire and demand new rights. Most dangerously, the Prussians' victory at Sedan left the rest of France open to invasion. The next twelve months were seared into French memory as *l'année terrible,* the "terrible year," which cost France 260,000 dead and subjected the country to a humiliating military defeat, the loss of an important part of its territory, a revolutionary uprising and a civil war that left much of Paris in ruins. The catastrophes of 1870–1871 would not be overshadowed until the world wars of the twentieth century.

THE GOVERNMENT OF NATIONAL DEFENSE

The provisional government set up in Paris in September 1870 had to choose between two fundamentally different ways of responding to the Prussian invasion. One was represented by the young republican Léon Gambetta, the new government's minister of the interior, the other by the seventy-three-year-old Adolphe Thiers, architect of the Orléanist takeover in 1830 and former leader of the conservative "Party of Order" during the Second Republic of 1848. Gambetta was determined to emulate the Jacobin republicans of 1792 and rally the country against the foreign invader. He promptly replaced most of the imperial prefects with republicans, charging them to uphold the central government's authority against challenges from any direction. Thiers saw military defeat as inevitable. He hoped merely to keep its cost in territory and indemnities as small as possible. The majority of deputies in the Chamber would have preferred to entrust the government to Thiers, but he refused to take responsibility for a defeat brought about by the Napoleonic regime he had so long opposed. In any event, the mass of the Parisian population insisted on a militantly republican regime. Gambetta and the other left-wing deputies who formed the government thought that establishing themselves in power was the only way to ward off a takeover by even more radical elements. Meanwhile, Thiers was dispatched on a fruitless tour of foreign capitals to seek diplomatic support against Prussia's demands.

France's military situation was already too compromised to give efforts to reverse the outcome of the war much chance to succeed. Sedan had destroyed the main body of the French army. The largest remaining element of it, Bazaine's force, sat surrounded in the fortress of Metz, where it eventually surrendered without a fight at the end of October. On September 20, Prussian forces encircled Paris, cutting it off from the rest of the country. While army troops and the Parisian militia, the National Guard, prepared to withstand a siege, Gambetta made a spectacular escape from the capital in a hot-air balloon. He hoped to organize resistance from the provinces. From Tours, southwest of Paris, he issued a ringing proclamation calling for a popular uprising against the occupiers. "Tied down and contained by the capital, the Prussians, far from home, anxious, harassed, hunted down by our reawakened people, will be gradually decimated by our arms, by hunger, by natural causes."[1] Gambetta did succeed in assembling a new army south of the Loire River, but the national uprising he had called for failed to materialize. Most of the French population, whose patriotism had saved the First Republic eighty years earlier, refused to join what appeared a hopeless struggle.

Only in Paris and a few big provincial cities was there strong popular support for continued resistance. During the Empire, the capital had become a stronghold of radical republican and socialist agitation. These left-wing groups now proclaimed themselves the true representatives of French patriotism and opposed any suggestion of capitulation. Blaming the Empire's repressive bureaucratic regime for France's catastrophic defeat, they called for the decentralization of power and the creation of a democratically elected

"Commune" to govern Paris. Meanwhile, the Prussian army settled down to starve the city into surrender. The French military commanders and members of the Provisional Government who had remained in Paris considered the situation hopeless, but they feared a popular uprising if they surrendered. As the siege dragged on, food and fuel began to run short. Newspapers published recipes for cooking dogs, cats, and rats, while the wealthy dined on the animals from the Paris zoo. In January, the Prussians began regular bombardment of the city. After a desperate attack on the Prussian lines failed to break the siege, the provisional government finally agreed to Bismarck's terms for an armistice in order to hold national elections for a government that would negotiate peace terms.

The elections, organized in a little over a week and held on February 8, 1871, pitted a republican movement identified with a policy of continued fighting against a broad and amorphous coalition of conservative forces that frequently identified themselves only as "the party of peace." The rural voters who dominated the population made an unambiguous choice: they voted for peace, for Thiers's policy rather than Gambetta's. Thiers himself received a strong personal mandate, being elected in twenty-six districts. Overall, the assembly initially contained over four hundred deputies who favored a monarchist restoration, as opposed to about two hundred republicans.

But the appearance of a conservative triumph was misleading. Many peasants who voted for an end to the war in February 1871 showed themselves firmly opposed to any effort to bring back features of the Old Regime in subsequent elections. Furthermore, the conservatives were not a solid bloc. Monarchists were divided between die-hard Legitimists, loyal to the comte de Chambord (heir of the Bourbon king Charles X, who had been overthrown in the Revolution of 1830); Orléanists, who wanted to bring back the dynasty installed in that revolution and the conservative, business-oriented regime it represented; and Bonapartists, loyal to the Empire that had just collapsed. Conservative Catholics, who blamed the Second Empire for encouraging an atmosphere of "sensuous self-indulgence," as one bishop put it, saw the defeat of 1870 as a divine warning to France to change its ways, but their strident calls for national repentance alienated much of the rest of the population. Thiers, who now became head of the government, understood the conservatives' weaknesses. As long ago as 1850, he had despaired of bringing the different dynasties' supporters together and had recommended a republican constitution because it was "the government that divides us the least." His first cabinet contained three moderate republicans but only one Orléanist. In order to assure himself broad support while he negotiated an end to the war, however, he postponed any debate about constitutional questions.

THE UPRISING OF THE COMMUNE

Cautious and skillful in his management of the monarchist-dominated National Assembly, Thiers was insensitive in his treatment of radical-dominated Paris. The siege and final surrender had left the city's population feeling betrayed by the rest of the country. The conservative Assembly's refusal to move any closer to the capital than Versailles irritated Parisians even further. The Assembly also angered Parisians by terminating the emergency measures taken during the siege to aid the poorer classes. By early March, it had ended a rent moratorium, cut off the pay of the National Guardsmen who had defended the city, and created a crisis for small businessmen by ordering the immediate payment of overdue bills. These actions were all the more dangerous because the Versailles government lacked real control over the city. The units of the National Guard, organized on a neighborhood basis,

still had their rifles and the cannon with which they had stood off the Prussians for four months.

Especially in the National Guard units recruited in the city's poorer neighborhoods, members of radical and socialist groups had found a strong base of support. The changes that had taken place in the city under the Second Empire favored the growth of such movements. Haussmann's rebuilding schemes had pushed workers out of the city's center and concentrated them in new neighborhoods where they lived isolated from the bourgeoisie. The growth of the economy had swelled the city's working population, and the gradual spread of schooling had made workers more literate. Finally, the labor movement that had grown up in the 1860s, and the flowering of political debate that followed the liberalization measures of 1867, had favored the circulation of radical ideas.

By 1871, many different revolutionary groups were competing for the support of the Paris population. The radical republicans, some of them veterans of 1848, blamed the Versailles Assembly for accepting Prussia's victory and feared that it would vote a monarchist restoration. But the republicans also had to compete with a variety of socialist and communist movements. There were mutualist followers of Proudhon, who favored the organization of workers' cooperatives and participatory local governments, and there were supporters of the veteran political conspirator Louis Auguste Blanqui, who preached the necessity of a determined revolutionary elite ready to seize power and use it to create a populist government favoring the common people. Then there were supporters of the International Working Men's Association, the "International," who had begun to absorb the ideas of Karl Marx and advocate a social revolution against capitalist property to accompany any political upheaval. All of these groups had organized clubs in the capital after the fall of the Empire, and they all had supporters in the National Guard, whose units had become seedbeds of political agitation. Radical National Guards had already participated in two unsuccessful attempts to overturn the moderate republicans of the Provisional Government in October 1870 and January 1871. An elected Central Committee of the National Guard gave the radicals a base from which to challenge the government.

On March 18, 1871, Thiers sent troops to try to seize the cannon that Paris's National Guard units had refused to give up after the end of the siege. In response to the government's action, crowds took over several government buildings in the capital, and killed two conservative army officers. Thus began the uprising of the Paris Commune, one of the most controversial episodes in modern French history. The initial popular movement had not been planned, and decisive action might have allowed Thiers's government to keep control of the capital. But Thiers, a veteran of the revolutionary upheavals of 1848, had long cherished a particular notion of how to react to such an uprising. He deliberately withdrew his forces from the city, allowing the radicals to take it over completely while he prepared a methodical military assault to crush the movement. The vacuum he left behind invited the radicals to set up a government of their own.

For the first few days, the radical movement seemed to have the initiative. The Parisians' call for the restoration of local autonomy and their appeal to patriotic sentiments set off sympathetic movements in several other cities, including Marseille, Lyon, Toulouse, and the factory towns of Saint-Etienne and Le Creusot. But these lacked the broad base of support that the Paris movement had and were all swiftly put down. In Paris itself, however, the experience of the siege had allowed radical ideas to penetrate both the working class and the petty bourgeoisie of small shopkeepers, businessmen,

and employees. In elections for a Commune, or citywide parliament, on March 26, some 227,000 voters out of 480,000 eligible chose delegates who represented various radical and socialist currents in the city. Abstentions ran high in the city's wealthy bourgeois neighborhoods, but the movement clearly enjoyed substantial support. Inside the capital and in many provincial cities, republican groups who opposed the Commune's socialist elements and its defiance of the national government nevertheless recognized the patriotic impulse behind it. They tried to get Thiers to negotiate a peaceful settlement. But Thiers and the conservative majority of the Versailles Assembly were determined to demonstrate that, despite its defeat by the Prussians, the national government still had the power to put down any domestic revolt.

During the two months it took Thiers to assemble his forces, the *Communards* offered the world the spectacle of a government attempting to legislate in the name of the working classes and common people. This, together with the brutality that accompanied the movement's eventual defeat, made the Commune's memory a rallying point for socialist and leftist movements in France and elsewhere. Karl Marx would subsequently proclaim that the Commune had been "a working-class government, the product of the struggle of the producing against the appropriating class."[2] The reality of the Commune was less clear-cut. Most of the *Communards* were neither proletarians nor doctrinaire socialists. Of the eighty-one deputies to the Commune council, at most thirty-five were genuine workers, primarily skilled artisans rather than factory workers; thirty were educated professionals of various sorts (including fifteen journalists); and most of the remainder could be classified as small businessmen. The social reforms they enacted were cautious for the most part and, like a decree allowing workers to take over shops whose owners had abandoned them, were often responses dictated by an emergency situation rather than attempts to restructure society in accordance with radical doctrines. The *Communards* were inspired as much by France's republican and revolutionary traditions as they were by socialist ideologies. The disagreements among them were one of the main reasons why the movement failed.

Nevertheless, the Commune did take steps that offered at least the suggestion of a world organized on very different principles from those of nineteenth-century French bourgeois society. It was the first French government in which workers actually held some important positions. If its actions were limited, its rhetoric was expansive. The Labor and Exchange Commission set up to deal with social problems announced its intention of "realizing the very aim of the revolution, namely the emancipation of labor, the abolition of monopolies and privileges, the end of industrial feudalism."[3] The Commune promised free public education, organized along scientific lines, and paid special attention to the problem of women's schooling, setting up an all-female Commission for Girls' Education and promising a network of day-care centers to help working mothers.

Women's participation was one of the Commune's most striking features. Women such as Louise Michel, a schoolteacher who had been active in radical circles during the 1860s, took part in political clubs and even formed groups of their own. Michel had been one of the leaders of the armed resistance to the seizure of the National Guard's cannon on March 18, 1871. Elizabeth Dimitrieff, a radical Russian exile, tried to set up women's workshops to make uniforms for the National Guards, arguing that if the Commune failed to provide gainful employment for women, they would have no choice but to support conservatism. Indeed, the Commune did encounter resistance from some women; in some neighborhoods, women opposed the closing of Catholic schools.

All of the Commune's social experiments were doomed to failure, however, by its inability to organize an effective defense of the city against the Versailles government's forces. The army brought fresh soldiers from the provinces and indoctrinated them to believe that Paris was in the hands of criminal anarchists. The Commune, hamstrung by the refusal of its National Guards to obey any central authority, did little to prepare for an assault. On May 21, 1871, the Versailles forces attacked the poorly defended fortifications on the west side of the city, rapidly occupying well-to-do bourgeois neighborhoods where support for the Commune was weakest. For the seven days of "the bloody week," from May 21 to 28, 1871, the *Communards* fought a losing battle on the barricades, making their last stand at the Père Lachaise cemetery. Its south wall, where the last armed defenders were shot, became the French left's most sacred monument. The Versailles troops treated their foes with terrible ferocity, shooting thousands of prisoners out of hand. The *Communards* retaliated by killing several prominent hostages, including the archbishop of Paris. During the fighting, fire destroyed a number of important buildings, including the Tuileries Palace and the Hôtel-de-Ville. The burning city impressed many observers as a vision of Hell, and conservatives spread the story that female incendiaries, the *petroleuses*, had deliberately tried to burn down all of Paris. At the end of the week of fighting, twenty thousand to twenty-five thousand had been killed, the overwhelming majority of them *Communards* or innocent victims. It was the largest toll in any civil conflict in Europe during the nineteenth century. The Versailles forces arrested some forty thousand prisoners, who were held under extremely harsh conditions for months afterward. Thiers's policy had prevailed, but at the risk of making France's political and social divisions more bitter than ever.

While the Commune uprising was under way, Thiers's government also had to deal with a major insurrection against French rule in Algeria. A series of natural disasters in the country in the late 1860s had driven the Muslim population to desperation. Their leaders recognized that the situation in France and divisions between the colonists and the French government offered them an opportunity. After the defeat of Sedan, the European colonists had effectively overthrown the military government. Their movement, headed by a French republican named Vuillermoz who had been exiled to Algeria in 1848 for his radicalism, insisted on fulfillment of promises made as long ago as 1848 that the colony would be "assimilated" to France, although they also assumed that only Europeans would have full citizenship rights. Gambetta's provisional government had promised the end of military rule, but stopped short of granting all the settlers' demands. The settlers resented its decision to grant French citizenship to Algeria's Jewish minority through the Crémieux law of October 1870; the colonists' antisemitism would help sustain anti-Jewish attitudes in France itself well into the twentieth century. With the Europeans divided among themselves, popular unrest spread among the Muslim population. A traditional Algerian chief, Mohammed el Mokrani, put himself at the head of the movement, and on April 8, 1871, a *jihad* was proclaimed. Up to a third of the colony's Muslim population joined the uprising, but their attacks on French settlements were poorly coordinated, and the death of Mokrani in early May deprived them of effective leadership. The Mokrani rebellion drove the European settlers and the French government back together. Heavy fines were imposed on districts that had rebelled, impoverishing the population, and large amounts of Muslim land were turned over to Europeans. The colonists achieved their dream of seeing French laws extended to the colony in ways that benefited them.

THE CONSERVATIVE REPUBLIC

The Commune uprising might have been expected to favor the monarchist movement, just as the June Days uprising of 1848 had played into the hands of conservatives. Paradoxically, it cleared the way for the success of republicanism in France. By liquidating the *Communards*, Thiers had demonstrated that a republican government could defend social order. In addition, the leaders of the various socialist and revolutionary groups that had participated in the uprising were either dead, imprisoned, or in exile, so that for some years the republicans faced no organized opposition on their left. Gambetta, who had resigned from the National Assembly in opposition to the treaty with Prussia, avoided compromising himself with the Commune movement and remained free to continue his political activities. At the end of April 1871, even before the end of the Commune, the republicans scored well in local elections, indicating the degree to which the movement had implanted itself in the country at large. In the Assembly itself, the various royalist groups still had a majority, but they proved unable to capitalize on it.

For the first two years after the Commune uprising, Thiers solidly controlled the Assembly, even though he had had to accept the harsh peace terms dictated by Bismarck and incorporated in the Treaty of Frankfurt. France lost the German-speaking province of Alsace and half of the heavily industrialized region of Lorraine. German troops were to remain in France pending the payment of an indemnity of 5 billion francs. Bismarck had exploited German national enthusiasm for the war to proclaim the creation of a new German Empire. France, reduced in size and economic strength, now for the first time in centuries faced a larger and more powerful continental rival. Nevertheless, public confidence in Thiers's leadership remained strong. A sale of government bonds to pay off the first installment of the war indemnity, held just a month after the defeat of the Commune, was a complete success. Elections to fill some one hundred vacant seats in the National Assembly in July 1871 were also significant; republican candidates won an overwhelming victory.

Reluctant to confront Thiers until the German troops were withdrawn in 1873, the monarchist majority of the Assembly sought to create conditions for an eventual restoration. At first glance, the problem seemed simple. The Bourbon pretender, the comte de Chambord, was aged and childless; at his death, the crown would pass automatically to the Orléanist candidate, the comte de Paris. But Chambord proved determined to claim his throne on his own terms or not at all. After a brief visit to France in early 1871, he retreated into exile again, announcing that he would only return if the country agreed to restore many of the features of the absolute monarchy and, above all, to abandon the tricolor flag for the traditional white flag of the Bourbons. "In the glorious folds of this stainless standard, I shall bring you order and liberty!" he promised his putative subjects, but only a small minority of diehard Legitimists were willing to support this symbolic rejection of everything that had happened in France since 1789.[4] Chambord's intransigent position ruled out any compromise with the Orléanists and allowed Thiers to paint the monarchists, rather than the republicans, as the main threat to political stability. "The Republic exists, it is the legal government of the country: to want anything else would be a new revolution," he warned them in 1872.[5]

In May 1873, with the war indemnity paid off and the German troops removed, the Assembly's conservative majority finally toppled Thiers. The Legitimist supporters of the comte de Chambord now had their opportunity to implement a restoration, but the Orléanists refused to accept a king who rejected constitutional government and the tricolor flag. By October 1873, it was clear that an immediate restoration was out of the question. As a stopgap measure, the Orléanist duc de Broglie—the leader of the ministry—persuaded the Assembly to install the conservative Marshal MacMahon as president for seven years. He would have extensive powers, including the right to dissolve the Assembly and call new elections. This was intended as an interim arrangement; many deputies hoped that the death of the aged Chambord would soon clear the way for the completion of an acceptable monarchist constitution. Chambord made a final effort to outwit them by traveling secretly to Versailles to persuade MacMahon to stage a royalist coup. But the general, despite his conservative views, refused to risk such an adventure, and the would-be "Henry V" returned to exile for the last time.

MacMahon, de Broglie, and the supporters of their "government of Moral Order" tried to use their power to halt the growth of the republican movement, but the pretender's intransigence fatally weakened their efforts. Many Legitimists blamed the Orléanists for sabotaging the chances of a restoration. In their fury, they were even prepared on occasion to vote with the republicans. As the two monarchist factions damaged each other, the Bonapartists staged a menacing recovery: by 1875, voters dissatisfied with the Assembly's squabbles had made them the largest conservative group in the Assembly.

Republicans Strengthen Their Base

Meanwhile, despite governmental efforts to harass them, the republicans continued to strengthen their political base. The "Moral Order" regime made censorship more oppressive than it had been under the liberal

Empire. Local republican officials were removed from office, and the police kept up the chase after republican symbols such as the female effigy "Marianne," who had come to stand for the republican movement. The "Moral Order" government maintained a close alliance with the Catholic church, which condemned the republican movement as atheistic and revolutionary. Government support helped the church build the huge basilica of Sacre-Coeur on the top of the Montmartre hill in Paris as a symbol of the nation's repentance for the moral sins that Catholics blamed for the defeat of 1870. To republicans, the new church represented a standing insult.

The "Moral Order" government proved unable to stem the rise of republican sentiment, however. The new values of democracy, secularism, and rationalist individualism that characterized the post-1848 republicans had sunk strong roots in the population by 1870. During the 1860s, the liberalization of the Empire had permitted the rise of a new generation of republican leaders, more realistic and pragmatic than those who had made the unsuccessful Revolution of 1848. Léon Gambetta was the most prominent, but he was only one of a group of talented and articulate militants who would provide the country much of its leadership well into the 1880s.

The republicans had found in school reform a central issue around which they could organize. The Alsatian schoolteacher-activist Jean Macé's *Ligue de l'Enseignement* (Education League), founded in 1866, served under both the Empire and the "Moral Order" government as an organizational framework for the movement as a whole. The demand for universal elementary education expressed the republicans' democratic convictions. Their insistence that this education be secular and based on science, rather than religion, expressed their devotion to progress and modernity and their opposition to the social and political influence of the Catholic church. Common schools, the republicans believed, would reduce the antagonisms between classes and thus prevent the growth of socialism. The Commune uprising made them all the more determined to establish a government which would head off the danger of a proletarian revolution.

They were equally determined to change the place of women in French society. Jules Simon, one of the most prominent republican leaders, had written a book denouncing the mistreatment of women workers under the Empire. Most republicans shared the conviction that women, as long as they were educated by Catholic teachers, would be a hostile force opposing progress in the country. While the republicans stopped far short of advocating civil equality for women—they were primarily concerned to make them better helpmates to their republican spouses—they nevertheless favored female education and some revision of the Code Civil's heavily male-biased provisions on divorce and property rights.

Despite the failure of his war policy in 1870, Gambetta had regained his position as leader of the republicans in the Assembly by 1872. His strategy was to take advantage of the monarchists' paralysis to win gradual acceptance for a republican constitution. Aware that they had to agree to new constitutional arrangements, the monarchists grudgingly came to acknowledge that there was no alternative to formal acceptance of republicanism. Gambetta, for his part, persuaded his followers to accept the establishment of an upper house or Senate to be chosen by the elected officials of France's municipalities, rather than directly by the voters. This arrangement violated the principle of direct popular sovereignty dear to the republicans. Conservatives had pressed for it because they expected to find support from the numerous village mayors who would dominate the voting. But Gambetta anticipated correctly that the republican movement could carry these rural voters.

On January 30, 1875, the Assembly took the crucial step. It passed, by a margin of one vote, a motion introduced by deputy Wallon providing that "the President of the Republic is elected by the plurality of votes cast by the Senate and the Chamber of Deputies." By its oblique reference to the form of the regime, the Wallon amendment established the fact that the new constitution would be republican. In contrast to France's two previous republican constitutions, that of the Third Republic was promulgated almost without fanfare. It included no preamble stating general principles and no declaration of rights. There was no reason to assume that the new constitution would prove to be France's most enduring since 1789, lasting until the defeat of 1940.

In Europe of 1875, however, the Third Republic's adoption of universal suffrage and its rejection of monarchy remained exceptional. Britain would not follow France's lead in instituting universal manhood suffrage until after 1900. The universal suffrage Bismarck had introduced in the new German Empire disguised the fact that real power remained in the hands of the emperor, the ministers, and the army. Only in two major countries, France and the United States, were democratic and republican institutions given a chance to prove themselves in the last third of the nineteenth century.

It remained for the republicans in France to capture the republic that the monarchist-dominated National Assembly had made. In 1876, the Assembly's five-year term ran out and the new Senate was to be chosen. Despite the "Moral Order" government's best efforts, the republicans—helped by the Legitimist minority, which struck a deal with Gambetta to exclude the Orléanists from the seventy-five Senate seats filled by the Assembly—won clear majorities in both houses. The conservatives' last hope was

that the powers of the president would be sufficient to resist the legislature. MacMahon named a moderate republican, Jules Simon, as prime minister, hoping that he and some of the republican deputies could be persuaded to abandon the core of their program. But Simon refused to do so. On May 16, 1877, MacMahon embarked on a test of whether he could overturn a hostile legislature. In a move widely condemned as a coup, he dismissed Simon and dissolved the Chamber of Deputies, appealing to the country to back him up. The republicans confidently accepted the challenge. Gambetta, their leader, wrote to his mistress, "We occupy the heights of the law, from which we can machine-gun just as we like the wretched troops of the Reaction floundering in the plain."[6] MacMahon summoned the prefects to make an all-out effort to influence the voters, but the verdict of the elections was clear-cut. The 323 avowedly republican deputies, led by Gambetta, strongly outnumbered the 208 supporters of the president.

MacMahon, a devoted monarchist but too cautious to defy such a clear expression of the popular will, gave up the struggle. Although he did not resign until January 1879, he made no further effort to exercise his constitutional powers. The outcome of the May 16, 1877, coup had clearly established the republicans' ascendancy.

NOTES

1. Cited in Michael Howard, *The Franco-Prussian War* (London: Methuen, 1981), 240.
2. Karl Marx, *The Civil War in France* (Chicago: Charles H. Kerr, 1934), 88.
3. Cited in Stewart Edwards, *The Paris Commune* (London: Eyre and Spottiswood, 1971), 276.
4. Cited in D. W. Brogan, *France Under the Republic* (New York: Harper Brothers, n.d.), 83.
5. Cited in Bury and Tombs, *Thiers*, 223.
6. Cited in David Thomson, ed., *France: Empire and Republic, 1850–1940* (New York: Harper & Row, 1968), 73.

CHAPTER 18

THE REPUBLICANS IN POWER

Only when the moderate republican Jules Grévy replaced MacMahon as president in January 1879 did the outcome of the events of 1870 finally become clear. France was to be neither a revolutionary republic, as the *Communards* had hoped, nor a conservative regime with Catholic overtones. It would be a political democracy. Universal manhood suffrage, inaugurated by the short-lived Second Republic in 1848 and maintained—despite distortions caused by an authoritarian government—throughout the Second Empire, had come to be regarded as an indispensable condition for political legitimacy. But the republican regime would be socially conservative. The bicameral legislature, with its rurally dominated Senate, was a safeguard against radical legislation. The electorate, dominated numerically by landowning peasants and members of the urban middle classes, was hardly likely to favor candidates hostile to the rights of property.

FRENCH PARLIAMENTARY DEMOCRACY

By the middle of the 1880s, the distinctive features of this moderate French-style democracy had begun to emerge. The new system's key institution was the Chamber of Deputies, the large and fractious assembly that represented the principle of popular sovereignty. Although the indirectly elected Senate supposedly had equal legislative powers, almost all laws were initiated in the Chamber. The president having been reduced to a largely symbolic role after MacMahon's failed coup of 1877, executive power fell to the Council of Ministers and particularly to its president or premier—the deputy designated by the president of the Republic to put together a team of ministers or cabinet.

The French system resembled the British one in that the cabinet had to resign if it could not command a parliamentary majority. But the two parliamentary systems actually functioned very differently because the French did not have a strongly rooted two-party system like the British. Throughout the Third Republic, French parties remained small and loosely structured. Deputies were elected from single-member constituencies, a system that favored candidates with strong local bases of support and made them largely independent of national parties. In contrast to Britain—where by 1870 the leader of the largest party in the House of Commons automatically became Prime Minister, and normally remained in office until his party lost an election—in France, several different politicians might be able to assemble a majority in the Chamber. In the absence of a strong party system, different coalitions could be put together, and the orientation of a cabinet did not necessarily have to reflect the results of an election. A cabinet could be overthrown at any time by a negative vote in the Chamber. No ministry ever lasted for the entire four-year span of a Third Republic legislature.

Over the decades, the seeming incoherence of French politics, with its rapid changes of ministries and sometimes prolonged periods of parliamentary crisis, gave the country a reputation for instability and ineffectiveness in the face of major problems. Throughout its existence, the Third Republic was the subject of regular criticism, but no major constitutional revisions were carried out before the regime's final collapse in 1940. One reason for this stability was that the Third Republic's political life was not as chaotic as it appeared on the surface. The frequent changes of ministries masked a high degree of continuity in leadership. The same politicians often reappeared in one cabinet after another. These *ministrables* made up a relatively small group and ensured a continuity of policies from one cabinet to the next. The stability of the top officials who served under the ministers in the major government departments (often for terms of ten years or more) also compensated for the rapid changes at the cabinet level. The centralized administrative system created under Napoleon, generally staffed by career officials with a strong sense of loyalty to the state, provided a balance to the constantly changing world of the Chamber.

The French parliamentary system had the virtue of flexibility. Ministers who could not find support for their policies were quickly eliminated, and periods of rapid turnover in ministries alternated with stretches during which one premier held office long enough to put through substantial programs. Historians in recent years have pointed out that the Third Republic's legislatures did pass important reforms in a number of areas, and that the regime's institutional weaknesses only became crippling in the face of unforeseen challenges that followed the First World War. No one can deny, however, that the system made the passage of controversial legislation difficult. The Assembly could always evade hard choices by overthrowing the current ministry. The entrenched conservatism of the Senate made it a graveyard for reformist ideas, especially if they involved taxes or limits on the rights of property owners. In the words of American political scientist Stanley Hoffmann, "The regime had plenty of brakes and not much of a motor."[1] But this situation suited a majority of the electorate, made up for the most part of voters who feared they had more to lose from change than they did from maintaining the status quo.

THE FERRY ERA

Once they had gained control of both houses of parliament and the presidency in 1879, the "Opportunist" republicans (as those who had followed Gambetta in arguing for acceptance of the 1875 constitutional compromise and pursuit of reforms that were "opportune" under the circumstances called themselves) were able to demonstrate that, under certain circumstances, the new system allowed rapid passage of fundamental legislation. Surprisingly, however, the triumphant movement denied its most prominent spokesman the chance to head the government. Léon Gambetta, whose parliamentary leadership had been instrumental in outwitting the conservatives throughout the 1870s, had made too many enemies among his colleagues. They banded together at this time to keep him out of office. Only in 1881 did Gambetta succeed in forming a government. By then, he was dangerously ill and no longer able to dominate his rivals. He held office for only sixty-seven days and died a few months after the collapse of his ministry.

The other Opportunist leaders lacked Gambetta's dynamism and ability to appeal to the common man. But they did push through programs designed to give the Republic strong roots in the country. The most prominent was Jules Ferry, a long-time rival of Gambetta's. Like the other leaders of the early Third Republic, Ferry had come of age as a member of the republican opposition during the Second Empire. Imbued with positivist ideas, he had also been a leading critic of its heavy-handed administration. Twice president of the Council in the early 1880s, he also held the key office of minister of education for most of the period from 1879 to 1885.

The most important legacy of Ferry's ministries was the series of "Ferry laws" that created a public school system intended to propagate loyalty to the nation and its new political institutions. The Ferry laws made elementary education free and compulsory for all children. Religious education in the public schools, introduced by the Falloux law in 1850, was abolished. Clergy were barred from teaching in the public schools, and the privileges granted to Catholic educational institutions—the establishment of a Catholic university had been permitted in 1875—were curtailed. The republicans made a particularly dramatic challenge to the church's traditional domination of women's education. Camille Sée's law of 1880 set up public secondary schools for women for the first time, and an 1881 law established a training college at Sèvres to provide teachers for them.

The Ferry laws were more than a mere change in the organization of schooling. They added up to a comprehensive political, moral, and intellectual program designed to achieve at long last what the revolutionaries of the 1790s had intended but had been unable to accomplish with their more violent methods—to transform the French into a people of republicans. Schoolteachers, male and female, were expected to represent the Republic and to form a network of loyalists capable of combatting the influence of the only other institution that was present in every community, the Catholic church. "You don't have to shout 'I am a republican' from the rooftops," teachers in one rural district were told in 1887, "but if anyone attacks republicanism in front of you, you must have the courage to defend it."[2] The "black hussars of the Republic," as the frock-coated teachers were dubbed by their conservative critics, were expected to lead model personal lives that would inspire respect for the regime they served, and to take an active civic role. In many small communities, they occupied key political positions as secretaries to the mayor. Their education made them local notables with considerable influence on public opinion.

The educational materials used in the schools were also designed to inculcate devotion to the new institutions. Madame Augustine Fouillée's geography text *Two Children's Tour of France*, one of the most popular elementary school textbooks introduced in this period, propagated the message that all French citizens were part of one big family. It glorified the country's great soldiers and thinkers, downplayed the role of religion, and denigrated the value of regional dialects and other potential threats to national unity. Educational methods were changed, supposedly in order to encourage independent critical thinking rather than blind acceptance of authority that was held to be typical of religious education. But this emphasis on the individual and his or her rights was balanced by a strong moral insistence on duties to the community. Boys were taught that they had an obligation to serve the country as soldiers; primary school textbooks for girls stressed their mission to serve others as wives and mothers. Although the curriculum stressed the equality of all citizens, Ferry's educational program was not meant to have revolutionary implications. Textbooks stressed the inevitability of social inequality and pounded home the message that those who accepted their lot in life were usually happier than those who tried to rise above their station. Boys and girls went to separate schools. Girls, who did not receive serious lessons in science or subjects that would prepare them for higher education, were supposed to absorb messages that would give them "love of order, make them acquire the serious qualities of a housewife, and put them on guard against frivolous and dangerous tastes," according to instructions issued in 1887.[3]

In the eyes of its authors, the Third Republic's educational program was the regime's greatest accomplishment. Modern historians have shown that its proponents sometimes claimed credit for achievements that were well under way before 1880. Literacy rates, for example, had increased steadily throughout the nineteenth century, and the compulsory schooling introduced after 1880 merely completed the process. Furthermore, the school reform program did not achieve all the goals its architects had had in mind. Despite governmental pressure against them, Catholic schools survived and continued to educate a substantial percentage of the population. The notion that pupils should be taught to think for themselves ran up against the inherently authoritarian nature of the classroom situation and the mandate to inculcate specific values. The reforms also had some unintended consequences. The universal literacy resulting from comprehensive schooling facilitated the spread of radical and socialist ideas. The introduction of schooling for women, and the possibility of a professional teaching career for educated women, led eventually to demands for a new status for women that had never been part of the legislators' intentions. Nevertheless, the school system created by the Ferry laws became a powerful engine for consolidation of the new republican regime. The introduction of a uniform school curriculum throughout the nation served to reduce regional differences and create a strong sense of national identity.

Remodeling Institutions and Replacing Symbols

Important as they were, the Ferry school laws were not the only major legislative initiatives taken in the years of Opportunist ascendancy. In every aspect of French life, the victorious republicans moved to remodel institutions in accordance with their principles and to entrench the regime in everyday French life. A series of legal changes, such as a law of 1879 stripping prefects of the right to deny authorization for opening of bars and cafés—a power long used to deprive republicans of gathering places—restrained authoritarian practices inherited from the Second Empire and earlier regimes. In 1881, laws restricting press freedom and imposing prior censorship on cartoons and on caricatures were abolished. In 1884, in the name of freedom of assembly, the organization of trade unions—tolerated since the 1860s—was finally legalized. A series of laws enacted between 1882 and 1884 gave cities and towns other than Paris (considered too much of a potential threat to the national government) the right to elect their own mayors and municipal councils. Divorce, prohibited since the Restoration, was made legal again in 1884, a reform seen as giving women greater individual freedom.

Another law passed in 1884 consolidated the triumph of the new system by declaring the Republic to be France's definitive system of government. This proclamation of what one historian has called the "absolute Republic" was intended to give the regime a more solid foundation than the 1875 Wallon

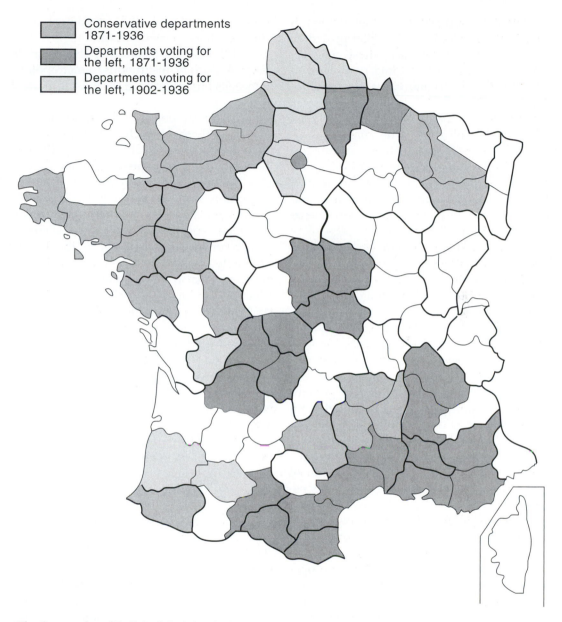

Conservative departments
1871-1936

Departments voting for
the left, 1871-1936

Departments voting for
the left, 1902-1936

The Geography of Political Opinion in France, 1871–1936
*Voting patterns during the Third Republic remained relatively stable. Republican and socialist senti-
ment, already strong in the south and center from 1871, spread to the industrial north during the period of the* Bloc républicain *after the turn of the century. Conservatives held strong blocs in the west,
the east, and the southern edge of the Massif Central.*

amendment, reluctantly adopted by a largely monarchist Assembly, had provided. As long as they were men, those who accepted the republican regime now enjoyed an extensive array of individual civil and political rights. The proclamation of 1884 was also a declaration that the regime would actively combat all those who challenged its basic values. Both groups that continued to believe in the monarchist and religious traditions of the past and those that questioned the individualist premises of liberalism and capitalism risked being stigmatized as enemies of the republican state.

To strengthen the regime, the republicans also created new symbols. July 14, the anniversary of the storming of the Bastille, became an official national holiday in 1880. In the early years, its celebration was an occasion for militant denunciations of the church and the vestiges of the past. Images of Marianne, the female personification of the Republic, which had been banned under the Empire and the "Moral Order" government, now multiplied in public squares and town halls. To promote political reconciliation, the Opportunist government pardoned the surviving participants of the Commune uprising. In 1882, the public celebration of civic funerals without religious elements became legal; the secular state funeral for the republican leader Gambetta provided an emphatic demonstration of the triumph of the new values.

Along with legal reform and the propagation of new symbols, the Opportunist republicans sought to prove that their regime would guarantee economic prosperity. A massive expansion of the national rail network to small towns all over the country, the Freycinet plan of 1878, was the keystone of this effort. It provided construction contracts and employment opportunities, and brought tangible evidence of the government's activities to many communities. The economic rationale for many of the new rail lines was

dubious, but the political impact of these "electoral lines" was significant.

Although the Third Republic consolidated democratic institutions in metropolitan France, its impact on France's most important overseas possession, Algeria, was quite different. After the defeat of the Mokrani rebellion in 1871, the French colonists, most of them vehemently republican, had obtained their demand to be treated as full French citizens, although with some privileges, such as exemption from certain taxes, because of their region's special situation. Algeria was no longer considered a colony. Its French population elected deputies to the French Assembly and had French courts, which applied laws that were very much at odds with Algerian traditions on such crucial issues as land ownership. Educated Muslims had the theoretical right to claim French citizenship, provided they explicitly renounced their rights under the Muslim law that continued to govern everyday life for their community, but few of them were willing to commit what they regarded as an act of apostasy. As a result, Algeria was run almost entirely in the interests of its small European population—which, in addition to settlers from France, included immigrants from Spain, Italy, and Malta—while the much larger Muslim population was excluded from participation in public life.

A New Colonial Policy

Overseas, the new republican government, particularly under Jules Ferry's leadership, took an activist stance with important implications for France's future. France's defeat in 1870 and the creation of Bismarck's unified German Empire had weakened the country's international position. Important reforms begun in the 1870s promised to give France an army better able to stand up to the Germans, but only the most optimistic imagined that France could successfully defeat its powerful new neighbor and regain the lost provinces of Alsace and Lorraine. Bismarck was able to use the threat of renewed hostilities to compel the French government to humiliating concessions in 1875, and the Republic was left out of important international conferences, such as the one that concluded the Russo-Turkish War of 1878. Within the country, opinion generally favored concentration on the goal of regaining equality with Germany.

During his terms as prime minister, however, Jules Ferry—in agreement with his rival Gambetta and with Catholic supporters of foreign missions on this issue—gave French foreign policy a very different orientation. Acting on his own, without parliamentary approval, he sent French troops to occupy Tunisia in 1881. In 1882, he and Gambetta pushed the Chamber to endorse the French explorer Pierre de Brazza's acquisition of extensive territories in western Africa for the Republic. In 1883–1885, Ferry proclaimed a French protectorate over the several kingdoms of Indochina (modern-day Vietnam, Laos, and Cambodia). In the scramble for African colonies, Ferry was even willing to cooperate with the Germans. To thwart British claims, he pushed Bismarck to convene a diplomatic congress in Berlin in 1884–1885 at which the European powers agreed on guidelines for the division of the African continent. By 1900, France had claimed most of West Africa and a number of colonies in the Congo region further south, as well as the large island of Madagascar off southern Africa's east coast and the territory of Djibouti on the Red Sea.

Assailed by critics who argued that these adventures in distant parts were distracting France from the task of preparing for a future clash with Germany, Ferry replied that· colonial expansion was vital to help France reassert its international standing and achieve economic prosperity. "Everywhere, in all matters where our interests and our honor are engaged," he said in 1882, "it is our will

and our duty to obtain for France the standing she deserves."[4] Because major countries were moving to protect their domestic markets by raising tariffs, Ferry argued, colonies were also a matter of economic necessity: France needed new territories as captive markets for its goods and outlets for investment. This aggressive imperialist policy was highly controversial in the 1880s.

More radical republicans denounced Ferry for "a policy that . . . repeats the mistakes of the Empire, engages our flag and spends our money on distant adventures," and for diverting attention from the duty of recovering Alsace-Lorraine.[5] Opposition to Ferry's colonial initiatives contributed to his final fall from office in 1885. Despite his critics, he left behind a much expanded empire that succeeding governments continued to enlarge. To modern eyes, the spread of French imperialism seems to reflect an unwarranted assumption about European racial and cultural superiority. There is no question that French rule was often imposed by naked force and maintained to facilitate economic exploitation of the native populations. Although the Third Republic institutionalized democratic freedoms for citizens of European France, it exercised arbitrary authority over its colonial subjects. The 1881 *indigénat* law allowed the authorities to imprison "natives" arbitrarily. They could be forced to work on French projects and to pay special taxes. French settlers and a few privileged natives were exempt from the *indigénat*, although they, too, often complained that they were not allowed to govern themselves. At the time, however, bringing the benefits of advanced civilization to the non-European world seemed, to many in France and elsewhere, almost a moral duty—or, in the common French phrase, a *mission civilisatrice* (civilizing mission). To leaders like Ferry, it was also a way of proving that France had recovered from the defeat of 1870 and of giving their fellow citizens faith in the nation's future. Only a handful of critics saw that the maintenance of the empire might some day come into conflict with the democratic principles of French republicanism.

THE SOCIAL BASES OF THE REPUBLIC

The greatest paradox of the Third Republic was that it combined democratic political institutions that struck contemporaries in many other countries as almost revolutionary with a profound social conservatism. The republicans who took office at the end of the 1870s had absorbed Thiers's conviction that the Republic would only survive if it could demonstrate that its institutions were compatible with existing social hierarchies and with the protection of the rights of property. The liquidation of the Commune uprising had been essential to assure small-town and peasant voters that the regime would have no truck with socialist ideas reminiscent of the doctrines of 1848. To be sure, the Republic was equally far from proclaiming that the rich had a natural right to special privileges. Gambetta coined one of his most famous phrases when he insisted that a democratic republic was necessary to incorporate what he called *"les nouvelles couches sociales,"* (new strata of society) into the political system. Deliberately vague, Gambetta's phrase nevertheless signaled that wealthy notables who had dominated French political life since the first Napoleonic Empire would have to share their hegemony with men of humbler origins. In practice, however, this broadening of political opportunities hardly extended beyond the middle classes. The newly enfranchised members of these groups joined with their social betters to maintain a social hierarchy that marginalized those below them. Furthermore, the old elites proved remarkably resourceful at finding ways to maintain their privileged social and economic status even in the context of a democratic political system.

The Third Republic's openness to men from modest middle-class backgrounds was most evident in electoral politics. The small, single-member districts from which deputies were elected allowed energetic local personalities to impose themselves. The landowners, lawyers, and wealthy businessmen who had dominated the parliamentary assemblies of the July Monarchy and the Second Empire slowly made way for deputies and local officials who were notaries, shopkeepers, or schoolteachers. The republic was sometimes said to be the regime of veterinarians and pharmacists. These small businessmen and modestly educated professionals represented the interests of small property owners in general, including the landowning peasants who continued to form the largest group in France's electorate. They faithfully reflected the parochial interests of their constituents, opposing measures that would mean increased taxes or additional government regulations imposed on them, and supporting policies that benefited shopkeepers and small farmers.

While the Third Republic thus accommodated the interests of small property owners, it also managed to protect the standing of wealthy elites who had prospered during the July Monarchy and the Second Empire. Aristocratic titles, although no longer officially recognized, still conveyed great social prestige. Descendants of the nobility still held a disproportionate share of positions in professions such as the army officer corps and the diplomatic service, whose criteria of recruitment included judgment of the candidate's ability to conduct himself in polite society. In areas such as western France, large landowners continued to dominate local affairs. Despite occasional rhetorical outbursts against the power of big business in the Assembly, the Republic was not opposed to the interests of large enterprises. Indeed, in the period from 1870 to 1914, big businessmen increased their fortunes at a much faster rate than the more modest entrepreneurs of the petty bourgeoisie. The introduction of universal free primary education had been meant to provide a minimum of education and opportunity to children from humble backgrounds, but the long-established dual school system screened out all but a few unusually talented children from poor families. Wealthy families who intended to send their children to the *lycée* for further study after the primary grades paid to enroll them in special elementary classes where they avoided contact with their social inferiors. Tuition was charged for secondary education. Many historians have seen the ostensibly democratic and egalitarian school system created by the Ferry laws as being in reality one of the main mechanisms through which social inequalities were maintained and transmitted from one generation to the next.

Within the bourgeoisie, certain groups gained more from the consolidation of the Republic than others. Middle-class members of France's Protestant and Jewish minorities were particularly at home in the new atmosphere. They welcomed the Third Republic's commitment to secularism and usually shared its leaders' faith in the importance of education. A number of leading republican politicians, such as Ferdinand Buisson, the longtime director of the educational system, came from Protestant backgrounds. So did a disproportionately large number of business leaders and prominent university professors. The ascent of the small Jewish community was less spectacular, but Jews achieved positions of prominence in journalism, academia, and the professions. The Jewish publisher Félix Alcan, for example, directed a prestigious series that put out almost all the serious publications in philosophy published in France at the turn of the century. He was typical of a prosperous Jewish elite that had completely assimilated French values and lifestyles.

Rural Decline

While the Third Republic thus offered new opportunities to some groups, others faced varying degrees of difficulty. The peasantry, solidly converted to republicanism in many regions of the country, derived some benefits from the extension of schooling and new access to the wider world provided by railroads, the popular press, and other new forms of contact with urban civilization. But the period was one in which many problems plagued agriculture. Even government sympathy to farmers' complaints could not provide them with protection against these economic crises. In response, the rural exodus which had affected only a limited number of regions in the first half of the century became more general. Between 1871 and 1914, sixty of France's eighty-odd departments lost population. While the pace of this rural exodus was slower than in Britain or Germany, it was sufficiently striking to create the sense that a traditional way of life, deeply rooted in the French past, was threatened.

The republican government, although not at all hostile to the economic interests of peasant farmers, was bent on transforming the culture of the countryside. Its schoolteachers were missionaries determined to root out such vestiges of backwardness as regional dialects, particularly in areas like Brittany where local customs were often associated with loyalty to church and opposition to the Republic. The experience of military service, made compulsory for all young men in the wake of the 1870 defeat, took peasant boys out of their native communities and exposed them to new values. The growing market economy, too, broke down regional isolation. All these processes contributed to the transformation of "peasants into Frenchmen," as historian Eugen Weber has shown. But memoirs like Pierre Jakes Hélias's *The Horse of Pride,* a highly readable account of a Breton village boy's life at the turn of the century, show that there was often a psychological cost to this imposition of new, fundamentally urban, values.

Urban Workers

The place of the urban workers in the new republican society was even more problematic. It was a basic tenet of the republican faith that workers did not form a class apart in French society, and that they would benefit from the changes the new regime introduced in the country. In fact, however, workers tended to live in distinct urban neighborhoods, and in conditions that set them apart from other groups in the population. Draft board records show that young men from working-class neighborhoods were shorter, on the average, than sons of bourgeois or peasant families, and that they more often suffered from debilitating illnesses. Public schooling did little to give the children of working-class families (who generally had to abandon their education at an early age to start earning a living) much chance for social mobility. To the extent that the Republic took cognizance of the specific problems that affected urban workers, its main policy was to encourage them to adopt values more in line with those of the bourgeoisie. Denis Poulot, the self-made entrepreneur whose book *Le Sublime* had offered a scathing indictment of the behavior of workers at the end of the Second Empire, was typical of these republican reformers in the 1880s. Elected mayor of Paris's eleventh *arrondissement,* a working-class neighborhood, he promoted the new secular schools for children and urged adult workers to educate themselves as well. In 1881, he founded a "Society for Civil Marriage" to encourage poor couples to legalize their unions and adopt the family pattern of the bourgeoisie. Poulot also patronized various schemes to encourage workers to save money and to form cooperative enterprises.

In the years after 1880, workers' styles of life did change to some extent along the lines that bourgeois reformers like Poulot had hoped. Stable marriages became more frequent, as working-class neighborhoods ceased to be composed primarily of young single men recently arrived from the countryside. Literacy rates rose as schooling became more widespread. The period after 1880 saw a gradual improvement in real wages and in living standards. Workers were able to afford a more diversified diet and, indeed, generally ate better than peasants. But the notion that, by saving and investing, workers could convert themselves into small property owners—and thus integrate themselves into the world that bourgeois republicans like Poulot had created—remained a utopian one. Rather than accepting such advice, many workers turned to movements that maintained that workers' interests were in fact opposed to those of the property-owning classes. Disrupted by the defeat of the Paris Commune, socialist groups began to reappear by the late 1870s. In 1879, a congress of workers' deputies in Marseille called for the creation of a workers' political party—testimony to a growing sense of identity and of isolation from the rest of society on the part of the more articulate members of the working class.

If the place of the working class in late nineteenth-century society remained marginal, there were also elements of the middle class whose role in the republic remained in question. The art historian T. J. Clark, in his essay on the social context of impressionist painters active in the 1870s and early 1880s, *The Painting of Modern Life,* has drawn attention to the way in which the paintings of Manet and others reflected the ambiguous status of a new and rapidly growing group of salaried bourgeois—such as shop attendants and office clerks. Members of these groups were bourgeois by virtue of their education and their style of life, but they lacked one of the essential attributes of classical bourgeois status. They did not live on income from individually owned property. Social critics complained that men of this sort lacked real taste and education. Impressionist paintings of the Sunday resorts around Paris reflected the swarming presence of these new members of the bourgeoisie and their aspiration to follow the cultural patterns of their betters. But in the course of their attempts, they threw into question the definition of the bourgeois elite and the grounding of its values.

The lifestyles of French citizens continued to vary greatly depending on their social class standing, but some social trends were common to the whole population. The period from 1870–1914 saw a gradual improvement in health conditions and life expectancy, due particularly to a decline in infant mortality and deaths in childbirth. French doctor Louis Pasteur's demonstration of the role of bacteria in spreading disease became the basis for measures to improve sanitation and limit the spread of many infectious diseases. The bourgeois model of family life gradually spread to other classes, as did the practice of birth control. Common in some regions before 1880, it tended to become a national habit after that date, although there were still important class differences, with workers tending to have larger families and bourgeois, office employees, and peasants limiting theirs more strongly. Men were supposed to control their households. Societal norms, strongly expressed in legislation and school textbooks, dictated that women should be submissive and devote themselves to domestic tasks. If they sought employment, it should be only to supplement the main breadwinner's income, and work was supposed to be only a temporary stage in a woman's life— one she would willingly abandon to raise her children. Few peasant or worker families, of course, could afford to follow this pattern; the percentage of women in the work force actually rose after 1870.

Women's Rights

Late nineteenth-century legislation gave women somewhat greater rights. Aside from the 1884 divorce law, in 1886 they gained the ability to open bank accounts without their husbands' consent. In 1893, single adult women were granted full legal rights, and in 1897, women obtained the right to testify in legal trials. It was during this period that women first began to enter the educated professions, although only in minuscule numbers. The first French woman to earn a medical degree graduated in 1875, and the first women doctors were permitted to work in French hospitals in 1885. By 1903, there were still fewer than a hundred female doctors in the country, but by 1913 women represented 10 percent of the medical students in French universities. Jeanne Chauvin became the first woman to earn a law degree in 1892, although it took eight years and the support of leading politicians before she was admitted to practice in 1900. The Ferry school laws, which set up a system of secular secondary schools for girls, created a new profession for educated women as teachers. The graduates of the *Ecole normale de Sèvres*, set up in response, provided a new model for female careers.

The Beginnings of the French Welfare State

During the early decades of the Third Republic, legislators passed several laws that expanded the government's role in promoting the personal well-being of many groups of its citizens. Such legislation departed from the traditional liberal premise that the functions of government should be as limited as possible and pointed toward the development of what would later be known as a "welfare state," in which national governments took responsibility for seeing that all citizens enjoyed adequate health care, living standards, and protection against such risks as unemployment and disability.

Traditionally, France was thought to have lagged behind the other major European countries in enacting welfare legislation, particularly because it was so slow in providing unemployment insurance. (National legislation for this purpose was not adopted until 1958.) Recent research has shown, however, that the Third Republic was a pioneer in many areas of welfare policy, especially with regard to protection of women and children.

Concern for the welfare of women and children was promoted, not primarily by women's groups, but by middle-class male reformers. Many of them were motivated by fear that France's national future was in danger because of its unusually low birth rate and its high rate of infant mortality. The military defeat of 1870 drew attention to the fact that Germany's population was growing faster than France's. The Roussel law of 1874 regulating wet-nursing, a practice condemned as exposing infants to unnecessary health hazards, was one of the first responses to this perceived problem. It was followed in 1889 by a law asserting the state's right to intervene in families to prevent child abuse, in 1893 by a law offering free medical care to expectant mothers, and in 1904 by legislation authorizing welfare assistance to children of poor families. Although republican ideology taught that women should remain at home to raise their children, French legislators recognized that, in fact, most poor women had to work. Many of them therefore supported activist Pauline Kergomard's campaign for public kindergartens or day-care centers, known in French as *écoles maternelles*, which were incorporated into public elementary schools in 1886. Ostensibly to protect families and children, legislators also passed laws in 1892 and 1900 limiting women's working hours. In her autobiography, the seamstress Jeanne Bouvier recalled that, before the 1892 law, her employer forced employees to work

"until two in the morning nearly every day, and without our having eaten, except for a small loaf of bread and a bit of chocolate at four o'clock."[6] Employers often found a way around the new rules, however, by hiring women to work in their own homes, where their hours could not be regulated.

One unintended consequence of the Third Republic's welfare legislation was the creation of government jobs for women as inspectors, to see that the newly enacted policies were being carried out. A few women had been employed in such roles as early as the 1830s, to supervise nursery schools and women's prisons, but the Third Republic's legislation brought the creation of new positions concerned with women's workplaces and the implementation of social assistance programs. Although the total number of these positions remained limited, they set an important precedent for the involvement of women in the public sphere. In increasing numbers, women were also starting to move into jobs in the service sector of the economy—selling goods in the department stores that flourished in the last decades of the century and working as office clerks and typists.

Many women, particularly those who were loyal to the Catholic church, did not accept the secular democratic values of the new regime. Catholic charity organizations, supported by middle- and upper-class women, frequently worked at cross-purposes with reforming efforts supported by men from the same backgrounds. Male republican spokesmen used the strength of women's commitment to the church as one of the main arguments for excluding them from voting.

The stability of the Third Republic was due in good part to the fact that the regime responded to the interests of groups whose members made up a majority of the electorate—members of the various elements of the bourgeoisie and middle classes, on the one hand, and peasants, on the other. This republican social coalition excluded the industrial working class, whose disaffection from the system was to become increasingly significant as time went on. Women, although excluded from politics, formed a less homogeneous group whose sentiments toward the regime are hard to assess. With its solid base of social support, the new political regime was able to put down stronger roots than any of its nineteenth-century predecessors.

NATURALISM, IMPRESSIONISM, AND MASS CULTURE

The consolidation of the Republic, a regime based on secular values, provided the opportunity for new cultural developments. In literature, the disillusioned realism of Flaubert evolved into the more explicit naturalism of Emile Zola and Guy de Maupassant. Zola's essay *The Experimental Novel* (1880) was the manifesto for the new literary movement. The fiction writer, Zola proclaimed, should see himself as contributing to the scientific study of man and society: "Scientific investigation, experimental reasoning, challenge one by one the hypotheses of the idealists and replace the novel of pure imagination by novels of observation and experiment."[7]

Zola applied his ideas in a series of novels meant to portray the French society of the late nineteenth century. Zola's methods were those of a social scientist. For his depiction of the new department stores that had become such a major feature of French life, *Au Bonheur des Dames*, he did extensive research on the operations of enterprises like the Parisian *Bon Marché*. His great novel of working-class protest, *Germinal,* was inspired by newspaper reports about miners' strikes in the 1880s, even though Zola set his story in the Second Empire period. The controversy that surrounded his work stemmed from his direct portrayal of aspects of life that were excluded from conventional bourgeois culture: poverty, class conflict, and sexuality. Influenced by biological research on the importance of heredity, Zola often gave his stories a fatalistic air. The calamities that befell his protagonists were described as the inevitable consequence of their ancestry, and the society he portrayed seemed to be in the grip of large forces beyond human control.

Zola was linked to the increasingly prominent group of impressionist painters by friendship and by a common aspiration to portray the world as it actually appeared. But the colorful canvases of Claude Monet, Camille Pissarro, Auguste Renoir, Edgar Degas, Paul Cézanne, and their friends—now become among the world's most popular artworks—shocked and offended art connoisseurs of the period as much as Zola's novels, with their emphasis on sex and suffering. The label "impressionist" was originally a critical one, derived from the title of one of the works Claude Monet exhibited at a group show in 1874. It meant to deride these artists' tendency to paint their impressions of what they saw, rather than giving their subjects a timeless and monumental quality. Zola defended his friends' works and gave the term a positive connotation. He argued that their efforts to capture "the impression of a moment experienced in nature" made them "the true representatives of our time."[8]

In their efforts to give a true rendering of what they saw, the impressionist painters abandoned traditional artistic rules about composition and style. Influenced by new scientific theories about the nature of vision, they painted using small touches of color, rather than mixing their tones on their palette. The Impressionists often worked in the open air, rather than laboring over their canvases in their studios. The subjects they chose—farm fields, unspectacular landscapes in the vicinity of Paris, scenes of daily life in the city's streets—lacked the grandeur and obvious significance of traditional artists' subjects. Their willingness to adopt ideas from other artistic traditions, particularly the Japanese, threw into question traditional assumptions about the inherent superiority of western art. In all these respects, the impressionists anticipated innovations that have come to be characteristic of modern art.

Only a sophisticated minority appreciated the impressionists' paintings at the time they were created. The mass culture that had begun to develop under the Second Empire and continued to flourish in the Third Republic had little contact with such avant-garde experiments. The steady rise of literacy allowed the new, cheap newspapers modeled after the *Petit Journal* to find an ever-increasing audience for their sensationalistic reporting. Using new technology to incorporate more illustrations, the press encouraged and exploited public interest in gruesome crimes, natural disasters, political scandals, and striking advances in science and technology. Circulation grew steadily, and by the early twentieth century, one French title had the largest daily circulation of any newspaper in the world.

Female readers devoured the "domestic novels" of writers like Josephine de Gaulle—grandmother of the future national hero—with their repetitive plots in which true love and devotion enabled female protagonists to bring order to homes and families menaced by chaos. The novels of Jules Verne, which mixed romantic plots with an emphasis on the possibilities of new scientific technology—submarines and space voyages—attracted young readers and promoted the development of a new literary genre, science fiction.

The culture of consumption that had begun to develop in the first half of the nineteenth century reached widening circles of the population. It was propagated above all by the development of the department store,

a new form of retailing that had appeared in France during the years of the Second Empire. Bringing together under a single roof a wide range of clothing and articles for the home, offered at set prices rather than being sold through a process of individualized bargaining, enterprises like *Bon Marché* and *Galeries Lafayette* democratized fashion and spread the habit of material acquisition. By permitting customers to make purchases on the installment plan after 1872, the owners of the *Samaritaine* department store opened up an even greater market for themselves. The democratization of consumer goods made possible by the department store developed in parallel with the political democratization of the period.

THE REPUBLIC'S WORLD'S FAIRS

The cultural aspirations of the Third Republic were most spectacularly expressed in the great world's fairs the regime sponsored in 1878, 1889, and 1900. The British had mounted the first great international exposition in 1851, but France, with its tradition of cultural universalism, became the most enthusiastic promoter of such events. Napoleon III's government had sponsored expositions in 1855 and 1867, broadening them from the British model of a display of technological achievements to include displays of art and exhibits devoted to social progress. The leaders of the Third Republic saw expositions as ways of demonstrating that, despite the defeat of 1870, France was more than ever at the forefront of progress and the center of world affairs. The 1878 fair had a special political point: opened just after the end of the crisis caused by Marshal MacMahon's "coup" in 1877, it was a chance for visitors from all over the world to see that the republicans were firmly in control of the country. To emphasize France's world role, the Third Republic's expositions were used as occasions for the convening of important interna-

AVENUE NICOLAS II

The international expositions of 1878, 1889, and 1900 were opportunities for Paris to underline its position as the "capital of Europe." Visitors from all over the world admired the elaborate pavilions and the exhibits of art and technology. The "Avenue Nicholas II," built for the exposition of 1900, honored the Russian Tsar, a gesture to cement France's alliance with Russia against Germany.
(Photo credit: Raymond Betts.)

tional congresses to discuss a wide variety of issues. Meetings held in conjunction with the 1878 world's fair included an International Congress on the Rights of Women, an international peace congress and a meeting of mountain-climbers. Victor Hugo chaired a conference on intellectual property rights that produced the first international copyright agreement, and another conference led to the creation of the Universal Postal Union, establishing global rules for the exchange of mail.

The 1889 world's fair was even more successful than that of 1878. Its date coincided with the centennial of the 1789 revolution, which led governments that were still monarchies to decline official invitations to participate, but this did nothing to reduce the flow of visitors: Thirty two million people came, twice as many as in 1878. A major function of the fair was to showcase the achievements of modern technology. French engineer Gustave Eiffel's three-hundred-meter-high steel tower, nearly twice as tall as any previous building, was the exposition's centerpiece. Denounced by critics, including most of France's leading artists and writers, as a "gigantic and hideous skeleton," it was initially supposed to be taken down after twenty years; instead, it has become the internationally recognized symbol of the country. Equally spectacular for fair visitors was the *Galerie des machines,* an iron-frame building whose girders supported a roof covering span of 377 feet, providing space for displays of the ever larger and more powerful machines that were the most visible symbols of modern man's conquest of nature. The fair was also an opportunity to publicize France's rapidly growing empire. The *Palais central des colonies* jumbled together reproductions of Algerian mosques, Cambodian temples and other unfamiliar architectural styles. Indoors, colonial "natives" performed in settings designed to emphasize the backwardness and strangeness of their cultures relative to that of France. Only one exceptional journalist reminded readers that "these are people and not exotic animals that we are watching behind the fences."[9] More than any previous fair, the 1889 exhibit stressed entertainment as well as education. The exotic belly-dancers in the Egyptian pavilion attracted more visitors than the industrial exhibits. Like the 1878 fair, that of 1889, which opened just after the Boulanger crisis (described in the next chapter), also served to reassure the public about the health of the Republic.

NOTES

1. Stanley Hoffmann, "Paradoxes of the French Political Community," in *In Search of France* (New York: Harper, 1963), 17.

2. Cited in Jacques Ozouf, *Nous les maîtres d'école* (Paris: Julliard/Gallimard, 1973), 175.

3. Cited in Linda L. Clark, *Schooling the Daughters of Marianne* (Albany: SUNY Press, 1984), 17.

4. Cited in Pierre Guillan, *L'Expansion 1881–1898* (Paris: Imprimerie nationale, 1984), 177.

5. Cited in ibid., 110.

6. In Mark Traugott, ed., *The French Worker: Autobiographies from the Early Industrial Era* (Berkeley: University of California Press, 1993), 372.

7. Zola, "The Experimental Novel," in Eugen Weber, ed., *Paths to the Present* (New York: Harper & Row, 1960), 171.

8. Zola, "Naturalism in the Salon," in Weber, ed., *Paths to the Present*, 186–87.

9. Cited in Lynn E. Palermo, "Identity under Construction: Representing the Colonies at the Paris *Exposition Universelle* of 1889," in Sue Peabody and Tyler Stovall, eds., *The Color of Race: Histories of Race in France* (Durham, NC: Duke University Press, 2003), 291.

CHAPTER 19

ECONOMIC DEPRESSION AND POLITICAL CRISES

The founders of the Third Republic, like Léon Gambetta, had assumed that a democratic regime would enjoy broad support and that its only serious opposition would come from groups loyal to the past, who were doomed to disappear as the new values promoted by the Republic spread. It soon became clear, however, that discontent with the republican regime came from many sources and that its success could not be taken for granted. Throughout the 1880s and 1890s, the parliamentary Republic faced repeated crises, rooted in economic difficulties and in its inability to win the loyalty of substantial groups of the population.

THE LATE-NINETEENTH-CENTURY "GREAT DEPRESSION"

One reason for the difficulties in the early decades of republican supremacy was the economic climate. After the period of prosperity and economic growth that characterized the Second Empire, especially in its first decade, came a prolonged period in which the French economy (together with those of the other industrialized nations) experienced a marked slowdown. This "Great Depression of the Nineteenth Century," lasting from 1873 to 1896, differed in important

ways from the more devastating depression that afflicted the world in the 1920s and 1930s. It entailed a slowing of growth, but not a severe economic contraction, and it did not affect living standards as strongly because unemployment was not as severe and prices of consumer goods actually fell faster than wages. It nevertheless colored the economic climate in France for two decades.

Among the hardest hit by the economic downswing were French farmers, for whom the period—in sharp contrast to the prosperity of the Second Empire—was one of multiple problems. The most devastating setback hit French winegrowers. From 1863, an insect-borne disease, *phylloxera,* had begun to spread in French vineyards. By the late 1870s, it had become a veritable epidemic, killing the vines that produced France's second most important crop. French wine production, which had reached an all-time high in 1875, dropped by more than two-thirds before bottoming out in 1887. Frantic experimentation showed that the most successful treatment was to pull up the affected plants and replace them with disease-resistant American grapevines. Healthy branches from French plants could then be grafted onto the new rootstock to produce the special varieties on which famous French vintages depended. While this procedure saved the wine industry, it required heavy investment that forced many small producers to abandon wine-growing. Production became concentrated in a few favored regions. Lower Languedoc, in the south, became the center of a heavily market-oriented wine industry, carried on by large-scale growers using hired labor, and producing cheap wines for mass consumption.

The *phylloxera* epidemic coincided with other agricultural difficulties. In the region around Lyon, silk growers found themselves swamped by cheaper foreign thread. Unlike the wine trade, their business never recovered. The same fate overtook the growers of plants used to make dyes for the textile industry, whose products were increasingly replaced by synthetic chemicals. Industrial de-

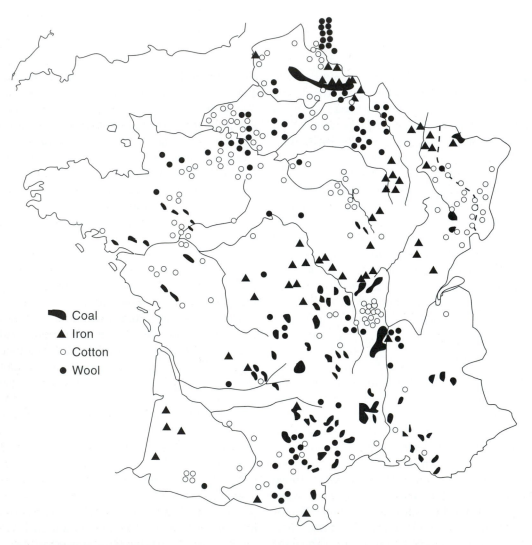

▬ Coal
▲ Iron
○ Cotton
● Wool

Industrial France, 1880
By the 1880s, the geographic pattern of French heavy industry was established along lines that would persist until the deindustrialization of the late twentieth century. The major centers were in the north, in Lorraine, and in the region around Lyon.

velopment threatened French grain growers, too. Cheaper transportation made foreign imports less expensive, driving grain prices down by 27 percent from 1871–1875 to 1895. France's peasant farmers, with their small holdings, lacked the resources to adopt efficient, mechanized methods.

For France's industrial sector, too, the period was one of difficulty. By the 1880s, French industry had established the geographic pattern it would retain until the late twentieth century. Mining and metalworking had replaced textiles as the most important industial sector. The embattled coalminers of Emile Zola's *Germinal* lived in the Nord, the region along the Belgian frontier, which was one of the main centers of production. Others were in Lorraine, where newly discovered deposits of iron ore made up for the loss of resources taken by Germany in 1871; in the region around Lyon and Saint-Etienne; and along the southern edge of the Massif Central. Rouen remained a major center of textile production, while the largest center of the chemical industry was in Lyon. Paris was a center for many kinds of light manufacturing and luxury trades. Regions that lacked the resources needed for modern industry or that had been centers of production dependent on old-fashioned methods that were no longer competitive, such as Brittany and the southwestern area around Bordeaux, suffered a relative and, in some cases, an absolute decline in prosperity and population. In a country where more than half the population was still rural, the agricultural depression meant a reduced consumer market which slowed the growth of manufacturing. The heavy spending on public works characteristic of the Second Empire tailed off under the Republic. This was especially true when the government had to curtail the expensive Freycinet railroad expansion plan in 1883, depriving business of an important stimulus. The collapse in 1882 of the *Union générale*, one of the country's most important banks, dealt a heavy blow to the credit market

and made lenders cautious about supporting business ventures.

International conditions prevented France from expanding its sales abroad to make up for the contraction at home. Foreign competitors were increasingly aggressive. In Bismarck's Germany especially, industry grew much faster than in France. Whereas the Schneider works at Le Creusot had probably been the largest industrial enterprise on the continent in the 1860s, by the end of the 1870s, Germany's factories surpassed the French. So did the growing industrial centers of the United States. As her competitors built larger factories and achieved higher levels of efficiency, French products proved to be too expensive to compete effectively. France, which had been the world's second manufacturing nation until 1870, slipped to a poor fourth place, far behind its rivals, by the end of the century.

The multiple problems besetting French agriculture and industry gave a strong impetus for reversal of the free-trade policy that Napoleon III had imposed in 1860 in an effort to promote economic development. A tariff law voted in 1881 and implemented the following year marked the abandonment of free trade, although the rates it imposed were relatively low. It also left the government considerable flexibility to negotiate agreements with other countries. Agriculturists and manufacturers who faced strong foreign competition kept up agitation for a stronger law throughout the 1880s. Their combined efforts were finally successful in 1892, when Jules Méline, a staunch defender of agricultural interests, guided a new tariff bill through parliament. The Méline tariff set considerably higher rates, from 12 to 30 percent, on imported products. It also forbade future governments from negotiating significant exceptions. It provided French producers with a well-guarded domestic market, and the principle of protection was not to be challenged again until the 1950s.

One argument used to support the demand for protection was the claim that tariffs would encourage French industrialists to invest in making themselves more efficient, since they would be able to rely on a guaranteed market for their goods. On the whole, however, the high-tariff policy failed to produce this effect. Freed from the threat of foreign competition, French manufacturers often saw little need to improve their methods. The relatively static French market gave them little incentive to expand production. France's low birth rate during the 1880s and 1890s deprived the economy of an important stimulus that encouraged industrial development in countries like Germany and the United States.

To the dismay of many contemporary observers, French capital was invested more and more heavily abroad after 1880. French investors purchased government bonds and underwrote the building of railroads in Russia and in many of the smaller countries of eastern and southern Europe. French overseas investments during this period were second only to those of Britain, and the country played a crucial role in financing the modernization of many regions around the world. In many cases, particularly with respect to investment in the Russian Empire, the French government strongly encouraged this process for diplomatic reasons. Overseas investment increased French leverage in strategic areas, and ties to Russia were particularly important after the two countries formed an alliance against Germany in the early 1890s. Argument has continued ever since as to whether this massive diversion of French capital beyond the country's borders weakened domestic industrial growth, or whether the economy as a whole benefited from the high dividends many of these investments earned until the First World War. The current scholarly consensus holds that the flow of capital abroad essentially reflected France's inability to employ its resources productively at home. Enough capital was available to underwrite domestic development where market conditions warranted it, but the overall structure of the French economy militated against rapid and widespread growth during this period.

THE BOULANGER AFFAIR

The legislative elections of 1877 and 1881 had been essential steps toward the consolidation of a republican majority. By the time of the next national elections, in 1885, a certain disillusionment with the new regime was evident. Discontent caused by hard times was one reason for this; the fact that the basically moderate Opportunist republicans had largely exhausted their political agenda after the enactment of the Ferry laws was another. As they settled into defending the new status quo, a more radical republican current began to assert itself and denounce their growing conservatism. The most prominent Radical deputy of the period was Georges Clemenceau. Trained as a doctor and thus imbued with a scientific outlook, Clemenceau had entered political life with the fall of Louis-Napoleon, winning election as mayor of the Paris suburb of Montmartre and trying to act as a mediator between the Thiers government and the Paris Commune. After the republican victory of 1877 had been consolidated, Clemenceau became a fierce critic of the Opportunist leaders, denouncing them in the Chamber and in his newspaper, *La Justice*, for abandoning the recovery of Alsace-Lorraine in favor of overseas expansion. He also criticized them for making no further effort to reform undemocratic aspects of the 1875 constitution (such as the role of the Senate), and for ignoring the problems of the lower classes.

With voters blaming the economic slowdown on the governing Opportunists, radical candidates were able to make strong gains in the 1885 elections. So did the right-wing opposition, producing a Chamber divided into three approximately equal blocks and making the formation of a stable ministry difficult. As the Chamber of Deputies bogged down in inconclusive debates, public opinion toward the new republican institutions began to cool. In 1886, the British ambassador to Paris wrote that the Republic had lasted sixteen years, "and that is about the time it takes the French to tire of a form of government."[1] By 1887, the Third Republic was facing the first of many crises that would punctuate its history, one in which powerful forces challenged the basic institution of parliamentary democracy.

The crisis that lasted from 1887 to 1889 crystallized around the person of General Georges Boulanger, a popular and outspoken military officer of radical republican views. The Radicals had engineered Boulanger's appointment as minister of war in 1886 as part of their price for a coalition with the moderates. Boulanger used the position as a platform to build a personal following. He posed as champion of the common man, improving the conditions of ordinary soldiers and flamboyantly encouraging military units sent to control strikes to fraternize with the workers. He also delighted patriotic opinion by provoking the Germans almost to the brink of war in 1887. Boulanger's recklessness and his growing personal appeal alarmed the cautious politicians who dominated the cabinet, and a ministerial reshuffle in 1887 led to his dismissal as war minister. The general's followers turned to the streets and to the ballot box. They put his name forward in several by-elections in the early months of 1888, and Boulanger scored a series of striking successes.

As Boulanger marched from one political triumph to the next, he united more and more of the groups who opposed the Third Republic behind his banner. The regime was in poor shape to defend itself. In December 1887, Jules Grévy, the moderate republican who had replaced MacMahon, had been forced to resign for tolerating scandals in his office. Initially, Boulanger's appeal had been mainly to the left. His first supporters had been Radical Republicans, and his populist rhetoric had won over many socialists, as well as workers and members of the petty bourgeoisie. His nationalism attracted supporters such as Paul Déroulède, the founder of the *Ligue des patriotes*—a movement launched with widespread republican support in 1881 that had increasingly identified French national interests with replacement of parliamentary government by a more authoritarian regime. But by 1888, Boulanger was also recruiting support from the conservative right, which saw in his mass appeal a chance to undermine the republicans' hegemony. Both sides sought to keep these contacts secret, but by 1888, the Boulangist movement was being largely funded by sympathizers from the monarchist camp.

In January 1889, Boulanger challenged the moderate republicans in the capital itself, which had been one of their electoral strongholds since the days of the Empire. Drawing votes from both the left and the right, he won a resounding victory for a parliamentary seat. His supporters now planned to nominate him as a candidate in every electoral district in France in the upcoming general elections, and thus put him in power in a virtual plebiscite. In the face of this challenge, republican parliamentarians, thoroughly alarmed, rushed through changes in the election laws to prohibit candidates from running in more than one district. Fearing that the government intended to move against him, Boulanger showed that he lacked the courage of a real conspirator. He abandoned his supporters and fled across the border to Brussels on April 1, 1889.

With its leader disgraced, the Boulangist movement rapidly disintegrated. The publication of documents about Boulanger's right-wing contacts dismayed his republican and socialist supporters, and Boulanger himself committed suicide at the grave of his mistress in 1891. Despite Boulanger's disappearance and the apparent victory of parliamentary republicanism, the two years of Boulangist agitation had profoundly altered the French political landscape. Historians have continued to differ in their assessment of Boulanger's personal political views and on the degree to which his support came from the left or the right. But there is no doubt that the growth of his movement revealed surprising weaknesses in the foundations of the Third Republic. The fact that a relative nonentity such as the general could cast himself for the role of Napoleon and come close to succeeding was disquieting. The participation of many socialists in the Boulangist movement marked their growing separation from the republican mainstream. From the time of Boulanger onward, the presence of an autonomous socialist movement critical of "bourgeois" republicanism became a permanent feature of the French political scene. In their disenchantment with Boulanger, however, the socialists and the republicans began to separate themselves from the ultrapatriotic nationalists, while conservatives learned from the Boulanger experience that nationalism could serve their purposes and win them a new mass base. Movements like Déroulède's *Ligue des patriotes*, originally oriented toward the left, now began to be counted as part of the right. The political shifts begun by the Boulanger episode and subsequently consolidated in the Dreyfus crisis of the late 1890s thus restructured the French political scene for decades to come.

Many of the republican parliamentarians who held off Boulanger did not have long to savor their success. Boulanger's remaining supporters, deprived of their hero, still held a weapon that allowed them to avenge themselves. In the midst of the Boulanger crisis, a French company formed to dig a canal in Panama had gone bankrupt. Large sums were at stake in the Panama affair, and those concerned had made payoffs to a number of republican deputies to protect their interests. In September 1892, the anti-Semitic journalist Edouard Drumont, a former Boulangist, exposed the scandal. After furious debates, the Chamber created a commission of inquiry, which found several dozen deputies (including many of the most prominent Opportunists as well as the Radical leader Clemenceau) to have been involved. The Panama scandal ended the careers of many of the first generation of republicans. More importantly, it contributed to a deep-seated distrust of the country's parliamentary leadership.

SOCIALISM, ANARCHISM, AND TRADE UNIONS

The 1893 elections disposed of many of the republican deputies tainted by the Panama scandal; the voters also elected some fifty socialist deputies. This new challenge from the left, and the question of whether it should be met by a broad union of conservative groups (including the Catholics against whom the republican regime had fought since its inception), dominated parliamentary life for the next few years. Most of the short-lived ministries that held office in the mid-1890s, as well as the more long-lasting combination put together by Jules Méline—the advocate of economic protectionism—from 1896 to 1898, leaned to the right. Panama had discredited the Opportunist label, but not that party's policies. A new set of moderate republican leaders, calling themselves Progressists, continued many of them. Under their leadership, the moderate republican synthesis seemed to have achieved renewed stability despite challenges from several groups excluded from the system. France also seemed ready to take on new challenges abroad.

To the left of the republican bloc, the socialist movement emerged as a major feature of French political life. Workers turned to socialism in response to economic hardship and to incidents such as the massacre at Fourmies in 1890, where nine workers were killed when soldiers opened fire on a demonstration. Socialism had particular appeal in heavily industrialized areas where workers were concentrated in large factories, such as the region of the Nord with its mines and textile plants. The first socialist political parties had developed in the early 1880s in response to initiatives from the national workers' congresses that had been held in the late 1870s. Instead of developing into one large, unified party, as in Germany, the French movement soon divided into several fractions, united only in their condemnation of the capitalist economic system and the liberal political institutions that had grown up with it. At a national conference in Saint-Etienne in 1882, the French socialists split into two groups. One was the *Parti Ouvrier Français,* headed by Jules Guesde, the French socialist most influenced by the ideas of Karl Marx, which he had encountered during his years in exile after the Commune uprising. Guesde maintained that there could be no cooperation between the industrial working class, the proletariat, and its bourgeois foes. The purpose of a socialist political party was to educate workers and organize them into a powerful political party that would ultimately carry out a revolution against the bourgeois capitalist order. For Guesde and his followers, participation in "bourgeois" politics was important only as a means of spreading the socialist message, whose triumph would inevitably occur as a result of the growth of the proletariat. Other forms of working-class activity, notably the formation of trade unions, took second place in the Guesdists' thinking, since—according to Guesde's interpretation of Marx—union activity could not make significant improvements in the condition of workers doomed to exploitation as long as capitalism existed. Guesde's movement appealed particularly to the downtrodden and relatively uneducated workers in France's northern textile cities. The department of the Nord, along the Belgian border, became its strongest bastion.

Guesde's rigid definition of socialism brought him into conflict with militants who came to the movement from different backgrounds, and who were less impressed with the authority of Marx's teachings. The 1882 split separated the Guesdists from a rival group that came to be known as the *Possibilistes*—a term invented by its main spokesman, Paul Brousse, to describe his policy of supporting whatever reforms proved possible under the existing republican system. Brousse, for example, urged socialists to seek local municipal offices, if necessary in coalition with the Radicals. He himself won a seat on the Paris city council in 1887. In opposition to Guesde's movement, the Possibilists formed their own party, the Federation of French Socialist Workers. In practice, as the Guesdists won local elections in areas like the Nord during the 1890s, they too began to put through practical reforms, and differences between them and the Possibilists were often more those of rhetoric and social style than substance.

Not all French socialists accepted the emphasis on political activity that the Guesdists and the Possibilists shared. An anarchist movement, inspired in part by the writings of Proudhon, turned its back on electioneering and on reformist trade union activity and urged workers to prepare for direct revolutionary action. "As far as I am concerned, only direct action in the streets can bring about the Revolution," the Lyon anarchist Toussaint Bordat proclaimed in 1886.[2] During the early 1890s, French anarchist militants, like those in other countries, sometimes turned to violent "propaganda of the deed," setting off explosives in public places and staging assassinations in the hope of inspiring workers to revolt against the established order. Their apparent total commitment to the cause of social justice won anarchist terrorists such as Ravachol considerable sympathy among artists and writers who shared a distaste for the hypocrisy of bourgeois society. The assassination of the republican president, Sadi Carnot, in 1894 marked the high point of these anarchist attacks. The government countered with repressive legislation, the so-called *lois scélérates*, which handicapped left-wing political activity and violated the liberal principles proclaimed by the regime. Anarchist violence gradually faded, but such direct action remained a temptation for extremist groups of the left and the far right. The anarchist critique of conventional political action led not only to individualistic violence; it also encouraged trade union organization and direct challenges to employers. In 1890, a number of members quit Brousse's Possibilist movement to follow Jean Allemane, whose *Parti Ouvrier Socialiste Revolutionnaire* emphasized such a policy.

The early 1890s saw steady growth in trade union activity. French workers had learned to use the strike weapon with increasing effectiveness during the 1880s, waiting for moments when employers had little choice but to make concessions. Taking advantage of the 1884 law that legalized such associations, unions—often born as strike committees—became more stable. Alongside the unions, the *bourses de travail*, or labor centers, set up in many industrial cities—often with the support of local governments—served as employment bureaus and defended working-class interests. In 1895, the organization of the *Confédération Générale de Travail (CGT)* gave the labor movement a national structure. Having grown out of the union movement and the experience of the *bourses de travail*, the CGT was heavily influenced by militants convinced that direct economic action was more important than participation in electoral politics. In contrast to the close connection of unions and political parties in Britain and Germany, the French union movement thus remained aloof from the socialist parties. Rather than achieving power through the ballot box, labor militants preached the notion of a general strike. If all workers quit their jobs at once, they could bring the entire bourgeois capitalist system to its knees. The myth of an apocalyptic general strike had a powerful attraction for French workers, who saw themselves excluded from the bourgeois society around them. Syndicalist rhetoric about *le grand soir* which would sweep away the capitalist system also stoked bourgeois fears and contributed to the tense social atmosphere of the period.

The divisions between the union movement and the socialist parties, and the splits among the latter, slowed the growth of all the left-wing organizations. They remained much smaller than in neighboring countries such as Britain or Germany. At the local level, however, the differences in doctrine that divided the various socialist, anarchist, and labor groups often became blurred. Labor militants usually worked together, and the majority of the parliamentary candidates who won election under the socialist label in the 1890s were "independents" who belonged to none of the organized groups, and who were often willing to collaborate with the more radical republicans. Ideological division thus proved less crippling to the growth of socialism and working-class movements than might have been expected.

OUTSIDERS: WOMEN AND CATHOLICS

In the first half of the nineteenth century, the French feminist movement had been closely associated with the development of socialism. After 1870, however, the two became increasingly separated. Some left-wing groups, particularly those influenced by Proudhon, were frankly opposed to an independent social role for women. Jules Guesde, consistent with his reading of Marx's teachings, argued that women's issues were peripheral to the central question of liberating the working class from capitalist exploitation. On the conservative side, the Catholic church continued to command many women's loyalties, but its teachings did not suggest any reconsideration of women's traditional roles. Within the church framework, laywomen were often active in charitable organizations, particularly those that emphasized the maintenance of established social hierarchies. The church also offered women who joined religious orders an alternative to married life. In 1878, nuns outnumbered male clergy, making up 58 percent of the church's personnel. Most of them were teachers in Catholic girls' schools; nursing was another common occupation for nuns. The strong association between women and the church was one reason many republicans and socialists opposed political rights for women. They feared female citizens would support conservatism.

The modern French feminist movement thus developed primarily in the space between the church and the far left. In 1878, just after the collapse of the "Moral Order" government, Maria Deraimes and Léon Richer established republican-oriented feminist groups—the Society to Improve the Condition of Women and Claim Their Rights, and the French League for Women's Rights. Both groups favored gradual reforms, such as the legalization of divorce and improvements in women's property rights. These two leaders opposed the combative Hubertine Auclert, the leading French advocate of voting rights for women. She asked why women should be obliged to pay taxes to a government in which they were not represented. At the 1879 workers' congress that led to the creation of France's first socialist party, Auclert successfully challenged the leaders of the new movement to adopt a feminist program. Despite their inclusion of women's rights in the socialist agenda, however, the socialist movements paid little attention to feminist issues, and women were relegated to a minor role in the parties of the 1890s. The French

feminist movement became primarily a bourgeois affair, in which the problems of working women were treated as secondary. Deraimes's and Richer's groups helped organize a widely publicized in-ternational congress on women's issues, held in conjunction with the Paris world's fair of 1889. In 1891, another bourgeois feminist, Eugénie Potonie-Pierre, organized the Women's Solidarity Group to address the problems of working women—with an eye to keeping them from turning to left-wing ideas. Another important initiative of the period was Marguerite Durand's publication of *La Fronde,* a journal written, edited, and printed exclusively by women which appeared in 1897. A second international women's congress was held in 1900. Bourgeois feminists thus succeeded in bringing "the woman question" into the public eye, but they were unable to overcome the gap between middle-class and working-class concerns—their repeated refusal to endorse proposals for a mandatory day off for domestic servants showed how deep this cleavage was—and the reforms achieved during the period were modest.

Like socialists and feminists, French Catholics remained on the margins of the political system, at least at the national level. During the 1870s, the hostility between the republican movement and the church had been overt and deep-seated. Catholicism was strongly identified with monarchism. Pope Pius IX, the head of the church, had condemned the basic principles of liberalism, democracy, and socialism as contrary to Christian teachings in his *Syllabus of Errors,* issued in 1864. After the republican victory in 1877, most of the Catholic hierarchy urged the faithful to have as little as possible to do with the new institutions. Women, who made up much of the church's base of support, were in any event excluded from political participation. Popular Catholic journalists like Louis Veuillot, whose paper strongly influenced the parish clergy, railed against the republicans and kept alive the hope of a restoration. The Ferry laws, which included measures banning the Jesuits and other Catholic orders that had never obtained government authorization for their activities in France, deepened the gulf between church and state, even though the republican legislators stopped short of an all-out assault on the church. Catholic schools continued to operate, and the Napoleonic Concordat was not abolished—partly in order to leave the government some means of control over the clergy. The fact that many conservative Catholics supported the Boulanger movement kept republican suspicions alive.

In the wake of the Boulanger crisis, Pius IX's successor, Leo XIII, decided that the time was ripe for a serious effort to promote a *ralliement*, or "reconciliation," between Catholics and the new regime. The occasion came when the archbishop of Algiers, Cardinal Lavigerie, was invited to speak to a luncheon of naval officers—most of them Catholic and monarchist in sympathies. The cardinal's words, cleared in advance with the Vatican, surprised his audience. He told them, "when the will of a people has been clearly stated, when the form of government . . . contains nothing in itself contrary to the principles which alone can give life to Christian civilized nations, when there is no other way of saving one's country from the disaster that threatens it than by adhering unreservedly to that form of government, then the moment has come . . . to put an end to our differences."[3]

Although the republican governments of the early 1890s tilted in a conservative direction and often adopted policies (such as the Méline tariff of 1892) that had a strong appeal to many Catholic voters, a genuine reconciliation between Catholics and republicans remained difficult. Educated in a separate school system by teachers who continued to warn against the atheistic tendencies of republicanism and to inculcate a general distrust of modern ideas in their pupils, French Catholics continued to form a world apart, hostile to the political system. Even with Leo XIII's blessing, the idea of *ralliement* failed to take hold.

A similar fate befell the effort of several prominent Catholic laymen and clergy to show that the church could offer meaningful solutions to the periods growing social problems. This Social Catholic movement had roots in the writings of Lamennais and in the philanthropic efforts of Catholics in the 1830s and 1840s who had condemned Guizot's liberalism for its indifference to the fate of the working class. In the 1880s and 1890s, Social Catholicism developed in two directions. An elitist version, led by wealthy noblemen such as Albert de Mun and the Marquis de la Tour du Pin, sought to convince the upper classes of their Christian duty to ameliorate the condition of the poor. At the same time, it tried to win workers away from socialist doctrines of class warfare. De Mun, a deputy, supported legislative measures to provide workers with insurance against accidents, illness, and unemployment at a time when most republicans remained resolutely hostile to what they saw as state interference with the individual rights of employers and workers.

Some supporters of la Tour du Pin's and de Mun's Social Catholic ideas recognized that the organizations they founded to promote them had a fatal weakness. Organized from the top down, they appeared to most workers as thinly disguised efforts to keep them under control. A few priests and the factory owner Léon Harmel urged the formation of genuinely worker-run unions and other organizations, such as youth groups, but the church hierarchy remained suspicious of initiatives not firmly under its control. Marc Sangnier, a charismatic young activist, gave this more democratic branch of Social Catholicism a new impetus at the turn of the century. His movement, the *Sillon* (Furrow), expressed sympathy for revolutionary movements, workers' cooperatives, and pacifism, and urged political cooperation with non-Catholic groups.

Sangnier influenced a generation of young idealists, many of whom would come to prominence after the First World War, but the *Sillon*'s radicalism and its openness to cooperation with non-Catholics led to its being condemned by the Vatican in 1910. The Social Catholic impulse to show that Christianity could contribute significantly to the resolution of modern social problems thus failed to produce real results in the prewar period.

THE FRANCO-RUSSIAN TREATY AND THE FASHODA CRISIS

Domestic issues were not the only ones concerning the French during the 1890s. The period was also a critical one for the definition of France's interests abroad. Decisions taken during these years would eventually lead France into the near-catastrophe of the Great War in 1914. The achievement of national security and defense of the country's standing in world affairs had preoccupied France's leaders ever since the defeat of 1870. The German annexation of Alsace and half of Lorraine was, of course, a painful loss for the French, and one to which public opinion never became fully reconciled. Schoolroom maps marked the "lost provinces" in black and textbooks like the immensely successful *Two Children's Tour of France*—whose child-heroes hailed from Alsace—transmitted the conviction to new generations that those territories were French. But by the 1880s, talk of a war of revenge to regain the lost provinces had cooled. French foreign policy was shaped by perceptions of what was needed to maintain national security and to sustain France's international position, not by an emotional crusade to regain Alsace and Lorraine.

The immediate aftermath of the Franco-Prussian War had left France isolated in Europe. Bismarck, the architect of German unification, worked skillfully to keep France without allies. He succeeded in bringing first Austria-Hungary and then Russia into a system of alliances with Germany, so that France faced a solid bloc of the major continental powers. He also carefully avoided provoking Britain. As long as Bismarck's system prevailed, French options were very limited. Jules Ferry's imperialist policy, justified partly as a means of showing that France could still play a dynamic role in world affairs, threatened to isolate the country even more. It was bound to cause disputes with Britain, the world's other major imperial power. Bismarck discreetly encouraged French overseas expansionism for precisely this reason, while trying to rein in the German colonial lobby to avoid such problems himself. French military planning after 1871 had to take the country's probable isolation in the face of a threat from Germany into account. It was therefore essentially defensive, concentrating on warding off an invasion from the east.

The breakdown of Bismarck's diplomatic system finally allowed France to end its isolation. The weak point of Bismarck's policy was the need to maintain friendly relations with two powers who were at odds with each other, Austria and Russia. The two empires' ambitions clashed in the Balkans, and Germany had to choose which one to favor. By 1887, the Germans made it clear that they would back Austria, and Berlin tried to pressure the Russians by blocking loans to them. The Russian government turned to the Paris market floating an initial loan there in 1888. The Russians at first held back on diplomatic contacts, however. France's democratic and republican constitution was anathema to the absolutist tsarist regime. But fear of isolation in the face of the German-dominated Triple Alliance—which linked Germany, Austria, and Italy—finally drove France and Russia together.

Diplomatic contacts between Paris and St. Petersburg began in 1890. The French fleet visited Russia in 1891, and in 1892, negotiators put together a military convention in which each country promised to come to the aid of the other in case of a German or Austro-Hungarian attack. Government-backed press campaigns, especially in the mass-circulation *Petit Parisien*, gradually moved French public opinion—initially hostile to the tsarist regime—toward acceptance of an alliance. In the French Chamber, deputies did raise questions about the secrecy shrouding details of the treaty, and about the extent of France's commitment (particularly if Russia became involved in a war with Austria over the Balkans, an area in which French interests were limited). But the advantages of the treaty seemed obvious. When Russian sailors visited Paris in 1893, an observer recorded that "the city trembled with joy. . . . There was a new feeling of security, after a long period of isolation."[4] The Franco-Russian Treaty, officially ratified in 1894, seemed to restore the balance between France and Germany. Between 1898 and 1902, the French followed up this achievement by negotiating a rapprochement with their Italian neighbors, with whom a conflict over influence in Tunisia and a long-running tariff dispute had embittered relations.

In the meantime, however, a France rendered more confident by its alliance with Russia had come very close to a war with its imperial rival, Britain. The two countries had had conflicting designs on crucial territory in Africa since the early 1880s. At that time the British had succeeded in gaining predominance in Egypt, a territory the French had had an interest in since Napoleon's day. British imperialists dreamed of acquiring a continuous strip of African territories "from the Cape to Cairo," and building a railroad that would link all their East African holdings. To do so, they needed to control the Sudan, the vast territory along the Nile south of Egypt where native resistance had halted their penetration. Meanwhile, the French (who in the 1880s had expanded their footholds on the West African coast into a

large sub-Saharan empire) sent an expedition to open an east-west route linking those holdings to the colony of Djibouti on the Red Sea. On September 18, 1898, a British expedition headed for the Sudan encountered the French Captain Marchand's small unit at the oasis of Fashoda. Both commanders had orders not to yield, and a showdown seemed inevitable. The press in both countries whipped up bellicose sentiment. In France, where a potent "colonial party" of business interests, publicists, and missionary groups had made imperialism more popular than it had been in the time of Ferry, a hit song hailed "the heroes who crossed Africa and planted the French flag on the banks of the Nile."[5]

Preoccupied by this time with the Dreyfus affair, the French government also recognized that it had dangerously overextended itself in foreign affairs. The country could not simultaneously take on Britain all over the globe and be ready to oppose Germany in Europe. The memory of 1871 ruled out the idea of an anti-British alliance with the Germans, and so the French government decided after several months to back down. An agreement signed in March 1899 recognized Britain's claim to the Sudan. It was the first major initiative of Théophile Delcassé, who was to remain French foreign minister until 1905, and who was to make reconciliation with Britain the centerpiece of French policy.

Notes

1. Cited in Eugen Weber, *Fin du siècle*, P. Belamare, trans. (Paris: Fayard, 1986), 139.

2. Cited in Yves Lequin, *Les Ouvriers de la région lyonnaise* (Lyon: Presses Universitaires de Lyon, 1977), 2:283.

3. Cited in David Thomson, ed., *France: Empire and Republic* (New York: Harper & Row, 1968), 245.

4. Cited in Pierre Milza, *Les relations internationales de 1871 à 1914* (Paris: Colin, 1968), 118–19.

5. Cited in Raoul Girardet, *L'Idée coloniale en France de 1871 à 1962* (Paris: Table Ronde, 1972), 149.

CHAPTER 20

THE TROUBLED YEARS OF THE FIN-DE-SIÈCLE

CULTURAL CURRENTS

Socialist and trade union movements, feminist groups, and conservative Catholics all challenged—in one way or another—the liberal, individualistic assumptions on which the Third Republic was based. By the last decade of the century, those assumptions were also coming under increasing intellectual challenge. The faith in the inevitability of progress, particularly scientific progress, so characteristic of the founders of the Third Republic no longer prevailed. Instead, artists and writers reflected a broader fear that French society, and perhaps the western world generally, had entered a period of decadence in which all values seemed increasingly uncertain.

Wherever they looked, observers of the French social scene in the 1890s claimed to find signs of moral and cultural degeneration. "Populationists" such as Jacques Bertillon lamented France's failure to match the birth rates in rival countries (particularly Germany) as a sign of declining national virility. The country was gripped by a veritable panic about the danger of venereal disease, whose spread appeared to many to threaten the very survival of the French "race." Doctors concurred that they were seeing increased numbers of patients with nervous ailments or "neurasthenia," a condition they diagnosed as a reaction of sensitive souls to the strains of modern urban life. This condition seemed to afflict primarily the wealthier classes, but the health of the poor seemed to be degenerating as well. One concern was the rising per capita consumption of alcoholic beverages, which doubled between the 1830s and the turn of the century thanks to the increasing availability of cheap, mass-manufactured products.

Was life really more difficult for most French men and women at the turn of the twentieth century than it had been fifty or a hundred years earlier? Modern historians who have tried to probe the inner lives of the population have come up with conflicting results. Objective indices show that the population was generally eating somewhat better, living in slightly improved housing, and enjoying a wider range of leisure activities. French historian Alain Corbin notes a growing sense of individual identity, particularly among the bourgeois classes. The spread of photography allowed ordinary people to preserve the record of their individual appearance, while changes in domestic architecture gave more family members private rooms and individual beds. The vogue for tourism, already in evidence during the

Second Empire but greatly expanded in the last decades of the century, showed an increased thirst for individual experiences beyond the routine of work and everyday life. The safety bicycle, popularized after 1890, provided a popular means of escape from a confining environment, as well as giving women justification for abandoning cumbersome corsets. Corbin even produces evidence to argue that both men and women were seeking and obtaining greater sexual pleasure by the end of the century.

These changes were not what impressed most observers at the time, however. To many writers and thinkers of the period, the visible social ills of the time were evidence that trends that had made France an increasingly rationalized, urban society had changed life for the worse. Maurice Barrès, one of the most influential of the new writers to come to prominence in the 1890s, was one of those who castigated the destructive influence of human reason on the healthy energies of the instincts, and deplored the uprooting of the rural population. He denounced the corruption of France's vigorous national instincts by philosophical skepticism—propagated, he claimed, by the Third Republic's secular school system. A more extreme vision of the decadence of modern society appeared in the novels of J. K. Huysmans, such as *A Rebours* and *Là-Bas,* whose protagonists lived in a claustrophobic and irrational atmosphere, cultivating their individual sensibilities to an extreme but separating themselves from the world around them. Like the Symbolist poets whose work Huysmans helped publicize and who achieved prominence at the end of the century—Mallarmé, Verlaine, Rimbaud—Huysmans drew inspiration from the earlier work of Baudelaire. But the new literature of the *fin-de-siècle* went beyond its forebears in the depth of its search for a reality beyond that of outward appearances. Jean Moréas's "Symbolist Manifesto," published in 1886, asserted that intuition, rather than

reason, was the artist's surest path to reality. But that reality could only be expressed indirectly, through symbols, a recipe for a difficult, allusive art that could only be understood by a small elite.

In their rejection of the visible and the rational, the Symbolists turned to mysticism and various forms of occultism which flourished in literary and artistic circles during the 1890s. The painter Gustave Moreau's pictures, which often strove to capture the intensity of visionary experiences, were the visual equivalent of Symbolist poetry. In music, the same tendencies were evident in the cult of the composer Richard Wagner who, despite his association with German nationalism, enthralled the Paris avant-garde with his evocation of a humanity in thrall to dark and mysterious forces. Turn-of-the-century French composers such as Claude Debussy also tried to convey some of the Symbolist message in their works, but they reacted against Wagner's influence by writing for smaller ensembles and using less elaborate orchestration.

Literature and art were not the only domains in which an increased interest in irrational forces could be detected during the 1890s. The sociologist Gustave Le Bon, whose *Crowd Psychology* became a best-seller, gave a gloomy analysis of the characteristics of modern mass society. The masses, he maintained, were fundamentally incapable of rational action, and were easily swayed by appeals to their lower instincts. His pessimistic ideas exercised a certain influence on many of the period's thinkers, including Sigmund Freud.

The greatest French social scientist of the period, Emile Durkheim, was considerably more subtle than Le Bon, and did not share the former's political conservatism. But his work, too, pointed in the direction of diminishing the importance of the individual and of rationalism in the understanding of social phenomena. Durkheim's analysis of religion as a social construct was not a return to traditional patterns of faith—he saw religious beliefs as essentially human in origin—but it cast doubt on the notion of society as a construct of autonomous individuals. Instead, society appeared an organic unity, imposing beliefs on the individuals who composed it. Durkheim's celebrated monograph on suicide, in addition to being an early model of the application of statistical methods to the study of social problems, also suggested the powerlessness of the individual in the face of society. His conclusion was that suicide was a result of *anomie,* or the experience of being isolated and not sharing the beliefs of the community around one. In both his methods and his conclusions, Durkheim was one of the founders of modern sociology. Personally, he was a loyal supporter of republican values, but the implications of his work undermined the faith in individual judgment that lay at the basis of the Third Republic's institutions.

No discussion of French cultural life at the end of the nineteenth century can omit mention of the tremendous burst of creativity in the visual arts that characterized the 1890s. By this time, impressionism was no longer at the forefront of experimentation in the visual arts. In some ways, such as their concern to paint reality the way it appeared to the human eye, the impressionist artists had shared the positivist outlook of the 1870s and 1880s. By 1890, some artists were striving to go beyond the impressionists' methods. These painters were not a cohesive group—in museums, they are usually vaguely labeled "postimpressionists"—but they shared an increasingly radical rejection of past methods, and their works retained an ability to shock that the impressionists had lost.

Paul Cézanne, an older artist of the impressionists' generation, had long been experimenting with canvases in which the objects portrayed seemed to dissolve into the simple geometric forms that underlay them. His work pointed toward the cubism and abstract, nonrepresentational art of the twentieth century, which has come to see him as one of the greatest innovators in the history of painting. Georges Seurat carried the impressionist technique of using small dots of pure color to an extreme, composing large canvases made up entirely of little flecks. This "pointillist" technique gave his works, such as *Sunday in the Park of the Grande Jatte,* a mysterious quality. Everyday scenes, frozen in immobility, took on a monumental air—suggesting some hidden, enigmatic message. The Dutch expatriate Vincent Van Gogh, who lived and worked in France in the last frenzied, creative years of his life, used bright color and emphatic brushstrokes to communicate a furious emotional intensity in his works. The contrast between the quiet serenity of Monet's landscapes and the violent tension suggested in Van Gogh's shows how strongly the new atmosphere of the *fin-de-siècle* differed from what preceded it. Van Gogh for a short time worked together with Paul Gauguin, who shared his interest in color. Gauguin became best known for his paintings of life in Tahiti, the French island colony in the Pacific. Often seen merely as celebrating the beauty and sexual freedom of a primitive people in contrast with the repressed civilization of Europe, Gauguin's work—like Van Gogh's—in fact reflected intense inner struggles, often religious in nature. In one way or another, the postimpressionist painters of the 1890s all reflected a sense of a world that seemed enigmatic and incomprehensible. A troubled spirit underlay the productions that are now regarded as the most original artworks of the period.

The connection between this outburst of creativity, which continued to the outbreak of the First World War, and the society of the Third Republic is anything but clear. The fact that painting had long been regarded as an important form of cultural activity in France (in contrast to the situation in the United States in the nineteenth century) was important. But the official art establishment certainly did not provide innovators with much encouragement. Republican officials patronized conventional painters who decorated public buildings with canvases repeating the tired clichés of neoclassicism or with uninspired history paintings. In the 1890s, conservative republicans supported an arts-and-crafts revival that looked to the delicate craftsmanship of the age of Louis XV for inspiration. Nevertheless, some aspects of French life did provide the basis for the flourishing avant-garde. Particularly in Paris, the network of galleries and dealers was extensive enough so that even the most radical innovators could find some financial backing. And the community of collectors was large enough to provide them with at least a small audience. The concentration of so many artists in one place favored the exchange of inspirations and spread of new ideas. If French society did not exactly embrace artistic experimentation, its respect for individual liberty at least gave it the opportunity to develop. In places like the Parisian neighborhood of Montmartre, artists, poets, and young people eager to flout social conventions clustered in such numbers that they constituted a veritable countersociety, a "Bohemia" in which new ideas could take root. By the end of the century, indeed, the existence of such an artistic milieu was a venerable tradition. The rebellious artist or poet was a long-established social type. "Bohemia" provided a tacitly tolerated escape from the restrictions of conventional society. Only occasionally—as when the young playwright Alfred Jarry had the actors in his play *Ubu Roi* open the show with the word *merdre* (shit) in 1896—did the denizens of Bohemia provoke their more conventional neighbors into a violent response.

DREYFUS

Many of the intellectual and cultural currents of the 1890s played a role in shaping the spectacular crisis that dominated French public opinion at the end of the decade—the Dreyfus affair. For months, France's fate seemed to depend on that of an obscure army captain named Alfred Dreyfus. Writers and artists were among those most engaged in the controversy, which pitted proponents of rationalism and individualism against those who proclaimed that the emotional ties of race and nation were all-important. The Dreyfus affair accelerated political transformations that had begun with Boulanger, and it affected much of French politics and intellectual life well into the twentieth century.

The Dreyfus case began without much fanfare in the summer of 1894, when a cleaning woman in the German Embassy in Paris found documents indicating a German spy had penetrated the offices of the French army general staff. Army investigators' suspicions quickly fastened on Captain Dreyfus, whose handwriting seemed to match that on the cover sheet, or *bordereau*, that the spy had passed to the Germans. There was nothing in Dreyfus's background to motivate such an act of treason, but one thing separated him from most of his fellow officers. They were predominantly Catholic, whereas Dreyfus was Jewish and—since his family came from Alsace—German-speaking.

The accusation that France's defense had been betrayed by a Jew seemed to confirm the warnings that critics of the Republic's liberal values had been spreading. Anti-Semitism had strong appeal to a variety of groups. The journalist Edouard Drumont's best-seller *La France juive*, published in 1886, had crystallized a new kind of prejudice against France's Jewish minority. To the traditional religious accusations against the Jews Drumont had added new assertions. Jewish bankers were the promoters of an exploitative capitalism that was destroying traditional French society, Drumont alleged. They were aliens who could never really form part of the French nation. They dominated the press and were poisoning the wells of French culture.

Drumont's ideas found an echo in much of the Catholic press, whose journalists found it easy to charge that Jews—along with other opponents of the church such as Protestants and Freemasons—were behind the Republic's anticlerical laws. To conservatives, nationalists, and many Catholics imbued with religious anti-Semitism, Dreyfus's "treason" confirmed that the liberal and republican principles of liberty and equality were leading the country to disaster. The Dreyfus affair revealed the extent of popular anti-Semitism. There were anti-Semitic demonstrations in at least seventy French cities in 1898 at the height of the agitation about the case. The most violent occurred among the French settlers in Algeria. It was his observation of anti-Semitic prejudice in France during the early stages of the Dreyfus case that led Austrian-Jewish journalist Theodor Herzl to conclude that Jews could never become truly accepted in predominantly Christian countries—even those like France whose laws accorded them civil equality. In 1896, Herzl published *The Jewish State*, a pamphlet advocating the establishment of an independent Jewish settlement that launched the modern Zionist movement of Jewish nationalism.

The anti-Semitic press noisily celebrated Dreyfus's conviction before a military tribunal and his sentence to life imprisonment on Devil's Island, a notorious prison off the coast of French Guiana. Initially, few outside of Dreyfus's immediate family questioned his guilt. Even the representatives of France's Jewish community, alarmed by the rise of anti-Semitism, carefully avoided appearing to come to the defense of a convicted traitor. But from the start, questions had been raised about the evidence used against Dreyfus and the conditions under which he had been sentenced. As months went by, a small group of determined supporters gained ground in their effort to get the case reopened. A Jewish journalist, Bernard Lazare, broke with the prevailing silence in his community and published pamphlets showing how flimsy the case against Dreyfus was. A republican senator, Auguste Scheurer-Kestner, undertook his own inquiries and began lobbying his colleagues to look into the matter. Within the army, an independent-minded officer, Colonel Picquart, became aware that some of the evidence against Dreyfus had been forged. Furthermore, a new suspect—Colonel Esterhazy—had emerged, whose handwriting resembled that of the spy. Esterhazy, burdened with gambling debts, fit the classic profile of a potential security risk much better than Dreyfus.

By the end of 1897, Dreyfus's conviction had become increasingly controversial. But powerful forces opposed a reopening of the case. The military high command justified its reluctance by claiming that an admission of such a serious error would destroy public faith in the army and thus undermine the nation's defense. Jurists and politicians insisted on the importance of maintaining the principle that legal decisions, once arrived at by the proper procedures, had to be upheld, lest the authority of the courts be subverted. And the case was ready-made to mobilize a variety of constituencies on the right. The fact that Dreyfus was Jewish, and that his most prominent defenders included non-Catholics such as Lazare and the Protestant Scheurer-Kestner, drove Catholics to oppose the "revisionists" who wanted to reopen the matter. Ultranationalists like Déroulède leaped to the defense of the army, "our last honor, our last recourse, our ultimate safeguard."[1] The nationalist writer Maurice Barrès defended Dreyfus's conviction in the name of "French truth, that is, what is most useful to the nation."[2]

While opposition to any revision of the Dreyfus judgment provided a natural rallying point for conservatives and nationalists, the demand for justice for Dreyfus gradually mobilized a movement as well. The trial of Esterhazy in January 1898, accused on the basis of considerable evidence of having been the real spy, proved a turning point in the affair. Dreyfus's supporters had been convinced that he would be convicted, which would automatically have forced a revision of Dreyfus's conviction (since Esterhazy was accused of the crime for which Dreyfus had been imprisoned). When the military court unexpectedly acquitted Esterhazy, however, the Dreyfusards had to adopt new tactics. On the day after Esterhazy's acquittal, the celebrated French novelist Emile Zola took the initiative in challenging the verdict. In a front-page editorial in *Aurore,* a daily paper edited by the veteran Radical Georges Clemenceau, Zola charged high-ranking army officers and magistrates of having knowingly participated in a perversion of justice. Zola's editorial, titled *"J'accuse,"* had an impact that few other newspaper columns have ever matched. As the novelist had expected, it provoked the government into bringing charges against him, which permitted a renewed debate over the case. It also served to generate a massive public mobilization in favor of Dreyfus, which was matched by an increasingly intense opposition.

Both sides contributed to the development of a new form of mass politics increasingly independent of conventional political parties. On both sides, leagues intended to influence public opinion rather than to run candidates for elections became the key organizations. Dreyfus's supporters joined such organizations as the League for the Defense of the Rights of Man. His opponents supported Déroulède's League of Patriots, the *Ligue de la Patrie française,* or a newly founded monarchist organization, *Action française,* which was destined for a long career in French public life. Both sides pressed their cause by mass rallies and intense press propaganda. And both sides were led largely by men who defined themselves in a new way—as intellectuals, a category destined to a special role in public affairs because of their education and intelligence, rather than because of their ownership of property or their social position. The politically committed intellectual, ready to risk himself for the sake of his moral principles as Zola had done, was largely a creation of the Dreyfus affair.

In the wake of Zola's initiative, the Dreyfus affair grew from a campaign against an act of injustice to a struggle over the nature of French society. The "Affair" dominated public life for months, dividing families and friends. For those who were active on either side, it was an experience of an intensity that would never be matched again. Although Zola was actually convicted of slandering the military court, the aftermath of his trial produced proof that some of the crucial evidence against Dreyfus had been forged. The forger, Captain Henry, committed suicide. Even after this, the army refused to absolve Dreyfus. He was brought back from Devil's Island and granted a new trial in 1899, which resulted in a renewed conviction. Many of his supporters urged him to refuse a presidential pardon and insist on having his name cleared, but Dreyfus—in broken health after four years of imprisonment—decided to accept the pardon while continuing to protest his innocence. He was finally cleared of all wrongdoing in 1906.

At the time, the Dreyfus affair seemed to be a victory for the ideal of individual rights. In the face of the combined opposition of the army, the church, the court system, and most politicians, the private citizens who had taken up Dreyfus's cause had launched the first modern crusade for human rights and had ultimately prevailed. The case attracted international attention and rejuvenated France's reputation as the homeland of the Rights of Man for decades afterward. Since 1945, however, historians have been more inclined to note the long-range impact of the groups that condemned Dreyfus. Unsuccessful in preventing the revision of the Dreyfus verdict, they nevertheless

A few weeks after the publication of novelist Emile Zola's fiery editorial, "J'Accuse," a popular Paris humor magazine showed a husband and wife quarreling over the Dreyfus affair. The husband has a portrait of Zola on his wall, the wife one of Major Esterhazy, the actual spy. The portrayal of the wife as an anti-Dreyfusard reflects the prevailing assumption that women were generally supportive of conservative groups, such as the Catholic Church. (Photo credit: Bibliothèque nationale, Paris.)

created a new model for right-wing, anti-democratic, and antiparliamentarist politics, and it has often been argued that republican France thus became the birthplace of twentieth-century fascism.

Anti-liberal tendencies associated with the Dreyfus affair scored a notable victory in Algeria, where anti-Jewish riots in 1898 had developed into a movement for autonomy on the part of the European colonists. To quiet these street protests, the French government announced in August 1898 the creation of an elected assembly that the European settlers would control. Two years later, French Algeria was given special legal status and its own budget. The Algerian colonists were thus largely free to run their own affairs and dominate the much more numerous Muslim population.

THE BLOC RÉPUBLICAIN

In metropolitan France, the main effect of the anti-Dreyfusard agitation in 1899 was to weld together a powerful prorepublican countermovement in response to outrages like a nationalist crowd's assault on the president of the Republic, Emile Loubet, in early 1899. In this atmosphere, republicans of all stripes and much of the socialist movement came together on a common platform of defense of republican and democratic institutions. Once again, as in the militant phase of the republican movement in the 1870s and 1880s, their supporters acted on the principle that there were "no enemies on the left," and that, in run-offs during parliamentary elections, socialist and republican voters should automatically unite behind whichever of their candidates had the best chance of winning—a tactic known as "republican discipline."

This common front on the left led to the formation in 1899 of a new cabinet, headed by Waldeck-Rousseau, dedicated to a policy of "republican defense." Waldeck-Rousseau's ministers reflected the full spectrum of groups that had come to see the anti-Dreyfusard agitation as an assault on the Republic itself. The Cabinet ran from General Galliffet, a conservative republican despised by the socialists as "the butcher of the Commune" because of his role in 1871, to Alexander Millerand, an independent socialist deputy who became the first member of that movement to hold ministerial office. Millerand's acceptance of office was controversial in the socialist movement. Followers of Guesde condemned him for cooperating with bourgeois politicians, particularly men like Galliffet. But the rising socialist spokesman Jean Jaurès, a more flexible tactician, quietly encouraged this experiment to see whether the democratic parliamentary system could be used to produce significant social reforms.

The Waldeck-Rousseau government was determined to face down antirepublican forces that had surfaced during the Dreyfus affair. It sternly repressed right-wing agitators in the streets and shook up the army officer corps, removing officers who had been willing to go to extremes to defend the Dreyfus verdict. But the government's main thrust was against the church. The Assumptionist order, whose popular newspaper *La Croix* had been one of the main channels of anti-Semitic and anti-Dreyfus propaganda, was dissolved in 1900. A new law on associations passed in 1901 tightened controls on the remaining congregations. In 1902, illness forced Waldeck-Rousseau to step down in favor of an even more militantly anticlerical republican, Emile Combes. Exasperated by the church's hostility, Combes eventually decided to completely change the ground rules of church-state relations. In 1904, his government broke relations with the Vatican. In 1905, the Assembly voted to nullify the Concordat which had governed church-state relations since Napoleon's day, and to carry out a separation of church and state.

Subsequent events were to prove that the separation enacted in 1905, rather than damaging the church, freed it from constant involvement in political controversy. In the combative atmosphere of the time, however, the enforcement of the separation law inspired intense resistance. The law forced the closing of numerous Catholic schools whose teachers were nuns, and it required the church to allow civil officials to make an inventory of church property. In strongly Catholic regions like the Nord and Brittany, supporters barricaded their churches to keep government officials out. There were armed clashes and even a few deaths. The violence subsided once the inventory process was concluded, but the struggle had served to reinforce the divisions in French life generated by the Dreyfus affair. Devout Catholics continued to feel alienated from the "godless" French state, while republicans remained convinced that the church formed a hostile bloc whose influence had to be kept to a minimum. Public school textbooks, which had given religion a rather neutral treatment since the 1880s, were edited to eliminate religious references altogether. The popular *Two Children's Tour of France* was revised so that its two heroes no longer visited the famous churches in the towns they passed through.

In carrying out their measures to restrict the church's public influence, the Waldeck-Rousseau and Combes ministries were able to count on solid support from both socialist and Radical deputies, who shared a common antipathy to the church. The atmosphere of republican militancy born in the Dreyfus struggle encouraged both these groups to organize themselves more effectively. In 1901, the Radicals—who up to that point had been nothing more than a loose network of deputies, journalists, and local clubs united on a vague platform of anticlericalism and loyalty to republican institutions—formed themselves into a cohesive political party. It was the first such modern, structured party in French history. The group's name, the Radical and Radical-Socialist party, showed that it hoped to appeal to a broad coalition ranging from factory workers to small businessmen, property-owning peasants, and small-town professionals who provided so many of its deputies.

The Radicals' program was never spelled out in detail, but its guiding spirit was the doctrine of "solidarism," articulated by one of the movement's senior figures, Léon Bourgeois. At the 1901 party congress, Bourgeois called for a society in which the rights of property were defended, but in which a democratically governed state intervened to make sure that the poor and the weak were not trampled underfoot by more powerful groups. He looked forward to what later came to be called the "welfare state," calling for government-provided social insurance programs and progressive taxation, so that members of all classes would realize they had a stake in the existing order. To ensure the spirit of national solidarity, the Radicals called for a unified elementary school system that would teach all French children their rights and their duties to the national community.

The Radicals' promise of gradual reform gave them a broad base of support. They occupied a pivotal position in the French political system down to the end of the Third Republic. But the very breadth and diversity of the party's support tended to dilute its effectiveness. The Radicals never imposed strict party discipline on their parliamentary deputies, who remained free to vote against laws implementing the reform promises in its electoral program—or to pursue their personal political ambitions at the expense of the party's agenda. To maintain its control in the Senate, dominated by small-town notables, the party frequently allied with more conservative groups to block progressive reforms. Eventually, the Radicals came to symbolize the political weaknesses of the French parliamentary system as a whole, and its inability to translate words into action.

In the first years of the new century, however, the rise of the Radicals seemed to offer an opportunity for significant changes in French society. Together with the deputies of the various socialist groups, the Radicals firmly controlled the Chamber of Deputies. The reformist cause found a powerful and attractive leader in the socialist deputy Jean Jaurès, who exercised a decisive influence. This was true despite the fact he did not even hold a deputy's seat between 1898 and 1902 and was never in the ministry. Jaurès's broad-minded conception of democratic socialism, his personality, and his death at the hands of an assassin in 1914 have combined to give him an aura unique among Third Republic politicians. Even for many outside France, his memory long represented all that was best in the progressive tradition.

In his own lifetime, Jaurès was a more controversial figure. Born to a modest bourgeois family in the southern town of Castres in 1859, Jaurès had come to socialism relatively late, after an educational career that had culminated in entry to the prestigious *Ecole normale supérieure.* There, he was part of a remarkable class that included the sociologist Emile Durkheim and the philosopher Henri Bergson. Returning to his native region as a schoolteacher, Jaurès entered politics in 1885, winning election as a republican deputy with support from local workers as well as bourgeois voters. In the 1890s, the increasingly intense conflicts between workers and employers that characterized his native region's mines and factories made him more aware of social problems.

It was during this period that Jaurès first read the writings of Karl Marx and became converted to socialism, but his ideas were considerably more supple than those of Jules Guesde. For Jaurès, socialism meant a crusade for moral justice as much as a struggle against economic oppression. In his view, the socialist movement needed to reach out to other classes besides industrial workers.

He urged socialists to articulate a program that dealt with the problems of small farmers, and to be ready to cooperate with members of "bourgeois" political parties to carry out progressive reforms. He argued that the apparatus of government could be used to carry out measures that would benefit workers, even without a total socialist takeover. A systematic refusal to work within the system, as the Guesdists advocated, would only harm workers' interests.

Jaurès's growing influence within the French socialist movement during the 1890s was due not only to his imaginative adaptation of socialist doctrines to French realities but to his powerful personality. Whether addressing striking miners at Carmaux in his home district or speaking in the Chamber of Deputies, he was a spellbinding orator, the embodiment of the fiery eloquence that the French often attribute to men from the *Midi.* Firm in defense of his own principles, he nevertheless avoided bitter quarrels with opponents. When the founders of the CGT rejected any link between political and union activity in 1895, Jaurès still kept up good relations with their leaders. He worked effectively with socialist leaders from other countries in the meetings of the Second International, founded in 1889, to unite socialists throughout the world.

Once converted to the Dreyfusard cause, Jaurès sought to bring the socialist movement as a whole into the campaign. At the same time, he used the opportunity to create a genuine alliance between socialists and republicans to bring about significant social reforms. The government of republican defense was the instrument through which Jaurès hoped to demonstrate the possibility of effective cooperation between socialists and republicans. After the 1902 elections, which saw Jaurès's return to the Chamber, socialist and republican groups formed a committee, the *Délégation des Gauches* (Delegation of the Left), to set policy.

Through the force of his personality, Jaurès largely dominated its activities. The Dreyfus crisis had thus created an almost unprecedented situation in the Third Republic's history. For once, a strong and cohesive coalition controlled the Chamber and was able to carry through a consistent set of policies.

The *Bloc républicain* was ultimately doomed by its members' inability to agree on a program that went beyond laws against the church and the strengthening of republican sentiments in the army. Jaurès's gamble was that the Radicals would be willing to transcend their characteristic narrow economic liberalism. Within the cabinet, the independent socialist Millerand had proposed measures that became a test of the Radicals' intentions. He sought to give labor unions more rights, and to have the government encourage collective bargaining as an alternative to strikes and labor violence. In the course of 1903 and 1904, it became increasingly apparent that these hopes were in vain. With the right-wing threat apparently under control, the Radicals and the moderate republicans saw no need to abandon their traditional emphasis on limitation of government involvement in economic matters. Millerand's proposals were also rejected by trade union activists faithful to the doctrine that unions should remain apolitical. Rather than coming closer together, as Jaurès had hoped, socialists and bourgeois republicans once more began to move apart.

Notes

1. Cited in Raoul Girardet, *Le nationalisme français* (Paris: Seuil, 1983), 177.

2. Cited in Zeev Sternhell, *Le droite révolutionnaire* (Paris: Seuil, 1978), 170.

CHAPTER 21

THE *BELLE ÉPOQUE*

The years from 1905 until the outbreak of war in 1914 have gone down in French memory as the *belle époque,* the "good period," remembered as a period of peace and prosperity sharply interrupted by the disaster of war. It is true that these years were a time of increasing economic prosperity and technological progress, but they were also marked by social conflicts and growing concern about international tensions. The retrospective glow that colors this period comes above all from the contrast with the years of war and depression that followed it.

THE SECOND INDUSTRIAL REVOLUTION IN FRANCE

By the first decade of the twentieth century, France was experiencing the impact of a series of new technological developments often labeled the "second industrial revolution." The first industrial revolution, which had reached France in the first half of the nineteenth century, had involved chiefly the exploitation of steam power, the mechanization of textile production, and the introduction of the railroad. The second revolution was characterized by the development of new industries that exploited the scientific advances of the nineteenth century, particularly in the areas of

electricity and chemistry, and new inventions such as the internal combustion engine, which made automobiles and airplanes possible. The Paris International Exposition of 1900 emphasized the wonders of electric lighting, and the need to transport the thousands of visitors whom it brought to the city led to the construction of the first lines of the Paris subway, the *Métro,* which used electricity to power its trains. Electricity and advances in chemistry were both essential for the development of the film and the projectors that made motion pictures possible. France was an early leader in this industry. The Lumière brothers showed the first movies in 1895, and another Frenchman, the pioneering filmmaker Georges Meliès, played a key role in demonstrating the possibilities of this new medium. The growth of the French motion picture industry from the 1890s to 1914 was one example of the way new technological advances marked the period. It owed much to the contributions of the Lumière brothers, manufacturers of photographic film who were based in Lyon. The Lumière brothers' original enterprise was a typical example of the new type of manufacturing, characteristic of the second industrial revolution. Filmmaking was a chemical process, and one heavily dependent on new scientific discoveries. Together with Thomas

Edison in the United States, the Lumières were among the first to develop methods for stringing multiple photographs together and showing them on a screen so as to give the illusion of motion. The new industry grew rapidly in the first decade of the twentieth century and, thanks to the Lumières and Georges Meliès, France held a leading place in it up to 1914.

French manufacturers were also highly successful in several other new industries. In 1913, France was second only to the United States in the manufacture of automobiles, another product made possible by innovations associated with the second industrial revolution. In this case, the innovation was development of compact, lightweight internal combustion engines starting in the 1880s. French firms such as Renault, which grew from making six cars a year in 1898 to producing 4,481 in 1913, were renowned for the high technological level of their products. French interest in automobiles was furthered by the Michelin tire company, whose familiar symbol, "Bibendum," a figure constructed out of rubber tires, was invented in 1898. By publishing guides listing hotels, garages, and tourist attractions, Michelin encouraged motoring; images in its advertising suggested that this was an activity through which successful men—women were never shown behind the wheel of a car—could assert their social status.

The French success in several important sectors of the modern economy demonstrates that the country was not inherently unable to compete in the new economic environment of the turn of the century. But it is easy to exaggerate the degree of French economic modernization in this period. French industrial development was very uneven. At the forefront in filmmaking and automobile manufacture, France lagged far behind other industrial nations in the adoption of other new technologies of the period, such as the telephone. And, unlike the American Henry Ford, the French auto manufacturers did not adopt mass production methods to bring down the prices of their products and open up a larger market for them. Indeed, the production of traditional luxury items—elaborate jewelry and expensive silk—remained a key sector of the French economy and helps explain the fact that many French enterprises remained small in scale, turning out goods that depended on a high degree of craftsmanship. French peasant farmers clung to their small properties and their preindustrial practices and, as a result, they failed to provide a dynamic domestic market for the country's manufacturers. New, productive industries were also highly concentrated in a few favored regions—notably in Paris (whose share of the total national population continued to grow), in the steel-making region of Lorraine, and around Lyon and Grenoble.

Economic expansion brought with it mixed consequences for the different groups in the French population. As businessmen saw new opportunities for expansion, the industrial workforce, which had stagnated since the late 1870s, grew rapidly. It expanded by more than 1,300,000 from 1896 to 1911 even though population growth remained very slow. The increase came mainly from more extensive employment of women and from immigration. Women made up more than half the workforce in the textile industry and in several other major trades, such as tobacco working. Often employed at home or in crowded sweatshops in urban areas, they were invariably paid less than men. The growing number of women in the industrial workforce inspired a major national debate. Middle-class reformers expressed dismay about a phenomenon which they blamed for taking women out of their proper sphere in the home and lowering the national birth rate. Male workers, particularly those in the more highly paid skilled trades that had traditionally barred women, also supported limitations on women's work, fearing their employment would lead to lower wages.

Foreign Immigration

The influx of foreign workers also caused debate and conflict. The French experience was part of a worldwide pattern in which members of poverty-stricken populations in Europe's less industrialized regions flowed to areas of economic growth. Just as poor Italians and East European Jews moved to the United States during this period, they also poured into France—along with Belgian migrants who settled primarily in the northern departments near their home country and Spaniards who concentrated in the *Midi.* The Italian workers, most numerous in the southeast, were often brought in to do poorly paid, exhausting manual labor that French workers were reluctant to perform. They encountered considerable prejudice and were sometimes targets of ethnic violence. French workers blamed them for undercutting wages, but the Italians often joined radical organizations and resisted employers' demands more vehemently than their French colleagues. The Jewish immigrants settled primarily in the poor neighborhoods of Paris and worked in artisans' trades, such as textiles. Their presence changed the nature of France's Jewish community. The new arrivals were considerably poorer and less assimilated than the long-established French Jewish population. The fourth *arrondissement* neighborhood where these Jewish immigrants concentrated, the Pletzl, has now become a Paris tourist attraction, although the Jewish population that now lives there is more often recent immigrants than descendants of the arrivals during the *belle époque.* Immigrants played an essential role in making economic growth possible, but the hostile reaction to their presence was the first sign of a pattern of nativist reaction that has reappeared as successive immigrant groups have settled in France.

For the working class in general, economic growth had paradoxical results. Workers' living conditions, which had remained stable or even improved slightly in the 1880s and 1890s because of falling prices, did not always improve in the years of expansion. The cost of living rose faster than wages from 1902 onward. After nearly a century of general price stability, France began to experience the steady inflation which—accelerated enormously by the First World War—characterized its economy until the 1980s. The Third Republic's legislators were not, as is sometimes alleged, completely indifferent to workers' problems. But the legislation they passed—an initial law on factory sanitation in 1894, a law making employers responsible for providing safe working conditions in 1898, a law limiting working hours to ten a day in 1900, an old-age pension law in 1910—came slowly. These laws were often passed years after comparable legislation in Britain and Germany, and enforcement was often inadequate. Meanwhile, the period's economic expansion certainly benefited the middle classes, and even more so the wealthy. Industrial profits rose sharply, and the very rich appropriated the largest share of this new wealth. In the short run, rather than easing social tensions, the economic growth at the beginning of the century set the stage for sharper confrontations.

THE YEARS OF PROTESTS

Although hindsight makes it clear that the French economic pie was growing in the years from 1905 to 1914, disputes about how it should be divided intensified for much of this period. Socialist militants, workers, and even a substantial fraction of the peasantry were now ready to take direct action to obtain their aims. On the other hand, the bourgeois supporters of the Radical party were now prepared to back a government that would firmly defend order and property, just as the more conservative Progressist republicans had in the early 1890s. As so often in French history, however, the dramatic gestures and rhetoric of the period did not tell the whole story. There were also some constructive compromises between rival social and political movements. At the moment when war broke out in 1914, it was uncertain whether France was poised on the brink of significant social conflict or significant reform.

The breakup of the Republican Defense coalition and the beginning of the new political period were precipitated by the end of collaboration between Jaurès's socialists and the government. This was a result of increasing frustration in the socialist rank and file with the results of Jaurès's reformist policy. The 1904 congress of the international socialist movement voted to condemn socialists who supported "bourgeois" governments, thus rejecting both Millerand and Jaurès. It sternly urged the French socialists, divided into a Jaurèsian reformist party and Guesde's "revolutionary" group, to unify themselves.

Rather than find himself outside the socialist movement, Jaurès bowed to these demands. He was then able to achieve another of the goals he had long sought. In April 1905, the longdivided French socialists for the first time created a unified party, the SFIO (*Section française de l'Internationale ouvrière*, or French Section of the Workingmen's International), commonly known as the Socialist party. Its program, promising "fundamental and unyielding opposition to the whole of the bourgeois class and to the State which is its instrument,"[1] was Guesdist in tone. But Jaurès was its principal leader and the party reflected his tendency to combine socialism and republican democracy. The party's increasingly diverse electoral base, which included not only industrial workers but also civil servants and schoolteachers who had a vested interest in the existing system, and peasants who were concerned with maintaining their small properties, ruled out a real revolutionary attitude. Internally, the SFIO had also adopted the procedures of parliamentary democracy. It accustomed its members to settling disputes through open debate and the casting of ballots. Increasingly, the revolutionary rhetoric of socialist manifestos was at odds with the party's reformist practices, a contradiction that was characteristic of French socialism throughout much of the twentieth century.

That the formation of the SFIO would in the end lead to a shift in the direction of reformism was certainly not clear in the middle years of the new century's first decade, however. From 1904 on, the number of strikes mounted every year. Employers and the government, freed from concern about the socialists' reaction, met these movements with increasing severity, and often the result was violence. In Limoges, a center of labor militancy, an employers' lockout in April 1905 set off a virtual insurrection, with workers building barricades in the streets. The army was called in to restore order, and one worker was killed. The strike wave brought hundreds of new members into the CGT, the national trade union federation founded in 1895. The CGT's call for a national general strike to demand an eight-hour working day on May 1, 1906 raised tension in the country to a peak. Union militants hoped, and timid bourgeois feared, that the protest would turn into the revolutionary general strike that syndicalists had long preached. In the end, it resulted in large demonstrations and scattered violence but no insurrection. In retrospect, its long-term impact was to strengthen the reformist tendencies within the union movement, parallel to those in the SFIO. Like that party, the union movement attracted growing numbers of members from groups who, in practice, had little to gain from revolutionary disruption. Unions representing groups such as postal workers, teachers, and employees in state-regulated industries such as the railroads became large components of the CGT by 1910. Although they occasionally staged significant strikes, their strategy was to generate political pressure on the government to grant their demands, rather than to destroy the capitalist economic system.

Revolutionary Syndicalism and the Action Française

One reaction against the CGT's drift toward reformism after the strike wave of 1904–1906 was the development of a new doctrine of revolutionary syndicalism. The leading figures in this movement were labor militants such as Gustave Hervé, who had been repeatedly jailed for his agitational activities. The idea of the general strike as a myth that could galvanize the working class was articulated most forcefully by the renegade anarchist Georges Sorel in *On Violence,* published in 1908. But his formulation had little direct impact on the labor movement. From the failure of the period's strikes, the revolutionary syndicalists concluded that the mass of the workers could never be mobilized against the existing social system through conventional forms of propaganda. Only a dedicated revolutionary minority, acting on its own, could provide the spark for a genuine social revolution.

Emerging on the extreme left of the French political spectrum, these antidemocratic and antirationalist ideas had a certain affinity with the outlook of the most extreme right-wing movements of the period, of which the most important was the *Action française.* Founded in 1899 to publish a conservative magazine, the group soon came under the leadership of a powerful ideologue, Charles Maurras, whose ideas guided it until its demise after the Second World War. Maurras preached a thoroughgoing rejection of republicanism and democracy. In their place, he called for a return to monarchy, not out of a traditionalist devotion to the French past, but because only an authoritarian leader could make France strong again. On this basis, Maurras constructed a cohesive nationalist doctrine, calling for the exclusion of foreigners, or *métèques* (he considered Jews the most dangerous), from the

country, the abolition of democratic institutions, and the total subordination of individual rights to national considerations.

Aware that his ideas could never command majority support, Maurras advocated violent means of agitation through which an activist minority could impose itself. These antidemocratic tactics, derived from those of the anti-Dreyfusard leagues of the 1890s, foreshadowed the methods of Mussolini and Hitler later in the twentieth century. In 1908 the movement, already in possession of a daily newspaper, created groups of armed toughs, the *Camelots du Roi,* who not only distributed its propaganda but fought street battles against its opponents. The *Action française* exercised a particular appeal to students and intellectuals, who often saw in it the only ideologically coherent alternative to left-wing radicalism. In the years before the war of 1914, *Action française* activists drove several Jewish professors from their classrooms at the Sorbonne and created a highly polarized atmosphere in the Paris intellectual world. Often tolerated or covertly supported by more conventional conservatives who criticized its methods but not its choice of targets, the movement kept the violent, anti-Semitic spirit of the anti-Dreyfus campaign alive for decades afterward. After the First World War, the rise of the Italian Fascist leader Benito Mussolini, formerly a left-wing socialist, demonstrated the dangerous significance of this fusion of extremes. In prewar France, however, revolutionary syndicalism remained a minority within the labor movement. Conservative groups, despite occasional gestures of sympathy toward the proletariat, never converted themselves into mass movements with a lower-class base.

Peasant Protests

The largest and most violent protest movement of these troubled years arose not among the urban working class, but in the wine-growing region of Lower Languedoc. After the *phylloxera* epidemic, this part of southern France had become a center of massive, industrial-style wine production, turning out a cheap, low-quality product for everyday consumption. Workers on the large grape plantations and the small independent growers who were still numerous shared a common interest in the price of their product. But overproduction and increased foreign competition caused an acute crisis after 1903. A charismatic café owner named Marcellin Albert (hailed as "the Redeemer" by his followers) and the socialist mayor of Narbonne, Ferroul, organized a protest movement whose rallies gathered as many as a half million supporters at their peak in the spring of 1907. Albert flirted with revolutionary rhetoric, urging his supporters to withhold taxes to obtain their demands. At moments, it seemed as if the government's authority was crumbling in the face of the wine revolt. One army regiment mutinied for fear of being ordered to fire on protesters, citizens of the same region from which the soldiers came. Government firmness, the discrediting of Albert, who had visited Prime Minister Clemenceau in Paris (and embarrassed his followers by allowing him to pay for his return train ticket), and measures that furthered a rise in prices after 1907 drained the movement of its militancy. Subsequent French governments down to the present, however, have repeatedly had to deal with militant peasant groups using direct-action tactics like those pioneered by Albert.

Coupled with disturbances caused by implementation of the laws separating church and state, the explosion of protests in the middle years of the twentieth century's first decade gave the impression that France was once again poised on the brink of a major crisis. The Radical government stood firm, however, and, as it became clear that strikes and demonstrations would not sway it, the social atmosphere gradually calmed down. The politician most closely identified

with the tempering of these protests was the veteran Radical leader Georges Clemenceau. His long period in office, from 1906–1909, was another example of the Third Republic's often underestimated capacity for generating strong leadership in critical situations. At the age of sixty-four, Clemenceau obtained a ministerial post for the first time under the colorless Jean Sarrien in early 1906. As minister of the interior, Clemenceau had to deal with numerous strikes sweeping the country's industrial regions. One was the miners' strike set off by the horrendous disaster at Courrières in the Nord in March 1906, in which some eleven hundred coal miners were killed. Although Clemenceau had a reputation as a man of the left, sympathetic to the problems of the lower classes, he quickly demonstrated that he belonged to the Jacobin tradition of leaders who believed the state's authority had to be maintained at all costs. He made free use of the police and the army to confront strikers. As the CGT prepared its nationwide strike on May 1, 1906, Clemenceau told its general secretary, Jean Griffuelhes, "Your method of action is to create disorder; my duty is to keep order."[2] He was as good as his word, and the result was several violent clashes between demonstrators and police, earning him the sobriquet "Top Cop of France" and the lasting hatred of the socialists and trade unionists.

The Sarrien government soon dissolved, and Clemenceau now received his chance to step up to the premiership. He came into office promising not only to continue his policy of containing protests, but also indicating he would introduce significant reforms along the lines of "solidarism" to deal with their root causes. His ministerial colleagues included many of the most promising young politicians of the day. Men such as Aristide Briand and Joseph Caillaux would occupy key positions in subsequent governments. He also created a new Ministry of Labor, entrusted to the independent socialist René Viviani, to indicate his determination to deal with workers' problems. Often hamstrung by the conservative sentiments of the Senate, however, Clemenceau failed to carry through major reforms. An example was the progressive income tax bill introduced by his finance minister, Caillaux, and voted by the Chamber of Deputies in 1907, but held up in the Senate until after the outbreak of the First World War.

If he failed to significantly alter the country's social stalemate, Clemenceau did demonstrate that the Third Republic's institutions were still sufficient to deal with labor militancy and social violence. After one particularly bloody clash between strikers and troops at Villeneuve-Saint-Georges in 1908, Clemenceau even had the leaders of the CGT arrested for provoking insurrection. The result of the government's stern attitude, continued by Clemenceau's successor Aristide Briand, who broke a nationwide rail strike in 1910, was to divide militant union leaders still committed to a policy of revolutionary action from the mass of their followers, who came to recognize the futility of violent agitation. Both in the southern wine country and in industrial regions, the social climate calmed considerably in the course of Clemenceau's premiership, which lasted until July 1909.

In the five years after the end of Clemenceau's ministry, the fate of domestic reform movements remained uncertain. The movement for women's suffrage was among those that seemed to be gradually moving toward success during this period. French women's groups, divided along lines of class and religion and smaller in numbers than those in the United States or England, nevertheless succeeded in obtaining increasing support and publicity for women's suffrage. In 1914, 500,000 women participated in a mail campaign to show support for a bill granting them the right to vote, and the first sizeable public demonstration for the cause was held just days before the outbreak of the First World War. From 1910 to 1914, political leadership alternated between conservative premiers like Aristide Briand and Raymond Poincaré on the one hand, and more reform-minded ministers such as Joseph Caillaux (chief proponent of a progressive income tax) and the independent socialist René Viviani (a strong advocate of women's suffrage who took office just before the start of the war). Whether the combination of a growing mass movement and sympathetic politicians would have been sufficient to pass a women's suffrage law had the war not intervened is uncertain. But the war crisis disrupted this and a number of other reform efforts.

The Republican Empire

The years from 1870–1900 had seen an enormous growth in the size of France's colonial empire. At the end of the Second Empire, France's colonies had occupied about one million square kilometers, with a total population of five million; by 1900, the figures were ten million square kilometers and more than sixty million people. France's colonial holdings were second only to those of Britain; they justified France's claim to be a major world power. Through much of the 1890s, the French had still had to struggle to establish control of their new territories in the face of opposition from the local populations. By 1900, the military stage of conquest was over in most of the colonies, and the French set up civil administrations and began thinking about these regions' futures. As a republican country supposedly dedicated to the universal principles of the French Revolution, France could not simply justify the acquisition of colonies as a matter of seeking wealth or glory. French leaders emphasized the country's *mission civilisatrice*, its duty to bring the benefits of civilization to the non-European populations of its overseas territories. Taken to its logical conclusion, the notion of the *mission civilisatrice* suggested that the ultimate goal of colonial policy should be one of assimilation: the populations of France's colonies should be taught the French language, should learn to live according to French laws, and should have the same rights and privileges as the inhabitants of the metropole. Assimilation implied that the French would accept members of other races as full members of their community—a radical notion compared to the practice of racial segregation that was spreading in the American South during this period or to the policies that the British followed in their overseas possessions.

The promise of assimilation was carried out to some extent in the colonies France had acquired before 1848. These territories lived under French laws and even elected deputies to the Assembly. The vast expansion of France's empire after 1880 led to increasing doubts about the practicality of assimilation, however. In Algeria, the French had already confronted the problem of a population that resisted giving up its own language and customs, and had concluded that only those individuals who deliberately adapted themselves to French ways of life could really be assimilated. The newly acquired colonies in Africa and southeast Asia posed even more daunting challenges. These possessions attracted very few French settlers: in 1914, the number of Europeans living in the colonies was about 850,000, of whom more than 600,000 were in Algeria. To deal with their new colonies, French politicians and colonial administrators adopted a new policy known as association. This meant that the French would not seek to impose their own values and customs on colonial populations, but would instead allow them to develop in their own way, while ensuring that their territories would remain connected with France. The leading proponent of such policies was Hubert Lyautey, a French army officer who served in Algeria, Indochina, Madagascar, and most famously

as governor of the French protectorate in Morocco from 1912 to 1925. Colonial service attracted Lyautey because it offered him scope for large projects which were impossible in France. Lyautey took a real interest in the cultures of the regions where he was posted, and thought French rule could be best established by winning over their local rulers. His vision of colonialism was in many ways an idealistic one. "Even if France derives nothing from this," he wrote, "we would not have been less the workers for providence on this earth, if we brought back life, cultivation, and humanity to regions given over to brigands and barrenness. . ."[3] Lyautey never doubted, however, that the introduction of European technology and trade constituted progress, and he had no qualms about imposing French control by military force. In France, Lyautey became a national hero who symbolized the positive side of colonialism, but when Morocco became independent in the 1950s, almost all monuments to him were removed.

Closely associated with the idea of France's *mission civilisatrice* overseas was the idea that the colonies needed to be developed economically, a policy known as *mise en valeur*. At first, the French thought that the building of transportation networks, and above all of railroads, would accomplish this goal. Energetic administrators such as Paul Doumer in Indochina and Ernest Roume in West Africa planned ambitious rail projects, some of which were still incomplete at the end of the colonial era. These undertakings produced profits for the French companies that provided the necessary equipment, and made the colonies a major outlet for French investment. Experience soon showed, however, that railroads alone were not enough to bring prosperity to the colonies' populations. French administrators complained that the "natives" in their territories did not have proper work habits; it was often necessary to use force to compel them to provide the labor the French wanted for projects such as the creation of rubber plantations in Vietnam. To make their colonial subjects into "useful men" fit for the modern world, the French also thought it necessary to teach them the French language, and to replace traditional local authorities such as Chinese-trained mandarin officials in Vietnam and tribal chiefs in West Africa. At the same time, however, the French worried that giving too many members of their colonial populations a European-style education would produce a discontented class of men with ambitions for higher-level jobs. On the eve of the First World War, the French empire was still far from fulfilling all the hopes colonial promoters held out for it, but optimism about its future remained strong.

THE ONWARD MARCH OF THE AVANT-GARDE

The artists, composers, and poets of the cultural avant-garde had little connection with the larger economic and social changes of the period. They continued to form a small but lively enclave in France's great metropolis which attracted talented and creative individuals from all over the continent. The explosion of artistic creativity continued unabated in the first years of the new century, moving ever farther away from the classical standards that had shaped western art since the Renaissance. Henri Matisse and the artistic group some critics dubbed the *Fauves* (the "wild beasts"), including Maurice Vlaminck and André Derain, conducted bold new experiments in the use of color. A few years later, the Spanish-born Pablo Picasso and his French colleague Georges Braque went beyond Cézanne's decomposition of images into geometric forms and created the style known as cubism—a giant step in the direction of modern abstract art. These rebels were all professionally trained artists, but they welcomed as a colleague the self-taught painter

Henri Rousseau and his dreamlike visions of strange beasts in exotic settings. The artistic innovations coming out of Paris attracted a large circle of foreign painters such as the Russians Marc Chagall and Natalia Goncharova—some of whom settled permanently in the country. Like the impressionists thirty years earlier, the *Fauves* and the cubists were roundly reviled by critics for destroying artistic traditions and producing "ugly" canvases. Like their predecessors, they relied for support on a small network of sympathetic dealers and collectors—many of them foreigners who came into possession of treasures French museums could only regard enviously.

The avant-garde painters formed part of a larger milieu that included practitioners of many other arts. They were frequently friends of equally innovative composers, such as Erik Satie, whose short compositions parodied "serious" music and made use of sounds of the industrial world (just as Picasso introduced mass-produced products into some of his collages). Foreign emigrés also contributed to the new trend in music. One example was the Russian Igor Stravinsky, whose daring *Rite of Spring* was the occasion for another of the theater riots that had punctuated the evolution of French culture since the time of Victor Hugo's *Hernani*. Much of Stravinsky's work was written for the Russian exile Serge Diaghilev's *Ballets russes*, a dance company that made Paris the center for experimentation in that art as well. The poet Guillaume Apollinaire, a close friend of Picasso, carried the period's spirit of experiment into yet another domain.

The evolution of prose literature was less radical, but there was a steady move away from the socially oriented naturalism of Zola's day. Anatole France kept alive the political spirit of the Dreyfus era in his satire of French history, *Penguin Island*, and produced the best French novel dealing with the Revolution, *The Gods Will Have Blood*. Sexuality, open and sometimes deviant, was a common theme in the novels of the period. The female author Colette celebrated women's sexual experience, and the novelist and essayist André Gide, strongly influenced by the nihilism of Friedrich Nietzsche, questioned the basis of conventional moral standards. His heroes were often characters who committed unmotivated crimes (*actes gratuites*) without remorse and without incurring punishment. *Le Grand Meaulnes,* by Alain-Fornier, a novelist whose career was cut short by the First World War, offered readers a curious combination of dream and reality. New literary trends were promoted in the pages of the *Nouvelle Revue Française,* destined to remain France's most influential literary journal throughout the interwar period. Gide was its most important contributor and the publisher Gaston Gallimard, who put out the works of many of the period's most original writers, underwrote it.

In philosophy, Henri Bergson, the most important French philosopher of his generation, continued the critique of positivist ideas that had begun to take shape in the 1890s. Bergson did not see himself as an irrationalist, and indeed he proclaimed his ambition to make philosophy a true science. But he argued that the content of human consciousness could not be accounted for solely by the rational analysis of sense data. In particular, the human experience of duration in time took place through a direct, nonrational experience of intuition, rather than through the use of reason and observation. In his *Creative Evolution,* published in 1907, Bergson elaborated on this effort to show that the natural sciences could not fully account for human experience. In this work, he introduced the notion of *élan vital,* or "creative energy," arguing that this force accounted for the human capacity for creative action, and attacking determinist theories of human nature. Bergson's writings and public lectures drew an audience well beyond the narrow circle of profes-

sional philosophers. He was popularly understood to be teaching that the nonrational power of intuition and *élan vital* allowed people to shape their own destiny. His criticism of scientific reason seemed to extend a hand to religion, and Bergson later converted to Catholicism. His ideas were cited by all those revolting against the constraints of an increasingly structured social reality.

The broad audience for Bergson's public lectures showed that his challenge to the powers of reason resonated with broader cultural tendencies. Many recent historians have seen signs of this movement in the growing appeal of psychological theories about the power of unconscious urges, the flood of journalism devoted to crime and violence, and even the craze for a sensual new dance, the Argentine tango, which was introduced to France shortly before World War I. Some have linked this feverish cultural climate to an emotionally tinged nationalism that helped push France into war in 1914. At the moment when the war broke out, French public opinion was riveted by the sensational trial of Henriette Caillaux, wife of a leading politician, who had shot and killed a prominent journalist for printing compromising private letters from her husband. Witnesses and attorneys at the trial had aired all the fashionable theories about the weakness of reason, especially women's reason, in the face of the passions, and Mme. Caillaux was in fact acquitted. Whether the same impulses that led to her acquittal were also behind France's involvement in the brewing conflict is less clear.

NOTES

1. Cited in David Thomson, ed., *France: Empire and Republic* (New York: Harper & Row, 1968), 284.
2. Cited in Jean-Baptiste Duroselle, *Clemenceau* (Paris: Fayard, 1988), 516.
3. Cited in William A. Hoisington, Jr., *Lyautey and the French Conquest of Morocco* (New York: St. Martin's Press, 1995), 11.

CHAPTER 22

THE COMING OF THE WAR

RISING TENSIONS

For decades before 1914, French elementary school textbooks had taught the nation's children that the country lived "under the threat of another war, possible at any time."[1] But from 1905 onward, that threat came to seem increasingly immediate. The settlement of the Fashoda crisis in 1898 had ended a period of dangerous confrontation with Britain. Théophile Delcassé, foreign minister from 1898 to 1905, had then set out to give France greater security by reaching a broader understanding with the British. The achievement of this "understanding," or *entente,* was not easy. French public sentiment remained anti-British for some time after Fashoda, while the British government—preoccupied by the Boer War in South Africa from 1899 to 1903—spent several years trying to negotiate a treaty with Germany. Only in 1902, when that effort had proved futile, did the British invite the French government to discuss issues dividing the two countries.

Delcassé and the French ambassador to London, Paul Cambon, enthusiastically embraced the idea. By the spring of 1903, the two governments had worked out an accord by which the French officially recognized British hegemony over Egypt, while the British endorsed France's control over Mo-

rocco. King Edward VII's well-publicized visit to Paris in May 1903 contributed significantly to converting French public opinion to a more anglophile stance. The French public, though republican, was dazzled by the glamorous foreign monarch. In April 1904, the two governments reached a general agreement resolving their remaining colonial disputes throughout the world. This Anglo-French *entente* was far from a formal defense treaty, but it indicated the two countries' decision to cooperate in international affairs.

Both the French and the British viewed the *entente* as a desirable reinforcement in the face of a Germany whose aggressive foreign policy under William II (emperor since 1888) inspired concern. To the Germans, however, it looked like the creation of a hostile alliance encircling them. Berlin lost no time in trying to show the French the risks such a policy involved. From the time William II had dismissed Bismarck in 1890, Germany had made strident complaints about not getting its fair share of overseas colonies. Abandoning Bismarck's policy of conciliation with Britain, the Germans had embarked on a massive expansion of their navy, which the British regarded as a direct threat to their security. In 1905, William II visited Morocco and encouraged the sultan to oppose French demands and to call for an international conference to regulate the country's affairs. Delcassé urged a firm response, despite the risk of war, but the Germans made their move at a clever moment. France's ally, Russia, just defeated in its war against Japan, could not offer support. The French government had to bow to German pressure. Delcassé stepped down, and a conference was convened at Algeciras to decide the fate of Morocco.

In the short run, this first Moroccan crisis seemed to be a diplomatic triumph for Germany at France's expense. But its long-range effects actually served to strengthen the Anglo-French *entente.* Germany's aggressive behavior increased fears on both sides of the Channel. The British supported France at the Algeciras conference, which ultimately endorsed most of France's demands, and the British agreed for the first time to informal military talks with the French about possible cooperation in the face of a German attack. The French also encouraged London to negotiate an understanding with Russia to end the many colonial disputes between the two countries. These talks were concluded successfully in 1907, making the *entente* a three-way arrangement. The Moroccan crisis also altered the tone of French public opinion. Charles Péguy, the eloquent essayist who had been one of the leading defenders of Dreyfus, was one of several prominent intellectuals converted from pacifism to vehement patriotism. "Everyone suddenly realized that the menace of a German invasion exists . . ., that it could really happen,"[2] he later recalled. From then on, he devoted himself to whipping up national spirit. It would be an exaggeration to claim that the French public became eager for war after 1905, but there was undeniably an increased sense that a conflict might be unavoidable.

One sign of the new atmosphere was the way in which the French left shifted its focus from revolution at home to opposition to war. With the failure of the strike agitation that marked the years around 1906, antimili-

tarism became the left's new rallying point. Jean Jaurès argued that the policy of diplomatic alliances, rather than protecting France against involvement in a conflict, was making war more likely. The country would be better defended by a Swiss-style citizen militia, prepared for defense but clearly not intended to wage offensive campaigns, he maintained. Jaurès hoped that socialist parties in different countries could cooperate to prevent an armed conflict; but if that failed, he still admitted that a defensive war would be justified. A small minority in the trade union movement, often inspired by anarchist principles, took an even more extreme position, advocating the sabotage of military installations and the disruption of mobilization plans in case of a war declaration. Socialist and left-wing antiwar agitation made French government leaders uneasy about the working class's loyalty in case of conflict, but the strength of the antiwar movement showed that only a part of the French public shared the bellicose nationalism of groups like the *Action française.*

With the consolidation of the Triple Entente among France, Russia, and Britain, the major European powers were clearly divided into the two camps that would go to war in 1914. For a few years, however, the Triple Entente made a German attack on France seem less plausible. Some French leaders, notably the Radical Joseph Caillaux, now thought that the two countries could collaborate in certain areas. France and Germany even signed an agreement on economic cooperation in 1909, although it produced few results. There was a renewed confrontation between them in 1911, when Germany triggered a second Moroccan crisis to protest French moves that extended its domain beyond what the Algeciras agreement had provided for. But this, too, was settled by a diplomatic compromise: in exchange for accepting France's control of Morocco, the Germans received a large part of the French Congo to add to their colony of Cameroon. Caillaux, the French prime minister of the moment, hailed the resolution of the crisis as the beginning of "a new era" in Franco-German relations, but he had misjudged the mood in his own country. Criticism of his handling of the affair brought down his government.

The Poincaré Government

The choice of Raymond Poincaré to replace Caillaux and Poincaré's subsequent election as president in January 1913 marked the end of the brief thaw in Franco-German relations. Poincaré, a conservative republican whose family had left their home in annexed Lorraine in the 1870s rather than live under German rule, had long been identified with a policy of firmness toward the Germans. He declared that France "does not want war, but she does not fear it."[3] Poincaré tightened military cooperation with France's allies. The British still refused to have their hands tied by written commitments to come to France's aid but, in 1912, the two countries agreed to a division of naval responsibilites in case of a general war. The French fleet would defend the Mediterranean, allowing the British to concentrate their forces in the North Sea. As the British were to recognize two years later, they had made themselves effectively responsible for protecting France's northern coast against German attack. Germany's decision in 1913 to enlarge its standing army by 200,000 men disquieted the Entente. The French responded in August 1913 by passing a law requiring draftees to serve for three years instead of two, keeping the French army approximately the size of its neighbor's. From the point of view of Germany's military leaders, the Triple Entente seemed determined to keep them hemmed in at all costs. Of their own allies, the Italians were visibly unreliable and the Austro-Hungarian Empire, menaced by nationalist secession movements, faced an uncertain future.

The Balkan crisis resulting from a Serbian nationalist's assassination of the Austrian Archduke Ferdinand on June 28, 1914, had little direct relationship to France's interests. But it revealed how the country's twenty-year quest for security through alliances had narrowed its options in such a situation. Encouraged by the Germans, the Austrian government quickly decided to use the situation to crush Serbia and put a stop to ethnic agitation that threatened the Dual Monarchy's future. Russia, traditionally hostile to Austria's pretensions in the Balkans, opposed them.

President Poincaré and the French Premier René Viviani happened to be returning by sea from a visit to Russia during the crucial days of the crisis and were thus largely out of touch with fast-moving developments. They left the Russian capital, St. Petersburg, on July 25, 1914, just before the Austrians issued their ultimatum to Serbia. By the time their ship reached France five days later, the Russians, despite French urgings to wait, had begun military mobilization. Poincaré tried to get the British to issue a clear declaration that they would join France in opposing any attack on Russia, hoping that such a move would deter the Germans, but the British government insisted on keeping its options open. When the German government sent a last-minute message to Paris on July 31, 1914, asking whether France would stay neutral in case of war between Germany and Russia, the French replied that the country would act "according to its interests." It has been argued that a clearer statement of support for Russia might have deterred the Germans, but in light of what is now known about German official thinking, this seems unlikely. On August 3, 1914, the German declaration of war took the decision out of France's hands. German troops were already entering neutral Belgium on their way to France, incidentally guaranteeing that Britain—bound by treaty to defend the Belgians against such an attack—would enter the war. The situation that France had feared and prepared for since 1871 had arrived; the question was whether the national community possessed the cohesion and the resources to withstand the German attack.

THE SHOCK

Even as war began in August 1914, few people in France could have imagined that it would come to mark a turning point in the country's history as decisive as 1789. The public and the press had been slow to appreciate the significance of the Serbian crisis until the last days of July 1914. When the conflict suddenly loomed as imminent, the country was not swept by war fever. Prefects' reports on the public mood show that the noisy demonstrations in a few cities after the announcement of mobilization reflected the attitudes of only a small minority of the population. But the German declaration of war ended all debate in France about the wisdom of entering the conflict. While there might have been some hesitation about fighting to defend distant Serbia, or even about coming to the aid of the repressive tsarist regime, the German action made the war one of self-defense.

Up to that moment, the French government had been concerned that a large sector of the population might not back the war effort. The highly vocal pacifist campaign led by some of the CGT's activists, and the SFIO's resistance to increased military appropriations and to the three-year draft law of 1913, had seemed to show that much of the working class opposed any military engagement. At Jaurès's urging, the SFIO in July 1914 had just voted that, in case of war, a general strike should be called to block mobilization—provided that their comrades in Germany did the same. Fearing the influence of left-wing antiwar activists, the police had drawn up a list of leaders, the so-called *Carnet B,* who were to be arrested in case of war to prevent them from disrupting mobilization. But the events of July 1914 created an unanticipated situation. On July 27, the German Social Democrats, swayed by the argument that Germany faced a hostile foreign coalition bent on its destruction, had voted to support their government. The premise underlying the French Socialists' antiwar strategy collapsed. Jaurès still hoped that some means could be found to halt the conflict, but as he and other French Socialist leaders gathered in a Paris café to discuss the emergency on the evening of July 31, 1914, a mentally unbalanced right-wing extremist fired two shots through the window, mortally wounding him.

Jaurès's death silenced the one man who might still have tried to slow the rush to war. It also dissuaded the government from carrying out the arrests of the left-wing activists listed in *Carnet B.* Coming on the heels of Jaurès's assassination, such an action risked provoking the resistance it was meant to prevent. In any event, the other Socialist and trade union leaders, recognizing that their followers were already rallying to the defense of the country, quickly responded to President Poincaré's appeal for a *union sacrée,* a "sacred union" of all French to defend the homeland. In an emotional scene in the Chamber, the veteran Socialist Jules Guesde embraced the Catholic conservative Albert de Mun. In view of the wartime emergency, the SFIO abandoned its policy of opposition. Guesde and another Socialist, Marcel Sembat, entered the government. Feminist leaders, whose campaign for votes for women had seemed to be on the verge of success in the Chamber, suspended their activities and threw themselves into war relief efforts.

Military mobilization was carried out smoothly, in contrast to 1870, and the strength of the initial consensus behind the war was shown by the fact that less than 2 percent of men liable for military duty failed to report. The initial reaction to the war seemed to show that the highly visible social and political divisions that had characterized the Third Republic's public life were less important than they had appeared.

Patriotic unity alone, however, was not enough to meet the German invasion. French military leaders had anticipated a war for many years, but the events of 1914 showed they had failed to grasp the nature of the German military threat or changes in the nature of warfare that modern weapons had introduced. Like their counterparts elsewhere, France's generals had anticipated a short war, culminating in one or more decisive battles. The troops mobilized in August would be home by Christmas. Confident that the conflict would resemble the fast-moving campaigns of Napoleon, the French had put their energy into developing weapons for mobile offensive warfare, such as their quick-firing 75mm field gun, pride of the French army. The military hierarchy rejected proposals to replace traditional French uniforms, with their highly visible red trousers, with anything resembling the Prussians' dull field gray. To do so, they claimed, would weaken the soldiers' fighting spirit.

The Germans, too, planned on a quick war, but they had prepared more systematically for it. Since the signing of the Franco-Russian treaty in 1894, the German general staff had assumed that any major war would involve its forces in a struggle on two fronts. It had responded with the Schlieffen plan, designed to deliver a knockout blow against France before the slow-moving Russian army could enter the fight. General Schlieffen's idea was to send a powerful striking force through neutral Belgium and to cut behind the French forces, concentrated along the northern and eastern borders. If the Germans moved fast enough, they could hope to roll up the entire French army in a matter of weeks, and then turn their attention to Russia.

In a general sense, the French knew the outlines of the German plan. German preparations, such as the building of extra rail connections to the Belgian border, could not be concealed. But French military planners underestimated the number of divisions the Germans could assemble for this attack and failed to take adequate measures to counter it. French rail lines were not extended toward Belgium. In any event, the French generals were wedded to an offensive strategy of their own. Joseph Joffre, appointed head of the French general staff in 1911, announced his intention to "organize a French offensive and not a defense or response to a German offensive."[4] Joffre's intentions, formalized in the French "Plan XVII" of April 1914, were simple. French forces would cross the border to liberate the lost provinces of Alsace and Lorraine, helped, he hoped, by a popular uprising. Their success would cut off the German invading force in Belgium from the rear. French planners discounted the fact that their troops would have to advance across hilly terrain, unfavorable for an offensive.

The optimistic "Plan XVII" collapsed in the first days of the war. The new weapons of the industrial age made old-fashioned attacking tactics obsolete. Machine guns and heavy artillery brought the planned French advance to a standstill. German forces in Alsace and Lorraine then mounted a menacing invasion of their own. But the greatest danger was in the north, where the powerful German columns pushed their way across Belgium with unanticipated speed. From August 19 to 23, in a series of combats (the "battle of the frontiers"), the Germans forced the French to retreat from Lorraine in the east and drove the combined Franco-British forces back from the Belgian border. The French public, kept in ignorance of the German advance by strict censorship—and encouraged to expect a quick victory by reports of Russian advances in the east—was stunned to learn on August 29 that a front had been stabilized "from the Somme to Vosges"—that is, deep inside France's frontiers. By September 2, German units were within thirty miles of Paris, and the French government was evacuated to Bordeaux while much of the civilian population fled the city.

Even as the army's prewar plans disintegrated, however, the French soldiers did not give up the fight. In the face of apparent disaster, the French commander Joffre refused to panic or even to alter his daily routine, with its prolonged afternoon nap. The Russian alliance also contributed to French survival. Despite inadequate preparations, Russian forces advanced into East Prussia and led the German High Command—sure that the campaign in France was won—to pull two army corps out of its attack force to meet this threat. The Germans won a smashing victory against the Russians at Tannenberg, but they may have let an even greater prize slip away in France.

Battle of the Marne

As the Germans neared Paris, the overconfident commander of the German First Army, the force meant to lead the encirclement of the French, made a fateful alteration to Schlieffen's plan. His forces were supposed to swing south of Paris, but as the French and British troops retreated north of the city, he turned to pursue them. As he did so, he exposed his army's flank to a hastily organized French Sixth Army which had been improvised for the defense of the capital under the command of the elderly general Gallieni. Gallieni and Joffre saw the opportunity this German maneuver offered them. Drawing up his forces on the Marne River northeast of Paris, Joffre prepared for a counterattack, to be aided by Gallieni's thrust against the German flank. To get his troops to the front, Gallieni called on the Paris taxi fleet. These "taxis of the Marne" became an indelible part of the French wartime legend. On September 7, the French and British struck the German troops, exhausted by more than a month of almost continual marching. To meet the French advance from Paris, the German First Army commander von Kluck shifted his forces south, separating himself from the German Second Army to his left. Joffre's

forces and the British advanced into this gap, and the Germans had to retreat. The Schlieffen plan had misfired, and there would be no repeat of the French collapse in 1870.

"The miracle of the Marne" saved France from defeat, but it was only the first act of the war. The French hope of following up their success on the Marne by driving the Germans back across the border proved vain. From September to December 1914, the two rival armies edged to the west in a "race to the sea," trying to outflank each other. The result was a line of fortified trenches marking a front through northern France and a corner of Belgium that would remain largely unchanged until 1918. German forces remained in control of a broad strip of northern France, including the industrial regions of Lorraine and the Nord. The short and decisive conflict the generals had anticipated had become a grinding struggle whose outcome no one could foresee.

THE ORDEAL OF THE WAR

French military leaders were slow to accept the new realities of the war. Well into 1915, Joffre continued to launch his troops against the well-dug-in Germans, hoping to achieve a breakthrough that would allow him to roll up the enemy lines from the rear. Again and again, the French troops found it impossible to advance in the face of barbed wire and merciless machine gun fire from protected positions. The French, who had lost 300,000 men between August 1914 and the end of the year, suffered higher casualties than the enemy in 1915, and Joffre's assurance that he would "wear them down" became increasingly unrealistic. The Germans' introduction of poison gas during the 1915 battles added a new element of horror to a war that claimed human lives on a scale never before dreamed of.

During 1915, the Germans maintained a defensive posture in France, devoting their main effort to an offensive against the

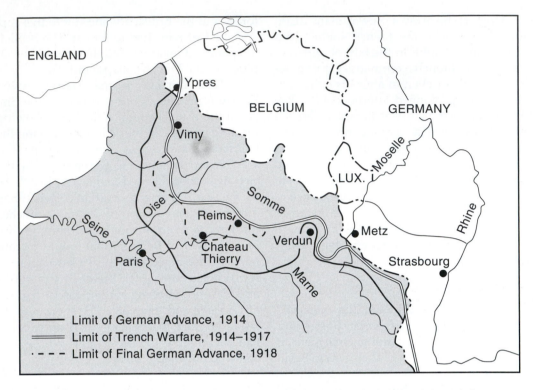

ENGLAND

Ypres

BELGIUM

GERMANY

Vimy

Moselle

LUX.

Somme

Oise

Reims

Seine

Verdun

Metz

Rhine

Chateau
Thierry

Paris

Marne

Strasbourg

——————— Limit of German Advance, 1914
═══════ Limit of Trench Warfare, 1914–1917
· – – – Limit of Final German Advance, 1918

France narrowly avoided military catastrophe in 1914, but it took four years of bitter fighting before the Germans were finally forced to surrender. Areas under German occupation for much of the war included many of France's important industrial centers.

Russians. When this failed to produce decisive results, the German High Command turned its attention back to the west. Falkenhayn, the head of the German general staff, no longer had any illusions about staging a sudden breakthrough. His plan instead was to drag the French into a battle of attrition that would "bleed them white." His chosen objective was the fortress-city of Verdun, a historic citadel whose abandonment the French would find psychologically impossible. Since the solidification of the front in 1914, the French position at Verdun had formed a salient sticking into the German lines and vulnerable to assault on three sides. From the strictly military point of view, the French would have been better off abandoning it when the German assault began with a massive artillery barrage on February 21,

1916. As Falkenhayn had calculated, however, the French were determined to hold their position. For the next ten months, the guns thundered day and night, turning the few miles of the Verdun salient into an inferno. In the early weeks of the fighting, the Germans captured several of the underground forts surrounding Verdun but, under the leadership of General Philippe Pétain, a stubborn and patient commander brought to the fore by this crisis, the French troops clung to their remaining positions.

For the front-line soldiers, the experience was one of almost unimaginable horror. Cut off from the rear by the constant shelling, cold, wet, often unable to bury the dead or evacuate the wounded, the men who survived returned "having lost even the strength to complain," one officer wrote. "In their eyes was an unheard-of depth of suffering."[5] Pétain, who did not want to push his troops beyond the limits of their endurance, insisted on rotating the forces engaged at Verdun so that, during the course of the battle, most of the French army suffered the nightmarish conditions there. A combined Anglo-French assault to the west along the Somme River, begun in late June, diverted some of the German pressure from Verdun, although it produced equally staggering casualty figures for minimal results. By the end of the summer, the German attack on Verdun had lost its momentum. German losses began to mount faster than those of the French, and Pétain's forces retook the fortresses lost at the outset of the battle. By the time the battle finally petered out in December, it had cost 163,000 French and 143,000 German lives and produced hundreds of thousands of wounded on both sides. As Pétain had promised, the Germans had not broken through. But the French army had been stretched almost to the breaking point.

Verdun was not just the supreme test of the ordinary French soldier's endurance. It also tested France's ability to organize its resources for a contest that depended as much on economic productivity and civilian morale as on military factors. Pétain, a cautious, defensive-minded commander, had held on at Verdun because he had understood that *"le feu tue"* (firepower kills) and had insisted on an ever-increasing supply of guns and shells to batter the Germans. To produce war supplies in sufficient quantities had required a considerable shake-up in the organization of French life. At the outset of the war, France had been as poorly prepared as any of the combatants for such a long and costly ordeal.

Prewar plans had foreseen a short conflict, and no attention had been paid to organizing war production. It had been assumed that the war would be fought with weapons produced beforehand. At the outbreak of hostilities, factories closed down, sending their male workers to the front and leaving the female ones unemployed and often destitute. In the crisis of August 1914, Joffre, the army commander, had assumed virtually autonomous power. The civilian government had retreated to Bordeaux, and the Chamber of Deputies and the Senate—adjourned after August 4, 1914—were not reconvened until December of that year. The battle of the Marne gave General Joffre immense prestige, and he showed little inclination to share power with mere elected officials. The entire country was put under military law, and army officers exercised powers normally reserved for civilian officials, including the right to arrest and try noncombatants. Strict censorship kept the public in ignorance of the military situation. Republican government seemed on the verge of becoming one of the war's casualties.

As it became clear that the war was not a passing crisis but a long ordeal, the civilian government gradually reasserted itself. Parliamentary deputies, many of them mobilized in August, began to criticize military deficiencies that threatened to undermine the war effort. Georges Clemenceau, then out of office, was one of the army's sternest critics. The censors seized his paper, *L'Homme libre (The Free Man),* for the first time on September 29, 1914. At that point, Clemenceau renamed it *L'Homme enchaîné (The Man in Chains)* and continued his campaign against the failings of the army's medical services and other shortcomings.

The failure of Joffre's offensives in 1915 emboldened critics, as did the generals' persistent failure to recognize the need to increase production of heavy artillery, machine guns, and other weapons needed for trench warfare. Within a few months, it had become evident that workers with special skills needed to be withdrawn from the front to maintain vital production lines. In the course of 1915, nearly a half-million soldiers were relieved for this purpose. With much of the prewar male workforce at the front, French factories had to employ increased numbers of women, who were put to work in many sectors previously closed to them. The French had discussed recruiting troops from the Empire even before the war, although little had been done to organize such units. Once the conflict began, the colonies were called upon not only for soldiers, like the famous *tirailleurs sénégalais* (Senegalese riflemen), but for laborers as well. By 1918, more than a third of the adult male population of Algeria was serving in metropolitan France, as were 200,000 troops from West Africa and 140,000 soldiers and laborers from Indochina. The war thus seemed to confirm earlier arguments about the Empire's value for France.

The war forced the Third Republic to abandon its practice of leaving the economy to its own devices. To increase war production and avoid wasteful competition for scarce raw materials, the government encouraged the formation of coordinating committees among leading enterprises in each branch of the economy. Albert Thomas, one of the socialists who had entered the government in 1914 as part of the *union sacrée*, emerged as the leading architect of France's war economy. Appointed undersecretary for artillery and military equipment in May 1915—partly in reaction to the army's persistent failure to give priority to the production of heavy weapons—and eventually named minister of armaments in December 1916, he sought to improve productivity. He also argued that the wartime crisis would bring about the state-controlled economy that socialists had sought before 1914. Thomas saw the wartime situation as an opportunity to win greater recognition for unions, and benefits for workers. Government intervention forced employers to grant workers' organizations some recognition, and the state encouraged manufacturers to yield to workers' wage demands to prevent strikes and interruptions of production. To some extent, the wartime experience seemed to confirm the arguments of prewar reformists in the labor movement that state intervention could give workers more recognition and a greater share of the benefits of industrialization.

Thanks in part to the organizing efforts of Thomas and others, French industry succeeded in expanding war production considerably, even though the invasion of 1914 had left the Germans in control of regions that had furnished 75 percent of prewar France's coal production and 61 percent of its steel. Whole new industries, such as aviation, grew to meet military needs, and firms that were able to respond to wartime demands—such as the auto manufacturers Citroen, Peugeot, and Renault—expanded tremendously during the war. French weapons, deficient at the start of the conflict, improved steadily during the war years. By the end of the struggle, France was equipping not only its own forces but those of many of its allies, particularly the United States. Impressive as this performance was, however, the French war economy was not as efficient in its use of scarce resources as the German or the British economies. French economic experts continued to deplore the multiplicity of small and medium-sized firms in most branches of industry.

The French government was considerably less imaginative about paying for the war than it was in encouraging war production. Some historians have remarked that the country's leaders were more willing to call on the citizens to sacrifice their lives than their money. Rather than raising taxes to meet the extraordinary expenses imposed by the conflict, the successive wartime governments relied primarily on the printing of additional currency and on borrowing. Massive propaganda campaigns encouraged the population to put its surplus savings into war bonds, which paid what appeared to be high interest rates. And the government borrowed extensively from the British and later from the United States, incurring war debts amounting to almost forty billion francs. Wartime conditions hardly permitted the maintenance of a balanced budget, but the government encouraged the belief that, once victory had been achieved, "the *Boche* will pay." It expected to extract reparations from the enemy that would allow it to reimburse its creditors without burdening the citizenry. Until the end of the fighting, wartime controls and support from the Allies made it possible to limit inflation. But after the armistice in 1918, France began to experience the severe inflation that was to become one of its chronic problems for the next seventy years.

NOTES

1. Cited in Eugen Weber, *Fin du Siècle,* P. Delamare, trans. (Paris: Fayard, 1986), 133.
2. Cited in Raoul Girardet, *Le nationalisme français* (Paris: Seuil, 1983), 251.
3. Cited in Pierre Miquel, *Poincaré* (Paris: Fayard, 1984), 272.
4. Cited in Pierre Miquel, *La Grande Guerre* (Paris: Fayard, 1983), 45.
5. Cited in Marc Ferro, *La Grande Guerre* (Paris: Gallimard, 1990), 167.

CHAPTER 23

CRISIS, VICTORY, DISILLUSIONMENT

THE END OF THE *UNION SACRÉE*

By the time the fighting at Verdun had died down in December 1916, the illusion that the war would be short and glorious had long since evaporated. As the casualty figures continued to mount, some voices began to be raised in protest against the apparent senselessness of continuing the struggle. At the outset of the fighting, one well-known writer, Romain Rolland, had taken refuge in Switzerland and condemned the conflict. But, at the time, he had been almost alone. All of France's political parties, the trade union movement, the Catholic church, and leading intellectuals of all tendencies had initially rallied to the policy of *union sacrée.*

The first organized opposition to the continuation of the war developed among minority groups in the left-wing movements that had denounced militarism prior to 1914. Louise Saumoneau, a longtime activist in the Socialist party, was one of the first to engage herself actively. She attended a women's peace conference convened in Switzerland by the German socialist Clara Zetkin in March 1915 and was arrested for circulating antiwar tracts in Paris later that year. Some bourgeois feminists, such as schoolteacher Hélène Brion, also broke away from the patriotic majority in their organizations and

sought to rebuild the international pacifist movement they had supported before the war.

Most socialists and trade unionists continued to support the war effort but, by July 1915, an organized group within the SFIO began to criticize the party's wholehearted support for the government and urge greater efforts to end the fighting. These "minority" socialists received less than 10 percent of the vote at the first wartime party congress in September 1915, but by the end of 1916, the "minority" represented nearly half of the party—losing a crucial vote in December 1916 by only 1,537 to 1,407. A similar current developed within the CGT. Two dissident French unionists participated in a socialist peace conference at Zimmerwald, in Switzerland, in September 1915. In 1916, the pacifists in the union movement formed a Syndicalist Defense Committee openly opposed to the continuation of the *union sacrée.* Wartime censorship limited public debate about the war, but did not entirely suppress it. In 1916, the writer Henri Barbusse (who had served in the trenches) was able to publish his grimly realistic novel, *Le Feu,* culminating with an appeal for peace. By July 1918, it had sold 200,000 copies—a figure considerably outweighed, it is true, by the patriotic literature encouraged by the war.

The events of the first half of 1917 raised much more serious questions about France's continuing participation in the conflict. The first months of the year saw two major changes in the international situation. In March (February according to the Julian calendar still used in Russia), a revolution in Russia overthrew the tsarist regime. A provisional government pledged to democratic reforms and to continuing the war took its place, but the disorganization caused by the revolution diminished Russia's contribution to the Allied war effort. On the other hand, in April 1917—in reaction to Germany's policy of unrestricted submarine warfare—the United States entered the war on the Allied side. The United States, with its minuscule army, at first added little to the Allied forces. But its large population and vast economic resources promised to be decisive in the long run.

Having outlasted the Germans at Verdun, the French high command believed the time was ripe for the long-dreamed-of counteroffensive that would break the German lines and decide the war. General Joffre, the hero of 1914, had been eased out of command by the end of 1916. He was replaced by General Nivelle, who had led the reconquest of key fortified positions at Verdun. Despite the skepticism of generals such as Pétain, who doubted that the German trenches could be so easily penetrated, and of many politicians appalled by the losses in earlier offensives, Nivelle planned a new attack in Champagne. He refused to alter his intentions, even when the Germans surprised their foes by withdrawing to a stronger defensive position in the weeks before the French attack.

The Army Mutinies

On April 16, 1917, the French soldiers went "over the top" along the Aisne, in an attack as futile as the bloody efforts of the preceding two years. In two weeks, Nivelle lost 147,000 men. For the *poilus* (front-line soldiers), the bloody failure of the Nivelle offensive was the last straw. A wave of disturbances, some amounting to outright mutinies, swept through the French units, affecting more than half the army's divisions. In a few cases, soldiers adopted revolutionary slogans and demanded immediate peace. But most of the protesters limited their actions to a refusal to obey orders to attack, and to demands for better treatment for ordinary soldiers. Still willing to defend their positions against the Germans, the war-weary infantrymen refused to waste their lives in hopeless frontal assaults on the enemy trenches.

Rigorous secrecy kept news of the army's disaffection from reaching the civilian population and, more importantly, the Germans. Nivelle was hastily replaced by Pétain, the hero of Verdun—respected by the troops for his concern about avoiding unnecessary casualties. Pétain restored army discipline, sending more than three thousand protest leaders before courts-martial and ordering the execution of at least forty-nine. But he also took positive steps to improve morale. Front-line soldiers were guaranteed better food. Home leaves became more regular, and soldiers were ensured of priority on trains so they could actually reach their families. Above all, Pétain kept the army on the defensive—waiting, as he put it, "for the Americans and the tanks"—and let the British carry the brunt of the fighting in the second half of 1917. The army responded to his combination of firmness and attention to soldiers' complaints because France's soldiers remained fundamentally loyal to the country. Unlike the soldiers of the Russian army, whose mass desertion after the revolution in their country in February 1917 showed that they had lost all attachment to the tsarist regime, the French *poilus* were willing to go on fighting once they were convinced that their commanders would not waste their lives for no reason.

Civilian Protests

The crisis at the front in the spring of 1917 coincided with growing unrest among the civilian population. Although overall casualty figures were kept secret, the mounting losses were evident. A young Norman bonnet maker later recalled, "Battles weren't fought on our fields; we weren't occupied; neither combatants nor wounded, nor ambulances nor munitions crossed our paths," but by 1917, she and her mother had made so many mourning hats for their clients that "every woman in Lisieux and the countryside had one."[1] Prefects' reports on the state of public opinion indicated a decline in home-front morale, particularly in urban areas where rising food prices added to complaints in the first half of 1917. Labor unrest, which had been negligible in 1915 and 1916 as workers gave their support to the war effort, began to mount. The antiwar Syndicalist Defense Committee drew 5,000 to 10,000 people to a Paris rally on May 1. Soon after, strikes—many of them staged by women workers in the clothing industry—showed that the national consensus behind the war effort was fraying. Protests against the war were not limited to metropolitan France. In 1916 and 1917, there were revolts against military recruitment and increased taxes in several regions of West Africa and in the Aurès region of Algeria.

France's political leaders were not immune to the concerns that affected soldiers and ordinary civilians. In the course of 1915 and 1916, the political unity achieved at the outbreak of war had faded and traditional political rivalries had begun to reassert themselves. None of the successive premiers in the first three years of the war managed to impose themselves as strong leaders capable of bringing the country through its ordeal. By early 1917, many leading politicians had become convinced that a military victory was unattainable. A German document concluded that "an important number of French politicians hoped for negotiations with Germany, without saying so publicly."[2] Joseph Caillaux (the prominent prewar premier who was still a leading figure among the Radicals), Aristide Briand, prime minister from July 1916 to March 1917, and Paul Painlevé (who held the post briefly in the fall of 1917), all had contacts of one kind or another with German representatives. Caillaux in particular became compromised by his encounters with several personalities whose activities crossed the line from searching for compromise to serving German interests. By September 1917, the Socialists decided to withdraw from the government, arguing that it was preventing efforts to find a formula for ending the fighting. Because the German government still refused to consider any agreement for ending the war that involved returning Alsace-Lorraine to France, contacts with them came to nothing. But the willingness of French leaders to engage in discussions showed that, even at the highest levels, there was doubt about the wisdom of continuing the struggle to the end.

THE HOME FRONT

The strike movements and other signs of protest in 1917 reflected the fact that the entire population had been affected by the continuation of the war. The impact was not the same, of course, in every region, and individuals suffered differently depending on their social class and their sex. But the first of the twentieth century's total wars had an impact broader than any event in France since the Revolution. An entire generation of young and middle-aged men were wrenched from their homes and families, and plunged into a violent existence far removed from the orderly routines of civilian life. In wartime propaganda, much was made of the way the common ordeal of military service broke down prewar barriers, such as those between Catholics and supporters of anticlerical secu-

The illustration on this card, printed by French prisoners of war held in Germany, reflects the loneliness and uncertainty endured by the thousands of soldiers captured during the fighting. Although prisoners were safe from the horrors of trench warfare, they suffered from separation from home and family and from worry about the outcome of the conflict.
(Photo credit: Karl Göllmann.)

larism. But the war experience also created new divisions, such as those between the *poilus* at the front and the *embusqués* (shirkers) who managed to find some way to avoid service. There was also a division between the civilian population in the regions occupied by the Germans—subjected to a harsh military regime, cut off from news, and affected along with their occupiers by the Allied economic blockade—and those living in areas far behind the lines who never saw physical effects of the conflict.

The coming of the war and the proclamation of the *union sacrée* had given workers

and the labor movement a degree of public recognition and political influence they had never enjoyed before. The war brought certain benefits to many skilled workers. Those in occupations considered vital to the war effort, such as miners and metalworkers, were exempt from front-line service. And the government pressured employers to improve pay and working conditions in order to prevent unrest in the factories. Hailed as essential cogs in the war machine, workers gained a new sense of self-importance and a correspondingly enlarged sense of entitlement. At the same time, however, the war undermined their position in certain respects. Economic regulation was not enough to keep wages from lagging behind rising prices. Although workers were better off than groups with fixed incomes, such as retirees, by 1917 they were acutely aware of their inability to keep up with the cost of living. Changes in the workplace also threatened the status of skilled male workers. Employers introduced new machinery that often simplified tasks, allowing them to replace skilled labor with women and less skilled men. Labor union officials opposed the employment of women and joined forces with conservative groups to make sure they were squeezed out of factory work when the war ended.

While workers gained some status as a result of the war, other social categories lost. The peasant farmers who still made up half the total population provided a disproportionate number of front-line soldiers and casualties. Women, children, and the aged had to replace them as best they could, and agricultural production fell during the war. Those who had surplus products to sell profited from wartime shortages, but families who lost their male breadwinner were often unable to keep their enterprises going. The petty bourgeoisie of shopkeepers and civil servants—a group that had grown considerably in the decades before the war—were not able to claim indispensability and avoid service as successfully as the proletariat. Women replaced many of them successfully, and this group also suffered financially as salaries lagged further and further behind inflation.

Much was written at the time, and more has been written since, about the war's impact on women. Necessity forced the breaching of barriers that had long limited their access to many occupations. Employers needed replacements for men, and women—unable to support their families on the meager allocations given to soldiers' families—needed sources of income. Some women were recruited for factory jobs, particularly in the munitions plants that mushroomed as a result of the war, although they never made up more than 15 percent of the industrial work force. War conditions allowed women access to many other jobs that had been previously been closed to them, however. Women became bus conductors, delivered mail, and replaced male colleagues as school directors. With their husbands gone, many peasant women had to take charge of family farms, making the business decisions that were normally a male preserve. The army had to overcome its long-standing prejudice against female nurses at the front. Like charity work at home, this was an occupation that fit conventional notions about proper sex roles. It was also one where class divisions between unpaid volunteer nurses from wealthy families and salaried nurses (often from more modest backgrounds) were painfully evident.

The evidence about women's participation in the war effort is clear. Whether this experience permanently altered mentalities is harder to determine. During the war, many women certainly learned to act more independently. They became accustomed to wearing less elaborate and less constraining clothing—the corset was one permanent casualty of the war—and to going out in public on their own. Popular mythology assumed that women came to enjoy greater sexual freedom. Cartoons and jokes expressed French soldiers' fears that their wives and girlfriends were taking advantage of the wartime situation—perhaps by enjoying the company of the thousands of American troops who began to arrive in 1917. Like factory workers, many women came to think differently about themselves. But prevailing male attitudes remained much more traditional, as the postwar period was to demonstrate. Male workers made it clear that they would not tolerate women in factories once the wartime emergency ended, and the conviction that woman's natural place was in the home remained strong. Even many women's groups shared the belief that, in view of the heavy losses caused by the war, women had a patriotic duty to have children.

The war also set in motion major changes in the relationship between France and its colonial populations. For the first time, large numbers of men from the colonies were brought to metropolitan France, where they were exposed at firsthand to both the attractions and the racial prejudices of European life. Although African-American troops sent to France with the American army felt that they were treated better than they were at home, French colonial troops and laborers often experienced discrimination. French soldiers at the front protested against the employment of colonial troops to keep order in factories where large numbers of French women were employed, for example. In spite of such difficulties, the war also presented possibilities for positive changes. Some French leaders encouraged expectations that the colonies' contributions to the war effort would bring rewards. Albert Sarraut, named as governor-general of Indochina in 1917, told a Vietnamese group in Paris, "I want to give you the instrument of liberation which will gradually lead you toward those superior spheres to which you aspire."[3] Inspired by similar hopes, Blaise Diagne, the black deputy from Senegal, volunteered to direct the recruitment effort there after the protests of 1917. He succeeded in enlisting sixty-three thousand men. Whereas Diagne looked forward to greater rights for colonial populations within the French empire, other men from the colonies were stirred by the American president Woodrow Wilson's talk of national rights to self-determination and by news of the Russian Revolution. The young Vietnamese Ho Chi Minh, the future leader of the Communist movement that would drive the French out of Indochina in 1954, first came into contact with radical ideas as a result of his wartime service in France.

CLEMENCEAU

Drained by the steadily mounting losses at the front, demoralized by a sense that the war would never end, and stressed by the social tensions mobilization generated, France by the middle of 1917 seemed close to the kind of breakdown that had forced Russia out of the war. When the Painlevé cabinet lost a vote of confidence in November 1917, the French president, Poincaré, decided that the time had come to abandon the effort to find a premier who could, through parliamentary compromises, hold together the increasingly fragile *union sacrée*. He turned instead to the seventy-five-year-old Georges Clemenceau, detested by the Socialists for his hard-line policy against social protests in 1906–1909 and by many of his fellow Radicals for his strident attacks against the way the war had been conducted.

Despite his age, Clemenceau brought a new vigor to the French government. The "Tiger of France" left no doubt about the policy he intended to conduct: "war, nothing but war."[4] Instead of giving ministerial posts to other leading politicians, Clemenceau appointed minor figures and made most decisions himself in collaboration with a few trusted aides. At home, he cracked down on the *demi-monde* of double agents with German contacts, several of whom were executed. He silenced political advocates of a compromise peace, such as Caillaux (arrested in January 1918), and the women's peace advocate Hélène Brion. To build army morale, he made frequent visits to the front, speaking not only to generals but to ordinary soldiers. For the first time since the war began, France had a leader with a clear policy and the personal authority to carry it out. Clemenceau's policy could only succeed, however, because the army and the population were ready to support him. Changes in the treatment of soldiers and civilian workers after the protests in mid-1917 had convinced members of both groups that their concerns had been heard. German intransigence showed that there was no possibility of a compromise peace on terms that France could accept. By the fall of 1917, much of the French public was ready for a "second mobilization," a grimly determined effort to see the war through to the end.[5]

Such leadership was sorely needed in the spring of 1918. With Russia definitely out of the fighting after the Bolshevik seizure of power in November 1917, Germany was determined to make an all-out bid for military victory before the growing American army could tilt the balance to the Allies. The German commander, Ludendorff, had a new formula for breaking the military stalemate. The German troops launched surprise attacks, rapidly penetrating the enemy lines. When their advances were halted, they broke off the fighting rather than bogging down in battles of attrition, and transferred the offensive to another sector of the front. Beginning in late March, the Germans launched a series of hammer blows that sent the Allies reeling. A new monster cannon, which the French dubbed "Big Bertha," shelled Paris from a distance of sixty miles, killing over two hundred civilians. In May, a German attack in Champagne brought the enemy to within thirty-five miles of Paris. The pessimistic Pétain, fearing a breakthrough, urged Clemenceau to move the government out of the capital.

Ludendorff's offensives battered the Allies, but did not break them. The initial attacks in March precipitated one critical decision. At a meeting on March 26, 1918, they agreed for the first time to create a unified military command controlling all their forces on the western front. Since the French army remained larger than the British or American forces, the post of commander-in-chief had to go to a French general. Pétain, as overall French commander, was the logical choice, but Clemenceau thought him too cautious. He swung his weight behind a general who shared more of his own aggressive instincts,

Ferdinand Foch. The first few months of Foch's command were a critical time. The German offensives continued to achieve substantial gains of territory and, behind the lines, a series of strikes in key munitions plants showed that French workers were increasingly adopting pacifist and defeatist sentiments. But time was running out for the German army. On July 15, for the first time, one of Ludendorff's attacks failed, and the momentum shifted to the other side.

On July 18, 1918, French and American forces, using a massed force of one thousand tanks (a wartime first), opened a counteroffensive against the extended German lines at Villers-Cotterets, east of Paris. By the end of August, the Allies had retaken all the territory lost during the spring. Foch was by no means confident of ending the war in 1918, but he continued to push the Germans back, first in one sector, then in another, sure that the growing American army would give him an ever-increasing superiority. Ludendorff had already concluded that defeat could not be prevented. On September 28, he told his government that it must conclude an armistice as quickly as possible.

Rather than addressing themselves to the French, the Germans turned to the American president Woodrow Wilson, whose widely publicized "Fourteen Points," issued in January 1918, had held out the prospect of a relatively moderate peace settlement. To the intense annoyance of the French and British, Wilson negotiated with the Germans without consulting them. Some French leaders opposed the granting of any armistice until Allied troops had actually entered German territory and made their victory unmistakable. But most, including Clemenceau, were willing to settle for a quick end to the war rather than pressing on to total victory. Foch, for his part, insisted that the Germans at least be forced to withdraw their forces behind the Rhine; that Allied troops be allowed to occupy several bridgeheads on the German side of the river; and that the Germans be compelled to turn over large quantities of weapons and supplies. Most of these demands were finally included in the armistice agreement; French concerns were thus not entirely shoved aside.

And so, at 11 A.M. on November 11, 1918, the war in France finally came to an end. The Assembly received Clemenceau with thunderous cheers and, in the streets of Paris, crowds danced with joy. At the front, one soldier wrote, "some hugged each other, others jumped up and down and danced, others tried to sing, while some cried. . . . My head hurt, and I wanted to laugh as much as I wanted to cry."[6] Battered and exhausted, France had nevertheless survived an ordeal without precedent. The institutions of the Third Republic appeared intact. When the need had been greatest, they had brought to the fore the statesman and the generals who led the country to victory. But the struggle had taken a heavy toll—one whose full extent would not be apparent until France once again faced a German invasion in 1940.

THE POSTWAR SETTLEMENT

The fighting had ended with German representatives accepting the armistice terms dictated by a French commander, and the negotiations for the peace were convened in France as well. At Versailles, the victorious Allies debated the treaty to be signed with their principal enemy, Germany. Negotiators housed in other historic palaces outside the French capital settled the postwar fate of the Kaiser's former allies. France thus appeared to hold the central role in the most sweeping rearrangement of Europe's frontiers since the Congress of Vienna. In reality, however, France's ability to impose its views was limited. The thunderous welcome Paris gave the American president, Woodrow Wilson, when he arrived in person to take part in the peace conference was in part a recognition that—

for the first time—the United States would play a major part in Europe's affairs. French enthusiasm for the high-minded American leader quickly cooled as it became clear that his ideas were far removed from those of French leaders and most of the French public. Britain and France had stood together through four difficult years, but old rivalries and differences of opinion now came to the surface. And far to the east, the new Communist regime in Russia—excluded from the peacemaking and fighting for its life against an array of foes, including a French expeditionary force on the Black Sea coast—offered the peoples of Europe a vision of a new society that would abolish war and exploitation.

In this highly charged atmosphere, the government of Clemenceau was bound to come into conflict with its allies in its efforts to obtain a postwar settlement with Germany which would help France recover from the devastating losses it had suffered and insure the country against any such catastrophe in the future. The French impulse to "make the *Boche* pay" and to keep Germany too weak to threaten France in the future ran counter to the need to maintain good relations with France's wartime allies. U.S. President Woodrow Wilson, in particular, meant that the peace that would conclude what he called "the war to end all wars" be a conciliatory one. The peace negotiations that began in January 1919 were thus controversial at the time and have remained so ever since. Within France itself, there was a division between those who wanted to see Germany permanently weakened—perhaps even split into several states—and those who doubted the possibility or the wisdom of so harsh a policy.

General Foch, the supreme commander of the Allied forces at the end of the war, was the leader of the hard-line party. He convinced Clemenceau to demand French control of all German territory west of the Rhine River—land that had been annexed to France during the Napoleonic period. Other French demands included the return of Alsace-Lorraine, already accomplished under the armistice agreement, control over the Saarland, whose coal mines were to compensate France for the damage done to its own mines, reparations to finance reconstruction, and permanent limits on Germany's military strength. In pushing for a "hard" peace, Clemenceau accurately represented most segments of French public opinion. Only the Socialists on the left openly favored a more conciliatory approach.

History has tended to present the peace conference as a duel between a vengeful but largely unsuccessful Clemenceau and an overly idealistic Woodrow Wilson. In fact, modern historical research has modified this traditional picture. The French were not as unsuccessful in pressing their demands as has often been claimed. They achieved not only a favorable distribution of the reparations demanded from Germany—52 percent of which were to go to France—but a list of other economic demands drawn up during the war and meant to favor expansion of French industry in the postwar period. Nor was the opposition between Clemenceau and Wilson as complete as it has often been made to appear. France did not oppose Wilson's cherished plan for a League of Nations to maintain the peace. In fact, the French representative to the commission which drew up the League charter—the venerable republican politician Léon Bourgeois—tried to give the League real substance by proposing it have an armed intervention force. When Wilson rejected the suggestion, French enthusiasm for what struck them as a plan without real teeth cooled.

Clemenceau also quickly realized that the Americans and the British would not accept either French annexation of the Rhineland or a separate French-sponsored state there. He had to settle for temporary Allied occupation of those territories, coupled with a promise from Wilson and the British prime minister, Lloyd George, to give France treaty guarantees against any future German aggression. Clemenceau's French biographer, Jean-Baptiste Duroselle, concludes that, far from systematically opposing Wilson, "Clemenceau sacrificed the full realization of his goals to the maintenance of an alliance which he considered more solid than it really was."[7] If Clemenceau yielded a good deal to the Americans in the negotiations, Wilson, for his part, was not totally hostile to French demands. He sided with Clemenceau against Lloyd George, who would have softened many of the treaty terms in the interests of helping the German government gain a solid base of public support in its struggle against the revolutionary movement in its own country. Neither man realized that the United States Senate would eventually reject any permanent American guarantee to France and any American participation in the League of Nations, thereby depriving Clemenceau of an essential aspect of what he had bargained for.

The final settlement agreed on at Versailles and accepted reluctantly by the German representatives thus took French interests into account. France recovered Alsace-Lorraine. To guarantee the country's military security, the Rhineland was to be occupied by Allied troops for fifteen years, and was to remain permanently demilitarized. Germany's army was limited to 100,000 men. Under the terms of the treaty, Germany could not possess tanks, military airplanes, or submarines. Other treaty provisions were meant to compensate France for its economic losses. Germany agreed to pay reparations, whose amount was to be determined in future negotiations. To make up for its ruined coal mines, France was to receive the coal production from the Saar for fifteen years, after which a plebiscite would determine whether the area returned to Germany. The Germans had to allow French exports into their country duty free, while the French were not required to reciprocate. Germany's colonies were distributed among the

Allies, France regaining the African territories it had ceded during the second Moroccan crisis. The postwar redistribution of the territories of the defeated Ottoman Empire—which had entered the war on Germany's side—brought further additions to the French empire. France was to administer Lebanon and Syria under mandates from the League of Nations, although the French public had little interest in these territorial gains.

The Versailles peace settlement, if it gave France less than some of the country's leaders wanted in the way of territories and guarantees against a German resurgence, thus paid a fair amount of attention to French concerns. Clemenceau, presenting the pact to the Assembly, reminded critics that France had not won the war alone, and had therefore had to compromise with its allies. The great question was whether the treaty would work as planned. The German government, compelled to accept under protest a war guilt clause alleging that Germany alone had been responsible for the outbreak of the conflict and a reparations bill whose full extent was not to be set until 1921, was bound to try to change the settlement. France's allies could not be counted on to help maintain it. France would have to rely on its own resources to make the treaty function as the French government thought it should.

NOTES

1. Bonnie G. Smith, *Confessions of a Concierge: Madame Lucie's History of Twentieth-Century France* (New Haven, CT: Yale University Press, 1985), 34.
2. Cited in Jean-Jacques Becker and Serge Berstein, *Victoire et frustrations, 1914–1929* (Paris: Seuil, 1990), 116.
3. Cited in William J. Duiker, *The Rise of Nationalism in Vietnam, 1900–1941* (Ithaca, NY: Cornell University Press, 1976), 128–9.
4. Cited in Jean-Baptiste Duroselle, *Clemenceau* (Paris: Fayard, 1988), 624.
5. This theme is strongly emphasized in Leonard V. Smith, Stéphane Audoin-Rouzeau and Annette Becker, *France and the Great War 1914–1918* (Cambridge: Cambridge University Press, 2003), the most recent overall treatment of the French war effort.
6. Cited in Leonard Smith, *Between Mutiny and Obedience: The Case of the French Fifth Infantry Division During World War I* (Princeton, NJ: Princeton University Press, 1994), 243.
7. Duroselle, *Clemenceau*, 758.

CHAPTER 24

FRANCE BETWEEN THE WARS

No matter how often one reads the figures for France's losses in the First World War, they remain starkly impressive. Almost 1,300,000 French soldiers killed—1 out of every 10 adult men in the population; over 300,000 men classified as *"mutilés,"* so severely injured that they could not work; 1 million more partially handicapped; 600,000 widows. In proportion to its population, no other major combatant nation was so severely stricken.

Certainly the memory of the war remained acutely vivid throughout the 1920s, a decade "when the memorials to the fallen were still new," as one historian born in the period has put it.[1] An entire generation had served at the front. In 1930, forty-five out of every one hundred adult males in the population were veterans. Like the American soldiers who served in Vietnam, these ex-*poilus* had difficulties digesting the horrors they had experienced. Many were haunted for years by the memories of comrades killed in the trenches, or the faces of enemy soldiers they themselves had shot. It would be easy to conclude from these facts—and from our knowledge of the disastrous defeat that France was to suffer in 1940—that the victory of 1918 was a Pyrrhic one, leaving the country too gravely scarred by its experi-

ence to recover. Such a conclusion would be too hasty, however. French society showed considerable vitality in coping with the war's impact during the 1920s. Its weaknesses were only to become glaringly evident in the face of the unanticipated problems of the 1930s, particularly the world economic depression and the triumph of Nazism in Germany.

Nevertheless, the challenges facing France at the end of the war were daunting. The impact on France's population was long lasting. With so many men absent at the front from 1914 to 1918, the number of births had fallen sharply. Since so many of those men never returned, these demographic losses were never made up. For decades, the French population pyramid was marked by the *classes creuses*, the abnormally small population cohorts born in the war years who were just entering adulthood when the Second World War broke out. France, already different from its neighbors before 1914 because of its low birth rate and its higher proportion of older people, became even more a country of old men and single women during the 1920s and 1930s. Many historians have explained the country's social conservatism and lack of dynamism in this period in terms of this population pattern. This picture must be modified, however, by taking immigration into account. At a time when countries that had traditionally been havens for immigrants (particularly the United States) were erecting barriers against newcomers, France welcomed an influx of laborers—mostly young men from Italy, Poland, and Spain—to fill the ranks decimated by the war. Employers' organizations systematically recruited these foreign laborers, many of whom eventually married French nationals and acquired citizenship.

The material costs of the war were as staggering as the number of lives lost. All across the northern departments, houses, factories, public buildings, roads, bridges, and rail lines had been destroyed. National monuments like the great Gothic cathedral of Reims were in ruins. The retreating Germans had flooded the coal mines in the occupied territories. Over five million acres of farmland were out of production, some of it so full of unexploded shells or poisonous chemicals that it could never be used again. (Even today, signs warn visitors to the Verdun war memorial against straying from the paved paths and possibly stepping on buried munitions.) And to cope with the task of reconstruction, France had limited resources. The extraordinary expenses imposed by four years of fighting had amounted to sixteen times the annual government budget of the prewar period. The situation was made particularly galling by the knowledge that, although Germany had also suffered heavy human losses in the fighting, it had never become a battlefield and had little physical damage to repair. In this respect, too, however, the situation was not as catastrophic as the bare statistics make it appear. As Germany and Japan were to demonstrate after the Second World War, the task of rebuilding was in some ways an economic stimulus—providing numerous jobs, especially in the construction trades.

THE DOMESTIC ATMOSPHERE

The peace negotiations were not the only preoccupation in France in the months following the end of the fighting. Social tensions that had built up during the conflict burst into the open afterward as well. By the last months of the war, a large number of workers had adopted revolutionary ideas, as the strike wave of May–June 1918 had shown. The little news that had reached France about the Bolshevik Revolution in Russia in November 1917 inspired labor and socialist militants, who had turned against the war and the bourgeois society that supported it, with aspirations to transform France. The government hoped to forestall working-class protest at the end of the war by conceding the eight-hour workday, a goal the unions had long pushed for. But passage of a law to this effect in April 1919 was not enough to end worker unrest. There was an extensive wave of protests and demonstrations in the spring of 1919, coinciding with agitation in other European countries (notably Germany). Some militants thought France was truly on the brink of revolution. The defeat of this strike wave frustrated left-wing militants, but they remained hopeful about the chances of emulating the Bolsheviks in Russia, whose success in 1917 provided the left all over Europe with inspiration.

Parliamentary elections had been postponed during the war. They were finally scheduled for November 1919. The SFIO, increasingly crippled by divisions between moderates and revolutionaries, went into the campaign having adopted a platform that ruled out election agreements with any of the "bourgeois" parties. At the same time, the Chamber had altered election procedures to give a bonus of seats to those parties that formed large coalitions. Most of the center and right groups joined in a *Bloc national* to take advantage of the system. They appealed to patriotic sentiment by putting up war veterans as candidates and used the fear of Russian-style revolution to win votes. A striking poster of a long-haired "Red" with a knife clenched between his teeth conveyed the message that the election was a choice between "voting against Bolshevism or voting for Bolshevism." As a result, the elections produced a clear defeat for the leftist parties that had dominated the Chamber from the time of Dreyfus to the outbreak of the war. Even though the SFIO actually drew more votes than it had in 1914, it won only 68 seats in the Chamber, down from 102 in the last prewar elections. The *bleu horizon* Chamber, so-called in reference to the sky-blue color of French soldiers' uniforms, was skewed further to the right than any previous French legislature of the Third Republic. As so often under that regime, the Chamber did not give an entirely accurate representation of public opinion. The SFIO's refusal to cooperate with their traditional Radical allies exaggerated the shift to the right. But French politics appeared polarized between a revolutionary minority on the left and a conservative majority.

One of the first casualties of the new political climate was Clemenceau, the "Tiger" who had led the country to victory. Catholic conservatives, who had provided many of the votes for the *Bloc national*, opposed him because of his lifelong anticlericalism. The left denounced his authoritarianism during the war, and rival Radical politicians were now ready to cut him down to size. He had hoped to be elected president in January 1920 in place of Raymond Poincaré, but the deputies rejected him in favor of Paul Deschanel. Clemenceau's defeat marked the resumption of French parliamentary politics as usual after the wartime hiatus. As prime minister, Deschanel appointed Alexandre Millerand, the one-time socialist who had by this time migrated to the center-right. When Deschanel's health

forced him to resign as president soon afterward, Millerand succeeded him, continuing to guide the *Bloc national* from his new office.

Millerand's government was immediately confronted with the largest wave of working-class protest the country had experienced since 1906. In the course of 1920, 1.3 million workers participated in strikes, often launched in support of revolutionary demands put forward by members of the network of Syndicalist Revolutionary Committees that grouped supporters of a Russian-style revolution in France. A general strike paralyzed the railroad system in February 1920, followed by lengthy work stoppages in the crucial coal mining regions in the north. On May 1, 1920, half a million marchers participated in the traditional parade in Paris, and fights with the police resulted in a death and numerous injuries. The holiday was the prelude to a further round of strikes. Millerand's government and France's employers reacted with severity. Fifteen thousand striking railroad workers lost their jobs, and numerous labor leaders went to jail. By May 21, 1920, the CGT trade union confederation, whose reformist leader, Léon Jouhaux, had been pushed into strike action by the revolutionary minority, called off the strike wave. As its failure became obvious, disillusioned workers quit their unions in large numbers. The defeat of 1920 demoralized organized labor for over a decade.

The war, the election debacle of 1919, and the failure of the 1920 strikes caused increasing tensions within the SFIO, the unified Socialist party created in 1905. The party leaders who had favored adhesion to the *union sacrée* throughout the war and a continuation of a reformist policy afterward had lost control of the party by 1918. The antiwar "reformers" now dominated the party and looked to the victorious Russian Bolsheviks for leadership. In July 1920, an SFIO delegation embarked for Moscow to apply for membership in the Third International, the Bolsheviks' international organization. To their shock, they discovered that adhesion to the Communist movement would require acceptance of the "Twenty-One Conditions" formulated by the Russian Communist leaders, which implied a complete repudiation of the French party's traditions of internal democracy.

At the SFIO's Congress at Tours in December 1920, the pro-Communist "reformers" divided, with a minority refusing the Soviet conditions and preferring to rebuild bridges with the group around Jaurès's successor, Léon Blum, who had never been tempted to embrace the Bolshevik program. A majority of the delegates to the congress, however, voted to accept the "Twenty-One Conditions" in the expectation that the French party—once it had joined the Communist International—could renegotiate the terms of its adhesion. The newly formed French Communist party (PCF) kept control of the SFIO's daily newspaper, *L'Humanité*. The socialists who refused to accept the vote followed Léon Blum, who promised to keep alive the spirit of the "old house" built by Jaurès. This group kept the old party name of the SFIO. Heavily outnumbered at the Congress of Tours, they nevertheless included most of the party's delegation in the Chamber of Deputies and most of its permanent officials.

The Communists' majority at the Congress of Tours was deceptive. Over the next few years, as the temporary burst of postwar revolutionary fervor faded, the SFIO succeeded in reestablishing itself as the larger of the two left-wing parties. But it was now less of a working-class party. Its rank and file and its votes were increasingly drawn from lower-level white-collar groups, such as government employees and schoolteachers. The PCF, repeatedly plunged into internal crisis by sudden shifts of leadership and policy imposed from Moscow, shrank during the 1920s to a small core of dedicated militants.

Apart from a few regions where it picked up peasant backing, its strength was primarily in the factory suburbs of the "red belt" around Paris. The split of the socialists was followed by a division in the French trade union movement. There, the pro-Communist minority abandoned the CGT to form its own organization, the CGTU (*Confédération générale du travail unitaire*), in 1922. Together with the formation of a small Catholic labor movement, the CFTC (*Confédération française des travailleurs chrétiens*) in 1919, the breakup of the CGT fragmented the union movement, which lost members steadily during the 1920s. The consequences of the divisions created in the French left at the beginning of the 1920s were still being felt fifty years later.

The Quest for Security

The divisions of the left allowed the *Bloc national* government to pursue the assertive foreign policy its leaders considered necessary to maintain France's security after the war. France at the beginning of the 1920s appeared to be the world's strongest military power. Even after the demobilization of most of the army in 1919, the country still had more men under arms than any other nation. The war and the Russian Revolution had at least temporarily eliminated Germany and Russia as military forces, and the Austro-Hungarian Empire had been permanently extinguished. A series of treaties with the newly created nations of central and eastern Europe—Poland, Czechoslovakia, Yugoslavia, and Romania—made France the patron of all those who had gained from the postwar treaties. The government encouraged French business investment in these regions to tie them even more closely to France.

The weakness of this activist policy was that France lacked the resources to sustain it. The fate of the Millerand government's use of force to maintain all the clauses of the Versailles Treaty against Germany demonstrated this. France reacted swiftly to German violations of the treaty clauses in 1920 and 1921, sending troops to occupy key German cities and openly encouraging separatist movements in the Rhineland. But the British and American governments refused to support these French initiatives. The French, frustrated by the American demand that France repay its war debts to the United States even when the Germans failed to make their reparations payments, decided on an even greater show of force at the end of 1922. To end German foot-dragging, Raymond Poincaré, the former wartime president who was then premier, sent troops to occupy the whole of the Ruhr industrial district in northwestern Germany in January 1923. The Germans responded with a program of passive resistance, which the French tried to break by importing workers to put the Ruhr's mines and factories back into operation, and by administrative measures to separate the occupied territory from the rest of Germany.

The French occupation and the consequent runaway inflation in Germany eventually forced the German government to the conference table. By then, Poincaré's policy had shown itself expensive for France as well. The Americans and British had brought financial pressure on the French government, and French investors themselves had speculated against the government. As a result, the French franc, already badly weakened as a result of the war, lost a further 46 percent of its value in the year following occupation of the Ruhr. France had to accept an international settlement of the reparations issues that had led to the crisis. It gained international guarantees that Germany would pay (thus partially achieving the goal Clemenceau had sought at Versailles of ensuring that France's wartime allies would help keep Germany under control) in exchange for accepting a reduction in German obligations. More significantly, the Ruhr crisis showed that France lacked the power to impose its interpretation of the postwar settlement on the rest of Europe.

By 1924, nationalist hopes for a French-dominated Europe had been dashed not only by the outcome of the Ruhr crisis but by other developments as well. The success of German enterprises thwarted the ambitious postwar *plan sidérurgique* (metal-industry plan) to use the economic clauses of the Versailles Treaty to make the French iron and steel industry dominant in the European market. In the military arena, the French generals had opted for Marshal Pétain's cautious defensive strategy in any future war with Germany, rather than for Marshal Foch's plan to punish any future German aggression by a swift advance onto enemy territory. Even before the 1924 elections brought the left back to power, French leaders were recognizing that the country's ability to control international affairs was more limited than it had appeared in the immediate aftermath of the war.

THE BRIAND YEARS

Having learned from the failure of their go-it-alone tactics in 1919, the Socialists agreed to an electoral pact with their traditional republican allies, the Radicals, in 1924. The Radical-Socialist *Cartel des Gauches* won 353 of the 610 seats in the Chamber. In domestic affairs, the ministry of the Radical leader Edouard Herriot was to suffer a resounding defeat. But by the time it fell in 1926, the *Cartel* government had redefined French foreign policy along lines that were to last well into the next decade.

The new course adopted in 1924 came to be identified with the name of the veteran politician Aristide Briand, who headed the Foreign Ministry from 1925 to 1932. Abandoning the policy of rigor toward Germany, Herriot and Briand sought to protect French interests by favoring international reconciliation, and above all by promoting a rapprochement with Germany. The French became leading proponents of strengthening the League of Nations, hoping that a larger international structure could contain German tendencies toward expansionism. In 1925, Briand accepted the German foreign minister Stresemann's suggestion of a treaty between Germany and its western neighbors guaranteeing their mutual frontiers. This Locarno Pact, an agreement among equals rather than a peace dictated to the defeated, seemed to promise a new era of peace for Europe, although the small states of eastern and central Europe—to which France had pledged protection—noted with concern that it included no assurances about German respect for their borders. In 1926, Germany joined the League of Nations, and Briand hailed the coming of a new international order. "Make way, rifles, machine-guns, cannon! Make place for conciliation, arbitration, and peace!"[2] Briand, by now internationally known as "the pilgrim of peace," lent his name to the Kellogg-Briand Treaty of 1928, by which the United States and France agreed to renounce the use of war in settling international differences. In following years, numerous other countries added their signatures to it. France, the country which had demanded the harshest terms toward Germany during the 1919 negotiations, had now become the leader of the movement to banish violence from international affairs.

In the wake of the Locarno Pact, France and Germany resolved their economic differences as well. An International Steel Agreement of 1926 consecrated the German lead in that field, but guaranteed French producers 32 percent of the European market. Numerous groups promoted youth exchanges between the two countries. Leading French intellectuals participated in programs to spread acquaintance with German literature and thought.

In 1929, France joined Germany and the other wartime powers in negotiations linking disarmament and German reparations. This led to the Young Plan, by which the Allies agreed to hasten the end of military occupation in Germany. From the French point of view, the most important aspect of the agreement was that the United States finally accepted the principle of a link between German reparations payments and French war debts.

After five years, France's policy of promoting international cooperation and reconciliation with Germany appeared highly successful. Briand's initiatives, culminating in a proposal for a European federation launched in September 1929, foreshadowed the successful process of western European integration undertaken in the 1950s. Tragically, just as Briand was suggesting the unification of Europe, Adolf Hitler began his rise to power in Germany. A quarter-century of catastrophes was to intervene before the initiatives of the late 1920s could bear fruit.

Colonialism in the Interwar Era

The interwar period was both the high point of the French colonial empire and the time when the forces that would break it up after World War II began to manifest themselves. The war had shown the value of the colonies, which had aided France with men and resources, and the peace settlement had awarded France new territories in Africa and the Middle East. Economically, the empire became even more important to France after the war than it had been earlier. The disruptions of the postwar period reduced international trade, and, as a result, the protected markets of France's colonies assumed a new significance. Exchanges with the colonies, 13 percent of France's overall commerce in 1913, grew to 33 percent in 1933, although most trade and investment went only to the colonies in North Africa and Indochina. Advertising images like the grinning, pop-eyed Senegalese soldier, the trademark of Banania, a popular children's breakfast drink, reinforced racial stereotypes, but they also made the empire a familiar presence in French homes. Whereas colonialism had been a controversial policy in the prewar period, by the 1920s only the small and unpopular Communist party openly campaigned against it. The 1931 Colonial Exposition in Paris, like the prewar world's fairs, attracted large crowds and encouraged visitors to identify with the "greater France" whose diverse peoples it displayed. Inaugurating the exposition, the minister of colonies Paul Reynaud reminded the public that metropolitan France was only 1/23rd of the Empire's geographic territory. Although the exposition emphasized the artistic achievements of non-European cultures, exhibits of advanced French technology being used overseas underlined the notion that France was still the source of all progress for its colonial territories.

Whereas the French public had come to take the colonies for granted, those who had to administer them found the task ever more complicated in the postwar period. Prewar optimism that France's republican values could easily be exported diminished as the years went on. Postwar French governments had less money to invest in the colonies, and ambitious schemes to replace traditional local leaders with French officials had to give way to an increased reliance on existing hierarchies, even if this meant abandoning the republican principle of social equality. Ironically, as the French became more familiar with the populations of their overseas territories, they became less confident of their mission to transform them. The ethnographic studies of Maurice Delafosse, the first great French expert on West Africa, revealed the richness and variety of the area's cultures. Delafosse supported colonialism and taught many of the administrators who were sent to govern the area, but his lessons raised doubts about the possibility or desirability of implanting French customs in such alien societies.

The greatest threat to the French empire, however, came from changing attitudes among the colonial populations themselves. The war had exposed them to heady rhetoric about democracy, national self-determination, and communist revolution. In their efforts to rally support from the colonies, French leaders themselves had made vague but alluring promises about increased rights for their populations. By the 1920s, there was a growing elite of so-called *évolués* in the colonies, who had received a French-style education. The first postwar governor of French West Africa warned that "the ideas of emancipation . . . are obviously destined to create illusions among the young educated blacks . . . and to incite them to dream of aspiring for themselves, to the exclusion of any foreign element, the role of educators and leaders of the indigenous societies."[3] Discontent with French policies did not always translate into calls for independence: in many cases, the initial demand of these educated elites was for fuller integration with France, which would give them increased legal and political rights and access to better jobs. When these demands were not met, however, members of the *évolué* groups began turning to nationalism and sometimes to communist ideas. The major anti-colonial revolt of the 1920s, Abd-el-Krim's rebellion in Morocco, could still be seen as a traditionalist attempt to drive out foreign occupiers, but the Yen Bay insurrection in Vietnam in 1930–1931 was organized by a movement that used the language of modern nationalism. In both cases, the French response was thoroughgoing repression, which strengthened resentment against their rule.

DOMESTIC POLITICS IN THE 1920s

The reorientation of French foreign policy was the most lasting legacy of the *Cartel des Gauches* victory in the 1924 elections. In domestic affairs the two years of the *Cartel*, from 1924 to 1926, proved to be an unhappy experiment that suggested France's parliamentary institutions were becoming increasingly unworkable. The centrist ministry of Raymond Poincaré, who held office from 1926 to 1929, appeared to demonstrate, on the other hand, that the Third Republic could, when necessary, pull itself out of political crises it periodically plunged into (as it had after Boulanger, the Dreyfus affair, and during the war). But Poincaré's term of office was the last time the regime was able to demonstrate such resiliency.

In domestic politics, the *Bloc national* governments had not only strongly repressed the revolutionary upsurge of 1920, but had reached out to conservatives with policies that broke with prewar republican tradition. The wartime experience had tempered the hostility between Catholics and nonbelievers, as members of both groups fought side by side to defend the country. From 1920 to 1924, the government gave Catholics satisfaction on several controversial issues. It tolerated the activities of Catholic religious orders that had been officially expelled from the country in 1901. In the recovered territories of Alsace and Lorraine, where the Separation Law of 1905 had never been applied, the 1801 Concordat was left in force as it had been during the German period. And in 1921, France reestablished diplomatic relations with the Vatican. With these measures, most of the gulf between the regime and its Catholic citizens was finally closed. The Republic no longer appeared as the agent of a militant anti-Catholic crusade, and Catholics in turn largely ceased to agitate for changes in the arrangements set up by the 1905 law.

The ministries of the 1920–1924 period were much less successful in dealing with another thorny problem, the reestablishment of France's public finances. The inflation spawned by the war had shocked a society accustomed to a currency (the "ger-

minal franc" established by Napoleon in 1803) that had remained stable for over a century. Several successive postwar ministers of finance promised that the immense debts contracted during the war could somehow be paid without weakening the national currency. The division of the government budget into so-called ordinary and extraordinary expenses—the latter supposedly to be covered by German reparations payments—disguised the size of the deficit. To promote postwar economic recovery, the government had to engage in still more deficit spending. To prevent the franc from losing its value, France had to borrow heavily abroad. The threat of withdrawal of these foreign loans was one of the major reasons Poincaré had to abandon occupation of the Rhineland in 1924. As part of this shift in policy, the conservative Poincaré was able to obtain new loans and shore up the franc in 1924, but his successor, Herriot, faced quite a different situation.

The 1924 election had seen the triumph of the left, but the government it produced had a shaky parliamentary base. Léon Blum's party adhered rigidly to the policy laid down at the time of the party's founding in 1905. Socialists would not accept ministerial offices in a government dominated by a "bourgeois" party. They would only support a Radical government as long as its policies were in accord with the Socialists' own program. The small businessmen and peasants who made up most of Herriot's own electorate responded to the Radicals' traditional attacks on the selfishness of the rich. But they had no sympathy for Socialist attacks on private property. The *Cartel* government thus had very limited room to maneuver. Herriot added to his problems by proposing to undo the concessions made to the Catholics between 1920 and 1924. In response, Catholic leaders organized a broad-based protest movement whose demonstrations attracted tens of thousands of followers. The success of this movement against the government's religious policy encouraged conservatives to resist its fiscal measures as well.

The left's apparent domination of the government after 1924 also inspired a resurgence of antiparliamentary, antidemocratic spirit on the far right, where some militants openly expressed their admiration for the way in which Benito Mussolini's Fascist movement had destroyed Italian democracy and implanted a dictatorial regime after 1922. The *Action française*, the most important of the surviving prewar right-wing leagues, remained active. But it faced competition from newly founded groups that found Maurras's organization too intellectual and insufficiently activist. Georges Valois's *Faisceau*, founded in 1925, borrowed its name and much of its symbolism from the Italian Fascists, as well as its pretension to synthesize ultraconservatism and syndicalism. The wealthy industrialist Pierre Taittinger bankrolled the *Jeunesses patriotes*, which imitated Mussolini's appeal to youth against a parliamentary regime dominated by old men. This "first wave" of French Fascist organizations failed to attract much of a following, however. France, which had won the war and which was enjoying economic prosperity in the mid-1920s, did not suffer from the conditions that had enabled Italian Fascists to recruit a mass following. The plethora of would-be leaders also weakened the extreme right. The *Action française* in particular suffered a major setback in 1926 when Pope Pius XI officially condemned the movement for its violation of basic religious values. The papal declaration weakened the tight bond that had connected Catholic faith and right-wing political extremism. Some Catholic intellectuals began to see that religious faith did not automatically entail the rejection of liberal and even socialist ideas.

The mid-1920s also saw the transformation of the French Communist party into a centralized and bureaucratically controlled organization modeled after the Soviet Communist party, and largely subservient to policy directives from Moscow. The PCF's opposition to occupation of the Ruhr had led to a repressive campaign against it, which hardened the remaining members' loyalty to the organization. Its agitation against the Herriot government's effort to maintain French colonial rule in Morocco by defeating the revolt led by Abd-el-Krim served to keep it at odds with the rest of the French political world. In 1927, the Soviets ordered the French party to adopt a policy of rigid opposition to the SFIO, extended even to voting against Socialist candidates on the second ballot in the 1928 elections. This was a violation of the strong French tradition by which the left-of-center parties aided each other against conservatives. This "class versus class" policy angered the Socialists and even many of the Communists' own voters, and kept the PCF demoralized and isolated.

In the 1920s, extremism of both the right and the left appeared to be only a minor challenge to the established political parties. But the winners of the 1924 elections had other problems of their own. The *Cartel* government was brought down by its inability to manage the nation's finances. By the spring of 1925, Herriot, the Radical premier, had had to exceed the legal limit for government borrowing from the privately run Bank of France. His Socialist allies' program for resolving the financial crisis—a tax on the savings and investments of the wealthy—was completely unacceptable both to his own supporters and to the country's conservative financial circles. After Herriot's government fell over this fiscal crisis in April 1925, his successors had equally little success in coming up with a plan that would reconcile left-wing voters and right-wing bankers. As the government drifted, the value of the franc began to drop with ever-increasing speed. Holders of government bonds tried desperately to cash them before they lost all value. Herriot, finally recalled in July of 1926 to make a last effort to reconstitute a government with a left-wing orientation, could not obtain a majority in the Chamber. The president, Gaston Doumergue, felt justified in offering the premiership to the conservative Raymond Poincaré, who succeeded in winning support from enough Radical deputies to break up the *Cartel* majority.

Poincaré and Financial Stabilization

More flagrantly than ever before, the Third Republic's parliamentary system had resulted in a government whose orientation contradicted the wishes expressed by the electorate. Yet a majority of the French public hailed Poincaré, who had "saved" the franc in 1924, as the only man capable of resolving the devastating fiscal crisis. Furthermore, Poincaré undertook to solve the fiscal crisis by demanding power to bypass the regular workings of the parliamentary system. The Chamber, aware of its own inability to resolve controversial issues, voted him the right to issue laws by decree. Although this was in one sense another example of the Third Republic's ability to meet crises, in another sense it was an admission that institutions created in 1875 were insufficient to deal with the complex problems of the postwar world.

Because he was personally popular with so much of the French public—the voters gave him and his conservative coalition a strong endorsement in the 1928 elections—and because his fellow parliamentarians realized there was no practical alternative to his policies, Poincaré was able to take measures to resolve the crisis that had paralyzed the *Cartel* government. In the course of his three years in office, Poincaré put through a number of important reforms. His government broadened access to the educational system by making secondary education tuition-free, and it passed France's first comprehensive social security law in 1928, providing a safety net of medical insurance and pensions for France's poorer citizens. But Poincaré's government was primarily hailed for restabilizing French government finances for the first time since the war. Poincaré's mere presence in office strengthened the franc, which nearly doubled in value against the British pound by the end of 1926. He pushed through a tax increase and trimmed government spending to reduce the budget deficit. Many of his supporters still hoped that Poincaré would somehow bring the franc back to its "true" value (the level of 1914), but by 1928 he had decided that the wisest policy was to accept that the cost of the war had entailed a permanent decline in the currency's value. The monetary law of June 1928 set the franc's value in gold at 20 percent of the prewar level, stabilizing it at approximately the rate it had reached on the foreign exchange market. Poincaré's measure represented an acceptance that much of the war's cost would have to be borne by France's savers, rich and poor, but it kept alive another illusion, namely the belief that France had finally come to the end of the period of instability begun in 1914.

NOTES

1. Raoul Girardet, "L'Ombre de la guerre," in Pierre Nora, ed., *Essais d'ego-histoire* (Paris: Gallimard, 1987), 139.

2. Cited in René Girault and Robert Frank, *Turbulente Europe et nouveaux mondes* (Paris: Masson, 1981), 148.

3. Cited in Alice L. Conklin, *A Mission to Civilize: The Republican Idea of Empire in France and West Africa, 1895–1930* (Stanford, Ca.: Stanford University Press, 1997), 190.

CHAPTER 25

THE ILLUSION OF NORMALITY

By the mid-1920s, France seemed to have recovered from the most immediate effects of the war. The country was once again enjoying prosperity and economic growth. Its position in the world seemed secure. Even when the American stock market crash of 1929 tumbled much of the world into a severe economic crisis, France appeared happily immune. For a few years, the stable, peaceful world of the prewar Third Republic seemed to have been regained.

ECONOMIC RECOVERY

The periodic newspaper headlines about the crisis of the franc during the 1920s gave a misleading impression about the state of the French economy in the postwar decade. In fact, as Raymond Poincaré recognized when he officially abandoned efforts to restore the currency to its prewar level in 1928, inflation and currency devaluation actually aided economic growth by reducing debts incurred by investors and making French products cheaper on foreign markets. It was not only the falling franc that stimulated French economic progress during the 1920s. Other factors were at work that allowed France to participate in the general surge of prosperity in the western world from

1921–1929, and (according to many statistical measures) put the country for the first time ahead of its rivals in terms of industrial growth. France's performance in the 1920s demonstrated that the economic development of the *belle époque* years had not been a fluke; it was a prelude to the even more impressive growth of the 1950s.

The first few years after the armistice were difficult ones in France as in the rest of the world. Social unrest, the need to convert factories from war production to civilian goods, and the problem of reintegrating the millions of demobilized soldiers into the workforce all caused economic disruption. Industrial production in 1919 was only 57 percent of its level in 1913, the last prewar year. By 1924, however, the industrial economy had significantly surpassed the prewar level. In 1929, on the eve of the worldwide economic crisis, the production index stood at 140. There were several reasons behind this economic upsurge. The postwar French government spent heavily to rebuild damaged areas of the north, giving work to the construction industry. Even in areas not directly touched by the war, government funds paid for new public buildings—schools, post offices, town halls—and government policies stimulated new housing projects and other construction. At Versailles, the French had negotiated for treaty provisions intended to promote the country's economic interests, and these were not totally without effect. From 1922 to 1928, France enjoyed a positive trade balance with Germany, a rare phenomenon in the two countries' relations. Through the 1920s, France's colonial empire provided a profitable captive market that helped to promote the country's prosperity.

As in the prewar period, the most technologically advanced sectors of the French economy led its growth. Iron and steel production expanded and modernized so that by 1929 France had, for the first time since the beginning of the industrial revolution 150 years earlier, reached the level of Britain. Growth in iron production resulted in a corresponding expansion of coal mining. Much of the country's iron and steel production went to the large factories of the fast-growing manufacturing sector. In 1929, the French automobile industry turned out 254,000 cars, making it the second largest in the world. (That status admittedly meant little in the face of the American industry's level of 5,300,000 vehicles.) The electrical industry also underwent dramatic expansion, exploiting the hydropower resources of the Alps and benefiting from government promotion of rural electrification. Modernization also penetrated parts of the commercial sector of the economy. Chain stores and credit sales, both developed in the late nineteenth century, expanded further in the 1920s. The domestic consumer market expanded as middle-class households began to acquire an increasing number of factory-made products, such as kitchen appliances and radios. Advertising became more pervasive and more imaginative. Seductive images of women were employed to sell an everincreasing range of products.

The modernization of some parts of the French economy was often seen as part of a phenomenon of "Americanization," the penetration into France of production methods and values pioneered in the United States. The expansion of American influence as a result of World War I and the tremendous growth of its economy made this a major issue for the first time. French commentators coined the words *fordisme,* to refer to the assembly-line methods copied from Henry Ford's auto factories, and *taylorisme,* in honor of American efficiency expert F. W. Taylor's time-and-motion studies aimed at raising worker productivity. Forward-looking industrialists, such as the owners of the Michelin tire company, were eager to show that they were keeping France competitive by adopting these new techniques. At the same time, however, they strove to give their enterprises distinctive French identities. Intellectuals were often more critical of American influence. Georges Duhamel's popular book, *America the Menace: Scenes from the Life of the Future,* articulated an image of America that has resurfaced repeatedly in France ever since. According to Duhamel, the United States was a soulless, mechanistic society, in which profit and efficiency were the only values. "What strikes the European traveler," Duhamel wrote, "is the progressive approximation of human life to what we know of the way of life of insects—the same effacement of the individual, the same progressive reduction and unification of social types."[1]

American models also had an impact on mass culture, which became increasingly associated with the electronic media. The French film industry suffered badly during and after the war, losing its initial supremacy to American silent film producers. But the introduction of talking films after 1927 and controls on the number of imports allowed it to revive during the 1930s. By 1933, there were over four thousand movie theaters in France, and the medium had largely replaced the music hall as the chief form of mass entertainment. Mass culture penetrated the home via increasing popularity of radio.

Regular broadcasting had begun in 1922. The annual Tour de France bicycle race was broadcast on radio for the first time in 1929, adding to the popularity of this distinctively French spectacle, which had been initiated in 1903 by a sports magazine. France hesitated for a long time between the American model of a broadcasting industry under private control and the British decision to entrust programming to a publicly controlled enterprise. During the 1930s, the state gradually took control, but with many delays which retarded the development of the medium. Private entrepreneurs evaded regulation by using "peripheral" transmitters located just outside France's borders. Some of them, particularly Radio-Luxembourg, founded in 1933, have continued to be major features of France's broadcasting system down to the present.

As in the prewar years, however, French economic development continued to follow a pattern in which—to a much greater extent than in other industrial nations—traditional sectors of the economy persisted alongside more modern ones. The rural economy was the most important example. During the war, the demand for farm products had been high, and the supply of consumer goods that peasants could buy with their money had been small. As a result, at the end of the conflict, many peasant families had accumulated considerable savings. Rather than investing in modern equipment or adopting new methods, however, they used this money to acquire new land. Despite the losses of the war, the rural population diminished only slowly during the 1920s, and there was little extension of improved agricultural methods. France's millions of small family farms continued to consume much of their own production, and to provide only a modest market for the country's urban industries. Through a generous tax policy and other measures, the governments of the 1920s also protected the hundreds of thousands of small shops and family businesses. These bakeries, hairdressers, and corner cafés might have been squeezed out by their economic inefficiency if larger enterprises had been allowed to take full advantage of their opportunities.

POSTWAR SOCIETY AND CULTURE

The economic growth of the 1920s thus did not threaten the position of major groups that had formed the social base of the Third Republic since its establishment: the business classes, large and small, the landowning peasantry, and the civil service establishment. The more humble strata of these groups were especially strongly represented in the numerous army veterans' organizations, which formed one of the most important social movements of the interwar decades. Originally concerned with obtaining proper compensation for the war-wounded and pensions for ex-soldiers, the veterans' organizations (which enrolled over three million members at their peak and far outnumbered political parties and trade unions of the period) represented the values of middle-class and peasant republicanism. Although their spokesmen reiterated that the war had been a necessary and patriotic endeavor, they were profoundly pacifist and sympathetic to Briand's conciliatory foreign policy. The mass veterans' movements rejected political extremism and, indeed, condemned conventional politics of all sorts, which they blamed for dividing the country. They argued that France's democratic society had provided the forces that won the war and that it therefore deserved to be preserved from either social revolution or transformations that unbridled capitalist development might bring about.

The dominant outlook among the war veterans was often similar to that of the extraordinarily influential newspaper columnist and philosopher Emile Chartrier, known as "Alain," who reached the peak of his fame after the war. Alain spoke for much of French society in his rejection of the all-powerful state and his defense of individual freedom. He urged his readers to be suspicious of all politicians and he considered the war to have been the ultimate proof of the stupidity inherent in organized political activity. If one had to attend a patriotic ceremony, he wrote in the early 1920s, "think of those blinded in the fighting, that cools the passions." Even the unbridled pursuit of economic progress struck Alain, the proponent of France's traditional society and its economy on a human scale, as misguided. "No, production is not an end in itself; a worthwhile life for everyone is the goal, the free individual is the goal."[2]

Immigrant Factory Workers

The industrial proletariat remained largely excluded from the organized veterans' movement, although large numbers of workers had certainly served in the war. And it was the working class that was most affected by economic changes of the 1920s. In fact, some recent historians have talked of a new working class, only remotely connected with the French workers of the 1890s. A good part of the working class was new because it consisted of immigrant laborers, two million of whom were recruited between 1921 and 1931. They were concentrated in certain sectors, such as mining, where immigrants, primarily Poles, were 42 percent of the labor force in 1930. "Outside the main gate," a visitor to the main Renault auto factory in the Paris suburb of Boulogne-Billancourt wrote in 1928, "a stall offers Armenian, Romanian, Czech, Hungarian newspapers, those from Vienna and Berlin, Italy and Spain."[3] The Renault plant was typical of the new, large factories that employed the biggest part of the postwar working class, in contrast to the smaller enterprises that had characterized the nineteenth century. The new proletariat generally lacked the special skills that had given the nineteenth-century worker a certain autonomy on the job. They were more likely to find themselves doing simple, repetitive tasks on the American-style assembly lines that dominated many of the new factories.

Around these new factories grew up new communities, such as the "red belt" of dreary suburbs surrounding Paris. Here, workers, uprooted from their homes in rural France or abroad, lived in physical isolation from the rest of society in hastily and shoddily constructed apartment blocks and small houses. Significantly, the Paris subway system, begun around the turn of the century and greatly expanded between the wars, did not penetrate into these communities until its expansion in the 1970s. Cut off from the rest of French life, the inhabitants of these working-class communities did not share in the prosperity of the 1920s. Average salaries rose only slowly during this period, not enough to make any significant improvement in living conditions. The Communist party found its strongest base in these areas. The CGT, dominated by unions of relatively well-off public service employees, did not offer these new factory workers much. Only the impact of the depression in the 1930s and the upsurge of the Popular Front would allow them to find effective forms of mass organization and make their voice heard in the rest of French society.

The Avant-Garde

While workers toiled in "Americanized" factories, those who were better off danced to the rhythm of American jazz bands. The vogue for the new American music, and for stars like the exotic African American dancer Josephine Baker, came to symbolize a revolt against the conventional culture and lifestyle of prewar bourgeois France. Victor Margueritte's best-selling novel, *La Garçonne*

(The Bachelor Girl), depicted the world of the jazz decade: corrupt, dissipated, avid for money, open to cultural experiments, and awash in alcohol and drugs. Only a tiny fraction of the population actually lived anything like the life *La Garçonne* portrayed, but some of Margueritte's themes evoked changes that, in less exaggerated form, affected larger parts of French society. Paris remained one of the world's great cultural centers. During the 1920s, it was home to a dazzling collection of foreign writers and artists, who found in *la ville lumière* a sense of freedom and excitement they missed at home. James Joyce, Gertrude Stein, Ernest Hemingway, exiled Russian intellectuals fleeing the Communist regime, and many others were among them.

Along with expatriates from foreign countries, Paris was a gathering point for educated elites from the French colonies. Thanks to the more liberal laws in the metropole and the sympathy they received from critics of colonialism, these exiles were often ahead of their compatriots back home in adopting new ideas and organizing protest movements. In Paris, a young Algerian, Messali Hadj, created the first movement for the independence of his country, the *Etoile Nord-Africaine*, in 1927, recruiting followers among immigrant workers. Paris was also the birthplace of the cultural movement known as *négritude*, which grew out of encounters between blacks from the various French colonies and African-American expatriates who transmitted the influence of Marcus Garvey's pan-African movement and the "Harlem Renaissance" of the 1920s. The leaders of the *négritude* movement, Aimé Césaire from Martinique and Léopold Sedar Senghor from Senegal, argued that people of African descent all shared a common culture, distinct from that of Europe. African civilization, Senghor claimed, had "the gift of emotion and the gift of sympathy, the gift of rhythm and of form, the gift of images

and the gift of myth, a communitarian and democratic spirit . . ."[4] Although Césaire and Senghor both made political careers in the French system, their writings helped inspire a new self-consciousness in black colonial populations.

The postwar decade was a lively one for French culture. The publication of Marcel Proust's masterpiece, *A La Recherche du Temps perdu*, the first volume of which had appeared just before the war, was completed in 1927, five years after its author's death. Proust's meditation on the distorting and creative power of memory continued some of the antirationalist trends of the prewar period. His complex, multilayered prose immediately established his work as a literary classic. André Gide, already well known in the prewar period, broke a major taboo in 1921 with the publication of his autobiographical *Si le grain ne meurt*, which explicitly discussed his homosexual awakening in pre-war Morocco.

The self-consciously avant-garde Surrealist movement, which attracted a number of artists and poets, took the prewar exploration of the unconscious and the irrational to new lengths. The poet André Breton, one of the group's main spokesmen, announced their intention to liberate the imagination by such techniques as "automatic writing" in which the author sought to put words on paper without subjecting them to any conscious shaping. In music, the most creative endeavors were those of "Les Six," a loose group of young composers (best known today are Darius Milhaud and François Poulenc) who brought to France the new atonal style pioneered before the war by the Austrian Schoenberg and the Russian Stravinsky. The period saw an important renewal of French theater, and the leading painters of the prewar avant-garde, such as Picasso and Matisse, continued to make new stylistic breakthroughs. Continuing the cubist tradition, Fernand Léger used machine-like shapes to create an art linked to the cult of industrial modernism, while Yves Tanguy's dreamlike landscapes reflected the influence of Surrealism.

Women's Roles

Victor Margueritte's *La Garçonne* reflected not only the period's interest in cultural experimentation but also its concern with new roles being adopted by women. Margueritte himself was a strong supporter of women's emancipation. His subsequent writings included a book advocating the right to abortion. His heroine, Monique, was an emancipated woman who lived a life as independent as that of any man—adopting the short skirts and close-cropped hair that were symbols of the new female freedom, and taking her sexual pleasure wherever she found it. But Monique—artistic creator and successful businesswoman—was hardly typical of the average French woman of the period. Even the period's major feminist movements continued to uphold conventional sexual morality. Radicals like Nelly Roussel, who campaigned for women's access to birth control, and Madeleine Pelletier, who dressed in men's clothing, were isolated figures.

The outbreak of war in 1914 had interrupted a campaign for women's suffrage that had been gaining increasing support. At the end of the conflict, women's groups thought that the important contributions women had made to the war effort and the granting of voting rights to women in other major countries, including Britain, Germany, the United States and Russia, would lead to similar action in France. Because they expected women to vote primarily for conservative causes, the Catholic Church and even Charles Maurras, the leader of the extremist *Action française,* supported this idea. The Chamber of Deputies actually passed a suffrage law in May 1919, only to see it blocked in the Senate in 1922. Conservative backing for women's suffrage led many senators

from the Radical Party to oppose the law; they feared that women would not support republican institutions. In addition, there were objections to granting women the vote because it would make them the majority of the electorate, since so many men had been killed in the war.

Women's groups continued to campaign for voting rights throughout the interwar period, pointing out, for example, that Joan of Arc had saved France in the 1400s but that she would have been barred from voting for a local city councillor in the 1920s. Despite several favorable votes in the Chamber of Deputies, the Senate continued to block all action on the issue. Nevertheless, the expressions support for women's suffrage in the Chamber convinced feminists that the Republic would eventually see the justice of their cause and discouraged them from adopting more militant tactics. Although women were barred from voting, they were able to influence public life in a number of ways. Women played a leading role in the pacifist groups that were among the most important public associations of the period. Twenty different women's peace groups were created during the 1920s. Women also had leading roles in the gradual expansion of social-welfare institutions that took place in the interwar years. Social services during this period were provided by a mixture of public and private agencies, and women philanthropists and social workers often had prominent positions in them.

Nevertheless, the sphere of women's activities was slowly being enlarged. The war itself made it inevitable that more women would have to live independent lives, since the heavy casualties suffered by the male population left the country with a permanent surplus of women. There was growing dissatisfaction with the limited curriculum of girls' secondary schools set up at the beginning of the Third Republic and an increasing trend for girls to demand a course of study identical with that offered to boys. In 1924, women were allowed to take the same *baccalauréat* exam as the men, giving them increased access to higher education. The number of professional women grew; women lawyers, with their experience in public speaking, played a prominent role in feminist organizations. Women schoolteachers obtained pay and privileges equal to men in 1919.

Although women gained more access to education and higher-level jobs, trends affecting sexual freedom were mixed. In 1920, driven by concerns about the country's low birth rate and by a reaction against the changes in traditional sex roles that had occurred during the war, the conservative *Bloc national* passed a draconian law that not only prohibited abortion but also outlawed any dissemination of birth-control information and sale of contraceptive devices other than male condoms. (This exception was justified on the grounds that men needed to be able to protect themselves from venereal disease.) Even the mainstream women's groups supported this law. Their leaders—mostly middle-class married women—accepted the patriotic argument that national strength required a larger population. They also feared that objections on their part would weaken support for women's suffrage and other reforms they favored. The development of Catholic women's groups in the 1920s represented a broadening of the women's movement, which had traditionally been dominated by laic tendencies, but the Catholic organizations added strength to opposition to abortion and birth control. The 1920 law had little effect on the birth rate, which remained low, and illegal abortions were common, but it emphasized the sharp difference between women's and men's positions in French society. Parallel to rationalization of the workplace, French women were urged to accept medical control of such basic functions as childbirth and to adopt

scientific principles of management in their homes. The percentage of Parisian babies born in clinics rose from 34 in 1920 to 68 in 1939, while home births dropped from 42 percent to 8 percent. Paulette Bernège's *On the Household System* (1928) became a standard guide to the efficient performance of household tasks. Other literature taught mothers how to provide a hygienic environment for their children, contributing to a continued decline in infant mortality.

The Descent into the Depression

As the 1920s neared their end, both France and the wider world seemed to have overcome much of the trauma of the Great War. It is true that the picture was not an unclouded one. Economic prosperity was not universal. Britain suffered from depression throughout most of the period, for example, and many of the new nations of eastern and central Europe had never overcome the difficulties of their new situation. But democracy still had solid foundations in France; and in Germany the new institutions of the Weimar Republic appeared to have taken hold. Only in hindsight, however, is it really possible to see how ephemeral the hopes of the 1920s were. Certainly no one in France in 1929 could have known that the country was headed for a grave economic setback and a period of political divisions worse than at any previous point since the foundation of the Third Republic.

For the world at large, the year 1929 was marked by the crash of the American stock market and the deep depression that followed. The American depression had immediate repercussions in many other countries, most notably in Germany, where the economic difficulties it caused gave Adolf Hitler's Nazi movement the opportunity to start its rise to power. Initially, however, France seemed to enjoy a certain immunity to the depression's effects. Less dependent on export markets than the Germans, French manufacturers still lived protected behind high tariff walls. For a time, French politicians and businessmen smugly asserted the fate of more industrialized countries like the United States proved "that French methods, often middling but always prudent, are best."[5] They argued that France's balanced economy, with its large peasant sector, was cushioned against massive shocks.

By the beginning of 1931, however, the depression had arrived in France. In statistical terms, it was less severe than in the hardest-hit countries. The percentage of unemployed French was kept low because employers who had recruited workers from abroad were sometimes able to send them back to their home countries, and because many French workers from rural origins returned to their native farms to eke out a living.

The depression was most severe for the more technologically advanced sectors of the economy. In 1934, the automobile manufacturer Citroën, known for introduction of new design ideas, had to declare bankruptcy. The less modern sectors of France's dual economy, those who had been slower to invest in new machinery in the 1920s, survived better. Manufacturers turned inward, away from a world market shrunken by protectionist policies of major governments, and relied on cartel agreements to prevent more efficient producers from driving out their domestic competitors. The colonies provided an outlet for French products, although manufacturers also had to buy colonial products at prices higher than world market levels. Some struggling enterprises were forced to turn to the state for aid. After a decade in which the French government had renounced the economic involvement of the war years, its role began to grow, albeit in a piecemeal fashion. In 1933, the country's privately owned air transport companies were forced to merge into a single enterprise, Air France, with the government as

minority stockholder. But there was no overall economic plan to combat the depression, and the slowdown remained persistent.

Poincaré had led a moderate and conservative coalition to victory in the 1928 elections, and it was left to his conservative successors to make the first efforts to combat the depression. Their policies, governed by strict economic orthodoxy, were uniformly unsuccessful. Higher tariffs were ineffective since consumers lacked money to spend, and measures designed to protect small businesses by allowing them to maintain high prices also reduced consumption. The government's dedicated defense of the franc's new value, established in 1928, made French goods more expensive on the world market when other governments devalued their currencies. To avoid budget deficits, the government reduced public employees' salaries, thereby reducing consumer demand even more. By the time of the 1932 elections, the voters were ready for a change. As in 1924, the Radicals and the SFIO formed an electoral alliance and made substantial gains. But the Radical leader Edouard Herriot, installed as premier, was as unsuccessful in combatting the depression as he had been in controlling inflation in 1924–1925. The Socialists' continued refusal to participate directly in the government weakened the left, and made a drift toward the right almost unavoidable.

Critics of the Government and Society

As usual under the Third Republic, the prolonged period of political instability in the face of a crisis situation provoked a wave of criticism of the regime. Not all of it came from extremist groups bent on using the crisis to destroy the Republic. The early 1930s saw numerous reform proposals aimed at preserving the best qualities of the republican regime by making it more functional. The conservative leader André Tardieu, the group of young Radical party members known as the "Young Turks," and dissident members of the SFIO were among those who offered proposals to pull the system out of the doldrums. Despite the political differences among the reformers, there were certain common themes in their proposals. All agreed on the need for a stronger, more effective executive branch of government, less dependent on the whims of a parliament that was widely condemned as unrepresentative of the country at large. The regime's critics asserted that the parliamentary system was especially unsuited to dealing with the realities of a complex modern economy. The idea of a national economic plan was widely discussed, and there were many proposals for creation of institutions that would represent different branches of the economy, a tendency known as corporatism. Many critics called for some form of centralized economic planning, directed by the government, to ensure efficient use of resources. This technocratic current, reminiscent of the Saint-Simonian movement of the first half of the nineteenth century, attracted a number of managers and engineers.

The political party system, too, came in for severe castigation. Tardieu tried to unite the many conservative groups into a broad-based conservative party. Meanwhile, a prominent socialist, Marcel Déat, split from his party in 1933 and founded his own neosocialist group in opposition to the SFIO's dogmatic Marxism and its reluctance to cooperate with middle-class political movements. These "political nonconformists" of the early 1930s were often men destined to play prominent roles in the politics of the next few decades—some as wartime collaborationists, others as members of the Resistance and the postwar governments. At the time, however, their reform proposals shattered against political party divisions and the inertia of parliament, whose members were not inclined to support changes that would reduce their power. Despite a lively and substantial debate about the need for fundamental changes in the political system, France continued to drift.

Although the intellectual debates of the period were not confined to politics, there was a strong tendency for writers and artists to turn from the concentration on personal problems characteristic of the 1920s to a preoccupation with public issues that seemed to have become so much more pressing. Emmanuel Mounier, one of the important intellectuals of the period, later described the generation that came of age after 1930 as "serious, solemn, occupied by difficulties, unsure of the future."[6] Mounier himself was a participant in one of the most important intellectual developments of the period, the renewal of French Catholic thought. The papal condemnation of the *Action française* in 1926 had loosened the identification between religion and ultra-conservatism, and permitted a revival of the more democratic and socially concerned Catholicism associated with Marc Sangnier's *Sillon* movement at the turn of the century. Mounier and other thinkers of the period, many of them Catholic, developed a doctrine they called "personalism," which attempted to define a middle way between individualist liberalism and the collectivist doctrines of fascism and communism. They stressed the importance of the socially committed individual and of a morally structured common life. *Esprit*, the journal Mounier founded in 1932 to spread these ideas, was one of the most important publications of the period. Simone Weil, a brilliant young Jewish woman who became a Christian mystic, faulted the Communists for claiming to free people from the burden of work rather than helping them find meaning in it. She called for a society in which "the worker would know . . . how his work fits into the factory's production, and what place his factory occupies in the life of the society around it."[7]

The Catholic novelist Georges Bernanos offered a different vision of personal commitment in his *Diary of a Country Priest,* published in 1936. It recounted a young clergyman's struggles to affirm his faith in the face of a largely indifferent society. Politically, he was at opposite ends of the spectrum from André Malraux, whose novels also exemplified the literature of commitment. Malraux's masterpiece, *Man's Fate,* set in China during the revolutionary upheavals of the 1920s, was one of several works drawing liberally on the author's own adventures. It told the dramatic story of the struggle and defeat of the Communist movement in Shanghai. The Spanish Civil War that began in 1936 inspired Malraux to an even more overtly political book, *Man's Hope,* which glorified the left-wing forces in that bitter conflict. While Malraux identified with revolutionary movements, Jean Giraudoux's popular 1935 play *The Trojan War Will Not Take Place* expressed a commitment to pacifism.

In the increasingly politicized atmosphere of the 1930s, not all leading writers identified with democratic or left-wing positions. Some of the most talented violently rejected what they saw as bankrupt humanitarian ideals, and turned to fascism or nihilism. The most troubling case was that of Louis-Ferdinand Céline, whose *Voyage to the End of the Night* (1932) and *Death on the Installment Plan* (1936) established him as perhaps the most creative user of the French language in the first half of the century. But his vehement detestation of what he saw as a rotten civilization expressed itself in denunciations of Jews, women, blacks, and all the conventional values of bourgeois society. Jean Giono's pastoral novels of life in his native Provence, several of them made into successful movies, expressed a more traditional lament about the impact of modernity on small rural communities. The wide range of views among the period's leading writers reflected the deepening cleavages in a society confronted with ever-more dramatic social and political issues.

The 1930s produced no striking new talents in the visual arts. The period foreshadowed the shift that would see Paris replaced by New York as the world's center of innovation in painting and sculpture. But it was in some respects a golden age for the French cinema, whose best filmmakers revealed an independence of spirit that distinguished their work from the flood of American films. (These latter nevertheless remained extremely popular with French audiences.) Jean Vigo's masterpieces, *Zéro de Conduite* and *L'Atalante,* expressed an anarchistic spirit that was too much for censors and commercial distributors. They were not seen in uncut versions until years later, when they became cult classics. Marcel Pagnol enjoyed great success with his sentimental trilogy of popular life in Marseille, *Marius, Fanny,* and *César.* Jean Renoir's *Rules of the Game* (1939) dissected the emptiness of upper-class life with memorable images that have made it an enduring classic.

NOTES

1. Cited in Jean-Philippe Mathy, *Extrême-Occident: French Intellectuals and America* (Chicago: University of Chicago Press, 1993), 59.
2. Cited in Georges Pascal, *Pour Connaître la pensée d'Alain* (Paris: Bordas, 1957), 21, 192.
3. Cited in Gérard Noiriel, *Les Ouvriers dans la société française* (Paris: Seuil, 1986), 151.
4. Cited in Raoul Girardet, *L'idée coloniale en France de 1871 à 1962* (Paris: La Table ronde, 1972), 249.
5. Cited in Richard F. Kuisel, *Capitalism and the State in Modern France* (Cambridge, UK: Cambridge University Press, 1981), 93.
6. Cited in J.-L. Loubet del Bayle, *Les Non-Conformistes des années 30* (Paris: Seuil, 1969), 23.
7. Cited in M.-M. Davy, *Simone Weil* (Paris: PUF, 1966), 115.

CHAPTER 26

FROM THE POPULAR FRONT TO THE WAR

THE CRISIS OF FEBRUARY 6, 1934

As the depression crisis deepened, extremist elements raised their voices in hopes of profiting from it. The far right was initially the most successful in exploiting public frustration with the government's inability to end the economic downturn, as a "second wave" of quasi-Fascist organizations developed. Whether these groups merit the label "Fascist" has been one of the most heated controversies among contemporary historians.[1] Some of them imitated the emphasis on uniforms, symbols, and mass meetings characteristic of Mussolini's and Hilter's movements, but others did not. Not all of these groups called explicitly for the overthrow of the republican regime. Some shared the overt antisemitism of Hitler's Nazis, but others condemned it. Since none of the many competing French groups ever came to power, it is impossible to say whether they would have attempted to make France into a totalitarian dictatorship and whether they would have been able to command enough support to carry out such a program. Collectively, they did create an atmosphere in which the possibility of a Fascist France seemed at least plausible.

One of the weaknesses of the French movements was the number of would-be *Führers* competing for power. Peasants in some regions followed the agitator Henri Dorgères's Peasant Defense Committee, which instigated violent incidents to protest falling prices. Small businessmen supported the demagogic Taxpayers' League, which blamed the crisis on wasteful government spending. François Coty, a wealthy perfume manufacturer who had supported earlier Fascist groups in the 1920s, tried to gain power through the press. His *Ami du Peuple* shot up to a circulation of over a million by 1930. A retired army officer, François de la Rocque, headed the *Croix-de-Feu*. It started out as a veterans' group but grew into a broad-based conservative movement whose penchant for mass rallies and antiparliamentary slogans was uncomfortably reminiscent of Fascist movements in other European countries. Marcel Bucard's *Francistes* paraded in their blue shirts and made no secret of their desire to emulate Mussolini and Hitler. In many cases, these right-wing groups' slogans and practices copied those of the anti-Dreyfus leagues of the turn of the century. But in the context of the international situation of the early 1930s and the discontent inspired by the depression, they were far more menacing.

After Italy in 1922 and Germany in 1933, was France ripe for a fascist takeover? The question came to a head in early 1934. The Radical ministry of Camille Chautemps was particularly vulnerable because of a recently exposed scandal. A financial swindler, Stavisky, had used his connection with some minor politicians from the governing Radical party to take control of the municipally owned bank in the small town of Bayonne and issue millions of francs of bonds in its name. The fact that Stavisky's lawyer was Chautemps's brother, and that he had succeeded in having legal proceedings against him postponed more than a dozen times, suggested that high-level Radical politicians had intervened on his behalf. When the swindler, pursued by the police, was found dead under mysterious circumstances in early 1934, the scandal became a national issue. The right-wing press strongly suggested that Stavisky had been killed to avoid revelations inconvenient to the Chautemps government. That government fell at the end of January.

On February 6, 1934, just after the formation of a new ministry, a broad assortment of right-wing groups called for mass demonstrations to converge on the Chamber of Deputies' meeting place (the Palais Bourbon) to protest parliamentary corruption. The Communists, equally antagonistic to the government, called for a simultaneous march of their own, as did the *Union Nationale des Combattants*, one of the largest veterans' movements. The result was a huge but uncoordinated crowd outside the parliament building. Some right-wing leaders undoubtedly hoped to provoke a violent assault on the Palais-Bourbon, while others (like de la Rocque's *Croix-de-Feu*) prudently kept their troops at a safe distance from the barricades. In the confusion, however, the beleaguered police finally opened fire on the demonstrators, killing fifteen of them.

The aftermath of the confrontation on February 6, 1934, was as confusing as the event itself. The forces of order had held firm against what appeared to be the most serious attempt to overthrow the regime since 1871. But the uproar against the gov-

ernment's use of force on demonstrators, including wounded war veterans, led the Radical prime minister Edouard Daladier to resign. For the first time in Third Republic history, street agitation had brought down a government. To many observers, France seemed in real danger of sliding down the slope toward a Fascist dictatorship. For the moment, the parliamentary right replaced the moderate left in power. The new premier, Gaston Doumergue, promised reforms to defuse popular discontent, but failed to accomplish anything of substance. Modern historians have tended to reject the belief, widespread at the time, that the riot on February 6, 1934, represented an organized attempt to overthrow parliamentary government and install a right-wing dictatorship. They point to the number of competing groups involved in the demonstration, the fact that many of them (particularly the *Croix-de-Feu*) showed no stomach for a fight, and the general acceptance of the moderate Doumergue ministry, which remained loyal to the country's republican institutions.

THE POPULAR FRONT

In contrast to the situation in Italy and Germany, the right-wing agitation of February 6, 1934, provoked a broad union of left-wing forces in France that temporarily consolidated the democratic republic. The first signs of this movement came within a few days of the riot. On February 12, 1934, supporters of the two long-divided left-wing parties—the SFIO and the Communists—marched together in a demonstration against fascism called by the CGT trade union confederation. Although both parties' leaders had reservations about working together (the SFIO because the Communists had denounced it for years for treason to the working class, the Communists because they had since 1927 faithfully followed the official party line of making Socialists their main target), their followers clearly wanted to see the two groups cooperate. Local "unity committees" threatened to bypass the regular party structures and, by July 1934 (the Communists having followed new instructions from Moscow to promote broad-based antifascist coalitions), the two parties agreed to work together.

The agreement between the SFIO and the PCF strengthened the left but, by themselves, they had no hope of winning a majority in the 1936 elections. The enlargement of the pact to include the Radicals seemed problematic in view of that party's commitment to defense of private property and small business interests that the Communists had always attacked. It was the Communists who reached out to the Radicals, however, abandoning many of their traditional positions, such as hostility to military expenditures. (The French Communists' surprising evolution on this issue reflected the Soviet dictator Stalin's preoccupation with the threat from Hitler, which had suddenly made a strong French army seem more attractive to him.) Local elections in May 1935 showed the effectiveness of this broad-based *Rassemblement populaire* or, as it has come to be remembered, Popular Front. The massive Bastille Day parade of July 14, 1935, in Paris, sponsored by the three parties under the slogan "give the workers bread, give the young work, and give the world peace," gave the movement the appearance of an irresistible tide. In January 1936, the three parties and several other smaller groups agreed on a common program, directed primarily against the country's wealthy elite (the so-called two hundred families who were accused of prospering while the mass of population suffered through the depression). Alongside the parties, a broad spectrum of other groups devoted to peace, the democratization of culture, and other causes swept thousands of ordinary citizens into the movement. The tide of unity also swept the labor movement. The two rival federations

that had fought each other since the Communists quit the CGT in 1922 reunited to form a single organization.

The looming Popular Front election victory drove some right-wing opponents to adopt the slogan "Better Hitler than Blum." In February 1936, *Action française* militants beat up the Socialist leader so severely that he had to be temporarily hospitalized. But the movement had developed too much momentum to be halted. Anticipation of a Popular Front victory paralyzed the existing government, and Hitler successfully defied the Versailles Treaty by remilitarizing the German Rhineland in March 1936, calculating correctly that the French would not respond. The May 1936 elections were, as expected, a sweeping triumph for the coalition parties. The SFIO came in ahead of the Radicals, for the first time achieving the status of the country's largest party. But the most sensational result was the rise of the Communists, who obtained 15 percent of the vote.

For more than forty years after its electoral breakthrough in 1936, the French Communist party would exercise a major influence on the life of the country. In many respects, the rise of the Communists seemed to be a new example of the familiar process by which new parties on the left had repeatedly replaced their predecessors, driving them toward the political center. The Communists differed from earlier left-wing parties, such as the republicans and the socialists, however, because they were part of a movement tightly controlled by a foreign government. The downfall of the Soviet Union in the early 1990s has allowed historians to study the archives of the Comintern, the international arm of the Communist movement, and document how closely French Communist leader Maurice Thorez followed the instructions relayed by its permanent representative in France, Evgen Fried. Furthermore, other French leftist parties governed themselves in a democratic fashion, choosing leaders and setting policies through open debate and elections, whereas the Communist party was a totalitarian organization whose numbers had no real influence on its direction. When it adopted its new policy in 1934–1935, the Communist movement reached out to new constituencies which were not exclusively proletarian, such as women and youth. It now proclaimed its loyalty to democracy and embraced the traditional symbols of French republican partiotism, such as the "Marseillaise," but even its Popular Front coalition partners remained wary of an organization capable of changing its orientation so rapidly and completely. Until the Communists' decline in the 1980s, France faced the problem of how to deal with an organization that enjoyed too much popular support to be ignored but that never fully accepted the values of democracy.

Léon Blum

Thanks to the SFIO's success, its leader, Léon Blum, undertook to form a cabinet in which his party would not only participate but take the lead. Blum, an assimilated Jew, had started his career as a literary critic before becoming converted to a democratic and humanistic socialism at the time of the Dreyfus Affair. Largely because of his Jewish background, Blum inspired a degree of hatred among the French right that was out of all proportion to his basically cautious and legalistic policies. When he made his first appearance before the Assembly as premier, the violently anti-Semitic deputy Xavier Vallat denounced him as "a subtle Talmudist." Blum courageously faced down such attacks, but he lacked the charisma to weld the left-wing forces that had supported the Popular Front behind him. Stiff in manner and somewhat dandyish in his dress, thoughtful and cautious in his speech, he did not have the potential to be a French Franklin Roosevelt.

Eminently respectful of democratic constitutional procedures, Blum refused to take office during the month separating the May elections from the convocation of the new parliament. To the dissatisfaction of many of the Popular Front's voters, he also took the position that his government (in which the Socialists were only one partner) had been given only a mandate for limited reforms. He made it clear that he would not try to implement the SFIO's own party program, which went beyond the Popular Front agreement. Blum's caution was realistic, given the constraints of the parliamentary system, but it unavoidably opened a gap between the government's policies and the aspirations of many of those who had voted for the Popular Front. Blum had hoped to have the broadest possible support for his ministry, but the PCF now adopted the position previously taken by the Socialists vis-à-vis the Radical governments of 1924 and 1932. The Communists would vote for Blum's measures, but would not take seats in the ministry. The CGT, true to its long-standing rule against direct participation in politics, also refused to formally join the government.

Wave of Strikes

While Léon Blum prepared to assume the premiership, the Popular Front movement boiled over into a nationwide wave of industrial strikes more extensive than those of 1906 or 1920. Government statistics counted 12,142 separate strikes in June 1936 alone. Buoyed by the Popular Front victory and the recent reunification of a union movement that had been virtually silenced in the 1920s, the workers in the big factories built since the war adopted a militant new tactic. Instead of simply staying away from their jobs, they occupied their factories. The dramatic break from the usual work routine and the long hours spent together during these sit-ins generated a festival atmosphere during the hectic weeks of May and June 1936. The strongest support for the strikes came from those workers who had been most neglected during the 1920s— the previously unorganized inhabitants of working-class suburbs around Paris and other cities where industry had implanted itself since 1914. Just as the Revolution of 1848 had given an earlier, more artisan working class a sense of identity, the 1936 strikes gave the new industrial proletariat a sense of strength and common purpose. The CGT, its ranks swollen by new members recruited in the heat of the excitement, had to scramble to gain control of a movement that had begun without any central direction. Even the Communists, the party closest to the factory workers, worried that the movement would go too far and scuttle the Popular Front experiment at the outset. "One has to know how to end a strike," the Communist leader Maurice Thorez proclaimed in June 1936.

By that time, Blum had taken office and convoked national negotiations between union representatives, employers, and the government. These meetings resulted in a set of agreements known as the Matignon accords, providing for substantial wage increases (especially for lower-paid workers), employer recognition of unions, and collective bargaining agreements. Although the Matignon accords were much less than a full-fledged social revolution, they substantially increased the bargaining power of organized labor.

The Matignon agreements were an improvised response to an emergency situation. But the Blum government also took a number of initiatives designed to make significant changes in French society. The *Banque de France*, which leftists blamed for undermining the *Cartel des Gauches* ministry in 1924, was brought under government control, although its policies remained largely unchanged. Blum's government nationalized the French armaments industry, the "merchants of death" whom leftist mythology blamed for pushing the country toward war

in 1914. In 1937, the financially ailing railroads were merged into a mixed public-private enterprise, the SNCF. The Popular Front thus increased the scope of the government's involvement in the economy, although not in a systematic manner.

Blum's ministerial cabinet also reflected a number of other innovations. Although the Popular Front did not raise the issue of women's suffrage—the Radical Party in particular continued to fear that such a reform would benefit the conservative opposition— Blum appointed three women as undersecretaries. His government was the first to address "the problem of leisure" and make the provision of cultural and recreational opportunities for ordinary people a public responsibility through appointment of ministers for sport and culture. Leisure seemed a pressing issue because the government's initiatives included a substantial reduction in the legal work week to forty hours, as well as implementation of the Popular Front's most enduring reform—paid vacations for all workers. In the summer of 1936, the industrial workforce for the first time joined the bourgeoisie in the trek to beach and countryside. The vacation law was the clearest symbol of the government's determination to redistribute the social privileges that had continued to mark French society.

In the troubled world of 1936, the festive atmosphere of the Popular Front's first few weeks could not last. The breadth of the strike movement that followed the elections masked the extent of opposition to Blum's government. Employers accepted the Matignon accords only grudgingly. Once the strike wave ebbed, they blamed the Blum government and their own representatives for compelling them to make hasty concessions, and began chipping away at the workers' new rights. The conservative press ridiculed the behavior of the new vacationers. More fundamentally, Blum's government proved unable to end the economic depression, and its attention was soon diverted by new threats to France's security.

The Matignon accords and the government's other measures had been intended to restart the economy by giving people more money to spend. Meanwhile, Blum tried to maintain business confidence by refusing to devalue the French currency. It had appreciated substantially against the dollar and the pound since the start of the depression, pricing French goods out of the world market. His policy was poorly thought-out from the economic point of view. For example, immediate implementation of the forty-hour week made it more difficult for factories to increase production to satisfy the new demand for many consumer goods that resulted from the Matignon wage increases. The economic policy, therefore, failed to achieve any of its objectives. Instead, the increase in wages caused inflation, and the government soon found itself with no choice but to devalue the franc. Nervous French investors transferred as many funds as they could abroad. Blum, not wanting to confront them or clash with the British and American governments, refused to impose exchange controls to stop the outflow. In March 1937, he announced a "pause" in the Popular Front's reform policies, hoping to reassure the business classes. He had little success; the "pause" served mainly to disappoint the Popular Front's own supporters and to fuel Communists' criticism of Blum's excessive moderation.

The Popular Front government also tried to head off the growing split between France and its colonial peoples. More explicitly than any previous French government, Blum's ministry recognized the contradiction between calling for greater democracy in France and maintaining arbitrary control over non-European populations abroad. In September 1936, the French negotiated treaties granting independence to the two Middle Eastern territories France had acquired as mandates after World War I, Syria and Lebanon, but the parliament refused to ratify them. The Blum ministry's main reform effort, also unsuccessful, concerned Algeria, whose population and economy had grown rapidly after the war. The benefits of this growth had been monopolized by the European settlers, however, and the Muslim population was increasingly attracted to nationalist movements such as Messali Hadj's *Parti du Peuple algérien* or to Islamic movements that rejected French ideas. There was still an important *évolué* group among the Algerians, represented by leaders such as Ferhat Abbas, who wanted to participate more fully in French life. The reforms proposed by Blum and his minister Maurice Viollette were designed to satisfy this group by allowing them to join the European settlers in electing deputies to the French parliament and giving them greater access to government positions.

Opposition to the Blum-Viollette proposal among the French Algerians was so violent that the French assembly never even debated the proposal. Algeria became a breeding ground for extreme right-wing movements; its local chapters of the *Croix de feu* movement, for example, were more overtly racist and anti-semitic than the movement as a whole. Representatives of Ferhat Abbas's group, on the other hand, drew the conclusion that France would never follow through on the promise of eventual assimilation and shifted toward a more radical nationalist position. The chances of converting the empire into a democratic system that the colonies could identify with were rapidly fading.

By June of 1937, the Blum ministry's difficulties, especially its inability to control the economic and financial crisis, had fatally undermined the high hopes with which the Popular Front government began. Unable to overcome the hostility of the conservative Senate, Blum resigned in place of a Radical-led cabinet pledged to continue the Popular Front's overall policies.

RESPONDING TO THE FASCIST THREAT ABROAD

Part of the Blum government's economic difficulties stemmed from the rapidly deteriorating international situation. Hitler's remilitarization of the Rhineland had tilted the military balance toward a rapidly rearming Germany. The Popular Front, many of whose supporters were profoundly committed to pacifism, found itself forced to undertake a costly military buildup. How to respond to the fascist threat deeply divided the Popular Front movement. The issue became acute in July 1936, when the Spanish colonel Francisco Franco began a military rebellion against the left-oriented Popular Front government of republican Spain. Blum's initial impulse was to lend aid to the Spanish government, the Loyalists, but this policy and the risk of war it implied incurred the hostility of many French Radicals for whom the Spanish Popular Front was too leftist. It also was opposed by the strong pacifist current within Blum's own SFIO. By the beginning of August 1936, the French government had proclaimed a policy of rigid nonintervention in Spain, cutting off most aid to the Loyalists, while fascist Italy and Nazi Germany sent arms and "volunteers" to aid Franco's forces. The French Communists vehemently opposed the nonintervention policy, which became a bone of contention among the Popular Front's supporters. Public demonstrations for "arms for Spain" became visible evidence of the disintegration of the Popular Front coalition.

Undermined by the failure of its economic policies and its internal divisions, the Popular Front parliamentary majority began to come apart. Many Radical voters and deputies had never been happy about joining a coalition with the Communists. The continuing labor unrest in 1937 and 1938—even though due more to workers' disillusionment with results of the 1936 accords than to

PCF or CGT initiatives—served as evidence of the need to end the Popular Front experiment. The French right had never reconciled itself to the left's victory in 1936.

Opposition to the Popular Front often took the form of virulent anti-semitism. There was considerable hostility to the wave of German Jewish refugees who came to France after Hitler took power in 1933. Unlike the working-class immigrants of the 1920s, many of these Jews were educated professionals. French doctors and lawyers, facing difficult conditions because of the depression, reacted violently to these potential competitors, often demanding the imposition of Jewish quotas. As the danger of war with Germany grew, Jews—who could hardly avoid opposing Hitler—were blamed for pushing France into an unpopular armed conflict. No anti-semitic laws were enacted in France before the German invasion of 1940—in fact, in April 1939, passage of a law forbidding incitement of racial and religious prejudice in the press allowed the prosecution of some zealous anti-semites—but the vocal attacks on Jews in the 1930s paved the way for measures against them after France's military defeat in 1940.

Opposition to the Popular Front was not limited to propaganda. An extremist group, the *Comité secret d'action révolutionnaire*, better known as the *Cagoule*, tried to organize a military putsch against the government. This effort failed, but hooded *Cagoule* assassins murdered several prominent leftists and created a climate of tension. The far-right press directed a stream of invective of unprecedented violence against the Blum government and all those associated with it. A defamatory campaign against the Socialist interior minister Roger Salengro, falsely accused of cowardice during the war, drove him to suicide in the fall of 1936. The Popular Front government banned several of the right-wing leagues and broke up the *Cagoule*, but it failed to stop the shift to the right. Colonel de la Rocque's *Croix-de-Feu* reincarnated itself as a political party, the *Parti Social Français,* which gained increasing numbers of adherents and appeared well on its way to becoming the first genuinely mass-based French conservative party.

The failure of Léon Blum's second attempt to form a ministry in the spring of 1938 cleared the way for the final end to the Popular Front coalition. His successor, the Radical Edouard Daladier, confronted the labor movement head on in August 1938 by revoking the forty-hour law passed in 1936. Daladier justified the measure by the need to increase weapons production. But revoking the forty-hour law inspired a new round of strikes which the Daladier government used force to suppress. Daladier's energetic finance minister, Paul Reynaud (appointed in November 1938), extended the offensive against the labor movement and the measures adopted in 1936. His policies, justified by the ever-more-threatening international situation and by failure of Popular Front measures to end the depression, had the effect of stimulating a genuine increase in industrial production in 1939. Thus it diminished any enthusiasm among the Radicals for a return to the left-wing coalition.

The Popular Front government lasted just over two years and broke up without having overcome the depression or guaranteed European peace—two of its main objectives. That its economic policies were misconceived is now conceded, even by historians sympathetic to Blum and his movement. French industry was not in a position to respond to increased consumer demand generated by the 1936 wage raises. And the sudden imposition of the forty-hour week made economic expansion even more difficult. The Popular Front was also weakened by its own internal divisions. The Communist movement was often ready to outbid Blum's government from the left, while the Radicals, officially part of the coalition, took advantage of their Senate position to under-mine many of its policies. Coming in the wake of failure of left-oriented governments elected in 1924 and 1932, the Popular Front's collapse raised a serious question about the French left's ability to govern the country. But Blum was not only a victim of his own mistakes and his movement's contradictions. The Popular Front's problems were aggravated by the vehemence of conservative opposition it confronted. By 1936, the degree of social and political consensus in France had become dangerously frayed. And the international situation France faced complicated the Popular Front's problems at every turn.

The threat of war loomed over the Paris World's Fair of 1937, whose organizers had meant to revive and update the tradition of the great international expositions of the late-nineteenth century. Visitors were most struck by the confrontation of the massive pavilions sponsored by the two hostile totalitarian regimes of Nazi Germany and the Soviet Union, which had been placed directly across from each other, and by the display of Picasso's *Guernica,* a painting expressing the violence of the Spanish Civil War.

Despite all this, the Popular Front was not a complete failure. If it didn't achieve the broad restructuring of French life that its more enthusiastic supporters hoped for, it did mark a significant step in integrating the industrial working class into the social and political system. In expanding the role of government in economic, social, and cultural life, it advanced a process that was to be carried even further by succeeding regimes. The broad-based social movement that underlay the election victory of 1936 also left a long-lasting heritage. The workers who had occupied their factories in 1936 were more self-conscious and militant than before. They recognized themselves in the propaganda of the Communist party, which succeeded in institutionalizing itself as the representative of the French working class for the next four decades.

FRANCE ENTERS HITLER'S WAR

As we have seen, the growing threat from Hitler's Germany was one of the difficulties that hung over the Popular Front government in France. Profiting from the unrest caused by the depression in Germany, the National Socialist leader Adolf Hitler had taken office in January 1933 and, within a few months, replaced the democratic institutions established there after the First World War with a dictatorship in which all opposition was eliminated. Hitler had repeatedly indicated his determination to overturn the Versailles peace settlement. He had embarked on a massive rearmament program as early as 1933, and had openly challenged the French by remilitarizing the Rhineland in March 1936. France had already accepted significant revisions of the Versailles pact in the 1920s, and its leaders were slow to recognize the difference between the German politicians of the Weimar Republic and Hitler. In any event, the unstable French governments of the mid-1930s were preoccupied with domestic problems, and any inclination they might have had to stand up to Germany was quashed by their British ally's determination to pursue a policy of appeasement, granting concessions to Hitler in the hope of moderating his policy.

French policy in the face of Hitler shifted erratically. In early 1935, a short-lived ministry headed by Pierre Laval, who would later collaborate with Hitler, signed a military agreement with the Soviet Union that revived the pre-World War I alliance. But this ran counter to France's system of treaties with the smaller countries of Eastern Europe—Poland, Czechoslovakia, Romania—which were all hostile to the Soviets. At the same time, Laval tried to improve relations with Mussolini's Italy. He was even prepared to tolerate the *Duce's* invasion of Ethiopia in 1935. But there was a tremendous public uproar when the terms of a proposed Anglo-French endorsement of Mus-

solini's aggression, the Hoare-Laval pact, became known. The Italians were driven into the arms of Hitler's Germany, whose ambition to annex Austria had initially antagonized Mussolini, and Laval's hope of creating a large anti-Hitler bloc crumbled.

Under these circumstances, France was unable to exert any significant influence on the course of events that was leading Europe toward a new war. From 1936 to 1939, Hitler went from one diplomatic triumph to another. France accepted the remilitarization of the Rhineland and confined itself to nonintervention in Spain, while Italy and Germany—now allied by the Axis pact—gave open support to Franco's forces. In March 1938, Hitler annexed Austria to his German Reich, enlarging his own war potential and menacing France's ally, Czechoslovakia. France renewed its promise to defend the Czechs but, in the absence of agreement with the British and the Soviets, the gesture was a hollow one. In the late summer of 1938, Hitler turned on Czechoslovakia, using the situation of the German-speaking population in the Sudetenland border as a pretext. The French followed the lead of the British prime minister Neville Chamberlain, who remained convinced that reasonable concessions would appease the German leader and proposed an international conference at Munich to work out a settlement. As Hitler raised the tension—threatening to attack Czechoslovakia if his demands were not granted—French public opinion remained predominantly pacifist, giving Daladier little encouragement to take a stand firm. At Munich on September 30, 1938, the two western powers granted Hitler control of the Sudetenland, leaving the Czechs (whom they had promised to defend) militarily helpless. French leaders knew what they were doing; Léon Blum referred to the "cowardly sense of relief and shame" they felt at the manner in which they had averted armed conflict, and prime minister Daladier himself considered it "an immense diplomatic defeat."[2] Nevertheless, they felt powerless to act otherwise. France, which had considered itself the dominant European power at the end of World War I, was now in a position of almost total helplessness.

The Munich crisis opened an angry debate about France's situation that showed the extent of the country's divisions. The new technique of public opinion polling, just introduced in France at the time, showed that 57 percent of the population approved the agreement, with 37 percent opposed. The question of how to respond to the German threat cut across the customary lines of political division. The *"Munichois"* included left-wing pacifists—35 percent of Socialists supported a pacifist resolution at the 1938 party congress—and moderates who considered that France could not afford another bloodbath on the scale of the first war. Most women's groups remained loyal to their commitment to peace and supported the agreement. On the far right, the Munich agreement had the support of those who considered Hitler the only serious barrier to the spread of Communism, and of fascist intellectuals like the novelist Drieu la Rochelle, who frankly admired Nazi vitality and considered his own countrymen "a dessicated people."[3] The opponents of Munich were equally varied. At one extreme, they included the French Communists, who had followed Stalin's orders since 1935 to support French military preparedness against Germany. At the other, there were conservatives such as the energetic Paul Reynaud, appointed finance minister in November 1938.

The debate following Munich led to a growing recognition of the German danger. By December of 1938, 70 percent of those polled opposed any further concessions to Hitler. The Popular Front government had already stepped up funding for rearmament. In March 1938, a greatly expanded plan for aircraft production had been adopted. After Munich, the planning expert Jean Monnet was sent to the United States to get American manufacturers to start turning out modern planes for the French air force. But this evidence of determination to be ready for the pending conflict came very late, and it was insufficient to counter the debilitating effects of earlier mistakes.

One of the most serious problems confronting France and Britain was their inability to reach agreement with the Soviet Union, which had been excluded from the Munich negotiations. The Soviet dictator Stalin increasingly suspected a western plot to abandon him to Hitler's mercy. In 1939, negotiations on military cooperation between the western Allies and the Soviets began, but neither side seemed determined to reach an agreement, and the Soviets were secretly seeking contact with the Germans instead. In any event, the smaller eastern European states refused to agree to the passage of Soviet troops through their territories, blocking any realistic plan. On August 23, 1939, the Russians and Germans stunned the world with the announcement of the Molotov-Ribbentrop pact, making them virtual allies.

For the French, as for the British, the Nazi-Soviet agreement was a severe blow, because war had visibly become imminent. Repeating the scenario he had used a year earlier against Czechoslovakia, Hitler demanded concessions from Poland. The two western powers responded by renewing their guarantees to that country. This time, there was no last-minute diplomatic evasion. On September 1, 1939, the Germans invaded Poland, and on September 3, with some visible reluctance, France followed Britain in declaring war. Even more clearly than in 1914, the French public was hardly eager for a fight. But the success of mobilization plans showed that the population was resigned to its necessity. The myth of a country too demoralized to make a military effort is exaggerated. But France had faced up to the necessity of the war too late to be well prepared for it.

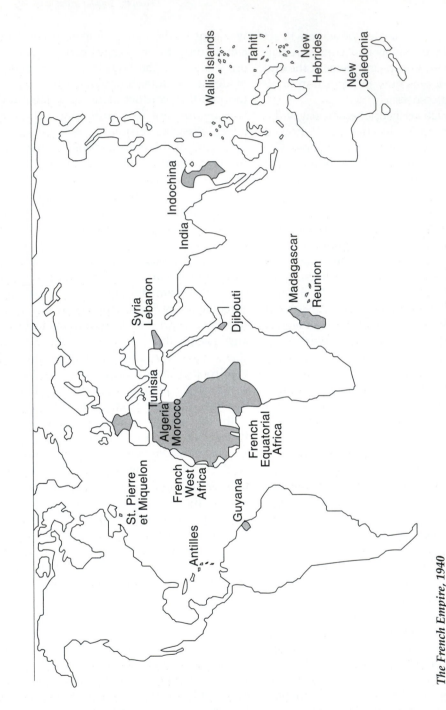

The French Empire, 1940
The French Empire reached its peak during the interwar period, sustaining the illusion that the country was still a world power. Native elites were already beginning to demand autonomy or independence even before the Second World War, however.

Wallis Islands

Tahiti

New Hebrides

New Caledonia

Indochina

India

Syria
Lebanon

Madagascar
Reunion

Djibouti

Tunisia
Algeria
Morocco

French
Equatorial
Africa

St. Pierre
et Miquelon

French
West
Africa

Guyana

Antilles

French military plans for another major conflict with Germany had been determined as a result of debates conducted in the 1920s. The lesson of the First World War, as interpreted by Philippe Pétain, the dominant figure in the interwar military, was the superiority of a defensive strategy. The failure of the Ruhr occupation in 1923 had underlined the difficulty for France of sustaining an aggressive military posture. By the end of the 1920s, France had decided to base its military planning on a system of elaborate fortifications along the German border. It was named the Maginot Line in honor of the minister of war who formulated the plan. The Maginot-line plan was never fully implemented: the line of fortifications stopped short at the Belgian border. The French could not decide whether to extend it all the way to the Channel, thereby leaving Belgium to the Germans' mercy, or to count on meeting the German advance north of their own borders.

One prominent French officer, a certain Colonel Charles de Gaulle, had raised public objections to Pétain's defensive strategy. In his *Toward a Professional Army*, published in 1934, de Gaulle urged the development of powerful tank divisions manned by well-trained career soldiers rather than citizen draftees and prepared for offensive operations—ideas already being adopted at that time by German military planners. De Gaulle won some converts to his ideas among the politicians of the late 1930s, but his criticisms angered the French military hierarchy, who clung even more firmly to their defensive plans.

With the declaration of war in September 1939, those defensive plans were put into effect. The French troops installed themselves in the underground forts of the Maginot Line. Meanwhile, fast-moving German armored units, supported by aircraft, demonstrated the effectiveness of their new *Blitzkrieg* (lightning war) strategy against the Poles, who were defeated in less than two months. In the west, there was no military action. For eight months, the two sides confronted each other without moving in the so-called phony war. French soldiers along the Rhine River were even ordered not to stir up trouble by firing at the Germans on the opposite bank. This period of inaction undermined French morale and raised new questions about the purpose of the war. It was too late to help the Poles and, in the absence of a German attack, there was no immediate threat to rally against.

Domestically, the situation was further confused by the Communist Party's change of policy. In response to the Nazi-Soviet pact, Stalin had ordered the French Communists to drop their support for the war. Daladier's government had responded by outlawing the organization. The CGT expelled its Communist members. Instead of a *union sacrée,* the war of 1939–1940 began with the creation of new divisions. The long months of the "phony war" exacerbated quarrels about policy. Daladier had wanted to offer military support to Finland, which had become embroiled in a war against the Soviet Union. Finnish resistance finally collapsed before the Allies decided whether to add a war against Russia to their war against Germany. But the issue brought Daladier's cabinet down in March 1940. He was replaced by the feisty Paul Reynaud, who was committed to a vigorous pursuit of the conflict, but who obtained only a narrow majority in the Chamber. On May 9, 1940, Reynaud's cabinet was defeated in its turn, but there was never time for a successor to be found. On May 10, the German invasion of France began.

NOTES

1. For a discussion of the debate about the nature and extent of French fascism, see Robert Soucy, *French Fascism: The Second Wave* (New Haven, CT: Yale University Press, 1995), Ch. 1.
2. Cited in J. B. Duroselle, *La Décadence 1932–1939* (Paris: Imprimerie nationale, 1979), 356.
3. Cited in Pierre Milza, *Fascisme français* (Paris: Flammarion, 1987), 220.

CHAPTER 27

FRANCE IN THE SECOND WORLD WAR

The four years of military defeat and foreign occupation France suffered between 1940 and 1944 form one of the darkest and most controversial chapters in the country's modern history. To this day, ordinary citizens and historians argue bitterly about who should bear the blame for the defeat, about the conduct of the population and the government during the war, and about the extent of resistance to the occupation. What one historian has called "the Vichy syndrome" is still a powerful presence in French life.

THE DEBACLE

The *drôle de guerre,* or "phony war," that had begun in September 1939 came to an abrupt end with a massive German offensive on May 10, 1940. The Germans' first moves were meant to convince the French and British that they once again, as in 1914, faced an attack through the Low Countries. In response, the Allied armies moved north from the French border into Belgium—and into the German trap. The real German thrust was being prepared further south, where General Heinz Guderian's armored divisions were snaking their way along the narrow roads of the hilly Ardennes through Luxembourg and southern Belgium, head-

ing for the point where the French Maginot fortifications ended.

Postwar historians exploded the belief, widely held in France at the time, that the attacking German army must have heavily outnumbered the Allied forces. The two sides had approximately the same numbers of troops and tanks, and the best French tank models were superior to those of the Germans. The Germans had some superiority in air power, although the Allies were rapidly closing the gap. The Germans' advantage was one of imagination. Hitler and his generals were determined to take the offensive, and they had recognized the potential of the new weapons at their disposal. Their strategy was built around the use of powerful concentrations of tanks and motorized infantry, closely supported by air power, to launch rapid breakthrough attacks and avoid the static warfare that had characterized the First World War. The French and British, by contrast, had anticipated a largely defensive conflict, and had counted on wearing the Germans down through an economic blockade. Their tanks were dispersed in small concentrations to support their infantry units, and their air forces were not coordinated with the ground troops. The French command structure was another weak point.

The overall commander, General Maurice Gamelin, was frequently at odds with his field commanders; and the various headquarters were separated from each other and often out of communication at crucial points in the battle. The success of the German *Blitzkrieg* in Poland made the Allies revise their plans somewhat. The French army began to create armored divisions similar to the Germans', but the process was still far from complete when the fighting began.

On May 15, the German armored divisions began to emerge from the Ardennes near the French city of Sedan, site of the disastrous French defeat in 1870. The French, confident that the terrain would prevent a German attack on this sector of the front, had never finished the fortifications intended to protect it. Sedan was held by second-line troops unprepared to meet an all-out assault. The Germans quickly routed these defenders, freeing their armored divisions for a dash across northern France to the sea. They reached the coast by May 20, cutting off the Allied forces that had entered Belgium from behind.

As the German high command itself knew, their strategy was risky. The narrow German spearhead was vulnerable to counterattack. If the French had shown the resilience Joffre had demonstrated in 1914, the breakthrough might have been contained. But this time, there was no "miracle of the Marne." At Gamelin's headquarters, panic and confusion spread rapidly. Reynaud, who continued as prime minister despite his loss of a parliamentary majority, reshuffled his cabinet, but the new recruits divided it more than ever. Some, like the recently promoted General Charles de Gaulle, urged continued resistance even if the government had to take refuge in the North African colonies. Others, like the aged hero of the First World War, Marshal Philippe Pétain—brought in to bolster the government's prestige—clearly considered the war already lost.

As the Germans advanced, the French population panicked. On June 10, the government abandoned Paris, which the Germans occupied on the 14th. Some six million civilians, terrorized by German bombing raids, fled as best they could, jamming the roads along which French units were trying to get to the front. The administration fell into chaos as local officials abandoned their posts. François Cavanna, a young mailman, was ordered from Paris to Bordeaux for emergency assignment—and told to travel by bicycle. By the time the ministers reassembled in Bordeaux on June 14, many of them had become as demoralized as the fleeing civilians. On the 15th, the cabinet voted to inquire about German conditions for an armistice. The next day, Reynaud resigned, and the defeatist Pétain took his place. Plans to continue the fight from a fortified position on the Brittany peninsula or from the North African colonies were quickly abandoned. On June 17, Pétain, by radio, informed the population that the fighting was over.

Armistice Terms

The German terms, imposed under humiliating circumstances (Hitler insisted that they be signed in the railway carriage used for the 1918 armistice negotiations), were harsh. As long as the war against Britain continued, the Germans were to keep the strategically important parts of the country—the entire Atlantic coast and the northern and eastern regions, including Paris, altogether three-fifths of France—under military occupation. The French government would retain sovereignty over the rest of the territory and nominal responsibility for civilian administration throughout the country. The French were to assist the Germans in maintaining military security. France was to pay the Germans a heavy indemnity for costs of the military occupation, calculated according to a formula very favorable to the Germans. This allowed them to use French funds to support their own war effort. French troops were interned in German prisoner of war camps pending the end of the conflict. France's one intact military asset, its navy, was kept out of German control, but was to remain in its home ports and not help the British. Originally foreseen as a temporary arrangement, due to be revised as soon as Hitler's lone remaining opponent, Britain, had been quickly defeated, the armistice terms became the framework for French life for the rest of the war. It put France in a unique position among the nations of occupied Europe—the only country whose government did not continue the war from exile, and which was not put under direct German administration. Pétain and his supporters thought that this arrangement would give France a better chance to protect its vital interests. The course of events showed that this was a dubious hope.

The defeat of June 1940 exposed the hollowness of prewar claims that the resources of France's overseas empire would enable it to stand up to Germany. Although the total population of the empire was one-and-a-half times as great as that of European France, less than 10 percent of the men France sent into battle came from the colonies. Pétain's refusal to move the French government to North Africa to continue the war showed that, as far as he was concerned, the defeat in Europe was all that mattered. In one way, however, the German occupation made the colonies more important than ever. Germany was unable to occupy France's overseas territories and depended on Pétain's regime to keep their resources from falling into British hands. From the French point of view, the colonies, together with France's undamaged navy, were the only assets the country had left with which it might be able to bargain with the Germans. Keeping control over its colonies was a major challenge, however. The catastrophic defeat of June 1940 seriously undermined French prestige in the eyes of its colonial populations, and encouraged nationalist groups eager to overthrow colonial rule.

THE VICHY REGIME

For most of the population, the end of the fighting came as an enormous relief, and the aged Marshal Pétain was hailed as a hero for having saved France from a repetition of horrendous losses suffered in the First World War. The armistice agreement allowed most of the civilian refugees to return home and resume their regular routines. It meant assurance that sons or husbands in the army would not be killed in a hopeless fight. Only a small minority of French fascist sympathizers really welcomed the German victory, but most of the population accepted Hitler's triumph as an accomplished fact. Britain, it was widely assumed, would have to make terms with him, too, or face an invasion it was poorly prepared to resist. Anti-British sentiment welled up in the wake of the defeat, as the French blamed their allies for giving them inadequate support. When the British, fearing that the Germans might gain control of the French navy, attacked their former ally's ships at Mers-el-Kebir in Morocco on July 3, 1940, and sank several of them with heavy loss of life, this feeling was strengthened.

Not only did most French welcome the end of the fighting, the majority also shared their new leader's conviction that the nation's defeat was the fault of men and movements that had governed the country during the 1930s. The institutions of the Third Republic were totally discredited. In a radio speech to the nation on June 20, 1940, Pétain blamed the defeat on deep-seated shortcomings in France's prewar society. "Since the victory [of 1918], the spirit of indulgence overwhelmed the spirit of sacrifice," he told his listeners. "People have made too many demands and showed too little willingness to contribute." The result of this spirit of egoism, as he pithily summed it up, had been "too few babies, too few weapons."[1] The moralizing tone of Pétain's speech was not all that different from that of the historian and future Resistance martyr Marc Bloch, who based his essay, *Strange Defeat,* on his experiences as a reserve officer called to duty during the campaign. Although he did not share Pétain's reactionary political views, he did agree that the French defeat was more than a military mishap. It reflected a pervasive failure of France's old governing classes, who had failed to prepare the country to meet the challenges of the modern world.

In this atmosphere, a broad cross section of the population was willing to give Pétain authority to restructure the country's institutions, even before the outcome of the war was clear. On July 10, 1940, by a majority of 468 to 80, the Third Republic's deputies gave Pétain a mandate to draft a new constitution, effectively terminating the regime under which France had lived since 1875. Pétain, titled Head of the French State—a designation which showed the new regime's desire to distance itself from the republican tradition—took up residence in the small provincial town of Vichy, a health resort in the unoccupied zone whose numerous hotels gave the government space to install itself. He appointed a cabinet made up primarily of conservative critics of parliamentary democracy who were determined to carry out a "National Revolution" against the forces responsible for France's defeat. What the French right had not been able to do through the ballot box for seven decades it would now attempt thanks to the German victory— the transformation of French life along hierarchical, antidemocratic principles.

Although the Vichy leaders were united in their contempt for the democratic republic they replaced, they agreed about little else. Some, like the marshal himself, were traditionalists who saw the National Revolution as a chance to restore France to its true roots by banishing foreigners, rehabilitating old artisan skills, and reinvigorating rural life. Others admired the technological modernity of Hitler's Germany and saw the abolition of the parliamentary republic as an opportunity to make France more efficient and up-to-date. At the outset, some saw the Vichy government as an opportunity to maintain a certain autonomy for France in Hitler's Europe, while others believed that the nation's survival depended on a wholehearted collaboration with the Germans. Torn between these contradictory impulses, the Vichy regime's policy remained incoherent and at the mercy of German pressures.

The regime's principal asset in winning popular support was Pétain himself. Vichy propaganda worked diligently to create a cult around him. Schoolchildren were taught to sing, "Marshal, here we are before you, Savior of France." For many, it was impossible to imagine that "the victor of Verdun" could possibly do anything contrary to the nation's best interests. Although it was Pétain more than anyone else who had pushed for the defensive strategy that led to the French army's defeat in 1940, he still commanded immense respect from the military. Many officers remained convinced that his policy of collaboration with the Germans masked a "double game" of secret preparation for a war of revenge when the time was right, as Pétain was to assert at his postwar trial. Ordinary people from all ranks of life made pilgrimages to Vichy to see Pétain emerge from his headquarters at the *Hôtel du Parc* for his daily walk, sometimes even kneeling to touch his coat as he passed. Until late in the war, much of the population retained its respect for him even as they became more and more hostile to his government.

Under cover of Pétain's popularity, the Vichy leaders sought to remodel the country, often along lines inspired by folklore or the Boy Scouts. For the republican motto, "Liberty, Equality, Fraternity," the regime substituted its own trinity, "Work, Family,

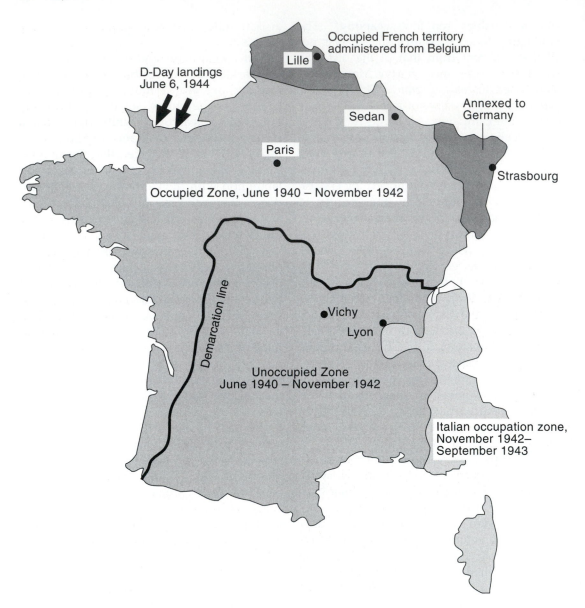

*Occupied French territory
administered from Belgium*

Lille

*D-Day landings
June 6, 1944*

Sedan

*Annexed to
Germany*

Paris

Strasbourg

Occupied Zone, June 1940 – November 1942

Demarcation line

Vichy

Lyon

Unoccupied Zone
June 1940 – November 1942

Italian occupation zone,
November 1942–
September 1943

France During World War II
*After the armistice of June 1940, more than half of metropolitan France was put under German mili-
tary occupation. The Germans took over the Vichy-administered unoccupied zone after the Allied
landings in North Africa in November 1942.*

Fatherland," emphasizing obligations to the community rather than individual rights. Vichy ostentatiously courted the support of the church, and conservative Catholics, long estranged from the Republic, eagerly welcomed a government sympathetic to their concerns. The regime preached a return to the traditional family structure and elaborated the system of family allocations that had been inaugurated just a few months before the war by the Daladier government. In response to conservative objections, Vichy repealed prewar reforms that had made secondary education free, thus restoring a system that favored wealthy families.

To get young people away from the debilitating temptations of city life, *Chantiers de la jeunesse* took urban adolescents to the countryside, where they were supposed to learn the pleasures of physical exercise and quasi-military discipline. A *Commissariat du sport,* headed until 1942 by the interwar tennis star Jean Borotra, continued efforts begun under the Popular Front to make French youth more physically fit. Some of the regime's initiatives, (such as the quasi-monastic *Ecole des cadres* set up at Uriage in southern France under the direction of inspirational army officer Pierre Dunoyer de Segonzac to train a new generation of leaders), reflected a genuine patriotic idealism. This spirit led many of the young Uriage participants to join the Resistance later in the war. Vichy propaganda celebrated the virtues of rural life and encouraged a return to the soil. In the economic sphere, corporatist policies promised to overcome the division between workers and employers. Government-sponsored *comités d'organisation* were created for each branch of industry.

The installation of the Vichy regime offered an opportunity for all those who

This propaganda poster for the Vichy regime's National Revolution contrasts the discredited Third Republic (shown lurching toward ruin because of the supposed domination of the Jews) with a solid France resting on foundations labeled "Work, Family, Fatherland." Native French traditions of anti-Semitism facilitated collaboration with the German occupiers.

(Source: Bibliothèque de documentation internationale et contemporaine, Paris.)

thought that the Third Republic had expanded women's rights too much and weakened traditional family structures. Emancipated women were blamed for turning away from motherhood and therefore weakening the country; public schools were castigated for encouraging young women to aspire to jobs that should be reserved for men. To encourage women to return to more traditional roles, Vichy made Mother's Day, introduced in France in 1920 in an effort to encourage larger families, into an official state holiday. Teachers were told to direct children on how to observe it, and Marshal Pétain himself emphasized its importance. Laws issued in October 1940 barred women, like Jews, from civil service jobs and ordered private employers to give hiring preference to married men with children. In April 1941, the divorce law passed in 1884 was amended to make the procedure more difficult, and in February 1942, abortion was defined as a crime against state and society. As in many other areas, Vichy's efforts to define gender roles were undercut by wartime conditions. With prices soaring and food in short supply, Vichy's own officials realized that women had to seek jobs if they and their families were to survive. When the Germans began demanding that France furnish laborers to work in that country in 1942, the laws discouraging women from working had to be suspended, and ultimately even married women were recruited to meet German requirements. Similarly, not much was done to ensure rigorous enforcement of the abortion law.

The corporatist reorganization of industry was another aspect of the National Revolution that, under the pressure of wartime necessities and German demands, turned out very differently from the hopes of Vichy's traditionalists. Rather than favoring a revival of traditional French craftsmanship, the war called for rational exploitation of France's economic resources. The *comités d'organisa-*tion became a means to favor the largest, most efficient manufacturers at the expense of both workers and smaller competitors. Within a few months of the armistice, German representatives were signing contracts with French businesses. The heavy indemnity payments required under the armistice agreement allowed the Germans to make the French themselves pay for this exploitation of their economy. Vichy's claim that it was protecting France from German exploitation was belied by the fact that the Germans extracted more resources from France than from any other conquered territory, and that the French standard of living was reduced below that of any of the other western European nations the Germans occupied.

Driven by wartime conditions to ration raw materials, the Vichy government steadily increased the state's economic role, continuing the trend begun in the Popular Front period. Key administrators like Jean Bichelonne, who became head of a new Ministry of Industrial Production in 1942, had the opportunity to implement many ideas about state-directed economic planning that they had formulated before the war. To be sure, Vichy did not follow the Popular Front's efforts to improve labor relations by giving unions an increased role. Its Labor Charter, issued in October 1941, prohibited strikes. But even in this area, Vichy took some modernizing initiatives, such as requiring employers to set up social committees with worker representation to oversee working conditions in factories. Paradoxically, the traditionalist-minded Vichy government thus accelerated processes of economic modernization begun under previous governments.

THE POLITICS OF COLLABORATION

One of the main disputes about the war period has been the question of whether collaboration with the German war effort was imposed on the Vichy government, or whether it represented a policy deliberately adopted by France's wartime leaders. When the Vichy leaders were brought to account after the Liberation, they naturally maintained that they had acted under duress. Historians have shown that this was often untrue: at least until the German occupation of the entirety of French territory in November 1942, Pétain and his colleagues actively sought possibilities for collaboration, sometimes offering to go further than the Germans wanted. Two of the best recent historians of the Vichy period remind us, however, that the wartime situation was a complicated one. Swiss historian Philippe Burrin writes that some accommodation with the forces occupying most of the country was inevitable, and British historian Julian Jackson remarks that "the history of the Occupation should be written not in black and white, but in shades of grey."[2]

The question of how to deal with the Germans dominated Vichy politics from the outset. Pétain's first prime minister, Pierre Laval, named in July 1940, was a veteran Third Republic parliamentarian firmly convinced that France's salvation lay in genuine cooperation with the Germans. He and the other Vichy leaders courted the Germans even in the face of clear signs that the latter had no interest in real collaboration. From the outset, German policy went beyond the armistice agreement. The Germans immediately annexed Alsace and Lorraine to the Reich and began expelling the French population. The department of the Nord was also detached from French authority and combined with occupied Belgium. The armistice agreement had promised that the French government could return to Paris, but the Germans never permitted this. The demarcation line between the occupied and unoccupied zones took on the character of a frontier, and French citizens needed German passes to cross it. The division of the country crippled the economy, and the punitive payments imposed on the French stood in the way of any real understanding between the two governments.

In the fall of 1940, Laval and Pétain made determined efforts to improve France's position by offering to assist the German war effort. Laval sought out sympathetic German representatives, such as Otto Abetz, a Foreign Ministry official stationed in Paris who had promoted Franco-German relations long before the war. In return for German concessions on indemnity payments and respect for France's territorial integrity, Laval hinted that France might even enter the war against Britain. Pétain was less enthusiastic about military cooperation, but he met publicly with Hitler at the French town of Montoire in October 1940 to discuss economic collaboration and other issues. In reality, Hitler had little interest in closer ties with the French, and neither Laval nor Pétain obtained significant concessions. German concerns were limited to insuring that Vichy was able to prevent the British from gaining control of the French colonies. Other than that, the one-sided armistice agreement served German interests too well for them to have much interest in altering it.

Laval's failure to obtain any meaningful agreements with the Germans was one of the main reasons why Pétain, who had no love for his subordinate, moved to dismiss him on December 13, 1940. The swift German reaction to this move showed how limited the Vichy government's authority really was. Laval's German friend Abetz descended on Vichy, accompanied by gun-wielding guards, to liberate the arrested prime minister and take him back to Paris. The German authorities refused to deal with Laval's first successor, Pierre-Etienne Flandin, a former appeasement advocate who had sent Hitler a well-publicized telegram in 1938 congratulating him on the Munich accord. They were only slightly more forthcoming when Pétain replaced him with Admiral François Darlan in February 1941. Like Laval, Darlan approached the Germans with proposals for cooperation in a number of areas, including possible military involvement. But the Germans limited their interest to details such as obtaining the right to use French bases in Syria for an unsuccessful effort to support an Iraqi revolt against the British in May and June of 1941.

While Hitler himself paid little attention to French affairs, individual officials like Abetz pursued their own policies. In Abetz's case, this meant continued lobbying for the reappointment of Laval as prime minister, a goal he finally achieved in April 1942. Laval continued the effort to prove the value of France's collaboration to the Germans. In response to German demands for laborers to keep their war factories running, he set up a scheme—the *relève*—under which the Germans were to release one French prisoner of war for every three workers who volunteered to go to Germany. Although Laval avoided the issue of French military participation in the war, he committed himself to the German cause more emphatically than any other French leader to date. "I hope for a German victory," he said in a speech in June 1942, "because otherwise, Bolshevism will take over everywhere."[3]

Vichy's policy toward the Jews was a particularly dangerous blend of autonomous French initiatives and collaboration with German policies, whose full intent French leaders did not recognize. The regime's first anti-Semitic measures were taken before the Germans even raised the issue. The Vichy *Statut des Juifs*, issued on October 3, 1940, had a stricter definition of Jewishness than Nazi Germany's own racial laws, and the Pétain government complained vigorously about the German policy of expelling Jews from the Reich to France. Jews who were not French citizens were interned in camps, where they were held under harsh conditions and were especially vulnerable when

the Germans began their program of deportations. In Algeria, which the Germans did not control, Vichy officials repealed the 1870 Crémieux law that had given the Jewish population there French citizenship. In June 1941, Vichy officials issued new anti-Jewish legislation, barring even French Jewish citizens from most civil service posts and professions, allowing confiscation of Jewish-owned property, and creating a centralized register of Jewish inhabitants. These measures reflected the long-standing anti-Semitism of French right-wingers such as *Action française* leader Charles Maurras, whose influence was also evident in Vichy's laws against Freemasons. Members of the Masons, traditionally active in republican politics, were accused of forming a secret conspiracy to dominate the country. Like the Jews, they were excluded from government positions and teaching posts.

In the course of 1942, when the Germans began to implement their "Final Solution" by deporting Jews from all over Europe to death camps, they were able to take advantage of Vichy's earlier measures which had made the French Jewish population easily identifiable. Most French Jews, accustomed to acting like law-abiding citizens of a country that had protected them since the time of the French Revolution, had obediently reported their addresses. Anxious to maintain the appearance of French sovereignty in the German-occupied zone, Laval agreed in June 1942 to have French police carry out the roundup of "foreign" Jews in Paris in July 1942—the *rafle* of the *Vélodrome d'Hiver,* an indoor bicycle-racing stadium used to hold the almost 13,000 victims before they were sent on to Auschwitz. Laval even insisted that the Germans take not only adults but Jewish children. He and Pétain did object to the deportation of Jews holding French citizenship, but they agreed to revoke the naturalization of Jews who had received that status during the 1930s.

The willingness to collaborate with the Germans was by no means limited to the Vichy leadership. Even after the end of the early honeymoon period of occupation, during which the French population rejoiced that Hitler's soldiers were so much better behaved than expected, French citizens from all walks of life were often willing to cooperate with the victors. French businessmen accepted German contracts without hesitation, encouraged by the Vichy authorities who saw this as a way of preventing German confiscation of French economic assets. In Paris, restaurants, theaters, and jewelry stores did good business entertaining the invaders. Leading actors and singers saw nothing wrong with such contacts.

A small but highly visible group of political and intellectual figures, concentrated mostly in Paris, went beyond pragmatic, personal collaboration and openly supported Hitler's "New Order." These French fascists sought German support to create movements modeled on the Nazi party and actively pushed for French participation on Germany's side in the war. They criticized the Vichy government for being too conservative and too cautious about backing the Germans. Among the most prominent of these collaborationists were several dissident leftists who had split with their parties during the 1930s and tried to found movements more attuned to what they saw as the realities of the times. Examples were neosocialist Marcel Déat and ex-Communist Jacques Doriot, whose *Parti Populaire Française* was the only one of the wartime collaborationist movements to have any popular success. Doriot himself volunteered for service with the German forces on the eastern front.

Other collaborationists came from the ranks of the extreme right, attracted by the Nazis' anti-Communist propaganda or by the mirage of a united Europe in which France would enjoy an honorable second rank. A number of prominent writers, such as Drieu la Rochelle and Robert Brasillach, convinced even before the war of the hopeless decadence of French culture, embraced what they saw as the youthful vitality of the Nazis. Ironically, the Germans gave these French admirers little real support. Recognizing how unpopular the extreme collaborationist groups were with most of their fellow citizens, the Germans kept them on a short leash. By using the threat of shifting support to them, the German authorities could extract concessions from the Vichy government. But only when German military defeat had come to appear inevitable did the Paris collaborationists obtain a foothold in the French government.

Changing Attitudes Toward the Germans

By the time Laval had publicly called for a German victory in the war, changes in German policy and in the world picture were making collaboration less and less acceptable to the French population. In the summer of 1940, German victory in the war had seemed inevitable, but by the middle of 1942, it looked at least uncertain. The unexpected resistance of the British under the leadership of Winston Churchill, the German failure to overwhelm the Soviet Union, and the entry of the United States into the conflict after the Japanese bombing of Pearl Harbor left Hitler to face a coalition whose potential resources far exceeded his own. Furthermore, the German occupation had become increasingly oppressive for the French. As more and more of France's food and industrial products were diverted to the Reich, French resentment against the Germans increased. The savage German repression following the first armed attacks on their troops in occupied France in the summer of 1941 shocked French opinion. So did the Vichy government's willingness to participate in the German-ordered execution of hostages through creation of "special section" courts in which normal legal safeguards were suspended. The measures imposed on Jews also contributed to the growing dislike for the Germans. Laval's appeal in April 1942 for volunteers to work in German factories was largely a failure.

The turn in the tide of the war in November 1942 decisively altered the situation in France. In that month, the Allies went over to the offensive on every front. In Russia, Soviet forces surrounded a German army at Stalingrad. In Egypt, the British under Montgomery defeated Rommel's Afrika Korps at El Alamein. And in North Africa, on November 8, American forces landed in French territory in Morocco and Algeria. The French forces stationed there, loyal to the Vichy government, put up some initial resistance, but the Americans quickly negotiated a ceasefire with the former Vichy prime minister Darlan, who had accidentally been in Algiers at the moment of the landings. To the outrage of the French Resistance movement, well developed by that time, the Americans recognized Darlan as the legitimate authority in French North Africa. Only his assassination by a Resistance activist on December 24, 1942, ended the awkward situation in which a leading Vichy official had the support of an Allied government. In the meantime, the Germans had reacted to Vichy's "treason" by putting the whole of France under military occupation on November 11, 1942. As the troops of "Operation Attila" neared the Mediterranean coast, the French scuttled their last major military asset—the battle fleet in the harbor of Toulon. Its destruction marked the failure of Vichy's effort to maintain a semblance of French autonomy in Hitler's Europe.

Notes

1. Cited in Jean-Pierre Azéma, *De Munich à la Libération* (Paris: Seuil, 1979), 70.

2. Julian Jackson, *France: The Dark Years, 1940–1944* (New York: Oxford University Press, 2001), 2.

3. Ibid., 197.

CHAPTER 28

THE ROAD TO LIBERATION

DAILY LIFE DURING THE WAR

By the time the Germans occupied southern France, the expectation of a short war ending in a German victory had long since been forgotten. As the war lengthened, living conditions in France became increasingly difficult. Despite the government's efforts to organize war production, shortages of vital raw materials and the reluctance of many workers to contribute to the German war effort led to a steady decline in industrial output. Food was also in short supply, as farmers could not obtain fertilizer and German requisitions skimmed off much of the crop. Food rationing had been imposed in September 1940 and allocations were repeatedly reduced. The population became uncomfortably familiar with the rutabaga, a vegetable normally reserved for animal feed. To supplement their rations, city dwellers took to their bicycles, invading the countryside on weekends to bargain with peasants, or depended on packages from rural relatives. If cases of outright malnutrition remained rare, it was largely thanks to the thriving black market where scarce items were available—but only for many times their legally fixed price. Fuel was also in short supply; the French shivered in the winter, and cars and buses had to be fitted out with bulging tanks that let them run on coal gas. In the absence of effective government controls, France suffered more severely from inflation than Germany, Britain, or the United States. Enforcement of regulations meant to equalize supplies was difficult in a situation where many considered evading the rules a manifestation of resistance to the Nazis.

For the first two years after the Armistice, most French who were neither Jews nor active members of the small Resistance organizations that had begun to develop were, nevertheless, not drastically affected by the war. While Britain suffered under German bombing and while much of Russia was laid waste by the German invasion, France enjoyed relative security. Even in the "occupied" northern zone, the Germans left most routine administrative tasks to French civil servants. Cultural life continued to flourish, despite a certain amount of censorship. Even writers who were later active in the Resistance, like Jean-Paul Sartre, continued to work without much interference. As Sartre later put it, "the Occupation was intolerable and . . . we managed to tolerate it well enough."[1] He was able to publish his major philosophical work, *Being and Nothingness,* in 1943. To escape temporarily

263

from the harsh realities of war and hunger, the population flocked to theaters and movie houses, whose audiences and profits soared. The war years brought a respite from the overwhelming competition of American-made films that had flooded French screens between the wars. Except for the many Jewish producers, directors, and actors, most French cinematists remembered the period as a virtual golden age. German production orders kept French factories running and unemployment was not an issue. But salaries did not keep up with inflation; employers often found it necessary to provide hot meals and other services to prevent discontent. Peasants who were able to conceal some of their production and sell it on the black market were frequently able to make modest profits during the war, as were small shopkeepers. But the real profiteers were the small minority who sold wholesale to the Germans.

While most of the population tightened their belts but were not otherwise dramatically affected by the war, certain groups felt the full brunt of Nazi policies. The most harshly treated were the country's Jews. Forced to give up their jobs and often robbed of their property, many were left with no means of support. In June 1942, the Germans required all Jews in the occupied zone to identify themselves by wearing a yellow star on their clothes, and, as we have seen, deportations to the gas chambers at Auschwitz began in July 942. After the German occupation of the Vichy zone in November 1942, Jews there were also in danger. As they came to understand the peril facing them, French Jews learned to be more wary and more willing to evade the laws designed to make them vulnerable. Nevertheless, it was a deep shock for Jews born in France to realize that their own country's government was discriminating against them, and that many of their fellow-citizens were willing to look the other way rather than try to help them. Of

the 300,000 Jews in France at the start of the war, over 75,000 were sent to the death camps, most via the sinister transit camp at Drancy outside of Paris. Compared to the Jews in other occupied countries, a relatively large percentage of those living in France survived the war, thanks to the complications injected into the deportation process by the existence of Vichy, the aid provided by French fellow citizens, and their own initiative in evading capture. But no other segment of French society paid such a heavy toll during the war.

The Jews suffered because German policies classified them as an inferior race. The populations of Alsace and Lorraine were singled out because they were considered racially German. Despite the armistice agreements, the region was effectively annexed to Germany in 1940. Much of the population was deported to the Vichy zone. The Germans invested heavily to make Strasbourg a great cultural center, and German colonists were imported to take over abandoned farms. The Alsatians were subject to German laws and to service in the *Wehrmacht*.

THE RESISTANCE AND CHARLES DE GAULLE

Although the majority of the French population initially accepted the defeat of 1940 and the Pétain government, a few isolated figures declared from the start that a German victory would mean the imposition of a morally and politically unacceptable regime. The most celebrated of these resisters was a junior member of Reynaud's last wartime cabinet, General Charles de Gaulle. As Pétain prepared to ask for an armistice on June 17, 1940, de Gaulle flew from Bordeaux to London. On the following day the BBC radio broadcast his speech, urging his fellow citizens to recognize that "France has lost a battle, but she has not lost the war," and to continue the struggle. In the chaotic conditions of the moment, almost no one in France heard de Gaulle's speech. It would be many months before he gained a real following within the country, and the French Resistance movement was never simply a response to de Gaulle's leadership. Without de Gaulle's efforts, however, the Resistance's significance would have been quite different.

De Gaulle's first achievement was to obtain British recognition as the official representative of French interests in the war. This he owed to Winston Churchill, who recognized his authority over the French forces that had refused to accept the armistice. The de Gaulle–Churchill relationship was to undergo many crises in the following years, but Churchill quickly recognized a kindred spirit in the young French general. Thanks to the British, de Gaulle was able to set up the skeleton of a government-in-exile. The British government provided him funds and a daily radio program on the BBC. A small but growing number of escapees from occupied France joined his cause, although political differences led some to remain aloof from his group. The United States, not yet involved in the war, gave de Gaulle the cold shoulder and recognized Vichy as the legitimate French government until 1942.

Just as the Vichy government saw the France's overseas colonies as its most important strategic asset, the Free French movement saw them as the one arena in which it could establish itself. De Gaulle called on their French administrators to follow him. The first to respond was Félix Éboué, the black administrator of the French colony of Chad, in central Africa, a member of the small *évolué* group that identified itself with France. With Éboué's help, De Gaulle was able to win over most of French Equatorial Africa; he could now claim to be more than just an exile whose territory was limited to Carlton Gardens, his headquarters building in London. But forces loyal to Vichy drove off a Franco-British naval expedition sent to Dakar, the capital of the larger and more strategically located colony of French West Africa, in September 1940. Despite this setback, de Gaulle was able to fly to Brazzaville, capital of French Equatorial Africa, and, on October 27, 1940, he announced the creation of the Council of Imperial Defense, the first step toward the creation of a counter-government opposed to the Vichy regime. By this time, he had also received support from some of France's other small colonies. In addition to West Africa, however, Vichy still had control of the critical French possessions in North Africa and Indochina.

De Gaulle responded to the weakness of his position by taking the most intransigent possible positions in defense of French interests. At several points in 1941 and 1942, de Gaulle, head of a minuscule movement of exiles, "alone in the midst of well-supported partners, terribly poor among the rich" (as he later wrote in his *War Memoirs*, one of the classic books to come out of the war), indignantly threatened to break off relations with the British Empire when he thought his allies were seeking to expand their influence in France's overseas territories. To him, "what was at stake was not only the expulsion of the enemy from [France's] territory, it was also its future as a nation and a state."[2]

De Gaulle's prickly treatment of the British reflected a calculated policy to defend what he saw as France's vital interests. But it was also consistent with the personality of the man who was to become the most important figure in French political life for the next three decades. De Gaulle's willingness to go his own way owed something to his family background. His family had strong intellectual roots—his paternal grandmother had been a noted writer of women's books—and also a strong Catholic heritage. Despite his attachment to the church, de Gaulle's father had defended Dreyfus's innocence and accepted the Republic. The son decided at an early age to enter the army, where his seriousness and his unusual height made him stand out. Wounded in August 1914, the young de Gaulle returned to combat as quickly as possible. Captured by the Germans at Verdun, he showed his devotion to what he conceived of as his duty by making repeated but unsuccessful efforts to escape. Ironically, it was Pétain himself who had recognized de Gaulle's abilities after the war and promoted his career, but rather than loyally defending his mentor's ideas, de Gaulle became one of the few critics of the defensive mentality Pétain had infused into the French army.

De Gaulle's Catholic background, his military outlook, and his views on the importance of leadership might easily have inclined him to join one of the many right-wing movements of the interwar period, but he remained aloof from them. The success of the German *Blitzkrieg* vindicated his own ideas about technological warfare. He was briefly able to apply them, leading one of the few French tank units into combat in the hectic days of May 1940. By then, it was too late to stem the German tide. His decision to fly to England on June 17, 1940, was of a piece with the character of a man who had long shown both his intense dedication to his country and his determination to follow his own ideas. De Gaulle's belief in himself and his cause was, of course, essential to the success of his wartime leadership, but it was at the same time a major obstacle in his dealing with others, who often experienced him as rigid and even dictatorial.

The Resistance in France

While de Gaulle struggled to impose himself as the legitimate representative of France's interests in world affairs, resistance to both the Germans and the Vichy government began to grow inside France. The earliest resisters appeared in the weeks immediately following the armistice, and their first gestures were largely symbolic—chalking anti-

German slogans on walls, or circulating hand-typed or mimeographed bulletins containing news from the BBC or exhortations to reject collaboration with the Germans. In the "occupied" north, where the German presence was direct, the choice between collaboration and resistance was clearcut. In the Vichy zone, matters were more complicated; for some time, many considered it possible to resist the Germans while serving a regime that claimed to be maintaining French sovereignty.

The brutal German repression of early Resistance groups, such as the circle led by several anthropologists at the Paris Museum of Man who founded one of the first Resistance periodicals, made it clear that the commitment to anti-German activism was a serious one. The earliest resisters tended to be young and had often participated in one or another of the numerous nonconformist movements of the 1930s. The movement attracted many supporters of the prewar left, but also activists from the social-Catholic and Christian-democratic milieus and even nationalists from the ranks of the *Action française* and the terrorist *Cagoule* group. French Jews were disproportionately represented in the Resistance, but most of them identified themselves as French patriots rather than as members of a distinct ethnic group. De Gaulle was not the only army officer who refused to accept the 1940 defeat. Henry Frenay, a young captain, became leader of *Combat*, one of the most important movements. Women were active in many Resistance groups from the start. Frenay's closest associate in *Combat* was his friend Berty Albrecht, a campaigner for women's right to birth control information in the 1930s. She took her own life after her arrest in 1943. Lucie Aubrac was one of the founding members of *Libération,* another important Resistance group in the southern zone. Marie Madeleine Fourcade, a charter member of the *Alliance* group (an important

source of secret intelligence for the Allies), took over the organization's leadership after the arrest of her male colleagues.

Germany's assault on the Soviet Union in June 1941 caused a major change in the composition of the French Resistance. The French Communist party, which, under Stalin's orders, had refused to back the war effort in 1939 and had referred to the conflict as a fight between "two gangsters" in 1940, suddenly reversed its policy. The party's shift was a relief to many of its rank-and-file members, who had never understood the pact between Hitler and Stalin, and it brought the Resistance the benefit of a well-organized movement with long experience in clandestine activities. The party could count on the loyalty of the numerous militants among immigrant workers in France, who were attracted by its internationalist orientation. Their movement, the Main d'Oeuvre Immigré, paid an especially heavy price for its Resistance activism.

The Communists' participation in the Resistance caused new strains in that movement, however. After their experience with the party's repeated policy reversals during the 1930s, many members of other groups had deep-seated suspicions of the Communists' motives. They also had a well-founded fear of Communist skill in penetrating and controlling other groups. In the fall of 1941, the Communists' decision to launch direct attacks on German occupation troops was opposed by all the Resistance groups. Communist killings of German officers, starting with the assassination of a naval lieutenant in the Barbès metro station in Paris in August 1941, brought frightful German reprisals. An example was the execution of twenty-seven hostages, including the seventeen-year-old son of a Communist deputy, at Chateaubriant in October. Both de Gaulle and most of the non-Communist resistance groups urged an end to such isolated attacks, which did little real damage to the

Germans but took a high toll in French lives. The Communists responded that the German repression would drive more of the population into resistance.

By 1942, the internal Resistance movements had lost some of their early, spontaneous character and were becoming more organized. Regularly printed newspapers—sometimes published at night using the same equipment that served authorized publications during the day—replaced typed and mimeographed bulletins. In the south, the Resistance movements created regional networks and special branches to provide forged documents, undertake sabotage missions, and gather intelligence. In the north, the Communist-dominated *Front national* created a host of special organizations for different social and professional groups. Whether or not they were affiliated with organized Resistance movements, a growing number of French actively opposed the regime and helped its victims. In the Massif Central, the inhabitants of the little Protestant village of Chambon-sur-Lignon hid hundreds of Jewish children in danger of deportation. Throughout the country, courageous housewives concealed downed Allied airmen and helped them make their way to the Spanish border and safety.

Both in France and in London, there was a growing sense of need for closer contact between de Gaulle's self-proclaimed government-in-exile and the groups working against Vichy and the Germans inside France. At the beginning of 1942, de Gaulle dispatched a representative, Jean Moulin, to enter France and try to organize the Resistance under his leadership. Initially, many Resistance activists were reluctant. Christian Pineau, head of *Libération-Nord* in the "occupied" zone, criticized de Gaulle's claims, saying, "We took action without him. . . . He isn't in the country, and he doesn't run the risks we do."[3] But he and other Resistance leaders eventually recognized the need for unity, as well as the advantages of having access to British-donated funds and equipment that only de Gaulle could supply. For non-Communist resisters like Frenay, de Gaulle also provided the assurance that the party would not dominate the movement, as it sometimes seemed bent on doing. By April 1942, Moulin had secured agreement from the major Resistance groups to set up a unified Secret Army to support the Allied liberation of France when it finally occurred. He also established an Information and Press Bureau to coordinate propaganda efforts and a General Study Committee to prepare position papers on the postwar reconstruction of France.

The Allied landings in French North Africa strengthened the bond between de Gaulle and the internal Resistance movements. The Americans, convinced that the troublesome Free French leader represented only himself, had refused to allow the Gaullists any role in the campaign. They had dealt instead with one of de Gaulle's rivals, General Henri Giraud, an army officer who had made a spectacular escape from a German prisoner-of-war camp but who had refused to make a clear break with the Vichy government. When they found Admiral Darlan on the scene in North Africa, the Americans promptly entered into negotiations with him that lasted until his assassination. Giraud had no support among the internal Resistance movements, which strongly backed de Gaulle, but American and British pressure forced the latter to accept an uneasy compromise with his rival. Confident that the Resistance's loyalty would eventually turn the situation in his favor, de Gaulle agreed to join Giraud in setting up a provisional government in Algiers, but the experience did nothing to improve his opinion of the "Anglo-Saxons."

In February 1943, Jean Moulin returned to France to hasten development of a structure that could eventually serve as the basis of a postliberation government. The German occupation of southern France, while it subjected the Resistance movements to more direct harassment from the Gestapo, had also clarified the political situation by making the Vichy government's subordination to the Germans unmistakable. Moulin was able to set up a National Resistance Council, including representatives of the major movements and of those political parties and movements that supported de Gaulle. The Germans arrested Moulin and several other top Resistance leaders in Lyon in June 1943, but the Council survived. Georges Bidault, a prewar Catholic activist, became its new head. The number of Resistance activists grew dramatically in the course of 1943 as thousands of young men sought to evade conscription for the *Service de Travail Obligatoire*, proclaimed by Laval in February 1943 in response to growing German demands for French labor. Rather than leave for Germany, many of those called up took to the woods in rural areas of France. These groups of *maquis*, so called in reference to the scrubby vegetation of the hills in southern France, provided the Resistance for the first time with a mass base. But they lacked food, arms, and training, which the Resistance groups had to scramble to provide.

By 1943, support for the Vichy government was rapidly eroding. Those collaborationists who had compromised themselves too thoroughly to change sides continued to support the Germans with bitter determination, however. In December 1943, the Germans forced Laval to bring three of the leading Paris collaborationists, Marcel Déat, Philippe Henriot, and Joseph Darnand, into his cabinet. The most sinister of the three was Darnand, the leader of the *Milice*, a French police force formed to assist the Gestapo. The *Milice* ruthlessly hunted down Jews and Resistance members and was often more brutal than the Germans themselves. Its activities exacerbated the enmity between those who supported the Resistance movement and those who opposed it, and created an atmosphere close to civil war in some regions. Meanwhile, in Algiers, de Gaulle gradually maneuvered the politically inept Giraud out of the picture. In September 1943, he convened a consultative assembly of representatives from the Resistance and prewar parties that had not participated in the Vichy regime. In June 1944, just before the Allied landings, the assembly proclaimed itself the provisional government of France.

As he looked ahead to creating a new government in France, de Gaulle also laid out plans for the future of the French colonies. Colonial support had made his movement possible, and he assumed that a restored empire would be an integral part of postwar France. At the same time, however, he recognized that the support he had received from men like Félix Éboué had been premised on the conviction that a liberated France would grant its colonial populations a greater role in governing themselves and the Empire as a whole. Furthermore, the war had created new pressures for the end of colonialism. To head off dissent in India, their largest colony, the British had already promised to grant it independence after the peace. The United States, whose forces were occupying French North Africa, openly encouraged talk about the eventual independence of those territories. At the end of 1943, after the threat of a German conquest of the Middle East had vanished, France recognized the independence of Syria and Lebanon, originally promised in 1936. In a speech in the Algerian city of Constantine on December 12, 1943, de Gaulle announced reforms to give political rights to a minority of French-educated Algerians, along the lines of the Blum-Viollette proposal of 1937. This opening came too late: Ferhat Abbas, leader of the *évolués*, joined with the more radical supporters of Messali Hadj and Islamic groups to form a united front demanding full autonomy. A confrontation between France and the Muslim population of its most important overseas possession was becoming inevitable.

The situation in sub-Saharan Africa appeared more optimistic. In January 1944, de Gaulle convened a conference on the future of France's African territories in Brazzaville, the capital of French Equatorial Africa. He proclaimed that "there will be no real progress if men in their native lands do not profit by it morally and materially; if they cannot raise themselves little by little to the level where they will be capable of participating directly in the management of their own affairs. It is France's duty to see to it that it shall be so." While de Gaulle's language seemed to point toward the eventual autonomy of the colonies, the official recommendations that came out of the meeting were more cautious, emphasized that there would be no break-up of the empire and that "the eventual creation, even in the distant future, of *self-government* for the colonies is to be set aside."[4] Education in the colonies was to be given only in French. Nevertheless, the Brazzaville conference promised that colonial populations would be consulted about their future, and it also committed postwar France to abolishing the *loi de l'indigénat* of 1881, which had allowed French authorities to impose arbitrary punishments on inhabitants of the colonies, and to ending the practice of forced labor. The Brazzaville conference excited new hopes throughout France's colonial possessions.

LIBERATION

For four years after the armistice of June 1940, the war raged in the Mediterranean, in Russia, in the Pacific, but not in France. Despite the activities of the Resistance and the determination of de Gaulle, it was obvious that the Germans could not be defeated until American and British forces landed on

French soil. Under the direction of the American general Dwight Eisenhower, the Allies spent 1943 and the first months of 1944 preparing Operation Overlord—the massive amphibious landing that would start the liberation of France. The French Second Armored Division, part of the army de Gaulle had reconstituted in North Africa and that had seen action in the 1943 Allied campaign in Italy, was transported to Britain to participate in the assault. But the French were kept in the dark about Eisenhower's plans. Even in the face of growing evidence of de Gaulle's popularity, the Americans considered installing an Allied military government in liberated France and postponing recognition of a French government until after elections could be organized. For de Gaulle, the long-awaited D-Day landing in Normandy on June 6, 1944, was thus another test of his ability to maintain French sovereignty, not only against the Germans but also against his own allies. But the problem, in de Gaulle's mind, was even more complex, for he also feared the Resistance itself. Rumors were rife that the French Communists would try to take power as the Germans were driven out.

The internal Resistance groups had planned long in advance to assist the Allies. Directed by radio messages from London, they knocked out railroad lines, disrupted German communications, and ambushed German units marching toward the Normandy battle front. Unfortunately, coordination with the Allies was less than perfect, and in some regions, the Germans inflicted heavy casualties on lightly armed *maquis* who had risen up in expectation of quick Allied support. Hundreds of Resistance fighters were killed in the mountainous Vercors plateau south of Grenoble in the bloodiest of these encounters. This added to the list of misunderstandings between the French and their wartime allies. French civilians suffered heavily, as well. Allied bombing raids before the landings, part of a plan to paralyze transportation behind the German lines, inflicted many casualties. And in the weeks just after the landings, German troops harassed by the Resistance committed some of the worst atrocities of the war. The entire population of one village, Oradour, 642 men, women, and children, were among the victims of these German reprisals.

In the Norman towns the Allied armies wrested from the Germans after the first landings, de Gaulle quickly made a triumphant appearance. He immediately implemented the provisional government's plan for restoration of French civil authority by installing *commissaires de la République*— delegates with sweeping authority—in the liberated areas. Despite misgivings in Washington, Eisenhower recognized the impossibility of trying to dispute de Gaulle's authority. But disagreements between de Gaulle and the Allies were by no means at an end. When Allied forces finally broke out of the narrow Normandy beachhead in late July and began a rapid advance across northern France, a new dispute developed about the fate of Paris. For military reasons, Eisenhower wanted to bypass the French capital. For political reasons, de Gaulle was determined to enter it as quickly as possible—before the Resistance forces, which he regarded as Communist-dominated, could install an independent government. When the Paris Resistance began an uprising on August 18, de Gaulle threatened to withdraw French forces from Allied command to rush them to the city. In the end, Eisenhower altered his plans. The French Second Armored Division and the first American forces reached Paris on the 24th of August. They found it largely intact, thanks in good part to the German commander Dietrich von Choltitz's refusal to implement Hitler's orders to destroy public buildings. On August 25, de Gaulle installed himself in the offices of the Ministry of War; on the 26th, he led a triumphal parade down the Champs-Elysées to Notre Dame Cathedral to celebrate the liberation. The war was still far from over—a fusillade broke out just as the general, whose height made him a conspicuous target, was entering the church—but there was no further doubt about who would head the new French government.

By the end of September 1944, the Germans had been driven from most of France. A second Allied landing, Operation Anvil-Dragoon, on the Mediterranean coast on August 15 launched a rapid campaign up the Rhône valley, linking up with the forces that landed in Normandy on September 12. The French First Army made up an important part of the Anvil-Dragoon force. In the meantime, Resistance units took control of much of the southwest and the Massif Central, abandoned by the Germans as they retreated. They also helped contain pockets of German troops who remained in several major Atlantic ports until the end of the war.

The battle front moved north into Belgium, and the retreating Germans installed Pétain, Laval, and the remaining French advocates of collaborationism in the south German town of Sigmaringen. In Paris, de Gaulle's provisional government could begin to grapple with the problems of France's second postwar reconstruction in a generation.

NOTES

1. Cited in Jean-Pierre Azéma, *De Munich à la Libération* (Paris: Seuil, 1979), 153.

2. Charles de Gaulle, *Mémoires de Guerre* (Paris: Plon, 1954), 2:1.

3. Cited in Jean Lacouture, *De Gaulle* (Paris, Seuil, 1984), 1:585.

4. Citations in D. Bruce Marshall, "Free France in Africa: Gaullism and Colonialism," in Prosser Gifford and Wm. Roger Louis, eds., *France and Britain in Africa: Imperial Rivalry and Colonial Rule* (New Haven, Ct.: Yale University Press, 1971), 716, 721.

CHAPTER 29

THE REVIVAL OF THE PARLIAMENTARY REPUBLIC

The euphoria that accompanied the liberation of Paris in August 1944 was the prelude to a third attempt in less than ten years to make fundamental reforms in French institutions and eliminate undesirable characteristics of the country's "stalemate society." Like the Popular Front and the Vichy regime, the leaders of what soon became France's Fourth Republic found this goal more difficult to accomplish than they had expected. Within a few years, the national consensus generated by the experience of German occupation had come apart, and the country—weakened by the ordeal of war—seemed as unable to cope with its problems as it had during the last years of the Third Republic. While its western European neighbors began to enjoy the benefits of peace, economic prosperity, and political stability that had eluded them between the wars, the Fourth Republic teetered from one crisis to another, beleaguered by colonial wars, inflation, and political crises, until its collapse in 1958. Charles de Gaulle, the charismatic leader who had tried and failed to set his mark on the Fourth Republic at the outset, and who replaced it with his own regime when it fell, did much to contribute to the postwar regime's reputation as a time of frustration and failure. In hindsight, however, it is clear that many of the suc-

cesses of the 1960s were built on foundations laid during the years from 1944 to 1958. The Fourth Republic lasted for half of the "thirty glorious years" from 1945 to 1975, during which France took its place among the prosperous, democratic societies of the advanced industrial world. However, the significance of the changes that began in the late 1940s and early 1950s only became evident after the Fourth Republic had disintegrated.

THE PROVISIONAL GOVERNMENT

Part of the reason for the rapid disillusionment with the Fourth Republic stemmed from the unrealistic expectations that prevailed at the time of the liberation. At the moment of de Gaulle's arrival in Paris, the country seemed united in its rededication to the fundamental republican values of liberty and social equality that had been so flagrantly disregarded by the Vichy regime. The mood in France was in tune with the atmosphere of the Allied crusade against Hitler, which had united the western democracies and the Soviet Union and raised hopes of a new era of world peace. Both in France and in the wider world, however, this apparent consensus concealed fundamental disagreements that had already become visible during the war years. These differences were rapidly exacerbated when the difficulties of postwar recovery became apparent.

In France, there was a virtually unanimous consensus to reject the leaders and institutions who had led the country to catastrophe in 1940 and during the war. A referendum in October 1945 showed that 96 percent of the voters opposed any return to the institutions of the Third Republic. These voters for the first time included women, who had been given the right to vote by de Gaulle's Provisional Government in Algeria in 1944. Politicians who had voted to give power to Pétain in 1940 were barred from office. The Vichy regime was even more discredited. As the Allied armies advanced across France, the population and Resistance movements settled scores with those who had sided with the Germans. This spontaneous "purification," exaggerated in later years by opponents of the left-wing movements that dominated the Resistance, resulted in the execution of about 10,000 members of Vichy's Milice and other collaborators. It was a figure far below the 280,000 French killed for opposing the Germans or Vichy during the war. The leading Vichy officials, taken to Germany in the last months of the war, were brought back and tried. De Gaulle commuted the death sentence imposed on the aged Marshal Pétain, but former prime minister Laval and a number of his colleagues were executed. Outrage at the way many leading industrialists had willingly worked for the Germans led to the expropriation of a number of large companies, such as the Renault auto company and the coal mines in northern France. The printing plants of newspapers that had continued to publish under German censorship were turned over to journalists from the wartime Resistance press.

The apparent unanimity that underlay this rejection of the Third Republic and Vichy did not extend, however, to the remaking of France's political and social institutions. The activists of the internal Resistance, many of them genuinely heroic figures who had risked their lives in the struggle, imagined postwar France as an extension of that movement. They dreamed of a new "hard and pure" republic, purged of corruption and inefficiency and committed to social justice. They wanted to see the spirit that had united Communists, Catholics, and socialists in the Resistance preserved, and the dreary political quarrels of the Third Republic buried. Many dreamed of creating a single party representing that movement and capable of directing the new government. Already before the end of the war, however, the unity of the Resistance had begun to unravel. The Communist party's tendency to take over the institutions created to unite the movement drove supporters of other views to revive their old parties or create new ones. Furthermore, even though its ranks had been swelled by thousands of "eleventh-hour resisters" who had waited until the last minute to commit themselves, the movement was far from representing the entire population.

Charles de Gaulle, the political outsider who had succeeded in imposing himself as the nation's unquestioned leader by the time of the liberation, was among those who distrusted the idea that militants of the Resistance should now run the country. He was convinced that the popular enthusiasm that had greeted his arrival in France gave him a mandate broader than that of the Resistance. He was also convinced that France needed above all a strong, decisive government, capable of defending its interests in the world arena. From the moment of his arrival in Paris—when he made a point of going first to the War Ministry offices before visiting the Hôtel-de-Ville (seat of the temporary city government set up during the uprising against the Germans)—de Gaulle emphasized his determination to put the restoration of authority first on his agenda. He did appoint a leading Resistance activist, the Catholic Georges Bidault, head of his Provisional Government, and selected ministers representing a cross-section of Resistance movements, including the Communists. However, de Gaulle often seemed more concerned with curbing the Resistance movements' pretensions than with rewarding them for their contribution to the country's liberation. He ordered the immediate dissolution of the armed French Forces of the Interior, whose members were either to join the regular army or return to civilian life. On a tour of the provinces in September 1944, he often snubbed Resistance activists and made it clear that the new government drew its legitimacy from the support of the whole French people, not just from an activist minority.

The main motivation for de Gaulle's policy was fear of the Communists. Particularly in some areas of the southwest where local Resistance forces had driven the Germans out on their own, Communist activists did dominate the new local administrations and act as though they planned to create a power base to challenge the provisional government. De Gaulle was able to outmaneuver them both because he enjoyed broader popular support and because Stalin soon made it clear that he opposed a Communist bid for power. Such a move would have run counter to his policy of conceding western Europe to the Americans and British while implanting Soviet- dominated regimes in the east. It would also have cost the French party the influence it expected to enjoy in the postwar government.

In foreign affairs, de Gaulle's main concern was to restore France to the rank of the major powers. For this reason, he made great efforts to see that French units participated in the remaining campaigns of the European war. To the long list of his grievances against his "Anglo-Saxon" allies, de Gaulle added the complaint that they were not quick enough to provide the equipment for the new divisions he wanted to create. He declared France's determination to retain all its prewar colonial possessions. To give himself more bargaining power with the western Allies, de Gaulle flew to Moscow in December 1944, hoping to revive the old alliance with the country he continued to refer to as "Russia." The French did succeed in getting themselves admitted to the Allied committee created to discuss the postwar fate of Germany, and they were promised an occupation zone and a seat on the council that was to administer Berlin. But de Gaulle was not invited to the meeting of the "Big Three" at Yalta in February 1945, at which the overall shape of postwar Europe was largely determined. Nor was he invited to the Potsdam conference in July 1945 following the German surrender. For all of de Gaulle's efforts, France lacked the resources to claim a full place in the Grand Alliance. The effort to regain the rank of a great world power was to drain the country's resources throughout the postwar period and eventually to put the fate of its democratic institutions in jeopardy.

Elections of 1945

Vital decisions about domestic policy had been postponed until the war had ended and elections could be held. The first postwar national elections in October 1945 produced a Constituent Assembly dominated by the three parties whose members had participated most actively in the Resistance, each of which won approximately 25 percent of the vote. The Communists came in slightly ahead of their rivals. They campaigned on a patriotic program, billing themselves as *le parti des fusillés* (the party of those sentenced to death). Their very real role in the

Resistance and their association with the Soviet Union and its great contribution to the defeat of Hitler had tremendously boosted their popularity. In addition, they had gained almost complete control of the CGT trade union confederation. There was nothing in the party's publicly avowed program to arouse controversy. Maurice Thorez, its leader, urged workers to participate in postwar reconstruction efforts, and abandoned the PCF's prewar support for independence movements in the colonies in order to endorse maintenance of the French empire. The Socialists (SFIO) also had a new momentum after the war. Aside from the elder statesman Léon Blum, the party had a new generation of leaders recruited during the Resistance, and broad support from voters who saw it as the best vehicle for defending both democracy and policies in favor of social equality. The two traditional left-wing parties now shared power with a new entrant on the French political stage, the *Mouvement Républicain Populaire* (MRP). Largely but not exclusively Catholic, it incorporated the Christian-inspired element of the Resistance, and its leaders were committed to working with the Communists and Socialists in the postwar system. Its diversified electorate, however, included a number of conservative voters whose commitment to this kind of alliance was slight. The other prewar parties, discredited by their acceptance of the Vichy regime, had virtually disintegrated, giving French politics a strong tilt to the left.

Relations between de Gaulle and the tripartite alliance that dominated the Assembly soon soured. De Gaulle, who refused to identify himself with any party, favored a system in which the president—elected by the Assembly—would have broad powers to set and carry out policy. At a moment when memories of the damage done by Pétain's authoritarian rule were so fresh, such ideas alienated not only the deputies with whom he had to work but many of the voters. The majority of the Assembly preferred a system dominated by an elected parliament. Assuming the large, cohesive political parties that had emerged after the war would remain powerful, they did not anticipate a return to the fragile ministries of the Third Republic. De Gaulle denounced this plan for "an all-powerful assembly, choosing a government to carry out its wishes,"[1] and, in January 1946, he challenged the parties directly by submitting his resignation. "I thought the French would soon call me back," he told a confidant a few years later.[2] Instead, the tripartite coalition reverted to the Third Republic practice of choosing a relatively undistinguished colleague to head the government—in this case, a Socialist, Félix Gouin. Opinion polls showed that the parliamentarians had considerable support. By a margin of 40 percent to 32 percent, the public regretted the departure of de Gaulle, but only 27 percent hoped to see him resume leadership of the government.

With de Gaulle gone, the professional politicians of the Assembly were free to draft a constitution that suited them. The two left-wing parties, loyal to a tradition of popular sovereignty dating back to the Convention of 1793, proposed a unicameral assembly with almost unlimited power. The MRP, noting that similar assemblies were becoming mechanisms for Communist domination in eastern Europe, wanted the plan to include a second legislative chamber and a president with some real powers. When these proposals were rejected, the MRP joined the small centrist and conservative groups outside the coalition in urging voters to reject the plan. On May 5, 1946, the electorate, by 53 percent to 47 percent, did so, forcing the election of a second Constituent Assembly. These elections showed the Communists holding their own, but the MRP attracting more votes from the right and surging past them to become the largest single party in France. The Socialists, many of whose members had had doubts about the constitutional plan, suffered a distinct setback. De Gaulle, who had remained silent during the earlier constitutional debate, made a dramatic intervention in the new one by proposing a presidential regime in which the elected parliament would have had severely limited powers. He failed to sway the deputies, whose plan retained a dominant Assembly, somewhat restrained by a Council of the Republic (a modified version of the Third Republic's Senate), and a president chosen by the two legislative bodies and authorized to nominate the president of the Council. The new plan incorporated a number of provisions meant to prevent the repeated overthrow of cabinets that had often paralyzed Third Republic governments. But in practice, they failed to function, and the Fourth Republic's political institutions ended up working much like those of its predecessor. The October 1946 referendum that approved this constitution showed, however, that many of the voters no longer believed that the design of the political system mattered much. Almost a third of the electorate failed to vote, and the new constitution received only 53 percent of the votes cast. De Gaulle, who had urged a "no" vote, had some reason to contend that the new system lacked a popular mandate: "A third of the French were resigned to it, a third rejected it, a third ignored it altogether."[3]

Reviving the Economy

By the time the new constitution was finally established, other issues—especially economic problems—dominated the public mind. The liberation had failed to stimulate a real recovery from wartime penury. The population continued to have to make do with inadequate rations of food and fuel, and industrial production in 1944 was only 38 per-

cent of its level in the last peacetime year, 1938. At the time of the liberation, it had been politically impossible to deny French workers significant and long-overdue wage increases, but these and the general shortage of consumer goods had unleashed runaway inflation. The Provisional Government had rejected its first finance minister Pierre Mendés-France's proposal for rigorous measures to control the amount of money in circulation at the end of 1945. Wartime destruction made the recovery process a slow one. Although the loss of human lives had been less than in 1914–1918—French casualties from 1939–1945 totaled around 600,000, including 170,000 combat losses and 430,000 civilian deaths—physical destruction had been much more widespread. Seventy-four departments were classified as significantly affected, as opposed to thirteen in 1918. Allied bombing, Resistance sabotage, and German demolitions had virtually paralyzed the nation's transportation system. France's damaged coal mines could not provide the fuel its factories needed. By 1947, industrial production had regained the 1938 level, but this was far from enough to satisfy the population's needs. In any event, workers' salaries were at least 30 percent lower than they had been before the war.

Already during the Vichy period, government experts had foreseen the need for a systematic reconstruction plan after the war. In this area, there was a strong element of continuity from the technocratic proposals of the 1930s to the postwar period. Jean Monnet, one of the prewar planning advocates, who had spent most of the war in the United States and witnessed firsthand the effectiveness of American wartime economic mobilization, became the key figure in directing postwar recovery. The liberation government had made him the head of a *Commissariat du Plan* in January 1946. Eschewing a centralized "command economy" on the model of the Soviet Union, Monnet instead emphasized voluntary cooperation of business and labor, whose representatives worked with government experts to establish economic priorities and overcome bottlenecks standing in the way of growth. From the start, Monnet was determined to see that the French economy was not just rebuilt but also significantly modernized. There would be no return to the self-satisfied mediocrity of the prewar "dual economy," sheltered from the world market by protectionist tariffs. The first plan, published in 1947, emphasized the economic infrastructure, setting targets for investment in energy, transportation, and heavy industry. It charted a promising path for French economic growth, but the benefits were to come only in the future.

The French government's ability to influence the economy was increased by the program of nationalizations carried out during the period of the Provisional Government. The first takeovers of large companies had been reactions to the wartime records of certain industrialists, but the subsequent ones were justified by the need to give the state control of sectors of the economy vital to the country's recovery. By early 1946, several major banks, the bulk of the insurance industry, the gas and electric networks, and the Paris public transportation system had been nationalized. This movement continued a trend toward increased state involvement in the economy begun well before the war, but it did not create a state-controlled economy along Soviet lines. The managers appointed to run the newly nationalized companies were usually experienced businessmen, and the companies—though state owned—continued to be run much like private, profit-making enterprises.

Alongside the program of nationalizations, the liberation government enacted several social reforms meant to implement Resistance hopes for a more just and equal society. Trade unions, repressed during the war, regained their freedom. Factory com-

mittees with worker representatives, set up under the Popular Front but abolished under Vichy, were reestablished. The new constitution incorporated a list of "social and economic rights" that promised all citizens health care, education, the right to a decent job, the right to "time for rest and leisure," and an adequate income for those unable to work. Influenced by developments in other western countries, such as Britain's decision in 1942 to create a government-run national health system, postwar France thus moved into the era of the comprehensive welfare state. Even before the war, there had been steps in this direction, notably the 1928 law creating a state-sponsored system of medical insurance and the inauguration of a system of family allowances in 1939. The postwar reforms greatly extended the range of benefits, however, even though it did not eliminate the complicated system of independent insurance programs to which many French citizens already subscribed. The result has been a system that covers almost all French citizens, but which is considerably more costly to administer than that of many other European countries. Critics have also noted that the French system generously subsidizes middle-class families and does little to reduce inequalities in income, in contrast to benefit systems in Britain and the Scandinavian countries.

THE TURNING POINTS OF 1947

As the year 1947 began, it was by no means certain that the French population would be patient long enough for Monnet's plan to succeed and for democratic institutions to take solid root again. Workers' strikes and housewives' street protests against rising prices became increasingly frequent. It was partly in this context that the postwar tripartite coalition finally broke apart. But the relations between the Communist party and its coalition partners had become strained for other reasons as well.

Throughout the world, the confrontation between the United States and the Soviet Union was hardening into a "cold war." In eastern Europe, Communist parties under Soviet domination had ousted non-Communists from new governments set up in 1945, while in the west, the Communists had already been evicted from postwar coalitions in Italy and Belgium. In March 1947, U.S. president Harry Truman denounced what he saw as a Communist bid for world domination. The French government, with Communist cabinet ministers but dependent on U.S. economic aid to carry out the ambitious Monnet plan, was in an awkward situation. Not that the Americans—as some French leftists subsequently alleged—directly forced the expulsion of the Communists from the French government, but their attitude favored such a course. When the Communist ministers (unwilling to openly oppose workers' protests) voted in May 1947 against the government's refusal to grant wage increases in the nationalized Renault factories, the Socialist prime minister Paul Ramadier expelled them from his government.

The breakup of the tripartite coalition, together with de Gaulle's resignation sixteen months earlier, marked the end of the liberation's direct impact on French politics. Both the man most identified with the Resistance and the party that had contributed the most to it were now in the opposition, and destined to remain there for the remainder of the Fourth Republic. Ramadier's government and its successors until 1952 labeled themselves representatives of a "Third Force," based on a coalition between the Socialists and the MRP and standing between the Communists on the left and the new movement—the *Rassemblement du Peuple Français* (RPF)—that de Gaulle launched in April 1947. The RPF, frankly anti-Communist, was bent on replacing the Fourth Republic with a presidentialist regime. The movement's devotion to a charismatic leader

and de Gaulle's condemnation of parliamentary democracy reminded many observers of Bonapartism or fascism, even though de Gaulle rejected any idea of taking power by extralegal means. For a brief moment in 1947, it appeared that he would win through the ballot box. In municipal elections, the RPF came in ahead of all other parties, installing its candidates as mayors of France's thirteen largest cities. But national elections were not due until 1951. In the interim, the RPF, which held few parliamentary seats, lost much of its momentum. Nevertheless, the potential threat of a Gaullist election success weakened the "Third Force" governments, caught between the Communists on the left and the RPF on the right.

The Marshall Plan

If the Fourth Republic avoided succumbing to these perils, the main reason was its success in overcoming the economic crisis of the postwar years—a success closely linked to the American decision to support European economic recovery. Jean Monnet's planning efforts had outlined the path to economic growth and modernization, but France was critically short of resources to implement his ideas. Ever since the liberation, France had had to borrow heavily from the United States to finance imports of food and raw materials. The massive trade deficit threatened to undermine the franc and block recovery. American secretary of state George Marshall's announcement in June 1947 of the foreign aid program that came to bear his name offered a solution to the French dilemma. In exchange for agreeing to economic cooperation with its western European neighbors, France was able to use American grants and loans to finance the beginnings of its economic revival.

To a remarkable extent, the American money came without entangling strings. The French government's Fund for Modernization and Investment provided some 60 percent of the credits invested in the economy from 1947 to 1950, emphasizing improvement of the transportation system, expansion of energy resources and the steel industry, and modernization of agriculture. Although the inflation that had begun with the war continued to plague the economy, by 1950 the physical damage caused between 1940 and 1944 had largely been repaired and key industrial sectors were ready for further development. Wages still lagged behind prices, and French workers had to make their own sacrifices to aid recovery by working longer hours, but a sense that economic conditions were on the road to improvement blunted the acute unrest of 1946–1947 and the potential threat to democracy that had accompanied it.

The Marshall Plan had originally been offered to all the countries of Europe, including the Soviet Union and its satellites, but the Communist countries had rejected it as a plot to extend American influence. In any event, it served to tie the western European countries that did participate more firmly into an American-led anti-Communist bloc. Within France, the growing divide between the Communist party and its former partners in the Resistance coalition had many repercussions. The trade union movement, precariously united in 1936 and again in 1944, splintered once more at the end of 1947. In April 1948, non-Communist unionists who had quit the CGT to protest Communist control founded a new labor federation, the *CGT–Force Ouvrière*, or FO. Schoolteachers, one of the largest unionized groups, set up their own independent *Fédération de l'Education Nationale* (FEN). The CGT remained the largest labor organization. Despite its revolutionary rhetoric, its leaders learned to negotiate successfully, especially in the large enterprises nationalized after the war. But the division of the union movement weakened workers' positions, and the CGT's identification with the Communists kept the most militant sector of the workforce isolated from the rest of French society.

French Foreign Policy

The effects of the cold war were equally evident in France's foreign policy. By the end of 1947, French leaders had to abandon the keystone of their independent foreign policy in Europe: the attempt to keep Germany weak and limit its economic redevelopment. The French occupation zone there was integrated with those of the American and British to form what soon became the Federal Republic of Germany, which had full autonomy over its own domestic affairs. The Soviets sponsored the rival German Democratic Republic in the territory they occupied. Although French spokesmen initially balked at American efforts to organize western Europe into an anti-Communist military alliance, the Soviet blockade of West Berlin in 1948–1949 made the Communist menace seem too threatening to be ignored. In July 1949, the Assembly ratified the North Atlantic Treaty, making France a member of NATO. Stepped-up American pressure following the outbreak of the Korean War in 1950 forced France to accept the creation of a West German army to assist in the defense of western Europe. The "Third Force" governments thus accepted France's position as a partner in a broad western alliance, led by the United States, in which a revived Germany played a major role.

Even before the beginning of German reunification, France and Germany had begun to move toward economic cooperation. As in the 1920s, the failure of efforts to keep Germany permanently crippled led French statesmen to adopt a policy of reconciliation with the former enemy in the context of a broader European community. The leading French architect of this change in policy was the MRP politician Robert Schumann, who occupied the Foreign Ministry in several successive cabinets from mid-1948 to early 1953. He found a responsive partner in West German Chancellor Konrad Adenauer, who was eager to end his country's isolation and anchor it solidly to the other western European democracies. In 1951, France, West Germany, Italy and the Benelux countries (Belgium, the Netherlands, and Luxembourg) formed the European Coal and Steel Community, allowing free trade in those crucial industrial commodities; it was the first step toward a broader common market. Cooperation in other areas proved touchier, however. Faced with the inevitability of German rearmament, French premier René Pleven had proposed in 1949 creation of a European Defense Community (EDC) with a common army as a way of avoiding the re-creation of an independent German military. Within France itself, the proposal proved violently controversial. The Communists denounced it as a plot against the Soviet Union, and a strong "neutralist" current, represented by the most influential of the new newspapers created after the war—the daily *Le Monde*—argued that France's security would be better assured by staying out of potential American-Soviet conflicts. De Gaulle and the RPF opposed the abandonment of French sovereignty over its own armed forces. In the end, opposition within France scuttled the plan, but not before it had served to undermine several successive ministries and highlight the Fourth Republic's inability to handle controversial issues.

The "French Union" and the Indochina War

At the start of the war, in 1940, the doomed Third Republic had issued a special postage stamp showing a map of "France overseas," emphasizing the importance of the colonies. The Vichy regime had reissued a stamp of the same design in 1941. In 1945, the Provisional Government released a third version of the same stamp, showing that it still saw France's overseas territories as vital to the country's future. But the war made it impossible to restore the old colonial system. North Africa's Muslim populations were increasingly impatient with French rule; in France's sub-Saharan African territories, the Brazzaville conference's promise of sweeping changes had created a new atmosphere. At the end of the war, France's colony of Vietnam had achieved independence: after the withdrawal of Japanese forces in August 1945, a nationalist movement led by the Communist Ho Chi Minh, which had received some American aid during the war, took control of the country. To retain France's colonies, the Fourth Republic had to find a way of convincing their peoples that democracy could be combined with an imperial system. Events were to show that this was an impossible challenge.

The Constituent Assembly that drew up France's new constitution in 1946 also proclaimed the transformation of the Empire into a "French Union" of supposedly equal peoples. Napoleon III's 1854 law excluding the colonies from constitutional protection was finally abrogated, and all inhabitants of France's overseas territories were declared to be French citizens with legal rights, including the right to vote for assemblies to govern their territories. This change abolished the 1881 *code de l'indigénat*. The autonomy promised by the statutes of the French Union did not include the right for overseas territories to declare themselves independent, however, and even before the new system went into effect, the French government had shown that it would use force to maintain its control over them. Anticolonial insurrections in parts of Algeria in May and June of 1945 were bloodily repressed. In Indochina, de Gaulle's Provisional Government dispatched troops who restored French rule in the southern part of the country. The

French officials sent to Vietnam differed sharply over how to deal with Ho Chi Minh and his Viet Minh movement. Jean Sainteny, a civil administrator, negotiated an agreement under which Ho Chi Minh would form a government in the northern part of the country, a referendum would be held in the southern provinces to decide whether they would accept Viet Minh rule, and Vietnam would remain in the French Union. Admiral Thierry d'Argenlieu, named governor-general of French Indochina, scuttled this plan, driving the Viet Minh to launch an attack on French forces in December 1946. Hostilities quickly escalated into a full-scale war.

From 1947 to 1953, French troops from the professional army and the Foreign Legion fought a frustrating struggle against the Viet Minh guerrillas. Like the United States in its own war in Vietnam fifteen years later, the French government tried to keep the war limited. Fearing the reaction of a public largely indifferent to the matter, it did not commit draftees to the fight. American financial aid kept the war from completely unbalancing the French budget, but it was a steady drain on national resources. Its purpose also became increasingly unclear. From 1948, the French had conceded the eventual independence of Vietnam, recognizing a native government headed by the non-Communist Bao Dai. But the French military, its prestige tarnished by the defeat of 1940, remained grimly determined to restore its reputation in the field. And French leaders agonized that concessions in Vietnam would force them to grant independence to colonies closer to home—particularly possessions in North Africa.

While the war in Indochina dragged on, the Fourth Republic also had to deal with resistance in other colonies. A nationalist uprising in Madagascar in 1947 was suppressed, at a cost of perhaps 80,000 deaths. Also in 1947, the French parliament passed a new statute for the government of Algeria. It foresaw the election of an Algerian assembly, half of whose members would be chosen by the French settlers and the small minority of Muslim Algerians who had qualified for French citizenship, while the other half would be chosen by the more numerous Muslim population. To safeguard the position of the French inhabitants, a two-thirds majority in this assembly was required to pass legislation. This gave deputies representing the 922,000 Europeans the power to veto measures supported by the representatives of the nearly 8 million Muslim Algerians. The rival Algerian nationalist movements all rejected this arrangement. To break their resistance, the French governor manipulated the elections to secure a loyal majority among the Algerian deputies, making it appear that Paris was willing to ignore democratic rules to protect the colonists. In sub-Saharan Africa, where there were few French settlers, postwar tensions were not as great, but educated members of the black population also began organizing to demand self-government.

INTELLECTUAL FEVERS AND OVERFLOWING NURSERIES

The heady experience of the Resistance, the liberation, and the confrontations accompanying the cold war stimulated intense, sometimes feverish activity among French intellectuals. In their own eyes, at least, Paris was once again the world's center of thought and debate. In retrospect, however, what is most striking about the thought of the "Sartre years" is the degree to which absorption in politics blinded French intellectuals to the important social and cultural changes taking place around them.

The Resistance activists had looked forward to a cultural and intellectual renewal as well as a political and social one. The liberation witnessed a violent reaction against the writers and performers who had collaborated with the Germans. Some notorious figures, such as author Robert Brasillach, were executed or—like the pro-Fascist novelist Drieu la Rochelle—committed suicide. All newspapers that had continued to publish under German rule were confiscated and their printing plants turned over to journalists from the underground Resistance press. The most lasting result of this measure was the creation of a new daily paper, *Le Monde*. It succeeded in giving permanent expression to the Resistance dream of a press independent of the economic interests and petty political concerns that had colored the prewar dailies, and that soon reasserted themselves in many postwar newspapers. Under the direction of a remarkable editor, Hubert Beuve-Méry, *Le Monde* became a fundamental feature of French life, respected for the thoroughness and honesty of its reporting and the independence of its political judgments. The postwar atmosphere was favorable to a renewal of some of the populist experiments of the Popular Front era. Theater producer Jean Vilar's *Théâtre national populaire* undertook to bring quality productions of important plays to a broad audience. Vilar also inspired the annual Avignon cultural festival, a tradition which continues today.

The most visible effect of the liberation, however, was to bring to prominence a new generation of intellectuals inspired by the ideal of political commitment. The most celebrated of the postwar generation was Jean-Paul Sartre, philosopher, novelist, and dramatist, who came to epitomize, in France and abroad, the notion of the committed intellectual. Before the war, Sartre had already published a novel and settled into a lifelong relationship with his companion Simone de Beauvoir. His prewar novel, *Nausea*, showed him wrestling with the problem of finding meaning in a world without purpose. The wartime years, which Sartre and Beauvoir experienced in occupied Paris, led him to define a doctrine of commitment: people, and especially intellectuals, must give meaning to their existence by their devotion to liberty and justice. Sartre defined his "existentialism"—the term and the philosophical tendency it represented had already begun to emerge in the interwar years—in a lengthy philosophical treatise, *Being and Nothingness*. But he expressed himself most effectively in plays laden with intellectual messages. He exalted the importance of intellectual activity—"The committed writer knows that words are actions,"[4] he proclaimed—and sought to make his life exemplify his thought through his active participation in political debate.

The existentialist group of which Sartre and the journal *Les Temps Modernes* (which he edited) were the center were—like most intellectual movements—loosely structured and frequently divided. The issue of how to translate commitments embraced during the Occupation into postwar political terms divided Sartre from his Resistance comrade Albert Camus, for example. Camus, who, like Sartre, wove his philosophical concerns into plays and novels, such as *The Plague*, came to fear that even the political currents of the Resistance era could become tyrannical orthodoxies. Sartre, for his part, remained engaged in an arduous effort to reconcile existentialism and Marxism. For Sartre, the committed intellectual was necessarily in opposition to bourgeois society. He was hostile to the American influence in Europe, both because it represented political domination and because American culture seemed to him imbued with mindless materialism. Anti-Americanism was not unique to intellectuals. The very extent of postwar France's dependence on the United States fostered a wider resentment of American influence. In the early 1950s, the Coca-Cola Company's attempt to introduce its product brought together an unlikely coalition that included both Communist militants and profit-minded wine growers who feared that soft drinks would reduce the market for the traditional French beverage. These opponents were able to obstruct the widespread marketing of this symbol of the American way of life for several years.

In retrospect, much of Sartre's thought has come to appear as closely tied to the troubled atmosphere of the postwar years as the exaggerated campaign against Coca-Cola. The writings of Camus, less directly political, and of the liberal social and political thinker Raymond Aron (a one-time classmate and longtime critic of Sartre's), now have greater appeal. So, too, does the most important work of Sartre's companion Simone de Beauvoir. *The Second Sex,* an analysis of the unique features of women's life experience and their consequences published in 1951, is one of the founding texts of modern feminism. This remains true even though its linking of biology and female destiny is frequently contested. There is no doubt, however, that Sartre dominated the French intellectual scene for a decade or more after the war.

Sartre's concerns were far removed, however, from the daily experience of most of the French population. The difficulties of daily life, such as the shortage of affordable housing and the fear of inflation, remained major preoccupations. In many respects, France continued to be as it had been before the war—a country marked by a sense of life's harshness and injustices. In one fundamental respect, however, the French population did change its attitude toward the future. Starting even before the end of the war, the French birth rate—which had remained at a level too low to sustain population growth since before 1900—began to show a marked rise. The increase accelerated after the liberation, despite the economic difficulties of the period. The country, which for decades had been characterized by a disproportionately elderly population, now experienced a sudden demand for baby clothes and kindergarten places. Foreign visitors who remembered prewar Paris where cafés stayed crowded and noisy until the wee hours of the morning lamented that the French were now too inclined to stay home with their children.

The population boom was encouraged in part by government policies, many of them extensions of measures first enacted in the 1930s or under Vichy. They included a program of family allocations to lessen the financial burden of child rearing and extended periods of maternal leave. But fundamentally the population increase reflected a general if inarticulate faith that a better future was in prospect for French society. In pursuit of that better life, the French were increasingly willing to change jobs and addresses. Occupational and geographic mobility reached record levels during the 1950s.

The growth of the population was one of the stimuli fueling France's postwar economic expansion. It created a larger market for innumerable products, and assured manufacturers that the number of consumers would continue to grow in the future. But France's move toward the consumer society advertised in the popular American films of the period (and reviled by most French intellectuals) was a slow one during the 1950s. In 1954, only 8 percent of French households had a refrigerator or a washing machine. In 1951, despite the introduction of low-cost auto models meant for a popular market—such as the Citroën 2CV with its canvas roof—French streets still needed to accommodate only one car for every seventeen people. The telephone, long an institution in American domestic life, remained a rarity. Although France had been a leader in experiments with television before the war, TV broadcasting developed slowly afterward. The fact that only a minority could afford the equipment that increasingly defined the "good life" made it difficult for most of the population to believe statistics purporting to show living standards were on the rise. The prevailing atmosphere was one of frustration more than contentment.

NOTES

1. Cited in Jean Lacouture, *De Gaulle* (Paris: Seuil, 1985), 2:230.

2. Cited in ibid., 2:249.

3. Cited in S. Berstein and P. Milza, *Histoire de la France au XXe Siécle* (Brussels: Complexe, 1991), 38.

4. Cited in Henri Lemaitre, *L'Aventure littéraire du XXe siécle* (Paris: Bordas, 1984), 577.

CHAPTER 30

FROM THE FOURTH TO THE FIFTH REPUBLIC

Only dimly aware of the extent of social and intellectual changes they were living through, the Fourth Republic's citizens were all too conscious of France's political difficulties. By the early 1950s, high hopes inspired by the liberation had evaporated. The Fourth Republic seemed to have inherited the worst characteristics of the Third, and its leaders were no longer wartime heroes but rather professional politicians. One example was the jovial Henri Queuille, who cheerfully explained that success in politics depended "not on solving problems, but on shutting up those who pose them."[1] Disillusionment with the changes made after the war paved the way for a steady shift toward more conservative ministries, culminating in that of Antoine Pinay in 1952. Pinay, a classic economic liberal, gained durable popularity with middle-class investors by emphasizing budget cuts and offering government bonds guaranteed against inflation. But his policies discouraged economic investment. Bedeviled by inflation and the exasperating debate over the European Defense Community, one ministry followed another without giving the country any sense of direction.

A humiliating defeat overseas in 1954 led to the elevation of a determined political leader who tried to set the Republic on a new course. The defeat came in Vietnam, where the French, frustrated by their inability to overcome Ho Chi Minh's forces, tried to lure their opponents into a set-piece battle around a fortified outpost called Dienbienphu, expecting to annihilate the guerrillas with air power and artillery. Instead, the Viet Minh troops overwhelmed the French with their Chinese-supplied cannon and forced their surrender in May 1954.

Dienbienphu plunged the government into yet another parliamentary crisis. Under its impact, a majority of deputies were willing to suspend their quarrels and support a leader with a clear policy for ending the war—the maverick Radical Pierre Mendès-France. PMF, the first French politician to be known primarily by his initials, had long stood out because of his honesty and his outspokenness. Of Jewish origins, he had been active in French politics since the early 1930s, but had always remained aloof from the major parties. A courageous member of the Resistance during the war, he had advocated a policy of rigorous austerity and concentration on industrial modernization after the liberation, and had repeatedly denounced the shortcomings of the subsequent governments. Unlike Charles de Gaulle, the other "strong man" waiting in the wings, Mendès-France wholeheartedly supported parliamentary government. He believed that the Fourth Republic's institutions could be made to function if it found leaders of sufficient energy and integrity.

Mendès-France became prime minister primarily on the basis of his promise to bring a quick end to the disastrous war in Indochina. On taking office, he promised to reach a negotiated settlement with the Viet Minh and their Chinese backers within thirty days or resign. The agreement reached in July 1954 at Geneva provided for the French to withdraw from Vietnam. That country was divided into a Communist sector north of the 17th parallel and an independent, non-Communist state south of that line. Even PMF's loudest French critics saluted him for disengaging the country from an impossible quagmire under relatively favorable conditions. The protection of the non-Communist south was left to a new patron, the United States, which confidently assumed its resources would enable it to achieve what France had been unable to. Determined to clear the decks of other nagging foreign policy problems so he could concentrate on domestic issues, Mendès-France also granted autonomy to Tunisia. And he let the Assembly vote on the European Defense Community, an issue so controversial that no previous Fourth Republic prime minister had been willing to submit it to parliament. The deputies killed the plan, ending several years of uncertainty. The French government then moved rapidly to negotiate an arrangement with its western partners that permitted German rearmament and participation in the NATO alliance, without the creation of a supra-national army.

Mendès-France had hoped not only to break the deadlocks on foreign affairs that had paralyzed France for years, but to give a new impetus to domestic institutions as well. Through personal addresses to the country on the radio (modeled after American president Franklin Roosevelt's "fireside chats" during the depression), he sought to build support for an aggressive program of industrial and agricultural modernization based on the successes of post-liberation planning and investments. In his desire to shake up a country which he regarded as still too comfortable with its old ways, he challenged widespread taboos. His denunciation of alcoholism and his effort to promote milk drinking inspired furious protests from defenders of the wine industry. For a generation of young French students and politicians, PMF's efforts to break with the past served as an inspiration. But the parliamentary institutions of the Fourth Republic made it an uphill struggle for him to enact his program. Once he had extricated France from the crises of Indochina and the EDC, traditional political patterns reasserted themselves. In February 1955, a vote of no confidence in the Assembly brought the Mendès-France experiment to an end.

Despite this setback, the seven months of Mendès-France's term in office had raised hopes that the Fourth Republic might be on the way to enjoying the stability and prosperity of the other western democracies. PMF's successor, Edgar Faure, continued many of his predecessor's initiatives in economic policy and negotiated settlements paving the way for independence of two of France's major North African colonies, Morocco and Tunisia. By this time, both French public opinion and most business interests were ready to accept the idea of independence for most of the former colonies. The era of imperialism was visibly coming to an end, and the colonies' economic importance was diminishing as France turned toward increasing its connections with its European neighbors. The Faure government gave renewed impetus to the process of European economic integration, which had made little headway since the establishment of the Coal and Steel Community in 1951. Negotiations set in motion in 1955 led to two important treaties ratified after the Faure government's collapse: creation of Euratom, a joint agency for the development of nuclear energy, in 1956, and the 1957 Treaty of Rome. The latter provided for the eventual establishment of a common market without tariff barriers among the six major western European countries belonging to the coal and steel association. These agreements linked France more closely to its European neighbors and made any retreat to the protectionist tariff policies of the Third Republic more difficult. The need to make French industries competitive with those of its neighbors provided a continuing stimulus to the process of economic modernization.

THE ALGERIAN WAR

In 1955, however, the consequences of European integration were still unclear, and the French public scene was dominated by other problems. The most important was the spreading nationalist revolt in Algeria. On November 1, 1954, a militant Algerian independence movement, the National Liberation Front (known by its initials in French as the FLN), launched an armed crusade to drive the French out with a series of coordinated bombings. The leadership of the movement came from young militants impatient at the lack of success of the older leader Messali Hadj. Hadj's movement still had considerable support, however, and bloody battles between these rival Algerian groups added to the horror of the war that grew out of the revolt. To the French, Algeria was different from their other colonies. It was close geographically, it had belonged to France for a longer period, and it had an important population of French settlers—the *colons* or *pieds noirs* (black feet), whose families had often lived there for several generations. Even Mendès-France, committed to separating France from Indochina, had swiftly proclaimed his intention to combat the uprising. "Algeria is France," he told the National Assembly.

By the end of 1955, the Algerian war had come to dominate French politics. Unlike the conflict in Indochina, the struggle against the FLN soon required the use of draftees doing their required military service, as well as of the soldiers of the professional army. The United States, long convinced of the inevitability of independence for the countries of North Africa, gave France no economic support; the expense of the war accelerated inflation to new levels. At home, the combined impact of war, inflation, and the efforts pursued by Mendès-France and Faure to make the economy more efficient, set off a new right-wing protest movement reminiscent of the quasi-Fascist leagues of the 1920s and 1930s. Its central figure was Pierre Poujade, a small shopkeeper from the poor and backward Massif Central region. He accused the government of favoring big business at the expense of small enterprises, and found broad support for his program of resistance to taxes and militant defense of French positions in Algeria. Once again, French democracy came under threat.

Hoping to obtain a mandate to deal with these issues, Edgar Faure called early parliamentary elections for January 1956. The results proved fatal for the Fourth Republic. The Communists remained the largest single party, the extremist Poujade movement obtained almost 12 percent of the vote, and the distribution of seats made it impossible to form a stable ministry. A large group of deputies supported the reappointment of Mendès-France, but the traditional parties blocked him and installed the leader of the SFIO, Guy Mollet, instead. Mollet represented a party with a long tradition of adherence to democratic values, but the policy he followed in Algeria contradicted them. In the face of *pied-noir* protests, he abandoned promises of reforms in favor of the Muslim population and gave the army free rein to put down the rebellion. The military leaders, humiliated by their defeat in Indochina and egged on by the majority of the *colons*, responded to the FLN's often bloody terrorist attacks with savage countermeasures. These included the systematic use of torture to force captured rebels to provide information. The civilian governments of Mollet and his successors did not dare confront the army, which opposed any effort at negotiations. In October 1956, the French violated international law by intercepting an airplane carrying several FLN leaders and imprisoning them in France. International opinion sided with the Algerian movement. France found itself even more isolated after it joined with Britain and Israel in November 1956 to launch an invasion of Egypt, whose leader Gamal Abdel Nasser had nationalized the Suez Canal earlier that year. The French had hoped to punish Egypt for supporting the Algerian rebellion, but combined American and Soviet opposition forced a quick end to the operation.

In metropolitan France, the government sought to smother growing protests against the use of methods uncomfortably reminiscent of those used by the Germans during the Second World War. The protest movement, which grew up largely outside the structure of established parties—even the Communists, normally anticolonialist, hesitated to engage themselves—took on the dimensions of another Dreyfus affair. Many of the protesters were leftists attracted to Marxism but disillusioned by both the Socialists (committed to pursuit of the war) and the Communists. The latter's image had been severely tarnished in 1956 by Soviet premier Nikita Khrushchev's revelation of Stalin's crimes and by the Soviet military intervention to put down the Hungarian revolt. Other protestors came out of the Catholic democratic tradition that had been so important in the Resistance. Together, these activists formed the origin of what came to be known as the "Second Left," a milieu committed to egalitarianism, social justice, and opposition to colonialism, but critical of the established political parties. Attempts to create a new party to represent this "Second Left" had limited success, but these tendencies had a noticeable impact on the press and the universities. Supporters of the war, an equally diverse group ranging from ex-Fascists to former Resistance members—who equated the defense of French Algeria with the defense of national independence—were equally active.

As the sense of crisis deepened, public confidence in the ability of the Fourth Republic's institutions to cope with it diminished. Opinion polls showed a steady decline in the ratings of all identified potential candidates for prime minister, and a steady rise in the number of citizens who favored recalling to office the wartime hero Charles de Gaulle. The former leader seemed to stand above parties and partisanship and to possess the qualities the situation demanded. After the failure of the RPF in 1951, de Gaulle had remained aloof from politics. He had published his memoirs of the Second World War, forcefully reminding the public of how he had rescued the honor of France in a previous crisis. His criticisms of the parliamentary system appeared increasingly cogent as the Algerian conflict and the economic crisis worsened.

Events reached a climax on May 13, 1958. Another parliamentary crisis had led to the announcement of a ministry headed by Pierre Pflimlin, who had indicated he would seek a negotiated settlement with the Algerian rebels. This news set off a revolt among the French colonists in Algeria, who stormed government buildings there. The army supported this uprising, and its leaders called for the naming of an emergency government in France. A confrontation between the civil government and its own armed forces had become inevitable. The supporters of de Gaulle had not organized the Algerian revolt, but they and their leader were willing to take advantage of it. In Algiers, Gaullist activists succeeded in inspiring calls for de Gaulle to take power, while in France, de Gaulle indicated his willingness to assume authority. Several weeks of tense negotiations were required to work out the details. Much of the French left was deeply suspicious of de Gaulle's motives. Was he not an army officer, an intransigent nationalist, and a man impatient with traditional democratic procedures, as his willingness to profit from the Algerian insurrection showed? But the army and supporters of a French Algeria were not entirely enthusiastic about de Gaulle either. He had never openly committed himself to the continued maintenance of French control in North Africa. De Gaulle's willingness to appear before the National Assembly and to accept a grant of special powers to govern the country for six months voted by its members proved just enough to overcome the hesitations of the deputies. They felt reassured that they were not signing away France's democratic liberties. This agreement, reached on May 29, 1958, came just in time to forestall a plan hatched among the hard-line officers in Algeria to land paratroopers in metropolitan France and stage a military coup. De Gaulle had succeeded in what one of his closest collaborators later called a "bluff."[2] He had obtained power on his own terms, without subordinating himself either to the politicians or the generals. The Fourth Republic had disintegrated, felled by its inability to master the twin challenges of adapting France to a new world and of modernizing the country's social and economic structures. Whether the new strong man could do better remained to be seen.

DE GAULLE'S REPUBLIC

Charles de Gaulle's return to power in 1958 opened a new chapter in French history. Under his direction, the country's political institutions were changed and a new regime, the Fifth Republic, inaugurated. The political stability resulting from the new constitution gave the country a chance to recognize the significance of the social and economic changes already begun before May 1958 but which became ever more apparent in the years that followed. To demonstrate that his recipe for a new republic could overcome the political paralysis that had brought him to power, however, de Gaulle first had to re-

solve the painful Algerian dilemma. On June 4, 1958, he flew to Algiers, where a huge crowd of *colons* waited for him to outline his policy. In a masterful exercise in ambiguity, de Gaulle stepped to the microphone and began, *"Je vous ai compris"* (I have understood you). His listeners heard what they wanted to hear: a promise to keep Algeria as an integral part of France. More thoughtful observers noted that the new president had carefully avoided any specific commitment, and he had not adopted the diehards' slogan, *"Algérie française"* (French Algeria). For the time being, de Gaulle succeeded in reestablishing authority over the army. He was able to return to Paris to take up the task of revamping the mother country's government.

The agreement worked out in May 1958 gave de Gaulle six months to design a new constitution, which would be submitted to a referendum for approval. In the meantime, the Assembly would be in recess and he would exercise emergency powers to govern. The new constitutional plan reflected many of the political ideas de Gaulle had outlined in 1946, but it incorporated some significant features of the parliamentary tradition as well. As de Gaulle had long urged, the office of the presidency was converted from a largely ceremonial one into a post endowed with broad powers. The president was to be elected, not by the members of the two assemblies, but by a vast electoral college made up of some 70,000 local and national officials. He could therefore claim that his authority rested on a broader base than that of the deputies. The president was to name the prime minister, and he could appeal directly to the nation on issues he regarded as vital by calling referenda. In times of crisis, the new constitution authorized the president to assume emergency powers.

The concept of entrusting so much power to a single person was largely alien to the French republican tradition. It called up memories of the Second Empire and the Vichy regime, and a number of prominent

Fourth Republic political leaders—including the reform-minded former prime minister Pierre Mendès-France and the future Fifth Republic president François Mitterrand—urged voters to reject de Gaulle's plan. But the new constitution retained some aspects of France's long tradition of parliamentary government. A directly elected National Assembly, balanced as usual since the Third Republic by a Senate chosen by indirect election, remained a key feature of the system. The prime minister, designated by the president, still needed the Assembly's approval to govern. On paper at least, it was by no means obvious whether the real direction of the government would be determined by the president or by the prime minister, who would be backed by the Assembly.

The fact that the Fifth Republic took on a clear-cut presidential character thus owed more to the personality of de Gaulle than to the letter of the new constitution. His behavior as head of the Resistance movement during the war and as president of the Provisional Government in 1944–1946 had already indicated that de Gaulle would exert strong personal authority. Once the voters had given their overwhelming approval to the new constitution in a referendum in November 1958, he proceeded accordingly. As ministers, he appointed capable men, but men who had distinguished themselves over the years primarily by loyalty to himself, rather than politicians possessing their own bases of power. He interpreted the constitutional text in a manner that gave him exclusive authority over a broad "reserved domain" of issues—particularly with regard to foreign and military policy. The parliamentary elections that followed the constitutional referendum were a triumph for the new Gaullist party, the Union for the New Republic (UNR). But this party served only to provide the president a solid bloc of loyalists, not to exercise any independent influence on policy. De Gaulle was to wait four years before calling on the voters

to give the presidential nature of the new republic its final consecration by approving an amendment to have the president elected directly by popular vote. But by then, four years of experience had familiarized the country with a new model of authority.

ALGERIA AND DECOLONIZATION

The great challenge of de Gaulle's first years in power was to settle the Algerian conflict and, more broadly, to disentangle France from an imperial heritage that had become more of a danger than an asset. In Algeria itself, he had to move cautiously. The French army, which had invested great effort in trying to bring the Muslim population under direct control, was repositioned to fight the guerrillas of the FLN's Algerian Liberation Army. In October 1958, de Gaulle appealed publicly to the FLN to accept a "peace of the brave" and enter into negotiations, without indicating what final outcome he expected from them. But the provisional government the nationalists had established in Tunisia rejected this overture. Unclear in his own mind about how far France would have to go to satisfy the demands of the Muslim population, de Gaulle adopted a waiting policy.

Even before the offer to enter negotiations with the Algerian rebels, de Gaulle's new government had set in motion sweeping changes in the rest of the French empire. As in many other cases, the Fifth Republic consolidated, completed, and obtained credit for changes that had begun under its predecessor. The leaders of the Fourth Republic had recognized the necessity of giving the native populations of France's colonies a greater voice in running their own affairs. The 1946 constitution changed the empire's name to the "French Union" and granted citizenship rights to the small French-educated minorities among the colonies' native populations. The colonies were represented in the French parliament and a few of their leaders—such as

African politicians Léopold Senghor and Félix Houphouët-Boigny—even rose to ministerial posts. Despite their French education and their active participation in French politics, this new generation of leaders increasingly identified themselves with their native communities and demanded reforms leading— not to greater assimilation with France— but toward autonomy and eventual independence.

French colonial policy, which in the years immediately after the war had concentrated on maintaining authority over the colonies, gradually shifted in the direction of accepting their autonomy. As we have seen in 1954, military defeat forced the granting of independence for the three Indochinese colonies, Vietnam, Cambodia, and Laos. The two North African protectorates, Morocco and Tunisia, obtained the right to govern themselves in 1956. In that same year, the colonies minister, Gaston Defferre, pushed through a law creating elected local institutions in all of France's sub-Saharan African colonies and increasing recruitment of civil servants from the local populations. In 1957, the former British colony of Gold Coast, renamed Ghana, became the first black African country to gain full independence. The direction of development was clear; the days of European colonial rule were drawing to an end.

The process accelerated with the installation of the Fifth Republic. Along with the new constitution, de Gaulle announced a referendum in all the French colonies (Algeria, considered an integral part of France, did not participate) on the formation of a "French Community" whose members would gain internal autonomy while the French government continued to decide military and diplomatic policy for the group as a whole. In recognition of the sovereignty of the colonies' populations, however, de Gaulle promised that any colony that voted not to join the Community would immediately be recognized as independent—although at the

price of losing all French aid. One colony, Guinea, took de Gaulle at his word. The others voted to remain associated with France. De Gaulle's hope that the French Community would succeed in keeping the former colonies from claiming full independence was soon disappointed, however. By 1960, all the African members had opted to become sovereign nations. Rather than abandoning them altogether, as had happened in Guinea, France retained close bilateral relations with its former colonies. French continued to be the language of higher education in most of them, French aid remained important, and the former mother country often retained important economic interests. This quick and generally peaceful adjustment to the end of the colonial era proved to be one of the Fifth Republic's most important achievements.

The path toward the independence of Algeria was a much more tortuous one. De Gaulle himself slowly recognized that the only way to bring the bloody conflict there to an end was to concede to the predominantly Muslim population the right to make a free choice on its own future. The majority of the population in metropolitan France was probably prepared to accept such a solution from the time de Gaulle took office. But he faced an arduous task in persuading his own supporters, many of whom had backed him on the assumption that the man who had fought to reclaim every inch of French territory in World War II would never yield Algeria. He also had to convince the army and try to persuade the *pieds noirs* to accept the inevitable. At the same time, he was determined to achieve a negotiated settlement with the FLN, which for its part remained equally determined to impose many conditions that de Gaulle initially regarded as unacceptable.

By September 1959, de Gaulle was ready to announce publicly that the Algerian population would be allowed to vote to determine its own future. In January 1960, the *pied-noir* population in Algiers rose up to protest de Gaulle's dismissal of General Massu, one of the leaders of the 1958 movement. A number of police officers were killed, and it took a week before the rebellion was put down. A visit to Algeria in December 1960 convinced de Gaulle that the Muslim population would never settle for less than full independence—a view confirmed by a referendum in January 1961.

As it became increasingly clear that France was preparing to concede Algerian independence, the diehard partisans of *Algérie française* became more and more desperate. On April 22, 1961, four generals opposed to de Gaulle's policy staged a military putsch in Algiers. Rumors of a planned parachute attack on Paris created an atmosphere of tension. While the rebellious generals tried to win over the troops stationed in Algeria, de Gaulle took to the airwaves. His appeal to rank-and-file soldiers to disavow "the little band of retired generals" who led the coup, his promise of firmness, and his final call to the people of France for their support— heard via transistors in barracks in Algeria— turned the tide against the rebellion.

The way was now clear for negotiations between the French government and representatives of the FLN. These culminated, after much hard bargaining, in a settlement announced in March 1962. The French negotiators had tried to obtain guarantees to permit the European population to remain in Algeria. But the bitterness inspired by eight years of conflict made these arrangements unworkable. The last-ditch supporters of *Algérie française,* the Secret Army Organization (OAS), waged a campaign of terror against both the Muslim population and French authorities who were attempting to carry out the government's policy. The violence of this *politique du pire* drove most of the European civilian population to flee to metropolitan France, ending the hope that a significant French community would remain in Algeria. In France itself, the OAS plotted to assassinate the man who had "betrayed" their cause.

De Gaulle narrowly escaped a bomb attack in September 1961, and an ambush in August 1962 during which his car was riddled with bullets. By then, however, Algerian independence had become an irreversible reality.

The independence agreement in 1962 marked the end, not only of French control of Algeria, but of the long era of French overseas imperialism. The remaining French overseas territories—known officially nowadays as the *départements* and *territoires d'outre-mer* (overseas departments and territories, usually abbreviated as the "DOM-TOM") and sometimes described as the "confetti of empire"— are, with the exception of French Guyana on the northeast coast of South America and research stations in Antarctica, small islands: Guadeloupe and Martinique in the Caribbean, Saint-Pierre and Miquelon in the North Atlantic, Réunion in the Indian Ocean (all of which were part of the "old" French Empire before 1789), New Caledonia, and the islands of French Polynesia in the South Pacific. Their inhabitants have the same rights as other French citizens, including that of voting in national elections. The fact that they receive French social benefits helps explain why there has been little agitation for independence in these territories. The DOM-TOM enable France to claim a presence in distant parts of the world, and some of them have practical value. Kourou in French Guyana, for example, is the European Space Agency's rocket-launching center, and, after the independence of Algeria, France used a remote island in the Pacific to test its nuclear weapons. Nevertheless, the residents of the DOM-TOM are far removed from the mainstream of French life and have not fully participated in the country's prosperity.

NOTES

1. Cited in Jean-Pierre Rioux, *La France de la Quatriéme République* (Paris: Seuil, 1980), 1:221.
2. Cited in Jean Lacouture, *De Gaulle* (Paris: Seuil, 1985), 2:230.

CHAPTER 31

A FRANCE "MARRIED TO ITS CENTURY"

In Charles de Gaulle's mind, the granting of independence to France's former colonies and the liquidation of the Algerian war were essential. This was not because France needed to accommodate itself to being one of several medium-sized European countries, but because the sequels of colonialism drained away resources the country needed to modernize. France needed to "marry its century," as he put it, to maintain its standing as a great power.

DE GAULLE'S GRAND DESIGN

As convinced as ever that glory was an indispensable aspect of France, the president of the Fifth Republic pursued an ambitious design to free the rest of the world from domination of the two superpowers—the United States and the Soviet Union. Militarily, this ambition found expression in the development of a nuclear arsenal. The monopoly on nuclear weapons that the United States had possessed at the end of the Second World War had already been broken by the Soviets, who exploded their first atom bomb in 1949. America's privileged ally, the British, also had nuclear weapons but France was the first medium-sized country to join the nuclear club largely through its own efforts. The development of the French bomb had begun

during the Fourth Republic, but the first successful test was not carried out until February 1960. In de Gaulle's eyes, possession of the bomb guaranteed the country's independence from both of the superpowers. Although France could hardly afford a military establishment equal to theirs, its nuclear-armed *force de frappe* (striking force) enabled the country to assert its own interests. The remark by one of France's top generals in 1967 that the missiles France was developing to carry its bombs could be pointed in any direction was a reminder to both the United States and the Soviet Union of the country's determination to follow its own course. De Gaulle also made good use of France's success in developing a supersonic jet fighter, the Mirage-III, in his diplomacy. The French sold the plane to a number of countries that did not want to be dependent on American arms and the restrictions that came with them. The Mirage thus served to export de Gaulle's own attitude of prickly national independence, as well as serving as a symbol of France's technological achievements.[1]

In reality, French military planning continued to be directed against the possibility of a Soviet attack on western Europe. But de Gaulle's foreign policy often gave the impression that he regarded the United States as the main threat to French autonomy. His

293

quarrels with the Americans dated back to his disputes with Roosevelt during the Second World War. But the real motivation behind his policy after 1958 was based less on settling old scores than on the reality that the American presence in western Europe was much more intrusive than that of the Soviets. To counter the weight of the United States, de Gaulle sought closer ties with France's old enemy, Germany. The close personal relationship he developed with West German leader Konrad Adenauer led to the signing of a friendship treaty between the two countries in 1963. It established the Franco-German alliance as the dominant factor in European politics, even though de Gaulle soon came to realize that West Germany, dependent on the United States for support against the Soviet Union, would never really embrace his dream of an independent Europe. On the other hand, de Gaulle claimed that the British were too subservient to the Americans and, in 1963, he vetoed their application to join the Common Market. De Gaulle's prickly nationalism had made the other western European governments fear for the future of that organization when he came to power in 1958, but the Common Market served his designs for modernization of the French economy too well for him to abandon it. De Gaulle nevertheless made it clear from the outset that he viewed the organization as an agreement among governments, not as a first step toward the creation of a larger European entity. During his years in power, French representatives opposed every initiative that smacked of "supranationality" and, at times, France came close to paralyzing the workings of the organization.

From the point of view of relations with the United States, de Gaulle's most significant action was to withdraw his country from the NATO military alliance set up in 1949 to meet the threat of Soviet aggression. In de Gaulle's view, participation in NATO subordinated French policy to American interests. Western Europe risked either finding itself engaged in a war because of American involvements elsewhere in the world, or else having the Americans abandon vital European interests in exchange for Soviet concessions in other areas. The American rejection of a 1958 French proposal to restructure the alliance and give it a three-way American-British-French directorate convinced de Gaulle of Washington's determination to retain effective control. The possession of nuclear weapons convinced him that France no longer needed to remain under the American "umbrella." The process of French disengagement was completed in 1966, when the last French units were withdrawn from the alliance and American troops left the country. From the French point of view, the move allowed their country to regain control over its own fate. From the American point of view, the French took advantage of the fact that the United States was bound to maintain its military presence in western Europe anyhow. France thus enjoyed protection from the Soviet bloc while remaining free to criticize American policy. Although French troops remained stationed in Germany, and France's commitment to the western world was never in doubt (as de Gaulle's outspoken support for U.S. actions during the 1962 Cuban missile crisis showed), diplomatic relations between Paris and Washington took on a sour tone that has never entirely faded.

American appreciation of French foreign policy was not facilitated by de Gaulle's efforts to give substance to the idea of France as main representative of those countries that wanted to remain independent of the two superpowers. His open criticism of American involvement in Vietnam, which he denounced in 1966 as an "unjust war . . ., a detestable war, since it leads a powerful nation to destroy a small one,"[2] outraged Washington. So did his evocation of the prospect of a Europe "from the Atlantic to the Urals," taking in European Russia but excluding the United States. Equally unappreciated in Washington was de Gaulle's criticism of the privileged role accorded to the dollar in the world financial system, and his proposal to return to the gold standard.

The United States was not the only country to take offense at de Gaulle's exploitation of his position as the world's least inhibited world leader. His call for "Free Quebec" in 1967 gave new visibility to the problems of Canada's French-speaking minority, but infuriated the Canadian government. The arms embargo he imposed on Israel at the time of its 1967 war against a powerful coalition of Arab states, and his subsequent remarks about "the Jews . . . a people . . . sure of themselves and overbearing," caused great controversy inside and outside of France. The line between the effective defense of French national interests and the deliberate provocation of controversies in order to separate France from other western countries became increasingly thin. In 1968, the brutal Soviet occupation of Czechoslovakia, whose leaders had attempted to reform the Communist system from within, showed that the countries of Europe had less room to maneuver between the two superpowers than de Gaulle had claimed. At the time of his resignation in 1969, the wisdom of his ambitious foreign policy, even from the point of view of French interests, was in doubt.

STRONG GOVERNMENT
AND ECONOMIC DEVELOPMENT

The Gaullist concept of politics involved not only establishment of an independent foreign policy, but also creation of a government capable of acting decisively in domestic affairs. For years, de Gaulle had denounced the paralysis of the parliamentary system, and the damage caused by conflicts among the multiplicity of political parties and groups that dominated it. The new constitution approved in 1958 incorporated many of his ideas, and elections for the new parliament at the end of that year

gave the president an overwhelming majority. Many prominent politicians who had opposed his ascent—particularly the spokesmen of the democratic left, such as Mendès-France and Mitterrand—lost their seats. The Communists were reduced to ten deputies. The Gaullist movement had a broad electoral base. It inherited most of France's conservative voters, apart from a small group still loyal to Pétain and irreconcilably opposed to de Gaulle. But de Gaulle also attracted many centrists and a significant number of voters whose normal loyalty was to the left, but who accepted his argument that France needed a more effective government.

The end of the Algerian war freed de Gaulle to turn his attention to other issues. The OAS assassination plots convinced him that the office of the president established in 1958 needed an important modification. To ensure that the practice of strong presidential government would continue even if he disappeared, he called a referendum to approve the election of the president through direct universal suffrage. The referendum campaign was a clear-cut contest between the Fifth Republic's strongman and the political forces identified with the Fourth Republic. From the Communists to the moderate centrists, all the non-Gaullist formations joined in a *"Cartel du 'Non'"* that called on voters to reject de Gaulle's proposal. The 62 percent vote to approve the change showed that the president's hold on public opinion had diminished somewhat with the end of the Algerian crisis—in 1958, 80 percent of voters had approved the new constitution—but it was still a solid endorsement of the new political order. Opponents could continue to protest against the excessive weight of the government in public affairs and against the systematic placement of Gaullist loyalists in key positions, but the future was clearly with those who decided to work within the new system.

The solid popularity of the Fifth Republic during most of the 1960s was due both to its success in ending the Algerian crisis and to its ability to provide conditions favoring economic prosperity. The Gaullist regime inherited from its much-maligned predecessor a functioning system of economic planning, and it maintained the crucial decision to participate in the Common Market rather than keep French business sheltered behind tariff walls. The economic consequence of the Algerian war, however, had been accelerating inflation, threatening the economic progress made in the 1950s. De Gaulle's government made the fight against inflation a major priority. Stiff budget cuts and the introduction of the new "heavy" franc, worth 100 "old" francs, marked a psychological break with the past and helped clear the way for resumption of rapid growth.

Even more decisively than the planners of the Fourth Republic, economic experts of the Fifth stressed the necessity to favor the most productive enterprises in order to prepare France for severe competition it would face when the free-trade area foreseen by Common Market treaties went into full operation at the end of the 1960s. The results were especially dramatic in agriculture. A series of laws enacted between 1960 and 1962 reversed the long-standing policy of protecting small farmers against market forces. Migration out of rural areas, already significant since the end of the war, accelerated sharply. But the remaining farmers were far more efficient, though rarely happy about government policy. From the early 1960s on, farm groups have staged periodic militant protests against what they see as inadequate subsidies. French agriculture, which had been unable to meet the country's food needs in the postwar decade, began to suffer from chronic overproduction, stimulated by generous government aid. By 1981, the country had become the world's second leading exporter of food products.

The modernization of agriculture paralleled the growth of manufacturing. Between 1959 and 1970, France emerged from the middle of the pack of leading industrial countries to achieve a growth rate second only to Japan. In this period, total production increased at an average annual rate of 5.8 percent. Governmental agencies continued to intervene actively to push private enterprises to become more competitive. They often promoted mergers that would produce firms large enough to stand up to foreign competitors, and guided efforts in areas considered especially important in maintaining economic independence, such as the development of computers. A similar push for productivity led to changes in patterns of commerce. The government ceased to protect small shopkeepers against the competition of bigger stores, and the first supermarkets opened in 1963. The regime put heavy emphasis on modernizing France's infrastructure, especially in areas where the country had lagged behind other industrial powers. The 1960s saw a great burst of highway construction, for example, as modern four-lane highways replaced the scenic but excruciatingly slow *routes nationales*. The road-building industry grew by an average of 16 percent a year during the decade.

De Gaulle saw success in technological competition as a way in which France could compensate for the loss of the empire on which its world standing had long depended. "Being the French people, we must reach the rank of a great industrial state or resign ourselves to decline," he announced.[3] Gaullist policy emphasized the development of distinctively "French" technologies, such as the gas-graphite design for nuclear-power plants that was put forward as an alternative to the light-water model developed in the United States. This policy made the regime attractive to engineers and technical workers, who strongly identified with the notion that their efforts were serving the nation. On the other hand, considerations of national prestige sometimes overrode calculations of profitability, as in the 1963 decision to invest heavily in development of the supersonic Concorde airliner—a technological success but a financial flop. The final balance sheet for the regime's economic policies in the 1960s showed that a decade of rapid and sustained growth had enabled France to close much of the gap between its standard of living and that of its European neighbors. On the European scale, however, French firms continued to be smaller, on the average, than their competitors, and less oriented toward the world market. The old habits fostered by decades of protectionism were difficult to root out.

A controversial best-seller published in 1967, Jean-Jacques Servan-Schreiber's *Le Défi américain* ("The American Challenge") revived debate about whether France's heavily state-driven economic policies could keep the country competitive with the economic giant across the Atlantic. Servan-Schreiber argued that the only way of warding off American domination was to adopt more of the American spirit of innovation, as he himself had done in creating *L'Express,* a newsweekly that borrowed ideas from American publications like *Time* and *Newsweek.* He also argued that France needed to seek greater cooperation with its European partners, rather than trying to stand up to the Americans by itself.

The Renewal of the Church

The birth of the Fifth Republic coincided with an important transformation in the Catholic church. For some time, French Catholics had been moving away from the hostility to the modern world that had long characterized the church. During the war, many Catholics had supported the Resistance and committed themselves to democratic politics. The war years had also seen the renewal of a controversial experiment, the movement of "worker-priests," ordained clergy who took factory jobs and sought to bring religion to a milieu that had long been cut off from it. Although the number of worker-priests was small, their effort to model a new relationship between the

church and society attracted worldwide attention, and conservative Pope Pius XII's directive suppressing the movement in 1954 aroused widespread opposition, even from loyal Catholics like the novelist and newspaper columnist François Mauriac. The 1950s were also a high point in the influence of Catholic lay movements, particularly the *Jeunesse agricole catholique* (Young Catholic Farmers), which attracted a generation eager to combine modern farming methods with the preservation of a rural culture threatened by aggressive capitalism. The Catholic student movement attracted many bright young people, although the church's conservatism often led them to switch to more leftist groups as they grew up.

Pius XII's successor, John XXIII, pope from 1958 to 1963, set a new direction for the Catholic church throughout the world. French bishops played leading roles in the Vatican Council that convened in 1961 and redefined the nature of church dogma and practices. For many French Catholics, John XXIII's *aggiornamento,* or updating of the church, was a liberation. French replaced Latin as the language of church services, and rituals were transformed to make them more participatory. An ecumenical spirit replaced the church's condemnation of Protestantism and Judaism, and the church firmly embraced the cause of human rights and democracy. Until John XXIII's successor Paul VI officially condemned all artificial birth control methods in 1968, there was widespread expectation that the church might accommodate itself even to changes in sexual practices. The changes enacted at the Council set off widespread ferment within the French church, sometimes going beyond what its leaders had intended. Some priests and nuns renounced their vows altogether, while others, supported by tradition-minded laity, resisted the reforms. The growing diversity within the church meant that it had become a mirror of the larger society around it, rather than a conservative bloc firmly opposed to the modern world.

A SOCIAL TRANSFORMATION

The political stability and economic prosperity of the decade following de Gaulle's assumption of power set the stage for profound transformations in French society. The new society was characterized by a dramatic increase in living standards, a steady shift to new forms of work, an increase in leisure time, and a change in patterns of personal and family life. Georges Perec's 1962 novella *Les Choses* (The Things), a story of a young couple obsessed with acquiring the ever-more-plentiful consumer goods they saw around them, depicted the period's atmosphere with painful intensity. The de Gaulle years were the time when the majority of French families were finally able to try to satisfy this yearning. Average personal income, adjusted for inflation, grew by 50 percent between 1959 and 1970. Families used this money to furnish their homes with consumer goods that had still been out of reach of most before 1958: washing machines, refrigerators, televisions, and private automobiles. By 1970, more than half of all French households owned each of these items. The homes in which they were installed were considerably more comfortable than the housing available a decade earlier. The period saw considerable progress in overcoming the housing shortage that had persisted since the 1920s. Much of the new housing was in large apartment complexes on the fringes of France's major cities, particularly Paris. Harshly criticized by urban planners for their dreariness and the lack of such social amenities as parks and gathering places, these complexes were nevertheless frequently regarded by their inhabitants as an improvement over the crowded and run-down quarters they replaced.

Not all the newly available resources went into the "things" of Perec's title. A significant fraction went to meeting the needs of the country's growing population of young people. The sharp increase in the birth rate after the war generated a demand for more teachers and more schools. The shift to a more technologically oriented economy encouraged the new generation to stay in school longer and demand more specialized instruction, so secondary education had to expand even faster than primary schooling. The age for compulsory education was raised from fourteen to sixteen in 1959. More and more students continued on from the *lycées* to the university level as well. The percentage of nineteen-year-olds enrolled in educational institutions more than doubled between 1954 and 1968. By the mid-1960s, France's institutions of higher education, many of them still housed in nineteenth-century facilities, were full to the bursting point.

Intellectual Trends

The new generation of students turned to a new generation of thinkers as their intellectual guides. Although many figures from the war years continued to write (notably Jean-Paul Sartre), the novelist and essayist Albert Camus's sudden death in a 1960 auto accident symbolized the passing of a generation shaped by the struggle against Fascism and the encounter with Communism. The new "structuralist" thinkers whose writings became popular in the 1960s reacted against their predecessors' stress on individual commitment and responsibility. The anthropologist Claude Lévi-Strauss used his analysis of primitive societies to suggest that all human interactions were governed by certain fundamental patterns or structures. His works implied that the notion of human freedom, so central to the thinking of Camus and Sartre, was essentially an illusion. The literary critic Roland Barthes took aim at the notion of the author as creative personality and the text as a reflection of social reality. He stressed instead the autonomy of writing and the presence of underlying patterns of meaning—inherent in the structure of language—that imposed themselves on writers of any period. In literature, the writers of the *nouveau roman* (new novel) school—such as Alain Robbe-Grillet and Natalie Sarraute—produced texts without identifiable characters or definable plots, and tried to eliminate any hint of an authorial presence.

New intellectual currents challenged leftist doctrines as well. The dissident Marxist philosopher Louis Althusser turned his back on Sartre's laborious effort to reconcile human freedom and Marxist analysis, and elaborated a "structural" Marxism. He argued that human beings were unable to transcend their place in the class hierarchy and the historical process derived from it. Frantz Fanon, originally from the West Indies, drew inspiration from the Algerian revolt to justify a worldwide revolt of people of color against the oppressive capitalist and imperialist civilization of the West. French students, like those in other western countries, were also attracted by calls for revolution emanating from Fidel Castro's Cuba and Mao Zhe-Dong's China. By questioning the notion of human autonomy central to the entire liberal tradition, and the Marxism that had grown out of it, all the influential French thinkers of the period contributed to a sense that western civilization was in the midst of a fundamental crisis. They attracted young followers flattered by the idea that they were destined to participate in the making of a new era.

Youth

Kept in school longer than their parents, the new generation that came of age in the 1960s was the first to have the leisure time and pocket money to develop a distinct "youth culture." Youthful audiences accounted for much of the success of a new generation of young filmmakers. Billed as the "New Wave," it was led by François Truffaut and Jean-Luc Godard, whose first major works reached the screen in 1959. Reacting against the elabo-

rately costumed historical dramas and imitations of Hollywood formulas that had dominated French cinema since the war, the "New Wave" directors brought a spirit of psychological realism and individualism to their art that influenced directors all over the world. New forms of music and entertainment reached an even broader audience than the movies. The media took notice of the phenomenon when a magazine devoted to music and other youthful enthusiasms, *Salut les copains! (Hello, Gang!)*, reached a circulation of over a million a year after its 1962 debut. The immense response to a public rock-and-roll concert sponsored by the magazine in June 1963 in one of Paris's public squares symbolized the triumph of the "yé-yé" generation. Audiences of all ages became increasingly addicted to television, which saturated the country during the 1960s. The number of sets in use went from 2.5 million in 1961 to 11 million in 1970. Programs became more diversified, with a second public channel being created in 1964; color broadcasting started in 1967. The introduction of commercial advertising in 1968 indicated a move away from the concept of broadcasting as a public service. In the meantime, the government's heavy-handed control over such a powerful medium had become increasingly controversial.

With the threat of military service in Algeria no longer hanging over the heads of its male members, the generation of the 1960s struck its elders as apolitical and preoccupied with private pleasures. One of the clearest differences between the youth of the sixties and their predecessors was in sexual attitudes and behavior. Film stars like Brigitte Bardot had already expressed a new openness about sexuality in the 1950s but, in the 1960s, practice began to catch up with theory. The introduction of the birth control pill in the middle of the decade coincided with a sharp and unexpected drop in the rates of both marriages and births. Sexual activity was increasingly separated from the formation of families.

Eroticism was part of the appeal of *Club Méditerranée*, a chain of vacation colonies that enjoyed great success in the 1960s. Customers flocked to the club's resorts, which offered an escape from the still-powerful conventions of French social life. In exotic and sunny locales, such as Morocco and Tahiti, club members were encouraged to "say goodbye to the weight of convention, leave everything and become another for two weeks . . ." by shedding their clothes for swimsuits and sarongs and addressing each other with the informal 'tu' rather than the formal 'vous.'[4] Few customers worried about the fact that their vacations were made affordable through the exploitation of low-wage local labor, an example of the persistence of unequal relations between France and its former colonies even after the end of imperialism.

Work

Despite the rapid growth of the French economy, finding a job was a major preoccupation for this younger generation. The nature of available employment possibilities was changing rapidly. The percentage of the population employed in agriculture plunged. The fraction of the workforce employed in industry grew slowly, reaching its all-time peak of 39 percent in 1968. But the most rapidly growing sector was that of "services," an amorphous category including all the varieties of white-collar jobs, which represented over 50 percent of the employment market by 1970. The best placed were those who emerged at the top of the highly competitive educational system—graduates of the prestigious *"grandes écoles"* such as the *École nationale d'administration*, which had been created after the Liberation to train up-to-date managers for French business and government positions. These wealthy *cadres* were often pacesetters in the spread of new lifestyles, such as overseas vacation travel. Most of those emerging from school had to settle for more modest positions, however, generally in large, bureaucratically struc-

tured enterprises. The number of small, independent, family-run enterprises (both farms and shops) tended to decline. The French middle classes' preoccupations changed accordingly, from a desire to maintain individual economic autonomy to a greater concern about opportunities for promotion and issues rooted in private life.

The industrial working class remained an important part of French society during the postwar period. Average living standards rose for them, as for most of the population, but at a slower rate. While many workers acquired some of the accoutrements of a middle-class lifestyle—by 1975, 74 percent owned their own car—their children still had a disproportionately small chance to obtain university degrees or rise in social status. Technological change was beginning to change the nature of work, creating a sharp distinction between unskilled positions (often filled by the growing number of immigrant workers whose arrival was openly encouraged by government policy) and positions demanding greater education.

The changing nature of the working class had its repercussions on the organized labor movement. The Communist-dominated CGT and the more moderate FO and FEN faced a dynamic new rival, the *Confédération française démocratique du travail* (CFDT). This confederation had grown out of the Catholic union movement. In 1964, it dropped the reference to Catholicism from its name and began a new life as a more innovative, reform-minded alternative to the CGT, with a special appeal to younger workers and the more marginal elements of the working class. While the CGT remained loyal to the Communist philosophy that a real change in workers' conditions could only come when representatives of the proletariat seized political power, the CFDT took an interest in ideas such as *"autogestion,"* the notion of workers taking over and managing factories on their own. Its growing influence was a sign of dissatisfaction, both with the capitalist industrial society of the time and with the rigidity of the Communist movement. The CFDT was close in spirit to the small political groupings of the "Second Left" that had grown out of the movement against the Algerian war—such as the Unified Socialist Party (PSU), which criticized the ideological rigidity of the Communists and the SFIO.

POLITICS IN THE GAULLIST REPUBLIC

The restlessness that came to the surface in some aspects of the labor movement and in the new youth culture found little expression in the official politics of the 1960s. Charles de Gaulle was solidly entrenched in the presidential office he had created for himself. As the decade advanced, however, the question of the eventual succession to de Gaulle (who had turned seventy-two shortly after the referendum introducing direct presidential elections) began to surface.

With the conclusion of the Algerian crisis in 1962, de Gaulle had marked the inauguration of a new period in domestic politics by replacing his first prime minister, Michel Debré, with Georges Pompidou. The choice revealed much about de Gaulle's conception of politics. Pompidou, originally a professor of literature, had never held an elective office and had spent most of his adult life in banking. He had served as de Gaulle's chief assistant during the first months of the Fifth Republic, before returning to the business world. His nomination as prime minister showed de Gaulle's determination to have a government headed by his own man and to reduce the influence of the Assembly. Pompidou was to remain in office for six years, an all-time record for French prime ministers and an indication of the difference between the institutional instability of France's parliamentary regimes and the steadiness of the new presidential republic.

The power exercised by the president in the Fifth Republic appeared so overwhelming that many critics questioned whether de Gaulle's system offered any possibility of a democratic alternative of power. In 1964, François Mitterrand—himself a future Fifth Republic president—denounced the system as a "perpetual coup d'état." Just a year later, however, he was able to show that there was a realistic possibility that alternative political forces could come to power within the new institutions.

The demonstration came in the first direct presidential elections, which occurred in November 1965. De Gaulle had anticipated an easy victory and hardly even deigned to campaign. Two major candidates emerged to challenge him, however, and both showed that there were unexpected weaknesses in the president's base of support. The various left-of-center groups, long divided by hostility between Socialists and Communists—and by the quarrels remaining from the period when the SFIO had supported the Algerian war while many non-Communist leftists had opposed it—produced a surprise by uniting behind François Mitterrand. Mitterrand (whose political career had begun during the Resistance, and who had served in several cabinets during the Fourth Republic) had the advantage of not belonging to any of the major left-wing parties. He had made his career as the leader of a small independent group. An outspoken critic of the Gaullist system, he had opposed the new constitution in 1958, but he was now willing to try his chances within it. Influenced by his contacts with members of the Democratic Feminist Movement, founded in 1961, one of the first feminist groups to appear since the granting of women's suffrage in 1944 had satisfied the principal demand of the movement in the first half of the century, Mitterrand made a conscious effort to appeal to women voters. His program promised the legalization of birth control, banned in

France since 1920, equalization of salaries and educational opportunities, and greater participation for women in politics. He was joined in the race against de Gaulle by a young politician named Jean Lecanuet, who put himself forward as a centrist and advocate of greater European unity as well as friendlier relations with the United States. Both positions were at odds with de Gaulle's aggressively nationalist foreign policy.

While de Gaulle maintained a dignified silence in the presidential palace, Mitterrand and especially Lecanuet adopted an aggressive, "American" campaign style. Lecanuet made especially effective use of television, which for the first time dominated the election. For the population, accustomed to broadcasting that was tightly controlled by Gaullist loyalists, the barrage of attacks on the government launched by the opposition candidates came as a shock and, in many cases, as a breath of fresh air. The election results themselves were even more of a surprise. De Gaulle received only 43 percent of the first-ballot vote, and Mitterrand's total of 32 percent showed that the united forces of the left could constitute a credible alternative to the regime. Under the new election system, a runoff was necessary, since no candidate had received an absolute majority. An aroused Charles de Gaulle demonstrated that he still had no master in the art of broadcast propaganda. He was reelected in the second round by 55 percent to 45 percent for Mitterrand. But the election had demonstrated that he no longer commanded overwhelming support, and that the Fifth Republic's institutions did not foreclose the possibility of an opposition candidate coming to power someday.

The political evolution that had begun in 1965 continued in the years afterward, as parties and leaders tried to position themselves for the post–de Gaulle future. Among de Gaulle's own supporters, a split emerged between those who continued to believe in the need for a strongly centralized government with extensive economic powers and a faction that favored a more liberal economic policy and greater openness to international cooperation. The leader of this liberal current was Valéry Giscard d'Estaing, a young and ambitious specialist in economic policy. On the left, Mitterrand had clearly established himself as the major figure. He continued his efforts to unite the quarreling non-Communist parties, but remained handicapped by the deep-seated hostility against former leaders of the SFIO stemming from the Algerian war. The national legislative elections of 1967 showed the effects of these developments. Giscard d'Estaing's Independent Republicans offered the Gaullists only qualified support. Their leader urged his followers to adopt a policy of "Yes, but . . .," toward the president and his policies. The Gaullist bloc emerged with only a bare majority, provided by the voters in France's small overseas territories. A gradual transition toward a more open political system and toward the era of post-Gaullism seemed well under way. But this gradual process of evolution was suddenly disrupted by a far more dramatic challenge to the system that had been set up in 1958.

NOTES

1. On the role of the Mirage, see François Leroy, "The Elusive Pursuit of *Grandeur* and Independence: Mirage Diplomacy, French Foreign Policy and International Affairs, 1958–1970" (Ph.D. diss., University of Kentucky, 1997).

2. Cited in Alfred Grosser, *Affaires extérieures: La politique de la France 1944/1984* (Paris: Flammarion, 1984), 214.

3. Cited in Gabrielle Hecht, *The Radiance of France: Nuclear Power and National Identity after World War II* (Cambridge, Mass.: MIT Press, 1998), 93.

4. Cited in Ellen Furlough, "The Business of Pleasure: Creating Club Méditerranée, 1950–1970," in K. Steven Vincent and Alison Klairmont-Lingo, eds., *The Human Tradition in Modern France* (Wilmington, Del.: Scholarly Resources, 2000), 186.

CHAPTER 32

MAY 1968 AND FRANCE AFTER DE GAULLE

THE EVENTS OF MAY 1968

Modern France has experienced many crises, but few as sudden and as unexpected as the "events" that erupted in May 1968. In a world filled with turmoil—massive campus protests against the Vietnam war in the United States, the "Cultural Revolution" launched by the Chinese Communist leader Mao Zhe-Dong, the "Prague Spring" in Czechoslovakia—France seemed to be an island of stability. President de Gaulle was about to embark on a visit to the dissident Communist nation of Romania, part of his unceasing effort to create a balance to the influence of the two superpowers. In a few short weeks, however, two long-neglected currents of unrest came together to set off an explosion: the frustrations of a generation of students unsure of their future, and the discontent of workers in offices and factories.

The first signs of the 1968 protest movement surfaced in the overcrowded universities of the Paris region, especially at the new campus in suburban Nanterre, a hastily constructed facility where students were packed together in isolation from the nearby capital. Small nuclei of activists, inspired by various currents of left-wing thought, succeeded in mobilizing wider student support for protests against degrading conditions on campus. They also protested against what had come to seem outmoded regulations on young people's lives, such as restrictions preventing men from entering women's dormitories. At the heart of the campus protest movement was a charismatic student agitator, Daniel Cohn-Bendit. When university authorities suspended "Danny the Red," his supporters spread the alarm to students at the main Paris campus—the Sorbonne in the heart of the Left Bank. Starting in the first week of May 1968, demonstrations in the neighborhood around the Sorbonne grew steadily larger, and led to violent confrontations with the police. Within a few days, the protests grew to enormous proportions. Reenacting scenes from Paris's nineteenth-century insurrections, the participants uprooted trees and iron grills surrounding them to build barricades blocking the streets. They greeted the police with barrages of paving stones and Molotov cocktails; the forces of order retaliated with tear gas and billy clubs. Appalled by the level of police violence, the residents of the area sided with the students, giving them shelter in their apartments, and sometimes adding to the chaos by pelting the police with flowerpots and garbage from their windows.

The authorities were slow to react. De Gaulle proceeded with his Romanian trip, leaving matters to the prime minister, Georges Pompidou, who thought that the movement would soon blow over. Instead, the insurrectionary spirit spread from campuses to factories and offices. Inspired by the students' occupation of the Sorbonne and other university campuses around the country, factory workers and civil servants took over their workplaces. By the middle of May, normal life in France had ground to a halt. In the occupied buildings and factories, a freewheeling atmosphere of debate prevailed. The dominant theme was the need for a complete restructuring of modern society, to break down hierarchical structures and provide greater opportunities for participation. Students challenged the authority of professors, workers demanded freedom from foremen and bosses, and state employees wanted a greater voice in directing policy. The walls of Paris were covered with inventive posters created by the students of the Fine Arts faculty, and with slogans that reflected the sense that anything was possible: "Be realistic, demand the impossible," "It is forbidden to forbid." The state-owned television system was paralyzed by a strike, as programmers and reporters demanded greater autonomy from political interference.

Returning from his trip abroad, de Gaulle tried to reassert his authority with a television broadcast promising a referendum on social reforms, but his effort was a failure. His prime minister, Georges Pompidou, attempted to end the nationwide strike wave through negotiations with union leaders, but they were unable to persuade the rank and file to accept wage increases and return to work. Although the organized forces of the left had had little to do with the spread of the movement, some of their leaders sensed the possibility of a power vacuum and prepared to fill it. On May 28, François Mitterrand announced that he was ready to step in as president, with Pierre Mendès-France as his prime minister. This initiative received

little support from the movement that had most often proclaimed its support for revolution, the French Communist party. Sensing that the spontaneous strike wave was threatening their control over the working class, Communist politicians and union leaders had tacitly allied themselves with the government in trying to restrain the movement or divert it toward traditional forms of action such as strikes for higher wages.

On May 30, France was stunned to learn that President de Gaulle had disappeared, leaving the capital for an unknown destination. A day later, he was back. At the time, it was not known that he had flown to headquarters of French forces stationed in Germany and consulted army commanders about the attitude of their troops in case armed intervention was required to end the movement. But before resorting to force, de Gaulle took to the radio to make another appeal to the population and to announce national legislative elections. This time, he obtained a massive show of support from the sectors of the population that had remained silent in the previous weeks, but that had now reached the limit of their patience. Within hours of his radio broadcast, a giant crowd formed on Paris's Champs-Elysées, shouting support for a return to order.

De Gaulle's maneuver broke the protest movement's momentum. In the days that followed, workers gradually evacuated the occupied factories and students, many of them suddenly remembering year-end exams, drifted back to their classrooms. Prime minister Pompidou orchestrated the election campaign, in which a conservative backlash propelled the Gaullist party to a record majority. The annual vacation season, beginning just after the elections, drained the last air from the insurrectionary balloon. The "events" of May 1968 thus ended without causing any tangible changes; the movement never turned into a true revolutionary crisis.

But the exaltation of those heady weeks of excitement remained in participants' minds, and even those who had been most aghast at the disorder had to admit that the extent of the movement showed the depth of dissatisfaction in the midst of France's prosperous and increasingly modernized society.

Among those most affected by the events of May was de Gaulle himself. Adamant about restoring the authority of the government, he nevertheless recognized in the movement a curious echo of his own preoccupations with breaking down old authority structures and blockages in French society and introducing what he called a greater sense of participation in public life. This put him at odds with conservatives who dominated his own party and who now had a majority in the Assembly. Along with the prime minister, their role in orchestrating the 1968 elections had been greater than de Gaulle's. The separation between the leader and many of his own followers became evident when he dismissed Pompidou, and replaced him with a ministry charged with implementing broad social reforms that many conservative deputies opposed. Frustrated by this opposition, de Gaulle resorted once again to a direct appeal to the nation, calling a referendum in April 1969. But he chose to campaign on a complex reform of the constitution that seemed to have little to do with the broad theme of participation, with which he had tried to identify himself. It has been suggested that he was deliberately preparing his exit from a situation he could no longer control. In any event, the voters for the first time rejected a Gaullist referendum proposition. On the following day, Charles de Gaulle issued a terse two-sentence letter of resignation and retired from public life. The sequels of the May "events" had brought to an end the extraordinary career of France's most important twentieth-century leader. He retreated to his country home, where he died in November 1970.

THE POMPIDOU PRESIDENCY

More than any other French regime since Napoleon's, the Fifth Republic reflected the personality of its creator. When he stepped down in 1969, the question of whether the system could be made to work by anyone else was still largely unresolved. Over the next twelve years, France cautiously edged out of de Gaulle's shadow. His first successor, Georges Pompidou, showed that a loyal follower could maintain the system. The second post-Gaullist president, Valéry Giscard d'Estaing, proved that the office could be occupied by a non-Gaullist who was nevertheless willing to govern in coalition with conservative forces that had backed his predecessors. Until 1981, however, the Fifth Republic had not yet withstood the ultimate test of a democratic constitutional system: an electoral triumph by the political opposition that had been out of power since the regime was founded.

De Gaulle's resignation in midterm in April 1969 forced the calling of an unscheduled election for the presidency. The unexpected nature of the situation sidelined several potential candidates who lacked the time to organize a bid, including two men who were eventually to win the prize—Giscard d'Estaing and François Mitterrand. The left-wing parties failed to agree on a common candidate; the centrists chose a little-known figure, Alain Poher, the president of the Senate, who had been thrust into the limelight as interim president when de Gaulle left office. The Gaullists turned to the man who had been de Gaulle's prime minister from 1962–1968, Georges Pompidou. Pompidou's relations with de Gaulle had soured in the last year of de Gaulle's reign, but he was still the obvious choice for most of those who had supported the general. Pompidou lacked his predecessor's ability to attract a significant portion of the centrist and left-wing electorate, however, and the

One of the many striking wall posters produced during the student protests of May 1968, this image provoked special outrage because of the way it equated the French CRS riot police (Compagnies républicaines de sécurité) with the German SS of the World War II era.

(Photo credit: Special Collections Department, University of Kentucky Library.)

Gaullist party under his leadership became a strictly conservative grouping.

In most respects, Pompidou continued the political policies of his predecessor; he took few bold initiatives of his own. The biggest exception was in the field of foreign policy. Without abandoning de Gaulle's insistence on French autonomy, Pompidou sought to reduce frictions with France's part-ners. In particular, he lifted the French veto on British entry into the Common Market. The European Economic Community thus grew from six to nine members (Ireland and Denmark accompanying the British) in 1972. Pompidou's first prime minister, Jacques Chaban-Delmas, was sympathetic to the idea of measures to respond to the frustrations that had led to May 1968. His program promised a "New Society," but the conservatism of the Gaullist party blocked any major changes. His successor, Pierre Messmer, suggested fewer new initiatives and was known primarily for his strict law-and-order measures. In domestic policy, Pompidou tilted more strongly toward satisfying the demands of big business. The argument that France needed large, profitable companies to survive the rigors of competition in the enlarged Common Market continued to justify government policies in their favor. The Pompidou years were also identified with the lifting of many long-standing restrictions on construction of modern buildings in Paris's older neighborhoods. To advocates, the shiny new structures represented a determination to keep Paris and France abreast of the modern world. To critics, they were a mutilation of the city's historic character. The most aggressively modernist of these structures, a contemporary art museum with walls made of glass and multicolored metal ducts—set at the edge of the seventeenth-century Marais neighborhood—now bears Pompidou's name.

Like de Gaulle's second term, Pompidou's presidency ended prematurely. Pompidou died in office in April 1974. This time, major politicians had anticipated the situation, and the two main contenders were well prepared. On the left, the disarray of 1969 was replaced by a new atmosphere of unity. The change was due to the startling renovation of the non-Communist left—due to the creation of a new, broad-based Socialist party in 1971, and to changes in the policies of the Communists. In 1969, the candidate put up by the SFIO had won barely 5 percent of the presidential vote, and the party had appeared moribund. The Communists, with their solid 20 percent of the vote, dominated the left. But their preponderance deterred middle-class and centrist voters from voting for the non-Communist parties of the left for fear that—if they won—they would be de-

pendent on Communist support. The non-Communist left's leading figure, François Mitterrand, was among those who concluded that the chances of ousting the conservatives from power depended on the creation of a new kind of leftist party, capable of holding its own against the Communists.

Although he had never been a member of the old SFIO, Mitterrand played a key role in the congress at Epinay in 1971, at which the new Socialist party (PS) was created out of the ruins of the older formation. The new party repudiated the old generation of SFIO leaders, identified with cold war anti-Communism and compromised by their support for the army during the Algerian war. Freed from this unhappy heritage, the PS absorbed several smaller groups from the "Second Left" and elected Mitterrand as its leader. At the same time, the French Communists had found new leadership and were striving to escape from the political ghetto in which they had been confined since 1947. Their longtime leader Maurice Thorez, a dedicated Stalinist, had died in 1964. His successor, Waldeck-Rochet, had tried to open up the party somewhat, but he died in 1969 before being able to institutionalize major changes. In 1970, the party chose a younger leader, Georges Marchais, who at first seemed dedicated to continuing internal party reforms. Under his leadership, the Communists and the newly strengthened Socialists reached agreement on a joint electoral program in 1972. In its details, this "Common Program" harked back to 1936 and 1945. It promised a sweeping program to nationalize major industries and incorporated anticapitalist rhetoric dating from before the years of postwar economic expansion. It reflected very little of the atmosphere of May 1968. But it had a dramatic effect on the political climate. In the 1974 presidential campaign, the joining together of the Communists, with their solid electoral base, and of the newly confident Socialists, able to reach out to voters whom the Communists could not attract, made the possibility of a left-oriented government realistic for the first time since the creation of the Fifth Republic.

On the right, the most important development was the success of a non-Gaullist personality against the self-proclaimed defender of the de Gaulle–Pompidou tradition. The Gaullist claimant was Jacques Chaban-Delmas, Pompidou's prime minister from 1969–1972. His rival was Valéry Giscard d'Estaing, an economic liberal who had been de Gaulle's finance minister from 1962–1966, but who had separated himself from many of de Gaulle's policies (and who had campaigned against de Gaulle's referendum in 1969). In the atmosphere of economic difficulties that had developed during the Pompidou years, Giscard d'Estaing's critique of the Gaullist tradition and his promise that a dose of economic liberalism would restore prosperity made him more attractive to conservative voters than his rival. He also benefited from the restlessness of a younger generation of Gaullists such as Jacques Chirac, impatient at the domination of "barons" like Chaban-Delmas, who owed their positions to their loyalty to the leader during the Second World War or the 1950s. The first round of the 1974 presidential election served as a primary for the right-wing candidates, and "VGE" scored a clear victory over his rival.

GISCARD D'ESTAING'S "ADVANCED LIBERAL SOCIETY"

The runoff round of the 1974 election was the closest and most bitterly contested in the history of the Fifth Republic. It was also the first in which the nature of the regime's institutions was no longer an issue. Both sides accepted the presidential interpretation of the constitution, but they differed drastically in their vision of how French society should be structured. The results showed a country divided in half. The right-wing candidate

won, but only by a handful of votes. The new president's reaction to this situation was to present himself as a reformer, eager to reach out to a number of groups that might have felt excluded by the preceding Gaullist governments. He opened his term with a number of symbolic gestures meant to mark a break with the past, and to reduce the distance between the presidency and the people. He walked up the Champs-Elysées to the presidential residence on foot after his inauguration, rather than riding in the traditional limousine. He had the national anthem, the *Marseillaise,* played in a slower and less martial rhythm, and he adopted the practice of making well-publicized visits to the homes of ordinary families on a once-a-month basis.

In the first years of his presidency, Giscard d'Estaing pushed through a number of significant reforms aimed at giving substance to his call for an "advanced liberal society." Eighteen-year-olds received the right to vote, and the government-controlled radio and television monopoly—long accused of being a propaganda tool for the party in power—was split into several independent (but still government-owned) parts. A new check on the powers of the government was also introduced by a law allowing sixty deputies in either the Assembly or the Senate to appeal any law to the Constitutional Council. That body of judges was charged, like the U.S. Supreme Court, with ensuring the constitutionality of legislation. But its role had previously been limited because only the president, the prime minister, or the presiding officers of the two legislative chambers could initiate an appeal. This reform, made it possible for the minority party in the legislature to launch an appeal. For the first time since the age of the *parlements* in the Old Regime, the judicial branch was given a real voice in the French political process. Another significant political reform was the decision to give Paris, the capital city, the right to elect its own mayor, ending a tradition of government supervision dating back to the Napoleonic era.

The Giscard d'Estaing presidency also began with important gestures toward women. Women's issues had become increasingly prominent after 1968 with the emergence of a new feminist movement—many of whose members were no longer content simply to demand formal equality with men. Its leaders were often young women who had participated in the 1968 student movement but who had discovered that "we do the cooking while they talk about revolution."[1] Abortion had become a central theme of public debate in 1971 with the publication of a declaration signed by 343 women, ranging from well-known celebrities like Simone de Beauvoir to young militants, admitting they had had illegal abortions and calling for the right for women to decide for themselves whether to terminate their pregnancies.

Women were an important part of the white-collar constituency that Mitterrand had tried to win for the Socialists. Giscard also tried to appeal to them. The new president appointed the first woman to hold a full-fledged ministerial office in the Fifth Republic, Minister of Health Simone Veil, and created a Secretariat on Women's Status designed to make recommendations on issues affecting women. Veil, a career politician with no links to the women's movement, nevertheless played a major role in pushing through several important laws affecting women. Three laws passed in 1974 and 1975 broadened access to contraceptives (whose sale in France had been strictly limited since 1920), liberalized divorce, and legalized abortion. The abortion law was the most controversial of the three. In fact, it became the first legislative enactment to be appealed to the Constitutional Council under the new procedure approved in 1974. The 1975 law, highly controversial in a Catholic country, marked a significant extension of individual autonomy and a new definition of women's rights. The "feminism" of the Giscard government should not be exaggerated, however. Françoise Giroud, a prominent journalist appointed to head the new women's Secretariat, found her advice ignored and quit in 1976. Women's rights activists came to see the left-wing parties as the only realistic vehicles for obtaining a real political voice.

Foreign Affairs

In foreign affairs, Giscard continued the effort, begun under Pompidou, to integrate French policies more closely with those of its European partners. He helped institute regular annual meetings of leaders of the European Community's member governments. He also pushed for establishment of the European Monetary System, under which the values of currencies of the major member states (with the exception of Britain) were linked together. Stable exchange rates promoted trade among the partners and pushed them to coordinate their economic policies. With France's consent, direct elections for a European Parliament were held for the first time in 1979. Although the Parliament's powers were strictly limited, this was a major step beyond the "Europe of Nations" that de Gaulle had favored.

Willing to go beyond the bounds of Gaullism in Europe, Giscard d'Estaing continued the Gaullist tradition of having France pose as champion of closer relations between Europe and the developing countries of the Third World. He led his European partners to sign the Lomé agreements of 1975, aimed at favoring trade between the European Community and former European colonies in Africa and the Caribbean. France became particularly active in selling weapons to Third World countries—a policy that benefited French industry but often aligned it with regimes with unsavory reputations.

Like his predecessors de Gaulle and Pompidou, Giscard continued a policy of French involvement in the affairs of its former African colonies. To maintain its influence in Africa, France frequently dispatched troops to support "friendly" governments, with little concern for their democratic credentials. Accusations that he had accepted a gift of valuable diamonds from Jean-Bedel Bokassa, the corrupt dictator of the Central African Republic, hurt Giscard's reputation. Under Giscard, France also seemed ready to accept the permanence of the hard-line Communist regime in the Soviet Union and eastern Europe. French public opinion chafed at the government's passive reaction to the Soviet occupation of Afghanistan in 1979, and its president's refusal to support the Polish Solidarity protest movement that developed after 1980.

FRANCE AND THE WORLD ECONOMIC CRISIS

Criticized at home for some of his foreign policy initiatives, Giscard lost even more of his popularity in the course of the 1970s because of his inability to master the country's continuing economic difficulties. In 1976, when the president replaced his first prime minister, the Gaullist Jacques Chirac, with Raymond Barre (a nonparty figure known for his economic expertise), he acknowledged that economic issues had become the country's top priority.

The long period of sustained prosperity that France enjoyed from the late 1940s to the early 1970s coincided with a worldwide trend. The subsequent downturn was also associated with changes in the larger world economy. The United States, the pivot of that economy during the postwar decades, had begun to experience slowed growth and rising inflation—a combination that was to become characteristic of the new period—at the end of the 1960s. By 1971, Washington was no longer able to maintain the fixed parity between gold and the dollar, whose value, fixed since 1944, was suddenly allowed to float. This introduced a serious element of instability into world trade. The 1973 Middle East war between Israel and the Arab countries of Egypt and Syria led the Arab oil-producing nations to strike at western industrial countries by drastically increasing the price of oil, unleashing new inflationary pressures. France, with no oil reserves of its own, was hard hit by this "oil shock." One response was a heavy investment in nuclear power plants. By 1990, France had become the country most dependent on this controversial technology, drawing nearly 75 percent of its electricity from nuclear energy.

By the mid-1970s, the French began to realize that their economic difficulties stemmed not only from external events over which they had little control but from domestic causes as well. The industrial plant built up in the 1950s and 1960s was beginning to show its age. In the face of a stagnating market and competition from more efficient producers in other countries, many French companies were no longer competitive. Such major industries as coal mining, steel, and automobile production suffered, and the French failed to gain a leading place in key high-technology areas (such as computers) to offset their decline. Giscard's answer to these economic challenges had been the promise of a dose of economic liberalism. He deemphasized the government-directed planning that had been a main feature of French life since the liberation. He also down-pedaled the Gaullist program of promoting investment in all major branches of industry, in favor of concentrating on a few areas where the country could be most competitive.

These policies failed to overcome the economic slowdown that had begun in 1973. Unemployment, marginal during the prosperous years of the 1960s, began a steady march upward—from 400,000 in 1974 to 1,600,000 in 1981. Unlike the strikes of May

1968, the labor struggles of the 1970s were desperate efforts to stave off the closing of factories like the Lip watch plant in Besançon, site of a highly publicized but ultimately unsuccessful worker takeover in 1973. The impact of the prolonged economic crisis fell especially heavily on regions that had long been centers of industrial production. These included the Lorraine steel-making basin and the coal-mining region of the Nord, where the closing of factories and laying off of workers threatened the social fabric built up over many decades. In previous periods, a slowdown in industrial production and a rise in unemployment had usually been accompanied by stable or falling market prices, but the peculiarity of the "stagflation" that set in during the 1970s was that inflation remained high. Despite the Barre government's program of rigorous budget austerity, prices rose by more than 10 percent a year from 1978–1980. Matters were not helped by the second "oil shock" of 1979, when petroleum prices quadrupled after a revolution overthrew the government of the shah of Iran.

THE INTELLECTUAL CLIMATE OF THE *"APRÈS-MAI"*

Since the Second World War, the tone of French intellectual life had been largely set by the left. One of the many paradoxical results of May 1968 was to undermine this hegemony. By 1981, when a left-oriented government finally took power, the divorce between that movement and the country's intellectual elite was almost complete. The rapid collapse of the 1968 movement caused a certain disillusionment with leftist ideas and a strong reaction against the Communist party, the embodiment of Marxist orthodoxy, which had opposed the student movement and limited the impact of the subsequent strike wave. The publication in the mid-1970s of the Russian writer Alexander Solzhenitsyn's devastating account of the

Stalinist prison camp system, *The Gulag Archipelago,* strongly affected French intellectuals. Many of them now converted to the view that totalitarian tendencies were inherent in any version of socialist ideology or revolutionary politics. A documentary about the Vichy years, "The Sorrow and the Pity," was made for television in the late 1960s but banned by nervous government officials. Finally released as a movie in 1971, it undermined the myth of the wartime Resistance, one of the main pillars of the leftist tradition. A student generation concerned about its economic future turned away from the small ultraleftist groups that survived after 1968 and, in some cases, turned toward aggressively right-wing tendencies.

The discrediting of the Marxist tradition went hand in hand with the rise of what has come to be known as "postmodernism" in philosophy and literary theory. Postmodernist thought proclaims its tolerance for diversity and contradiction; it is therefore hardly surprising that the label has been applied to a variety of thinkers whose ideas cannot always be harmonized. The movement has been an international one, but many of its key figures have come from France. The philosopher and historian Michel Foucault was one of the most prominent. His specialty was the unmasking of the relations of domination and oppression concealed in the structures of everyday life and language. Its effect was to call into question the traditional values of both right and left (the direction in which Foucault's own personal sympathies lay). The psychoanalyst Jacques Lacan developed an original interpretation of Freud's theories that undermined conventional notions about autonomy and rationality of the individual. The name of Jacques Derrida, philosopher and literary critic, became synonymous with the literary-critical trend known as deconstructionism. It denied the possibility of finding a single core meaning in any literary text, and questioned the manner in which certain works had been consecrated as "classics" while others were banished from the canon of literary studies. Deconstructionism, like Foucault's writings, had ambiguous implications and, indeed, glorified ambiguity. It seemed to rule out the possibility of meaningful political commitment. Derrida and many other deconstructionists were also characterized by a complex and difficult writing style, full of neologisms—which indicated a turning away from any effort to reach the general public. Foucault, Lacan, and Derrida had a profound impact on women seeking to find ways to *penser autrement* (think otherwise) and escape from the tyranny of "masculinist" modes of expression. Feminist philosophers like Julia Kristeva, Luce Irigaray, and Hélène Cixous made France a center for new thinking about women's issues.

The deconstructionist and feminist theorists continued France's long tradition of posing cultural issues in universal terms, and their works have found an audience among academics throughout the world. But less esoteric forms of French literature and culture seem to have lost the broader appeal they had in the 1950s and 1960s. Very few contemporary French novelists have found an audience extending beyond the country's borders—Marguerite Duras is one exception—and not many French films of recent years have found an international audience.

The difficulties surrounding successive efforts to reform the French educational system, whose shortcomings had been so vividly demonstrated in May 1968, added to the general sense of intellectual disorientation in the years that followed. Ambitious efforts to democratize higher education, launched by minister Edgar Faure during the last months of de Gaulle's presidency, sought to modernize the curriculum and give students and younger faculty more of a voice in decision-making. But the results were mixed. In the years that followed, suc-

cessive governments tried one formula after another, but the long-range effect has been primarily to alienate all groups concerned: faculty, students, and parents.

As the end of Giscard d'Estaing's presidential term neared, the "advanced liberal society" he had promised in 1974 seemed to have defaulted on its promises. The reforming thrust of his first year in office had long since exhausted itself. A sputtering economy and a foreign policy that seemed to lack guiding principles had undermined the president's popularity, and he seemed at a loss as to how to respond to the changed intellectual climate. But it was by no means clear that discontent was strong enough to cost the conservative coalition the presidency. The left-wing opposition was itself mired in difficulties. A period of euphoria had followed the near-miss in the 1974 elections. The Socialist party continued to gain support, and Georges Marchais's Communists appeared willing to go farther than ever in breaking with the Stalinist heritage that had made many French voters unwilling to let them participate in governing. The high point of this flirtation with a reformist "Euro-Communism" came in 1976, when Marchais announced that his party no longer saw the need for a "dictatorship of the proletariat" to overthrow capitalism, and announced its commitment to a "socialism in the colors of France." Within a year, however, the Communist leadership decided that the danger of being overshadowed by their coalition partners was greater than the danger of keeping the right in power, and the left alliance set up in 1972 fell apart. The split cost the former coalition partners the chance to win the 1978 legislative elections, and appeared to ruin their chances in the presidential election due in 1981.

NOTE

1. Cited in Hervé Hamon and Patrick Rotman, *Génération* (Paris: Seuil, 1988), 2:223.

CHAPTER 33

THE MITTERRAND YEARS

THE ELECTIONS OF 1981

The election of the Fifth Republic's first left-wing president in 1981 set the stage for a decade of striking and often unexpected political developments. In view of the breakup of the left-wing coalition in 1977, the fact that the left-wing candidate won in 1981 was a surprise in itself. The apparent disarray of his opponents undoubtedly gave Giscard d'Estaing a false sense of security as the election approached. His inability to end the economic crisis and a sense of lack of direction—the reforming energy of the first years of his term had long since faded—cost him critical votes. So did the rivalry between his supporters and the Gaullist backers of his former prime minister, Jacques Chirac.

For his part, the Socialist party candidate François Mitterrand may have benefited from his party's split with the Communists. The old tradition of "republican discipline" ensured that their voters ended up in his column in the second round of the election anyway, while he was able to attract centrist votes by showing the Socialist party's independence from Moscow. Campaigning on a slogan of "calm strength," he struck voters as more capable than his rival, worn down by seven years in office. The

electorate gave Mitterrand a narrow but clear victory, by a vote of 52 percent to 48 percent. For the first time in the history of the Fifth Republic, the country's most powerful office was given to a member of the left-wing opposition that had long denounced such a dangerous concentration of power in the hands of one person.

For the half of the country that had voted for the left, the significance of Mitterrand's election went beyond everyday politics. Happy crowds in the streets revived memories of 1936 and 1968, and showed the depth of expectations raised by the Socialists' promise they would bring about far-reaching social transformation. Business circles and conservative groups were correspondingly alarmed. Prices on the Paris stock exchange fell so sharply after the election that it had to be closed for two days to prevent a panic. But conditions in 1981 were quite different from what they had been in 1936. There was no large-scale popular movement like the wave of strikes that had forced the Blum government into hasty action and terrified conservatives, and right-wing opposition remained within institutional channels.

Mitterrand immediately showed his willingness to make use of broad powers of the Fifth Republic presidency (whose creation he had opposed in 1958) in order to consolidate his victory. "These institutions weren't designed with me in mind," he told an interviewer, "but they serve my purposes very well."[1] He dissolved the Assembly and called new elections. With many discouraged right-wing voters staying home, the Socialists and their small centrist coalition partners won an absolute majority of parliamentary seats. Installed in office for seven years himself, and with a solid legislative majority assured for the next five, Mitterrand was in a position completely different from that of the left-wing governments of 1936 or 1945.

For the first few months of his term, the new president profited from what he called "a state of grace." Public opinion welcomed the first complete change in political personnel since the creation of the Fifth Republic in 1958. New faces, many of them relatively young, were installed in all key offices. The inclusion of four Communist ministers in the cabinet led by Pierre Mauroy caused shock waves in other western capitals, particularly in Washington, D.C. (where the conservative Republican Ronald Reagan had just taken office). But Mitterrand judged that it was better to have their party's support than its opposition, and he soon convinced the wary Americans he would make no concessions to the Soviet Union. In fact, in foreign policy, Mitterrand proved to be closer to the Americans than his conservative predecessors. During the final flare-up of East-West tensions that marked the first half of the 1980s, he strongly supported the American decision to match a Soviet buildup of medium-range nuclear missiles with installation of similar forces in NATO countries. Franco-American relations in general were smoother under his presidency than at any other time during the Fifth Republic.

Foreign affairs were secondary in the French Socialists' minds to domestic changes,

however. The festival atmosphere that followed the presidential elections was reminiscent of 1968, but the program the party put forward was closer in spirit to the ideas of 1936 and 1945. It included the nationalization of a wide range of businesses and industries, and a redistribution of income in favor of the lowest-paid groups. This was accomplished through a large increase in the minimum wage and a generous social welfare program. Mitterrand's supporters argued that these measures would enable the government to overcome the economic crisis that had dogged France since the mid-1970s by putting more spending money in consumers' hands and by channeling investment more efficiently. They optimistically promised to revive even the most depressed of France's heavy industries, and to make quick inroads against unemployment. The Socialists' program also included reforms in many other areas: an increased voice for workers about factory conditions, the abolition of the death penalty, the delegation of important powers to elected regional councils, and the reduction of administrative powers of the prefects. Even the title of prefect was abolished for several years. Giscard's powerless Secretariat on Women's Status was turned into a full-fledged Ministry for Women's Rights, and women were named to several other cabinet posts.

The new government also devoted considerable energy to cultural issues, although it found itself out of step with an intellectual community whose long-standing enthusiasm for left-wing ideas had diminished considerably during the 1970s. The budget for the Ministry of Culture, first created by de Gaulle in 1959, was doubled, and its charismatic minister, Jack Lang, broadened its programs beyond the traditional support for museums, orchestras and theater to include pop music and public festivals. One of the most successful of his initiatives was the establishment of the *Fête de la musique* ("Festival of Music"), an annual event that draws crowds into the streets of French cities every June for a night of free performances by ensembles of all sorts. Lang's enthusiasm for Third World cultures made Paris the center for the development of an increasingly intercultural "world music," mixing European, African, and American elements. Breaking with a long tradition of state-controlled broadcasting, the new government legalized independent radio stations in 1982, allowing an unprecedented diversity on the airwaves; France's first privately owned television channel was established in 1984. Few of the Mitterrand government's cultural initiatives were as successful as the bold decision to modernize the Louvre museum by building a starkly geometric glass pyramid in the central courtyard of one of the world's most famous historic buildings. After tremendous initial controversy, the project has generally been acknowledged to have resulted in a happy marriage of the old and new.

THE "U-TURN" OF 1983

In the face of a worldwide economic recession that was just reaching its lowest point, the Socialists' ambitious economic program soon ran into difficulties. France's main economic partners had all taken an opposing course, cutting government expenditures. As a result, the effect of French policy was to unleash rapid inflation without producing any upsurge in production or employment. By June 1982, Mitterrand and Mauroy had to change direction. They imposed a freeze on wages and prices, promised not to raise taxes any further, and cut the public budget. This first round of measures proved insufficient and, in March 1983, the Socialist government reached a turning point. France either had to try to buffer itself from the wider world economy by leaving the European Monetary System set up in 1979—and po-

tentially breaking up the European Economic Community—or it had to adopt a full-scale program of economic austerity. This meant abandoning the effort to save uncompetitive industries, and adapting to the rules of a world economy in which the uncompromising free-enterprise policies of "Reaganomics" were dominant.

Mitterrand's decision to choose the second path had far-reaching consequences, both for the French economy and for the political atmosphere. The decision to concentrate on making France fully competitive within the framework of a capitalist economy was a rejection of hopes that had sustained French socialism—in both its democratic and its Communist versions—throughout the twentieth century. The government's new course won some praise from business circles, where it was recognized that the Socialists were facing up to difficult decisions that the conservative governments of Pompidou and Giscard had avoided. The Socialists, for example, finally controlled the inflation that had characterized the French economy for decades. But it deeply disappointed trade unionists and others who had voted in 1981 for a rupture with capitalism. The replacement in 1984 of Mitterrand's original choice for prime minister, the veteran Socialist Pierre Mauroy, with Laurent Fabius (a young graduate of the elitist *École nationale d'administration*), and the Communist party's withdrawal from the governing coalition, underlined the shift from a government identified with the world of labor to a more technocratic orientation. Feminist critics charged that the government's new policies were especially costly to women, who found themselves being urged to accept part-time jobs to make the economy more flexible instead of benefiting from earlier promises to equalize men's and women's salaries.

Having concluded that a rupture with the capitalist world economy was not a realistic possibility, Mitterrand made the promotion of a closer union between France and its European partners the highest priority of his remaining years in office. He took a key part in resolving a long drawn-out dispute over the terms of Britain's participation in the European Community in 1984, which cleared the way for passage in 1985 of the Single European Act. It committed the members of the organization to the removal of all obstacles to the free movement of goods, money, and people within western Europe. The new arrangements, put into effect at the end of 1992, made it exceedingly difficult for any European country, including France, to adopt an independent economic policy.

In domestic politics, the Socialist change of course in 1983 also set major changes in motion. The Communist party, a major feature of the political landscape since the 1930s, was unable to adapt to the new climate. The Communists withdrew from the governing coalition in 1984, in protest against the policy of economic rigor adopted the year before. But this return to opposition did not revive their electoral fortunes. The drastic decline of industries whose workers formed its electoral base, and the end of any prospect for creation of a noncapitalist economy in France, virtually eliminated the party as a political force. This happened even before the collapse of the Soviet Empire in the late 1980s. Communist candidates have polled less than 10 percent of the vote in all nationwide elections after 1988.

At first, the Communists' decline benefited the Socialists. Their share of the vote topped 30 percent in national elections from 1981–1988, making the PS the largest single party in France. In reality, however, the Socialists were also faced with a dilemma. Having rejected their traditional anticapitalism, they lost their distinctive message, and the difference between their policies and those of traditional right-wing parties became increasingly blurred. The relatively open atmosphere that had characterized the party during its rise to power gave way to an emphasis on supporting the government, even at the price of suppressing internal debate. It also led to a scramble among party leaders to promote their own careers; Socialist "elephants" began to acquire the same unsavory reputations as the Gaullist "barons" of a generation earlier.

At the same time, the political landscape was altered by the rise of a powerful party on the extreme right, the *Front National* (FN), which first gained attention by scoring striking successes in local elections in 1983. In the beginning, Mitterrand and the Socialists were not unhappy about the FN's appearance. They expected it to take votes from the traditional conservative parties, which would be embarrassed by the question of whether they would accept support from a group that appealed to racist ideas. Before long, however, it became clear that the FN was also winning votes from former working-class supporters of the Communists. The FN steadily increased its score in national votes from 11 percent in the 1984 elections to the European Parliament to just under 15 percent in the 1992 regional balloting. Its gains were made by exploiting widespread concern about the number of non-European immigrants in France and the rise of crime and insecurity in many of its urban areas. Under its charismatic leader Jean-Marie Le Pen, the FN became the longest-lasting right-wing extremist movement in modern French history.

The traditional right-wing parties also benefited from public disenchantment with the Socialists, and particularly with discontent aroused by a school reform proposal intended to bring Catholic schools under increased government control. The Socialists, pushed by the schoolteachers' union (the FEN), introduced such a proposal in 1984. To the astonishment of most observers, the proposal revived the long-dormant quarrel over the role of the Catholic school system that had marked French life since the 1840s. A series of rallies against the government's plan in 1984 drew what were probably the largest crowds in French history, and forced the withdrawal of the measure. In a society where less than 15 percent of the population still attended church regularly, the issue was no longer one of religion versus republicanism. The mobilization against the government's plan reflected, above all, a discontent with bureaucratized institutions and a demand for pluralism. The FEN and the Socialists, with their warnings about the dangers of rival school systems, seemed to be caught in the past—still fighting the battles of the Jules Ferry era.

A MULTIETHNIC FRANCE

During the early years of the Mitterrand presidency, the situation of the rapidly growing part of the French population whose ethnic origins were not European became an increasing concern. Immigrants were nothing new in France, which absorbed large numbers of Italians, Belgians, Spaniards, and Poles early in the twentieth century, and a substantial influx of Portuguese in the 1960s and 1970s. These groups shared a certain cultural background with most of the French population, and they accepted the principle of assimilation, which offered them entry into national life in exchange for adopting the French language and social customs. The large-scale influx of non-European immigrants began during the economic expansion of the 1950s and 1960s, when French governments encouraged the importation of workers, particularly from the former colonies, to meet the booming demand for labor. Initially, most of these migrants expected to eventually return home; consequently, they made little effort to adapt to French ways. By the early 1980s, however, it was becoming clear that many of them

were permanently installed in France. Many Algerians in France, for example, gave up hopes of returning to that country as its post-independence government turned increasingly dictatorial and its economy failed to develop. A new generation of children born in France to immigrant parents or mixed families complicated the situation: would they be accepted in French society, or stigmatized as "foreigners" even though they had never lived anywhere else?

The end of the "thirty glorious years" of rising prosperity in the mid-1970s made the integration of these new populations more difficult. As unemployment began to rise, accusations that foreigners were taking jobs that should have gone to native French workers became more common. The economic situation made life more difficult for most immigrants as well. Most of them lived in crowded, run-down neighborhoods on the outskirts of France's cities. The sense of hopelessness that gripped many of them provided conditions for the spread of crime and other social problems. In the early 1980s, several riots in these suburban ghettos thrust their problems onto the front pages of French newspapers. The Muslim groups from North Africa faced the strongest obstacles to acceptance in France, because of their desire to maintain some aspects of their distinctive religion and culture. In the early 1980s, *beurs,* the French-born descendants of this community, became a highly visible group, with a distinctive identity centered around institutions such as *Radio Beur,* a station founded after the end of government controls on radio broadcasting.

The immigrant issue was politicized by the rise of the *Front National.* The party's platform blamed non-European immigrants for causing crime and unemployment, and revived the old *Action française* slogan "La France aux français." Prejudices against immigrants whose appearance and behavior clearly revealed their origins were not limited to followers of Le Pen, however. A sociological inquiry at the end of the 1980s concluded that a substantial part of the population considered non-European immigrants a threat to France's national and cultural identity. Interviewees told the researchers that immigrants were too noisy, that "they take French people's jobs," that "they speak their own language and you don't understand anything," and that they took unfair advantage of France's welfare system.[2] In response to a wave of racist incidents in the early 1980s, the Mitterrand government helped promote *SOS-Racisme,* a movement for civil rights that was particularly successful with younger people and the media, but its slogans did little to change underlying attitudes.

From "Cohabitation" to Confusion

The five-year mandate of the legislature elected in 1981 ran out in 1986, and voters disillusioned with the Socialists gave the right-wing coalition a majority. The election results subjected the institutions of the Fifth Republic to a new test: "cohabitation" between a president from one side of the political spectrum, and a prime minister representing the other. Jacques Chirac, the popular Gaullist mayor of Paris, became prime minister. He pledged to adopt policies that would reduce government interference in the economy, and bring France in line with Ronald Reagan's program in the United States and Margaret Thatcher's in Britain. He cut tax rates and reprivatized some of the companies nationalized after 1981. In a break from a decades-old tradition, the Chirac government even sold one of the public television channels to a private owner, giving commercial interests control over what many French citizens had long considered a public service.

There had been much speculation as to how François Mitterrand would react to a situation in which day-to-day policy making was in the hands of one of his chief political opponents—indeed, his anticipated rival in the upcoming presidential election. The "cohabitation" episode showed that the man many French had come to dub "the Florentine," because of his evident relish for Machiavellian political intrigue, knew how to use institutions created by de Gaulle more skillfully than de Gaulle's own political descendants. Restricting himself to foreign and defense matters and to occasional comments on domestic policy, Mitterrand managed to saddle Chirac with the blame for most of the country's difficulties, particularly the continuing malaise of the economy. Meanwhile he reaped credit for his dignified conduct and his sense of long-term national interests.

"Cohabitation" under institutions of the Fifth Republic thus turned out to be a trap for Mitterrand's opponents. In 1988, the voters rejected Chirac and rewarded Mitterrand with a second seven-year term. But the election was really a success for the man who had come to be recognized as the most skillful politician of the post–de Gaulle era, rather than for the Socialist party. Legislative elections called immediately after Mitterrand's reelection gave the Socialists just enough seats to reclaim the prime ministership. A cabinet headed by Mitterrand's main rival within his own party (and would-be successor), Michel Rocard, resumed the modernizing and technocratic orientation adopted in 1983—and interrupted from 1986 to 1988 by the more aggressively probusiness policies of the Chirac government. Rocard, a longtime activist in the PSU (the splinter party that had represented the spirit of the "Second Left" in early 1960s), moved the Socialists even further away from their old Marxist traditions.

After 1988, however, the Socialist government was clearly losing momentum and was unable to achieve much. Rocard did successfully defuse a major crisis in New Caledonia, one of France's few remaining overseas possessions, where a radical independence movement had taken a group of

French gendarmes hostage. The New Caledonia crisis was the only time in recent decades that a problem in any of France's overseas territories dominated the national news. Rocard, whose ambition to succeed Mitterrand was no secret, was often at odds with the president. Mitterrand reshuffled his cabinet in 1991, appointing the first woman prime minister in French history, Edith Cresson, but she failed to stem either the government's decline in the polls or the steady erosion of Mitterrand's own personal popularity.

In the early 1990s, the Socialists were rocked by a number of major scandals. An inquiry into their fund-raising practices led to a humiliating police search of the party's headquarters, and several ministers were eventually convicted of having stalled the adoption of an American-manufactured process for detecting AIDS-contaminated blood products in order to favor a French competitor, thereby allowing the disease to spread among French hemophiliacs. In elections for regional governments in March 1992, the Socialists' share of the vote fell to 18 percent, the level from which the party began its rise to power in 1971. Mitterrand dropped Cresson after a term of only thirteen months in favor of Pierre Bérégovoy, a former finance minister popular in business circles. Mitterrand also tried to revive his government's popularity by calling a referendum on French adhesion to the treaty for European union, negotiated with great fanfare at Maastricht in 1991. This move backfired when the proposition passed with only a bare majority in September 1992. Legislative elections in March 1993 completed the rout of the Socialists. Their conservative opponents won 80 percent of the seats in the Assembly. The defeated prime minister Bérégovoy's suicide in May 1993 seemed to underline the collapse of the Socialist party's fortunes.

Mitterrand's presidential term still had two years to run after the Socialist election defeat in 1993, but the magnitude of the right-wing victory made it clear that his successor would be a conservative. Unwilling to risk a repetition of the embarrassment Mitterrand had inflicted on him during the first period of "cohabitation," Jacques Chirac let Mitterrand appoint one of his longtime supporters, Edouard Balladur, as prime minister. His government resumed the selling off of publicly owned enterprises started in 1986 but suspended after Mitterrand's reelection in 1988. The right-wing legislature passed a set of strict new measures designed to limit immigration and to diminish the appeal of the *Front National*, a goal that was not achieved because the extremist party continued to gain supporters. Mitterrand's last years in office were marked by a series of revelations about his personal past that cast a retrospective pall over his entire presidency. The admission that he had pressured his doctors to conceal the fact that he had been diagnosed with prostate cancer as early as 1981 made many French citizens wonder if they had ever really known the man who led their country longer than any other president of the Fifth Republic. The public proved relatively tolerant of the discovery that he had maintained a long-running extramarital relationship and fathered an illegitimate daughter, but the fact that he had deliberately covered up the extent of his involvement with the right-wing *Croix-de-Feu* movement in the 1930s and his support for the Vichy regime in the early years of the Occupation made many of his former supporters doubt that he had ever sincerely embraced the values of the Socialist party.

Mitterrand's admissions about his personal involvement with Vichy were linked in the public mind with a slow and painful process of coming to terms with the extent of collaboration during the war, and especially with French government officials' complicity in the deportation of Jews to the death camps. A series of widely publicized trials, beginning with the prosecution of the former German SS officer Klaus Barbie in 1987, produced testimony showing that several prominent French figures who had gone on to long public careers after the war had been involved in these crimes and that politicians, including presidents Pompidou and Mitterrand, had intervened on behalf of men like Paul Touvier, a leader in the wartime *Milice*, and René Bousquet, who had organized the roundup of Jews at the Vélodrome d'Hiver in 1942. The 1998 conviction of Maurice Papon, another Vichy official who had held high office after the war, for his part in shipping Jews to Auschwitz, constituted an official recognition by the French courts that the country's governing elites had colluded in covering up wartime crimes. The reputation of Mitterrand, who had remained a personal friend of René Bousquet's long after the accusations against him had become public, suffered from this reevaluation of the past. Mitterrand's reputation took a final battering in 1994, when France, true to its policy of supporting almost any French-speaking government in Africa regardless of its policies, stood by while the Hutu regime in Rwanda launched a genocidal attack on the Tutsi minority there. France had trained some of the forces that took part in the massacres, and provided arms to the Hutu regime, but it made no effort to use its influence to prevent the killings.

The scandals and revelations of his last years in office were painful for a man who had been determined to leave his imprint on his country. His often-criticized penchant for costly architectural monuments in Paris (in addition to the glass pyramid at the Louvre, he sponsored a new opera house on the Place de la Bastille, a striking new building for the Ministry of Finance along the Seine, and a gigantic new National Library, which now bears his name) dramatically changed the landscape of the capital. His final place in history will depend heavily on the future success of the project of European integration to which he committed himself so strongly after 1983. At the beginning of his two presidential terms, Mitterrand believed that France still retained the autonomy to set its own social and economic policies. By the end of his presidency, the country had tied its destiny so strongly to the European Union that the options open to its national government were greatly reduced. Many of the groups that had supported Mitterrand in 1981 were disappointed by his subsequent policies. Although inflation was brought under control and economic growth was stronger than under Giscard d'Estaing, unemployment continued to climb throughout Mitterrand's presidency, growing from 1.6 million in 1981 to levels of over 3 million in the early 1990s. Few of the promises he had made to women voters in 1981 were fulfilled; in particular, the Socialists did little better at opening important political offices to women than their conservative predecessors. Mitterrand's skillful political maneuvering permanently weakened the Communist party, whose strength had long prevented a regular alternation between right- and left-wing governments in France, but the right-wing *Front National* took the Communists' place as a disturbing presence on the French political scene. Whereas the legacy of Charles de Gaulle's years in power was clear and unambiguous, Mitterrand's impact on France was much more mixed.

Notes

1. Cited in Jacques Chapsal, *La vie politique sous la Ve République*, 4th ed. (Paris: Presses universitaires de France, 1989), 235.
2. Michel Wievorka, *La France raciste* (Paris: Seuil, 1992), 10–3.

CHAPTER 34

AN UNCERTAIN START
TO THE NEW MILLENNIUM

At midnight on December 31, 1999, television audiences all over the world gasped in awe at the fireworks display set off around France's national symbol, the Eiffel Tower. The French celebration of the beginning of the new millennium was one of the most spectacular anywhere on the planet, and seemed to symbolize the country's confidence about entering a new era. The carefully planned event also showed, however, that French leaders knew they were living in an increasingly competitive global world, in which special effort was necessary to make their country stand out. Two years later, in April 2002, France was once again at the center of world attention, but this time news reports cast the country in a much less positive light. First-round balloting in that year's presidential elections made Jean-Marie Le Pen, the leader of the extreme right-wing *Front National* party, one of the two finalists. Although Le Pen was overwhelmingly defeated in the second round of voting in May 2002, his success in knocking Socialist prime minister Lionel Jospin, who had governed the country since 1997 with a fair degree of success, off the final ballot raised serious questions about the state of French democracy. In early 2003, France made world news again when its government led opposition to the United States's decision to go to war against Iraq. Irritated American politicans responded by rewording menus in the U.S. Capitol cafeteria to change "French fries" into "freedom fries." Although France refused to join the American effort to transform the Middle East in Iraq, its relations with its own Muslim population made headlines in 2004, when a law forbidding the wearing of Muslim headscarves (*foulards*) in public schools was enacted. The four events that have drawn the most attention to France in the new millennium show that the country, like the rest of the world, faces both new hopes and new uncertainties.

The dramatic and unexpected events since 2002 followed a decade in which many observers had concluded that France was successfully adjusting itself to a new place in the world. After many years of rising unemployment and slow growth, economic trends in the second half of the 1990s had been generally positive. Doubts about the process of European unification, which led almost half of French voters to oppose François Mitterrand's referendum on the issue in 1992, had given way to a general consensus on the process's benefits. France played a leading role in planning for the creation of a common European currency, the euro, which was successfully introduced at the beginning of 2002.

In July 1998, France hosted the World Cup soccer competition, and the national team set off a wave of euphoria by winning the championship for the first time. The fact that the team's hero, Zinedine Zidane, was the son of Algerian immigrants and that several other players, all of them French citizens, had roots in Africa or in other European countries, was cited as evidence that the country had outgrown racial and ethnic prejudices and now accepted the diversity of its population. The French team's dismal performance in the 2002 World Cup, in which they were eliminated in the preliminary round, like the Front National's strong showing in the 2002 elections and the angry confrontation with the United States in 2003, have shown that neither consensus at home nor France's place in the world can be taken for granted.

Politics After Mitterrand

Although the events of 2002 and 2003 have overshadowed the developments of the 1990s, the years following the Socialist Party's election defeat in 1993 were anything but quiet ones. Although François Mitterrand's term lasted until 1995, the aged and ailing president played a much smaller role during this second period of "co-habitation" with a right-wing prime minister and legislature than he had from 1986 to 1988. The Socialists seemed so discredited after 1993 that a right-wing victory in the 1995 presidential elections appeared inevitable. The big question was whether the winner would be the man Mitterrand had defeated in 1988, the Gaullist Jacques Chirac, or Chirac's longtime supporter Edouard Balladur, who Mitterrand had named as prime minister in 1993. Once he found himself in office, Balladur developed presidential ambitions of his own. Balladur's economic policies were popular with conservatives. Chirac therefore needed to appeal to centrist voters, which he did by presenting himself as a candidate concerned about social inequality, an issue previously identified with the left-wing parties. As a stalwart of the Gaullist party, Chirac had long been critical of France's commitment to European union, but he also had to reassure a business community now firmly wedded to that process, which Balladur supported.

By general consensus, Chirac ran a successful campaign, representing himself on television as a family man with strong roots in the rural region of the Corrèze, his electoral fief. When he finally pulled ahead of Balladur in the opinion polls, few expected that he would have trouble defeating Socialist candidate Lionel Jospin, chosen by his own party at the last minute after several other better-known politicians had declined to run. Jospin surprised everyone, however, by finishing ahead of both Chirac and Balladur in the first round of the election. With most of Balladur's supporters voting for him, Chirac won as expected in the runoff, but Jospin's strong showing boosted the morale of the left and began a duel between Chirac and Jospin that dominated French politics until the unexpected result of the presidential elections in 2002.

Like his predecessor, Mitterrand, Chirac was a veteran politician more committed to becoming president than to any firm set of beliefs, and, like Mitterrand, he had also shown great resiliency in recovering from setbacks. Despite the folksy tone of his 1995 campaign advertising, he had had the typical education of a modern French politician, with degrees from the elite Institut des Etudes politiques ("Sciences po") and the Ecole nationale d'administration. He joined the Gaullist movement in the early years of the Fifth Republic, and distinguished himself as a collaborator of Georges Pompidou during the May 1968 crisis. Chirac obtained his first ministerial post during Pompidou's presidency in 1973, but in 1974 he supported Valéry Giscard d'Estaing for president rather than the official Gaullist candidate. As a reward, Giscard made Chirac prime minister at the relatively young age of 42, only to dismiss him after two years as the economic malaise of the 1970s worsened. Chirac found a new role in French political life by becoming mayor of Paris, a post he held from 1977–1995; his popularity with the city's residents gave him a power base that survived even the Socialist electoral landslide of 1981.

As prime minister in the first period of "co-habitation" from 1986–1988, Chirac abandoned the traditional Gaullist emphasis on state guidance of the economy and pushed aggressive neo-liberal policies like those advocated by U.S. president Reagan and British prime minister Maggie Thatcher at the time. As we have seen, Mitterrand and the Socialists were able to exploit his government's inability to lower unemployment and recover control of the Assembly in 1988. Still recognized as the leading figure on the Right at the time of the Socialists' defeat in 1993, Chirac decided not to risk a repetition of his previous experience in "co-habitation" with Mitterrand. When Edouard Balladur successfully claimed the neo-liberal, pro-business position, however, Chirac had to reinvent himself by promising to do more for the poor and disadvantaged, and, as we have seen, he also distanced himself from his earlier criticisms of the process of European unification. Because of his many shifts of position over the years, when Chirac finally won the presidency in 1995, voters had no clear sense of what policies he would adopt.

Chirac's first two years in office seemed to confirm the impression of a man more successful at winning elections than at governing. His new government, headed by Prime Minister Alain Juppé, reacted to problems that had arisen during France's participation in the 1991 Gulf War by phasing out France's long republican tradition of linking citizenship with participation in the armed forces. Instead of requiring all young men to perform a year of military duty, France went over to a professional army. The measure sparked some controversy, but it was generally accepted that an army of poorly trained draftees who, by law, could not be sent on missions outside the country, was not adequate to protect national interests in the modern world. Chirac's insistence on conducting a series of nuclear-weapons tests in the South Pacific in 1995, however, caused protests throughout that region. At a time when the United States and Russia were reducing their nuclear arsenals, France's actions risked legitimizing other countries' efforts to acquire such weapons. France finally ended its tests and signed a treaty against nuclear proliferation in 1996.

More damaging to the right-wing government was Juppé's effort to reduce the cost of France's social security system, which had grown steadily since the end of the Second World War and was running large deficits. Juppé's proposal to trim benefits to some government employees aroused strong opposition. Railroad and subway workers took the lead in launching a massive strike wave that paralyzed much of the country for several weeks in November and December 1995. The number of strikers approached that recorded during the strikes of May 1968, although most private enterprises continued to function. The reforms were along the lines of measures enacted in a number of other countries facing the same problems during this period, but Chirac and Juppé were unable either to convince the public to support them or to control the chaos caused by the strikes. Eventually, Juppé withdrew his more ambitious proposals, seriously undermining the government's credibility.

The 1995 strikes were a warning that the conservative government's popularity was less solid than the 1993 and 1995 election results suggested. Fearing further erosion of support, Chirac decided to exercise the presidential power to call for early legislative elections in May 1997. Although he expected that the right-wing parties would lose much of the huge edge in legislative seats they had gained in the landslide year of 1993, he hoped they would still have a majority in the Assembly for the remaining five years of his term. Instead, voters turned power over to a coalition headed by Lionel Jospin's Socialists and their allies, the Communists, the ecologists (*les verts*, or "the Greens"), and several other small parties. Rivalries among the leaders of the various right-wing parliamentary factions hurt Chirac's own coalition badly. The right also suffered from the policy of the *Front National*, which punished the traditional conservative parties for refusing to make agreements with it by withholding support from their candidates in the second round of the elections. The *Front National*'s insistence on participating in "triangular" runoff contests rather than withdrawing in favor of the best-placed right-wing candidate allowed the left-wing coalition to win many seats with less than 50 percent of the popular vote.

Few had expected the Socialists, so thoroughly discredited just four years earlier, to return to power so quickly. Although his coalition, dubbed the "pluralist left" because of its multiple constituents, had only a narrow majority, Jospin proved adept at managing it and soon established himself as a popular and competent leader, despite his rather stiff and stand-offish personality. Jospin's government was the Fifth Republic's third and longest experiment with "cohabitation," the coexistence of a president from one side of the political spectrum and a prime minister from the other. Confident that Chirac would not risk calling premature legislative elections after his humiliation in 1997, Jospin also benefited from favorable trends in the global economy during his first years in office. The unemployment rate, which had been 12.5 percent in 1997, fell to below 10 per cent by 2001. Jospin avoided the unrealistic economic experiments of the

first Mitterrand government in 1981; in fact, he went further in selling off shares in state-owned businesses than any previous French government. France remained firmly committed to the process of European unification, and kept a tight rein on public spending in order to meet the standards imposed by the agreement setting up the new common currency, the euro.

Jospin's signature issue in the economic domain was the reduction of the standard French work week from thirty-nine hours to thirty-five with no loss of pay, a reform intended to give workers more free time, encourage more flexible working arrangements, and generate new jobs. France's business community strenuously opposed this measure, claiming that it would raise costs and make the country uncompetitive. The complicated "Aubry laws," named for their architect minister Martine Aubry, one of several prominent women cabinet members under Jospin, nevertheless were gradually implemented between 2000 and 2002. The effects on job creation were limited, but the laws did not cause the drastic problems some opponents had predicted. Since working hours could be averaged over a year, for example, employers were often able to give workers extra time off during slack seasons, rather than finding themselves short-handed when they needed peak production.

In addition to passing the thirty-five-hour laws, the Jospin government distinguished itself from the right-wing cabinets of 1993–1997 in its handling of social issues. Some of the harsh measures against illegal immigrants passed during those years were repealed, and legislation was passed to allow unmarried couples, including those of the same sex, to enjoy the same legal benefits as married ones by forming a "civil partnership," known by its French acronym as a "PACS" (*Pacte civil de solidarité*). In the 2001 municipal elections, Bertrand Delanoë, an openly gay Socialist candidate, was elected as the mayor of Paris, one of the country's most visible political offices. The Jospin years also saw the culmination of a campaign launched in the early 1990s to increase the number of women elected to public office. In 1992, several prominent female political figures had issued a manifesto, *Au pouvoir citoyennes! Liberté, égalité, parité,* ("Take power, women citizens! Liberty, equality, parity") which called for a requirement that half of all elected officials be women. A constitutional amendment to promote such "parity" was finally passed in June 1999, although it fell considerably short of these demands. Legislation passed in 2000 set quotas for the percentage of women candidates that parties had to nominate, rather than for the number of women who were to actually hold office, and women have continued to find themselves nominated primarily in situations where their chances of winning are meager. The number of women actually holding public offices has increased, particularly at the local level, but France continues to lag behind other western countries in this respect.

The "plural left" government's first few years were generally serene, and polls regularly forecast that Jospin would defeat Chirac if the two men were the candidates in the 2002 presidential election. In 1999, the right and left collaborated to push through a long-discussed constitutional reform reducing future presidents' terms from seven to five years. The idea was to make presidential and legislative elections coincide and reduce the probability of "co-habitation." The reform was generally seen as a weakening of the presidency, and Chirac's agreement to it as an acknowledgment that he was not cast from the mold of his more charismatic predecessors. Chirac's popularity did recover somewhat as time went by, and he was able to prevent any other political figure from challenging him as the recognized leader of the French right, even though he was dogged by persistent accusations of financial miscon-

duct. His chances seemed enhanced when dissident members of Le Pen's *Front National* tried unsuccessfully to oust its founder in 1999, and then quit to found their own party. It was widely assumed at the time that this would reduce support for the extreme right-wing movement, and that many of those who had voted for it would back more conventional conservative candidates. The end of the rapid rise in world stock markets in 2000 dampened the economic climate that had buoyed Jospin's popularity, and, after four years in office, his coalition suffered losses in local elections in 2001. Nevertheless, as the 2002 presidential election campaign began, no one anticipated that the prime minister would fail to reach the final round.

The assumption that Chirac and Jospin were bound to be the candidates on the ballot in the second round of voting in 2002 had the effect of encouraging a record crop of small-party candidates to enter the race. As was traditional in French politics, these candidates did not expect to affect the final outcome; instead, they ran to show how much support their factions had within the larger right- and left-wing coalitions or to register a protest. Among the sixteen candidates were three representatives of the Trotskyist extreme left, a black woman from French Guyana whose candidacy promoted attention to race relations in France, and representatives of the many segments of Jospin's "plural left" coalition. Chirac also faced several right-wing rivals, and the two halves of the *Front National* both fielded candidates. The issues stressed by the various campaigns seemed predictable and unlikely to sway most voters. The left ran on its generally positive economic record and its claim that it was protecting France against the undesirable effects of globalization; right-wing candidates denounced the thirty-five-hour week and what they called an alarming increase in crime and insecurity.

As the election neared, polls showed Chirac with a narrow lead over Jospin, but the last surveys before the vote showed an unexpected development: *Front National* founder Jean-Marie Le Pen was moving ahead of Jospin into second place. Voting results on April 21, 2002, confirmed this: Chirac, with 19.9 percent of the vote, was in first place, although he was the choice of less than one out of every five voters, while Le Pen, with 16.9 percent, edged out Jospin, at 16.2 percent, for the second spot on the run-off ballot. Although the combined vote for all the left-wing candidates was well over 40 percent, their coalition had been so splintered that it would not have a representative in the final vote. There was little danger that Le Pen would actually be elected president, but his strong showing rearranged the French political landscape. Politicians with similar programs had scored well in parliamentary elections in several other European countries, but the focus on the presidency in the Fifth Republic's system made his success particularly visible. His barely veiled racist, anti-immigrant, and anti-semitic beliefs, his hostility to European integration, and his tolerance for violence—Le Pen had been barred from office for several years in the 1990s for physically assaulting a rival candidate—made Le Pen's place on the ballot an embarrassment for most French citizens. To register their opposition to Le Pen, even voters who disliked Chirac had no choice but to rally to him. The final result was an anti-climax: Chirac made a record score of 82.2 percent, more than Charles de Gaulle had ever received, and Le Pen's percentage of 17.8 showed that he had not picked up any voters beyond those who had supported the two halves of the *Front National* in the first round. Le Pen had, however, thoroughly disrupted the usual workings of the French political system.

Even though his score in the final round of the presidential election hardly represented real enthusiasm for him, Chirac was able to use the extraordinary situation to win an overwhelming majority in the na-tional legislature, for which elections were held just a month after the presidential campaign. A hastily constructed new party, the *Union pour une majorité présidentielle* (UMP), imposed unity on the long-fractured parties of the conventional right. The "plural left" coalition was literally leaderless, Jospin having resigned his post and quit politics immediately after the first round of the presidential election. Support for Chirac's allies was so strong that Le Pen's followers had no chance to play the spoiler's role as they had in 1995. The UMP won 355 of the Assembly's 577 seats. Among other things, the results indicated a break with the voters' tendency to impose "co-habitation" on the politicians by choosing assemblies at odds with the president, as had happened three times in the previous seventeen years. To run the government, Chirac chose Jean-Pierre Raffarin, a younger conservative politician with a reputation for good rapport with the public.

FRANCE, AMERICA, AND GLOBALIZATION

France's 2002 elections had taken place in the new world climate resulting from the spectacular terrorist attacks on New York and Washington on September 11, 2001. The French public and the nation's leaders had reacted with horror to the destruction of the World Trade Center. The country's most respected newspaper, *Le Monde*, normally regarded as critical of the United States, had editorialized, "Nous sommes tous des américains" ("We are all Americans"), and the French government had accepted American president George W. Bush's decision to invade Afghanistan and overthrow the Islamic Taliban government, which had provided sanctuary for the Al-Qaeda organization that carried out the attacks. In the fall of 2002, however, as the American government began a campaign to win diplomatic support for an attack on Iraq, France became the most vocal of several European governments that op-

Jean-Marie Le Pen, the candidate of the extremist Front National party, shocked the French public by making the run-off round of the 2002 presidential elections against the conservative Jacques Chirac. Opposition to Le Pen inspired massive demonstrations, such as this rally of 600,000 in Paris on May 1, 2002. Most of the marchers had supported one of the left-wing candidates in the election's first round, but Le Pen's success left them no alternative to voting for Chirac.
(Photo credit: David Popko.)

posed the idea. The threat of a French veto effectively killed the Bush administration's hope of getting the United Nations Security Council to endorse the pre-emptive strike it finally launched in late March 2003. Explaining France's position, Jacques Chirac said, "France . . . regards war as always the worst solution, to be used only when there truly are no others . . ." An economic embargo enacted after the 1991 Gulf War and United Nations weapons inspectors had effectively restrained Iraq's dictator Saddam Hussein from threatening his neighbors, the French argued, and, as President Bush had to concede several months after the start of the war,

there was no evidence of Iraqi involvement in the terrorist attacks on the United States.

Although the French position had wide support elsewhere in the world, American leaders were particularly irritated by France's role in opposing the Iraq campaign. Prowar commentators popularized the epithet "cheese-eating surrender monkeys," and politicians evoked the memory of American soldiers who had died fighting for French freedom in the two world wars. (They conveniently ignored the heavy losses France had sustained in World War I and the role that American isolationism had had in making the German invasion of 1940 possible.)

Americans also pointed out, accurately, that France had criticized the economic embargo imposed on Iraq after the 1991 Gulf War, and that French companies had been building up a privileged position in that country in anticipation of the end of those restrictions.

To some Americans, French opposition to the invasion of Iraq looked like part of a larger current of anti-Americanism in France. It was also often interpreted as evidence of France's reluctance to adjust to the realities of an increasingly globalized world, in which the efforts of a medium-sized country to maintain a distinctive identity were doomed to failure. In France, criticism of excessive American influence was often closely tied to a critique of a world economy dominated by American economic influence. For many on both sides of the Atlantic, the symbol of French resistance to Americanization and globalization was peasant activist José Bové's highly publicized trashing of a McDonald's outlet in the small southern town of Millau in August 1999. The media-savvy Bové, who was not a traditional peasant but rather a veteran of the May 1968 movement who had moved to the countryside after its failure, charged that American fast food was both un-French and unhealthy. In the name of profit, large corporations were imposing *malbouffe* ("bad eating") on the population. Bové's action made him an icon for the worldwide anti-globalization movement that was spreading rapidly at the time.

Although Bové was eventually brought to court for his actions, they evoked considerable support in France and even abroad. The transformation of world politics following the collapse of the Soviet Union in 1989–1991, which left the United States as the world's only superpower, revived concerns about the imposition of American values in France and in many other parts of the world. As Hubert Védrine, French foreign minister under Jospin, put it, globalization favored Americans' interests "because of their economic size; because globalization takes place in their language; because it is organized along neo-liberal economic principles; because they impose their legal, accounting and technical practices; and because they're advocates of individualism."[1] In response, French policy was to try to regulate world issues through multilateral agreements, and to insist that the laws of the marketplace should not be the only factors considered in determining policies. When George W. Bush became American president in January 2001, he quickly made it clear that the United States was no longer favorable to such an approach. Even before the crisis of September 11, 2001, America had rejected international rules meant to slow global warming and proposals for a world court to try human-rights violators. For many in France, the American decision to invade Iraq without United Nations authorization was an extension of this tendency to equate might with right. In French eyes, their opposition was not anti-Americanism but a defense of the idea that world problems need to be regulated within a framework of agreed-upon laws.

Although many in France have been critical of Americanization and globalization, the notion that the country has tried to wall itself off from the world is misleading. Economically, France has become considerably more open to foreign trade and investment than the United States: by the end of the 1990s, foreign trade was equal to 49 percent of the country's gross domestic product, nearly twice the proportion in the U.S. Foreign investors held 40 percent of the shares of companies traded on the French stock market. French companies have pursued opportunities abroad, showing that they can compete effectively in a global marketplace, even if the most aggressive French entrepreneur of recent years, Jean-Marie Messier, whose Vivendi company surprised Americans by buying Universal Studios in December 2000, suffered a spectacular reversal just two years later, when his overextended empire collapsed and he was forced out of his job. French consumers were slow at first to turn to the Internet, in part because the country had its own, more primitive national online network, the Minitel, introduced in the 1980s, but by the beginning of the new millennium, Internet use was taking off. José Bové's attack on McDonald's garnered considerable public sympathy in France, but it was French consumers themselves who had made the company successful. Bové's gesture did nothing to diminish the popularity of the now-ubiquitous storefronts selling Chinese food microwaved on demand, as well as the sushi bars, falafel stands, and Mexican restaurants that have proliferated in French cities in the past decade.

DOMESTIC ISSUES IN THE NEW MILLENNIUM

While French attitudes toward the United States and toward globalization have preoccupied Americans, the attention of the country's population and its leaders has often been concentrated on other problems. The large vote for Le Pen in the 2002 presidential elections was a reminder that the integration of France's large population of recent immigrants remained a burning issue. The extensive publicity given to the ethnically mixed 1998 World Cup championship team generated a short-lived optimism about the assimilation of the immigrant groups whose situation had generated so much debate since the early 1980s, but a "friendly" football match in Paris between the French and Algerian national football teams in October 2001 showed that sport could lead to increased tensions as well. The crowd, made up mostly of fans of Algerian descent living in France, booed the *Marseillaise* and the French players; prime minister Jospin, who was at the match, was widely criticized for not having insisted that something be done in response. The rising tensions in the Middle East were reflected in France itself, as radical Islamist movements won supporters in the dreary working-class suburbs where many immigrants lived; they were blamed for a wave of anti-Jewish incidents that reflected passions stirred by the violent conflict between Israel and the Palestinians.

Concern about Muslims in France expressed itself above all in a seemingly endless controversy about whether Muslim schoolgirls should be allowed to wear headscarves or *hijabs* (called *foulards* in French) while attending public schools. Longstanding French rules barred students from wearing external signs of religious or ethnic identification. Those who opposed toleration of such symbols included not only conservatives but also a number of prominent figures identified with the French Left. Their argument was that democracy in France has depended on the creation of a single, universally shared, set of national values, and that tolerance of students wearing *foulards* in school would open the way to the division of the country into subgroups with nothing in common. French feminists often denounced the headscarves a symbol of Islamic discrimination against women. Interviews with the schoolgirls at the center of the original *foulard* affair in 1989 suggested that they were not trying to flaunt their religion; instead, they were trying to find a compromise that would persuade their traditionalist parents to let them attend French public schools and prepare themselves for life in the wider society around them. In the 1990s, French governments backed away from a total ban on the headscarves, but in December 2003, a commission appointed by the Chirac government recommended prohibiting all symbols of religious or ethnic identification in schools and other public institutions, and a law to this effect was passed in March 2004. Bernard Stasi, the commission's chair, told the press, "There are indisputably Muslims or . . . groups seeking to test the resistance of the Republic, . . .

that want France to no longer be France." A young Muslim's response was, "Today, they forbid us from wearing veils. Tomorrow, they'll forbid us from being Muslims."[2] Both comments indicate the seriousness of this French version of a cultural war. Although there were reasons for concern about ethnic tension, these years were also saw a new level of honesty about French conduct during the Algerian war of the 1950s and early 1960s. Candid memoirs by several retired generals openly admitted that the French army had routinely tortured Algerian prisoners, and a process similar to that which had led the French government to admit its complicity in the deportation of Jews in the Vichy period was clearly under way, as official archives began to be opened and a fuller picture of events emerged.

The condition of France's complicated social security system was another major preoccupation for the Chirac government. Like all western countries, France now faces a demographic conundrum. The sharp fall in the birth rate since the introduction of modern contraceptives in the mid-1960s means that the number of working-age people has shrunk relative to the large cohort of those from the post-World-War-II baby boom who are reaching retirement age. France's problems in financing old-age pensions are exacerbated because it went further than other countries in encouraging early retirement, which the Socialist government of the 1980s in particular hoped would help open up jobs for younger workers. In addition, rather than a uniform pension system for all citizens, France has guaranteed state employees and a number of other professional groups special benefits which have now become so costly that taxpayers have to help pay for them. Although cutting social benefits is never easy, in France or elsewhere, the Raffarin government forced through some changes in retirement rules in the spring of 2003, raising retirement ages for a number of groups.

France also faces growing difficulties paying for its generally excellent healthcare system. As this is written, in 2004, various proposals for raising fees and cutting costs are under discussion. All are likely to cause considerable anguish in a country accustomed to universal health coverage at reasonable prices. Another area of concern is the educational system, a huge bureaucracy that runs all of the country's public schools and universities. Public dissatisfaction with the schools, especially those in poorer neighborhoods, has been increasingly evident in recent years, and teachers have been equally unhappy with classroom conditions. Universities are also underfunded and overcrowded. Several decades of failed attempts to significantly reform the system warn against any expectation for rapid change. The cost of maintaining France's very large state sector, which takes almost 50 percent of the country's gross domestic product every year, is creating strong pressure for restructuring, however. Both the Jospin and Raffarin governments agreed that the country's tax burden was too high and enacted modest tax cuts, with the result that France's budget deficits currently exceed the 3 percent limit imposed by the rules the country agreed to when it joined the euro bloc. The fact that other major euro countries, particularly Germany, were in a similar situation in 2003 gave France enough allies to prevent the European Central Bank from forcing the government to raise taxes or cut expenses, but the credibility of the new currency depends on member countries' willingness to impose fiscal discipline on themselves.

At the start of the new millennium, the people of France, like those of the rest of the world, thus find themselves wondering what the future holds for them. France today is certainly one of the privileged parts of the globe. Most of its citizens enjoy a high standard of living, with social benefits that Americans often envy, but the French are increasingly aware of the difficulties of maintaining this level of prosperity, and of the considerable part of the population that has not fully shared in it. The fact that so many of France's poor are also members of incompletely assimilated immigrant groups adds to the stresses the country faces in dealing with the changing ethnic makeup of its population. Since the end of the Algerian war in 1962, France has experienced one of the longest periods of peace in its history, but the upsurge of violence in the world in the past decade, which led to the involvement of French forces in the 1991 Gulf War and in peace-keeping operations in the former Yugoslavia, has been a reminder that tranquility cannot be taken for granted. Whether the tensions that have arisen in the past few years between France and the United States will fade remains to be seen. France's role in Europe is also bound to change as the European Union completes the integration of the ten new member countries, most of them former parts of the Soviet bloc, who became official members of the group in 2004. As one of twenty-five participating countries, rather than one of fifteen, the French are finding it more difficult to defend some of their special concerns, such as the privileged status of the French language in the Union's affairs.

From the revolutionaries of the 1789 through the technocrats of the twentieth century, modern France has produced many utopian visionaries who tried to persuade their fellow citizens that their country could, if it wished, enjoy permanent peace and prosperity. The spectacular fashion in which

France celebrated the beginning of the new millennium at midnight on December 31, 1999 was part of that tradition. Today, such soaring hopes are out of fashion, sometimes replaced by dystopian predictions of looming social or environmental disasters. In facing the uncertainties of the future, however, the French can still draw on many resources: a modern and productive economy; a rich cultural tradition; schools, hospitals and other institutions which, despite their problems, are still far better than those available to the overwhelming majority of the world's population. As Jean-Marie Le Pen's second-place finish in the 2002 elections showed, some French citizens are angry about the state of their country and fear for its future. The rather lackluster Jacques Chirac's overwhelming triumph in that election, however, demonstrated that more than four-fifths of the electorate retains its faith in the country's basic democratic principles. Whatever new challenges the coming years may bring, it is not unreasonable to expect that France and its people will succeed in meeting them, and in making their own distinctive contributions to the shaping of our planet's future.

NOTES

1. Cited in Philip H. Gordon and Sophie Meunier, *The French Challenge: Adapting to Globalization* (Washington, D.C.: Brookings Institution Press, 2001), 111.
2. Cited in Lexington, KY., *Herald-Leader*, 13 Dec. 2003, 1.

APPENDIX A

FOR FURTHER READING

This short bibliography is meant to direct students to reference works that will help them find more specialized readings, to some of the more general books in the field, and to a selection of specialized monographs of particular interest. It has been updated to include works published up to 2004. With a few exceptions, it is limited to titles available in English. References to works in French can be found in the bibliographies of most of the books listed here.

BIBLIOGRAPHIES, JOURNALS, AND GENERAL REFERENCE WORKS

The *Bibliographie annuelle de l'histoire française* (1963–), published yearly, provides the most comprehensive bibliography of recent scholarly books and articles on French history, in both French and other languages. There are several scholarly journals in English devoted to French history: *French Historical Studies, French History, Modern and Contemporary France*, and the *Proceedings of the Western Society for French History*. Many other historical journals also publish articles in this field. An increasing amount of information about French history is available on the World Wide Web. One good way to get recommendations for useful websites is to post

a query on H-France, the international French historians' e-mail list. As of 2004, the e-mail address to subscribe to H-France is H-France@lists.uakron.edu.

The series of *Historical Dictionaries* published by Greenwood Press are useful reference works, containing short articles on most major historical personalities and topics. See Samuel Scott and Barry Rothaus, eds., *Historical Dictionary of the French Revolution*; Owen Connelly, ed., *Historical Dictionary of Napoleonic France*; Edgar Newman, ed., *Historical Dictionary of France from the 1815 Restoration to the Second Empire*; William Echard, ed., *Historical Dictionary of the French Second Empire*; Patrick Hutton, ed., *Historical Dictionary of the Third French Republic*; and Wayne Northcutt, ed., *Historical Dictionary of the French Fourth and Fifth Republics*. David Bell et al., eds., *Biographical Dictionary of French Political Leaders Since 1870*, gives short profiles of prominent French politicians from the Third Republic to the 1980s.

GENERAL HISTORIES

Few historians have tackled the challenge of providing a general overview of modern French history. The great French social and economic historian Fernand Braudel died before completing his *The Identity of France* (1988); the two volumes he finished put modern French social and economic history in a perspective stretching back to the Stone Age. Gordon Wright, *France in Modern Times* (5th ed., 1995), is a solid and comprehensive textbook. Martin Alexander, ed., *French History Since Napoleon* (1999), offers thematic essays, mostly by leading British historians. The essays in Pierre Nora, ed., *Realms of Memory* (1996–1998), and *Rethinking France* (2001–) (two sets of translations from Nora's French project, *Les Lieux de mémoire* (1984–93), include many fascinating discussions of how the French memory of the past has been shaped. Useful syntheses covering a more limited period are Roger Magraw, *France 1815–1914* (1983), a Marxist perspective; Charles Sowerwine, *France since 1870: Culture, Politics and Society* (2001); Maurice Agulhon, *The French Republic, 1879–1992* (1993); and Maurice Larkin, *France Since the Popular Front* (1988), on the years since 1936.

Most of the volumes of the *Nouvelle histoire de la France contemporaine,* a series of high-level syntheses by leading French scholars, published beginning in the 1970s, are now available in English; though varying in quality, they generally provide a good overview of the periods they cover. See Michel Vovelle, Marc Bouloiseau, and Denis Woroneff, *The French Revolution* (3 vols.) (1983–1984); Louis Bergeron, *France Under Napoleon* (1981); André Jardin and A.-J. Tudesq, *Restoration and Reaction 1815–1848* (1983); Maurice Agulhon, *The Republican Experiment* (1983); Alain Plessis, *Rise and Fall of the Second Empire* (1983); Jean-Paul Mayeur and Madeleine Rebérioux, *The Third Republic from Its Origins to the Great War* (1983); Philippe Bernard and Henri Dubief, *The Decline of the Third Republic* (1985); Jean-Pierre Azéma, *From Munich to the Liberation* (1984); and Jean-Pierre Rioux, *The Fourth Republic* (1987). In France, Philippe Bernard's volume covering 1914–1929 has now been replaced

by Jean-Jacques Becker and Serge Berstein, *Victoire et frustrations* (1990), and Serge Berstein has published two volumes on the Fifth Republic: *La France de l'expansion I. La République gaullienne* (1989) and *II. L'apogée Pompidou* (1995). The series was completed in 2002 by the publication of Jean-Jacques Becker, *Crises et alternances 1974–2000.* David Thomson, *France: Empire and Republic, 1850–1940* (1968), is a useful collection of translated political documents. Olivier Wieviorka and Christophe Prochasson, *La France du XXe siècle. Documents d'histoire* (1994), includes selections dating from the 1870s to the mid-1990s.

For those who read French, the relevant volumes of the many multivolume thematic histories published in France in the past three decades are very useful. They generally include contributions by leading French scholars in the fields concerned. See Fernand Braudel and Ernest Labrousse, eds., *Histoire économique et sociale de la France* (1970–1982), on economic and social history; Georges Duby and Armand Wallon, eds., *Histoire de la France rurale* (1975–1976), on agriculture; Georges Duby, ed., *Histoire de la France urbaine* (1983), on city life; Jacques Dupâquier, ed., *Histoire de la population française* (1988), on demography; Gérard Cholvy and Yves-Marie Hilaire, eds., *Histoire religieuse de la France contemporaine* (1985), on religious life; Roger Chartier and Henri-Jean Martin, eds., *Histoire de l'édition française* (1983–1986), on publishing and reading; and Claude Bellanger et al., *Histoire générale de la presse française* (1969–1975), on newspapers and journalism. Two series available in English that cover western civilization as a whole but that give special attention to their subject in a French context are Philippe Ariès and Georges Duby, eds., *History of Private Life* (1990), and Georges Duby and Michelle Perrot, eds., *History of Women in the West* (1992–). A multivolume semiofficial diplomatic history of France is in publication; the four volumes currently available are Pierre Guillen, *L'Expansion 1881–1898* (1984), Jean-Baptiste Duroselle, *La Décadence 1932–1939* (1979) and *L'Abyme 1939–1944* (1985), and Pierre Gerbet et al., *Le Relèvement 1944–1949* (1991).

Broad Chronological Perspectives

For the last half-century, French historians have insisted on the importance of viewing historical phenomena over long periods of time. It has not been easy to apply this recipe to the event-filled history of the last 250 years. Most attempts to do so have emphasized economic and social history. Economic history has been a somewhat neglected field in recent years; the major works in English are now rather dated. See David Landes, *The Unbound Prometheus* (1969). François Caron, *Economic History of Modern France* (1979), more technical in approach, also covers the entire period. Roger Price, *Economic Modernization of France 1730–1880* (1975), is useful for the first half of the period covered in this book. Rondo Cameron, *France and the Economic Development of Europe, 1800–1914* (1961), looks at the French contribution to industrialization beyond its own borders. Charles Kindleberger, *Economic Growth in France and Britain 1851–1950* (1964), stops just short of the country's greatest surge of development. Tom Kemp, *Economic Forces in French History* (1971), also takes a long view.

Georges Dupeux, *French Society, 1789–1970* (1976), is a general overview of social history. Annie Moulin, *Peasantry and Society in France Since 1789* (1991), and Gérard Noiriel, *Workers in French Society in the 19th and 20th Centuries* (1990), are good surveys of these topics. Theodore Zeldin, *France 1848–1945*, 2 vols. (1973, 1979), is a vast, sprawling essay that covers politics, culture, and social history. It is often fascinating but hard to follow. Charles Tilly, *The Contentious French* (1986), explores patterns in collective behavior over the past three centuries. René Ré-

mond's *The Right in France* (1969), although limited to one side of the political spectrum, proposes a general theory about the structure of French politics applicable to the period from 1815 to the present. Peter Sahlins's *Boundaries: The Making of France and Spain in the Pyrenees* (1989) revises accepted ideas about the formation of national identity in the period from Louis XIV to the Second Empire. Paula Hyman, *The Jews of Modern France* (1998), is a brief history of a significant minority group.

Specialized Titles: Select Bibliography

1750–1789

A classic interpretation of the connection between the Old Regime and the Revolution, still valuable for its many brilliant insights, is Alexis de Tocqueville, *The Old Regime and the Revolution* (1955; orig. 1856). Two general overviews of Old Regime society and institutions are Roland Mousnier, *The Institutions of France Under the Absolute Monarchy, 1598–1789*, 2 vols. (1979, 1984), and Pierre Goubert, *The Ancien Regime* (1973). Colin Jones, *The Great Nation: France from Louis XV to Napoleon* (2002) elegantly summarizes recent research on Old Regime politics. French- and English-speaking authors have both contributed extensively to recent research on social history of the eighteenth century, particularly the lower classes; many of the best studies extend into earlier or later periods. An invaluable source from the period is J.-L. Ménétra, *Journal of My Life* (1986). A sample of recent monographs includes Daniel Roche, *The People of Paris* (1987); Cissie Fairchilds, *Domestic Enemies: Servants and Their Masters* (1984); Robert Schwartz, *Policing the Poor in 18th Century France* (1988); Olwyn Hufton, *The Poor of Eighteenth-Century France* (1974); Michael Sonenscher, *Work and Wages: Natural Law, Politics and the Eighteenth-Century French Trades* (1989); Steven Kaplan, *Provisioning Paris* (1984); Timothy Tackett, *Priest and*

Parish in Eighteenth-Century France (1977); and Kathryn Norberg, *Rich and Poor in Grenoble 1600–1814* (1985). Jeremy D. Popkin, ed., *Panorama of Paris* (1999), is a selection of translated excerpts from an eighteenth-century book about everyday life in Paris, Mercier's *Tableau de Paris.* Studies devoted to the elites are much rarer. See the older work of Bernard Groethuysen, *The Bourgeois: Catholicism vs. Capitalism in Eighteenth-Century France* (1968; orig. 1927), David Garrioch, *The Formation of the Parisian Bourgeoisie, 1690–1830* (1996); Guy Chaussinand-Nogaret, *French Nobility in the Eighteenth Century* (1985); Samia Spencer, ed., *French Women and the Age of Enlightenment* (1987), includes sections on social history.

The period's intellectual life has attracted numerous scholars. Peter Gay, *The Enlightenment: An Interpretation* (1966–1969), puts French contributions in a European context. Daniel Roche, *France in the Enlightenment* (1998), is a leading contemporary French historian's overview of the movement's impact on French society. Roger Chartier, *Cultural Origins of the French Revolution* (1991), is shorter and more selective. Robert Darnton, *The Forbidden Best-Sellers of Pre-Revolutionary France* (1994), is a readable study of underground books and publishers. Darrin McMahon, *Enemies of the Enlightenment* (2001) considers opposition to the movement. Major studies of individual authors include Arthur Wilson, *Diderot* (1972); Jean Starobinski, *Rousseau: Transparency and Obstruction* (1988); and Keith Baker, *Condorcet* (1975). Works linking culture and politics at the end of the Old Regime include Thomas Crow, *Painters and Public Life in Eighteenth-Century Paris* (1985); and Sarah Maza, *Private Lives and Public Affairs* (1993). Dena Goodman, *The Republic of Letters* (1994), emphasizes women's role in the Enlightenment, and Nina Gelbart, *The King's Midwife* (1998), celebrates one woman's contribution to medical progress.

Interest in the period's politics has revived strongly in recent years. Dale Van Kley has examined the role of the *parti janséniste* in *The Religious Origins of the French Revolution* (1996) while Steven Kaplan's *Bread, Politics, and Political Economy in the Reign of Louis XV* (1976) deals with issues concerning economic modernization. David Bell, *Lawyers and Citizens* (1994), examines the role of one key professional group. The Old Regime's final attempts to change itself are analyzed in P. M. Jones, *Reform and Revolution in France, 1774–1791* (1995). The impact of the political crisis resulting from Louis XV's final attempt to silence the parliamentary opposition is the subject of many of the essays in Keith Baker, *Inventing the French Revolution* (1990). Michael Kwass, *Privilege and the Politics of Taxation in Eighteenth-Century France* (2000) and David Bell, *Cult of the Nation: Inventing Nationalism 1680–1800* (2001) offer two very different perspectives on how royal policy helped prepare the way for the Revolution. Munro Price, *Preserving the Monarchy* (1995), traces French foreign policy in the era of the American Revolution. Alan Williams, *The Police of Paris* (1979), studies the day-to-day administration of the capital. Sue Peabody, *"There Are No Slaves in France"* (1996) considers legal debates over slavery in pre-revolutionary France.

The Revolution and the Napoleonic Period

There are several recent general histories of the Revolution in English: Simon Schama, *Citizens* (1989); William Doyle, *Oxford History of the French Revolution* (1988); and Donald Sutherland, *French Revolution and Empire: The Quest for a Civic Order* (2003). Two older works that are still worth consulting are the synthesis by the leading French historian of the twentieth century, Georges Lefebvre, *The French Revolution,* 2 vols. (1962); and the exceptionally clear narrative of Norman Hampson, *Social History of the French Revolution* (1963). François Furet and Mona Ozouf, eds., *Critical Dictionary of the French Revolution* (1989), includes topical articles on a number of personalities and themes of the revolutionary era. Three useful collections of translated documents are Paul Beik, *The French Revolution* (1970); J. H. Stewart, *Documentary Survey of the French Revolution* (1951); and Laura Mason and Tracey Rizzo, *The French Revolution* (1999).

On the origins of the Revolution, see Georges Lefebvre, *The Coming of the Revolution* (1947) and *The Great Fear of 1789* (1973); William Doyle, *Origins of the French Revolution* (3rd ed., 1999); and Keith Baker, ed., *The French Revolution and the Creation of Modern Political Culture*, Vol. 1 (1988). The second volume of that series, edited by Colin Lucas under the title *The Political Culture of the French Revolution* (1988), contains contributions dealing with many aspects of revolutionary politics. Timothy Tackett, *Becoming a Revolutionary* (1996), follows the evolution of the National Assembly, and his *When the King Took Flight* (2003) shows the significance of the king's failed attempt to flee in 1791. Malcolm Crook, *Elections in the French Revolution* (1996), explains another key aspect of revolutionary politics. Isser Woloch, *The New Regime* (1994), shows the movement's impact on civic institutions. Alison Patrick, *The Men of the First French Republic* (1972), deals with the deputies of the National Convention. Timothy Tackett, *Religion, Revolution, and Regional Culture in Eighteenth-Century France* (1986), and Suzanne Desan, *Reclaiming the Sacred* (1991), examine the social bases underlying the religious conflict, whose stages are recounted in John McManners, *French Revolution and the Church* (1970). Paul Hanson, *The Jacobin Republic under Fire* (2003) looks at the conflict between Paris and the provinces in 1793. David Jordan, *The Revolutionary Career of Maximilen Robespierre* (1985) argues that the leader of the Montagnards was not a monster, while Colin Haydon and William Doyle, eds., *Robespierre* (1999) brings

together a number of perspectives on its subject. R. R. Palmer, *Twelve Who Ruled* (1943), makes sense of the Committee of Public Safety's policies. R. B. Rose, *Gracchus Babeuf* (1978), looks at one of the most extreme revolutionary thinkers, while Jacques Godechot, *The Counter-Revolution* (1964), covers both thought and action. Stanley Loomis's highly readable *The Fatal Friendship* (1972) is the best work on the royal family and its fate; David Jordan, *The King's Trial* (1979), is another gripping account.

François Furet's essay *Interpreting the French Revolution* (1981) opened a new era of historiography, focused on the Revolution's political culture. Lynn Hunt, *Politics, Culture and Class in the French Revolution* (1984), and Mona Ozouf, *Festivals and the French Revolution* (1988), offer stimulating explorations of this subject. Jeremy Popkin, *Revolutionary News* (1990), and Jack Censer, *Prelude to Power* (1976), deal with the newspaper press; Joan Landes, *Visualizing the Nation* (2001) discusses the use of visual imagery in revolutionary propaganda, Daniel Roche and Robert Darnton, eds., *Revolution in Print* (1989), surveys all the major media of revolutionary propaganda, and Emmet Kennedy, *Cultural History of the French Revolution* (1989), covers the entire range of cultural activities. Patrice Higonnet's *Goodness Beyond Virtue* (1998) is a provocative new look at the Jacobin movement and its ideology.

With the dissolution of the Marxist paradigm, there is no convincing synthesis of the complex social history of the revolutionary period. Peter Jones, *The Peasantry in the French Revolution* (1988), gives an overview of the Revolution in the countryside, and John Markoff, *The Abolition of Feudalism* (1996), uses quantitative methods to explore this subject more deeply. Charles Tilly, *The Vendée* (1967), uses the counterrevolutionary peasant revolt to build a general model explaining social protest. The urban revolutionary movement is the subject of Albert Soboul,

The Sans-Culottes (1964); George Rudé, *The Crowd in the French Revolution* (1959); and Richard Cobb, *The Police and the People* (1970). David Garrioch, *The Making of Revolutionary Paris* (2002) is a new look at the interaction between the Revolution and France's capital. Much new work has recently appeared on women during the Revolution. See especially Dominque Godineau's social history *The Women of Paris and Their French Revolution* (1998) and the documentary collection of Darline Gay Levy et al., *Women in Revolutionary Paris* (1979); the provocative interpretation offered by Joan Landes, *Women and the Public Sphere in the Age of the French Revolution* (1988); Sara Melzer and Leslie Rabine, eds., *Rebel Daughters: Women and the French Revolution* (1992); Olwyn Hufton, *Women and the Limits of Citizenship in the French Revolution* (1992) Suzanne Desan, *The Family on Trial in Revolutionary France* (2004) and Carla Hesse, *The Other Enlightenment* (2001). Madelyn Gutwirth et al., eds., *Germaine de Stael* (1991), treats the epoch's most important female writer. Alan Forrest has examined two important groups in the revolutionary period in his *The French Revolution and the Poor* (1981) and *Soldiers of the French Revolution* (1990). Laurent Dubois is the author of two recent studies of the Revolution in the Caribbean colonies: *Avengers of the New World* (2004), on Haiti, and *A Colony of Citizens: Revolution and Slave Emancipation in the French Caribbean 1787–1804* (2004).

On the Directory period, see Martyn Lyons, *France Under the Directory* (1975), a good overview; Isser Woloch, *Jacobin Legacy* (1970), which looks at the period's left-wing movement; and Harvey Mitchell, *The Underground War Against Revolutionary France* (1965), and Jeremy D. Popkin, *The Right-Wing Press in France, 1792–1800* (1980), on royalist intrigues. James Livesey, *Making Democracy in the French Revolution* (2001) is a controversial attempt to rehabilitate the Directory's democratic credentials.

Martyn Lyons, *Napoleon Bonaparte and the Legacy of the French Revolution* (1994), and Geoffrey Ellis, *Napoleon* (1997) are good recent overviews. Louis Bergeron's *France Under Napoleon* (1981) emphasizes the experience of the French people rather than Napoleon's life; Felix Markham, *Napoleon* (1963), is a reliable biography. J. C. Herold, *The Mind of Napoleon* (1955), gives selections from his letters and memoirs. Robert Holtman, *Napoleonic Propaganda* (1950); Gunther Rothenberg, *The Art of Warfare in the Age of Napoleon* (1979); Owen Connolly, *Blundering to Glory* (1987), and Isser Woloch, *Napoleon and his Collaborators* (2001) cover various aspects of the reign. Alan Forrest, *Napoleon's Men: The Soldiers of the Revolution and Empire* (2002) takes a new look at the "Little Corporal's" armies. Peter Geyl, *Napoleon: For and Against* (1949), and Frank Kafker and James Laux, eds., *Napoleon and His Times* (1989), document historians' changing views of Napoleon over time; the latter title has a good bibliography.

1815–1870

In recent decades, social historians have taken the greatest interest in this period, which saw the beginnings of French industrialization and the consolidation of bourgeois society. Roger Price, *Social History of Nineteenth-Century France* (1987), is a general introduction. Important monographic studies include Louis Chevalier, *Laboring Classes and Dangerous Classes* (1973), a classic account of the problems of urban life; John Merriman, *The Red City* (1985), an excellent study of a provincial city; William Sewell, *Work and Revolution in France* (1980), which looks at the development of working-class identity; and Maurice Agulhon, *The Republic in the Village* (1982), which links rural social change and new political ideas. Bonnie Smith, *Ladies of the Leisure Class* (1981), shows that notions about the bourgeoisie must be changed to take women's experience into account. Other recent works on women's history in this period include Rachel Fuchs, *Poor and Pregnant in Paris* (1992), Whitney Walton, *Eve's Proud Descendants: Four Women Writers and Republican Politics in Nineteenth-Century France* (2000), and Lenard R. Berlanstein, *Daughters of Eve: A Cultural History of French Theater Women from the Old Regime to the Fin de Siècle* (2001). On men's roles in nineteenth-century bourgeois culture, see Robert Nye, *Masculinity and Male Codes of Honor in Modern France* (1993), William Reddy, *The Invisible Code: Honor and Sentiment in Post-Revolutionary France 1814–1848* (1997), and several of the essays in Jeffrey Merrick and Bryant Ragan, eds., *Homosexuality in Modern France* (1996). Mark Traugott, *The French Worker* (1993), contains excerpts from nineteenth-century workers' autobiographies. William Reddy, *The Rise of Market Culture* (1984), emphasizes workers' resistance to the imposition of capitalist norms. Gay Gullickson, *Spinners and Weavers of Auffay* (1986); Tessie Liu, *The Weaver's Knot* (1994); and Judith Coffin, *The Politics of Women's Work* (1996), all examine the sexual division of labor in manufacturing. Robert Bezucha, *The Lyon Uprising of 1834* (1974), is about the first major workers' revolt of the century, and Jeremy D. Popkin, *Press, Revolution, and Social Identities in France, 1830–1835* (2002) looks at the role of the media in the period's social conflicts.

Works on political history tend to be divided by regime. Two exceptions are Maurice Agulhon, *Marianne into Battle* (1981), an innovative study of the development of nineteenth-century political symbolism, and Robert Goldstein, *Censorship of Political Caricature* (1989), a well-illustrated history of political cartooning. On the Restoration, G. Bertier de Sauvigny, *The Bourbon Restoration* (1966) is a standard overview. Sheryl Kroen, *Politics and Theater: The Crisis of Legitimacy in Restoration France, 1815–1830* (2000)

demonstrates that this period had an important participatory political culture. Alan Spitzer, *The French Generation of 1820* (1987), deals with intellectual elites' activities in that decade; David Pinkney, *The French Revolution of 1830* (1972), describes the fall of the regime; and Peter Sahlins, *Forest Rites* (1994), uses an anthropological approach to the rural aspects of this event. Douglas Johnson, *Guizot* (1963), is a life of the figure most identified with the July Monarchy; J. P. T. Bury, *Thiers* (1986), examines the career of a figure whose activities spanned the regimes from 1830–1873; while David Pinkney, *Decisive Years in France, 1840–1847* (1986), argues for the period's crucial importance in understanding French history. Pierre Rosanvallon's *Le moment Guizot* (1985) marks a turning point in evaluations of the period's liberalism. Edward Berenson, *Populist Religion and Left-Wing Politics in France, 1830–1852* (1984), treats another dimension of the period's atmosphere. Michèle Riot-Sarcey, *La démocratie à l'épreuve des femmes* (1994), shows the significance of women's issues in the evolution of democratic and republican thought; Lawrence C. Jennings, *French Anti-Slavery: The Movement for the Abolition of Slavery in France, 1802–1848* (2000) treats the campaign against slavery.

The literature on the 1848 Revolution and the Second Republic is copious. Karl Marx, *Class Struggles in France* and *The 18th Brumaire of Louis Bonaparte,* and Alexis de Tocqueville, *Recollections* (1970), are contemporary accounts that greatly influenced subsequent historians. Roger Price, *The French Second Republic* (1972), is a reliable narrative; the same author's *1848 in France* (1975) is a useful documentary collection. Ted Margadant, *French Peasants in Revolt* (1980), studies the rural insurrection of 1851; Mark Traugott, *Armies of the Poor* (1985), and Roger Gould, *Insurgent Identities* (1995), examine urban conflict. Mary Lynn Stewart-McDougall, *The Artisan Republic* (1984), deals with the revolution in Lyon, France's second city.

Roger Price, *The French Second Empire* (2001) is the most recent overview of this important period. Sudhir Hazareesingh, *The Saint-Napoleon: Celebrations of Sovereignty in Nineteenth-Century France* (2004) offers a new perspective on relations between the regime and the public. Theodore Zeldin, *The Political System of Napoleon III* (1958), explains the evolution of political structures during the period. Philip Nord, *The Republican Moment* (1995), tells the story of the Empire's republican counterculture. David Pinkney, *Napoleon III and the Rebuilding of Paris* (1958), and David Jordan, *Transforming Paris* (1996), deal with Haussmann's tranformation of the capital, while Sandra Horvath-Peterson, *Victor Duruy and French Education* (1984), examines the scope and limits of the period's reform efforts.

The period's many movements for social reform have generated another large body of studies. Frank Manuel, *The Prophets of Paris* (1962), is a classic introduction to the French Utopian socialists; Jonathan Beecher, *Charles Fourier* (1986), is a detailed study of the most imaginative of them. The feminist movement is the subject of Claire Moses, *French Feminism in the Nineteenth Century* (1984), while Dominique Desanti, *A Woman in Revolt* (1976), recounts the life of Flora Tristan, who combined socialist and feminist agitation. Christopher Johnson, *Utopian Communism in France* (1974), analyzes Cabet's Icarian movement. K. S. Vincent, *Pierre-Joseph Proudhon and the Rise of French Republican Socialism* (1984), is a sympathetic portrait of the not always likable prophet of mutualism. Ellen Furlough, *Consumer Cooperation in France* (1991), tells the story of a movement that had important practical results.

For the period's intellectual and cultural trends, the detailed narrative in F. W. J. Hemmings, *Culture and Society in France 1789–1848* (1987), is a useful starting point.

André Jardin, *Tocqueville* (1988), is a life of the period's major social thinker, and Renée Winegarten, *Double Life of George Sand* (1978), recounts the career of the period's best-known woman writer. The characteristics of the Parisian counterculture are analyzed in Jerrold Seigel, *Bohemian Paris* (1986), and radical ideas about art are the subject of Neil McWilliams, *Dreams of Happiness* (1993). Dominick LaCapra's *"Madame Bovary" on Trial* (1982) is both an analysis of the clash between cultural innovation and social conservatism and a plea for new approaches to cultural history. Jan Goldstein, *Console and Classify: The French Psychiatric Profession in the Nineteenth Century* (1987), looks at the development of one of the learned professions. Thomas Kselman, *Miracles and Prophecies in Nineteenth-Century France* (1983), is about popular Catholicism, and the same author's *Death and the Afterlife in Modern France* (1993) deals with attitudes toward one of the fundamental features of the human condition.

1870–1940

The great crises that repeatedly shook France during the Third Republic have always guaranteed political history a larger place in the study of this period than of the one preceding it. D. W. Brogan, *France Under the Republic (1870–1939)* (1940), provides a lively narrative, written under the influence of the regime's collapse; David Thomson, *Democracy in France Since 1870* (5th ed., 1969), offers a more analytical approach. For those who read French, the classic work of François Goguel, *La politique des partis sous la IIIe République* (1946), and the more recent treatment of the regime's institutions in Jean-Marie Mayeur, *La vie politique sous la Troisième République* (1984), give indispensable analyses of the Republic's durable characteristics.

On the origins of the Third Republic and the Paris Commune uprising, see Michael Howard, *The Franco-Prussian War* (1967), stressing military aspects; Stewart

Edwards, *The Paris Commune 1871* (1971), a balanced account; Karl Marx, *The Civil War in France* (1974; orig. 1871), a contemporary analysis that laid the basis for the interpretation of the Commune as the first "worker's state"; and Sanford Elwitt, *The Making of the Third Republic* (1975), which rehabilitated the founders of the "bourgeois" Republic. Gay Gullickson, *Unruly Women of Paris* (1996), probes the significance of gender in the uprising. Katherine Auspitz, *The Radical Bourgeoisie: The Ligue de l'Enseignement and the Origins of the Third Republic* (1982), fills in the Republic's ideological background. J. P. T. Bury, *Gambetta and the Making of the Third Republic* (1973), covers the most important republican of the period; the same author's *Gambetta: The Final Years* (1982) covers the brief period of his ministry.

For the period from 1877–1914, there are many studies centered around the political crises of Boulangism and the Dreyfus affair. These include Michael Burns, *Rural Society and French Politics: Boulangism and the Dreyfus Affair* (1984); Frederick Seager, *The Boulanger Affair* (1969); and William Irvine, *Boulanger Affair Reconsidered* (1989), arguing for the importance of the movement's conservative connections. Jean-Denis Bredin, *The Affair: The Case of Alfred Dreyfus* (1986), supersedes older narrative accounts; Robert Hoffman, *More Than a Trial* (1980), looks at the effects of the crisis; and Norman Kleeblatt, ed., *The Dreyfus Affair* (1987), examines artists' involvement. Eugen Weber, *Action française* (1962), follows the development of the most important of the right-wing movements to emerge from the affair. J. H. Jackson, *Clemenceau and the Third Republic* (1946), gives a somewhat dated account of its subject's life; a more recent study of the first half of Clemenceau's career can be found in Jack Ellis, *The Early Life of Georges Clemenceau* (1980), while Harvey Goldberg, *The Life of Jean Jaurès* (1962), is a classic biography of the great socialist leader. Michael Burns ap-

proaches the subject through a study of Dreyfus's family in *Dreyfus: A Family Affair* (1991). Burns has also edited a book of documents: *France and the Dreyfus Affair* (2000). John McManners, *Church and State in France, 1870–1914* (1972), is a straightforward account of the campaign against the church.

Few periods have benefited as much from the recent upsurge of women's history as this one. Among the major monographs are Patrick Bidelman, *Pariahs Stand Up!* (1982), on the early stages of the feminist movement; Steven Hause and Anne Kenney, *Women's Suffrage and Social Politics in the French Third Republic* (1984), and Steven Hause, *Hubertine Auclert, the French Suffragette* (1987), on the bourgeois republican component of the movement; and Charles Sowerwine, *Sisters or Citizens? Women and Socialism in France Since 1876* (1982), on women in the socialist camp. Jo Burr Margadant, *Madame le Professeur* (1990), treats the development of the teaching profession, while Linda Clark, *Schooling the Daughters of Marianne* (1984), examines the girls' school curriculum of the period. Women's issues were vital to the development of the French welfare state, as Elinor Accampo et al., *Gender and the Politics of Social Reform in France, 1870–1914* (1995), and Mary Lynn Stewart, *Women, Work, and the French State* (1989), have shown. The "new women" of the period are the subject of Mary Louise Roberts, *Disruptive Acts: The New Woman in Fin-de-Siècle France* (2002).

The history of France's Jewish community has become a thriving subfield in its own right, with the Dreyfus era occupying a central position. Major contributions include Phyllis Cohen Albert, *Modernization of French Jewry* (1977), and Paula Hyman, *Emancipation of the Jews of Alsace* (1991), on the period before Dreyfus; Michael Marrus, *The Politics of Assimilation* (1971), on the Dreyfus era; and Paula Hyman, *From Dreyfus to Vichy* (1979), on the first decades of the twentieth century. Other immigrant groups have received little study in English; a good survey is Gérard Noiriel, *The French Melting Pot* (1996), which puts the issue in the context of current debates about national identity.

For an overview of the French imperial experience in this period, see Robert Aldrich, *Greater France* (1996). Alice Conklin, *A Mission to Civilize: The Republican Idea of Empire in France and West Africa, 1895-1930* (1997) is a major new assessment of French colonialism. An older standard work on the subject is Henri Brunschvig, *French Colonialism 1871–1914: Myth and Realities* (1966). The road from the defeat of 1870 to the outbreak of war in 1914 is explained clearly in John Keiger, *France and the Origins of the First World War* (1983). Keiger has recently published a more extended work on French foreign policy, *France and the World since 1870* (2001).

Leonard Smith et al., *France and the Great War* (2003) is the most up-to-date overview of the ordeal of 1914–1918. Alistair Horne, *The Price of Glory* (1962), evokes the horrors of trench warfare in unforgettable terms. Jere King, *Generals and Politicians* (1952), explains the politics of the war, and Jean-Jacques Becker, *Great War and the French People* (1986), covers the home front. Leonard Smith, *Between Mutiny and Obedience* (1994), brings new insights to the question of why French soldiers endured this ordeal. On women and the war, see Margaret Darrow, *French Women and the First World War* (2000). Antoine Prost, *In the Wake of the War: Les Anciens Combattants and French Society* (1993), is a condensation of a fundamental French study of postwar veterans' groups, and Daniel Sherman, *The Construction of Memory in Interwar France* (1999) looks at the institutionalization of war memory.

Politics in the interwar period are not well represented in the English-language literature. Diplomatic issues are treated in Walter McDougall, *France's Rhineland Diplomacy 1914–1924* (1978); Stephen Schuker, *The End*

of *French Predominance in Europe* (1976); and Marc Trachtenberg, *Reparation in World Politics* (1980). Charles Maier, *Recasting Bourgeois Europe* (1975), is a comparative study that addresses French domestic politics in the 1920s. Socialist leader Léon Blum gets a sympathetic hearing in Joel Colton, *Léon Blum: Humanist in Politics* (1966), while his party is subjected to harsher treatment in Tony Judt, *Marxism and the French Left* (1986). Robert Wohl, *French Communism in the Making 1914–1924* (1966), deals with the origins of the new left-wing party. The early Fascist movements are the subject of Robert Soucy, *French Fascism: The First Wave 1924–1933* (1986); the same author's *French Fascism: The Second Wave, 1933–1939* (1995); and Zeev Sternhell's controversial *Neither Right nor Left: Fascist Ideology in France* (1986). Traditional conservatism is dealt with by William Irvine, *French Conservatism in Crisis* (1979). There is a well-balanced treatment of the Popular Front in Julian Jackson, *The Popular Front in France* (1988), and agrarian protest movements are the topic of Robert Paxton, *French Peasant Fascism* (1997). Stéphane Courtois and Marc Lazar, *Histoire du Parti Communiste Français* (1995), explains what the opening of the Soviet archives has revealed about the French party's subordination to Moscow.

Social historians have found the period up to 1914 at least as rich as the preceding one. Eugen Weber, *Peasants into Frenchmen* (1976), offers a broad argument about the changes in rural life and mentalities, a process recounted in personal terms in Pierre-Jakez Hélias, *The Horse of Pride: Life in a Breton Village* (1978). On urban workers, see Lenard Berlanstein, *The Working People of Paris, 1871–1914* (1984), which explodes the image of a unified working class concentrated in large factories; Michael Hanagan, *The Logic of Solidarity: Artisans and Industrial Workers in Three French Towns 1871–1914* (1980); and Kathryn Amdur, *Syndicalist*

Legacy (1986), on the impact of rival visions of unionism. Regional studies include, in addition to John Merriman's *The Red City* (see above), Joan Scott, *The Glassworkers of Carmaux* (1974), and Donald Reid, *The Miners of Decazeville* (1985), while Edward Shorter and Charles Tilly look at patterns of strikes over a long period in their *Strikes in France 1830–1968* (1974), and Michelle Perrot examines the strike phenomenon in detail for the period 1870–1890 in *Workers on Strike 1871–1890* (1987). Comparable studies for the period from 1914 to 1940 are fewer, but Herrick Chapman, *State Capitalism and Working-Class Radicalism in the French Aircraft Industry* (1991), which goes from 1930 to the 1950s, breaks new ground in this area. Tyler Stovall, *The Rise of the Paris Red Belt* (1990), deals with the implantation of Communism in the Paris suburbs. Two books that let French women recount the experience of the twentieth century in their own words are Bonnie Smith, *Confessions of a Concierge* (1985), and Emilie Carles, *A Life of Her Own* (1991).

Not all work in social history has focused on the lower classes. Norma Evenson, *Paris: A Century of Change 1878–1978* (1979), looks at changes in France's largest city and extends well into the twentieth century. Aspects of bourgeois life are touched on in Michael Miller, *The Bon Marché: Bourgeois Culture and the Department Store* (1981); Alain Corbin, *Women for Hire* (1990); and art historian T. J. Clark's influential study *The Painting of Modern Life* (1984). Bourgeois mentalities and fears feature in one way or another in such works as Susanna Barrows, *Distorting Mirrors: Visions of the Crowd in Late Nineteenth-Century France* (1981); Robert Nye, *Crime, Madness, and Politics in Modern France* (1984); Rosalind Williams, *Dream Worlds: Mass Consumption in Late Nineteenth-Century France* (1982); Leora Auslander, *Taste and Power* (1996); Edward Berenson, *The Trial of Madame Caillaux* (1992); Matt Matsuda, *The Memory of the Modern* (1996);

and Debora Silverman, *Art Nouveau in Fin-de-Siècle France* (1989). The petty bourgeoisie's political orientation is the subject of Philip Nord, *Paris Shopkeepers and the Politics of Resentment* (1986). Stephen Harp, *Marketing Michelin: Advertising and Cultural Identity in Twentieth-Century France* (2001) and Kolleen Guy, *When Champagne Became French: Wine and the Making of a National Identity* (2003) both show how commercial advertising helped shape national culture. Nicola Cooper, *France in Indochina: Colonial Encounters* (2001) explores the cultural impact of France's Asian colonies. Two important contributions to the history of French social policy are Paul Dutton, *Origins of the French Welfare State* (2002) and Sian Reynolds, *France between the Wars: Gender and Politics* (1996). Christine Bard's *Les Filles de Marianne: Histoire des féminismes 1914–1940* (1995) covers interwar feminist movements.

F. W. J. Hemmings, *Culture and Society in France 1848–1898* (1971), is a straightforward narrative that places the leading writers in their historical context. Michael Curtis, *Three Against the Third Republic* (1959), treats the emergence of modern antidemocratic conservatism. Stephen Lukes, *Emile Durkheim, His Life and Work* (1972), is the standard study of the great sociologist, while William Keylor, *Academy and Community: The Foundation of the French Historical Profession* (1975), looks at academic professionalization. Roger Shattuck's *The Banquet Years* (1955) brings the turn-of-the-century avant-garde to life. George Weisz, *The Emergence of Modern Universities in France* (1983), looks at the development of modern intellectual institutions. For the interwar period, H. S. Hughes, *The Obstructed Path* (1966), offers an overview that extends into the postwar period. Mary Louise Roberts, *Civilization Without Sexes* (1994), shows how the war affected gender issues. Carole Fink, *Marc Bloch: A Life in History* (1989), treats the historian who made France a world leader in that discipline. Charles Rearick, *The French in Love and War* (1997), deals with popular culture, and Shanny Peer, *France On Display: Peasants, Provincials and Folklore in the 1937 Paris World's Fair* (1998) shows how the exposition shaped cultural identities. Tyler Stovall, *Paris Noir: African-Americans in the City of Light* (1996) is about a very distinctive expatriate community's interactions with France. Sue Peabody and Tyler Stovall, *The Color of Race: Histories of Race in France* (2003) brings together essays on the black experience in France over the past two centuries.

1940 to the Present

Robert Young, *France and the Origins of the Second World War* (1996), explains the policy background to the conflict, and popular historian Alistair Horne's *To Lose a Battle* (1969) ably recounts the military debacle. Marc Bloch, *Strange Defeat* (1968), is a classic analysis by a participant who was also a leading historian. Robert Paxton, *Vichy France: Old Guard and New Order* (1972), opened the modern era of scholarship on the Vichy regime, demolishing many myths jealously defended by both participants and opponents, a process continued in Michael Marrus and Robert Paxton, *Vichy France and the Jews* (1983). Philip Burrin, *France Under the Germans* (1996), and Julian Jackson, *France: The Dark Years, 1940–1944* (2001) synthesize the current scholarship on this controversial period. Bertram Gordon, *Collaborationism in France During the Second World War* (1980), looks at the organized collaborationist movements. John Sweets, *Choices in Vichy France* (1986), and Robert Zaretsky, *Nîmes at War* (1995), are regional studies. Two recent books on women under Vichy are Miranda Pollard, *Reign of Virtue: Mobilizing Gender in Vichy France* (1998) and Francine Muel-Dreyfus, *Vichy and the Eternal Feminine* (2001). Renée Poznanski, *The Jews in France during World War II* (2002) looks at the French experience of the Holocaust from the victims' perspective.

Journalist David Schoenbrun's *Soldiers of the Night* (1980) is a readable chronicle of the Resistance. H. R. Kedward, *Resistance in Vichy France* (1978), is a more scholarly account. Charles de Gaulle, *The Complete War Memoirs* (1955–1960), is a magisterial narrative from a very particular point of view; the first volume of Jean Lacouture, *De Gaulle: The Rebel* (1990), fills in the Resistance leader's earlier life and nuances his account of the war. Henri Frenay, *The Night Must End* (1977), is a gripping account of the domestic Resistance. Women's contributions are highlighted in Margaret Rossiter, *Women in the Resistance* (1985). Eric Jennings's *Vichy in the Tropics* (2001) broadens our picture of the war to include the colonies. Peter Novick puts the controversial sequel to the liberation in perspective in *Resistance Versus Vichy* (1968). Annie Cohen-Solal, *Sartre: A Life* (1987), is a biography of the dominant intellectual figure to emerge from the war; Tony Judt, *Past Imperfect: French Intellectuals 1944–1956* (1992), is highly critical of Sartre and his followers. Richard Kuisel, *Seducing the French* (1993), looks at the contradictory French responses to American influence after the war. Jean-Philippe Mathy, *Extrême-Occident* (1993) concentrates on French intellectuals' attitudes toward the US. Sarah Farmer, *Martyred Village* (1999) examines the construction of postwar memory.

Stanley Hoffmann's essays, inspired by the experience of the Fourth Republic, are fundamental for an understanding of the French republican experience as a whole: Stanley Hoffmann et al., *In Search of France* (1963), and Hoffmann, *Decline or Renewal? France Since the 1930s* (1974). Robert Gildea, *France Since 1945* (1996), is a good overview of the postwar period. Philip Williams, *Crisis and Compromise* (1964), is a classic analysis of the malfunctioning of the postwar republic. Irwin Wall, *The United States and the Making of Postwar France* (1992), revises accepted notions about the origins and impact of

American involvement in French affairs after 1944. Journalist Alexander Werth's *France 1940–1955* (1956) captures the day-to-day atmosphere of the postwar period, while another talented journalist, Bernard Fall, conveys the bitterness of the Vietnam conflict in his *Street Without Joy* (1961). The French version of the second volume of Lacouture's *De Gaulle* (1985) includes valuable chapters on the Provisional Government and de Gaulle's years out of power which are omitted from the abridged English translation. The same author's *Pierre Mendès-France* (1984) treats the Fourth Republic's most innovative premier.

Richard Kuisel, *Capitalism and the State in Modern France* (1981), looks at the origins of economic planning and its eventual triumph after the war. Gordon Wright, *Rural Revolution in France* (1964), and Peter Amann, *The Corncribs of Buzet* (1990), examine the postwar agricultural revolution in two different stages. Anthropologist Lawrence Wylie's *Village in the Vaucluse* (orig. 1957), an analysis of life in a small village at the beginning of the 1950s, has become a scholarly classic; the additional chapters added to successive editions give important insights into the social changes from the 1950s to the 1970s. Claire Laubier, *The Condition of Women in France, 1945 to the Present* (1990), is a valuable documentary collection (texts in French, commentary in English). George Ross, *Workers and Communism in France from the Popular Front to Eurocommunism* (1982), covers the evolution of one segment of postwar society. Kristin Ross, *Fast Cars, Clean Bodies* (1995) is a provocative reading of the cultural trends of the 1950s. Gabrielle Hecht, *The Radiance of France: Nuclear Power and National Identity After World War II* (1998) explains how modern technology was used as a basis for asserting national identity.

John Talbott, *The War Without a Name* (1980), is the best account of the Algerian war. David Schalk, *War and the Ivory Tower* (1991), compares the antiwar movement to the American protests against Vietnam. Charles

S. Maier and Dan S. White, *The Thirteenth of May: The Advent of de Gaulle's Republic* (1968), is a documentary collection about de Gaulle's return to power, an event recounted from the general's point of view in his *Memoirs of Hope and Renewal* (1971) and, from a less one-sided perspective, in Jean Lacouture, *De Gaulle: The Ruler* (1992). Philip Cerny, *The Politics of Grandeur* (1980), explains the motives of de Gaulle's foreign policy.

Alain Schnapp and Pierre Vidal-Naquet, eds., *The French Student Uprising* (1971), reprints documents from the 1968 movement. Raymond Aron's *The Elusive Revolution* (1969) is a polemical assault on the movement's pretensions. Keith Reader, *The May 1968 Events in France* (1993), and Kristin Ross, *May '68 and its Afterlives* (2002) offer cultural interpretations. J. Frears, *France in the Giscard Presidency* (1981), recounts the unhappy presidency of "VGE." The emergence of the new Socialist party can be studied in D. S. Bell and Byron Criddle, *The French Socialist Party* (1988). Journalist Jane Kramer's *The Europeans* (1988) includes insightful essays on social and cultural trends of the early 1980s, while Jill Forbes and Michael Kelly, eds., *French Cultural Studies* (1995), provides an overview of modern French culture. Françoise Gaspard, *A Small City in France* (1995), is a first-hand account of how the *Front National* gained power in one French community. Alastair Cole, *François Mitterrand* (2nd ed., 1997), and Julius Friend, *The Long Presidency: France in the Mitterrand Years* (1998), are accounts of what turned out to be the longest presidency of the Fifth Republic. Claire Duchen, *Feminism in France* (1986), examines the formative stage of that movement; Jane Jenson and Mariette Sineau, *Mitterrand et les françaises* (1995), looks at the politics of women's issues from the 1960s to the 1990s. David Looseley, *The Politics of Fun* (1995) treats cultural policies in the Mitterrand years. *New Yorker* magazine correspondent Adam Gopnik collected his lively essays on French life in the 1990s in *Paris to the Moon* (2000).

Index